MIDDLE EAST POLITICS:
THE MILITARY DIMENSION

Middle East Politics: The Military Dimension

J. C. HUREWITZ

PUBLISHED FOR THE

Council on Foreign Relations

by

FREDERICK A. PRAEGER, *Publishers*

New York · Washington · London

FREDERICK A. PRAEGER, PUBLISHERS
111 Fourth Avenue, New York, N.Y. 10003, U.S.A.
5, Cromwell Place, London S.W. 7, England

Published in the United States of America in 1969
by Frederick A. Praeger, Inc., Publishers

Library of Congress Catalog Card Number: 68–30937

Printed in the United States of America

For my devoted harem,
who suffered in vocalized agony
through the prolonged gestation.

PREFACE

The Middle East, however defined, is a diverse region with states of widely varying size and description. One of its prominent features is the country with a plural society, which in the Middle East connotes a society of culturally discrete communities that split along linguistic, religious, and ethnic lines. The communal, or vertical, divisions in such states are often more significant for research in the social sciences than are the class, or horizontal, divisions. In states with plural societies, membership in a particular community counts even more than membership in a particular class. Since the communal and the class cleavages crisscross one another, the patterns of analysis become complex and resist simple generalization derived deductively, which has often characterized studies in the social sciences on the Middle East as on other nonindustrial regions. The only valid hypotheses about social phenomena in the Middle East are commonly subregional hypotheses.

For these reasons, I have deliberately chosen the inductive method of inquiry—structuring the hypotheses to fit the evidence. But even the empirical method is no more useful than the available evidence. Ideally, each state under analysis should first have been thoroughly studied by the scholars, so that their monographs might provide the needed, and proved, testimony. This happy condition rarely exists, and in the Middle East the number of available monographs on the individual states and their quality are far from uniform. Where the monographs were nonexistent, I have had to marshal the data myself. Moreover, the best experimental research is usually first done for a professional audience. Later, with the jargon sifted, the analysis refined, and the prose enlivened, the product is presented to the public at large. In this work, I have skipped the first stage, for, despite the book's experimental quality, I have directed it toward the nonprofessional reader, hoping nevertheless that the specialist would also find it valuable and running the risk of satisfying neither.

From the outset, I felt that a broad-gauged analysis, despite the difficulties of research, would yield more valuable returns than a more restricted one. I therefore adopted a generous definition of the region to encompass North Africa and non-Soviet Southwest Asia—the contiguous Muslim sovereignties from Morocco to Afghanistan and Pakistan, plus Lebanon and Israel. Omitted are Cyprus, which at the time of my research hovered between sovereignty and external condominium, and the People's Republic of South Yemen, which won its precarious independence too late for inclusion. The Middle East thus defined numbers eighteen states, enough to furnish many varieties of political experience and, in my analytical framework, to obviate single-entry categories. But, to keep track of developments in so many states, all undergoing rapid change and several suffering prolonged and inconclusive civil war, demanded a juggling act better suited to team than to individual research. Now that the work is done, I am pleased that I stuck it out despite the frustrations of research.

The book was conceived as an inquiry into the causes and consequences of military intervention in the postwar politics of the Middle East. An understanding of the causes of military coups d'état, however, required examining not only those states where the soldiers became rulers but also the others, where they did not, so as to ascertain the precise conditions that seemed to invite military seizure of power. The inquiry thus grew into a comparative analysis of the political systems in the Middle East. The focus on civil-military relations helped provide a basis for classifying the systems and made it possible to include all states—new and old, Arab and non-Arab, Muslim and non-Muslim.

The Middle East political systems, when classified according to the domestic political role of the armies, fell initially into those states in which the soldiers had destroyed civilian regimes (Syria, Egypt, Iraq, Pakistan, Sudan, Turkey, Algeria, and Yemen) and the others, in which the civilians continued to govern. The military-political systems, in turn, divided into the military republics (Chapters 7–9), wherein the soldiers did not return to the barracks, and the military-civilian coalitions (Chapters 10–11), which largely reactivated civilian politics. These coalitions, I discovered, represented two contrasting styles of partnership. The coalitions with soldiers as senior partners differed in kind from those with civilians in command, and the latter in the postwar Middle East constituted a stage preliminary to full military take-over.

The republic in the Middle East is an imported political system that made its regional appearance in Turkey after World War I. The classical Islamic political system was the monarchy. In the 1960s, tribal armies were the mainstay of three of the eight surviving kingdoms. Elsewhere among the kingdoms, modernized armies were brought into being to reinforce the authority of the crown. On the manifest assumption that military structures, and consequently civil-military relations, reflect the societies from which the officers and men are recruited and which they are supposed to serve, I called those with tribal forces the traditional monarchies (Chapters 12–14) and the others the modernizing monarchies (Chapters 15–19). The overthrow of modernizing monarchies in Egypt and Iraq in the 1950s led to the creation not of new dynasties, as would certainly have occurred in earlier centuries, but of republics. By contrast, the attempted overthrow of the traditional monarchy in Yemen led to civil war, for the social structures in that isolated, traditional society could not yet sustain an alien system.

The final category consisted of the three non-military republics (Chapters 20–22), whose political systems share little more than the civilian management of the armed forces and an unlikely candidacy for military coups d'état.

The Middle East, as a region, is nonindustrial—a term I use in the social, political, and military as well as in the purely economic sense for states that are in the early stages of industrialization. I prefer to call these states nonindustrial rather than new or non-Western or underdeveloped or even developing. All Middle East states, even the traditional monarchies, are changing. The pace, of course, differs from country to country, and the reasons are multiple. In nonindustrial states, it is often difficult to tell where the initiative comes from in the process of institutional change. In the country analyses (Chapters 7–22), I explore the relation of armies to the process of political change. In Chapter 23, I take a critical look at the prevailing hypotheses on the role of modernizing armies in the process of social and economic change.

One of the features of nonindustrial states is their dependence on the industrial states for modern military equipment. This explains the extra-regional participation in the military politics of the postwar Middle East. I therefore examine the imperial and post-imperial techniques of the industrial states in offering or denying modern military weapons as a means of influencing the policies of their military clients (Chapter 5). One of the side effects of the superpowers' rival military aid policies in the Middle East has been the stimulus to arms races (Chapters 24–25).

The analysis is essentially limited to developments since 1945. A work of this size, however, would appear unfinished without a historical introduction outlining the military-political continuities with the Islamic and European imperial past (Chapters 2–4). The cut-off date for individual chapters is variable. In the Arab-Israel zone, it is June 1967, since political developments after the Six Day War remain, for obvious reasons, obscure. Elsewhere, internal developments determine the date; in no instance does the detailed analysis go beyond 1967.

Finally, I have brought together in tables statistical data on the individual countries, illustrating the postwar growth of population, force levels, government expenditures (including defense), and GNP. Because of the prevailing inflation and the constantly shifting rates of exchange, I decided to keep the fiscal data in most of the tables in local currencies, so as to reduce possible distortions. Despite the care that I have used in selecting the data, I must caution the reader that the reliability of the demographic and financial statistics, to say nothing of those relating to the military establishments, varies from state to state. In offering the tables, I hope to provide the reader with, at best, an accurate guide and, at worst, a relative guide to the patterns of growth.

J. C. HUREWITZ

New York City
November 1968

ACKNOWLEDGMENTS

A work of this size and complexity requires the help of many people in many places. The search for information on a theme that touches the security interests of rival states invites defeat. Those men who know, as a rule, will not talk; those who do not know usually talk too much. For assistance in surmounting obstacles that might have been frustrating, I am especially indebted to officials of the United States and other governments and of intergovernmental agencies with whom I have discussed these matters.

A large number of academic friends, at home and abroad, criticized individual chapters, calling attention to errors of fact and interpretation. For their assistance, I am deeply grateful. At every stage in the making of the book, I profited from the stimulating exchange of ideas with my colleagues at Columbia University, particularly in the School of International Affairs and in the regional institutes. I am most appreciative of the generous aid given by John S. Badeau, Charles Issawi, Juan J. Linz, and Herbert Passin, who permitted me to impose on their friendship. Among the foreign scholars to whom I am highly indebted for sharing with me a deep understanding of their societies are Mordechai M. Bar-On, Hafez Farman-Farmaian, Shaykh Muhammad Ikram, Ömer Celâl Sarç, and Costi Zurayk.

The Columbia University libraries were indispensable sources of background literature. The libraries of other major institutions, in this country and elsewhere, were always open to my quest for materials on military politics. In London, I owe many obligations: to Noble Frankland, the Director of the Imperial War Museum, and to its principal librarian, Rose E. B. Coombs; to B. W. King, the chief librarian of the Ministry of Defense library, and his deputy B. N. P. Fabian; to the Royal Institute of International Affairs and particularly its press librarian, Elisabeth Campbell; and to the Institute for Strategic Studies, where David R. Wood, as research associate, attended to my research needs. I should also like to record my obligation to the Institute's quality publications on all aspects of military affairs.

The book originated in a discussion group at the Council on Foreign Relations, which met in 1963–64 to explore military politics in the Middle East, under the chairmanship of Kermit Roosevelt. The group consisted of Frank Altschul, Hanson W. Baldwin, James P. Baxter, Col. Donald S. Bussey, USA, John C. Campbell, James E. Cross, Col. Donald Decker, USMC, Russell H. Dorr, Lawrence S. Finklestein, Col. Robert N. Ginsburgh, USAF, Manfred Halpern, Col. Fred Haynes, USMC, Donald R. Heath, Charles Issawi, John H. Kaufmann, Harry F. Kern, Jeffrey C. Kitchen, Hal Lehrman, Walter J. Levy, Derwood W. Lockard, Kennett Love, Richard H. Nolte, Don Peretz, William R. Polk, Dankwart A. Rustow, James Spain, Harold R. Spiegel, Brig. Gen. Eugene L. Strickland, USAF, Phillips Talbot, Champion Ward, Donald N. Wilber, and William Witman, 2d. I benefited greatly from the meetings, where I was able to test the preliminary findings with men of established *expertise* who helped clarify and explain the evolving phenomena. Early in 1965, John C. Campbell presided over a meeting at the Council to review a sample chapter assessing the state of literature on military politics in the Middle East and other nonindustrial regions. This meeting, at which the exchange of ideas was most valuable, was attended by Harry J. Benda, Cyril E. Black, John K. Cooley, John Devlin, Col. Edward P. Foote, USAF, George Gilder, Manfred Halpern, Col. Fred E. Haynes, USMC, Roger Hilsman, Samuel P. Huntington, Merle Kling, William R. Polk, Dankwart A. Rustow, K. H. Silvert, and Jonathan D. Stoddart.

My deepest obligation is to John C. Campbell, who, as research advisor at the Council, encouraged me at every stage and saved the book from many errors. Also helpful were my intellectual companions at the Council, William J. Barnds and Richard P. Stebbins.

The members of the Council staff, the participants in the Council meetings, and all the others who came to my assistance are not responsible for the contents of the book or its deficiencies. I alone am wholly accountable for the statements and interpretations of fact and for the conclusions.

Warmest thanks are due to the Council and to George S. Franklin, Jr., its Executive Director, and David W. MacEachron, its Deputy Executive Director, for generous support before, during, and after a residence research fellowship. To Grayson Kirk, as President of the Council and of Columbia University and as chairman of the Council's Committee on Studies, I am beholden for unflagging cooperation. I am also profoundly obligated to Andrew W. Cordier, then Dean of the School of International Affairs, Columbia University, and to Philip E. Mosely, the Associate Dean, for research assistance from the School's Ford Foundation grant to complete the book after the expiry of the Council fellowship.

Donald Wasson, a selfless librarian, and Janet Rigney, a dedicated assistant librarian, indulged me above and beyond the call of duty, enabling me to make the most effective use of the Council's superlative clipping files and invaluable collection of works on world politics. To them and their staff I cannot adequately express my gratitude. I wish also to thank Helen Caruso, for placing at my disposal her uncanny talent for uncovering relevant evidence; Helena Stalson, for expert guidance in structuring the tables; William Jaber, for making unusually fine maps; and Mary Lynne Bird for allowing nothing of importance to escape her index. It is a rare pleasure to acknowledge my indebtedness to Robert W. Valkenier, whose skills as an editor are exceeded only by his warmth as a person, and to Carol Kahn, his assistant, who tirelessly and even enthusiastically checked and rechecked the details of the text and tables.

My thanks are also due to the following for permission to quote from books they have published: Sampson Low, Marston & Co.; Harvard University Press; and Clarendon Press, Oxford. Full acknowledgement is given in the section "Notes." Chapters 3 and 21 first appeared in much different form in the *Middle East Journal*; similarly, Chapter 2, in the *Journal of the American Oriental Society*; and Chapter 20, in the book *The Military in the Middle East*, edited by Sydney N. Fisher and published by Ohio State University Press in 1968. I am deeply grateful to the original publishers for permission to use this material.

I should also like to thank, among the many who helped prepare the manuscript for publication, Leanora Dreisinger, Martha Hollins, Sylvia Kowitt, and Isabel Ludeman.

J. C. H.

CONTENTS

Maps appear on pages 4–5, 76–77, and 469.

LIST OF TABLES

MIDDLE EAST POLITICS:
THE MILITARY DIMENSION

1

AMERICAN ENTANGLEMENT IN THREE-DIMENSIONAL POLITICS

The Six Day War in June 1967 riveted world attention on the huge quantities of sophisticated weapons that the Arab East states and Israel had amassed in their arsenals. Among the rich assortment were supersonic planes, tanks of all standard sizes, armored personnel carriers, Soviet assault guns, and American self-propelled howitzers and guided missiles of many types (ship-to-shore, air-to-air, air-to-surface, anti-aircraft, and antitank, though not the 200- to 500-mile range surface-to-surface missile sought by both sides). The postwar arms traffic in the Middle East contrasted sharply with similar traffic in Latin America, another region with a tradition of recurrent military coups d'état.

The two regions are roughly comparable. As defined in this book, the Middle East comprises eighteen states, stretching from Morocco to Afghanistan and Pakistan; embraces an area of more than 5 million square miles; and supports a swiftly growing population that by the mid-1960s passed 300 million, more than one-third of whom were crowded into Pakistan. The twenty states of Latin America (excluding the four Caribbean republics that won their independence in the 1960s), though larger in over-all area (nearly 8 million square miles), were smaller in over-all population (about 250 million). On the basis of estimated American market value for related items, the eighteen states of the Middle East procured military hardware probably worth more than $11.0 billion in the two postwar decades ending in 1965. By contrast, the nineteen states of Latin America, excluding Cuba, imported in the same period weaponry that probably did not exceed $1.5 billion in estimated American market value. In fact, according to one informed estimate, while the rising Latin American defense budgets totaled slightly more than $1.5 billion in 1963–64, less than 10 per cent of the sum constituted investment in hardware.[1] In that same period,

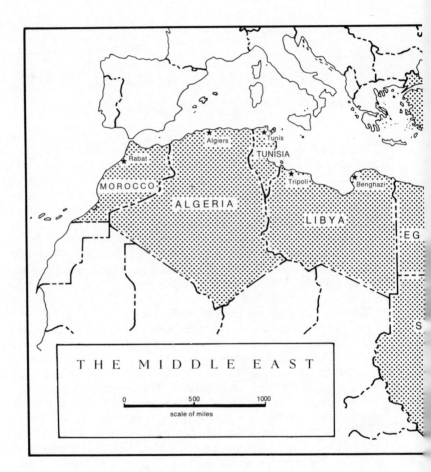

THE MIDDLE EAST

0 ——— 500 ——— 1000
scale of miles

Egypt or Israel alone procured military equipment worth more than the total reaching all Latin American countries (Cuba again excluded). As late as 1967, none of the Latin American armed forces (Cuba excepted), even in the major countries, could yet point in their weapons inventories to supersonic planes, medium or heavy tanks, or other than ship-to-air guided missiles.

From these bare statistics, we must not draw hasty conclusions. The safeguard lies in an assessment of the political systems of the individual countries of the Middle East to ascertain the character of civil-military relations in all states, whether under military rule or not. Yet even such a study yields many surprises, and the investigator is well advised to avoid the booby traps that litter the field. The most vigorous democracy in the Middle East, Israel is also the state that arms most vigorously, and though it has established a garrison democracy, it is not a militaristic state. The defense budget of the military regime of Sudan, minuscule to begin with, rose only moderately in the six years of its existence, reflecting a modest enlargement of the armed forces. Like democratic Israel, Sudan under military rule could hardly be labeled militaristic. In brief, armament on an elaborate scale does not necessarily militarize the sponsoring regime; nor does a military regime invariably favor the armed forces.

The study of military politics in nonindustrial states is a good deal more complicated than scholars, policy-makers, and journalists, to say nothing of laymen, seem ready to admit. Interest in the subject was nurtured by the long history of military interventions in Latin American politics and then broadened, after 1950, as soldiers seized political power in a growing number of newer, and even in a few of the older, states of Asia and Africa. As a rule, studies of military coups are limited to the individual countries immediately affected or to a comparative evaluation of the causes and consequences of military rule.[2] Such works, useful as they are, hardly go far enough to answer many basic questions. In the comparative study of armed forces and political change in the postwar Middle East, we must therefore examine civil-military relations in all the states, including those that have not fallen under military domination. This should help explain why army officers were able to seize political power in some countries but not in others, despite comparable social, economic, and political circumstances.

The only signals we receive are the coups d'état staged either by soldiers alone or by coalitions of soldiers and civilians. Since the traditional political systems in the Middle East were military in origin and later development, the question of how to classify the present-day Islamic kingdoms arises. Are their regimes to be viewed as civilian or military? Moreover, even the traditional monarchies have all begun to modernize, and one of the distinguishing features is the progressively more elaborate administration, as discrete ministries and bureaucratic institutions come into being. Such political systems imperceptibly lose their martial qualities, until they start modernizing their armed forces, which then can be used to impose the will of the ruler on his subjects more efficiently than at any time in the past. The determination of the dividing lines between military and civilian regimes is hardly a semantic one.

The analysis thus grows steadily more complicated, since the influence of military rulers in the postwar Middle East tended to spill over national boundaries into the politics of neighboring states. Thirteen of the eighteen Middle East states are Arab states, and ever since 1955 the Arab military republics have been trying to subvert or, in their favored cliché, to "liberate" the monarchies and the nonmilitary republics. The overturn of the Hashimi dynasty in Iraq in 1958, if not sparked by such appeals, was nevertheless strongly influenced by them. So, too, was the replacement of the civilian regime in Sudan a few months later. Even more directly attributable to such action was the near destruction of the Hashimi dynasty in Jordan in the preceding year. The soldier-rulers in Cairo sharpened their skills in attempted long-distance suborning of other Arab governments and regimes through the use of the mass media, the export of teachers and military technicians, and the import of political refugees.

The study of military politics thus necessitates a consideration of regional influences. Each time an army overthrows or tries to overthrow a Middle East monarchy, all the surviving monarchs take a deep breath and a close look at their own armies and tighten the screening procedures for officer loyalty. All the kingdoms in the postwar Middle East became the targets of intensifying political attack, from without and from within. If the kings were to keep their thrones and save their dynasties, they had no choice but to improve the quality of their armed forces. Yet they responded to the mounting challenge in differing ways.

The kings of Saudi Arabia and Libya, for example, continued relying on tribal troops for internal defense. They simply standardized and modernized the equipment and the training and supplemented the irregular ranks by creating wholly modern regular units, including air and naval arms. The tribal forces, however, still served as the mainstay. Other monarchs, such as the shah of Iran and the kings of Jordan and Morocco, abandoned the tribal levies altogether, except for purely local police duties or for emergency call-up. King Hasan of Morocco, after committing his army to the border war with Algeria in the fall of 1963, also mobilized tribal troops. For the most part, however, these monarchs had come to place full trust in their regular armies. In brief, they modernized the military organization as well as the equipment and the training.

These differences often had little, if anything, to do with ability to pay for modern armies. The Saudi Arabian and Libyan kings seemed in no rush to give up their tribal troops even after the two desert kingdoms had become major oil producers. Following the settlement in 1954 of the oil dispute with the British concession-aires, the shah of Iran received increasingly bounteous oil revenues that might have been diverted to the armed forces. Yet, in practice, for a decade longer, he continued to lean heavily on the United States for military aid, just as the king of adjacent Afghanistan, without any oil revenues, managed to modernize his armed forces in less than a decade by accepting, after 1955, large-scale military aid from the U.S.S.R. Those regimes whose armed forces remained partly tribal were the traditional monarchies. The others, with wholly modernized forces, were the modernizing monarchies.

The very diversity of the Middle East helps explain why much of the literature on the region's military politics is characterized by overgeneralization. It is one thing to develop theories about the nonmilitary role of armies on the basis of inherent logic; it is something else again to demonstrate the applicability of such theories to a region that abounds in plural societies and widely differing political systems. Scholars who analyze the problems of modernization —that is, the problems of social change induced by imported technology—seem especially prone to the facile generalization. According to a common contention, military modernization in nonindustrial states automatically stimulates economic and social, to say nothing of political, modernization. It is also often argued that the technical skills learned in military service are later transferred to civilian use; such transferability, however, takes place slowly under career armies, and because twelve of the eighteen armies in the Middle East are career armies, the personnel rotate at a snail's pace.

Not all military intruders into politics, assuming that they are motivated by social protest and have thought out the details of reorganizing the economy and the society (both rash assumptions), are given the opportunity to become social innovators. Syria and Iraq were excellent examples of retrogression, while Sudan under military rule best illustrated static military-political leadership. Even those political sociologists who believe that a study of the social origins of army officers will shed light either on their likely political ambitions or on their social policies, if they have seized power, run into difficulty in the Middle East, particularly in those countries with plural societies, such as Lebanon, Iraq, Iran, and Afghanistan. In such countries, ethnic, sectarian, and linguistic origins may be more pertinent. As a rule, the only generalizations that stand up against the evidence are subregional. But even these limited generalizations need more than superficial study to be established.

The pattern of comparative inquiry into postwar Middle East military politics becomes even more complicated by the need to assess the interplay of domestic and regional with international politics. The sophisticated weaponry that filled the arsenals of the Middle East states in the postwar years was not manufactured there. It had to be imported. Admittedly, Israel developed an elaborate military industry which nearly, but not quite, gave it a self-generative capability. All other states in the area lagged far behind. Egypt, for example, entertained aspirations for an independent military-industrial capability. But the ambitious research and engineering program for the manufacture of supersonic jet planes and guided surface-to-surface missiles upon which Egypt embarked with the aid of foreign scientists and technicians ended in costly failure. As a major consequence of the Egyptian experiment, Israel was spurred into proliferating its own military industry.

Almost all the heavy equipment available to the Arab East states and Israel in June 1967 carried Soviet, American, French, or British manufacturers' labels. Arms watchers in the importing states kept track of the types and amounts of equipment that their neighbors were getting; arms watchers in the exporting states kept track of one another's shipments to the Middle East. The weapons traffic, moreover, received continuing notice, often exaggerated, in the press of the importing and exporting countries alike, further quickening the traffic.

Even after the Arab-Israel hostilities in June 1967, the Soviet-American Cold War in the Arab-Israel area seemed unresponsive to the thaw on the European continent. The U.S.S.R. continued pouring sophisticated equipment—even new items, such as ship-to-ship missiles with a homing device that sank an Israeli destroyer in

the following October and short-range surface-to-surface missiles—
to make up for the losses sustained by its clients. Except for Cuba,
Latin America never became a zone of Soviet-American rivalry in
military aid, as had the Arab-Israel area after 1955.

The Cold War manifestly conditioned military politics in the
postwar Middle East. Without the competitive military aid, which
became more and more generous, Iran and Jordan in the 1950s
might well have turned into military republics, and republican
Yemen in the 1960s would never have served as host to a third or
more of the Egyptian army. Without such aid, the Middle East
might well have become the scene of other separatist movements
on the model of the Kurds of Iraq. Instead, in most states of the
region the rulers proved able, for the first time in history, to procure the means for permanently imposing central authority on the
tribal districts and even creating more homogeneous societies. Nor
did it make any difference whether the weapons came from the
United States or the Soviet Union; they were put to similar use.
The aid itself represented, in effect, the fallout of American-Soviet
mutual deterrence.

The results of such activity in a heterogeneous region, as might
be expected, have varied. Westerners have tended to assume that
Soviet military policies in the Middle East were inescapably uniform because of the monolithic Soviet state and the doctrinaire
Communist ideology. But in the politics of military aid, Communists proved to be as much guided by expediency as are non-
Communists. At the international level, military politics consisted
in the use by extra-regional powers of military aid for the attempted enhancement of their political influence. The suppliers on
both sides were trying to serve contradictory Cold War goals. The
United States, for example, deliberately kept certain Middle East
regimes alive: the Pahlavi monarchy in Iran after August 1953, the
Hashimi monarchy in Jordan after April 1957, and the confessional
democracy in Lebanon in 1958. The U.S.S.R., for its part, took the
opposing side in these crises and gave military aid to the republicans who overturned the monarchy in Iraq in 1958, to those who
staged the uprising in Yemen four years later, to the Algerians after
the short-lived war with Morocco in the fall of 1963, and to Egypt
after June 1967. In taking these steps, each antagonist in the Cold
War was trying to bar its adversary from access to the Middle East
states concerned.

In an area already studded with its own cold wars, the lines of
influence of any one type of external policy were not always

straight or clear or durable. At times the overlap of interest between aider and aided proved sustained, as in the American and
Turkish opposition to the U.S.S.R. or in the Soviet and Egyptian
opposition to the United States and the West in the multiple Arab
crises. At other times, the common purpose dissolved before a client relationship could develop, as in the tentative military assistance from the United States to Lebanon late in the 1950s or from
the U.S.S.R. to Morocco early in the 1960s. The study of military
politics in the postwar Middle East, it is clear, remains incomplete
without probing into the military policies of the Cold War antago-
nists.

Arms races, it is true, arise from regional tensions. The quarrels
from which they stem normally predate the involvement of the
interested extra-regional powers. But in a region like the Middle
East, where in the postwar years Britain and France abandoned
their dependencies one after another, the United States and the
U.S.S.R. could hardly have failed to become rivals. In the opening
postwar decade, the United States tried to shore up the position of
its trans-Atlantic allies by offering jointly with them military aid to
the successor states as a political lever. They tried to use it to curb
rather than promote regional adventurism. In retrospect, this was a
mistaken policy, since it not only whetted the appetite of the Middle East states for modern equipment, but also encouraged the
U.S.S.R. to step in as a competitive supplier. But, from the outset,
particularly in the Arab-Israel area, the U.S.S.R. used arms aid lav-
ishly and for partisan purposes to destroy Western positions in the
Arab countries by precipitating crises of brinksmanship. The
U.S.S.R. had no inhibitions about siding with the Arabs in their
dispute with Israel and about encouraging Soviet military clients to
appeal for overthrow of the "conservative" Arab regimes that were
clients of the West. The United States, on its side, tried to establish a neutral position on the Arab-Israel dispute and to support its
own Arab clients and Israel against the tactics of Soviet military
aid. Moreover, the United States sought to avoid direct participation as a major supplier in this area by encouraging Britain and
France to furnish most of the requisite weapons. The bewildering
arms races that resulted from entwining supplier and client competition compounded the confusion of military politics at the regional and domestic levels.

It is to the interplay of domestic, regional, and international politics, with a primary focus on the military dimension, that the present book is addressed. At the domestic level, the political systems

in the postwar Middle East fall into five classes: republics under military rule, republics under military-civilian coalitions, traditional monarchies, modernizing monarchies, and nonmilitary republics. A study of the differing systems should enable us to assess the role of the military in each class in balanced perspective. Before we turn to that study, however, we must first examine the region's Islamic and European imperial legacies, for both have durably molded military politics in the Middle East.

Legacies

2

THE ISLAMIC TRADITION*

Military politics in the Middle East in the first two postwar decades is usually assessed on the basis of contemporary evidence, which is not always clear or convincing. The longer perspective of history can, however, add clarity and discernment to the discussion. Islamic political systems, before the advent of European imperialism, could almost uniformly be classified as varieties of military authoritarianism, commonly with the strict alternative of autocracy under a strong monarch and praetorianism or tribal supremacy under a weak one. Military authoritarianism persisted in most Muslim lands under European rule, although it was often disguised or cushioned by an imperial bureaucracy made up of technicians or by native bureaucracies used to administer the dependencies. In either case it was military rule. What is remarkable, in the circumstances, is not that the military in the first two postwar decades seized power in eight Middle East states, but that a larger number of civilian regimes did not vanish in these years.

The general community of Muslim states was still relatively free from the subordinating influence of European imperialism at the turn of the eighteenth century. At that time the area of the Middle East, as we have broadly defined it, comprised four large Muslim dynastic states—the Ottoman (Turkey), the Safavi (Persia), and the Mughal (India) empires, and the 'Alawi kingdom of Morocco. There were, in addition, many small tribal principalities in the Arabian Peninsula and North Africa into which the Ottoman and 'Alawi realms faded at their extremities.

The Ottoman Empire, it is true, had just suffered its first decisive defeat in Europe. The Treaty of Carlowitz (1699), which brought to an end a decade and a half of fierce fighting that had ranged Austria, Poland, Venice, and Russia against the Islamic

* This chapter appeared in somewhat different form as "The Islamic Military-Political Tradition," in *Essays in Memory of E. A. Speiser*, edited by William W. Hallo (New Haven: American Oriental Society, 1968), pp. 96–104.

realm, deprived the Sultan of territory north of the Danube that he never regained. Despite its manifest weakness, the Ottoman Empire was not easily shoved out of Europe, and by the end of the eighteenth century it still clung to most of its possessions there. Nor had Persia been reduced to wardship, despite the political anarchy through which it passed in the half-century preceding the Napoleonic wars. Shielded by geographic isolation, Persia escaped the European expansive pressure until tsarist forces began bearing down on the Caucasian principalities just "reconquered" by the emergent Qajar dynasty that finally reunited the shahdom. Meanwhile, the maritime powers of Western Europe at the start of the eighteenth century were still clutching insecurely the margins of India, many European-held ports significantly being out of Mughal reach at the southern tip of the subcontinent. Few observers at the time would have predicted that in less than a century the Mughal Empire would disappear.

The Muslim State System

The Muslim dynasties of the day were military and tribal in origin, as were most Muslim states, large and small. Islam itself had emerged from a tribal society, so that the tribal influence became durably imbedded in the Islamic religious political system. More than that, the *dar al-Islam*, or territory under Islamic rule, encompassed far-flung tribal districts, which kept spawning new military dynasties.

Writing in the fourteenth century, 'Abd al-Rahman ibn Khaldun attributed the desert beginnings of Muslim dynasties to the military superiority of the beduin tribesmen. They "provide their own defense and do not entrust it to, or rely upon, others for it," declared the renowned Arab historical sociologist, whereas the settled townsmen and villagers "have entrusted defense of their property to the governor and ruler who rules them and to the militia which has the task of guarding them." Yet ibn Khaldun acknowledged the inferiority of "desert civilization . . . to urban civilization." The urbanization of a successful dynasty, he continued, first lifts it to heights of glory by yielding "leisure and tranquility in which the fruits of royal authority are enjoyed," and then thrusts it downward to the stage of "waste and squandering," when it "is seized by senility and the chronic disease from which it can hardly ever rid itself, for which it can find no cure, and, eventually, it is destroyed." [1]

Had ibn Khaldun been present at the opening of the eighteenth century, he would probably have characterized the three imperial dynasties as senile. Indeed, Safavi rule in Persia expired in 1722, followed four decades later by the end, for all practical purposes, of Mughal rule in India. The Ottoman dynasty at Istanbul, however, contrived to limp along with declining energy until it was rescued in 1839–41 by the intervention of the European concert seeking to preserve the balance of power on the continent that might have been upset by the sudden disappearance of the sprawling Muslim empire. These three dynasties and the 'Alawi dynasty of Morocco were hardly fly-by-night phenomena. Safavi and Mughal rule endured for more than two centuries each, and Ottoman rule for more than six centuries, an enviable record in history. The 'Alawi dynasty of Morocco entered its fourth century in the mid-1960s, having barely survived more than fifty years of French overlordship in the twentieth century.

Despite political divisions, the Islamic world in 1700 still viewed itself as one society, and in some respects it was. The sovereign Islamic states were still bound together by the principles and customs of a generalized Islam under the supremacy of a common religious law. Insofar as a Muslim owed wider allegiance than to his tribe, his locality, or his guild, it was to the Muslim *ummah*, or community. The *shari'ah*, or sacred law, protected his personal rights, and each Islamic polity in its total experience seemed a replica of the next. This preserved transdynastic institutions and related activities, most notably those connected with religious law and the court system that served it, which functioned in all states, large and small. The few Muslims who travelled from one dynastic jurisdiction to another up and down the dar al-Islam thus felt thoroughly at home. A trained *qadi*, or judge of the sacred law, for example, could find employment anywhere in the dar al-Islam, and sometimes did. Ibn Khaldun, a native of the Maghrib (northwest Africa) could serve as judge in Cairo, the seat of authority of another Islamic state. His contemporary fellow Maghribi, Muhammad ibn 'Abdallah ibn Battutah, famous for his travels in Asia and Africa, held comparable offices in India and the Maldive islands.

The universality of the sacred law kept alive the theory of a universal Islamic state, implicit in the concept of the dar al-Islam, long after the start, in the eighth century, of the political fragmentation of the 'Abbasid Caliphate (750–1258), the last state to embrace almost the entire Muslim community. An Islamic state system, slow to emerge, seemed embryonic by contrast to the European state system. Administrative law varied from state to state; and religious doctrinal quarrels, it is also true, provided criteria for identifying mutually discrete states in both systems. The Safavi dynasty, for example, established the Ja'fari rite of Shi'ah (schismatic) Islam as the state religion of Persia at the start of the sixteenth century. Yet until the twentieth century Persia had no fixed territorial boundaries with its Sunni (orthodox) Muslim neighbors. Those Muslim countries that held on to their sovereignty did not begin to exchange permanent diplomatic missions with one another until the mid-nineteenth century. Nor did anything that even remotely resembled the balance of power in Europe take shape within the Islamic zone before the close of World War II.

The absence of fixed rules of succession was the important generator of military politics in Islam. The principle of primogeniture, almost uniformly applied in Europe, was not recognized in Islam, least of all among the Muslim dynasties of the seventeenth and eighteenth centuries. All male members of an extended royal family were acceptable candidates for the throne—brothers, nephews, cousins, and uncles as well as sons and grandsons. In theory, the successor was elected, but a mode of orderly election never became institutionalized. As a consequence, Islamic polities, hovering between hereditary and "elective" monarchies, became inured to violent and disorderly succession whenever the reigning monarch's wishes were not honored after his death. The "electoral college" consisted of the wives and the concubines in the harem and their attendant eunuchs, the advisory and administrative imperial staffs at the palace, the religious leaders (particularly in the Ottoman Empire), and the princes—all acting in varying combinations. Each combination sought alliance with top military commanders, for the ultimate decision favored that candidate with the strongest military support. Military intrusion into politics was thus built into the succession process, and whether or not the soldiers continued to play decisive political roles under the new monarch depended on his capacity or the capacity of the civilian manipulator behind the throne (whether a queen mother in the Ottoman Empire or Safavi Persia or a civilian consortium) to seize and hold the political leadership. The military-civilian combinations thus constituted loosely organized interest groups which became especially competitive at the time of succession and during the reign of a weak monarch.

In an effort to assure an orderly succession, the monarch usually designated as crown prince one of his male relatives, most often a son. A powerful dynast took precautions to try to make his choice stick. He might attempt to groom the crown prince for later responsibilities by naming him governor of an important province close to the capital or by having him serve an apprenticeship in the palace. A not infrequent complementary step was the dispatch of ambitious princes as governors to provinces remote from the capital. But such precautions were not always foolproof. Again and again, succession crises threatened to wreck each of the four dynasties under review, even the most powerful. The first ten Ottoman sultans from Osman to Süleyeman I (died 1566), it is generally agreed, were "able and intelligent men rare if not unique in the annals of dynastic succession." [2] Yet even then the dynasty suffered three major crises in the transfer of the crown from one sultan to the next. The Mughal dynasty was in full vigor in the seventeenth century, yet consider the turmoil of 1657–58, while Shah Jahan, best known for his Taj Mahal, still sat on the throne. He had named as heir his oldest son, Dara Shukoh. But the youngest, Awrangzib, was the most ambitious of the four princes, who did not even wait for their father to die; they jumped the gun when false word of the emperor's death reached them from agents at the palace. The war of succession, which lasted more than a year, finally brought Awrangzib to the throne, his three brothers to defeat and death, and Shah Jahan to imprisonment for the remaining eight years of his life.

Before examining the role of the military in resolving succession crises, we must first consider the nonmilitary measures devised to check the princely rivalry, if not eradicate it altogether. How better to remove the rivalry than to remove the princely rivals? Muslim dynasties, if they lasted long enough, could be expected to engage in fratricide. In the Ottoman Empire Fâtih Sultan Mehmed II (1451–81), the conqueror of Constantinople, allegedly gave legal sanction to fratricide "by strangulation with a silken bow-string . . . to the end that blood should not be let." [3] The practice continued until after the death of Mehmed III (1595–1603), who had executed nineteen brothers soon after accession and two sons in later years, or about a fourth of the total number of known royal executions in the dynasty's history, nearly destroying the ruling family altogether. After a reign of more than a half-century, Shah Tahmasp I of Safavi Persia left nine living sons on his death in 1576. Within two years only one remained. The bloodletter, the dissolute Shah Isma'il II, wore the crown for only eighteen months.

Following the death of Mehmed III, the Ottoman dynasty introduced a benign alternative to fratricide. All princes older than seven, except the sons of the ruler, were locked up in the *kafes* (cage), or special quarters, of the Topkapi palace at Istanbul. There they stayed for life, unless chosen as sultan, receiving little if any formal education as youngsters, permitted female companionship as they reached adulthood, but denied the right to have children, leading a purposeless, indolent existence. The institution of the kafes inhibited royal rebellion. But it also guaranteed that heir pollution would place on the throne political incompetents lacking the capacity to develop executive leadership, although in theory the imperial government remained as personal as it had always been, with the sultan as the sole decision-maker. The reigning sultan even lost the right to name his successor. The real sultan-makers in the seventeenth and eighteenth centuries were the self-constituted "civilian-military" coalitions formed by the inmates of the harem and the palace (including at times the *ulema*, or religious elite) with the principal military officers in the capital, who commanded rival military forces of Janissaries and *Sipahis*, or feudal gentry-cavalry.

In Safavi Persia, meanwhile, the shah adopted the Byzantine custom of maiming the princes. Blindness was viewed in Persia "as an absolute disqualification from the exercise of regal functions." [4] In fact, Shah Tahmasp's oldest son, Muhammad Khudabanda, renounced the throne in 1576 because of partial blindness. The condition later enabled him to escape death at the hand of the sanguinary Isma'il. Upon the latter's death, Muhammad Khudabanda, as the sole living brother, ascended the throne and, after a lackluster decade, abdicated under pressure in favor of his son, 'Abbas I, in whose 42-year reign the Safavi dynasty reached its full power and splendor. Shah 'Abbas promptly rendered his two younger brothers politically harmless by blinding them, and later murdered his oldest son and blinded another.

Military Politics in the Dynastic States

Violent succession was the corollary of the refusal to honor the reigning monarch's choice of a political heir. Violence could be invoked only with the support of the army, which meant the support of army commanders. The struggles for succession were mostly settled by civil war and by coup d'état, with the outcome generally as closely related to the structure of the military command as to the prevailing political environment. Yet even when the royal contenders were political misfits, the dynasties were not overturned, since it was much easier to legitimize a new incumbent of an established line than to try legitimizing a new dynasty.

The theory of Ottoman succession in the empire's prime, prior to the mid-sixteenth century, seemed to rest on the assumptions that a prince who had undergone an apprenticeship would make a better sultan than one who had not, and that the crown would pass from father to the most meritorious son. The sultan in that period, moreover, was not a nominal but an executive ruler and served as his own commander in chief. To provide governing experience and determine regal talent, the sultan appointed his sons viceroys of the major provinces and gave them field commands in the recurrent wars, and the consistently high quality of imperial leadership in the early centuries attested to the soundness of the selection procedure.

While the Ottoman procedure brought forth effective rulers, it also tended to breed wars of succession, chiefly because it failed to provide dignified political employment for the unsuccessful candidates. According to custom, the acceding sultan's brothers, treated as expendable, were simply set aside to enable the new generation of princes to move up the ladder of candidacy. The alternative for the princely apprentices could hardly have been more sharply delineated: either the highest office in the realm or political oblivion. Little wonder that the selection procedure invited violence.

Those Ottoman princes who gained experience in military statecraft, which was the essence of Ottoman imperial and provincial politics, almost invariably developed ambitions, nurtured by mothers and others who stood to benefit from a prince's triumph. The rebellious spirit among the aspiring princes grew steadily more vigorous as the dynasty aged. When princes rebelled in the lifetime of their father, the sultan had no choice but to dispose of the offenders to hold the state together. In the Ottoman Empire this meant, not blinding the rebels, as was the Safavi practice, but killing them. Bayezid II (1481–1512) began his reign in a civil war with his younger brother, later poisoned two rebellious sons, and finally abdicated against his will at the climax of a three-year war of succession among the three surviving sons. It was the youngest who seized Istanbul in 1512, proclaimed himself Selim I, and defeated and executed his older brothers. By the time such monarchs subdued their royal opponents, they had manifestly become seasoned warriors. Thus in 1516–17 Selim the Grim, as he became known to posterity, swallowed up the Mamluk Empire consisting of Egypt and the Arab districts north of the Arabian Peninsula.

The Mughal theory of succession with princes assigned to provincial apprenticeship paralleled the Ottoman, and so too did the consequences. From the death of Jahangir in 1627 the outcome of civil wars invariably determined the inheritor of the crown. Except in tribal districts such as the Pushtu-speaking north (on both sides of the present-day Afghan-Pakistan frontier), the provincial armies were essentially mercenary, and the soldiers (among them non-Muslims) salaried. The princely rivals prepared for the contest (or rebellion, for often an ambitious prince did not bide his time) by hoarding money and jewels in the provincial treasuries to pay the armed forces and to distribute largesse to principal political advisers. Those princes triumphed who commanded their own troops, mustered the largest armies with the lure of well-paid employment and the prospects of booty, and won initial battles, for mercenary soldiers rarely sustained allegiance, except in victory. Not uncommonly the mercenary armies melted away overnight after a defeat in battle or merely in fear of such a defeat.

Consider, for example, the abortive rebellion of Awrangzib's third son, Akbar, in 1681. For the scheme to usurp the throne, Akbar had assembled some 30,000 troops. The night before the expected decisive battle Awrangzib ensnared the commander of Akbar's army and killed him. Learning of their commander's death early the next morning, Akbar's officers simply withdrew their contingents without informing Akbar, leaving behind for him "a faithful band of 350 horse." [5] The rebels and conspirators, then as now, sought credentials of legitimacy. Four 'ulama on Akbar's staff issued a statement on the eve of the expected military showdown accusing Awrangzib of forfeiting the throne by violating the shari'ah. Nearly a quarter of a century earlier, Awrangzib himself had tried to legitimize the deposition of Shah Jahan by having him declared "infirm and intellectually unfit for governing the realm," a condition that required, in defense of the faith, "government by a pious and vigorous man" such as Awrangzib. In later correspondence with the imprisoned Shah Jahan, Awrangzib justified his actions by noting that "kingship means the protection of the realm and the guardianship of the people. . . . A king is merely God's elected custodian and the trustee of His money for the benefit of the subjects." [6]

From the Ottoman and Mughal theory of succession the Safavi and 'Alawi practices in Persia and Morocco veered away. The Ottomans and the Mughals kicked over their tribal traces in the process of erecting imperial states that expanded the dar al-Islam by absorbing large infidel-populated districts. The Safavis and 'Alawis, by contrast, preserved the classical Islamic character of their dynastic states by building political systems that made pri-

mary use of the inherent military power of martial tribes. Such
tribes are prone to dissipate their power in rivalry, a condition that
was transcended only when rival tribes could be enlisted in a sectarian cause.

The Turkman tribes that figured prominently in the founding of
the Safavi state had begun to affiliate with a Sufi or mystic order
that produced a Shi'ah sect at the start of the fourteenth century,
under the leadership of Shaykh Safi al-Din (c. 1250–1334). Shaykh
Safi gave the dynasty its name, but the dynasty's founder was his
descendant, Shah Isma'il I (1501–24). Isma'il's sectarian Turkman warriors were collectively known, because of their scarlet
headdress, as the Qizilbash (red head) tribes. It was the propaga-
tion of the Ja'fari rite of Shi'ah Islam that united the nine tribes behind Isma'il in the opening quarter of the sixteenth century in the
conquest of what became the Safavi empire and in the establishment of their sect as the state religion. The Qizilbash tribes, at the
start of Isma'il's reign, came mostly from Azarbayjan and adjacent
eastern Anatolia, and perhaps even from as far west as Syria. They
spoke Turkish dialects, as opposed to the Persian and Persian-
related dialects spoken by most of the indigenous population elsewhere in the empire.

These seminomadic Turkman warriors accepted Isma'il as their
military, political, and religious leader, believing him endowed with
divine attributes. From Azarbayjan Shah Isma'il diffused the Qizilbash tribes through the northern and central provinces, giving
them large tax-free tracts of choice lands and investing their chiefs
with lifetime governorships. Livestock breeders and warriors by
profession, the tribesmen also became professional Shi'is spreading the faith throughout the newly fabricated realm. Thus, the
Safavi dynasty and the Qizilbash tribes became mutually dependent. Dynastic influence reached into the provinces through the
tribes, yet no single tribe could aspire to the crown, for such an
ambition was bound to stir the jealous hostility of the remaining
Qizilbash tribes. Still, so long as these tribes continued to pull in
religious harness, to acknowledge Safavi leadership, and to enjoy a
monopoly or near monopoly of military power, they formed a military political aristocracy. Beyond that, the Qizilbash amirs had pre-
empted the provincial governorships from the outset, so that when
the early Safavi shahs sent their sons to the provinces, the princes
could become no more than nominal governors. From such offices
they could hardly gain experience in military-religious rulership.

This system meant, in effect, that in the best of circumstances the Qizilbash chief became a protector and a protagonist of his princely charge, in the hope that he would continue his custodial or advisory role when the prince became shah. Thus, military-political competition sharpened, because the Qizilbash tribes were automatically drawn into the process of selecting the new shah and keeping him on the throne. In the final analysis, the Safavi princes faced the same stark alternative that the Ottoman and Mughal princes faced, either the crown or probable maiming or execution, with this major difference: the Safavi prince did not command his own troops but leaned instead on the Qizilbash forces. Yet the dynastic line was assured so long as it could provide male issue and did not have to parry a major threat from outside the Qizilbash system.

The working of the system became manifest after the death of Tahmasp I in 1576. In the dozen years of weak imperial leadership that followed, the influence of the Qizilbash tribes steadily expanded, and they were becoming inured to their praetorian role. 'Abbas I (1587–1629), however, set out to contain the tribal influence, starting in the first year of his reign by suppressing a Qizilbash uprising. Despite lack of prior training, 'Abbas developed on the throne into a ruler of executive and military talent, taking into his own hands supreme authority. He reorganized the military institution, not by destroying the Qizilbash contingents, but by diluting their ranks with fresh recruits loyal to the crown, called the *shah-i sevan* (the shah's friends). To supplement and counteract the Qizilbash provincial military power, 'Abbas also created new nontribal units paid by the shah and directly reliant on him: the *qullar* (slaves) of the shah, recent converts to Islam mostly of Caucasian Christian origin, trained as musket-bearing cavalry, who became the shah's elite troops; Persian-speaking peasants trained as mounted infantry who were issued swords and daggers as well as muskets; and an expanded artillery corps armed with heavy guns. Moreover, as Qizilbash governors died, 'Abbas replaced them with slaves of the palace service whose devotion to the crown was unquestioned. Nevertheless, at the end of his reign, five of every six provincial amirs were still Qizilbash chiefs.

Despite the military and administrative innovations, 'Abbas inhibited the normal development of the dynasty by removing his immediate heirs. For his own lifetime, he built well. He curbed the rebellious tribes; he created a detribalized imperial, as distinct from the tribal provincial, military power; and he enlarged the realm. But on his death in 1629, the tribal groups still enjoyed enough power to reassert their roles as shah-sustainers, if not also shah-makers, throughout the life of the dynasty for nearly a century longer, forming varying coalitions, often with harem inmates, to run the empire from behind the throne. Even after the extinction of the Safavi dynasty, the Qizilbash tribes remained a primary force in the country, for from their ranks came the stillborn Afshar dynasty of Nadir Shar in the middle decades of the eighteenth century and the long-lived Qajar dynasty at its close.

The military-political system of 'Alawi Morocco, like that of Safavi Persia, was tribal. The 'Alawi dynasty was established in the 1660s on the ruins of the century-old Sa'di principalities based at Fez and Marrakesh, which in turn had formed in religious resistance to infidel conquest of the Moroccan coast by Portugal and Spain, starting as early as 1415. The Sa'di sharifs, or claimed descendants of the Prophet, contrived to organize and defend the Moroccan hinterland against further European encroachment, but to the end the twin states remained rivals. Isma'il (1672–1727), the second ruler of the 'Alawi line of sharifs, finally fused the territory into a single kingdom and drove the Europeans from almost all their coastal strongholds. The secret of the success of the long-lived *mawlay* (master), as the 'Alawi monarchs styled themselves, lay in his reorganization and enlargement of the *gish* (military) tribes.

Isma'il doubled the number of gish tribal federations to four. He infused loyal 'Alawi retainers into the original Sheraga (easterners) federation, taken over from the Sa'dis, and reassembled from scattered localities the Sudanese tribesmen, known as the *'abid al-Bukhari* (Bukhari's slaves) or the Bwakhir, originally brought into Morocco as slave-soldiers. Of the two new federations, the Sherada and the Udaya, the latter was built around the tribe of his maternal uncles, giving the federation its sobriquet, "uncles of the mawlay." The gish tribes, primarily Arabs or Arabized Berbers and Negroes, were settled in the fertile plains west of Fez and Meknes in the north and of Marrakesh in the south. In return for the tax-free use, and sometimes possession, of the land, the tribes were required to provide soldiers to the state at the mawlay's pleasure.

Isma'il failed to fix the succession, and on his death the gish tribes, joined after a while by Berber mountain tribesmen, got out of hand in playing the praetorian game. No fewer than fourteen incumbents sat on the 'Alawi throne in thirty years, as varying combinations of tribal commanders in disorderly rotation selected and deposed Isma'il's sons. Fortunately, the gish tribes did not exhaust the candidates, for Isma'il's sons were said to exceed fifty in number. Stability was not restored until the death in 1757 of Mawlay 'Abdallah, who had reigned at least five times and who was followed by his son, Muhammad III. From the death of Muhammad in 1790 through the mid-nineteenth century the gish tribes, particularly the Sherada and the Udaya, resumed their role as mawlay-makers.

Meanwhile, in the declining Ottoman Empire of the seventeenth and eighteenth centuries, praetorianism had become a favorite pastime of the once impressive Janissary (*Yeni Çeri*, or new force) Corps. The Janissaries were originally a product of a carefully elaborated program of recruitment and training that had made the Ottoman Empire the most professionally administered state of the day. The recruits were enslaved Christian youngsters, either captured in the newly conquered districts (chiefly of southeastern Europe) or later periodically conscripted there. As slaves of the sultan, they were first Turkified and Islamized and, after several stages of screening, the ablest were enrolled in special palace schools where they received intensive instruction for periods of two to eight years in Islam, designated crafts, and military skills. The graduates passed immediately into the imperial service: the central administration, the sultan's workshops, or the elite units of the armed forces. Most of the last were destined to become Janissaries. The Janissaries thus constituted at the time the most literate, best trained, and most carefully screened military force in the world, and they were intensely loyal to the crown and to the dynasty. Their commander sat in the imperial council as the principal military adviser to the sultan and as police chief of the imperial capital.

Murad III (1574–95) debased the Janissary units by doubling their size mostly with untrained free-born Muslims. Before the mid-seventeenth century the palace schools were gradually abandoned, and so, too, largely was the conscription of Christian youngsters. From elite troops the Janissaries were swiftly reduced to a privileged force of scarcely any military value. The Janissary commander, however, was almost invariably involved in the conspiracies for the making and breaking of sultans. Under the first ten Ottoman sultans, who ruled for some 270 years, the crown passed in vertical succession from father to son. The next twenty sultans, from Selim III (1566–74) and Mahmud II (1808–39), reigned for a total of 273 years, and the crown passed in each generation horizontally from brother to brother. In this period eight sultans abdicated, almost all forcibly, and half of these were murdered. In the conspiracies that led to the coups d'état, the princes who were designated sultans did not participate.

3

THE BEGINNINGS OF
MILITARY MODERNIZATION*

In the eighteenth century the European imperial powers began encroaching on the Muslim world. As the Mughal Empire crumbled in the first half of that century, France and then Britain began to pick up the pieces. Before the century's end, Britain, after virtually eliminating France as a rival, became the dominant power in the subcontinent. If, in Africa, Morocco escaped scot-free, it could be attributed to the state of advanced political decline of Portugal and Spain, while the remaining European maritime powers were distracted or, perhaps more correctly, attracted by the much greater opportunities farther afield in the Western Hemisphere and in Asia. The same distraction helped prolong the sovereignty, but not the territorial integrity, of the Ottoman and Persian empires.

European imperial encroachment was an uneven process. It started at the farthest end, moving southward toward or westward from the Indian Ocean rather than eastward across the Mediterranean. After France anchored itself on the Algerian shore in 1830, the spreading European domination of the Muslim world grew into an enveloping activity that reached its climax in the years between the two world wars of the twentieth century.

As the surviving Muslim regimes—Persia, the Ottoman Empire, Egypt (an Ottoman province that hovered on the brink of independence in the fifty years preceding the British occupation in 1882), and Morocco—came to recognize the transcendent power of the European states in the nineteenth century, they attributed it to military superiority. The Egyptian viceroy therefore tried to win his sovereignty, and the other Muslim rulers to uphold theirs, by employing Western military technicians and importing modern

---

* This chapter appeared in somewhat different form as "The Beginnings of Military Modernization in the Middle East: A Comparative Analysis," in *The Middle East Journal*, vol. 22 (Spring 1968), pp. 144–58.

weaponry. In their dependencies the European powers at times recruited natives for service in imperial armies and at others created local forces on the European model. Either way, by native initiative or by imperial action, military modernization was accelerated. Muslim military practices of the type that prevailed before the coming of European imperialism endured into the twentieth century. Such pockets of tradition survived almost intact beyond World War II in those countries least affected by the European incursion: Afghanistan, Saudi Arabia, Yemen, and Libya. Elsewhere, even after the start of military modernization, the newly independent Muslim states occasionally fell back on traditional practices in time of crisis, as in the mobilization of untrained irregulars by Arab states in the Palestine war of 1948 and by Morocco in its war with Algeria in 1963.

In so heterogeneous a region as the Middle East, whose peoples underwent such vastly differing experiences, the scope and the pace of change were bound to differ from locality to locality and from time to time. And everywhere in the Middle East, military modernization raised questions of organization, training, and supply that have not yet been resolved.

In many ways Mehmed Ali in Egypt undertook the most spectacular modernization in the Middle East before World War I. He appeared to have unlocked the puzzle of effective modernization, and this appearance later contributed to his downfall. But before we examine his failure, let us first explore his early triumphs.

"Integrated" Modernization in Egypt

Napoleon's seizure of Lower (northern) Egypt in mid-1798 from the Mamluk beys, the quasi-sovereign rulers of the Ottoman province, loosened their grip on the district. The French troops Napoleon left behind in 1799 capitulated two years later to a combined Anglo-Ottoman force and were allowed to return to France under the armistice terms. Following the British retirement in March 1803, three contenders moved into the military-political void: the surviving Mamluk beys (who were divided into two rival groups), the sultan's appointee as provincial governor, and the commander of the Albanian troops who was murdered within two months. The command fell to Mehmed Ali, a native of Macedonia and a onetime tobacco tradesman who had gone to Egypt in 1799, at the age of thirty, as a senior officer of the Albanian unit. With a combination of skill, courage, and unscrupulousness, the enterprising adventurer played one party off against the other, destroying each in turn; in June 1805 the Sublime Porte accredited him governor of Egypt, with the title of pasha.

The Albanian irregulars, profiting from the plunder they were allowed, became the pasha's loyal troops. In the next half-dozen years he established himself as master of Lower Egypt. He contrived in 1811 to ambush and murder many leading Mamluk commanders of Upper Egypt, a task his son finished in the following year. While consolidating his hold in Upper Egypt, Mehmed Ali also sent his Albanian troops to the Arabian Peninsula on the sultan's instructions, to break the power of the Wahhabiyah, a Muslim revivalist order whose warlike tribesmen were ravaging the sultan's provinces in Asia.[1] The slow progress of the campaign drained the enthusiasm of the Albanians. When Mehmed Ali in 1815 proposed modernization for the first time, the soldiers mutinied. But he persevered. Indeed, as early as 1809 he had begun sending to Europe, chiefly to the Italian city-states, small groups of Ottoman and Circassian students for officer instruction and for the study of shipbuilding, engineering, and printing. Late in 1816 he opened a preparatory school in Cairo for the military and general education of young Mamluks, whose ownership he had acquired after the removal of the beys.

After the victory in Arabia in 1818, Mehmed Ali was determined to replace his refractory Albanian forces with what he termed a *Nizam-i Cedid* (new system),[2] comprising freshly recruited officers and men who were to be organized and trained in the European manner. The original plan seemed simple enough. The European-trained Ottoman and Circassian officers would fill the top command slots and European instructors would work alongside. The young Mamluk graduates of the preparatory school in Cairo would provide candidates for further training as commissioned and non-commisioned officers. Captured Sudanese slaves would form the lowest ranks. Among other purposes, Mehmed Ali began the conquest of Sudan in 1820 to assure the plentiful supply of soldiers; but within three years he abandoned the further use of Sudanese slaves, because of the high mortality rate, and turned instead to press-gang conscription of *fallahin* (peasants) in Upper Egypt.

Mehmed Ali entrusted the training program to Joseph Sève, a former captain in the French army, who, after conversion to Islam, adopted the name of Süleyman and received the title of Ağa (commander). Aided by a handful of European instructors, mostly French and Italians, and by the Ottoman officers trained in Europe, Süleyman Ağa by the end of 1823 built the Nizam-i Cedid into a force of 24,000 officers and men, comprising six infantry regiments, with five battalions of 800 men each and equipped with French rifles. Mehmed Ali deployed the first regiment in the Arabian Peninsula, the second in Sudan, and the remaining four— under the command of his son Ibrahim—in Morea or southern Greece, on the urgent appeal of Sultan Mahmud II to help suppress the Greek rebellion.

Mehmed Ali, however, kept one battalion of each of three regiments in Egypt as the training nucleus for three new regiments. Because of the demands of the Greek war, the new Egyptian army expanded rapidly, with the sultan's sanction. Many more European instructors, civilian and military, were hired, mainly from France. By the summer of 1825 three more regiments were shipped to Morea, and the innovative provincial governor had placed his first orders in Italy and France for fully equipped naval vessels. Even before delivery of the French ships in July 1826, Mehmed Ali had already hired French technicians to help him organize a navy and instruct its officers and men.

Mehmed Ali began developing an elaborate military school system to produce officers for the infantry, artillery, cavalry, and navy and to furnish the armed forces with engineers, doctors, pharmacists, veterinarians, and even buglers. At the apex, a staff college gave promising officers advanced education in higher mathematics, physics, chemistry, and foreign languages (Arabic, Persian, and French), as well as strictly military subjects. Only Circassian Mamluks and Ottomans (among them Albanians, Kurds, and Greeks) qualified for command training, while at first Egyptian cadets were recruited wholly for the noncombatant services, which helps explain why Mehmed Ali did almost nothing for elementary and secondary education, for the Egyptians were graduates of traditional mosque schools and of al-Azhar, from which the religious leaders came. The only secondary institutions that the viceroy sponsored were the Mamluk preparatory school and a military high school for the sons of the ruler and of his principal aides. Though selectively trained in the 1830s for combat assignment, Egyptian officers were nevertheless not allowed to rise above the rank of major.

As part of the progressively more ambitious plans for military reorganization and expansion, and largely to pay for it, Mehmed Ali put into effect political, economic, and social reforms that cumulatively took the shape of a comprehensive development program. Mehmed Ali abolished the tax farms assigned to the beys, centralized the administration, reassigned the massive estates to relatives and retainers, and gave the peasants de facto title to small tracts of land. He had put to use his experience as a businessman when he formed his first commercial monopoly as early as 1808 to buy wheat from the fallahin and sell it to the British. Gradually he built up an inclusive monopoly over the external, and the related domestic, commerce of the province.

Spurred on by the empire-builder's impulse and the businessman's instincts, Mehmed Ali had the imagination to exploit opportunities and to plunge into industrial modernization as well. With the aid of foreign advisers, mostly from France, Mehmed Ali introduced in 1821 the cultivation of long-staple cotton, which prospered in the rich alluvial and sun-baked soil and which found an insatiable market in the spreading textile industries of England and France. To expand the area of cotton planting, channels for perennial irrigation were dug. To expedite the flow of exports and imports, the harbor of Alexandria was modernized and linked by canal to the Nile, thus facilitating communication between the interior cities and the province's major port. Mehmed Ali imported European machinery for the multiplying industries, which manufactured textiles, chemicals, sugar, leather, glass, and paper, as well as weapons and ammunition. He built foundries for the production of artillery, spare parts, and even simple industrial machinery. The total investment in manufacturing by 1838 was estimated at the equivalent of £12 million, and the number of industrial workers rose to well over 30,000, or more than 1 per cent of Egypt's population.

Meanwhile, Mehmed Ali continued adding to his armed forces. On behalf of the rebels in the Greek war, the naval units of Britain, France, and Russia shattered the combined Ottoman-Egyptian fleet, which included Mehmed Ali's entire navy, at Navarino in October 1827. With the return from Greece of the combat-hardened soldiers and sailors, the viceroy swiftly enlarged his army beyond all earlier levels and acquired for his navy new and larger ships, building many—including ships of the line mounting 100 guns or more—in his own dockyards with the aid of French advisers. When, at the end of 1831, he sent his son Ibrahim to seize Syria from Sultan Mahmud II, the Egyptian armed forces comprised close to 100,000 men. The sultan could not raise an adequate defense against such a formidable force, and by February 1833 the Egyptian troops pushed deep into Anatolia. Only Russian naval intervention, requested by the sultan, saved the Ottoman dynasty. Under the Ottoman-Egyptian settlement in May 1833

Mehmed Ali kept Syria (as the western Arab provinces north of the Arabian Peninsula were then known), conscripted its peasants into his army, and exploited its natural resources, particularly the trees for shipbuilding and for charcoal to make gunpowder. The start of the second Syrian war in 1839 threatened even greater disaster to the Ottoman dynasty than had the first.

The collective intervention in 1840–41 of the major European powers (except France) cut Mehmed Ali to provincial size. The powers stripped the viceroy of Crete, Syria, and Arabia, and put an end to his military and supporting economic modernization programs. The imposed settlement of 1841, to which France in the end reluctantly subscribed, compelled Mehmed Ali permanently to reduce his army to no more than 18,000 men, or less than one-tenth its prior maximum size, and prohibited him from building war vessels. But, above all, it put into effect in Egypt the Anglo-Ottoman commercial convention of 1838, under which the viceroy's monopolies of domestic and external commerce were abolished. Within a year the Egyptian industries, civilian and military, withered.

Thus, Mehmed Ali's plans for military and economic modernization ended in failure. Still, the over-all development thrust in the two decades preceding the intervention of the European concert in 1840 was remarkable, considering that it was taking place at roughly the same time as the opening stages of industrialization in Western Europe and the United States.

Mehmed Ali's initial success could be ascribed to a number of factors. Until the final reckoning in 1840–41, he enjoyed the almost continuous support of France, where most of his technical advisers came from. As an autocrat, he erased the line between his personal interest and the state interest. The personal monopolies became state monopolies, in effect, and the program as a whole took the form of state capitalism. Moreover, since decisions were exclusively his, he gave all projects—military, economic, and social—his personal attention and endowed the total with an inner consistency. He was an efficient, if also brutal, coordinator, and for so long as the European powers did not intrude he made his program work.

Mehmed Ali and his successors never recovered from the effects of the European intervention, although his grandson Isma'il came closest to emulating the dynasty's founder. Isma'il enlarged his army, with the sultan's approval, to an estimated 100,000 by 1870, in return for doubling the annual tribute to the Sublime Porte. Isma'il also pushed the Egyptian conquests deeper into Sudan with the aid chiefly of American officers—veterans of the Union and Confederate armies—employed to command as well as to instruct the troops. Despite the impressive growth of exports, particularly cotton, and the corresponding rise in foreign currency earnings in his reign, Isma'il borrowed heavily and at ruinous discounts and interest rates for his elaborate schemes of military, economic, and social modernization. As a result, Egyptian debts multiplied from an estimated £3 million in 1863 to nearly £100 million in 1879.

In that year the khedive, the title Isma'il assumed for himself in 1867, was deposed at the request of Britain and France, which came to exercise a dual control over Egypt's finances under the authority of a public-debt commission. The rigid economies of the controlling powers weighed most heavily on the Egyptians, particularly the civil servants and the military officers whose salaries were withheld for months at a time; their policy compounded the resentment of Egyptian officers and higher civil servants who were already chafing under the preferential treatment of Europeans employed by the government and of Ottomans and Circassians who constituted the bureaucratic and military elite. Egyptians were not allowed to fill the top civil service posts, and Egyptian officers could never receive a rank above that of colonel. In September 1881, a group of disgruntled officers under the leadership of Colonel Ahmad 'Urabi, an officer of fallah origin, staged a coup d'état and forced the khedive to appoint an all-Egyptian cabinet. In the months that followed, the Egyptian military-civilian coalition, by working toward the possible overthrow of the viceregal dynasty and the creation of a constitutional regime, and by giving evidence that foreign debts would be repudiated, achieved wide popularity. After mounting crisis, Britain finally backed into the occupation of Egypt in July 1882, without precipitating war in Europe. For more than sixty years thereafter Whitehall decided the fate of the Egyptian army.

Ottoman Modernization in a Closed Circuit

The Ottoman experience bore only a moderate resemblance to the Egyptian. The Egyptian program in its most flourishing phase under Mehmed Ali, whatever the secondary effects, was designed to fulfill only one purpose: to expand the military and political power of the empire-builder. By contrast, the Ottoman program was framed to save a contracting empire and its aging dynasty. Both had to uproot the inherited systems before the imported ones could become workable. What Napoleon began by assaulting the Mamluk institution, Mehmed Ali finished by wiping it out altogether only to discover that he had to wipe out his own Ottoman force as well. The job took precisely two decades to complete. In the Ottoman Empire the beginnings of the assault on the Janissaries and on the provincial feudal cavalry are hard to date. Two things are clear: The Ottoman Empire had borrowed military technology and technicians from Europe all along; and in the period of Ottoman decline, when such exchanges grew steadily feebler, particularly in the eighteenth century, each scattered effort to graft European practices on the fossilizing Ottoman military establishment could be viewed as an attack on that establishment.

Until the 1790s such efforts focused almost wholly on the development of an artillery corps and on the production of cannon, with marginal attention also to improving the instruction of naval officers. The experiment of Selim III (1789–1807) with the Nizam-i Cedid undeniably represented the first attempt to fashion a Europeanized army, and it is often hailed as the effective beginning of Ottoman modernization. Yet the Nizam-i Cedid, begun quietly in 1792, ended in disaster less than a decade and a half later, thanks to the determination of the Janissaries (with the help of the ulema) to save their institutional skins. The break with the past thus did not occur until Sultan Mahmud II (1808–39) destroyed the Janissary corps in 1826 and, five years later, the remaining tax-exempt *timars*, or military fiefs, on which the dynasty had relied since the beginnings of the empire for *sipahis*, or provincial cavalry. On paper, Mahmud had reached the stage of durable innovation in 1831, about a dozen years later than had his Egyptian vassal. Like Mehmed Ali before him, Mahmud began sending army and navy cadets to Europe for training as early as 1827, but the total number remained small in his reign. On their return, a few became instructors in the officer training "schools" that the sultan opened in and around Istanbul with the aid of European technicians, chiefly from Britain, Prussia, and Austria.

Significantly, Mahmud sent no civilians to Europe for technical training, since he sponsored no economic development projects. He was economically hobbled, even in the predominantly Muslim districts, by an imperial and dynastic tradition that reserved the commerce of the empire for the non-Muslim minorities and for the European factors resident in the principal ports and interior trading centers. The imperial government raised revenue not by developing the economy but by raising the taxes, which meant raising the payments exacted from the provincial tax farmers, who in turn exacted more and more arbitrary payments from the sultan's subjects. The modernization program in the Ottoman Empire was essentially a program for the modernization of the government: the armed forces, the diplomatic service, the bureaucracy (or imperial administration), the judiciary, education, and, as the century wore on, communications.

Even if the urge to develop the Ottoman economy had sharpened after 1840, that urge would have come too late. By then the European powers had, by concerted intervention, harnessed the Ottoman and Egyptian agricultural economies to the industrializing European economies, with the familiar pattern of commerce based on the exchange of raw materials for industrial goods. As a result, in the Ottoman Empire even more than in Egypt the emergence of domestic industry and of a Muslim middle class was checked. Instead, non-Muslim minorities and the enlarging European resident communities performed middle-class functions. The absence of economic reform in the Ottoman Empire thus closed the circuit of innovation. The new secular educational system promoted primarily the interests of the new class of military officers, civil (imperial) servants, diplomats, and teachers who by 1870 formed a new urban educated elite. Their influence in domestic politics outlived the empire and, indeed, the First Republic.

In the Ottoman Empire it was Mahmud II who created the necessary conditions for durable change. Driven to reorganize the armed forces, Mahmud was nevertheless denied the time to do the job well. The last decade of his reign was a period when the Eastern Question became murky, when his quarrel with Mehmed Ali interlocked with another over Ottoman affairs between Russia and Britain, with Austria supporting Russia, and France Mehmed Ali. Faced with this awesome menace from within and without, the sultan accelerated the speed of military change.

By 1837 the sultan had brought into being twenty-five regular regiments of four battalions each, totalling roughly 40,000 men and comprising fifteen regiments of infantry, six of cavalry, three of artillery, and one of engineers. Almost an equal number of reserves was also available, enabling the sultan for the first time to call up trained men instead of having to fall back, as in the past, on untrained and undisciplined irregulars. The primary obstacle was the paucity of new officers, despite training schools inherited from Selim and the new ones Mahmud opened. Yet the standards of instruction were much lower than those in Egypt, and the graduates too few for the duties given them, especially with the two Syrian crises of the 1830s. Nevertheless, Mahmud laid the foundation of a new officer-training system, under European technical direction, that educated the cadets along European lines using French as the language of instruction. He enlarged the navy and expanded the naval officer school. By the end of his reign, his warships equalled Russia's Black Sea fleet in number. As in the past, a British naval mission supervised the naval training program.

Meanwhile, in desperation, Mahmud also resuscitated Selim III's abortive experiment in reciprocal continuous diplomacy. One of the first fruits of the new diplomacy was Ottoman participation in the European settlement of 1841, which guaranteed the sultan his sovereignty and relieved his regime of anxiety over its survival, as distinct from continuing anxiety over its territorial integrity. As part payment for the reintegration of his domain, the sultan had to accept what amounted to Europe's collective custodianship over his realm. Nor were the concert's guarantees empty ones in the early years of Ottoman reciprocity. This was amply demonstrated by the Anglo-French intervention (1854–56) on the Ottoman side in the Crimean War and the pressure on France to withdraw its troops from Lebanon in 1861.

An unplanned benefit of the new diplomacy was the discovery of talented Muslims who, after roving diplomatic apprenticeships in the major capitals of Europe, came back to Istanbul to take charge of the nonmilitary reform projects. Of greater long-range significance was the early rivalry between the devotees of civilian reform and those of military reform. The first civilian reformers could observe European institutions and practices directly. The first military reformers could not. They were chosen, not because of special competence in the reforms they were expected to inspire and to manage, but because of loyalty to the crown. Husrev Paşa, the first (1827–36) to hold the office of *Serasker* (commander in chief and principal military adviser to the sultan), was illiterate and his successor underwent no advance training for the office. While primarily dedicated to the nonmilitary program, the civilian modernizers did not resist the reorganization of the armed forces. Until after the Crimean War, however, the military modernizers who flourished under reactionary grand vezirs, particularly in 1841–45 and 1852–53, vigorously opposed civilian reforms. As a result, the *Tanzimat*, as the modernization program was known, bifurcated, with the military and the civilians each going their separate ways. By the early 1870s, when the modernization process had become self-perpetuating, two discrete types of leadership had emerged, producing for the first time in Ottoman history a civilian bureaucracy.

The first schools to appear were the officer-training schools for the armed forces and "professional" schools for civil servants. The several officer-training facilities in and around Istanbul were fused into a single *Mekteb-i Harbiye* (War College) in 1846. Many instructors were European and the cadets in the two-year cycle, in addition to the usual military courses, studied mathematics and foreign languages (French from the outset and, after the mid-1880s, also German). Starting in 1848, general staff officers were also admitted to the War College for their own course of study. The corresponding institution for training civil servants for employment in the imperial (or provincial) administration was the *Mekteb-i Mülkiye* (Civil Service College), founded in 1859 after two decades of experimentation with other institutional types.

Not until 1869 did the Sublime Porte approve the plan for a comprehensive network of primary and secondary schools throughout the empire. The number of cadets graduating from the Harbiye multiplied from an annual average of about 25 in the 1840s to more than 100 in the 1870s and some 500 at the turn of the century. The first class to leave the Mülkiye in 1861 numbered 33; the graduating class 25 years later had risen to nearly 400, and three-fourths of them were boarders, signifying that they had come from the provinces. More and more jobs opened up in the imperial service following the provincial reorganization. A quarter-century in the making, the new scheme was embodied in the vilayet law of 1864, which standardized and centralized the administration. The imperial government appointed the officials at all levels, who, with the exception of those in the villages, were viewed as part of the bureaucracy.

The armed forces were reorganized and enlarged under successive laws. The first comprehensive law in 1843 laid down that the army would comprise five corps. The imperial guard and one other corps were deployed in Istanbul, and the others in Rumelia, Anatolia, and the Arab Asian provinces. A sixth corps, created in 1848, was assigned to Baghdad. The infantry, cavalry, and engineer units were structured on French models, and the artillery on Prussian. By 1850 there were 150,000 officers and men in the army, 10,000 in the navy, and nearly 100,000 in the army reserves. Under the law of 1869, all branches of the army were reshaped along German lines. In conjunction with the envisioned reconquest of Yemen, a seventh army corps was created and stationed there. The armed forces were steadily expanded, so that in the war with Russia of 1877–78 the sultan could place in the field 750,000 men. Moreover, Sultan Abdülaziz took a special interest in the navy, which he steadily enlarged until it was reputed at the close of his reign in 1876 to be the third most powerful in the world. This was a dubious distinction, since naval vessels at that time became obsolescent soon after they were commissioned. The large navy simply encumbered the Sublime Porte with high expenditures for purchase and upkeep, because Ottoman dockyards could no longer produce modern warships. Non-Muslims, in theory, were subject to conscription as early as 1856 when the *cizye* (military exemption tax) was abolished; but they were not in fact inducted until 1909. Quite apart from the mutual hostility that separated the religious communities, the Sublime Porte was unwilling to give non-Muslims military training for fear that they might use the skills in the nationalist movements for independence in their provinces.

The more the urban educated elite imitated Europe, the more they tried to centralize the imperial administration and to modernize the armed forces. The more they succeeded, the more they became aware of their failure, for the models that they followed became antiquated before the Ottoman modernizers could put their versions into effect. Thus at each stage of military development, on the eve of the promulgation of each new major law between 1843 and 1909, the proponents of the legislation called attention to the urgent need for reorganizing the armed forces. In 1876, when for the first time in nearly seventy years coups d'état occurred (two sultans being replaced within three months), significantly it was the new urban educated elite, civilians and soldiers, who staged them. Moreover, because of greater political experience, the civilians were the senior partners of the civilian-military coalitions.

Abdülhamid's countercoup restored the sultan's absolute rule early in 1878, and he kept it for three full decades. Under a repressive regime, he continued to modernize the armed forces, the bureaucracy, and the foreign service. No powers were delegated to his vezirs who were reduced from policy-making to policy-management. The junior military officers who took the lead in creating the Committee of Union and Progress which staged the overturn of the repressive Hamidian regime in 1908 did not themselves seek direct power, but preferred to undergo a period of apprenticeship. They too started out as junior partners in a civilian-military coalition. After suppressing the counterrevolution in April 1909, the military officers gradually seized power and held it through World War I. In theory, the officers had reinstated the constitution of 1876, with its provision in amendments for a parliamentary regime. In practice, the military officers had instituted their own form of military authoritarianism.

Although the Ottoman Empire had acquired a modernized army and navy by the eve of World War I, it could hardly be claimed that Ottoman military capability had become self-generative. For all heavy equipment and for warships the Sublime Porte had become more dependent than ever on European sources of supply. Still, by contrast with Persia and Morocco, Ottoman military modernization was substantial.

Marginal Modernizers in Persia and Morocco

Persia and Morocco, like the Ottoman Empire, turned to military modernization for defense and survival. Since Persia lay in the path of Anglo-Russian advance, the shahdom came perilously close to losing its sovereignty in 1907, when an Anglo-Russian convention divided the country into spheres of influence. Five years later, Morocco became a protectorate, with France getting the lion's share and Spain most of the rest and the city of Tangier set aside as an international enclave. Whereas Mehmed Ali and Mahmud II had to destroy the traditional military structures before undertaking modernization, the Persian and Moroccan monarchs of the nineteenth century continued to rely, as in the past, principally on tribal forces. The very existence of such forces impeded military modernization.

The start of military modernization in Persia is usually ascribed to 'Abbas Mirza, the crown prince in the first third of the nineteenth century and governor of the province of Azarbayjan, whose modern force was intended to defend Persia against Russia. During the short-lived alliance between France and Persia (1807–8), the training program was entrusted to a French military mission, but Napoleon's failure to support Persia against Russia abruptly ended the mission.

Under the renewed Anglo-Persian alliance in 1809, British officers and NCOs were reassigned from India as advisers to 'Abbas, primarily for training infantry and artillery. Britain also furnished modern weapons and munitions, and British technicians built and ran a foundry at Tabriz for making guns and powder. By 1815 the new force was said to number some 12,000 infantry, recruited chiefly among the tribes, in addition to a brigade of cavalry with about 1,200 men, and a unit of horse-drawn artillery equipped with twenty field pieces. 'Abbas Mirza sent a few young Persians to England for study and training, but only after 1845 did the practice of sending young men to Europe for professional education become standard, although their numbers remained small.

When Persia and Britain broke diplomatic relations in mid-1836, following a Persian attack on Herat (Afghanistan), Britain suspended military aid to Persia and did not resume it until the eve of World War I. Apart from individual British officers who remained in the private employ of the shah, the Persian government turned to the Italian city-states, France, Austria-Hungary, and Russia for military advisers. The Italians, who reached Persia in 1852, remained for about a dozen years. Austria sent two separate missions, one in the 1850s consisting chiefly of noncombatant technicians, and a somewhat larger mission in the 1880s to assist the shah in creating a force, no larger than 6,000 men, organized in seven battalions for duty in western Iran. Meanwhile, a small mission from France with fewer than a dozen men apparently accomplished little in the two years (1859–61) that it served the shah. Many of the European officers were used as instructors in the *Dar al-Funun* (polytechnic institute), founded in 1852. The forerunner of the University of Tehran, the Dar al-Funun remained the principal officer-training school until the opening of a durable military academy in 1885, also staffed in part by European officers.

The first modernized formation that took root was the Persian Cossack Brigade, and even that force developed haltingly. Begun in 1879 with Russian assistance, the regiments of the brigade consisted on paper in 1891 of an estimated 1,800 officers and men. In fact, however, it numbered fewer than 300, all *muhajirs* (immigrants), descendants of Transcaucasian Muslims who had resettled in Persia at the beginning of the nineteenth century and who were reassigned as a detachment from a "regular" cavalry unit. The handful of Russian officers and NCOs, who served as instructors and commanders, still belonged to the tsar's forces, although they were in the shah's pay. The Russian personnel in 1906–7 included one colonel, one major, two captains, and six sergeants. By then the Persian Cossacks may have numbered as many as 1,200. For more than a decade and a half, their only activity consisted of drill and parade. Following the assassination of Nasir al-Din Shah (1848–96) in May 1896, the brigade became essentially an imperial guard for protecting the monarch and the dynasty. When Muhammad 'Ali Shah tried by counterrevolution, with the support of the

Persian Cossacks and a contingent of Russian troops, to abrogate the constitution of 1906 and to dissolve the Majlis (legislature) for which it provided, Bakhtiyari tribal troops marched on Tehran compelling the shah to abdicate in favor of his son Ahmad (1909–25). Indeed, the irregular tribal cavalry, enlisted as needed with little or no drill or discipline, remained more powerful than the Cossack Brigade until World War I.

Conceived as a paramilitary establishment, the gendarmerie, or provincial police, financed by Britain and instructed by Swedish officers, was created in 1911. The so-called Swedish gendarmerie, by the outbreak of war three years later, numbered about 3,000 officers and men and, as a fighting force, was superior to the Cossack Brigade. The gendarmerie was assimilated in November 1916 into the South Persia Rifles, who were recruited, trained, and commanded by British officers and sustained by British subsidies.

Mirza Husayn Khan, educated in Europe and an experienced diplomat, was appointed Grand Vezir in 1872. In manifest imitation of Ottoman practice in modernization, he created discrete ministries and named himself to the new post of *Sipahsalar A'zam*, or minister of war and commander in chief of the army. But his efforts to civilianize the provincial administration were less successful, principally because no provision was made, as in Istanbul, for separate training facilities for the army and for the civil service.

In Morocco, Mawlay 'Abd al-Rahman (1822–59), after defeat by the French forces in Algeria in 1843, recognized the need to create a modern army. No action, however, appears to have been taken until after his son Muhammad IV (1859–73) ascended the throne. An edict of 18 July 1861 called for comprehensive military reorganization, and the basic technical assistance was eventually entrusted to French officers. The creation of the *'asker*, or standing army on the European model, reduced the political influence of the most important gish leaders. The 'asker resembled the Cossack Brigade in forming a force for protecting the royal family.

At the same time, Mawlay Muhammad also tried to reorganize the gish tribes on a more rational basis. The tribal troops were divided, in theory, into regiments (500 men), companies (100 men), and groups (20 men) of standard size and were given a modicum of formal drill. The tribal forces continued to excel in horsemanship and constituted the best cavalry in the kingdom. The mkhaznis, or gish soldiers, eligible for service in the military-civilian bureaucracy, could rise to the highest posts; the pasha of the Bwakhir served as governor of Meknes, and the pasha of one of the Sheraga tribes as governor of New Fez.

The Widening Technological Gap

The experience of Egypt and the Ottoman Empire with military modernization demonstrated that effective change could not take place until the traditional military institutions were substantially extirpated. Neither Persia nor Morocco freed itself from the grip of its tribal forces. Military modernization in each consisted chiefly in creating a small Europeanized unit of elite troops with the explicit mission of safeguarding the dynasty. The two monarchies also tried to rationalize the structure of their tribal forces, to update the weaponry, and to give the tribesmen the benefit of formal drill. But the recurrent efforts were short-lived and the cumulative results marginal. From reliance on such informal, undisciplined, and largely uncoordinated forces, the shift to a unified army required the taming of the tribesmen. This goal was not reached in Persia until the rise, after World War I, of a single-minded military leader who, though establishing a new dynasty in the traditional manner, nevertheless used his office to modernize the army. Morocco had to wait until it regained sovereignty in 1956. The European imperial masters had earlier broken the military power of the tribes once and for all in the process of "pacifying" the protectorate.

The modernizing armies in the Middle East, meanwhile, were shooting at moving targets. The very armies that were serving as models were themselves swiftly changing, as Western Europe became steadily more industrialized. The Egyptian experiment might have become self-generative if left to run its course in a Middle East setting free from any European threat. But the European powers, after the start of the French conquest of Algeria in 1830, had begun to close in on the Middle East, and against the rapidly industrializing states of Europe no Middle East dynastic state could have been expected to hold its own. As late as the second quarter of the nineteenth century the issue was still blurred. The industrial revolution had not yet overtaken the manufacture of military weapons. The technological gap, in brief, was still a civilian gap. Thus, with the advisory aid of European engineers, Mehmed Ali could construct foundries for the manufacture of cannon, plants for the manufacture of rifles and ammunition, and even dockyards for the building of warships. The end products were probably as good, or almost as good, as weapons and vessels made in Europe.

The breakthrough in military industry occurred after mid-century, starting during the Crimean War (1853–56). The switch from immobile to increasingly mobile artillery, from fixed gun tubes to those equipped with cradle suspension and automatic recoil mechanisms, from round ball to elongated projectiles, from inaccurate single-shot small arms to machine guns and repeating rifles, from densely smoking to smokeless powder, from pigeons and fire-signallers and personal messengers to telegraph and telephone, from horse-drawn vehicles and animal-pack carriage of supplies to bulk and rapid transport by railroad, from sail to steam in naval propulsion, and from wood to iron and then to even tougher steel in naval construction—all these changes, and many more, began to revolutionize military industry in the second half of the nineteenth century. As a major consequence, the rapidly changing military industry in Europe progressively shortened the life-span of each new generation of weaponry. The Middle East rulers could no longer realistically hope to catch up with military technology in Europe. They might buy modern weapons, but they could not be certain that their troops would use them easily. No longer could the Middle East rulers hope either to manufacture the proliferating family of weapons or to stand alone in the increasingly complex industrializing world.

The revolution in weapons and weapons technology accelerated the changes in the type, the size, and the organization of European armies. Indeed, such changes had antedated the military industrial revolution; but the revolution quickened the tempo. Mercenary troops had finally disappeared by the close of the eighteenth century and large standing armies, either professional or cadre-conscript, became the norm. These were highly trained, strictly disciplined, and intensely nationalistic armies. By the early nineteenth century, moreover, the combat forces consisted chiefly of infantry supported by cavalry and artillery. The Middle East armies at that time were for the most part degenerate versions of armies that once had thrived on *ad hoc* enlistments in time of crisis and that relied almost exclusively on cavalry, with only marginal artillery support and almost no infantry. Meanwhile, after mid-century, the service troops in European armies became progressively more elaborate to include such special branches as communications, engineering, medicine, supplies, and finance, while the commanding staffs became more and more professional. As the European models grew steadily more intricate, the armies in the Middle East lagged farther and farther behind.

Military modernization in the Middle East in the nineteenth century thus raised many problems. Even if the industrial states of Europe were willing to share their military technology, the Muslim dynastic states could not have mastered the new skills without simultaneously changing their societies and their economies. In Europe the scientific revolution had preceded the industrial revolution, which, in turn, had preceded its application to the needs of war. In the Middle East the military modernizers were trying to reverse the process. Even when the process works in reverse, the rates of diffusion differ. Still, it has become fashionable among scholars to claim that modernizing armies in pre-industrial and industrializing societies invariably become agents of economic, social, and political modernization. The claim rests on the premise that the skills developed in the care, use, and repair of modern weapons are transferable to nonmilitary economic and social purposes in the society at large—in brief, that "a new soldier" becomes "a new man" in the nonindustrial states. It also rests on the further premise that many military investments in overhead, such as road construction, harbor improvement, airport development, and the introduction of new communications systems, cater also to nonmilitary purposes—in brief, that military investment in overhead almost always contributes to economic and social development. This thesis, as we shall see in subsequent chapters, has had only limited and variable validity.

In view of the widening technological gap, it is less relevant to evaluate military modernization in the Middle East on Western than on local standards. Any assessment made on the basis of the performance of the European models is bound to show the achievement in the Middle East in a poor light. A more meaningful measurement can be made by considering the contrast with the performance of the displaced armies. Whatever the mode of military assessment, modernizing Middle East armies transformed the conditions and the consequences of military politics, although the results were far from uniform in the several Middle East states.

One result, however, seemed almost universal. The Middle East states in the nineteenth century commonly sought military aid from more than one European supplier. As early as the 1830s, Helmuth von Moltke, then a junior Prussian officer in Ottoman employ, described the modernizing Ottoman army as one founded "on the European model with Russian jackets, French regulations,

Belgian weapons, Turkish caps, Hungarian saddles, English swords, and instructors from all nations." [3] "In addition to the Russian officers," wrote a British authority on Persia late in the century,

> relics of the successive waves of foreign military importation . . . still survive in Persia in 1891 in the person of seven Austrian officers, six of whom are generals, and one a major, a French bandmaster dignified with the rank of a general, an Italian and a Bulgarian chief of instructors, an Italian head of police, and two Prussian officers, acting as professors in the Royal College. This is the flotsam and jetsam that the receding tide of polyglot military influence has left stranded upon the dubious shore-line of Teheran.[4]

A French specialist described the modernization effort in Morocco at the turn of the century as consisting "of a regiment commanded by an English officer, of a French mission of military instruction, of a factory of arms at Fas directed by an Italian officer and of the building at Rabat of a fort by a German engineer." [5] The importation of instructors and of weapons from many European countries undoubtedly compounded the confusion of modernization in each Middle East state. Yet the reasons for the practice were primarily political. It was precisely because European technological superiority had become an instrument for subordination of the technologically backward states, particularly in the age of European imperial expansion, that the Middle East rulers tried to protect themselves by seeking military assistance from many European powers rather than from only one.

4

EUROPEAN IMPERIAL STYLES

Military modernization in the Middle East between the wars took place, for the most part, under alien rule. The Middle East in 1965 comprised eighteen sovereign states; forty years earlier there had been no more than five. Indeed, European imperial influence in the Islamic world reached full sway in the three decades between 1914 and 1945. World War I and the peace settlement finally destroyed the Ottoman Empire, and its non-Turkish Asian provinces became European dependencies. The Fertile Crescent plus Egypt and Sudan in adjacent northeast Africa represented essentially a British preserve with only a marginal French presence in mandated Syria and Lebanon; northwest Africa, essentially a French preserve with only a marginal Spanish presence in Morocco and an international presence in the city of Tangier. Libya, which fell between the two, became the sole Italian colony in the Middle East.

The only Middle East states to escape European rule at the time were located in Asia. For three years, Turkish nationalists had to fight against France, Italy, and British-backed Greece to rescue Turkish-speaking Anatolia from the expiring polyglot empire and to reintegrate it. A military coup d'état in February 1921 enabled Iran to escape an unequal alliance with Britain. Afghanistan also managed to wrest full liberty over external affairs from an exhausted and overextended Britain. Two other states were just emerging to independence in the Arabian Peninsula: Yemen and what was to become Saudi Arabia. Both were embryonic traditional dynastic monarchies, and both asserted their sovereignty on the disappearance of Ottoman authority. Both were inward-looking, and before 1939 their external interests hardly reached beyond the peninsula. Not until 1926 did either state win its first European recognition, the still expanding Saudi kingdom from the U.S.S.R. and Yemen from Italy.

The sovereign states enjoyed freedom of accepting or rejecting foreign military aid. Until the eve of World War II, Saudi Arabia felt little need for military modernization and did not actively seek it. After all, King 'Abd al-'Aziz conquered most of the peninsula with tribal forces and in 1934 easily defeated Yemen, in the one interwar challenge. Imam Yahya of Yemen desired limited quantities of modern light weapons, but turned his back on offers that Fascist Italy thrust upon him, for he was supremely suspicious of outside help and hesitated to enter into intimate relations with any single European power. Instead, he sent officer candidates to Baghdad for training in the 1930s, soon after the mandate's end, when Iraq took over the management of its army. In the north, Turkey, Iran, and Afghanistan dealt with many European suppliers to avoid heavy dependence on any one, thus continuing the practice of the nineteenth century. While Iran's Reza Shah sent officer candidates chiefly to France but also to Germany and the Soviet Union for training, Afghanistan preferred to entrust the training of its army officers to a Turkish military mission, though for the creation of an air force, the Afghan monarchy successively enlisted the aid of the major European powers.

In military dealings with Europe there was a marked distinction between the sovereign states and the dependencies. In the latter, the army became a symbol of future independence and a possible instrument for winning it. Nationalists were therefore prone to demand the creation of armies where none existed or, where such armies were already in being, the nationalization of their officer corps. For the same reasons the imperial powers were reluctant to relinquish the military controls. The native army thus tended to become a focus of dispute between an imperial power and its ward. Such disputes were bound to differ in intensity, and often in kind, from country to country in view of the heterogeneity of the Middle East.

Alien political institutions, on the other hand, were being fashioned under alien rule, and these in time influenced the course of military politics. Among the new trends in the interwar years was the appearance of the Islamic republic. Turkey, the first such republic in the Middle East to survive, did not arise under alien rule but in rejection of it. The Turkish nationalists, having destroyed the imperial government on the eve of the Lausanne conference in November 1922, enshrined their provisional republican institutions in a formal constitution promulgated in 1924, just after the dissolution of the caliphate. The four other sovereign states were dynastic monarchies in the traditional image. Among the dependencies, however, the republican movement was unmistakable, even though in some instances the institutions were still rudimentary. Syria and Lebanon under French mandate became incipient republics. Palestine, too, seemed likely to grow into a republic, if it were ever to become sovereign—an outcome less from imperial design than from the rationally insoluble quarrel of Arabs and Jews over the political future of the country. Sudan's status turned obscure after 1924, when Britain took over sole management of the Anglo-Egyptian condominium and expressly withdrew Egyptians from the military units and the administrative service. As part of metropolitan France, Algeria was being republicanized, even though its political future remained in doubt as late as 1945.

Meanwhile, the technological gap between the industrial and the nonindustrial states was steadily widening. The European powers generally assumed in the interwar years that they had come to the Middle East to stay. European military technology between the wars, admittedly, was not innovative: the industrial powers were still trying to recover from the depletion of their human and natural resources in World War I, and the majority of the people in the victorious democratic countries seemed to favor disarmament and small armies. In any case, even without innovation, the industrial powers still had to assimilate the new weapons systems invented in World War I. The tank, the airplane, the ever larger and more mobile guns had not passed beyond the experimental stage by 1918. As the automobile, the truck, the telephone and the radio were being adapted to military use, they were changing the structure and the military doctrines of the armed forces in industrial countries. Thus, despite the slowdown of innovative research and engineering in the interwar years, the newfangled gadgetry was steadily improved. Tanks became heavier and more efficient and were equipped with more powerful engines. Military aircraft also gained in versatility and speed. The inability of any Middle East country to produce such sophisticated equipment lulled the European imperial powers into a state of complacent superiority, reinforcing their assumption that their influence in the area would continue indefinitely into the future.

There was thus no direct threat from the dependencies, merely annoyance which grew more stubborn as the nationalists organized in one Middle East country after another. Only rival European powers could challenge British and French hegemony. Despite its expansionist Communist ideology, Soviet Russia pursued a defensive policy in the interwar Middle East. The U.S.S.R. remained sensitive to the presence of major powers in the neighborhood as a potential danger to Soviet security. In the very first treaty that Communist Russia concluded in 1921 with Persia, as Iran was then known, it was expressly laid down (Article 6) that third powers would be prohibited from using the kingdom as a base of operations against Russia; and that if the Persian government, following Russian notification, could not prevent it, Russia reserved the right to move "troops into the Persian interior for the purpose of carrying out the military operations necessary for . . . [Russian] defence." [1] This was the first of a cluster of treaties that the U.S.S.R. framed between the wars with its next-door Muslim neighbors to reconstruct, as in an earlier century, a buffer separating the Russian and British empires. The Soviet Union also sent diplomatic missions to Saudi Arabia and Yemen late in the 1920s but gave the new states no military aid. Elsewhere the imperial powers simply excluded the Soviet Union from any kind of formal relationship, even consular.

More serious was the competition from Italy and Germany, particularly after the mid-1930s. The zone of free competition consisted of the contiguous sovereign states in the Asian Middle East, but none of these states seemed willing to play the game of attaching itself to a single European supplier. Elsewhere, military aid took the form of gun-running to nationalists, and the Arab East seemed to offer the challengers the most attractive possibility. But, in retrospect, neither Italy nor Germany really succeeded in the interwar years in undermining the military supremacy of either Britain or France.

Britain and France employed differing styles of military aid in the dependencies. Britain modernized the military structures, while France modernized the soldiers.

The British Wards

Britain's military development policies in its Middle East dependencies were far from uniform. They were, it is true, inspired by the Indian experience, but that experience was itself long and varied. Natives were recruited in the seventeenth century for the defense of company property, and in the eighteenth for the acquisition and subsequent defense of an incipient empire. In the nineteenth century, natives in the Anglo-Indian forces were employed for the extension and consolidation of that empire and for the defense of British possessions beyond the subcontinent, and in the twentieth for helping Britain win two world wars. The structure of the Anglo-Indian army meanwhile underwent parallel changes. Until the end of the nineteenth century the native recruits were organized into three presidency armies. After the sepoy rebellion of 1857, which had as one consequence the termination of the East India Company and the transfer of administrative responsibility to the crown, certain "races" were declared "martial" and thus eligible for service in the armed forces. Among the "nonmartial races" were the Bengalis, whose sepoys had run amok. The exclusion of Bengalis after 1857 basically shaped the Pakistan army 90 years later, since almost all soldiers inherited by the new Muslim state were West Pakistanis, and even there the "martial races" were basically Punjabis and Pathans. The presidency armies, in the interim, had been dissolved and a single Anglo-Indian army created in their place. This program was carried out in the dozen years before World War I. In both world wars, the Indianization of the officer corps was pressed forward.

The date of introduction of the Indian precedents into a Middle East country thus influenced the policy that Britain pursued. Clearly, the Indian precedents of the 1880s, when Britain took over management of Egyptian military affairs, differed from those in the 1920s, when Britain created armies in Iraq and Sudan, and these in turn from those in World War II when Britain formed armies for Transjordan, Libya, and the Jewish National Home in Palestine. Moreover, because the Middle East itself was so heterogeneous and the circumstances of conquest so varied, local realities had to be accommodated, and the accommodations were reflected in the policies.

By 1914 the Anglo-Indian army had become a unified force, with a peacetime strength of the fighting units slightly in excess of 150,-000 in all ranks. Some 2,000 British officers and NCOs held the top positions. Under the pressure of the demands in World War I, close to 900,000 Indians entered into active service, and half of them were sent abroad. The very size of the contribution to the imperial war effort gave the nationalists an opportunity to demand the Indianization of the officer ranks. Previously, Indian officers qualified for viceroy commissions only. Before the war's end they became eligible for honorary king's commissions as captains and second lieutenants. Immediately after the war the policy was inaugurated of annually selecting ten Indians as cadets for training at Sandhurst for king's commissions. Still, Indianization slowed down between the wars, as the small peacetime army, fixed at 200,000 officers and men, was largely neglected along with the neglect of the ground forces in Britain itself.

Anglo-Indian troops had been used in World War I in the conquest of Mesopotamia, as Iraq was then known, and British officers from that army were later seconded to the military mission that was charged with creating the Iraqi army. Iraq was one of the Class A mandates that Britain acquired after World War I. Article 22 of the Covenant of the League of Nations stipulated that the mandatory power was to lead its ward to self-government. From the start of the civil administration in 1920, Iraqi nationalists began to request a national army. Because of nationalist opposition, the British officers formally relinquished executive responsibility but in reality exercised strong informal influence on organization, training, and policy. The first Iraqi officer recruits were veterans of the former Ottoman army and graduates of the staff college in Istanbul. The British military mission in 1924 founded a military college for the training of Iraqi cadets and four years later a staff school for higher officers. By then, the initial steps had also been taken to establish an air force. The first five cadets were sent to the RAF college in England for pilot training, while twenty volunteers from local technical schools were assigned to the RAF units in Iraq for training as mechanics. The British mission under the mandate never exceeded forty officers, headed by a major general.

More closely analogous to the Indian model was the Sudan Defense Force (SDF), which came into being in January 1925. Until then, Sudanese units formed an integral part of the Egyptian army. All Egyptian formations and their Egyptian officers had been withdrawn from Sudan immediately after the murder in the preceding November of Sir Lee Stack, the British *sirdar* (commander) of the Egyptian army. The Sudanese troops remaining behind were then reorganized as the Sudan Defense Force, which from the outset the British kept at a peacetime strength of just under 5,000 NCOs and privates and fewer than 100 commissioned officers. All the command positions were vested in some 70 British officers. Mechanization began as early as 1926–27 with the formation of motorized machine-gun batteries. Each SDF company was commanded by two officers, seconded from the British army. Native officers received governor-general's commissions, some by promotion from the ranks and others after training as cadets under a special program. Enlistment in the force was voluntary, but recruitment took place chiefly in the Arab provinces, where 80 per cent of the personnel came from; the others were pagan tribesmen from the three southern provinces.

In Palestine, where the complexities of the Arab-Zionist dispute precluded the promotion of self-governing institutions, the British nevertheless created a local force that was designed to provide quasi-military services to the mandatory with non-nationalist regional manpower. This was accomplished by the establishment in 1926 of the Transjordan Frontier Force (TJFF), as a replacement for the Palestine gendarmerie. Financed and managed by the Palestine government, the TJFF was commanded by British officers and organized along British army lines. It comprised at first three cavalry squadrons and one camel squadron and was conceived as supplement to the Arab Legion (or police force) of Transjordan and to the Palestine police. It was called at the time the "Foreign Legion" of the Fertile Crescent, since it included Muslim and Christian Arabs from Palestine and Transjordan, Jews, Druzes, Circassians, Sudanese, Armenians, Greeks, Indians, and Egyptians, and even German and Russian residents of the mandate. Each company was commanded by a British major with a British captain as second in command; by 1934 there were twenty-four British officers under the command of a lieutenant-colonel. The TJFF was gradually mechanized in the 1930s but always kept small, consisting in the mid-1930s of some 750 privates and about 100 NCOs. Border patrol duties apart, the force was given primarily a domestic security mission. Meanwhile in Transjordan, British officers also commanded the Arab Legion, a paramilitary force charged with domestic police duties. In 1938 the over-all strength of the force probably did not exceed 1,200, and of these, one-fourth, constituting the desert section, was partly mechanized.

When the British occupied Egypt in 1882, they found a local army of more than 45,000 officers and men. The foreign officers in Egyptian military employ were dismissed, and the army was placed under the command of British officers. Thereafter the British kept the Egyptian army weak; by 1914 the army had been reduced to some 10,000 officers and men. During the war, even after Britain declared Egypt a protectorate, while the army doubled in size, most of the new recruits entered the transport and labor battalions and the fighting units remained essentially unchanged. British enthusiasm for modernizing the Egyptian army after the war was dampened by the Egyptian nationalist agitation that led to the termination of the protectorate in 1922. Following the separation of the Sudanese contingents in 1925 the army continued to decline. In the next dozen years of Anglo-Egyptian diplomatic stalemate the army received little fresh equipment, nor did the British relax their grip. The British Inspector General (1927–36), Major General Sir Charlton W. Spinks Pasha, served in all but name as the supreme commander and, from his seat in the War Council, could also manage military policies. Assisted by fifteen to twenty British officers holding ranks between brigadier and major, the Inspector General could check attempts by Egyptian officers to take basic decisions inimical to British interests.

The French Wards

The experience in Algeria conditioned French military policies in North Africa and, later, in the mandate for Syria and Lebanon to an even greater degree than had the Anglo-Indian experience in Britain's sphere. In North Africa uniformity could be achieved because the countries were contiguous, the populations comparable, and the spurts of expansion spaced to allow for the consolidation of French power. In developing a policy for the recruitment of natives into its military service, France fumbled in the early years in Algeria with mixed French and native formations. The need for such troops arose from the fact that the commander of the invasion forces in 1830 discovered that France had effectively won no more than a beachhead, the three coastal towns of Algiers, Bône, and Oran. The conquest or, to use the European imperial euphemism of the day, the pacification of Algeria still lay before the victors. It took four decades to pacify the populated north, as distinct from the sparsely inhabited Saharan south which was gradually added in later decades.

Muslim soldiers participated in the French conquest of Algeria, but they represented less than 10 per cent of the total forces under French command. Algerian Muslims later took part in the seizure and pacification of Tunisia in the 1880s, when the French began recruiting Tunisians into the French army. On the eve of World War I, Algerian and Tunisian soldiers fought alongside the French soldiers in the subjugation of Morocco. Military recruitment in Morocco began almost at the start of the protectorate, and by the end of 1913 the number of Moroccans in the French North African army numbered almost 14,000.

In the three North African dependencies, all native military units formed part of the metropolitan army and were accordingly liable to foreign duty. As early as 1855, for example, units of the Algerian *Tirailleurs* (Rifles) popularly known as Turcos, fought in the Crimea and were used in its occupation. Algerians also participated in the Franco-Prussian War in 1870–71 and, along with Tunisians, in the French conquests south of the Sahara toward the end of the nineteenth century. North Africans qualified for commissions, but unless they were naturalized French citizens they could not rise higher than captain, and only a handful ever reached that rank. Muslim officers, in principle, were entitled to executive powers, yet in practice they were denied the right to command mixed French and Muslim ranks. Similarly, they were excluded from top administrative posts in the armed forces, always reserved for French officers. Naturalized Muslims, however, received the same treatment as Frenchmen. But in Algeria, where Napoleon III as early as 1865 specified the rules for naturalization, the requirement that Muslims accept the validity of French civil law and, in effect, abandon Islam reduced to a trickle the flow of those seeking French citizenship, and of these, fewer still became soldiers. The metropolitan army remained distinct from the colonial army, which consisted wholly of troops from the sub-Saharan colonies or Indochina. In the metropolitan army all officers and men, including North African Muslims, received the best instruction and equipment available.

Approximately 250,000 Algerian Muslims and 75,000 Tunisians served in the French army in World War I, some two-thirds assigned to combat duty, many on the western front. Very few Moroccans saw service in France in World War I, since the pacification of the new protectorate had just begun. The contraction of the metropolitan army between the wars resulted in a corresponding decline in the number of Muslim soldiers. The pattern of military organization, however, continued intact. Muslims in the three North African dependencies entered all branches of the armed forces. The infantry and cavalry brigades tended to be homogeneous. Thus, the Muslim infantry brigades formed the Algerian, Tunisian, or Moroccan Rifles, while the Zouaves consisted exclusively of Frenchmen born in North Africa. Similarly, the cavalry consisted of separate brigades for Muslims and Frenchmen, the Muslims known as *Spahis* and the French as *Chasseurs d'Afrique*. The artillery, on the other hand, comprised mixed units, with the Muslims furnishing the drivers and the French the gunners; the transport units were made up mostly of Muslim soldiers under French officers and NCOs.

The French military administration of Lebanon was instituted at the end of 1919, and of Syria in the next summer, after the formal assignment of the mandate to France. Units of the metropolitan and colonial armies were deployed there for establishing French rule and later for defense and security. The French forces in the mandate were designated the *Troupes du Levant*, to which were attached local troops called auxiliaries, which the mandatory began to organize early in the 1920s. On the eve of the outbreak of the Druze rebellion in 1925, before French reinforcements arrived, metropolitan soldiers in Syria and Lebanon numbered just over 14,000 officers and men, and the auxiliary troops just under 5,000, of whom about 1 per cent were native officers. The auxiliaries were commanded by 164 French officers, assisted by 300 French NCOs. The mandatory power opened a military school for Syrian and Lebanese cadets in 1924. In 1932, the French started calling the local recruits the *Troupes spéciales du Levant*, which reached a peak of 13,500 officers and men by the end of that year. Thereafter the force grew smaller until it was fixed at approximately 10,000 officers and men, remaining at this level until the expiry of the mandate. Officers and men were recruited disproportionately from the minority communities.

The Special Troops underwent less sophisticated training than the North African units in the metropolitan army, and, since they were troops in countries under mandate, were not sent abroad. Throughout the mandate the French cadre assured French domination. The mandatory in 1937 enrolled one Syrian and one Lebanese officer in the École Supérieure de Guerre in Paris, the only ones schooled in France in the interwar years.

The Challenge from Italy and Germany

Italian influence in the Middle East was anchored in Libya, in which the Fascist regime promoted Italian colonization only after the pacification of Cyrenaica in 1932. By the eve of Italy's entry into the war in 1940, two Libyan divisions with 8,000 men each belonged to the Italian 10th Army stationed in Cyrenaica. The only other Italian holdings in the Mediterranean were the Dodecanese Islands, just off the southeast corner of Turkey. These islands, too close for comfort, largely accounted for Turkey's unabated suspicion of Fascist Italy. This ruled Turkey out as a country in which Italy might seek to expand its influence.

The Fascists therefore sought other outlets for their expansive interest in the Middle East. As early as 1926, Italy concluded with Imam Yaḥya of Yemen a treaty of amity and commerce. The imam had invited the arrangement, after the breakdown of his negotiations with Britain over conflicting claims to tribal districts on the undemarcated frontier between his kingdom and Britain's Aden protectorate. However, the supplemental secret agreement in the following year was framed on Italian initiative. It hinted in the preamble at an alliance, and it defined the terms of Italian arms and associated military technical aid to the imamate. Despite the two agreements, the imam refused to receive a permanent Italian diplomatic mission in San'a, to say nothing of exchanging such missions with Italy. Italy accordingly relied on technicians and doctors to advance its political influence. The doctors proved more popular with the imam than the military technicians, whom he manifestly distrusted. Little wonder that he rejected Italian proposals on the eve of World War II to enlist Yemenis in the Italian colonial forces in Somaliland and Eritrea. Starting in 1937, Italy elicited somewhat more positive response from Afghanistan, where it entered the small-scale competition with other European powers (Britain, Russia, and Germany) for the creation of an air force.

The interest of Nazi Germany focused initially on the trio of sovereign states that separated the U.S.S.R. from the zone of Anglo-French hegemony in the Asian Middle East. The Nazis sought markets for commercial exports to the three Muslim countries and developed a relatively brisk trade toward the end of the 1930s. This was supplemented in Iran by the sale (along with other European suppliers) of military equipment and by technical assistance in the manufacture of small arms and ammunition. The Nazis offered credits to Afghanistan for the purchase of planes and modern military equipment, more generous than those of the other European powers, including Czechoslovakia, which sold machine guns and artillery.

Late in the 1930s, as King 'Abd al-'Aziz grew dissatisfied with Britain, his customary supplier, Saudi Arabia also began to show an interest in the purchase of arms from Germany. An agreement was finally reached in July 1939, when Germany undertook to sell modern arms to the Saudi monarch and offered him 4,000 rifles as a gift along with 2,000 rounds for each piece. Saudi Arabia was authorized to buy on credit arms worth up to R.M. 6 million, but the war broke out before the agreement could be executed. Nor were Yemeni efforts to buy captured Polish equipment from Germany in the fall of 1939 at all successful. It is doubtful that Germany gave high priority to the sale of arms to either Arabian monarchy, and in any case, after August 1939 Germany could hardly have contemplated running the British blockade.

The Italian invasion of Ethiopia in September 1935 alarmed Egypt almost as much as Britain and thus helped break the impasse in Anglo-Egyptian treaty negotiations. The instrument signed in August 1936 was a treaty of preferential alliance such as had already been concluded with Iraq on the termination of the mandate in October 1932, when Iraq became a member in the League of Nations. Egypt, too, joined the League in May 1937.

The preferential alliances were unequal instruments, although, admittedly, Britain transferred domestic sovereignty. But they resurrected the sphere of influence, a concept that had been popular in the century preceding 1914. Iraq and Egypt promised not to adopt in foreign lands "an attitude inconsistent with the alliance" and agreed that the British ambassadors would enjoy precedence over all other diplomats in Baghdad and Cairo. More concrete were the military rights given to Britain, which retained two air bases in Iraq and air, ground, and naval bases in Egypt. In the event of war, Britain was to enjoy all the facilities and assistance of the two Arab states, including in Egypt the right to impose martial law and censorship. Most important, Britain received the exclusive right to instruct and equip the Egyptian and Iraqi armies. The two Arab states, it was obvious, were junior partners. As members of the League, they exercised external sovereignty but only insofar as that would not impair the senior partner's transcendent strategic interests.

Britain had always stated that it viewed the Suez Canal as a "vital" British imperial interest. In Article 8 of the 1936 treaty, Britain recognized that the Suez Canal was "an integral part of Egypt." Egypt, in turn, acknowledged that the canal "is a universal means of communication as also an essential means of communication between the different parts of the British Empire." But in going on to stipulate that Britain's right "to station forces in Egyptian territory in the vicinity of the Canal" would last only "until such time as the High Contracting Parties agree that the Egyptian Army is in a position to ensure by its own resources the liberty and entire security of navigation of the Canal," the 1936 treaty, in effect, could hardly fail to press the Egyptian government into framing plans for accelerating the modernization of its army.[2] This, indeed, was one of the major consequences. In December 1938, Egypt's Supreme Defense Council approved a five-year military development plan for the acquisition of new weapons for an expanded army and air force, at an estimated cost of $200 million.

The development plan was manifestly unrealistic, since under the alliance the hardware had to be purchased in Britain, which could ill spare the quantities sought—some 500 fighters and bombers and comparable sophisticated weaponry for ground forces—at a time of its own urgent need for rearmament in a growing international crisis. But the failure to comply with the Egyptian request simply kept alive among Egyptians the conviction that Britain was deliberately withholding the weapons, as it had done in the long period of disagreement preceding the alliance. Moreover, since in Egypt, as in Iraq, the armies were placed under the command of native officers and under the civilian management of the two Arab governments, Britain was unable to prevent the framing of such plans. Built into the alliance, then, were all the elements for later conflict, as the Egyptians even more than the Iraqis came to resent and resist British attempts to use its monopoly of the arms import markets as a form of political influence on the preferential allies.

While Britain continued its close if indirect supervision of the local armies, it nonetheless did not interfere in peacetime in the internal politics of the two countries. Thus, in Iraq, the army overthrew the civilian government in 1936 and established a new cabinet responsible to a military junta, which still professed loyalty to the king. Over the next five years the military, either alone or in coalition with civilians, staged six more coups d'état. In Egypt the army took over supervision of the military academy and revamped its recruitment policies and curriculum.

A fifty-day general strike by nationalists in Syria and the announcement of the renewal of Anglo-Egyptian negotiations encouraged France to conclude preferential alliances with Syria in the spring of 1936 and with Lebanon the following fall. To each treaty was attached a military convention which proposed assigning to Syria and Lebanon contingents recruited from their respective countries for service with the Special Troops. To each government France agreed to send a military mission to assist in the training, equipment, and further development of the armies along French military lines. Syria and Lebanon in return obligated themselves "to engage only Frenchmen in the capacity of instructors and specialists," who were to be responsible to the chief of the French military mission. The officers of the French mission, it was laid down, might "be called upon to exercise temporarily an actual command" in the local armies "on request addressed to the representative of the French Government and approved by him." Syria and Lebanon also pledged to buy military hardware only in France, and France in turn to supply "arms, ammunitions, ships, aeroplanes, materials and equipment of the most recent model" on request from the two Arab states. France was to retain two air bases in Syria and air, ground, and naval bases in Lebanon.[3] However,

France did not ratify the treaties and, as we shall see, its effort to reactivate the draft instruments after 1942 proved abortive.

Speedup of Military Modernization in World War II

After the defeat of France in World War II, Britain began mobilizing its dependencies in the Middle East for the war effort. Britain strengthened the local armed forces already in being and created new ones. The process of nationalizing these forces was also accelerated, as Britain tried to enlist their aid. Once again India led the way. Nearly two million men, one-third of them Muslims, volunteered for military service, many going abroad to theaters of war in Asia, the Middle East, and Europe. The Indianization of the officer corps was once again accelerated, yet on transfer of the armed forces to the successor governments in 1947, Pakistan invited continuing British military command until the end of 1950.

The Sudan Defense Force was put on a war footing immediately after Italy declared war. The SDF took part in the Eritrean and Ethiopian campaigns, thus becoming combat-hardened and skilled in handling modern weaponry. In Transjordan, the participation of the Arab Legion in the brief Syrian and Lebanese campaign in the summer of 1941 provided the basis for converting the Legion (then essentially a police force) into a regular army. The success of the tiny mobile force—it did not exceed 1,350—in the brief campaigns in 1941 encouraged Britain to enlarge the Legion's military arm for war service. By 1945, Transjordan had 8,000 men under arms, the police included. Though modernized, the enlarged army was deprived of battle experience, because war had receded from the Middle East by the time the new units were trained. Nevetheless, at the war's end, the Legion constituted an integral part of the imperial forces under the British Middle East Command, for it was the best-trained and best-equipped Arab army of that time. Its top command and basic cadre were British officers under contract to the ruler of Transjordan.

In Palestine, the mandatory power had been reluctant to develop a positive military policy before the outbreak of war in 1939. The military urges of the Arabs and Jews in Palestine were therefore satisfied by the creation of irregular forces. Palestine Arab nationalists, with the cooperation of nationalists in the neighboring lands, had organized guerrillas to stage a revolt that started in April 1936 and dragged on inconclusively for more than three years, finally petering out in the fall of 1939. During the Palestine Arab revolt the British trained Jewish supplementary police and paramilitary units to help defend the Jewish community. That community, meanwhile, had already formed an underground militia, called *Haganah* (defense), which marked the beginning of what later developed into the citizen army of Israel.

Most Palestine Arab nationalists after September 1939 did not identify with Britain's war effort, for they were convinced that the mandatory power favored the Jews and that a British victory would be detrimental to Arab nationalist interests. The Palestine Jews by contrast had no choice but to align themselves with Britain in the war against Nazi Germany. The differing attitudes were reflected in the enlistments for the British forces in the two communities in the first half of the war. By December 1942 some 27,000 Palestinians had volunteered for service, and of these only one-third were Arabs, even though the Arab community was twice the size of the Jewish community. What is more, the military experience of the Palestine Arabs later dissipated itself in the absence of a stable political system to serve. In the Jewish community no opportunity was lost to persuade and pressure the mandatory power to approve step by step the formation of a self-contained Jewish fighting force. It took five years, but finally, in September 1944, Britain authorized the creation of a Jewish Brigade Group.

The Palestine Jews and their supporters abroad beat down British opposition. At the outset the mandatory power permitted the recruitment of Arabs and Jews in equal numbers for noncombatant service. After the defeat of France in the spring of 1940, Britain abandoned the rule of numerical equality in noncombatant enlistments, replacing it with a policy of recruiting an equal number of Arab and Jewish companies for an infantry regiment, called the Palestine Buffs. As Britain's military position deteriorated further, the mandatory power in the spring of 1941 dropped the parity principle for infantry companies. By August 1942, with Axis forces only seventy miles from Alexandria, the Palestine Buffs were converted into the Palestine Regiment and existing companies were used to form separate Arab and Jewish infantry battalions for general service in the Middle East. The mandatory power also gradually slackened its requirements of accepting only Palestine citizens, first by admitting Jews who had not yet been naturalized and later by admitting Jews who had entered the country illegally. As early as October 1940, Prime Minister Churchill had approved in principle the formation of a Jewish Division, to be recruited in Palestine and elsewhere, under the general command of British officers, but with Jewish junior officers. Even though a British commander had been named and talks on the official communiqué announcing its formation had been started, the Zionist leaders were informed in March 1941 that there would be a delay of six months. By October, the Colonial Office decided that in the existing circumstances there would be no prospect of carrying such a proposal into effect. The Zionist leaders redirected their pressures from the closed doors of government departments to the open forum of public opinion. The Zionist campaign for a Jewish fighting force lasted nearly three years longer, until Whitehall finally reached a positive decision.

The Palestine Jews clearly knew what they wanted. They were determined to have their own combat-hardened army, which they believed they would put to effective use after the war, when they hoped to create their own independent state. By 1945 the number of Palestine Jews in the British armed forces and those in the paramilitary and police units in Palestine numbered altogether some 60,000 men and women. Almost all belonged to the still illegal Haganah, which had been forged during the war into a well-organized, if still underground, army with a striking force, a static defense force, and reservists. Among the armies in the British sphere outside the subcontinent, Haganah thus became the largest and the most highly experienced force.

After Italy became a belligerent in 1940, Britain began raising a Libyan refugee force among Cyrenaican Arabs who had taken asylum in Egypt during the Italian pacification in the 1920s. This force was raised with the cooperation of al-Sayyid Muhammad Idris, the leader of the Sanusi movement (a Sunni mystical order) and of the Cyrenaican refugees in Egypt. In 1940 the first four battalions, consisting of more than 600 Sanusi officers and men, were placed under the command of 21 British officers and 29 British NCOs. The Sanusi force received mostly noncombatant experience. In 1941 the British captured almost intact the two divisions of Libyans, mostly Cyrenaicans, who had been conscripted into the Italian army; some of these were later screened for reassignment to the British-commanded Libyan Arab Force (LAF). After the Italian and German armies were driven out of Libya in 1943, a British military administration governed Cyrenaica and Tripolitania, and a Free French administration governed the district of Fazzan. At that time, the British demobilized three LAF battalions and transformed the two others into a gendarmerie. The Cyrenaica Defense Force (CDF), as the gendarmerie was known, consisted in 1945 of about 900 Arabs commanded by some 50 British officers. Meanwhile, the Sudanese Defense Force sent a number of units for garrison duty in Tripolitania, or western Libya, until the local police force could be formed. When Libya finally reached independence in December 1951, it was the CDF that constituted the military mainstay of the new kingdom.

Once again mutual suspicions kept Britain and Egypt apart in World War II. The less than enthusiastic interest of the Egyptian government and the nationalists in the British war effort deepened the mutual hostility, so that the Egyptian army was neither expanded nor modernized. The only units that received combat experience were the anti-aircraft companies in 1940–42, when Egypt was subject to occasional air raids. Still, the military academy continued turning out officers who became dedicated to liberating their army from all residual British controls.

Despite the preferential alliance, Britain had virtually lost its influence over the Iraqi army after the outbreak of war. Top officers had been involved in the many coups d'état since 1936. The civilian-military coalitions that ran the kingdom after September 1939 responded more openly to the courtship of Germany and Italy. After Britain's restoration of its supremacy, the British military mission closely supervised Iraqi military affairs. Apart from the purge of the anti-British officers, no attempts were made to modernize or enlarge the army, and the army did not take part in the war.

Meanwhile, in the negotiations between Britain and the Free French on the eve of the Syrian campaign, General Charles de Gaulle and his colleagues left no doubt that they intended to uphold French supremacy in the two mandated countries by means of preferential alliances. Churchill assured de Gaulle in June 1941, on the eve of the joint overthrow of the Vichy regime in Syria and Lebanon, that Britain sought "no special advantages in the French Empire" and had "no intention of exploiting the tragic position of France for our own gain," to which de Gaulle replied that Free France would "proclaim and respect the independence of the Levant States on condition of a treaty with them enshrining the rights and special interests of France." [4] Throughout the rest of the war the Free French leaders, in their dealings with Syria and Lebanon, seemed preoccupied with efforts to conclude preferential alliances, modeled on those that Britain had framed with Iraq and Egypt in the 1930s. As a means of bringing pressure to bear on the two Arab states, the Free French simply refused to hand over to them the command of the Special Troops, making such a transfer contingent on the signature with France of the desired treaties.

In North Africa, France treated its possessions as interdependent and administered them accordingly, despite the governance of Algeria as an extension of the French mainland and of Tunisia and Morocco as protectorates. Local units from North Africa were sent to France for military service until the armistice of June 1940. As part of the armistice arrangement, the French were allowed to retain up to 120,000 officers and men in North Africa (55,000 in Morocco, 50,000 in Algeria, and 15,000 in Tunisia), 70 per cent of them Muslims. Their weapons and equipment were in short supply and generally obsolete even at the time of the armistice. As the war unfolded, their military capacity declined even further, since North Africa was cut off from the new generation of weapons. Following the Allied liberation of North Africa in 1943 the North African forces participated along with other branches of the metropolitan and colonial armies in the Italian campaign and later in the liberation of France. The Syrians and Lebanese, by contrast, received no field experience in the war.

Under the impact of World War II the buffer that the Soviet Union had erected to separate the Russian and British empires broke down in Turkey and in Iran. In Turkey the treaty of neutrality and nonaggression was replaced by a treaty of alliance with Britain and the acceptance of a British military mission, which was still in the country at the war's close. In Iran, Britain and Russia simply occupied the kingdom. The United States with the occupiers' acquiescence sent military and gendarmerie missions to the kingdom in 1942, and the missions were still there in 1945. Only Afghanistan stuck to its neutrality throughout the war. In October 1941, Afghanistan complied with requests from the U.S.S.R. and Britain to expel Axis agents from the country; its later wartime search for aid in military modernization went unrequited. Afghanistan was all that remained of the Soviet Union's interwar buffer; as a result, by 1945, it appeared that the U.S.S.R. might replace Germany and Italy as the principal foe of Anglo-French hegemony in the Middle East.

At the war's close, there was no reason to assume that Britain and France would be unable to withstand the challenge of the Soviet Union, if it developed, less successfully than they had withstood the challenge of Italy and Germany. By 1945 the imperial powers had amassed in the Middle East an amount of military equipment more massive than ever before and vastly more than they would require in peacetime. It would manifestly be both economical and convenient to distribute such equipment to the local governments in return for political favors. Whether the use of military aid could effectively check the advance of nationalism and preserve the imperial supremacy was a question that would be resolved after the war. For the time being, Britain and France seemed able to reassert their domination of the Middle East arms traffic. Their past practices, formalized by written and unwritten conventions, seemed to bar freedom of action in the area to the United States; for that matter the U.S.S.R., with its massive problems of domestic reconstruction and organizing its new allies in Eastern Europe, did not seem on the verge of developing a military aid policy for non-Communist countries.

Postwar Politics

5

MILITARY POLITICS AND THE LINGERING COLD WAR

The European imperial powers—primarily Russia, Britain, and France—had gobbled up the Muslim world in the century and a half preceding the close of World War I. What the tsars seized, the commissars never gave up, for the Soviet empire assimilated the Muslim districts of the Crimea, the Caucasus, and Central Asia that lay in the old Russian empire. As late as 1945 the Asian Middle East and adjacent northeast Africa to Libya fell within the British pale and throughout the area Britain bore an exclusive or primary responsibility for defense. Only northern Iran, occupied by Russia and the two primitive Muslim kingdoms of Afghanistan and Yemen, lay outside the British bailiwick. Beyond its varied traditional Middle East empire Britain now occupied southern Iran and French-mandated Syria and Lebanon, established a military administration over Libya after the expulsion of the Italians, and maintained military training missions in Turkey and Saudi Arabia. Northwest Africa remained French throughout the war, although it took an Anglo-American expedition forcibly to transfer administrative title from Vichy to the Free French. Within twenty years France lost all its imperial possessions in the Middle East, and Britain's dependencies were cut back to a string of protected tribal shaykhdoms along the southern and eastern littorals of the Arabian Peninsula.

The Russians continued to hold their Muslim dependencies after World War II and even sought to expand them. When Stalin tried to seize the Turkish Straits and tear Iran apart in 1945–46, he gambled on accomplishing it in the turmoil of transition to peace, and he lost. The attempted seizure of the Straits, followed by a Russian claim to a naval base in the Dodecanese Islands and to a trusteeship over one of the other former Italian colonies, either Libya or Eritrea, recalled similar Russian maneuvers in the days of

Napoleon to break out of the Black Sea and establish a foothold in the Mediterranean. In the century and a half between the two, the tsars had tried again and again to satisfy their aspirations at the Straits, only to face frustration at every trial. The latest effort of the Russians to force their way into the Mediterranean and the Middle East raised the hackles of the Western powers. The recurrence of thrusts by tsarist autocrat and Communist dictator convinced the United States that the Russian urge to reach the Mediterranean was deep-seated and, under communism, had acquired an ideological cast. It could be checked only by erecting a solid wall of defense.

Clash of Interests and Strategies

As early as 1947 the United States therefore offered to uphold the independence and integrity of all states beyond the Soviet ambit against the threat of direct or indirect Communist aggression; or, in the idiom of the Truman Doctrine, "to support free peoples who are resisting attempted subjugation by armed minorities or by outside pressures" and to assist these peoples "to work out their own destinies in their own way." [1] Between the enunciation of such a principle and its application in the Middle East lay the realities of a region over much of which Britain and France still ruled. The Soviet threat to the region's sovereign states was bound to strengthen Western prestige in them. The same threat to the British and French empires in the Middle East was bound to curry favor among local nationalists struggling for independence.

The Soviet leaders held the stiff Western response to their initiatives in Turkey and Iran as testimony of "capitalist encirclement." Yet throughout the remaining years of Stalin's rule the U.S.S.R. persisted in its diplomacy of bludgeon and bluster toward the Middle East and continued using the local Communist movements as a clandestine spearhead for the promotion of Soviet influence. As soon as the U.S.S.R. sensed the weakness of Britain and France, the Kremlin developed a strategy for ridding the Middle East of the established political, economic, and military interests of the two Western European powers and for preventing the United States from moving in. Moscow therefore championed every move that would hasten the British and French withdrawal and shut the United States out. But the harder the Soviet Union pressed Britain and France, the more it pushed the United States into building military power in the Middle East and accepting political commitments and leadership. Suspecting clandestine Soviet participation

in every demonstration, riot, and uprising that attended the be-
deviling process of transferring sovereignty from Britain and
France to the regional successor regimes, the United States tried to
take precautions to keep Soviet influence from reaching the new
states.

The strategy of containment thus gave the United States an inclusive regional interest: that of hemming the Soviet Union in at
its Middle East frontier. Surprisingly small at the outset, the actual
American military commitment in support of this interest grew
slowly and fitfully, from crisis to crisis. Among the sovereign
Middle East states, Turkey was the lone beneficiary of the Truman
Doctrine for more than a half-dozen years. The primary American
interest was also shared with Britain and France, which were striving to hold the imperial line at least long enough to salvage whatever political, economic, and military investments they could. The
continuing pervasive British and French presence, in fact, represented an American asset. Many of the major Middle East strategic
routes by land, sea, and air on which the United States and its
allies depended for repelling the Russians passed through allied dependencies. The bases and staging areas along these arteries housed
garrisons and stockpiled equipment that could be marshaled for
the common cause and made available to American forces in an
emergency.

These assets, however, were turning into growing liabilities in
the protracted British and French imperial retirement. Britain was
forced to negotiate with Egypt (1946–54) for the evacuation of the
giant Suez Base which fell under constant Egyptian pressure, tied
down some 80,000 troops, and required massive supplies for a half-
dozen years at a probable annual cost to the exchequer in excess of
$300 million.[2] Many times more costly to the metropolitan power
was the Muslim war for independence in Algeria (1954–62); in the
last four years the guerrillas immobilized some 400,000 of the most
experienced French forces. Egypt and Algeria were the linchpins
of the British and French imperial systems in the Middle East. In
the decade and a half that it took to arrange the disengagements,
the two European powers surrendered most of their remaining
Middle East dependencies, at times with violence, as in Palestine
and Cyprus, and at other times with relative calm, as in Sudan,
Morocco, and Tunisia. In the sticky transition from imperial rule
to political sovereignty, the effectiveness of the containment strategy rested largely on the Western powers' preserving, wherever
possible, their rights of access to routes and bases. This proved a

losing proposition. Britain procured, in the settlement with Egypt in 1954, a seven-year right of re-entry to the Suez Base, only to lose it two years later at the time of the Anglo-French fiasco at the Canal. Similarly, the prolonged Algerian war first compromised and then foreshortened French rights to bases in Tunisia and Morocco, long before their intended expiry.

When such bases disappeared, the Western powers tried to develop substitutes. With the loss, in 1956, of transit and servicing facilities for notified RAF flights in Egypt, Britain opened an alternative southern air route from Libya through Sudan to Aden, which lasted until the overturn of the military regime in Sudan late in 1964. Cyprus, originally conceived as replacement for Suez in the eastern Mediterranean, never met the requirements of the British army or navy although its airstrips proved valuable to the RAF, more, it seems, as a staging area for Southeast Asia than for the Middle East. The civil war after 1963 vitiated even this limited role. The versatile base at Aden became Britain's main military anchor in Southwest Asia after the loss of Suez and the fizzle of Cyprus.

As the West gradually surrendered rights and bases, particularly after 1956, the balance of commitment and power within the Western security system shifted from Britain and France to the United States; concurrently, Western deterrence of a Soviet military presence in the Middle East shifted from reliance on conventional, manned, and largely land-based weaponry to reliance on nuclear, automated, and increasingly sea-based weaponry. The United States, it is true, acquired air bases in Morocco, Libya, Saudi Arabia, and Turkey. But fundamentally such mainland positions were eschewed, since they might be construed as territorial aggrandizement that might tempt nationalist anti-American agitation. American military power was therefore concentrated in a steadily enlarging fleet that was placed under its own command and stationed in the Mediterranean. Equipped with an air arm and marine battalions, the fleet could summon immediate American troop reinforcements from Europe in a crisis and, as air transport improved, also from the United States. All three services, for example, took part in the American landing in Lebanon in 1958, and ground troops were drawn from American units in Germany. With this capability, the United States assumed the major responsibility for choking off Soviet efforts directly or indirectly to inherit abandoned Western facilities, which, in turn, dictated the insulation of Middle East regimes against possible seizure by groups hostile to the West. In August 1953 the United States delivered Muhammad Reza Shah in the nick of time from probable overturn in a situation in which the Tudeh Party might well have seized the armed forces. The Eisenhower Doctrine at the start of 1957 was expressly designed to furnish the United States a basis for military action in defense of Middle East states "against overt armed aggression from any nation controlled by international Communism"; it was less than four months later when the United States rescued King Husayn of Jordan.

By contrast with the progressive disappearance of French and British rights to bases and arteries for military transport, one Western European interest grew steadily in the postwar years: oil. Apart from marginal participation by domestic and Japanese companies, the oil industry in the Middle East was wholly operated by Western concessionaires. Although American nationals commanded nearly three-fifths of the total production, the United States imported less than 10 per cent of its crude from the Middle East. British, French, and Dutch companies controlled only about a third of the Middle East output, but three-fourths of the oil consumed in the rapidly expanding Western European market came in the mid-1960's from the Persian Gulf zone and from North Africa. The rapid expansion of the Middle East oil industry after 1947 was deliberately tied first to the economic recovery of Western Europe and then to fueling the armies and the economies of the European NATO members. This was done to help the trans-Atlantic allies of the United States conserve hard currency by enabling them to import from a nondollar area most of their crude, which was refined in Europe, also as part of an integrated NATO plan for further dollar savings. One gauge of the expansion of the oil industry in the Middle East was the massive growth of published proved reserves from about 2.5 billion tons in 1945 to over 30 billion tons twenty years later, or three-fifths of the world's total.

Until 1956 the Middle East industry was confined to territories washed by the Persian Gulf; but the Suez crisis of that year demonstrated the vulnerability of the routes of supply, so that new discoveries in Algeria and Libya were swiftly brought into production. For these multiple reasons, the safeguard of the strategic industry became a common Western concern, which, however, was never spelled out explicitly. After 1956 the United States, in effect, assumed primary responsibility for defense of the industry west of Suez; by default, Britain retained primary responsibility east of it. Indeed, this proved to be Britain's last military outpost in the Middle East, one that it finally began to dismantle when it surrendered Aden in 1967 and announced its withdrawal from the Persian Gulf no later than 1971.

The view from Moscow naturally looked different. The Asian Middle East abutted "the soft underbelly" of southwest Russia, though the only states that shared common borders with the U.S.S.R. were Turkey, Iran, and Afghanistan. The problems of Russian defense could have been eased by sweeping the interests of third powers out of these non-Arab Muslim countries. Russia's sensitivity to the presence of major powers in the neighborhood, representing a potential danger to Soviet security, harked back to the early days of the Soviet regime.

Under the impact of World War II the buffer broke down in Turkey and Iran. The Soviet Union's inbred sensitivity helps explain its expansionist pressures in 1945–46 that significantly were directed to Iran, where Britain occupied the south and the United States maintained military and gendarmerie missions; and to Turkey, Britain's wartime ally and military client; but not to Afghanistan, which had nursed its neutrality throughout the war. The Kremlin had been distraught over the wartime pan-Turanist appeal in Turkey to disaffected Turkic-speaking people in the Soviet Union, especially when a number of these and related smaller Muslim communities in the Caucasus and the Crimea cooperated with the Nazi military administration. After the reconquest of these districts, as early as 1944, Stalin banished to remote Soviet provinces the Balkars, Chechens, Ingush, and Crimean Tatars. Afghanistan, like Turkey and Iran, had lost territory to Russia in the nineteenth century, and the division of peoples and tribes and districts vexed both sides. Far-fetched as it may seem to outsiders, the U.S.S.R. may well have viewed Turkey and Iran at the war's close as posing a threat to its security in the combination of latent irredentist grievances and major-power presence.

If Russia had succeeded in subordinating Turkey and Iran, with or without the trusteeship over Libya or Eritrea, it might have been able to thrust Soviet naval and air power into the Mediterranean and Arabian seas. It might then have challenged the supremacy of the West on both sides of the Suez Canal and could have met any threat to Soviet security in Southwest Asia more effectively than in the past. As events turned out, instead of obtaining forward Russian bases, Russia faced proximate hostile bases. In an age of ever faster planes and longer-range unmanned delivery systems, moreover, the military presence of the adversary even in North Africa became too close for comfort.

However, in the Arab Middle East the U.S.S.R. enjoyed psychological advantages. No Arab state bordered on the Soviet Union, so that the Arabs, unlike the Turks and Iranians and Afghans, had never experienced Russian imperialism. The postwar struggle for Arab political emancipation therefore focused on the two principal allies of the United States. As a result, in many parts of the Arab world, the United States came to bear the onus of guilt by imperial association. Its problems in finding Arab allies were compounded by American friendliness to Zionism, since the political leaders of the Arab East had persuaded themselves and their publics that Israel could never have come into being or long endured without American sponsorship. It was the Arab area that gave the U.S.S.R. its major opportunities for acquiring military and political influence in the Middle East, although the breakthrough did not occur until the start of the second postwar decade.

Meanwhile, the United States had steadily built up its military capability in the region. In 1952 Turkey became the only Middle East member of NATO and immediately opened its facilities to its allies, particularly to the United States, in organizing the defense of Western interests in the eastern Mediterranean. Under the NATO agreement, Turkey permitted the erection of radar screens, the only elaborate Western air-defense system so close to the U.S.S.R., which consisted also of a network of air bases that could accommodate planes of every variety, including strategic bombers. As Jupiter intermediate-range ballistic missiles rolled off the assembly line at the end of the 1950s, fifteen were fixed to pads in Turkey within reach of major Soviet targets. The United States also was allowed to launch U-2 flights from the bases in Turkey and from Pakistan and to procure bases in Saudi Arabia, Libya, and Morocco. As protecting power, France issued base rights in Morocco in 1951; the United States continued using these bases for its Strategic Air Command (SAC), with the subsequent acquiescence of sovereign Morocco, until 1963. In the period before missiles, the SAC bases gave the U.S. Air Force "big feet," enabling its long-range bombers to deliver nuclear weapons to primary Soviet targets, thus assuring the United States effective retaliatory power against nuclear attack by the U.S.S.R. Britain, as military administrator, permitted the United States in 1948 to reactivate Wheelus Field in Libya, initially for the air transport service and later for more extensive military use. Independent Libya in 1954 formalized the arrangement in a seventeen-year agreement, which also authorized use of the field for NATO training and for refueling. Because

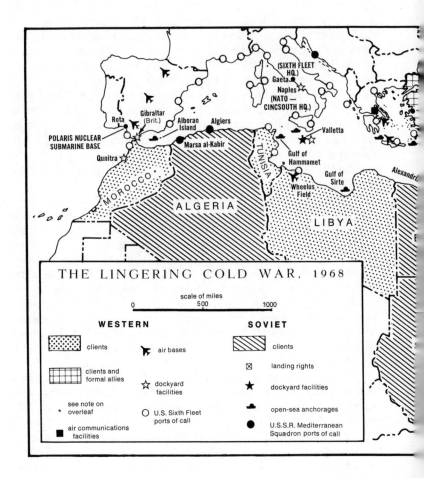

THE LINGERING COLD WAR, 1968

scale of miles

0   500   1,000

WESTERN   **SOVIET**

clients   air bases   clients

clients and   landing rights
formal allies   dockyard
                  facilities   dockyard facilities

see note on
* overleaf   U.S. Sixth Fleet   open-sea anchorages
                 ports of call

air communications   U.S.S.R. Mediterranean
facilities   Squadron ports of call

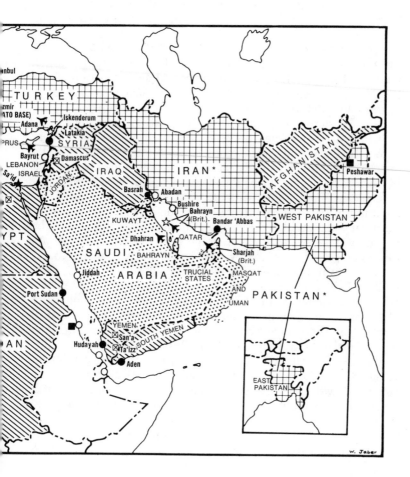

of touchy Arab-American relations over the Arab-Israel dispute, the Dhahran field in Saudi Arabia, constructed in 1945, never fulfilled the original American hope of becoming a fully developed United States air base but remained available only for transit and support activities.

For the most part, however, the United States relied on its Sixth Fleet in the Mediterranean in the 1950s. The fleet served as a roving base that projected American naval and air power throughout the Mediterranean and the Middle East. The United States removed its Jupiter missiles from Turkey in 1963 when security planners in Washington decided that the political disability of the launching pads outweighed their military value, since the sites, known to the enemy, had become " 'lightning rods' that attract attack" and more particularly, since they could by then be replaced by nuclear submarines firing Polaris missiles, which were becoming available for regular duty with the Sixth Fleet. As the central element in the Western security system in the Middle East, the Sixth Fleet had largely replaced British and French bases throughout the region after 1956. But because of the failure to bring Egypt into the system, the Suez Canal was no longer freely available to the Western naval powers. The shortest route between the Sixth Fleet in the Mediterranean and the Seventh Fleet in the Western Pacific, it was a tenuous link at best, resting as it did on the sufferance of Egypt. This raised many questions of Western defense east of Suez, where the United States maintained a small naval squadron in the Persian Gulf, stationed at the British-protected principality of Bahrayn. For the rest, the United States leaned heavily for defense and peacekeeping in that Middle East zone on the British command with headquarters at Aden, which became, for little more than a decade after 1956, Britain's principal base in Southwest Asia.

West of Suez, Britain's Middle East Command was reduced to the streamlined bases in Libya and Cyprus. The French military

---

Note to Map on Two Preceding Pages: The only formal Middle East allies of a superpower were Turkey, Iran, and Pakistan. Steady arms purchases from one side in the Cold War, however, revealed preferences. Iran became a marginal arms customer of Russia in 1967, and Pakistan a more substantial one in 1968; neither repudiated its bilateral alliance with the United States. Similarly Morocco, a Western—increasingly American—arms customer, experimented in 1961 and 1967–68 with supplemental purchases from Russia. The situation in the Middle East in 1968 was clearly transitional.

decline in the Middle East was no less dramatic and final. In the prolonged counterguerrilla warfare in Algeria, France irreparably destroyed its preferential military position in Tunisia, weakened it in Morocco, and salvaged only temporary nuclear-testing sites and a naval base in Algeria—all abandoned well ahead of treaty schedule. Moreover, long before France withdrew from the military activities of NATO, it had largely ceased its military coordination with the United States and Britain in the Middle East.

The U.S.S.R. looked with alarm at the growing power of the United States in a region that the Soviet Union continued to regard as its back doorstep. The more the United States built up its military capability in the Middle East, the louder the Soviet Union complained against the "aggressive, imperialist blocs." Contiguity to the Asian Middle East gave the U.S.S.R. a short-term advantage of being able to shore up its military power on Soviet soil out of enemy sight, but that power could not be used to compete effectively with the United States for influencing peacetime military-political decisions in the area. In consequence, Stalin's successors alternated the hard line of frightening Middle East governments into submission with a soft line of enticing them into cooperation. In its strategy of containment the United States sought the commitment of Middle East states to the Western side in the Cold War. As a riposte, the U.S.S.R. adopted the strategy of peaceful coexistence, which catered to noncommitment. In the Middle East, peaceful coexistence was launched as early as 1953 in Turkey and Iran with Soviet assurances of a desire for friendly relations, and then in the independent Arab states with Soviet endorsement of Arab claims in the dispute with Israel. This was promptly followed by offers of material favors such as economic and military assistance to those Middle East governments that were prepared to proclaim their neutralism in the Cold War, and in these countries the U.S.S.R. bypassed the local Communist parties, even acquiescing in their suppression. The United States and its allies, which until then had pre-empted almost all forms of foreign aid in the Middle East, suddenly had to face a challenger. Thus, in the second postwar decade, Cold War strategies, shaped by the dominant members of the two major coalitions, actually became competitive in the region.

Let us first examine the unfolding of United States military aid policies toward the Middle East before the Soviet Union entered the contest.

Western Monopoly

Containment called for commitment, and in the Middle East the United States started out with an overwhelming initial advantage. Britain and France were already committed, in principle, at the time of the issuance of the Truman Doctrine and, by alliance, when NATO came into being two years later. They fervently welcomed containment as a means of keeping the U.S.S.R. at bay, while they attempted to come to terms with the nationalists by adjusting the status of their dependencies to postwar realities. But the effort by the metropolitan powers to hold on to their political paramountcy sharpened the disputes with the nationalists across the region. The spreading conflicts weakened the effective commitment of Britain and France to the Western cause, as one important military facility after another was tied down in disuse by nationalist siege. In its leadership, the United States seemed bent on finding a compromise formula that would satisfy the imperial powers and the nationalists and thereby keep open, or reopen to the West, the primary bases and strategic routes. Fundamentally, these were problems that attended the transfer of sovereignty from the imperial powers to the successor states. The NATO allies' efforts to anticipate the difficulties in the negotiations for withdrawal had varying results.

Dealing with the region's long-standing sovereign states proved no less baffling. The logical candidates for alliance with the West were Turkey, Iran, and Afghanistan, all lying in the direct line of possible Soviet expansion. Yet even the erstwhile buffers could not be easily or wholly assimilated into the emerging Western alliance complex in the Middle East. Turkey alone responded promptly and neatly. Until 1953 the best that the United States could accomplish in Iran was its denial to the U.S.S.R. Afghanistan, presumably denying itself to its northern neighbor, was simply ignored. With the Palestine problem in crisis and with mounting pressures for independence, the Arab East seemed the least likely source of candidates, actual or prospective, for alliance with the West. Since only four states in the zone were sovereign in 1947, there was still time for maneuver. Worrisome to the West but hemmed in by pro-Western Turkey and the British military presence in adjacent Arab lands, Syria and Lebanon nevertheless required watching. Saudi Arabia and Yemen were far enough removed from the Soviet Union in time as well as space to cause the least anxiety.

As a primary means for attempting to align the unaligned, the United States and its major trans-Atlantic allies turned to military aid. Economic aid consisted of either grants or loans. Military aid was more broadly defined. It included grants and technical instruction in the use and care of military weapons and vehicles and also the sale of such equipment for cash, by discount, or on credit—hence, the variable practices of the purveyors who doled out modern arms or withheld them, sold them at market prices or at generous discount, or gave them away altogether. The market in martial hardware in the postwar Middle East, as elsewhere in Asia and Africa, operated under its own unique rules. If the rules appeared irrational at times, the reason lay in the confusing interplay of political, emotional, commercial, and fiscal factors at the patron and client levels. Military and economic aid were sometimes considered complementary. Both could serve as modernizing agents in the receiving state, and this was what the United States occasionally claimed was happening. Yet military aid and economic aid tended to work at cross-purposes. American economic aid placed growing emphasis on self-help by the recipients. Military aid was rarely conceived in these terms by Soviet-bloc or Western donors. Investment in military industry, assuming that the receiving state has the technical capacity to run such plants and a use for the products that would warrant the investment on economic grounds, requires an initial high capital outlay. Besides, if the receiving state became militarily self-sustaining, the assisting state lost some of its options and therefore much of its advantage. Unless a project meets sound technical and economic standards, it will end up as a net drain on the developing economy. Military aid almost always cultivated expensive habits, the effects of which were delayed, however, whenever the patron absorbed much of the immediate cost, with the result that such clients were mortgaging their economic future.

The United States conducted a lone and, by later standards, minuscule military aid program in the Middle East in 1945: the military and gendarmerie-training missions to Iran. After the tardy evacuation of the Red Army units from the north in 1946, the United States also made small amounts of war surplus available. Yet the missions and the munitions were charged to the Iranian account. When Turkey in 1947 became the second American military client, the United States established itself as a leading arms supplier in the region. In postwar Europe, the United States grew from the great provider into the great coordinator, and its decisive leadership made NATO an early reality. By contrast, the United

States did not attempt immediately to perform the same functions in the Middle East, despite its expanding obligation to protect Western interests. Throughout World War II the United States had accepted British military leadership in the Middle East. In the first postwar decade neither Britain nor France seemed prepared to surrender its hegemony in military, political, or economic affairs in its area. Britain expected, as in the past, to continue to dominate the Western defense system in the Arab East, permitting the United States to play a role somewhat larger than in World War II, but still only secondary. In the Arab West, France simply did not invite the United States to play any military or economic role whatsoever, except for making bases available in Morocco for direct use by American forces, with indirect economic benefits for the French and the Moroccans. Little wonder that allied defense planning, which had started out as tripartite, progressively narrowed in the 1950s to an Anglo-American enterprise.

British and French military policies varied from place to place according to whether the receiving country was sovereign or dependent. The two imperial powers accredited advisory missions to sovereign states: Britain to Turkey and Saudi Arabia; France to Syria and Lebanon. The four states were clients, not wards, and paid for their military hardware. So, too, did Iraq and Egypt, whose armies in the 1930s had been placed under native commands, which, however, were subordinated to tight British surveillance in World War II. The British military missions to both were formally withdrawn soon after the war, but the United Kingdom continued its close regulation of the quantity and the quality of arms exported to the two states. The Arab Legion in Transjordan and the Defense Forces of Sudan and Cyrenaica were commanded by British officers and financed by the British exchequer. The French in North Africa simply recruited natives into the French forces. The British followed this practice only in Palestine; but the Jewish Brigade and the fewer Palestine Arab units were demobilized before the formal inauguration of containment.

Britain and France could be expected to adhere to these policies as long as possible, and wherever nationalists were not too obstreperous, the United States did not press for change. As the United States became engaged, it developed its own policy preferences, avoiding direct command and close supervision, to say nothing of direct recruitment. It favored instead advisory and training missions and early in the 1950s perhaps even an integrated command, provided some kind of workable collective security system could be invented to bring together in partnership the United States, its Western European allies, and the sovereign Middle East states.

With the Middle East arms market remaining a Western monopoly until 1955, the three powers had little trouble in regulating the flow of arms into the region, for they were essentially working toward the same larger goals. The text of the Truman Doctrine hardly said a word about the nature of American military aid to states threatened by the Soviet Union. But the specific shape of the aid program to Turkey eloquently disclosed that military grant aid was primarily intended and that the amounts would be generous. The message came through loud and clear to Turkey's Middle East neighbors: Declare yourself under threat of Soviet or Communist aggression, place yourself in the custody of the United States, and you will find no more certain way of acquiring modern arms as a gift or at nominal cost, with free training thrown in for good measure. This was the preferred line of reasoning in extending American military aid.

The American preference by 1950 was blended with established British and French practice in a Tripartite Declaration which came the closest to setting forth Western principles of military aid. The statement was expressly addressed to the Arab governments and to Israel, but it also had region-wide application. All states, it was recognized, "need to maintain a certain level of armed forces to assure their internal security and their legitimate self-defense." All applications for such purchase could expect favorable consideration. Moreover, those states volunteering "to play their part in the defense of the area as a whole," that is, to join the Western coalition for the containment of the Soviet Union, could, by definition, expect treatment *à la turque*. The three powers set forth the conditions of their offer. They opposed "the development of an arms race between the Arab states and Israel"; the purchasing state had to pledge not "to undertake any act of aggression against any other state"; the Western allies announced "their deep interest in and their desire to promote the establishment and maintenance of peace and stability in the area and their unalterable opposition to the use of force or threat of force between any of the states in that area"; and they warned that any violation of frontiers or armistice lines would give rise to the sponsors' immediate "action, both within and outside the United Nations, to prevent such violation." [3]

The Tripartite Declaration, in effect, infused American largesse into the traditional British concepts of defense and peacekeeping in the Middle East with the composite aims of containing the

U.S.S.R. and maintaining British supremacy in the Arab East. The policy worked well for five years because the United States was identified with it (the outbreak of the Korean War precisely one month after the issuance of the Declaration strengthened the credibility of American willingness to use force, if necessary); Moscow's hard line in these years proved counterproductive for Soviet interests in the Arab East; and the continuing pervasive military presence of the British kept the local nationalists preoccupied with local issues. This was particularly true in Egypt, where even the military junta did not elect to dissipate its resources on regional issues until the settlement of the dispute with Britain. The only major threat to interstate peace came from the infractions along the Arab-Israel armistice lines, which settled down to a pattern of small-scale Arab raids from Egypt (and the Gaza Strip), Jordan, or Syria, followed by Israel's "massive" retaliation. But even these raids and counterraids did not get out of hand. So long as British ground, air, and naval bases honeycombed the Arab East, British military might served as a deterrent at the international and regional levels, performing the roles of defender and peacekeeper.

However, the European imperial departure, though still in its early stages, was already upsetting established regional defense arrangements and threatening to create problems of intraregional security. The roles of defender and peacekeeper were interrelated but not identical. If the quarrels among the sovereign states in the Middle East could be kept below the threshold of war, the problem of regional defense was eased, but there were no guarantees of automatic cooperation by all Arab states with the United States and its allies within the Middle East and outside it, as they took steps to protect the area against rising Soviet influence. Still, it could not be denied that the ability of the three powers to defend Western interests in the Middle East derived largely from their success in preserving peace, or in restoring peace when it had broken down, for actual hostilities and the disputes from which they sprang invited external interference. In the Tripartite Declaration, the United States was thus assuming, jointly with its allies, the police function in the Arab-Israel zone, although it did not exercise this obligation outside the United Nations until after British power in the area had been discredited in the Suez crisis of 1956.

The decline of British power in the Middle East in the first postwar decade represented a contraction of military as well as political influence. Ever since the end of World War I, Britain had reacted to nationalist pressure, wherever it manifested itself, by relinquishing visible political controls in favor of less visible ones while preserving its military rights essentially intact. This was best illustrated in the device of the preferential alliance which had superseded the mandates in Iraq (1932) and Transjordan (1946) and the military occupation in Egypt (1936). Britain hoped after the war to transform the interwar preferential instruments into "equal" alliances under which Britain would no longer maintain garrisons in Egypt and Iraq in peacetime but would enjoy the right of re-entry in an international crisis. Such alliances would also provide for close cooperation and military planning between the signatories, with Britain undertaking to train and equip the local armed forces and assist them in maintaining the important military bases in a state of readiness for instant use. Above all, such alliances would have relieved Britain in peacetime of the steep costs of permanent military posts and of the burdens of local nationalist irritation to which the presence of foreign troops invariably gave rise. But the two treaties of equal alliance, signed with Egypt in 1946 and with Iraq in 1948, were repudiated by the Arab governments.

It was at this juncture of British frustration, indeed a month before Britain and Egypt reopened their treaty negotiations, that the Tripartite Declaration was framed, and the reference to participation "in the defense of the area as a whole" was intended as a gentle hint that those states opting to align with the West would be rewarded with generous military aid. Following the breakdown of Anglo-Egyptian negotiations in July 1951, the British security planners must have believed that nationalist objections in the Arab East might be dissolved if Britain abandoned the search for a bilateral formula in favor of a multilateral one enshrining the principle of equality. Egypt was chosen for the decisive test because the other Arab states could be expected to follow the lead of the largest and most influential one, as they had done in the negotiations of the armistice system in 1949, and, even more, because the Suez Canal and the giant base that the British had constructed there in World War II would contribute substantially to the defense of Western interests in the region. During the war the base had served as regional arsenal, repair shop, military industrial site, and training ground for the three arms of the imperial forces, and had furnished them airstrips, naval stations, and garrisons as well. In 1947 it became the operational headquarters of the British Middle East Command. But the fate of the base hung in the balance as

Egyptian nationalists intensified the pressure on Britain, following the abortive negotiations of 1946, to evacuate its forces and terminate the preferential alliance of 1936.

To overcome Egyptian hostility the United States, France, and Turkey joined Britain in inviting Egypt in October 1951 to become a founding member of an Allied Middle East Command modeled on NATO. The transformation of the British base into an allied base with Egyptian participation in an integrated command would, it was hoped, prove less noxious to Egypt. Instead, the failure to consult Egypt in framing the proposal pressed on the nerves of the nationalists, who especially resented any suggestion that their country continue as host to foreign troops under a British commander. The presence of British forces, London had frequently reminded Cairo, was essential for the adequate defense of the Suez Canal.To Egyptian nationalists this could only mean Britain's deliberate pursuit of a policy of political domination for the purpose, among others, of retarding Egyptian military development. Not only were British troops still on Egyptian soil, but the British were recommending the addition of American, French, and Turkish forces as well. Even diminutive Lebanon and fragile Syria could boast the retirement of French and British garrisons as early as 1946, while backward Yemen had never undergone European occupation and had become sovereign as early as 1918. To the Egyptian nationalists the proposal represented not progress but regress. The Egyptian government rejected the plan out of hand and unilaterally repudiated the 1936 treaty.

The four powers responded by issuing in November 1951 a fresh set of principles under which any Middle East state might voluntarily adhere to the projected Middle East Command. In the latest statement, the Western powers were less oblique in referring to military aid: "Requests for arms and equipment made by states in the area willing to join in its defense to sponsoring states in a position to assist in this connection," the statement read, "will be filled by them to the extent possible following the coordination of such requests through the Middle East Command." It was also suggested that as a continuing objective the command would aim "to reduce such deficiencies as exist at present in the organization and capacity for defense . . . so that the peacetime role of the states of the area in Middle East defense will progressively increase, thus permitting the peacetime role of states not territorially part of the Middle East to be decreased proportionately." [4]

The offer of military aid seemed to tempt the military junta in

Egypt even less than it had the monarchy. "The heart of the trouble" in Egypt, reported Secretary of State John Foster Dulles in the spring of 1953,

> is not so much the presence of British troops, for both sides agreed that they should be withdrawn, but the subsequent authority over and management of this gigantic base. . . . Experienced adminis-trative and technical personnel is needed to keep the base in operat-ing efficiency and the provision of this personnel causes difficulty. The matter has an importance which goes beyond Egypt, for the base serves all Near Eastern and indeed Western security.[5]

Although Dulles admitted that a Middle East Defense Organiza-tion was "a future rather than an immediate possibility," he never-theless sensed among "the northern tier of nations" an "awareness of danger" from the Soviet Union and

> a vague desire to have a collective security system. . . . While await-ing . . . [its] formal creation . . . the United States can usefully help strengthen the interrelated defense of those countries which want strength, not as against each other or the West, but to resist the common threat to all free peoples.

The United States accordingly signed military aid agreements with Pakistan and Iraq in 1954, as a prelude to the formation in the following year of the Baghdad Pact which brought together these two Middle East countries with Turkey, Iran, and Britain. Though a sponsor, the United States did not formally join the new organization. From the outset the Baghdad Pact demonstrated the limited value of attempting to bring into harness major members of NATO and Middle East states for Cold War purposes. The only Middle East member that fully identified itself with the pur-poses of the Western alliance was Turkey, and it already belonged to NATO. The participation of Pakistan alienated India and Af-ghanistan. The presence of Iraq in the scheme, it was hoped, would constitute an entering Arab wedge. Instead, it intensified Arab hostility, as Egypt became an outspoken foe of the pact. "After the success of the [Egyptian] revolution in 1952," 'Abd al-Nasir later recalled,

> Britain and the USA began to ask us to ally ourselves and come to an agreement with them. . . . Our reply . . . was that we could not conclude an alliance with them . . . [but only] with Arab States. I

asked them. . . . would the views expressed by Egypt count with Britain? If we sit at one table—Mr. Eden representing Great Britain and I representing Egypt—how can a great Power ally itself with a small State like us? This would not be an alliance—merely subordination. . . . We can co-operate with you on equal terms; we can come to an understanding; we can be friends—but we will on no account agree to being an appendage or subordinate.[6]

The Baghdad Pact itself never really developed into a military organization, nor did it ever create an integrated command.

The attempted consolidation in the Baghdad Pact of allied military policies along the Soviet frontier with those in the Arab zone by the promise of lavish military aid to those Middle East states that might affiliate with it had an effect the reverse of that intended. Instead of opening the door to wider Middle East membership in the Western system, it opened the door to Soviet military aid to the angered countries.

Peaceful Coexistence vs. Containment

In 1955 Egypt became the first Soviet military client in the Middle East. In less than a year Syria and Afghanistan followed, with Yemen not too far behind; the U.S.S.R. picked up the arms accounts of four of the sixteen sovereign states in the region at the time. The United States and its allies were caught flatfooted, their monopoly broken unexpectedly and with ease. Their postwar arms-supplying policies had been framed on two premises: that the Soviet Union would probably not make military equipment available to non-Communist governments; and that, even if it did, no non-Communist state in the Middle East, or elsewhere in Asia and Africa, would be likely to accept the offer because of the attendant political risks.

In retrospect, it is hardly astonishing that the U.S.S.R. became a major arms purveyor in the Middle East. All governments need arms, and new governments need them more than others. The manufacture of modern weapons is highly specialized, costly, and beyond the capacity of any but the industrial countries, so the new states without exception had to import such weapons. In postwar economic planning the U.S.S.R. had given special consideration to producing military goods, even at the expense of civilian goods. But the manufacture of weapons became thoroughly discombobulated because of the technological revolution that overtook conventional as well as nuclear systems. To this disarray, electronics, aeronautics, and rocketry were the primary contributors. Never before in history were such expensive and such highly sophisticated military weapons systems so short-lived. No sooner did intricate instruments of war roll off the assembly line than more efficient and entirely new ones were being readied for production, while still more efficient ones had already reached the drawing boards. Before the end of the first postwar decade it became manifest that only the United States exceeded the U.S.S.R. as a producer of modern armaments. Far behind the two giants tagged the industrial countries of Europe and the West. All the remaining producers were the pygmies of the military industry. Both giants had armaments to spare; for them and their industrial allies, the weapons underwent swift obsolescence; in the rest of the world the obsolescing arms were highly coveted.

In brief, military goods, in brisk demand in the new states, crammed Soviet shelves by the mid-1950s, at a time when Russia could begin to turn from its preoccupation with Europe and the Far East to a consideration of other regions. The U.S.S.R. could hardly have escaped the role of military supplier. Indeed, military aid was easier to provide than economic aid, in view of the chronically short supply of consumer and even capital goods—to say nothing of primary agricultural products. However much and loudly the traffickers denied it, the traffic in arms was more political than economic; and to make Communist arms politically acceptable in the long run, the Soviet Union also became an economic as well as a military-aider, thereby depriving its own citizens and its Communist allies of needed material resources.

On the receiving side, Gamal 'Abd al-Nasir expressed the anger, fear, confidence, and aspiration that had fused to impel him and his colleagues to conclude the first arms deal with the Soviet bloc. "You know that heavy weapons are controlled by the big powers," explained the Egyptian Prime Minister to his people in September 1955, when he advertised the agreement with Czechoslovakia, and

that the big powers have never agreed to supply our army with heavy weapons except with conditions and with stipulations . . . [which] we refused . . . because we are jealous of our true freedom and . . . of our independent policy. We are anxious . . . [to] have a strong independent policy so that we may make of Egypt a new independent personality which will really rid itself of imperialism . . . of occupation . . . [and] of foreign domination in all its aspects.[7]

'Abd al-Nasir left no doubt of his conviction that the political benefits of becoming a buyer of Soviet arms more than outweighed the political risks. "When I hear someone say that this opens the way for Russian or foreign influence in Egypt or the Middle East," he noted,

> I think of the remote past and I say that this commercial agreement . . . means the eradication of the foreign influence which so long depressed and dominated us.
>   My brothers, when we are able to equip our army with the necessary arms without conditions or restrictions, we destroy foreign control—that control which I . . . and you have felt in the guise of equipping our army and . . . of providing it with arms. Those who talk to us about foreign influence know that they themselves have no intention of seeing foreign influence wiped out.

Each Soviet military client in the Middle East admittedly had its own reasons for taking the plunge. But basically all subscribed to 'Abd al-Nasir's belief that Soviet influence could be held in check.

At the time of the Soviet breakthrough in 1955 neither the Egyptians nor the Russians could predict the reaction of the United States and its allies. This accounted for the special precautions taken in negotiating the first agreement. By prearrangement, it was announced as a Czech-Egyptian agreement, and the first shipment of arms reached Egypt before the public disclosure of the deal. Soviet military aid to Middle East states, moreover, was no less pragmatic than American aid, for obvious reasons. In the first postwar decade, the United States became an arms supplier in the Middle East to prevent Soviet expansion. At the start of the second decade, the Soviet Union became an arms supplier to inhibit the further growth of American influence in the region. Moscow's decision to support non-Communist underdeveloped countries broke sharply with traditional Soviet policy. Before the death of Stalin, the U.S.S.R. dispensed neither economic nor military aid to the non-Communist world. Israel, the lone exception in the Middle East, had bought heavy equipment in 1948 from Czechoslovakia, with the Kremlin's blessings; but the arrangement, though important to Israel at the time, did not last longer than a few months and was never renewed. Not until seven years later did the Soviet Union enter the military aid business on a sustained basis to wean selected Middle East countries away from dependence on the West and to deny their facilities in the containment of communism. It was hardly surprising that the U.S.S.R.'s first military clients in the region were the foes of the Baghdad Pact: Egypt, Syria, and Afghanistan; although, to attract these countries as customers, Russia bid higher than the West.

The U.S.S.R. boasted that its military aid had no strings attached. Peaceful coexistence was an appeal to neutralism, and thus there was no insistence that recipients of Soviet military aid join the Communist alliance. The U.S.S.R. did not restrict the shopping list to defensive weapons, as did the United States in sales to nonallied clients in the Middle East. Soviet customers were allowed to pick and choose among almost the entire range of conventional weapons, strategic as well as tactical—MiG 15 fighters, self-propelled assault guns, antitank guns, anti-aircraft cannon, electronic communications gear, mobile radar stations, torpedo boats, minesweepers, and even submarines. It did not matter that most of the weapons, particularly in the early years, were obsolescent or surplus. Nor did the supplier rigidly fix the amounts. The customer could request matériel in any quantity, and the orders were promptly filled. These were sales, it is true. But so, too, were Western arms that went to nonaligned Middle East countries. Unlike the Western powers, however, the U.S.S.R. and its satellites did not demand payment in hard currency on delivery; instead, they accepted local currency for later purchase of local primary products and a flexible schedule of deferred payments including long-term, low-interest credits. But, above all, as 'Abd al-Nasir noted, "These arms were entirely unconditional. We simply had to pay their cost. There was no restriction or condition." [8]

Despite differences in style, Soviet military aid to Middle East countries was just as pragmatic as American military aid, to which it was reactive. Contrast, for example, Soviet policies toward the Arab states and toward Afghanistan. In Egypt and Syria, as later also in Iraq, Algeria, and even Yemen, Soviet military aid seemed designed to encourage economic and social revolution at home and hostility abroad, particularly to those neighbors that were Western military clients. The planners of Soviet military aid to Afghanistan must clearly have been looking over their shoulders at Turkey, Iran, and Pakistan for purposes not of arousing Afghan enmity to the allies of the West, but of demonstrating to them that even military aid from the U.S.S.R. need not be feared. Afghanistan had become a Soviet arms customer in 1956 at a moment of Afghan pique not only over the Baghdad Pact but over the United States military aid agreement with Pakistan after an earlier American rejection of overtures from Kabul for military and gendarmerie missions and modern weapons. Western observers freely predicted the suborning of the tribal kingdom and an early Communist take-over. Nothing of the sort occurred. The U.S.S.R. bought with arms the usual tactical advantages: Afghanistan became dependent on the Soviet Union for spare parts and replacements, to say nothing of new equipment; the Afghan army adopted Soviet military doctrine; Afghan officers trained in the Soviet Union and Soviet technicians and instructors in Afghanistan cemented official and personal relations at all officer levels; and Russian became the military language of the new Afghan army. Yet the Russians did not appear to exploit these advantages. The Soviet Union, in brief, made no attempt to overthrow the Afghan regime and seemed unperturbed by Communist sponsorship of a prenationalist, traditional, absolute monarchy.

The West, complacent until the Soviet arms agreement with Egypt, became anxious thereafter. The old policies had demonstrably become outmoded; yet no new ones were immediately framed. The West had lost the monopoly of the Middle East arms market and could no longer restrain the region's governments simply by threatening to withhold modern weapons. The real effect of Soviet military aid to the Arab states and Afghanistan on the Great Power military balance in the Middle East was not easy to evaluate. It became clear, after a time, that the U.S.S.R. was not seeking immediate military rights in client countries. Military technicians and advisers were not the same presence as troops; and the building of airstrips and submarine pens for receiving countries did not entail the use of these facilities by Soviet planes and submarines. Still, the United States and its allies suspected the worst—that the Russians might be amassing arms at strategic points in the client states for later Soviet use in the event of a showdown with the West; or infiltrating agents in the guise of military technicians or advisers to plot the Communist seizure of power; or engaging in indirect aggression by encouraging their clients to promote subversion in neighboring lands friendly to the West. Yet the strategic status quo was not basically changed until the Suez crisis of 1956, after which the West irrevocably lost assured access to the Suez Canal zone when it was most required. What was denied the West, however, was also denied the U.S.S.R., both in the canal zone and in strategically less valuable real estate belonging to the other clients. The net effect was a Soviet gain, of course, but only a limited gain, to which the West could accommodate.

After Stalin's death, it is clear, the Soviet Union altered its strategic doctrine for the Middle East but not its strategic objectives. Under Stalin the strategic doctrine consisted of the traditional Communist appeal for a proletarian revolution against existing bourgeois regimes which were tied to the imperial powers by the oil monopolists and Wall Street. The strategic objectives aimed at installing "people's democracies" and assuring domination. Stalin's successors altered the doctrine to one of peaceful coexistence that appealed to the uncommitted nations, whether or not they were Communist, or whether their rulers were proletarians or progressives, so long as they were working to quicken the departure of Britain and France from the Middle East and keep the United States out. The Soviet leaders had elected to work with and through the "nationalist bourgeoisie" in these countries to reach the strategic goals which remained fixed, except that the balance of power had changed. The British withdrawal was well advanced in the Arab East by 1955. Similarly, the French position in the Arab West was greatly weakened, although few would have predicted at the time a total political retirement from North Africa in less than a decade. The United States presence, meanwhile, was becoming more and more visible.

The strategic doctrine of the United States, by contrast, remained unchanged. It was still summed up in the concept of containment, calling for the union of the free—that is, non-Communist—world behind the Western security shield. The strategic objectives of the Truman Doctrine aimed at keeping the Russians out of the Middle East altogether, allowing them no opportunity to gain an entering wedge. Under President Eisenhower, the strategic objectives had to be modified, since the Soviet Union had by then acquired military clients in the Middle East. The United States now had to make certain that these clients were not converted into satellites and that the Russians did not establish military bases in these countries.

In supplying economic and military aid to non-Communist states, the U.S.S.R. was adopting Western policies, while adapting them to Soviet capabilities and objectives. It promptly lifted many of the restraints on the quantity and quality of weapons that it was prepared to make available to its clients. The United States, in turn, was forced to adopt the Soviet policies of offering sophisticated hardware even to states that did not join the Western collective security system. A new formula had to be framed to enable the United States to persuade governments which looked as if they might be falling under Soviet influence, direct or indirect, to accept

American economic and military aid. More than that, the new formula could no longer insist on alignment with the West as the price for obtaining offensive weapons.

This was the meaning of the Eisenhower Doctrine, which found its way from the text of a formal presidential address to the Congress in January 1957 to embodiment in a joint resolution two months later. The Congress strengthened the President's proposal by stipulating that "the United States regards as vital to the national interest and world peace the preservation of the independence and integrity of the nations of the Middle East." The resolution authorized the President to give economic assistance and "to undertake in the general area of the Middle East military assistance programs with any nation or group of nations . . . desiring such assistance." At presidential discretion, moreover, the Congress declared that the United States would be "prepared to use armed forces to assist any such nation or group of nations requesting assistance against armed aggression from any country controlled by international communism." [9] Any Middle East state, in short, qualified for economic and military aid simply for the asking, without having to endorse containment. Caution was thrown to the winds. The President had received a blank check from the Congress, enabling him to match or exceed Soviet aid in sophistication or amount and even to employ American military power in support of any Middle East regime requesting it—thus going beyond the Soviet capacity to compete under the existing military balance.

The U.S.S.R. could hardly have failed to protest against the Eisenhower Doctrine as a device for unilateral American military intervention in internal Middle East affairs, and to contrast this with its own allegedly high-minded foreign policy, which "does not aspire to have military bases or any concessions in the Near and Middle East countries for the purpose of extracting profits and does not aspire to receive any privileges in this region. . . ." Embedded in the propaganda in the first of a series of Soviet exchanges with the United States on the Eisenhower Doctrine was a concrete proposal which exposed some of the motivation of the Soviet military aid policies. The U.S.S.R. would be willing to swap its export of arms to Middle East countries for a reciprocal arms embargo by the Western powers, for their renunciation of efforts "to involve these countries in military blocs with the participation of the Great Powers," and for their liquidation of "foreign bases" and their withdrawal of "foreign troops from the territory of Middle Eastern countries." For good measure, the Russians also proposed that the Soviet Union and the three Western governments subscribe in principle to "noninterference in the internal affairs of the Middle Eastern countries, and respect for their sovereignty and independence." [10] The Russians were thus saying, in effect, that they would give up their military aid policies toward the Middle East only after agreement with the West on the military neutralization of the region.

The Russian price was obviously too high, and the state of mutual confidence too low, for an American-Soviet détente. The United States, in its opening reply, rejected the Russian proposal, finding "cause for considerable doubt as to the seriousness of the Soviet Government's invitation to . . . the United States to join it in cooperation in the Middle East," in view of the continued Soviet vilification at the United Nations of American Middle East policies. "When it comes . . . to such matters as 'military blocs,' the liquidation of foreign bases and the withdrawal of foreign troops," the American reply continued, ". . . the United States . . . must point out that the Middle Eastern states are fully capable of deciding what cooperative efforts are required to enable them to play their part in the defense of the area." The United States "has always kept in mind," the note insisted,

> the need to encourage stability and foster progress toward lasting peace and security there. It therefore regrets the Soviet Government, on the contrary, saw fit to effect massive shipments of arms into the area at a time when regional disputes there had become sharply exacerbated.[11]

The United States applied the Eisenhower Doctrine almost before the ink dried on the joint congressional resolution. In the Jordan crisis of April 1957, which in the Washington view was largely inspired by Egypt, the White House announced that the President and his Secretary of State had accepted King Husayn's judgment that "international communism" threatened the independence and integrity of his kingdom. Units of the Sixth Fleet were therefore ordered to the eastern Mediterranean, and the United States inaugurated its program of supporting assistance to Jordan, which to all intents and purposes replaced the former British military subsidy. In the Syrian crisis in the summer of 1957, the United States began signaling to the U.S.S.R. that it might have to intervene. A field report by the Deputy Under Secretary of State had persuaded Eisenhower and Dulles that Syria's Arab neighbors had become jittery over "the apparently growing Soviet domination . . . and the large build-up there of Soviet-bloc arms . . . [unjustified] by any purely defensive needs." These neighbors had grown concerned "over border incidents and intensive propaganda and subversive activities directed toward the overthrow of duly constituted governments." Dulles left no doubt in his annual speech to the United Nations General Assembly in September 1957 that in his view Soviet military aid to the Arab states was designed by

> intensive propaganda . . . to incite [them] . . . to believe that with Soviet arms, with Soviet technicians, and with Soviet political backing they could accomplish extreme nationalistic ambitions.
>
> This Soviet Communist effort had made progress in Syria. There Soviet-bloc arms were exultantly received and political power has increasingly been taken over by those who depend upon Moscow. True patriots have been driven from positions of power by arrest or intimidation.

A month later at the General Assembly, Ambassador Henry Cabot Lodge continued hammering away at the massive exports:

> There is no question whatever of challenging any country's right to acquire arms. Let me make that clear. But we are entitled to inquire regarding the motives behind sending such large quantities of arms into a potentially explosive area at a particularly tense moment because such shipments in such circumstances inevitably heighten tensions.

Lodge accused the U.S.S.R. of "creating an artificial war scare" in Syria to further Soviet "expansionist purposes and, in accordance with [the Soviet] . . . historic aim, reduce the Middle East to the status of the captive nations of Eastern Europe." [12]

The Syrian crisis demonstrated that the United States was interpreting the consequences of Soviet arms sales to the Arab states as falling within the scope of the implied definition of indirect aggression in the Eisenhower Doctrine that the Doctrine was expected to check. While few, if any, Syrians could wax enthusiastic over the Eisenhower Doctrine, many would nevertheless have agreed that the massive Soviet arms deliveries were related to the drift of their country toward communism, for in February 1958 a majority of the Syrian political leaders chose union with Egypt as the means of escape from a possible Communist take-over. The Syrian crisis was thus resolved. But the crisis in American-Soviet confidence deepened. The overturn in July 1958 of the Western allied Hashimi monarchy in Iraq, to which Egyptian inflammatory propaganda had contributed, led to the landing of American troops in Lebanon and the return of British troops to Jordan, both on invitation of the Arab regimes. In this connection, the United States never quite claimed that its intervention in Lebanon represented action under the Eisenhower Doctrine, for while the Department of State could prove that the Lebanese civil war was one in which the two regions of the U.A.R., Syria and Egypt, were both intimately involved, it could not prove that the U.A.R. itself was "controlled by international communism."

By this act the United States established its reputation as captain of the gendarmes in the Middle East, for the unilateral intervention in Lebanon was carried out without a single casualty, despite the vehement protests of the U.S.S.R. and its Arab arms clients. Although the President and the Secretary of State would have been hard put in a legal hearing to prove that the landing of troops accorded with international law or even with established American policy, the peacekeeping mission was a complete success, and the success could be attributed to roughly equal proportions of power and of skill, perseverance, and luck. The American intervention, which ended when the troops were withdrawn four months later, meanwhile facilitated the transfer of power, by regular election and with the unanimous approval of the Arab League states, from the pro-American president who had invited the American landing to a neutral president who was pleased to see the American forces go. The U.S.S.R. profoundly resented its exclusion from any peacekeeping role in the region. "The Soviet Government," Gromyko had informed Secretary-General Hammarskjold in October 1957 at the time of the Syrian crisis, ". . . is prepared to take part with its forces in suppressing aggression and punishing the violators of peace." In August 1958, Khrushchev, in a letter to Eisenhower on the Lebanese crisis, was reaffirming the same principle when he wrote that "No state which is genuinely concerned to protect the independence and security of the small countries can arrogate to itself the right to intervene in those countries' affairs and proclaim this or that 'doctrine' with such an end in view." [13] In other words, if the U.S.S.R. could not participate in peacekeeping, it was determined to deny the United States that right.

The Soviet Quest for Strategic Mobility

In retrospect, it seems clear that in the series of Middle East crises from Suez to Lebanon, the U.S.S.R. was deliberately increasing the tension and threatening to intervene so as to frighten the United States and its allies into giving Russia a seat on the region's peace-keeping directorate. The landing of American troops in Lebanon underlined the willingness of the United States to use military power in the cause of regional peace. For more than eight years thereafter the U.S.S.R. stopped resorting to brinkmanship as a form of diplomatic pressure. One may assume that the Russians did not want to get the United States into the habit of sending troops, or the Middle East states into the habit of receiving them. If it happened too often, the Soviet leaders may have reasoned, the troops might one day remain. In any case, the presence of American troops in Lebanon tended to call attention to the Soviet lack of strategic mobility.

The American–Soviet rivalry in military policies toward the Middle East had reached an impasse by the end of 1958. The United States could not prevent the Soviet Union from pursuing its military aid programs as it wished or from encouraging its clients to sponsor the "liberation" of their neighboring lands—that is, the overturn of regimes friendly to the West. Still none of the clients became a satellite, nor did their number grow rapidly. The Soviet Union had obtained four arms accounts in 1955–56; to these were added only two others in the next ten years: Iraq in 1958, and Algeria in 1963. However, the Soviet Union did not lose any clients either, since that relationship, for obvious reasons, tended to be durable.

The U.S.S.R. was unable at this stage to modify the strategic status quo in the Middle East. That this remained uppermost in the minds of the Soviet security planners could be seen in October 1962, at the height of the second Cuban crisis, when Chairman Khrushchev proposed to President Kennedy a reciprocal and simultaneous withdrawal of Soviet missiles from Cuba and American missles from Turkey. "You are worried over Cuba," observed Khrushchev.

> You say that it worries you because it lies at a distance of 90 miles across the sea from the shores of the United States. However, Turkey lies next to us. Our sentinels are pacing up and down and watching each other. Do you believe that you have the right to demand

security for your country and the removal of such weapons that you qualify as offensive, while not recognizing this right for us?

You have stationed devastating rocket weapons, which you call offensive, in Turkey literally right next to us. How then does recognition of our equal military possibilities tally with such unequal relations between our great states? This does not tally at all.[14]

It was shortly after the second Cuban crisis that the U.S.S.R. turned its efforts to establish a continuous naval presence in the Mediterranean. Toward the end of the 1950s Albania had permitted the Soviet Union to erect berths at Valona for a handful of submarines, only to terminate the arrangement in 1961, when, in the hardening dispute between Russia and China, Albania sided with the latter. Early in 1963, the Russians began gradually to amass in the Mediterranean a mixed naval force of surface vessels and submarines. From a level of some 20 vessels, reached by the end of 1966, the size of the force was enlarged to 30 on the eve of the Six Day War in June 1967, and then by half as much again immediately following the war. The Soviet Mediterranean fleet, fixed roughly at 30 vessels by the close of 1967, included submarines, surface combat vessels (among them, guided-missile frigates and destroyers and landing craft), electronic trawlers, and logistical support ships (tenders, oilers, and tugs). The fleet selected as anchorages more than a half-dozen protected bights in international waters off islands and the mainland from one end of the Mediterranean to the other. Copying the American practice, it used the anchorages for refueling, replenishment, and repair at sea. Even before the Six Day War, Soviet units called at Yugoslav, Algerian, Egyptian, and Syrian ports. After the war, Soviet combat ships anchored more often and in larger numbers at Alexandria and Port-Sa'id, using the calls for supplies and repairs. (See Map 2, p. 76.)

Of potentially greater significance were the signs of Soviet efforts to procure air-base rights in Egypt. Before the Six Day War, Soviet air power had been shut out of the Mediterranean and the Middle East because Soviet planes could not in peacetime, without prior consent, overfly third countries that were not Soviet allies. The airlift of arms to Egypt, via Yugoslavia, in the summer of 1967 represented a new departure. This was the route later used in the demonstration flights to Cairo of Soviet bomber squadrons in December 1967 and January 1968. Such flights, followed in the spring by Soviet pilots flying Soviet-made planes with Egyptian markings from Egyptian bases on recurrent Soviet reconnaissance missions, must have awakened visions in the Pentagon of Soviet access to Egyptian airfields. If regularized, such an arrangement, even an informal one, might compensate for the lack of seaborne airpower in the Soviet navy, which has always depended on a land-based air arm. The rearmament of Egypt after the June war as payment for formal or informal, open or concealed, landing and take-off rights—if established—would certainly cost less than the construction of aircraft carriers and their assimilation into the Soviet navy. If successful in Egypt, the U.S.S.R. might be expected to seek comparable rights: in Algeria and Syria for greater strategic mobility in the Mediterranean; in Republican Yemen and South Yemen for air-naval superiority at the southern entrance to the Red Sea; and in Iraq for a checkmate against the West in the Persian Gulf after the British withdrawal in 1971.

The Soviet-American rivalry in the Middle East, in the final analysis, focused on strategic advantage. Time and again after 1955, the U.S.S.R. publicly warned the United States that it viewed the Middle East, west and east of Suez, as the Soviet backyard and that it would not tolerate American military and political paramountcy there. The Sixth Fleet, however, vividly symbolized American military primacy in the Middle East west of Suez. Accordingly, the Soviet government seemed to proceed from the premise of the need to remove from its immediate southern vicinity all competitive power, to the logical conclusion that it must neutralize the Sixth Fleet, or overtake it, or drive it out of the Mediterranean altogether. Viewed in this light, the Soviet insistence on continuing the Cold War in the Middle East seemed to reflect a belief that such policies offered the U.S.S.R. the brightest hope of achieving a Soviet-American strategic stalemate in the region. This goal helped explain why the U.S.S.R. encouraged every act that barred the Sixth Fleet from Mediterranean ports or otherwise weakened American ties to the littoral states, such as the action by Russia's Arab arms clients in severing diplomatic relations with the United States in June 1967.

Indications were already appearing in 1968 that the naval competition might spread east of Suez after the British retirement from the Persian Gulf. There, in the 1970s, the Soviet Union could be expected to try to keep the United States from replacing British naval power. Even without that prospect, the Soviet buildup in the 1960s of a continuous naval presence in the Mediterranean had already opened a new phase in Soviet-American rivalry. Manifestly, the U.S.S.R. was capable of maintaining such a fleet in the Mediterranean, and the United States could not prevent it any more than it had earlier prevented the Soviet sale of arms to Middle East states. Yet it could also be said that the Soviet force did not by itself represent an immediate threat to United States naval supremacy in the Mediterranean. Nor could the U.S.S.R. really hope to bar the United States Navy from the Persian Gulf, if it should seek entry.

Meanwhile, the primary activity of the Soviet Mediterranean force in 1967–68 was to trail the Sixth Fleet—at times so closely as to interfere with replenishment and even maneuvers. By the same token, the training exercises of the Sixth Fleet basically were concerned with reconnaissance of Russian naval activity. The two "snooper powers" used all available devices—sonic, photographic, and radar—so that each charted the other's changing components and shifting positions.

Still, by adroit moves before and after the Arab-Israel war in June 1967, the Russians strengthened their bargaining position and potentially their strategic position in the Middle East. The Soviet policy thrusts seemed to be spaced a decade apart, and the two earlier challenges of the same genre gave rise to periods of creative American policy response. One extended through the middle years of the first postwar decade, which yielded the Truman Doctrine as a global directive and the Tripartite Declaration as a regional one. The other embraced the opening years of the second postwar decade, when the Soviet breakthrough and the American reaction resulted in an ever-sharpening competition between the two superpowers in the distribution of modern military weapons among their Middle East clients. Would the Soviet quest for strategic mobility and its potential threat to American strategic supremacy in the Mediterranean and the Middle East prod the United States into framing new policy principles? If so, there were no clues in mid-1968.

This much, however, was clear: The imperial retirement of Britain and France and their replacement by the Soviet-American military competition in the first two postwar decades conditioned military politics in the Middle East.

6

ARMIES IN POSTWAR POLITICS

Diversity best describes military politics in the postwar Middle East. The military structures were as variable as the states that they were supposed to serve. To begin with, the military establishments under review were primarily armies. Almost all Middle East governments aspired to develop air forces, but by and large these remained relatively small. Smaller still were the navies, wherever they existed. Consequently there was little if any interservice rivalry in postwar Middle East military establishments of the type that characterized such Latin American armed forces as those of Brazil and Argentina, where naval officers sometimes competed with army officers for political power. In the late 1960s it was still premature to say that interservice political rivalry was close at hand in the Middle East; thus, in most states it was fair to speak of the army as referring not merely to the ground forces but to all branches of the military establishment.

In the study of military politics the military tradition must be examined to ascertain whether the army was of alien or native origin. If the state were a former dependency, alien influences in military organization, training, and doctrine were bound to survive long after the imperial withdrawal. Admittedly, once Egypt took the plunge in becoming a military client of the U.S.S.R., it made every effort to exorcise all traces of British influence. But Egypt was a regional exception. In considering the military tradition, it is also necessary to evaluate earlier efforts at modernization, wherever these might have occurred. In Turkey, for example, the nineteenth-century tradition of military modernization, which transformed army officers into members of the urban elite, conditioned the behavior of the military who staged the coup d'état of 1960. Tribal armies persisted into the third postwar decade in the traditional monarchies with relatively large beduin populations, and the kings relied more heavily on these forces than on the so-called modern armies that were brought into being, often against their will and better judgment. Military politics in these states were conducted in the Islamic tradition, for the line of military-political development was basically uninterrupted until the twentieth century.

Nevertheless, despite the conservatism of the traditional monarchs, their regular armies were gradually gaining ground, since in the prevailing mood of the postwar Middle East a modernizing army was one of the marks of sovereignty. Even in such countries as Tunisia and Lebanon, where a military career was held in low esteem, the armies began to fall under the spell of the regional fad by the start of the third postwar decade. Military modernization in the region was clearly a function of the Cold War, which gave opportunities to many states, particularly after 1955, to modernize and expand their armed forces at irresistible prices. Turkey, Iran, and Pakistan, by allying themselves with the United States in the Cold War, qualified for military and economic grant aid. In the Arab-Israel zone, armies "modernized" at a hectic pace, as the states were drawn into bewildering, interlaced arms races. Sparked by regional rivalries and hostilities but fed by the superpowers and their respective Cold War coalitions, these races easily became the most intense in the Middle East—indeed, in the nonindustrial world. Alongside them, the arms race that started in the mid-1960s among France's three former dependencies in North Africa looked like child's play. Nonetheless, wherever these races occurred, the investment in military modernization quickened.

The professionalization of an officer corps, some social scientists have argued, insures against the politicization of an army. This may well be true in the industrial countries. In a nonindustrial region such as the Middle East there were a few armies whose officers might be accurately described as professional—those of Iran, Israel, Pakistan, and Turkey. Yet Pakistani and Turkish officers seized political power. In addition to denoting specialized competence, "professional" also relates to career employment. Largely in the second meaning were there professional armies in the Middle East, which therefore might preferably be called career armies. All armies are built around career cadres by the addition of conscripts, wherever conscription is practiced. Among the eighteen armies in the postwar Middle East approximately a third were cadre-conscript. The rest consisted wholly of volunteers who entered the army for employment. In such career armies there is a slow turnover of personnel and the likelihood of a more rigid hierarchical structure than in the cadre–conscript armies.

Social scientists who study military politics have often found it useful to investigate the social origins of the officers and men as an essential part of the evaluation of the political role of a military establishment. Thus it is held that if army officers are recruited from the same class as the rulers of a state, both share an interest in the established system and each supports the other. If this is viewed as an invariable rule, however, it fails to explain why the generals in Pakistan and Sudan seized power from the civilian politicians, since both came from the same social class. It does explain, however, why these generals were clearly not radical reformers and why in both cases they did not attempt to destroy the existing social and economic institutions. On the other hand, if army officers are recruited from an underprivileged class, as were the Free Officers of Egypt who destroyed the monarchy in 1952, they might be expected to try to improve the status of the class from which they came. Yet, although this made sense in a homogeneous country like Egypt, most Middle East states have plural societies, and vertical divisions among ethnic, religious, or linguistic communities are more significant than horizontal economic and social divisions.

The career army of Pakistan, for instance, recruited its officers and men in the Punjab and among the Pathan tribesmen in the former Northwest Frontier province. Inherited from British India, the practice of recruiting primarily West Pakistanis gave the East Pakistanis yet another grievance against the government for alleged discrimination. At the western extremity of the Middle East, in Morocco, a majority of the population were Arabs or Arabized Berbers, but nearly four-fifths of the soldiers of all ranks were Berbers. Arab officers and men from the northern provinces predominated in the Sudanese army, in which non-Arabs from the south were severely restricted in number and almost shut out from the command slots in the officer corps. After the coup d'état of 1966, the Syrian army fell under the domination of officers from the 'Alawi community, a small schismatic and underprivileged group. In Israel, Druzes and Circassians were subject to conscription, whereas Christian and Muslim Arabs were not even permitted to volunteer for military service until the mid-1960s. Jews in all Arab countries were, by the same token, debarred from military service. Even among the most homogeneous countries of the region, similar discriminatory practices prevailed. Muslim Turks tended to relegate Muslim Kurds to secondary roles, while in Egypt the Muslim Arabs disallowed Coptic Christians from achieving any primacy in the forces.

The extreme heterogeneity of the Middle East emerges clearly from the statistical indicators for 1965, as set forth in Table 1. Judged by population alone, the eighteen countries of the region ranged in size from Kuwait with only a half million inhabitants to Pakistan with more than 100 million. More than half of the countries had populations smaller than 7.5 million, while Pakistan's population exceeded those of the next three—Iran, Egypt, and Turkey—put together, whose populations ranged between 23 million and 31 million. In countries of such variant sizes, the armies might also be expected to lack uniformity. Only five countries had force levels above 100,000 (Egypt, Iran, Pakistan, Israel, and Turkey), and five others, below 20,000 (Kuwait, Lebanon, Libya, Sudan, and Tunisia). More significant were the relative numbers serving in the armed forces. Among the lowest force levels per thousand inhabitants were Sudan (1.4), Pakistan (2.5), Tunisia and Algeria (4), Lebanon (5), and Egypt (6). The highest was Israel's citizen army (144), followed by Jordan (22.5) and Kuwait and Turkey (15).

Egypt spent more on its armed forces than any other Middle East country. Turkey was not too far behind, with Israel and Iran coming next, but at a much lower level of investment. Once again, however, in view of the great variations in living standards from country to country, the per capita investments were more meaningful. The two highest per capita spenders were Kuwait ($153.50) and Israel ($121.50); the three lowest were Afghanistan ($1.92), Pakistan ($2.77), and Tunisia ($3.02). The sums spent on defense might be compared with the sums given to development. In 1965 all but three countries for which such data was available were allocating more money to development than to defense. The share of the government's total budget set aside for defense in that year varied from 47 per cent in Jordan, 34 per cent in Iraq, and 33 per cent in Syria to 6 per cent in Tunisia.

Perhaps the most revealing statistics related to the GNP. The per capita GNP ranged from $3,670 for Kuwait and $1,308 for Israel to $100 for Sudan, $104 for Afghanistan, and $110 for Pakistan. Clearly, some countries were better able to afford expensive military habits than others. Yet it is also instructive to see that the percentage of the GNP consumed by defense ranged from as little as 1.6 in Tunisia and 1.8 in Afghanistan to as much as 12.7 in Iraq and 12.0 in Jordan. Indeed, with the exception of Lebanon, which had one of the lowest percentages in the region as a whole, all

TABLE 1. The Middle East, 1965: Force Levels, Government Expenditures, and GNP

	Population (millions)	Force Levels		Defense Expenditures	
		(thousands)	(per 1,000 population)	Total (millions $ U.S.)	Per capita ($ U.S.)
Afghanistan	12.0	90	7.5	23.00e	1.92
Algeria	11.7	65	5.5	101.00f	8.63
Egypt	29.6	180	6	461.84	15.60
Iran	23.4	185	8	315.51	13.48
Iraq	7.4	82	11	243.60	32.92
Israel	2.6	375b	144b	315.93	121.50
Jordan	2.0	45	22.5	58.80	29.40
Kuwayt	0.467	7	15	71.70	153.50
Lebanon	2.4	13	5	29.35	12.23
Libya	1.6	18.2c	11	61.34	38.34
Morocco	13.0	42	3.2	101.77	7.83
Pakistan	102.9	253	2.5	284.70	2.77
Saudi Arabia	3.2	45d	14	131.00e	40.93
Sudan	13.5	18.5	1.4	59.64	4.42
Syria	5.6	60	11	95.47	17.05
Tunisia a	4.6	17.5	4	13.90	3.02
Turkey	31.4	480	15	440.19	14.02
Yemen	4.1				

	Development			Total Budget		GNP		
	Total (millions $ U.S.)	Per capita ($ U.S.)	As % of defense	Total (millions $ U.S.)	Defense as % of	Total (millions $ U.S.)	Per capita ($ U.S.)	Defense as % of
Afghanistan				159g	14	1,250e	104	1.8
Algeria	794	26.8	171	895g	11	2,630e	225	3.8
Egypt	731	31.2	231	2,084	22	5,060	171	9.1
Iran	182	24.6	75	1,487	21	5,830	253	5.4
Iraq	338	130.0	106	715	34	1,919	259	12.7
Israel	28	14.0	48	1,457	22	3,401	1,308	9.3
Jordan	131	281.0	183	126	47	504	252	12.0
Kuwayt	62	25.8	211	591	12	1,714	3,670	4.2
Lebanon	243	151.9	249	171	17	887	370	3.3
Libya	156	12.0	153	464	13	1,196	748	5.1
Morocco	284	2.8	100	415	25	2,605	200	3.9
Pakistan				1,939	15	11,010	110	2.6
Saudi Arabia	89	6.6	149	691g	19	1,521e	475	8.6
Sudan	106	18.9	111	310	19	1,352	100	4.4
Syria	88	19.1	629	292	33	1,084	194	8.8
Tunisia a	383	12.2	87	218	6	881	192	1.6
Turkey				1,673	26	8,776	279	5.0
Yemen								

SOURCES: Data from tables that follow; also ACDA, Economic Bureau, *World-Wide Military Expenditures and Selected Data, Calendar Year 1965* (Washington, Dec. 1967); David Wood, "The Armed Forces of African States," *Adelphi Papers*, No. 27, Institute for Strategic Studies (London: April 1966); AID, *Summary of Basic Data*.

a 1964 conversion rate.
b Citizen army.
c Roughly two-thirds were tribal forces.
d Roughly half were tribal forces.
e ACDA statistics.
f *Adelphi Papers*, No. 27, p. 5.
g AID, *Summary of Basic Data.*

other states in the Arab-Israel zone ranked highest in the portion of the GNP that they assigned to their armed forces.

The basic diversity of the Middle East inescapably yields diverse results. Most of the meaningful generalizations on military politics, therefore, are necessarily subregional. Middle East political systems, when classified by the domestic political role of the armies, divide in the first instance into those countries in which the military overturned civilian regimes and the others, which remained under civilian rule. On closer scrutiny, it becomes clear that while the military interveners in Turkey and Pakistan later restored a substantial measure of civilian rule, the others continued to be dominated by military officers. This raises the obvious question why some military politicians seem impelled to reactivate civilian politics, while others do not. The military-political systems thus fall into two classes: the first carries the label of military republics, and the second, that of military-civilian coalitions.

The classical form of Islamic state is monarchical, and before the rise of European imperialism those Middle East states that were not dynastic were semisovereign oligarchies, such as the Barbary states of North Africa, which in the eighteenth and early nineteenth centuries were still tied to the Ottoman Empire. Turkey, the first Muslim republic, was a product of the twentieth century. Military republics were thus a new state form in Islam. Nor is it accidental that two of the three non-military republics—Israel and Lebanon—are also not Islamic states. The three nonmilitary republics manifestly form a separate category, yet they hardly resemble one another, except that the civilian rulers preserve their hegemony over the armed forces. The three states also seem unlikely candidates for early military rule.

This leaves the monarchies. In three of the eight surviving monarchies, tribal forces still played a principal role in upholding the regime in the 1960s. In the five others, which also had had tribal forces until the recent past (Iran was the only one to eliminate its tribal army before World War II), tribal forces had given way to modernized armies. The monarchies therefore fall naturally into two groups, one traditional and the other modernizing.

Before examining in later chapters the political systems and the character of civil-military relations in Middle East states, we should first familiarize ourselves in outline with the several patterns of military intrusion into politics. After 1949, armed forces successfully took part in the overturn of eight civilian regimes in the Middle East: Syria (1949); Egypt (1952); Iraq, Pakistan, and Sudan

(1958); Turkey (1960); and Algeria and Yemen (1962). In Syria and Iraq, the regimes of the military were plagued in turn with recurrent coups mounted by their colleagues. Although the military regime in Sudan after six years of rule was itself overthrown by a civilian uprising, Sudan enjoyed the further distinction of being the only military republic in the Arab world that did not become a Soviet military client; it became one only after the resumption of civilian rule. In none of the eight could it be said at the start of 1968 that the soldiers had carried out their avowed political programs, reinstated civilian rule, and returned to the barracks—not even in Sudan, where civilians literally drove the soldiers back. The two non-Arab military regimes, Turkey and Pakistan, framed new constitutions and placed the routine operations of government in civilian hands; yet the military leaders, as we shall see, retained a custodial responsibility for the republican institutions that they had fashioned. Military officers, in brief, have found it simpler to seize political power than to relinquish it—or to use it effectively.

The Pattern of Take-over

It is necessary at the outset to demarcate the stage at which it may be said that the military have intervened in politics. That stage is reached, it seems to me, when the soldiers cast aside civilian restraints on the military establishment—that is, when the armed forces become truly autonomous. Anything less than autonomy subordinates the soldiers to the civilian rulers. Insofar as the autonomous armed forces tend to confine their political activity to managing the military affairs of state, the intrusion of soldiers into politics may be characterized as minimal. In the postwar Middle East, Pakistan (1953–58) and Algeria (1962–65) best illustrated this unstable condition. At the other extreme is full military rule that is reached when civilian cabinet ministers are almost invariably technicians and, whether technicians or not, are nevertheless subordinate to the military ruler(s). This condition obtained in Syria under Za'im (1949) and Shishakli (1952–54), Egypt under 'Abd al-Nasir (from 1954), Iraq under Quasim (1958–63), Pakistan in the opening years of Ayub's rule (1958–62), Sudan (1958–64), and Turkey (1960–61).

The techniques of the military seizure of power in the Middle East after 1945 were relatively uniform. In each typical instance the military conspirators, in advance of the overturn of the regime, suborned key officers of elite garrisons posted in the capital or its outskirts. With the help of such garrisons, or after their neutralization if the help were withheld, the plotting officers entered the capital with armored units in the predawn hours. They placed the head of state and the members of the cabinet in custody, stationed troops and tanks at strategic points throughout the city while mobile forces in battle regalia policed its principal streets, took over the broadcasting station and other communications centers, and announced the end of the regime, the establishment of a new one, and the temporary imposition of martial law. These were essentially bloodless seizures of government. Even the savagery that attended the death of the Hashimi dynasty of Iraq in July 1958 did not cost many lives, despite the riotous demonstrations and the murder of the king, the regent, and the prime minister.

The joint civilian-military coup de'état in Algeria in 1962 was the slowest-motion coup in the postwar Middle East. The conspiratorial coalition grew naturally out of the Muslim rebellion that dragged on for more than seven years. In guerrilla warfare the line that separates political from military functions disappears; the distinction between politicians and soldiers is not sharp. The French, moreover, simply laid down political sovereignty on 3 July 1962. They did not transfer it directly to the Muslims; indeed, they seemed to believe, if the appointment of the Algerian Temporary Executive Council was an accurate guide, that the independent Algerian government would represent the European settlers no less than the Muslims. The Muslims maintained at Tunis their own political executive, called the Provisional Government of the Algerian Republic (GPRA), that had managed the rebellion after September 1958. They had even earlier formed an embryonic legislature, the National Council of the Algerian Republic, to which the GPRA was responsible. The GPRA was generally expected to uphold and promote the Muslim interest in the creation of a sovereign Algeria. At the head of a small group of politicians Ahmad Ben Bella, who had sat out most of the Algerian rebellion in a French prison (from October 1956 to March 1962), joined forces with Colonel Houari Boumedienne, the commander of Muslim Algeria's External Army that French counterguerrilla measures had kept in a state of total inactivity. After flouting the authority of the GPRA, Ben Bella, Boumedienne, et Cie. proceeded in the chaotic inaugural weeks of independence to demolish the GPRA altogether. Then, in September 1962 they rigged the election of deputies to the first National Assembly so as to insure a pliant majority in the legislature.

In Yemen, too, a civilian-military alliance tried at the end of the same month to overthrow the imamate. The conspirators captured San'a, destroyed the Imam's palace, and killed many of its royal inmates and their attendants. But Imam Muhammad al-Badr, who had just ascended the throne a few days before, escaped and rallied loyal tribesmen to resist the rebels. The incomplete coup d'état grew into a full-scale insurrection, thanks to the indispensable military, technical, and administrative assistance of Egypt. Almost from the very outset the soldiers gained the upper hand over the civilians in the Yemeni republic. When the United States, in December 1962, recognized the government of the Yemen Arab Republic as the lawful one, it was recognizing an insurrectional government that had not yet fulfilled, even on the most generous reckoning, its claimed purpose of destroying the traditional Muslim monarchy, let alone establishing the new regime's authority over the entire country. The Zaydi tribesmen of the northern interior highlands remained faithful to the institution of the imamate, if not always to the current incumbent; but even the Shafi'i tribesmen of the coastal plains and southern highlands proved far from enthusiastic supporters of the republican rulers. In the civil war that pitted republicans, to whose cause Egypt eventually committed more than 70,000 troops at one time, against royalists, who received material and moral support from Saudi Arabia and initially also from Jordan, the outcome was by no means certain, even after the evacuation of Egyptian troops in December 1967.

The rationalizations that the military regime-topplers adduced to justify their actions were standard. Their reasoning rested on two premises: that the former guardians of the national welfare had betrayed their trust; and that the army serves the nation or the state but not the government or the regime of the day. In throwing the office-holding rascals out, the soldiers claimed that they were performing the highest duty to the nation. They were cleansing the country of corruption, tyranny, and selfish interest. In tearing up constitutions, deposing or even slaying monarchs, arresting cabinet members, dissolving legislatures, suppressing political parties, and introducing martial law, the military officers insisted that they were simply putting an end to sham parliamentary democracies whose manipulators had kept themselves in office through fraudulent elections and infringement of the laws. The Yemeni imamate, of course, had neither a written constitution nor a parliamentary system. There the military-civilian coalition asserted that it was rescuing the people from unspeakable poverty and degradation and from a despotic regime that terrorized and humiliated its subjects by primitive methods of torture and punishment.

In every instance, the soldiers stated that they had intervened in politics reluctantly and for the sole purpose of setting public affairs in order. They promised to refashion the political system, insulate it against any recurrence of the former evils, and make it responsive to the popular will. They harbored no political ambitions, they said, and sought only to restore honesty, honor, and freedom to the land and efficiency to public administration and to reassert the rights of the people. Once this mission was accomplished, the military rulers pledged to hand over the reins of power to elected representatives and to retire from politics.

The logic in this line of reasoning springs ultimately from the assumption that the army, as caretaker of the nation's military capability, is the best arbiter of the nation's needs. Custodianship of military capability is held to be the equivalent of political wisdom and moral rectitude. This assumption is a risky doctrine for the emergent military, no less than the subverted civilian, regimes. Who indeed are the final arbiters? The particular officer groups that had overthrown the old regimes? May they not also in time be labeled incompetent, self-seeking, or despotic by competing officer groups? This was basically what happened in Egypt, Turkey, Pakistan, and Sudan, even though it was rarely acknowledged as such.

Major-General Muhammad Nagib—the first president of the Egyptian Republic, the president of the Revolutionary Command Council (RCC), the prime minister, and the commander-in-chief of the armed forces—was a generation older than his junta colleagues, who viewed him as no more than their front man. But he did not view himself in that light, and to the Egyptian masses General Nagib became the embodiment of the popular military regime. The younger officers resented the high esteem in which he was held no less than his habit of taking decisions on affairs of state without consulting the RCC. The junta's first endeavor to brush him aside late in February 1954 turned into a fiasco, for in the face of tumultuous demonstrations in Cairo, the officers had to reinstate him within three days as president of the republic and a week or so later also as prime minister and as RCC chief. Only after the general suffered an emotional and physical breakdown a few weeks later did the RCC finally remove him. Even then, chastened by the first failure, they did so in two stages, stripping him first of the premiership, the junta leadership and the supreme military command, and at the year's close, of the presidency as well.

In Turkey, the National Unity Committee (NUC), the junta that had in May 1960 put the First Republic out of the misery of its declining years, lost mastery over the armed forces to the Supreme Military Council (SMC) by June 1961, when Lieutenant General Irfan Tansel, the commander of the Air Force, successfully resisted dismissal and reassignment to Washington. From that time on, the SMC, an essentially military agency bequeathed by the First Republic, also performed the nonmilitary custodial and decision-making functions of the NUC, thereby effectively displacing it. Membership in the second junta, moreover, was not fixed, since changes in the top military assignments each August brought changes in the SMC, although General Cevdet Sunay, its primary spokesman, continued beyond the customary period, for he served as Chief of the General Staff from August 1960 to March 1966, when he was elected president of the republic.

If Turkey's second coup was the quietest on the postwar Middle East record, Pakistan's was the quickest. A military-civilian combination, headed by President Iskander Mirza, terminated Pakistan's First Republic on 7 October 1958, removing the cabinet and abolishing the constitution, the central and provincial legislatures, and all political parties. The successor regime became thoroughly militarized a scant three weeks later when General Muhammad Ayub Khan, the commander-in-chief of the armed forces and chief martial law administrator, compelled Mirza to resign and himself assumed the presidency.

In Sudan, too, the military junta headed by General Ibrahim 'Abbud, the army's chief commander, was reshuffled following a second coup in March 1959, when two area commanders holding the rank of brigadier literally forced their way into membership of the Supreme Council of the Armed Forces. From the crisis this body emerged with ten members instead of thirteen, as a result of the dismissal of three generals (including the junta's deputy commander) and of its two colonels. A further attempted coup in May proved abortive, and the two brigadiers, once again implicated, lost their seats in the Supreme Council, as did also a third brigadier a few weeks later. Then comprising the seven top officers of the armed forces, the military directorate withstood another attempted coup in November 1959, and its membership continued unchanged until the return of civilian government five years later.

Under a constitutional order issued at the time of the initial coup in 1958, the Supreme Council vested in itself full executive, legislative, judicial, and military powers, which it delegated to General 'Abbud. The Supreme Council took all basic governmental decisions; the generals also sat in the cabinet which co-opted a number of civilian technicians to manage such ministries, as those for foreign affairs, finance, commerce, education, and justice.

Syria and Iraq alone among the Middle East eight underwent more than two coups, the initial ones wholly military, most later ones partly civilian. The first military regime in Syria, led by General Husni al-Za'im, met an inglorious end in less than five months (30 March 1949—14 August 1949). Colonel Sami al-Hinnawi, who had staged the second coup, tried to restore civilian government but was himself removed from the army command before the year expired (19 December 1949). No subsequent regime appeared able to strike vigorous roots. General Adib al-Shishakli's military dictatorship (29 November 1951—25 February 1954), even including the opening phase of indirect rule, did not celebrate its third anniversary; nor did, for that matter, the U.A.R.'s military quasi-protectorate over Syria (February 1958—September 1961) reach its fourth. Instead of erecting a robust military regime, the army officers in Syria had created an irrepressible military condition.

When army officers joined politicians to overthrow General 'Abd al-Karim Qasim on 8 February 1963, a Ba'th-dominated military-civilian coalition was established to govern Iraq. In mid-November Colonel 'Abd al-Salam Muhammad 'Arif's abrupt removal of Ba'thi officers and politicians from the regime confirmed the new pattern of Iraqi politics. Nor was this astonishing, since Iraq could boast multiple military coups (1936–41) until the United Kingdom in the stress of World War II invoked its preferential alliance to reoccupy the country and resuscitate, under British patronage, strong civilian rule in the name of the monarchy.

What is remarkable is not the recurrence of military risings in Syria and Iraq but the fact that such a military-political condition did not become endemic in most, if not all, Middle East countries that succumbed to military rule. Under a military regime, army officers are prone to become politicized, as their opportunities for nonmilitary public service multiply. Repeated coups in any country tend to fracture its military establishment and to bring rival officer groups together with rival civilian political groups. And the principle that might makes right, if tested and proved effective in the same country more than once, threatens to become habitual.

Legitimizing the Regime

To discourage further regime-toppling, the stagers of coups d'état customarily try to legitimize their rule. On the very day of the coup d'état (27 May 1960) the military junta in Turkey named a body of seven professors to draft a new constitution. Meanwhile the National Unity Committee (NUC) issued in mid-June a provisional constitution giving itself full legislative powers. The professorial committee, later enlarged, split into factions, and in December the NUC reassigned the task to a Constituent Assembly that, on the first anniversary of the coup, approved the text which was then adopted by referendum on 9 July 1961.

The military junta in Egypt that had forced King Faruq to abdicate on 26 July 1952 set up a Regency Council a week later to serve, in theory, as the custodian for the infant King Ahmad Fuad II. Under this umbrella of legitimacy the new military rulers proceeded in December to jettison the monarchical constitution, to suspend parliamentary life for three years, and, in the following month, to liquidate all political parties except the Muslim Brethren (which survived until the end of 1954). Prime Minister Nagib issued in February 1953 an interim constitution that vested supreme authority, under his leadership, in the Revolutionary Command Council. By June 1953 the RCC felt secure enough to terminate the monarchy altogether and with it the Regency Council, but waited three years longer before resorting to referenda for approval of the "definitive" constitution and for election to the presidency of Gamal 'Abd al-Nasir, who had succeeded Nagib as head of the RCC and prime minister.

The military junta in Iraq destroyed the monarchy outright, and therefore established a Sovereignty Council on which sat representatives of the three major communities (the Sunni Arab, the Shi'i Arab, and the Kurdish) to "carry out presidential duties until there is a general plebiscite."[1] Within a fortnight the junta promulgated a provisional constitution; the promised definitive constitution was never presented for plebiscitary acceptance. The Sovereignty Council lasted as long as Qasim but remained to the end an honorific body.

The steps by which Ben Bella and Boumedienne moved from usurped authority to legitimacy in nascent Muslim Algeria furnishes a classic illustration. In replacing the GPRA early in August 1962, the Ben Bella–Boumedienne group did not label itself a provisional government, although it attempted to conduct itself as one.

The group insisted that it was simply the Political Bureau of the National Liberation Front, the title given the popular movement of the rebellion. With no public mandate, the self-styled Political Bureau devoted less time to administering the country than to organizing the election of the constituent National Assembly. This it proceeded to do by naming a single list of candidates, offering the public the alternatives only of endorsement or protest. With the election concluded on 20 September 1962 and the obedient deputies' confirmation of the Cabinet selected by the Political Bureau on the following day, Ben Bella became the legitimate Prime Minister of Algeria, and Boumedienne the legitimate commander of the National People's Army.

Engineered legitimacy, it is clear, at times takes hold and at others does not. The multiple reasons will be explored in later chapters. Here it suffices merely to call attention to the relatively uniform procedures that army officers follow in seizing political power and in attempting to entrench themselves.

Use of Usurped Power

Variety begins to appear in the uses to which the militarized regimes put their political power. In this connection it has been suggested that coups d'état in Latin America, Asia, and Africa, where unconstitutional political change is related to the modernization process, fall into three classes: the governmental or "palace revolution" that changes the rulers without appreciably modifying the social structure; the truly revolutionary take-over that convulses the country by the radical transformation of its economy, society, and politics; and the reform coup that introduces only gradual changes in the body politic and its supporting social and economic institutions. According to this analysis a coup d'état corresponds to a democratic election, for each provides a mechanism for changing rulers and policies. "In underdeveloped areas of the world the governmental coup was the traditional means by which leadership was changed," it is asserted. What is more, "Reform coups tend to follow a dialectical process resembling the swings in the political pendulum in a constitutional democracy." The reformers, it is argued, tend to set in motion a series of coups alternately managed by radicals and conservatives, each giving way to the other, when the pace of change loses its momentum.[2]

When we try to fit this inventive hypothesis to the postwar experience of the Middle East, we see at once that the analogy between military coups and democratic elections has been drawn too closely. Elections may bring new leaders and new lines of government activity; but, in addition, military coups nearly always alter the political system, and sometimes also the social, economic, and political institutions. As a result, much takes place in reverse. In a democracy the uncertainty usually ends with the counting of the ballots or, if the incumbent party loses, with the consequent transfer of government to the victors. After a coup, however, the period of uncertainty starts immediately and endures at least until the new regime is formalized, often until its sponsors have contrived its legitimacy and not uncommonly even longer. The stagers of the coup do not campaign in advance, for as conspirators they must conceal their identity until the actual seizure of political power. Thus the "campaigning" occurs after the old regimes have been smashed and while the new ones are still taking shape. In fact, declarations that accompany the coup and that enunciate its "principles" and aims constitute an appeal for popular support and hence compare with the platforms that American political parties nail together at their pre-election conventions.

Furthermore, the division of coups into three classes—the non-changers, the modest changers, and the major changers—is too rigid for the conditions that have prevailed in the postwar Middle East, where modernization as such is something that all governments, whether regularly or violently constituted, formally subscribe to. Even Yemen began late in the 1950s to lower its barriers to technical improvements, by accepting a military training mission from the U.A.R. and road-building missions and grants from Communist China and the United States. A verbal endorsement of modernization in a coup manifesto is often no more than simple rhetoric. Technological change and, in its wake, economic and social change are occurring in all Middle East countries, and the special contribution of military regimes to the process cannot always easily be gauged.

Indeed, statements issued in the white heat of take-over by soldiers who have no prior experience in politics or in the management of extramilitary programs are not reliable guides to motives or intentions; and the degree of reliability may have little or nothing to do with the sincerity of the authors. At the hour of the political triumph, all army officers in the postwar Middle East have claimed to be card-bearing reformers. Conservative military rulers may be expected not to espouse radical policies; but radical military rulers may be prevented from launching the programs they favor. The interplay of stubborn realities separates intention from accomplishment, and the outcome can rarely be foreseen. In brief, the ability and training as well as the social and ethnic origins of the governing army officers are not brought to bear in a vacuum. The new military elites must grapple with many of the same unyielding conditions that plagued the displaced civilian elites: the condition of the local society, whether relatively homogeneous as in Turkey and Egypt or plural as in Iraq, Pakistan and Sudan; the condition of the local economy, whether pre-industrial and substantially peasant and pastoral as in Yemen or swiftly urbanizing as in Syria; the condition of regional politics, whether in the main a relatively regulated projection of European international politics as was typical until 1955, or a near-chaotic freedom of behavior among a group of fledgling states as became typical a decade later; the condition of international politics, whether essentially one of integrating or disintegrating bipolar alliances, East and West; and a host of other factors, among them just plain luck.

Finally, whenever military officers demolish civilian regimes they inescapably transform the political system. These changes do not necessarily constitute reforms in the normal sense of betterment through the elimination of abuse, corruption, and inefficiency or through the redistribution of land among the peasants and the shift of economic and political opportunity from the traditional oligarchies to the rising middle classes. The forcible overturn of the monarchies in Egypt and Iraq, for instance, yielded military republics. Whereas the Republic of Egypt established itself from the outset as dedicated to reform, the Republic of Iraq became on balance a socially retrograde personal dictatorship in the first four and a half years and then required another eighteen months and two more military regimes before embarking on a series of radical economic and social policies.

It can be easily shown that the avowed purposes of each coup cannot be taken at face value and that the consequences cannot be judged, as a rule, with any finality until the regime established by the coup is supplanted by another. How, for instance, should the Egyptian coup of 1952 be designated? If the changes attending the transformation of the monarchy into a republic are set aside the junta proceeded very cautiously with only moderate reforms. This could be ascribed in part to the inexperience of the military officers who were undergoing their apprenticeship as reformers and as rulers simultaneously and in part to the distractions of the dispute with Britain over the preferential alliance and the Suez Base. The replacement of Nagib in 1954 represented a palace revolution in the beginning at least, since the Revolutionary Command Council under 'Abd al-Nasir did not frame intrinsically fresh policies until 1955. Even then, Egypt tested radicalism on foreign policies before attempting to apply it to domestic affairs. 'Abd al-Nasir's participation in the Bandung Conference in April 1955 marked a turning point that led subsequently to the arms deal with the U.S.S.R. and then, step by step, to the nationalization of the Suez Canal Company in July 1956, the Sinai-Suez crisis in the fall, and the sequestration of British and French property in January 1957. Five years more were to elapse before the bundle of doctrines, pragmatically formulated and progressively applied, were assembled under the general title of Arab socialism and presented to the public in May 1962 as the Charter of National Action. By then it could be said that the military regime in Egypt had become revolutionary.

The weary and worrisome years of Qasim's dictatorship brought few, if any, durable reforms in Iraq. Qasim started out with zeal and wide popularity. But as he removed one political rival after another, his policies became increasingly arbitrary. He changed his mind more than once on the licensing of selected political parties, precipitated war with the Kurds, and ultimately became more concerned with personal and political survival than with public policy and national interest. Toward the end he characteristically imprisoned himself in his office-apartment at the Ministry of Defense until he had almost to be bombed out by the Ba'th-dominated coalition that executed the coup of February 1963. His predecessors, Nuri and the monarchy, had initiated their development plans in 1950 and gradually adopted a comprehensive scheme, prepared and partly supervised by an international consortium. Without question the Hashimi dynasty invested more in basic economic and social projects than did Qasim, who never endorsed firm, long-range plans and who lost the services of many skilled Iraqi technicians by his own dismissal practices. Even the Ba'th-managed coalition that governed Iraq from February to November 1963, despite espousal of a Socialist ideology, did not begin to fulfill its revolutionary promise. Its leaders were sidetracked by the abortive Arab unity negotiations in Cairo in March and April, by the renewal of the fighting with the Kurds in June, and by internal dissensions within the party in November that enabled 'Arif to step into the breach. The Qasim dictatorship was succeeded by a collegial authoritarianism that did not last long enough to acquire its own contrived legitimacy, so that in retrospect the Ba'th-led coup represented a simple governmental change. 'Arif's rise to power brought new policies: pruning Ba'thi influence, reaching a truce with the Kurds, and in July 1964 nationalizing the banks, insurance companies, and selected industries. These were the opening steps of what was intended to unfold into a form of Arab socialism on the Egyptian model.

There is no way of knowing whether the contagion of military rule in the postwar Middle East has been checked or will continue spreading. The period under study, little more than two decades, is far too short for conclusive judgment. Latin America in a century and a half underwent alternating periods of expansion and contraction of militarized politics. The number of military regimes there began declining before World War I and reached a low of six in 1928 only to start climbing abruptly once more after the onset of the depression, so that a decade later soldiers were playing key political roles in all but five of the twenty countries. In the Middle East, after all, there is a much older tradition of military rule than in Latin America. It is therefore safe to conclude that military regimes in the Middle East are here to stay, although the precise number, as in Latin America, might be expected to expand and contract in the long run. A close look at the military republics should enable us to evaluate their similarities and differences.

Military Republics

EGYPT: MILITARY RULE IN
A RAPIDLY CHANGING SOCIETY

Many factors mold a military regime: the structure of society, the nature of the replaced civilian political system, the prior absence or presence of military rule, the rate of social and economic change, the degree of the military regime's sponsorship of such change, and the character of the military establishment before and after the seizure of political power—to list the most striking components. Each of the military republics in the postwar Middle East reflected its own mixture of the contributory factors, and the particular combination must be borne in mind as we try to ascertain the general pattern.

Experts often do not recognize a military regime when they see one, and in such instances they may sharply disagree among themselves. Consider the case of Egypt. Many close observers accepted at face value the junta's contention that its regime became civilianized in June 1956, when all those members who continued to hold ministerial portfolios in the new government under the newly approved republican constitution adopted civilian dress as a public earnest of their formal retirement from the army. This act, it was declared, civilianized the political system, despite the one exception, Major General 'Abd al-Hakim 'Amir, the commander-in-chief of the armed forces, who continued as minister of defense. While the uniforms of a junta that constitutes a government leaves no doubt of its military quality, the switch to mufti and even the formal surrender of commissions do not necessarily herald the civilianization of a military political system.

Continuity and Discontinuity

The dynasty of Egypt collapsed in the opening months of 1952. It began with "Black Saturday" (26 January) when mob violence that King Faruq had a hand in fomenting resulted in widespread destruction of life and property, not all of it British, even though the riots were ostensibly organized in protest against British policies; and as a result the king dismissed the elected Wafd government and proclaimed martial law. In later weeks, he dissolved parliament, indefinitely postponed elections, and ruled by decree. His capacity to enforce the royal will rested, ultimately, on the loyalty of the security forces, particularly the army. When the Free Officers executive (the military officers who organized and led the conspiracy) finally moved early on the morning of 23 July, all they had to do to topple the monarchy was gain control over elite army and air force units and then roll the well-padded dissolute off his throne.

Officer promotion in the armed forces under the monarchy had been determined more by birth and girth than by merit. The top echelon consisted largely of men from the privileged upper class which, though substantially Egyptianized, could trace its origins to the Ottoman-Circassian elite of the nineteenth century. By contrast, the military junta were Egyptians from the lower middle class, almost to a man. These officers were the first beneficiaries of the new program at the military academy in Cairo, inaugurated in 1936 immediately after the treaty with Britain gave the army greater internal freedom. The academy at that time waived membership in the privileged class as a basic requirement for admission. In fact, all the members of the junta graduated from the academy before World War II and, with the exception of the front man, Major General Muhammad Nagib, were under the age of forty. The new officer recruitment program continued throughout the war and early postwar years, so that by 1952 the Free Officers executive, consisting of men holding the rank of major, lieutenant colonel, or their equivalent, could count on the support of most of their juniors with whom they shared a common social background.

The junta swept away the dynasty that Mehmed Ali had established a century and a half earlier, its quasi-democratic scaffolding erected in the interwar years, and the senior echelon of military officers who remained loyal to the monarchy. The parliamentary system, when allowed to function, constituted a device primarily for safeguarding and promoting the interests of the landed and commercial oligarchy who together with the king governed the kingdom. The only party with a mass following and a national organization reaching into the provinces was the Wafd, which had originally come into being in November 1918 to protest the continuance of the British protectorate. Once the protectorate was termi-

nated in 1922 and a democratic constitution promulgated, the protest movement grew into a political party and remained thereafter
the monarchy's only real party. The other political groups were
little more than factions organized by clusters of politicians who
failed to gain a mass following. The *Ikhwan al-Muslimun* (Muslim Brethren), the sole exception, was not a true political party but
a religious movement with political overtones. Precisely because it
was a mass movement, it represented, under the monarchy, a long-
run threat to the Wafd. As it turned out, in every free election
between 1924 and 1950, the Wafd Party won resounding victories.
The rhythm of politics in these years was fixed, finally, by the
changing relations among the three main actors—the king, the
Wafd, and Britain.

The junta's structural sweep was clean, since without the king
and the Wafd the British presence remained essentially a problem
of external relations. The new regime that replaced the old, though
slow to take shape, nonetheless seemed solidly built. It was dy-
namic, innovative, reckless, yet durable. The original thirteen
members of the Free Officers executive constituted the exclusive
policy-makers in the political system. Though a handful of selected
military officers were later given important assignments, their influence and authority stopped short of sharing executive power. In
domestic policy, the Egyptian military rulers broke sharply with the
old regime; but in foreign policy, they introduced changes in style
rather than substance. The five guiding principles of external policy
under the monarchy in the postwar years had been the termination
of Britain's military presence, leadership both in the Arab unity
movement and in the Arab hostility to Israel, neutrality in the East-
West Cold War, and swift military modernization. These also became the guiding principles of the military junta.

In the opening years, the military rulers became obsessed with
replacing the preferential alliance by an equal relationship with
Britain. The Anglo-Egyptian treaty created the formal basis of such
a relationship in October 1954; but it came too late to last, and two
years later blew up in the Suez crisis. Whether royalists or republicans, Egyptians, from the start of their participation in the unity
movement, acted as if it were their destiny to lead Arab affairs. To
them the Arab League, founded in 1945, represented a means of
organizing the support of the Arab states for the conduct of Egyptian foreign policy, while pursuing the objective of Arab unity.
With the rise of 'Abd al-Nasir to uncontested power late in 1954,
the Arab unity cause, which suffered from indecisiveness in the

League, found purposive, flamboyant leadership. 'Abd al-Nasir galvanized the Arab masses into a crusade against imperialism under the banner of "positive neutralism," a concept he brought back to Egypt in April 1955 from the Bandung Conference where he met with Nehru, who had already established his mark as a practitioner of noncommitment in the Cold War. Positive neutralism fitted well into the world outlook of Arab unity partisans, who were demanding the final eradication of the residual European controls in all Arab territories. They insisted that the Arab zone had to become wholly self-reliant in political and economic affairs, and that the defense of Arab countries had to rest upon an Arab collective security pact and unified command. Military association with an outside great power could only signify the continuance of imperialism in disguise. The royal Egyptian government, it will be recalled, had stuck to neutrality in the Korean war; earlier, it had also led Arab resistance to the creation of Israel in 1947–48. 'Abd al-Nasir came to symbolize Arab hopes for the redemption of Palestine by the eventual defeat and destruction of the Jewish state.

Finally, the engrossment of the junta with military modernization and expansion was a policy and a mood also inherited from the monarchy. At the time of the overthrow of King Faruq, the military managers of the new regime were persuaded, as had been their civilian predecessors, that the British government was deliberately subordinating the Egyptian armed forces so as to preserve British military hegemony. This suspicion of Britain ran deep in Egypt. Ever since the British occupation in 1882, Egyptian military and political leaders had been convinced of Britain's determination to keep Egypt militarily weak. The most recent frustration grew out of British promises in the 1936 Treaty to transfer responsibility for defense of the Suez Canal to the Egyptian army at such time as the army could "ensure by its own resources the liberty and entire security of the navigation of the Canal." [1] The transfer had not yet taken place in 1952, and Britain was denying Egypt modern weapons as a means of influencing it to continue giving Britain special military rights. Obviously, in retrospect, the military government would seek with ever greater determination than the monarchy to modernize and expand the armed forces. But first, the political system that the military junta created must be examined.

The Junta's Apprenticeship

For less than two years, from September 1954 to June 1956, the eleven members of the Revolutionary Command Council (RCC), as the Free Officers executive renamed itself after the coup d'état, sat in the cabinet, where they outnumbered the civilians. The RCC members retained their military commissions, wore their uniforms, and used their military and ministerial titles interchangeably. The RCC did not share primary policy-framing powers with other military officers or with civilian administrators. More than that, its ranks then and later were closed to all newcomers, except for Major General Muhammad Nagib. No one doubted the military character of the regime at that time. Even the junta acknowledged it.

In the first year of the revolution, only General Nagib stood in prominent display as commander-in-chief of the armed forces, prime minister, military governor, minister of defense, and minister of the interior. The impressive array of titles did not suggest a Pooh-Bah. The Egyptian general spoke the language of the people with his articulate and warm manner and cut a father figure. Nagib's attractive personality and leadership provided everything that King Faruq and the politicians of the monarchy did not.

The RCC meanwhile underwent its political apprenticeship. Each military officer attached himself to a particular ministry, but only civilians carried ministerial titles. The RCC chose with care the civilian ministers, who as a group were highly talented technicians. The army officers could watch and experiment and learn without responsibility. In theory, they served as liaison officers with the several ministries. Yet they also created a mixed committee that brought them together with trusted civil servants, and through this device the politically inexperienced army officers participated in policy formulation at the ministerial level. Accordingly, they could claim the credit and avoid the blame. They observed one another and molded themselves into a compatible and cooperative team by ousting the discordant and less able colleagues in the RCC. The new generation of army officers, as reflected in the junta, created in the inaugural months of the military-political system a public image of selfless devotion to the national interest.

Lieutenant Colonel Gamal 'Abd al-Nasir had received his first ministerial post in June 1953, eleven months after the coup d'état, when he relieved Nagib of the ministry of the interior and became deputy prime minister as well. At the same time Nagib surrendered the ministry of defense to Wing Commander 'Abd al-Latif al-Baghdadi and the supreme command of the armed forces to Major 'Abd al-Hakim 'Amir (promoted to the rank of major general without a seat in the cabinet), while Major Salah Salim became minister of national guidance and Sudanese affairs. The rest of the RCC members entered the cabinet one or two at a time over the next fourteen months.

In the first two years of the transition period, as in the second two, no one questioned the military quality of the regime. The RCC preserved martial law, which had been almost continuously in effect since September 1939, superimposing on the normal legal process special military tribunals to try those charged with political crimes, broadly defined to encompass corruption, graft, and treasonous acts against the revolution. They dissolved the political parties, confiscated party assets, placed the leading politicians under arrest or administrative detention, and imposed a rigid censorship on the press. All civilian ministers were technicians or former civil servants who performed top-level management duties only. Policy-framing remained the exclusive preserve of the RCC, which met as a supreme executive and ruled by decree, thereby merging the legislative with the executive function. Nagib presided over the RCC until the crisis of the opening months of 1954, which was precipitated by the struggle for power between the popular president, who embodied the revolution in the public mind, and the revolutionaries who had staged the coup and wanted to take public part in governance and in shaping the future.

The outcome of the power struggle is a matter of public record. In retrospect, its coincidence with the conclusion of the drawn-out Anglo-Egyptian negotiations bought time for the still politically inexperienced officers. The clause in the 1954 Anglo-Egyptian treaty stipulating the phased evacuation of British troops from the Suez Base within 20 months shored up the prestige of the RCC. On the other hand, the further clause that the deactivated base would nevertheless remain available to the United Kingdom in certain circumstances kept alive the junta's fear that British imperialism had not yet been thoroughly eradicated. Soon after the signature of the accord, Egyptian counterintelligence agents seized an Israel spy ring that was planning to incite American-Egyptian ill will by blowing up the USIS building in Cairo. The Israel destruction two months later of an Egyptian police headquarters in the Gaza Strip underscored the urgency of the RCC's efforts to modernize the weaponry of their armed forces and accumulate a stockpile for the eventual showdown with their hated northern neighbor. The fact that Israel viewed its measures as a form of retaliation against Egyptian acts of aggression, such as the closure of the Suez Canal to Israel shipping and the mounting Arab raids across the armistice line, made no impression on the junta.

Meanwhile, the difficulties with Israel became intertwined with American and British attempts to persuade Egypt to join the Western collective-security system in the Cold War. Such a system appeared to the young officers as a fresh entangling alliance and a form of neo-imperialism. Affiliation of this sort seemed to them too high a price to pay for more generous purchases of modern military equipment than were allowable to Egypt under the Tripartite Declaration that the United States, Britain, and France had issued in 1950. 'Abd al-Nasir and his colleagues therefore challenged the Western monopoly of the military hardware market in the Middle East by entering in mid-1955 into an agreement with Russia, originally disguised as an arms deal with Czechoslovakia. In the months that followed, American mishandling of the Aswan Dam negotiations, first pleading with the RCC to accept the aid and then peremptorily withdrawing it, triggered the nationalization of the Suez Canal Company. With the Israel invasion of Sinai, the abortive Anglo-French military strike at the Suez Canal, and the seizure of British and French financial, commercial and cultural establishments in Egypt, the crisis over Suez reached its peak. Not until the spring of 1957, however, could it be said that the crisis had passed.

It was in this period that 'Abd al-Nasir won his reputation as an infallible leader, at home in Egypt and abroad in the Arab world. In the final analysis, it was 'Abd al-Nasir who inspired the major policies that challenged Western supremacy in the Middle East. His decision to buy arms from the Soviet Union broke the Western monopoly of the modern arms market in the region. His subsequent protracted delay in accepting the offer of economic and technical assistance for the construction of the Aswan Dam from the United States, Britain, and the World Bank revealed his skill in dealing with the Great Powers; and when the Western offer was withdrawn, his riposte in nationalizing the canal company was prompt. By the winter of 1956–57 when, with the help of the United States and the Soviet Union, 'Abd al-Nasir converted Egypt's military defeat in the Sinai-Suez war into a political victory, the Egyptian president had risen head and shoulders above his colleagues in the junta. From then on, there was no doubt about who was taking the final political decisions in Egypt. Yet it was part of 'Abd al-Nasir's genius that he managed to preserve the loyalty and the cooperation of his colleagues in later years, for he continued taking all basic decisions only after consultation with his colleagues and his staff.

The preoccupation in the first five years with the struggle against imperialism eased the RCC's problem of winning broad public support. Even the displaced politicians could not quarrel with the junta's policies, particularly since from the Egyptian standpoint these policies yielded such handsome dividends. By contrast, the RCC paid next to no attention at this time to domestic reforms. Its major innovational act, the agrarian reform law of September 1952, was moderate. Nor did the regime take any further steps for nine years to arrange for a more radical redistribution of holdings. "A study of the government's actions in the economic and social field between 1952 and 1956, when civilian influence was predominant in that field," writes a leading authority, "shows that it proceeded with great caution, and along highly orthodox lines, to restore economic stability, develop production, and bring about some measure of social welfare." [2] For the rest, the military rulers devoted themselves to neutralizing their domestic opponents by removing the residual pockets of political interest and power inherited from the monarchy.

The RCC destroyed the political parties, especially the Muslim Brethren. The junta placed the politicians and their associates under arrest or administrative detention and foiled recurrent schemes for countercoups. The officers made a public spectacle of those found guilty of graft and corruption; and they began to undermine the position of the minorities and, by extension, of the Muslim religious opposition, by closing all religious courts in January 1956. In brief, the RCC removed the political props that upheld the landed oligarchy and its satellite mercantile, industrial, and conservative religious interest groups without, for the time being, assaulting their economic and social privileges. In fact, the military government granted modest pensions to those politicians who had served as cabinet members under the monarchy and were not later charged with political crimes or corruption.

Union with Syria and the Consolidation of Military Rule

The turning point came with the promulgation in June 1956 of the first republican constitution at the time of the much heralded termination of the "transition period," a term which was, in the RCC's manner of speaking, a synonym for military rule. The junta discarded all the external military symbols of the regime. They terminated martial law, lifted press censorship, released all political prisoners, and announced the formal termination of the RCC. Except for Major General 'Amir, all members of the RCC gave up their military commissions, no longer appeared in uniform, and sat in the cabinet as civilians. The junta gave all other officers in the ministries a choice of returning to the army or remaining in the civil service; and if they chose the latter, they also had to cut their formal ties to the armed forces and put their uniforms in mothballs. With the disappearance of the outward trappings of the military regime, 'Abd al-Nasir and his fellow revolutionaries cultivated the impression that their government had become civilianized and that the Egyptian republic was a civilian republic.

The coming of the Suez crisis within a month of the approval of the constitution and the election by popular referendum of 'Abd al-Nasir as president delayed for about a year the creation of the envisioned "civilian institutions," such as the National Union and the National Assembly. No sooner had these institutions begun to function than the merger with Syria in February 1958 demanded their replacement by others that were to embrace the two regions of the United Arab Republic. The application to the U.A.R.'s northern region of the ground rules for politics that 'Abd al-Nasir and the junta had already established in the southern region, dictated the suppression of the political parties, including the Ba'th, whose leaders had taken the initiative in bringing Syria into the union with Egypt. With the cooperation of the Syrian armed forces, the central government of Cairo introduced into Syria the same repressive policies as had already been tested and proved in Egypt, employing as directors of security in the two regions the same personnel: Field Marshal 'Abd al-Hakim 'Amir and Zakariya Muhyi al-Din, both members of the original RCC. There was no escaping the conclusion that the junta had entered a new transition period, and that the U.A.R. regime was merely the military regime of Egypt under a new guise. At all events, with the dissolution of the political parties in Syria, the junta created, under the constitution for the U.A.R., a new National Union for the two regions in 1959 and a new National Assembly a year later.

With the consolidation of the junta's paramountcy throughout the U.A.R., the military oligarchy in Cairo embarked upon an ambitious program of state socialism. The adoption of socialism proved an easy step after the nationalization in 1957 of British, French, and Jewish firms, soon followed by the seizure of Greek and Italian properties and finally by discriminatory measures against the indigenous Copts. The growing centralization of the U.A.R.'s political system was epitomized late in the summer of 1961 by the bringing to Cairo of Colonel 'Abd al-Hamid al-Sarraj, the military ruler over domestic affairs in Syria, to be one of the five vice-presidents of the U.A.R. but instead of assuring the junta's supremacy in the northern region, the step destroyed it by removing the local agent through whom Cairo dominated Syria, thus making it possible for the Syrians to withdraw from the Union.

Reorganization for the Socialist Revolution

Once embarked on a course of radical socialism, the junta drafted yet another constitution, phrased in appropriate jargon and creating new institutions to serve the new goals of the state. Before releasing the new organic law in March 1964, the military rulers took a series of preliminary measures. They had convened a National Congress of Socialist Forces in Cairo in May 1962, to accept formally the National Charter that embodied the socialist doctrines set forth in the context of a socialist interpretation of Egyptian history and contemporary Arab affairs. Of the 1,750 participants, half represented "the working forces of the peoples": the peasants (mainly drawn from the rural middle class) and urban labor (including many professional people).

The Charter announced the prospective formation of an Arab Socialist Union as the political vehicle of the revolution that would "constitute the authority . . . [of] the people and the driving force behind . . . the Revolution and the guardian of the values of true democracy." [3] In September 1962 the junta overhauled the structure of government. A constitutional proclamation of the president brought into being as the supreme policy-making organ a Presidential Council of twelve consisting of eight of the revolution's founding fathers (among them President 'Abd al-Nasir and the five vice-presidents), two other former military officers, and two civilians. The former Council of Ministers, now called an Executive Council (instead of a cabinet), was shorn of policy-making powers. It was merely assigned the task of implementing the Presidential Council's policies and administering the government. 'Ali Sabri, one of the former military officers in the Presidential Council, headed the Executive Council of 29.

Before the constitution finally appeared in March 1964, the junta had once again reorganized the structure of government, eliminating in name the Presidential and Executive councils. Still, the constitution (Article 107) invested the president with the right to "appoint one or more Vice-Presidents and relieve them of their posts." 'Abd al-Nasir chose four of his junta colleagues to serve as vice-presidents and, in effect, to sit as an abbreviated and informal presidential council with exclusive policy-framing powers. For the first time since the 1952 coup, the 1964 constitution provided for presidential succession by stipulating (in Article 110) that

> In the case of the President's resignation, permanent disability or death, the First Vice-President temporarily assumes the Presidency. The National Assembly then proclaims, by a two-thirds majority vote, the vacancy of the office of President. The President is chosen within a maximum period of sixty days from the date of the vacancy of the Presidential office.

Significantly, 'Abd al-Nasir had already designated as First Vice-President Field Marshal 'Amir, thereby reaffirming the army's role as protector of the revolution. The 1962 Charter, in fact, had earlier stressed the point when, in commenting in the socialist idiom on "the peasants' rebellions against the tyranny of feudalism," it observed that

> The greatest thing about the revolution of July 23rd 1952 is that the armed forces . . . who stage[d] it were not the makers of the Revolution, but its popular tool. . . .
> The needs of our country were such that it was not enough to patch up the old and decaying building, try to keep it from falling by means of supports and give the exterior a fresh coat of paint.
> What was needed was a new and strong building resting on firm foundations and towering high in the sky. . . .
> To their national army they [the Egyptian people] assigned the task of safeguarding the building operations.[4]

Five of the thirteen in the junta that had seized power in 1952 were still wielding it twelve years later. In the absence of an effective legislature, all laws appeared in fact, if not always in name, as presidential decrees that either originated in or required the endorsement of the informal presidential council, whose membership might vary at the pleasure of the president but whose first candidates at least were chosen only from the original junta. Three of the five who formed this extraconstitutional body in March 1964 were the anchor men of the revolution, performing the same roles that they had performed from the time that the RCC had thrust Nagib aside in 1954.

'Abd al-Nasir was still uncontestably the leader, a presidential dictator under the constitution but in practice still listening to his colleagues, though with declining frequency. As military commander, 'Abd al-Hakim 'Amir furnished the vital link with the armed forces. He assured the loyalty of the officer corps by drawing on it to supply the ministries and proliferating government agencies and industries with many of the regime's administrators, managers, and—where civilian technicians continued serving in such posts—guardians of the revolution. These guardians of the revolution formed part of an elaborate militarized internal security system that Zakariya Muhyi al-Din designed and directed to keep the regime's opponents under strict surveillance, particularly after the start of the junta's second decade when it was already well launched on its career of social and economic radicalism. This was confirmed as early as 1961 when more than 3,400 of the 4,100 employees in the ministry of the interior were either active military officers or men who had resigned their commissions after transfer from the armed forces. Throughout the remaining ministries at that time, there were about 300 men of military background. Furthermore, at least 22 of the 26 provincial governors, as late as 1964, were active or retired officers of the security forces, among them three lieutenant generals and six major generals.[5]

The two remaining founding fathers of the military republic who did not lose seats in the 1964 reshuffle had been given varying duties over the years: Husayn al-Shafi'i most recently had been given custodianship over the Arab Socialist Union in Cairo, and Hasan Ibrahim in Alexandria. In addition, Anwar al-Sadat, who had floated in and out of the inner cohesive circle of policy-makers, became in March 1964 the speaker of the National Assembly, the third such legislative body (and the second over which Sadat presided) that the junta had created under each of three constitutions in less than eight years. Like its prototypes, the third model did not show any visible signs of becoming a true legislative organ. Still it provided the regime with a transmission belt for conveying the latest slogans of the revolution to the rural and urban masses from whose ranks half the deputies came.[6]

Moreover, a former army officer, though not a member of the junta, 'Ali Sabri, became the prime minister in March 1964, in which capacity he performed essentially the same functions that he had performed in the preceding eight years: those of trusted confidant of 'Abd al-Nasir and coordinator of presidential affairs.

The military regime, like the monarchy before it, faced the same massive problems that derived from a seemingly irrepressible population pressure. Only 15,000 square miles, or less than 5 per cent of the total land area of Egypt—the Delta and the narrow band along the Nile—were cultivable. Into this restricted area was crowded almost the entire population of the country, so that with 2,000 people per square mile in the inhabited zone, Egypt was one of the most densely populated countries in the world. Even the rural areas had a population density perhaps as high as 1,500 per square mile. Under military rule, the Egyptians multiplied in a decade and a half from 21.5 to nearly 31 million. Despite the growing concern and the experiments in family planning, the military rulers by the mid-1960s could hardly claim to have reduced the annual population growth rate of 2.5 per cent.

It is in this context that the social and economic achievements of the military regime must be assessed. In 1952, perhaps no more than 35 per cent of the children between the ages of six and twelve were registered in schools under the compulsory education law. Fifteen years later, despite the substantial rise in school-age population, some 80 per cent of the qualified children were attending classes. In the same period, government health centers were opened in more and more villages and urban slum districts. Under socialism, the government established a wide assortment of factories for the production chiefly of consumer goods such as transistor radios, TV sets, refrigerators, and even a plant for the assembly of automobiles. Much less attention was paid to the production of goods required by the peasants, who after all constituted the vast majority of the population. Thus, the government failed to invest in the manufacture of insecticides and agricultural tools (except the assembly of tractors), although it did expand to full capacity the fertilizer plant built in the final years of the monarchy and began building another at Aswan. Costly, too, was the steel factory which processed imported iron and for which the coal also had to be imported.

Despite the uneven record, the Egyptian economy grew under military rule. This was reflected in the expansion of the GNP in current prices from an estimated £E 905 million in 1952 to an estimated £E 2,400 in 1966; the per capita GNP in the same period rose from £E 42 to £E 79, although the real value of the Egyptian currency by the mid-1960s had declined considerably (see Table 2). The accomplishment might well have been far more impressive, had the military regime not diverted so much of the national resources to military modernization and expansion.

TABLE 2. Egypt: Force Levels, Government Expenditures, and GNP, 1952/53–1966/67

	Population (millions)	Force Levels [b] (thousands)	Government Expenditures (millions of Egyptian pounds)			GNP (millions of pounds at current prices)	Defense Expenditures (as % of GNP)
			Defense (including internal security and justice)	Development	Total		
1952/53 [a]	21.4		48.3	24.6	206.0	905	5.3
1953/54	21.9		52.8	47.6	197.5	963	5.5
1954/55	22.7		63.2	56.9	228.1	1,014	6.2
1955/56	22.9	80	99.9	87.6	275.6	1,072	9.3
1956/57	23.4		98.8	66.6	280.5	1,125	8.8
1957/58	24.0		81.8	59.0	276.5	1,195	6.9
1958/59	24.7		94.0	77.6	304.5	1,256	7.5
1959/60	25.4		95.5	155.0	341.6	1,372	7.0
1960/61	25.9	100	104.6	172.3	482.8	1,467	7.1
1961/62	26.6		104.3	196.5	517.6	1,550	6.7
1962/63	27.3		146.9	214.6	612.4	1,685	8.7
1963/64	28.0		214.1	369.4	862.3	1,894	11.3
1964/65 [c]	28.9		201.1	307.2	825.5	2,058	9.8
1965/66 [d]	29.6	180	200.8	345.4	906.1	2,200	9.1
1966/67 [d]	30.3		215.7	364.6	978.7	2,400	9.0

SOURCES: Based primarily on Statistical Department, *Annuaire statistique*; National Bank of Egypt, *Economic Bulletin*; and IMF, *International Financial Statistics*.

[a] Fiscal year ends 30 June.   [c] Provisional.
[b] Excluding police and other paramilitary forces.   [d] Budget estimates and GNP projections.

Military Modernization and Expansion

Ever since the 1936 treaty, it will be recalled, the Egyptian government appealed to Britain for the purchase of modern weapons. The military development program of 1938–39 was frustrated by the mounting international crisis and Britain's inability to spare the equipment that the Egyptian military planners were seeking. The war brought further delays, and serious negotiations could not be resumed until 1946, when the first postwar attempt at treaty revision failed. The distractions of the Palestine war then delayed the reopening of talks until 1950, when the Egyptians once again stepped up their efforts to arrange simultaneously for the termination of the preferential alliance and the procurement of modern weapons. The military junta later hewed to the same line until Egypt and Britain finally patched together their agreement of 1954, largely on Egyptian terms.

As early as 1950 Britain placed Egypt on the privileged list for buying current models of heavy armaments such as jet planes and Centurion tanks. Egypt immediately ordered 16 Centurions, depositing 80 per cent of the price on signature of the contract. The opening round of Anglo-Egyptian talks, after eleven weeks, ended in a stalemate late in August 1950. The next month the British Ambassador in Cairo notified Egypt that his "Government had decided that the North Atlantic powers and the British Commonwealth should receive priority, and delivery of these arms to Egypt must reluctantly be postponed for a time." [7] In the weeks that followed, the Labor Government wavered, until it finally acquiesced in pressure from both sides of the House to suspend delivery indefinitely. Two years later, Prime Minister Muhammad Nagib, as spokesman of the junta, was still trying to persuade Britain to fill the 1950 order and to resume the sale of other heavy weapons. The Conservative Government proved no more accommodating than its predecessor, making it clear to Egypt that the purchase of heavy weapons would have to await Egypt's integration into the Western defense system of the Middle East. The Egyptians were, in fact, kept waiting until the conclusion of the treaty negotiations in 1954.

The United States, meanwhile, had quietly served as good officer in the protracted Anglo-Egyptian exchanges, prodding Britain and enticing Egypt, for Washington impatiently sought, especially after the start of the Korean War in 1950, to integrate Britain's wide-ranging bases in the Middle East into the Western collective security system. At the same time, to strengthen Britain's hand

and perhaps also to allay the fears of the American partisans of
Israel, the United States rejected direct approaches from Egypt for
military equipment that it failed to get from Britain. Still, the
United States let it be understood that Egypt might expect a favorable hearing once an Anglo-Egyptian settlement was reached. The
United States also associated itself with proposals for an Allied
Middle East Command or an alternative regional security system
on the model of NATO which would bring the Western powers
into partnership with Middle East states, including some, if not all,
of those in the Arab East.

In postwar British military planning for the Middle East, there
was no substitute for Egypt if the United Kingdom were to remain
the paramount power in that region and bear its "responsibilities
[there] . . . on behalf of the rest of the Commonwealth and the
Western allies as a whole.[8] The massive investment in workshops,
stores, and military installations in the Suez Base and its strategic
location made the base ideal for the headquarters of the British
Middle East Command, the jurisdiction of which stretched from
Malta to Pakistan and from Turkey to Kenya. The Suez Base was a
relic of World War II, but it was there and was paid for. Britain
could neither replace it nor afford to relocate it, even if a suitable
alternative site could be found.

It was Britain's promotion of the Baghdad Pact and of Iraq's
Arab leadership in it in 1955 that pushed Egypt and the U.S.S.R.
together. The Soviet-Egyptian arms deal of that year offered Egypt,
for the first time since the 1830s, an opportunity for acquiring massive supplies of military equipment. The military leaders of Egypt
in 1955 were even more convinced than their royalist predecessors
that the weakness of the Egyptian army could be ascribed to a deep-
seated British, and Western, imperial plot to keep Egypt submissive. The Egyptians refused to believe that Israel achieved its military superiority largely by its own efforts and ingenuity and not, as
they insisted, with the collusion of the Western powers. 'Abd al-
Nasir saw the arms problem of Egypt arising primarily from mod-
ern-weapons starvation. Enrich the military diet, he prescribed, and
the symptoms of starvation will disappear. He also suffered from a
morbid fear of external domination. As a revolutionary, 'Abd al-
Nasir did not hesitate to take risks greater than the royalists had
ever contemplated.

Observers were prone to overlook the realities of international
politics in the Middle East when 'Abd al-Nasir first bought modern arms from the U.S.S.R. That decision represented an act of

defiance against the three Western powers, which had stated un-equivocally five years earlier that they would not tolerate arms races in the region and that they would give special consideration in plans for military modernization to those Middle East states that were prepared to join a Western-sponsored regional defense system. 'Abd al-Nasir had no way of knowing in advance how the Western powers might react to the challenge to their monopoly or to the rejection of the offer to take part in their collective security system. Yet he was determined to build up the military might of his country. His was a military government, and he could not long abide the Egyptian army's reputation for backwardness. Like his articulate countrymen generally, and even like his political predecessors, he believed in instant modernization.

On the outbreak of the Palestine war in May 1948, the Egyptian armed forces probably did not exceed 30,000 officers and men. During and immediately after that war, their number was nearly trebled to 80,000, remaining constant until the conclusion of the arms deal with Russia. The army then slowly expanded, reaching 100,000 by 1960; the rate of expansion was thereafter accelerated, so that by 1965 there were an estimated 180,000 officers and men in all branches of the Egyptian armed forces. Precise figures on Egyptian outlays for defense are not available. The defense column in Table 2 includes expenditures for internal security and justice, which represented roughly one-fourth of the total. Such a sum was manifestly far too high for the operation of the law courts, the prisons, and the police service; clearly subsumed in this category are all expenditures on domestic security, which trebled in this period. Since the armed forces assumed major responsibility for the enlarged domestic security network which furnished the lifeblood of the military-political regime that the junta had erected, the expenditures on domestic and external security would provide a more realistic estimate of over-all defense costs. Even then, the combined figures probably did not reflect the total sums that the Egyptian government was spending for defense, particularly after 1960.

For one thing, considerable sums were set aside for research and development of sophisticated weaponry, notably jet planes and surface-to-surface missiles. The cost of the programs rose steadily in the 1960s until it probably reached an annual level of somewhere between £E 25 million and £E 50 million. It was very likely that this item, along with others of a comparable nature, such as investments in new military industries, were entered in the column labeled "Development" in Table 2. Moreover, after 1962 the cost of the war in Yemen mounted steadily. Part of this was probably incurred on the basis of a deferred-payment plan by arrangement with the U.S.S.R. as the primary weapons supplier. By 1966 the total Egyptian military debt to the U.S.S.R. was estimated as ranging between £E 150 million and £E 175 million, and it was reported that the U.S.S.R. had relieved Egypt of repayment for about two-thirds of the indebtedness, partly as a Soviet contribution to the war in Yemen. Estimates of the cost of that war to the Egyptian exchequer have ranged between £E 25 million and £E 75 million per year. This may not have represented the total cost of the war, to which Egypt by 1966 had committed about one-third of its military manpower. A portion of these outlays, too, may not have been reflected in the total defense expenditure; if so, it is hard to determine where these sums might have been placed. If this reasoning is sound, the size of the defense expenditures in relation to investments in development, the total budget, and the GNP are understated in the table. With the indicated adjustments the probable real expenditures for defense in 1966 may well have reached £E 300 million, or some 12.5 per cent of the estimated GNP. The impact of such high defense expenditures on the economy was cushioned in the first half of the 1960s by Soviet aid and also by American aid.

'Abd al-Nasir's Loss of Flexibility

One of the keys to 'Abd al-Nasir's success in the first dozen years of military rule was his ability to steer a middle course in the Cold War between the U.S.S.R. and the United States. Admittedly, his policies after 1955 were tipped in favor of the U.S.S.R., but he continued to elude full identification with the Soviet Union. Even in the period when Egyptian hostility to the United States and the West reached high intensity, culminating in the Lebanese crisis of 1958, 'Abd al-Nasir left no doubt that he was fundamentally a nationalist leader and that Egypt had not become a Soviet satellite. A public controversy with Prime Minister Nikita Khrushchev in 1959 opened the door to rapprochement with the United States. Between 1961 and 1964, 'Abd al-Nasir became the major Middle East beneficiary of the Cold War, receiving guns from the U.S.S.R., grain from the United States, and economic aid from both superpowers and from some of their respective allies.

Following the overturn of Khrushchev in October 1964, 'Abd al-Nasir antagonized his principal Western benefactors. The crisis in relations with West Germany was precipitated by its secret sale of arms to Israel. It seems hard to understand why 'Abd al-Nasir went as far as he did in his attack on West Germany. The moment the Egyptian president made his complaint public, the West German government cancelled the contract with Israel. In an earlier year, 'Abd al-Nasir would have accepted this as a victory and then repaired relations with West Germany by procuring additional loans. In 1965, instead, he threatened to recognize East Germany, thereby inducing West Germany to recognize Israel, an act that the Arab League states had successfully prevented since the early 1950s.

Far more serious were the consequences of the quarrel that he picked with the United States. By intemperate speeches, which reflected progressively less moderate policies, 'Abd al-Nasir helped to bring to an end the flow of agricultural surplus from the United States. In the Kennedy Administration and the first year of Johnson's presidency, the export of food to Egypt was worth (even at a fraction of its market price in the United States) more than $700 million, payable in local currency. In addition, the United States issued to Egypt more than $500 million in loans. Even if President Johnson had been more sympathetic to Egypt than he was, his hands would nevertheless have been tied by congressional opposition, for sentiment in both houses hardened against the continued sale of agricultural surplus, which in any case was dwindling, to a country whose president appeared ungrateful for past favors. Since relations with Britain and France had never been restored to normal after the Suez crisis of 1956, the simultaneous alienation of the United States and West Germany made Egypt more dependent than ever on the U.S.S.R. and the Communist countries of Eastern Europe.

Meanwhile, by midsummer of 1965, 'Abd al-Nasir's compounding difficulties at home could no longer be concealed. At the funeral in August of Mustafa al-Nahhas, the leader of the former Wafd Party, the mourners staged massive anti-government demonstrations, which the police suspected had been organized by the outlawed Muslim Brethren and which threatened to get out of hand. Coming so soon after an alleged attempt at the life of 'Abd al-Nasir by the same group a month earlier, the demonstrations manifestly persuaded the president to tighten domestic security measures. Early in October he called to the prime ministry his trusted aide on internal security, Zakariya Muhyi al-Din, who retained personal control over the interior ministry. Following large-scale arrests, begun before Muhyi al-Din became prime minister, hundreds of Muslim Brethren were brought to trial; between 300 and 400 police officers were discharged; some 50 high officials in the interior ministry were pensioned off; and nearly all security chiefs in the provinces were dismissed. At the same time, Muhyi al-Din was assigned the further task of checking social unrest by devoting more public funds to housing and curtailing the investment in new industrial ventures. He proved a better security officer than an economic and social administrator, however, and in September 1966 he was replaced as prime minister by Sidqi Sulayman. Trained as a military engineer, Sulayman had reached the rank of colonel in the early days of the revolution. Then assigned to help establish military factories, he rose by 1962 to head the ministry for the Aswan High Dam and to sit in the National Production Council. Since Sulayman, like Sabri before him, was a Marxist, while Muhyi al-Din was not, it was commonly interpreted at the time that the government's policies reflected the ideological preferences of the prime ministers. The fact remains, however, that the policies were fundamentally those of 'Abd al-Nasir.

'Abd al-Nasir's difficulties extended even to relations with his Arab neighbors. After imaginatively uniting the Arab League states early in 1964 on a common program of action against Israel over the Jordan River waters dispute, he contributed in 1965 to the destruction of that unity. 'Abd al-Nasir failed to persuade all Arab states to sever diplomatic relations with West Germany. Thereafter, the Egyptian president pursued policies that tended to isolate his country from the rest of the Arab world.

His military investments in this period, meanwhile, continued to run high. Egypt imported more and more expensive equipment, and persisted in its ill-fated research and development for the manufacture of supersonic fighters and intermediate-range missiles. National resources were further squandered in the inconclusive war in Yemen, and the failure of his troops to defeat the ill-organized and poorly armed royalists drained Egyptian prestige throughout the Arab world. Given this combination of disastrous and costly policies, 'Abd al-Nasir and his regime had reached the lowest ebb in domestic and external status by the spring of 1967. Undoubtedly this contributed to 'Abd al-Nasir's incautious policies toward Israel in May.

'Abd al-Nasir, meanwhile, finally took over personal rule in name as well as in fact on 19 June 1967. Now that he was running scared, he could hardly allow the Arab Socialist Union to become a true political party, since it might easily develop into an opposition party. Still genuinely popular among the city masses, 'Abd al-Nasir could, as earlier, summon popular demonstrations, a skill he proved by engineering his popular recall after resigning in the Six Day War. But with the removal and later probable suicide of Field Marshal 'Amir, the president's strongest bond to the armed forces was dissolved. Its officer corps in any case had returned from Sinai and Yemen beaten, splintered, and demoralized. Unless that corps were reintegrated, its morale restored, and its confidence in 'Abd al-Nasir's leadership rebuilt, the president would be compelled to find another mechanism for training and recruiting reliable managers and servants in the expanding bureaucracy. As the functions of government multiplied under socialism, the mounting need for competent and loyal personnel was satisfied by the reassignment of military officers to nonmilitary duties. Undeniably, the junta and many other former officers who chose government employment in preference to military careers became progressively civilianized, as army officers divorced from military duties were bound to become. But in civilian employment they showed a high degree of solidarity and, of greater importance, loyalty to the president and his program of Arab socialism. As long as 'Amir remained in office, his supreme command assured close identification of the officer corps with the junta, binding the men on active duty to those who had left the armed forces for the civil service.

It took little imagination to appreciate the deep trouble into which 'Abd al-Nasir was plunged. With the political parties demolished, the politicians removed, the former landed and mercantile oligarchy disfranchised and dispossessed, the civilian technicians and bureaucrats unorganized, no alternative mass political party created—with a total absence, in brief, of any organized opposition —the inactive and active military officers in nonmilitary government employ, whose ranks were constantly infused with new recruits from the armed forces, constituted the only effective political group in the country up to June 1967. The likelihood of 'Abd al-Nasir's resuscitating its effectiveness seemed slim after the defeat by Israel.

In many respects 'Abd al-Nasir had swung full circle, for his position after June 1967 closely resembled that of King Faruq fifteen years earlier. The Egyptian army once again was a demoralized, defeated army. For all practical purposes, 'Abd al-Nasir had replaced collective rule with personal rule. This, in the final analysis, rested on the continued loyalty of the armed forces and of the internal security system to his leadership. Even after June 1967,

'Abd al-Nasir was still a more popular ruler than Faruq on the eve of his overturn. 'Abd al-Nasir's taking over the premiership and the secretary-generalship of the Arab Socialist Union revealed the little confidence he placed in his colleagues. Whether these steps would save him remained uncertain in the war's immediate aftermath. After his resignation speech, he made only two others in 1967, one in July and a second in November, attesting to his state of political shock.

'Abd al-Nasir made no headway, even a year after the war, in restoring relations with the United States. He needed to keep the living standards of his people from dropping; he needed to check their rate of rapid growth; he needed grain more than he did guns. To commit the United States once more to a program of aid to Egypt, he would have to make a convincing case that he had changed his manners as well as his policies. Whether 'Abd al-Nasir, with his authority at home and his prestige in the Arab world still in question, was capable of such a gesture remained dubious. Yet, without it, he was probably doomed to building alternative bridges to the West. That France and Britain, with their cordiality to Egypt rewarmed, might become an adequate substitute seemed unlikely even after a number of West German firms agreed in January 1968 to resume sales to Egypt on long-term credit. Unless the Western European states or the United States or both helped rescue the Egyptian economy, 'Abd al-Nasir would be at the mercy of the Soviet Union.

For the first time, Russia seemed determined to press its advantage by exacting a price for swiftly rearming Egypt, even to the extent of airlifting equipment there after the disaster in Sinai. Egypt's location, after all, was still strategically valuable to a superpower whether or not the Suez Canal was reopened. 'Abd al-Nasir must have pondered the significance of the replenishment and repair of Soviet naval vessels in Egyptian ports, the comprehensive role of Soviet technicians in the armed forces, the disguised Soviet air-base rights, and the pressures for less guarded alignment with the U.S.S.R. All these activities 'Abd al-Nasir would have viewed a decade earlier as a violation of Egyptian sovereignty. It could safely be assumed that he was still searching for national self-esteem and would still be inhibited from going all the way. In mid-1968 he seemed no longer able to extricate himself. Yet he still could not be written off, for he remained what he was at the outset, a superlative pragmatist.

8

MILITARY ROULETTE:
SYRIA AND IRAQ

The advent of soldier-politicians in Egypt led to the creation of a durable regime; in Syria and Iraq it led to the creation of what might be termed durable conditions. Could the difference be attributed simply to historical accident? Or were there underlying forces in each that influenced the course of military politics? A comparison of the experience of Syria and Iraq under army rule with that of Egypt should indicate an answer to these questions.

Military politics in the three Arab lands possessed a number of traits in common. Before military rule, all were experimenting with democratic institutions, which had been diverted into serving the privileged interests of the oligarchies of wealthy landowners, businessmen, and—in Syria and Iraq—tribal and communal leaders. The collapse of the civilian regimes in advance of the military intrusion into politics lightened the task of take-over. At the start of military rule in Syria and Iraq, as in Egypt, the army officers stepped into situations for which they were unprepared. None had received practical training in government and politics, or in economic and social planning, let alone in the mechanics of executing development programs. In the three states, too, once the soldiers became politicians, the civilians never regained mastery of the armed forces or of the machinery of government. After 1961, the Egyptian political system was dominated by an ideological military oligarchy; after 1963, the successive military oligarchies that held sway in Syria and Iraq also claimed the espousal of socialism. Finally, the soldier-politicians of Syria and Iraq, like those of Egypt, placed a high emphasis on modernizing and expanding their armed forces and enlarging their arsenals for the pursuit—especially by Syria—of assertive foreign policies. Once the U.S.S.R. entered the Middle East as an arms purveyor in 1955, the ruling officers in Egypt and Syria and later in Iraq sought to make up for lost time under Western imperial and postimperial restrictions on the easy flow of modern weapons into the region.

Far more significant than the shared qualities, however, were the basic differences in the political systems of the military rulers. As has been seen, the junta in Egypt, step by step, fashioned its own rules and institutions of governance under the uncontested leadership of 'Abd al-Nasir, who still enjoyed the support of some of his original co-conspirators, even after June 1967. In the two other Arab states, instead of long-lived juntas, personal dictatorships emerged and, on becoming arbitrary and oppressive, were overthrown, thus establishing the military coup as a normal means of changing rulers and policies.

Syria was the first Middle East state to fall under military rule after World War II. Colonel Husni al-Za'im, who started the process in Syria in 1949, wasted little time in naming himself president of the republic and in seizing all powers of state. But a disgruntled faction of officers, headed by Colonel Sami al-Hinnawi, abruptly terminated Za'im's dictatorship less than five months after its start and sought to restore civilian government under a new constitution. Hinnawi himself, however, was expelled to Lebanon in less than four months by yet another army cabal, which nevertheless permitted the drafting and adoption of a fresh organic law in 1950. For two years civilian politicians went through the motions of managing public affairs, but behind them stood the Syrian general staff exercising a close watch on the several short-lived governments and imposing at will the powers of veto it assumed. Colonel Adib al-Shishakli, the chief of the general staff, removed the civilian façade in December 1951, and for half a year the army ruled directly without a formal government. To all intents, Shishakli was already a military dictator, although he did not become president and prime minister until July 1953 under a new constitution.

Between the overthrow of Shishakli in February 1954 and the merger with Egypt four years later the seven cabinets that functioned under the resuscitated 1950 constitution came as close to restoring civilian government as Syria was to go, although even then the military factions played varying roles as government-makers. With the formation of the U.A.R., the ruling Egyptian junta progressively weeded Syria's civilian politicians out of the central and regional government and groomed the regional minister of the interior, Colonel 'Abd al-Hamid al-Sarraj, as local military "dictator" in 1960–61. In the series of regimes that followed

the breakup of the U.A.R. in September 1961, the military conspirators increasingly dominated Syria's politics.

On this, however, close observers did not agree. Some argued
that once the Ba'th (resurrection) party formed a coalition with
the faction of army officers who had staged the coup d'état in
March 1963, the officers no longer acted wholly in their private
interest but in the interest of an ideological party. The Ba'th—as
its full name, the Arab Socialist Ba'th party, indicated—formed a
branch of the socialist movement that had been created in Syria in
World War II by two French-trained Damascus teachers, Michel
'Aflaq, a Greek Orthodox Christian, and Salah al-Din al-Bitar, a
Sunni Muslim. The Ba'th merged in February 1953 with the
Syrian Socialist party of Akram al-Hawrani, a maverick politician
who won young army officers to the socialist cause and with their
backing contrived to remain on friendly terms with the early military regimes. The enlarged Ba'th later spread to other Arab countries, including Iraq. By 1963, 'Aflaq and Bitar had fallen out with
Hawrani, who left the party. The central Ba'thi doctrines were
blended into a program of action that called for socialism at home,
political unity in the Arab world, and anti-imperialism in the international community. These doctrines were enshrined in a provisional constitution, which the military-civilian coalition promulgated in April 1964. As card-bearing party members, the military
officers in the coalition, it was said, faithfully subscribed to the
Ba'thi political ideology. The military-civilian relationship persisted
under the new coalition that seized power in February 1966 and
that forced 'Aflaq and Bitar into exile. The difference lay in the
type of party leadership. The old coalition consisted of urban, intellectual, middle-aged, moderate socialists who were prone to seek
'Abd al-Nasir's cooperation on their terms. The new coalition consisted primarily of young extreme socialists of rural and nonintel-
lectual background and of irreconcilable hostility to 'Abd al-
Nasir's leadership.

A second interpretation seemed more plausible. According to
this thesis, the officers in the coalition that had seized power in
March 1963 so militarized the regime in the next three years that
the Ba'th Party became in effect the private property of the military junta. The 1964 constitution, it is true, replaced the National
Council of the Revolutionary Command (NCRC), as the military
junta had styled itself, with a much larger National Revolutionary
Council (NRC), in which the 17 military officers of the NCRC
continued to sit but only as a minority of less than 20 per cent. The

enlarged NRC was designed, on paper, as a parliament to exercise sovereignty in the name of the Syrian people. Also under the constitution, the Presidential Council (PC), named in theory by the NRC from among its own members, shared executive power with a cabinet of the PC's choice; and the two branches of the executive were responsible to the parliament. Yet, in fact, the roles were reversed, for the NRC as well as the cabinet were appointed by the PC and accountable to it. Moreover, until his removal in February 1966, Lieutenant General Muhammad Amin al-Hafiz dominated the PC over which he presided. In addition, he served as head of state, military governor, and chairman of the NRC and also for a time as prime minister. Major General Salah Jadid, the strong man of the junta that overturned Hafiz, held the leftist contingent of the Ba'th Party even more tightly in his grip.

In Iraq, 'Abd al-Karim Qasim started out in July 1958 by sharing the leadership with 'Abd al-Salam Muhammad 'Arif and other Free Officers who had planned the coup and by enlisting the cooperation of prominent politicians who had opposed the monarchy in its final years. Qasim removed 'Arif by the fall of 1958. Simultaneously, Qasim began suppressing one after another the remaining Free Officers who resisted his leadership and the political groups that had collaborated with him at the start, gradually entrenching himself as military dictator. Personal compassion toward 'Arif, who escaped execution and was released after three years of detention, contributed ultimately to Qasim's own undoing. The military-civilian coalition that seized power in Baghdad in February 1963 formed a National Council of the Revolutionary Command (NCRC) through which as a mixed junta they exercised their real governing authority. The civilian politicians and most of the officers of the NCRC were recruited from the Iraqi branch of the Ba'th Party. The junta named Colonel 'Arif president of the NCRC, but he did not himself become a Ba'thi.

'Arif was manifestly modeling himself on 'Abd al-Nasir. The first nine months of 'Arif's presidency under Ba'thi rule served as a kind of apprenticeship. He let the Ba'this become entangled in domestic and intraparty squabbles before pushing them aside. His work was eased by the excesses of the Ba'thi politicians during their brief period in office. The pretext for expelling the Ba'th came in mid-November 1963, when the party leadership split over the question of the status of the party's paramilitary organization, the National Guard, which threatened to get out of hand in Baghdad and thereby challenge the supremacy of the armed forces.

'Arif's purely military coup resulted in cleansing the government of Ba'thi civilians and the armed forces of almost all officers attached to the party. Besides retaining the presidency of the republic, 'Arif took over the supreme military command and the chairmanship of the reorganized and now wholly military NCRC, composed of the deputy commander and the five divisional commanders. He immediately announced the dissolution of all political parties and declared that his "new government had been formed on the basis of efficiency and equality and consisted of personalities chosen to that end." [1]

Following the promulgation of a provisional constitution in May 1964, the NCRC was replaced by a National Revolutionary Council (NRC) with a membership limited to twenty under 'Arif's presidency. A special law vested in the NRC full legislative and executive powers during the three-year "transitional" period, but then went on, as an "exceptional" act, to transfer these powers to President 'Arif for one year with the right of renewal at his discretion. An Arab Socialist Union (ASU), established in the summer of 1964 with Brigadier 'Abd al-Karim Farhan, the minister of guidance and culture, as secretary-general, became the sole legal political party in the country and included among its members many politicians of the monarchical period. Like its namesake in Egypt and for essentially the same reasons, the Iraqi ASU failed to grow into a true political party.

The top military officers themselves divided over cooperation with Egypt. There were those who urged full military and political unity with Egypt, while others favored a less intimate arrangement. Although 'Arif went on record as an advocate of the first position, he seems privately to have inclined toward the second, to judge from the unfolding record. For this, he had to pay by keeping close watch on the pro-Egyptian officers in his ruling entourage, who on at least three occasions attempted to overthrow the 'Arif regime. When 'Arif himself was killed in a helicopter accident in April 1966, the vigor of his regime was confirmed by the ease with which the National Defense Council (which included all the army officers in the old NCRC plus the commanders of the air force, the navy, and the Baghdad garrison) selected as the new head of state 'Arif's older brother, 'Abd al-Rahman, a major general in the army and the acting chief of staff. It was in this period that the military regime experimented with a civilian prime minister, the first one since the overthrow of the monarchy in 1958. The new President 'Arif finally acquiesced in the organized opposition of his military colleagues to the continuance as prime minister of Professor 'Abd al-Rahman al-Bazzaz, despite the many achievements in his eleven months in office (September 1965–August 1966), most notably the basis for a settlement with the Kurds.

The rotation of rulers in Syria and Iraq took place by tank and not by ballot. The sudden changes of regime undeniably interrupted the continuity of policy and on occasion altered the structure of government. But clearly power passed from one group to another, not because of large-scale rebellion, but because of small-scale scheming by coteries of dissatisfied army officers acting at times alone and at others in partnership with civilian politicians. The essential ingredient, however, was the participation of the soldiers, for once the precedent was fixed of changing rulers by force, it became difficult to break the habit. In these two countries, the institutionalized coup, it might be said, became the accepted form of political change.

Division of Officers into Rival Factions

The cohesion of the officer corps or the lack of it helps explain why the experience of Egypt under the military diverged from that of Syria and Iraq. In modern times, it must be remembered, Egypt could claim a longer military tradition than its two northern neighbors, a tradition that traced back to Mehmed Ali in the first half of the nineteenth century. But under the Ottomans, as later under the British, native Egyptian officers could not rise to the top of the military hierarchy. The revolt led by Ahmed 'Urabi in 1881–82 aimed, among other purposes, to replace the Ottoman-Circassian and foreign military elite with native Egyptian officers. The highest staff and command appointments remained the preserve of the landed oligarchy which, though progressively Egyptianized, still reflected Ottoman-Circassian strains in its background even as late as World War II. By then the younger graduates of the Military Academy in Cairo, whose admissions policy was liberalized at the time of the 1936 Anglo-Egyptian treaty, found inspiration in the memory of 'Urabi and his devotion to the Egyptian national interest.

Moreover, the visible presence of an alien power, its reluctant withdrawal, and its later threatened forcible return kept the morale of the politically inexperienced officers at a high pitch and furnished them a built-in program for uniting the Egyptian public behind their leadership. While undergoing their non-military training, the young military politicians of Egypt thus escaped the divi-

sive consequences of attempted domestic reforms and, probably
without fully realizing it at the time, found a unique opportunity
to weld their intimate group into a purposeful team. What is more,
the triumph in the contest with the British and the French won for
the junta a reputation for leadership, which they put to effective
use in governing the country. Thus, by the time they became articulate domestic reformers at the end of the first decade in office,
they had also become good governors, versed in the art of collective
leadership by a small and exclusive committee.

The same type of military brotherhood did not obtain in either
Syria or Iraq. The external enemy in each of the two countries at
the time of the military take-over was more imaginary than real.
Foreign troops had withdrawn from Syria three years before the
first military intrusion into politics. Similarly, Britain's preferential
alliance with Iraq had been terminated in 1955, three years before
the monarchy's demise, and the Baghdad Pact brought benefits as
well as obligations. Still, anti-imperial slogans continued to arouse
the most vigorous sentiments of hatred among the people at large,
as among the army officers. Even more extreme were the feelings
against Zionism. Yet European imperialism did not represent a
concrete danger to Syria nor did Zionism to Iraq; overuse had
transformed the two bogies into little more than abstract crusaders'
cries.

The Free Officers of Iraq did not long remain united. Almost
immediately they precipitated a struggle for power and lost a
chance of developing collective leadership and the techniques of
group decision. Within two months of the republic's founding,
Qasim and 'Arif quarreled; within three, 'Arif lost his political
posts; and within four, his initial attempt to oust Qasim proved
abortive and 'Arif ended up, not as president, but as prisoner.
Once the chief conspirators fell out among themselves, so too did
their subordinates; and most others were less fortunate than 'Arif,
for as a result of losing patience with Qasim they also lost their
heads. Qasim then grew more and more suspicious of the men
around him, particularly after the attempted assassination of "the
sole leader" in October 1959. To this, his recluse existence in the
ministry of defense bore eloquent testimony; it was an apartment
equipped with bullet-proof windows, and a door connecting bed-
room to office had a peephole focused on his desk. As against the
smooth succession from the younger to the elder 'Arif in the spring
of 1966 must be weighed the abortive military coups in the
months that followed and his overthrow in July 1968.

What accounts for the failure of the Syrian and Iraqi officers to preserve their solidarity? For one thing, the Iraqi army did not have to look far back into history for its origins, since the British had brought it into being under the mandate (1920–32). For another, after the United Kingdom reasserted its primacy in 1941, the Iraqi armed forces once again became a British appendage, until 1955 under the preferential alliance and thereafter under the Baghdad Pact, so that all officers trained at the Military College in Baghdad underwent a double screening by the British military mission and by Nuri Pasha al-Sa'id, the principal author of Iraq's pro-British policies in the last decade and a half of the monarchy.

The situation in Syria was no more promising. There the first military coup had taken place without prior planning. It was the work, not of a conspiratorial group, but of a single individual, the chief of the general staff responding to an invitation from civilian politicians to help restore domestic order. Colonel Za'im therefore felt no compulsion to share political power with other officers once he had seized it. The overthrow of Za'im by Hinnawi fractured the officer corps, which became further divided by Hinnawi's removal and the gradual entrenchment of Shishakli as personal dictator. It must be remembered that, at the time the military first intruded into politics, the army itself with fewer than 10,000 officers and men was still minuscule. Its officers, moreover, had not been selected or trained under a nationalist system. The top commanders had received formal military education from the Ottomans, and all other officers from the French. Under military rule the army steadily expanded to about 35,000 in 1960 and over 60,000 in 1965. Not until the late 1950s could the alumni of the Military Academy at Homs have begun to demonstrate an effective group spirit. But by then the officers were drawn to rival political ideologies. As one coup followed another after 1949, each brought new officers to political prominence, and many of their military opponents, personal and political, were purged. Since precisely the same group has never been given a second chance, the net effect over time, as we shall see, was to change the complexion of the officer corps.

Plural Societies

A major reason why neither the Iraqi nor the Syrian officers contrived to work as a team could be found in the heterogeneous societies of the two states, which contrasted with the relatively homogeneous society of Egypt. The soldiers who reached the highest political office in Cairo after 1952 were Sunni Arabs only, as were also nearly all the cadets at the military academy. The non-Egyptian minorities in Cairo, Alexandria, and elsewhere in the Delta did not serve in the armed forces, and even the native Copts, who constitute less than 8 per cent of the population, were substantially underrepresented in the officer corps and probably also in the armed forces as a whole. Furthermore, 'Abd al-Nasir's policy after Suez of expelling foreigners from the country had its domestic parallel in the displacement of Copts from public office and from primary roles in the economy and in the discouragement of their entering upon military careers.

France's policy as mandatory in Syria seemed to favor the recruitment of minorities in all ranks of the *Troupes spéciales,* out of which later grew the armies of Syria and Lebanon. The wealthy Sunni Arab landowning and commercial families reinforced this policy. As leaders of the nationalist movement, they opposed sending their sons for military training, even as officers, particularly in a force that they viewed as serving French imperial interest. The French therefore selected officer candidates in the minority communities, usually from the leading families. It was thus perhaps not wholly accidental that in the first five years under military rule, apart from the brief Hinnawi interlude, personal dictatorships were established by Kurdish officers—Za'im and Shishakli—who represented a non-Arab community no larger than 5 per cent of the total population. In the purge that followed the ejection of Shishakli in February 1954, Kurdish officers were removed from the highest positions. After the French withdrawal in 1946, the Military Academy at Homs had opened its doors to candidates from the lower middle class, as in Egypt a decade earlier. Even after independence, the Sunni Arab upper middle-class families did not encourage their sons to choose the army as a career. Over time, the purges that followed the successive coups, particularly after the secession from the U.A.R. in 1961, steadily reduced the number of Sunni Arab officers. Meanwhile, as the minority officers, chiefly 'Alawis and Druzes, became numerically dominant (according to one estimate, perhaps exaggerated, 70 per cent of the officers were 'Alawis), they moved into more and more command positions and tended to favor applications from co-sectarians for admission to the army, navy, and air academies.

'Alawis and Druzes were for the most part mountain peasants, although those who qualified for officer training commonly came from the urban or semi-urban branches of the two communities and usually also from the lower middle class. The 'Alawis, adherents of a Shi'i or heterodox Muslim sect representing little more than 10 per cent of the Syrian population, were bunched in the district of Lataqiyah in the northwest. Roughly a third the number of the 'Alawis, the Druzes, belonging to a post-Islamic sect, lived for the most part along the frontiers of South Lebanon and Israel. Of the two communities, the 'Alawi was the more depressed. The 'Alawi officers, in turn, were divided into two rival groups, one consisting of native-born Syrians and the other of immigrants from the vilâyet of Hatay, as the district of Alexandretta became known after its assimilation by Turkey in 1939. Of these two groups, the immigrant officers, coming from families that were more urbanized and a notch or two less impoverished, filled the superior posts. Thus, paradoxically, in republican Syria, the traditional Islamic pattern of military-political dominance of the total population by its most illiterate section, usually tribal, had become fixed in Syria as a result of the recurrent coups d'état. Young 'Alawi and Druze officers played a prominent role in the coup of March 1963 and presumably intended to use as a front man General Hafiz, a Sunni Arab who at 52 was considerably older than his fellow conspirators. But with the support of the army command and the Ba'th party organization, Hafiz played 'Alawi and Druze officers off against one another and then managed to seize supreme power and retain it for nearly three years.

Personal rivalry among the officers, by then endemic in the Syrian army, acquired a communal quality after September 1965, when Major-General Salah Jadid, the 'Alawi chief of staff, was dismissed. With the cooperation of other ambitious officers, chiefly 'Alawis in and out of the Hafiz junta, Jadid organized the plot by which Hafiz was expelled in February 1966. For the first time, 'Alawi officers wrested control over the army and through it over the government. The top civilian positions, it is true, went to Ba'thi leftists—as it turned out, to three doctors of medicine. Nur al-Din al-Atasi, a member of one of the best known Sunni Arab families in the country, was named head of state, an honorary office in the regime, clearly intended to placate the Sunni Arabs; and Yusuf Zu'ayyin, a Sunni, and Ibrahim Makhus, an 'Alawi, were named premier and foreign minister respectively. The common assumption that the ruling junta after February 1966 was a genuine civilian-military coalition, dominated by the Ba'thi leftists, missed the main point.

Precisely because the 'Alawi officers came from the lower middle class and from a small and underprivileged minority, they were prone as a group to favor the social reforms advocated by the Ba'th Party and to oppose the privileged upper middle class, particularly the Sunni Arab upper middle class. This was hardly ideological, although there may even have been class-conscious Marxists among the 'Alawi officers. The voice was the voice of the Ba'th, but the hand was the hand of the 'Alawi officers. Under these officers, Ba'thi doctrines guided government policy but were far from sacred. The real head of the Syrian regime after the coup of February 1966 was General Jadid, who, representing the minority 'Alawi community and a minority political party, espoused extremist positions on foreign as well as domestic policies. This helps account for Jadid's cooperation with the Ba'thi leftists and his uncompromising opposition to union with Egypt for fear that the army would once more be dominated by Sunni Arabs. It also helps account even more for its high dependence on the U.S.S.R. in the international community. The U.S.S.R., in turn, found the vulnerable government of Syria a useful means of exerting influence in the Arab world, as attested in the spring of 1967 in the developments culminating in the Six Day War.

At the time of the destruction of the monarchy in Iraq in 1958, the three main Muslim communities—the Shi'i Arab, the Sunni Arab, and the Sunni Kurdish in descending order of size—were proportionately represented in the armed forces, even though the Sunni Arab officers held the choice posts, as did their counterparts in the civilian establishment. Moreover, even before Qasim rose to power and to a greater degree than in Syria, officers and enlisted men owed primary loyalty, not to the state, but to their respective communities. The diverse ethnic and religious origins of the officers, in fact, went a long way toward explaining the lack of solidarity. Underprivileged despite its numbers, the Shi'i Arab community resented Sunni dominance in the army as in the society at large. But the two communities were nonetheless Arab and accordingly could agree on many policies, domestic and external. The Kurds, however, generally lacked confidence in their fellow Muslims, whether Sunni or Shi'i.

The junta encountered no resistance at the birth of the republic in enlisting the support of those politicians whose parties Nuri Pasha had suppressed in 1954 and to whom he had later denied participation in politics. These politicians represented a majority of the total, as well as all shades of political belief. Qasim's early cabinets typically comprised Shi'is and Kurds as well as Sunni Arabs, in the manner of the cabinets under the monarchy. The junta also made a point of stressing communal balance in the Sovereignty Council that it created and advertised as performing the function of the chief of state but invested with only nominal authority. It consisted of a Sunni Arab as head (Najib al-Rubay'i, a retired general), a Shi'i (Muhammad Mahdi Kubbah, the head of an outlawed party), and a Kurd (Khalid al-Naqshbandi, the military commander of Baghdad).

Qasim went to great pains to persuade the Kurds that they were taking part in a social revolution that would fully integrate them into Iraqi society and its "Arabic and Kurdish Republic." As an earnest of the new spirit, the Iraqi Republic in October 1958 welcomed back Mulla Mustafa al-Barzani and some five hundred of his tribesmen who had spent a dozen years in the U.S.S.R. with their families. Mulla Mustafa himself was given Nuri Pasha's villa in Baghdad, a government pension, and a car. Even after disarming a Kurdish unit for having joined Kurdish civilians in attacking Iraqi Turkmans in Kirkuk in March 1959, Qasim still consented to the assignment of most Kurdish troops and officers to Kurdish towns, as part of the Arab-commanded second division that was customarily stationed there. When Qasim permitted the controlled restoration of party political life in January 1960, he issued licenses to only three parties, one of them being the Democratic Party of Kurdistan with Mulla Mustafa as president.

Qasim began to reverse his Kurdish policy late in 1960 by declaring the Democratic party illegal, arresting many Kurdish officials, closing several newspapers, and depriving Mulla Mustafa of his special perquisites. These measures formed part of Qasim's effort to curb the Communists throughout the country. He seemed to have regarded the Barzanis as Soviet agents, since Mulla Mustafa himself had attended in Moscow the November 1960 anniversary celebration of the Bolshevik Revolution. In his dealings with the U.S.S.R., however, Mulla Mustafa was himself walking the same tightrope as Qasim. If anything, the redoubtable Kurd grew more stubbornly nationalist over the years. Those Sunni and Shi'i Arabs politically disfranchised as the dictatorship became securely ensconced were thrown together in mounting hostility toward "the sole leader" and started clandestinely to plot his overthrow. The nationalist Kurds, for their part, came to believe that their progressive political disqualification represented a form of communal discrimination. In the last year of his rule, Qasim alienated the Shi'is too.

Qasim's ill-fated Kurdish policy became manifest in 1961: incitement of Kurdish tribes that had scores to settle with the Barzani tribesmen, the transfer of Kurdish troops of the Second Division to the south and the import of Arab forces into Kurdistan, attempted frontal assaults on Barzani guerrillas in their mountain strongholds, the use of the Iraqi air force for terrorizing villages that cooperated with Mulla Mustafa, and the wholesale arrest of more than 4,000 Kurds. Mulla Mustafa rallied to his cause many tribes and even urban intellectuals who would not otherwise have endorsed the Kurdish rebellion. The Barzanis drove refractory tribes across the frontiers into Iran and Turkey. By early in 1963, the Barzanis held Kurdistan in their grip more firmly than ever before. The government was spending, it was estimated, the equivalent of more than $150,000 a day upon its fruitless campaign that led neither to military victory nor to negotiated settlement. The Ba'this concluded a cease-fire with the Kurds at the time of the overthrow of Qasim in February 1963. By then, however, the Barzanis had crystallized their demands: full territorial autonomy, an equitable share of public revenue, the withdrawal of Iraqi troops from Kurdistan, and the stationing of Kurdish units there. These terms proved unacceptable to the Ba'thi regime, which resumed full-scale military operations against the Kurds in June 1963, with token military assistance from Syria in the fall. President 'Arif negotiated a fresh truce in February 1964, which again broke down soon thereafter. Prime Minister Bazzaz negotiated yet another truce in June 1966, based on an offer of autonomy to the Kurds, and three Kurds were named to the cabinet formed in August, none, however, a partisan of the Barzanis. The fighting stopped, but the mutual confidence among the communities would take years to rebuild, if indeed it could be done at all. Equally remote was the restoration of communal balance in the political system, upset by Qasim and never later redressed by the 'Arif brothers.

Finally, the nationalists in Syria and Iraq, while still subscribing to the concept of Arab unity nevertheless split on ways of carrying it into effect—in marked contrast with the wholly unambiguous Arab policy framed by the military junta in Egypt after 1954. It took for granted Egyptian leadership in the Arab unity movement. The military officers, 'Abd al-Nasir even more than the others, entertained no doubts that the early realization of unity depended on their initiative and example. In Syria the proponents of a merger with Iraq in a united Fertile Crescent state vied with those who endorsed joining Egypt in some alternative scheme. The formation of the United Arab Republic in 1958 strengthened those elements in Syria that upheld the merger with Egypt. The failure of the experiment in 1961 later encouraged the growth of sentiments advocating fusion with Iraq. Comparable divisions in Iraq itself gave rise to comparable results. Syrian and Iraqi officers gravitated to the rival cliques, thereby undermining the resolve of the military governments in both countries even in the handling of Arab affairs.

Consequences of Recurrent Coups

Syria and Iraq, like Egypt, gave high priority to military modernization. This was reflected in the rising cost of defense in the two Asian Arab lands. From an acknowledged £S 39.4 million allocated to the ministry of defense in 1953, Table 3 shows that Syria progressively enlarged the armed forces budget to £S 364.8 million in fiscal year 1965, more than a ninefold increase in a dozen years, and the later figure is probably low. In each of the years, except 1965, for which such data is available, public funds devoted to security overtopped those devoted to development. The Syrian government acknowledged spending close to 9.0 per cent of the GNP on defense (including internal security), but the real proportion was undoubtedly higher.

In Iraq, the number of officers and men in the armed forces had grown from fewer than 50,000 in 1958 to over 80,000 seven years later (even after the defection of perhaps as many as 10,000 Kurds). Defense and security expenditures grew at about half the Syrian rate in the same period, increasing from DI 19.7 million to DI 87.0 million in the dozen years ending in 1965–66. Probably not fully reflected in these figures were the mounting costs of the Kurdish war. Starting in 1963–64, the sums invested in defense and security began to exceed the sums allocated to the development budget. Even with rising oil revenues, as Table 4 reveals, the government spent 11.6 per cent of its GNP on defense in 1964–65 and 12.7 per cent in 1965–66.

From the outset, the military elite in Egypt took deliberate steps against the politicians of the old regime, first denying them the right to hold public office, then depriving them of their parties, and finally confiscating their wealth. By contrast, the succession of military rulers in Syria and Iraq never systematically uprooted the old-line politicians—a failure which multiplied the opportunities for rival military and civilian factions to join forces in planning conspiracies. Nor had the opportunities vanished after 1965 when

TABLE 3. Syria: Force Levels, Government Expenditures, and GNP, 1953–65

	Population (millions)	Force Levels[a] (thousands)	Government Expenditures (millions of Syrian pounds)			GNP (millions of Syrian pounds at current prices)	Defense Expenditures (as % of GNP)
			Defense (including internal security and justice)	Development	Total		
1953	3.7		39.4		196.8 e	2,092	1.9
1954	3.8		89.9		219.2 e	2,244	4.0
1955	3.9	25	104.9	63.1 f	323.7	2,023	5.2
1956	4.0		166.4	63.1 f	406.1	2,757	6.0
1957	4.1		277.5	63.2 f	478.7	2,882	9.6
1958 b	4.4		144.5	31.5 f	244.4	2,276	6.3
1958/59	4.7		268.4	80.8	531.2	2,595	10.3
1959/60	4.8		288.9	185.5	677.0	2,665	10.8
1960/61	5.0	45	295.3	248.9	749.5	2,886	10.2
1961/62	5.2		300.2	229.7	748.7	3,622	8.3
1962/63 c	5.3		516.7	313.1	1,217.4	3,741	9.2 g
1964	5.5		355.3	198.9	843.0	4,120	8.6
1965 d	5.6	60	364.8	403.6	1,114.2	4,141	8.8

SOURCES: Primarily Syrian Arab Republic, *Statistical Abstract*; and Central Bank of Syria, *Bulletin*; and IMF, *International Financial Statistics*.

a Excluding police and other paramilitary forces.   c 18 months fiscal period ending December 31.
b Six months fiscal period ending 30 June.   d Budget estimates.
e Total same as ordinary expenditures as no independent data on development expenditures are available.
f Estimated expenditure for development for calendar years 1955 through June 1958 £S 220.9 million; this sum was arbitrarily divided into proportionate amounts for the three and a half year period.
g Based on an estimated defense expenditure in calendar 1963 of £S 344 million, or two-thirds of the outlay for the 18-month period.

TABLE 4. Iraq: Force Levels, Government Expenditures, and GNP, 1953/54–1965/66

	Population (at mid-year in millions)	Force Levels[c] (thousands)	Government Expenditures (millions of Iraqi dinars)			GNP[a] (millions of dinars at current prices)	Defense Expenditures (as % of GNP)
			Defense (including internal security and justice)	Development	Total		
1953/54[a]	5.7		19.7	12.3	62.5	287.0	6.9
1954/55	5.8	40	20.1	20.8	74.6	330.0	6.9
1955/56	6.0		20.0	34.0	84.9	342.0	5.8
1956/57	6.2		28.6	45.0	115.2	389.0	7.4
1957/58	6.2		30.4	45.4	124.1	413.0	7.4
1958/59	6.4		34.4	56.6	142.3	436.2	7.9
1959/60	6.5		40.1	65.7	165.9	453.0	8.8
1960/61	6.7	70	47.1	47.6	161.8	502.8	9.4
1961/62	6.8		45.1	66.9	186.1	557.3	8.1
1962/63	6.9		49.3	59.3	187.7	600.8	8.2
1963/64	7.1		61.3	54.2	203.2	587.6	10.4
1964/65[b]	7.2		73.0	60.0	230.0	628.7[e]	11.6
1965/66[b]	7.4	82	87.0	65.0	255.5	685.3[e]	12.7

SOURCES: Primarily Central Bank of Iraq, Statistics and Research Department, *Annual Report*; and IMF, *International Financial Statistics*.

[a] Fiscal year ends March 31.
[b] Provisional.
[c] Excluding police and other paramilitary forces.
[d] Calendar years 1953 through 1965.
[e] Preliminary estimates.

nearly all the old-line Syrian politicians went into exile, since most of them congregated in nearby Bayrut where they enjoyed the freedom of assembly.

Instead of merely supplementing the military ministers with civilian technicians and civil servants, as the Egyptian officers had done, the Qasim and Ba'thi regimes in Iraq invited civilian politicians to sit in the cabinets also. The purely military ruling cliques of the 'Arif brothers, after November 1963, tried to introduce the Egyptian practice. The military juntas that acquiesced in the brothers' leadership seemed to work compatibly. Their opposition to Bazzaz as the one civilian prime minister in republican Iraq, even though the only civilians in his cabinet were technicians, suggested that the military rulers were not prepared to compromise their stand. Moreover, while Kurds began sitting in the cabinets again in the summer of 1966, no Kurdish military officers were admitted to the inner sanctum of the regime. The absence of the Kurds betokened trouble, pending a stable settlement of the Kurdish dispute. So, too, did continuing Shi'i dissatisfaction with the Sunni domination of the army and politics.

Also in Syria, after the separation from the U.A.R., old-line politicians staged a comeback in the three successive coalitions that usurped governmental authority. But the Ba'th Party, which was instrumental in 1963 in banning the other political parties, was itself later tamed by the army officers to serve the political will of the military junta and to help it carry into effect the Ba'thi socialist program. The very military methods of rule contributed to the regime's unpopularity. Even more unpopular was the leftist Ba'thi regime, dominated by the 'Alawi officers, who seized power in February 1966. These conditions increased the probability of further military coups.

Of no less significance was the difference in style between the durable military regime and the durable military condition. Perhaps even without consciously understanding the process, the former military officers in Cairo learned that governments, like armies, have their own rigid rules of management and conduct. The longer the Egyptian officers ran the government, the more they fell into the pattern of performing these functions as other rulers of nonmilitary background performed them. The junta, in time, overhauled the society and the economy of Egypt as well as its government; but in doing so they adopted the accepted ways of governance. Meanwhile, new officers fresh from the armed forces steadily streamed into the bureaucracy and, because the regime was a socialist one, into the multiplying industries owned or dominated by the state as well as into the cooperatives sponsored and regulated by the state. In a word, the closed ranks of the makers of policy became more and more civilianized, while the open ranks of the executors and guardians of that policy remained militarized because of the continuing replenishment by fresh recruits from the officer corps. In effect, two bureaucracies (in the extended state socialist sense) came into being: one civilian and one military, the first subordinated to the second. It was this very device that made the military regime in Egypt perhaps one of the best examples in the postwar world of a modernizing army becoming a modernizing agency in the economy and in the society at large. But the example of Egypt was unique in the Middle East. No other military government either copied the Egyptian model or developed another of comparable efficacy in using the army for training nonmilitary leadership.

In Iraq and Syria, on the other hand, the process was reversed. The replenishment of active army officers occurred at the policy-framing summit as each new faction replaced an old one. The new leaders removed the old and promptly promoted themselves to the top military commands and political offices, retaining an active interest in the army and the government to prevent rival factions from supplanting them. But they did not, as a rule, hold on to power long enough either to suffuse the civilian bureaucracy with loyal military officers or to establish a transcendent military bureaucracy. In Syria there were signs of the gradual transformation of the civil service from one that was overwhelmingly Sunni Arab to one that was increasingly staffed with minorities. The failure to militarize or to subordinate the civilian bureaucracy partly explained the failure of the socialist regimes in the two countries after 1964 to put their socialist policies to productive effect. In brief, the military regimes in Syria and Iraq could hardly demonstrate that they had become successful sponsors of non-military modernization.

9

SUDAN: MILITARY INTERRUPTION OF CIVILIAN RULE

A military republic is almost invariably regarded as militaristic, as bent on military expansion at the expense of other essential public activities. The three military republics considered in the preceding chapters undoubtedly fit this description. Sudan under military rule emphatically did not. Though as populous as Syria and Iraq put together, Sudan had an army in 1964, the last year of military rule, only one-seventh the combined size of the Syrian and Iraqi armies. Or to put it differently, the population of Sudan was nearly half that of Egypt but maintained in military uniform in 1964 only one-tenth the number of men.

Despite the military interruption of civilian rule for a half-dozen years (1958–64), Sudan avoided radical policies. In large measure this could be ascribed to the high standards of the civilian bureaucracy; the quality performance of the British officials during the condominium carried over into independence. But British policy had been fundamentally paternalistic, and the development of autonomous political institutions came too late to acquire solidity. Nine of every ten Sudanese, at independence, could not read or write. The population, living in a preindustrial economy, was overwhelmingly rural and tribal—Arab Muslim in the north, and pagan and Christian in the south. Even if neighboring Omdurman and greater Khartum were lumped together, the combined population in 1956 hardly exceeded 200,000. No other towns at that time had a fourth that number of inhabitants. Democratic institutions in a largely illiterate plural society can hardly be expected to work effectively. What was remarkable, therefore, was not the breakdown in 1958 of the experiment in democracy, but its attempted revival by chastened politicians six years later, after the overthrow of the military junta. After, as before, military rule, the democratic experiment was limited to the Muslim Arab north, comprising six of the nine provinces and perhaps 70 per cent of the close to 14 million people in the country in 1966. This was the homogeneous segment of the population, containing most of the country's trained manpower, entrepreneurial skills, and political leadership. The 4 million pagans in the three southern provinces with their small but growing Christian communities were splintered into rival tribes speaking perhaps as many as 80 languages and dialects. The south was represented in the government, but the government itself was managed by the north, where the traditional politicians with the powerful backing in the rural areas of large Sufi orders kept the urban educated elite in harness.

Thus it was the plural society that was preventing the later democratic experiment from taking vigorous hold. The northerners were simply not learning how to live with the south. They seemed as determined as ever to dominate it, which forced the northern rulers to enlarge their armed forces and the sums that they set aside for its modernizing weaponry. The amounts allocated to that purpose had not yet become excessive in 1967, but the civilian rulers were unmistakably heading in that direction.

The Legacy of the Condominium

The Anglo-Egyptian condominium that lasted for more than a half century was a condominium in name only. Britain governed the territory as a British dependency. British officials filled all the top positions; only below the level of district officers did Egyptians qualify for employment in the bureaucracy and for comparable ranks in the army. Such influence as Egypt could bring to bear in the opening decades of the condominium was finally erased late in 1924. Britain retaliated for the murder by Egyptians of Sir Lee Stack, the governor general of Sudan, by forcing the withdrawal of Egyptian civil servants and army units from the country. The progressive Sudanization of the bureaucracy at the intermediate level started at that time.

The British administration of Sudan was unique, since it was accountable not to the Colonial Office but to the Foreign Office. For that reason British technicians who volunteered for posts in Sudan were not rotated among the British dependencies, as were those in the colonial service. They tended, as in India, to remain in Sudan for a lifetime career, often becoming dedicated servants of the country. The senior British personnel became devout advocates of Sudan's political development and established high standards of public conduct and performance which their Sudanese juniors emulated. Over time, this had the effect of fashioning a European-ized civil service where none had existed before.

Although the beginnings of nationalism in Sudan traced back to the 1930s, the first opportunity for fruitful political pressure came after the outbreak of World War II. In response, Britain gradually created autonomous institutions in the northern provinces, and finally in 1948 a partly elected Legislative Assembly with a respon-sible Executive Council.

The nationalist movement, meanwhile, split into rival political "parties," which had their roots in traditional religious politics. Two powerful Sufi orders of nineteenth-century origin still at-tracted a considerable Muslim Arab peasant following. Those in the east were largely *ansar*, or followers of the self-proclaimed Mahdi, the leader of a militant Islamic revivalist movement that won "independence" for Sudan in the early 1880s. The Mahdiyah survived its founder's death in 1885, and the leadership of such mystical orders was by custom hereditary. The Ummah (nation) Party, the secular political group associated with the Mahdiyah, called for the gradual attainment of sovereignty through coopera-tion with Britain. Ranged against it was the Khatmiyah, a rival Sufi group whose predominantly peasant membership lived mostly in the northwest. Urban leaders of the Khatmiyah established the secular Ashiqqa (brothers) Party basically to compete with the Ummah for popular support. The Ashiqqa favored union with Egypt and demanded the termination of the condominium. It was during the stalemate in Anglo-Egyptian negotiations, partly over Sudan, that Britain unilaterally created the autonomous institu-tions in the north. Precisely because of Egyptian opposition, the Ashiqqa refused to take part in the elections, enabling the Ummah to dominate the Legislative Assembly and the Executive Council.

The coming of the military regime to Egypt broke the Anglo-Egyptian impasse over Sudan with an agreement in February 1953 on a self-government statute for the condominium and the assur-ance of independence within three years. In preparation for the election of a bicameral legislature in the fall, the Ashiqqa changed its name to the Nationalist Union Party (NUP) to stress its close identity with Egypt. The NUP victory brought Isma'il al-Azhari to the premiership of a one-party government that supervised the Su-danization of the bureaucracy and the administration. After the expiry of the condominium on 1 January 1956, sovereign Sudan continued functioning under the self-government statute, which parliament amended to enable a five-man Supreme Commission to serve as a collective head of state. Executive power for the actual conduct of government was vested in a council of ministers.

After independence, Sudanese preference for Nagib rather than 'Abd al-Nasir, and Egyptian demands for modification of the boundary with Sudan, weakened NUP ties to Egypt. The leaders of the Mahdiyah and the Khatmiyah united in February 1956 to compel Azhari to form a coalition cabinet. Soon thereafter the Khatmiyah broke away from the NUP altogether to form its own People's Democratic Party (PDP), which joined with the Ummah in July 1956 to replace the Azhari government with another under the premiership of 'Abdallah Khalil of the Ummah Party.

In the first election after independence, in February 1958, the Ummah, while winning a plurality, failed to procure a majority in either house and joined the PDP in yet another coalition. The Ummah's primary dependence on the ansar gave it greater strength in the rural than in the urban areas, and it became the party that advocated cooperation in the Cold War with the United States, the West, and their Arab friends. Meanwhile, following the separation of the Khatmiyah, the NUP turned into a secular, urban party, with headquarters in Khartum and branches in the northern towns. Azhari and his colleagues promoted economic radicalism, close relations with Egypt, and neutrality in the Cold War. The PDP never became an integrated political party, nor did it develop effective leadership, despite its Khatmiyah ties.

Perhaps the most stubborn problem facing the politicians of sovereign Sudan was the chronic conflict between the north and the south. The Muslim Arabs, taking advantage of their homogeneous society, numerical preponderance, and higher level of education, tried to impose their language and their religion on the pagans of the south. This competed with an on-going program of Christian missionaries who, under the condominium had made some headway in converting tribesmen to the several denominations, principally Roman Catholicism. The paternalistic policy of the British throughout the condominium had also, in effect, preserved the traditional cultures. Moreover, with the relatively swift withdrawal of the British officials during Sudanization, the autonomous government sent northerners to fill most of the vacancies. Their appearance in August 1955 touched off a mutiny in the army, which was accompanied by anti-northern riots in the three provinces; the security forces restored order before the British laid down their authority. But the southerners continued to hold the Muslim Arabs in deep suspicion. Nor was the restiveness in the south allayed by the grant of at least two seats in each cabinet, starting in 1953, since the southern politicians believed that they were entitled to no less than one-third of the total.

The continuing quarrel between the north and the south contributed to the paralysis of the new parliament and of the Ummah-PDP coalition cabinet in the summer and early fall of 1958. The parties and politicians seemed incapable of making the parliamentary system work, and charges of corruption brought it into disrepute. To compound the troubles, the country was beset by an economic depression brought on by the continued sluggishness of cotton exports, the largest earner of foreign currency. The coalition was visibly falling apart, as leaders of the three principal parties engaged in drawn-out but fruitless bilateral negotiations to construct a stable combination. During these exchanges, the PDP and NUP leaders met in Cairo in October with 'Abd al-Nasir, giving substance to fears in the Ummah ranks of a possible Egyptian-engineered military coup d'état. These fears were reinforced by the unabating U.A.R. propaganda attacks on the Sudan government for its alleged pro-Western policies. Given these conditions and the failure of parliament to frame a permanent constitution, the prestige of the civilian politicians simply withered away.

Before entering politics in 1948, 'Abdallah Khalil, the prime minister, had been a career officer in the army for 38 years and held the distinction of being the first Sudanese to rise to the rank of colonel. He seems to have decided in the fall of 1958 that the army would provide much more decisive leadership for the country than the civilian politicians. A week before the military seized power, Khalil reportedly shared his views with a former junior colleague, Major General Ibrahim 'Abbud, commander-in-chief of the army. When the officers, led by 'Abbud, staged their coup on 17 November, they apparently did so without advance notice to Khalil or any other civilian politician.

Military Non-changers

The officers who ran the Sudanese government for the next half-dozen years were skimmed off the top of the military hierarchy. Under the leadership of 'Abbud, the Supreme Council of the Armed Forces (SCAF), as the junta was called, set itself up as an exclusive policy-framing directorate. Like the military junta in Egypt, the SCAF proved hardy, for it was not replaced by any subsequent military coup. Nevertheless, following three abortive military coups in the first year of its rule, the SCAF by November

1959 was trimmed in size from eleven to seven, thereafter remaining unaltered during the life of the regime.

The SCAF retained direct command over the military establishment, took over the powers of the legislature, and kept an eye on the judiciary. All the officers, while sitting in the cabinet, continued parading their uniforms. So, too, did the officers next in rank who went out as provincial governors, one for each of the six northern provinces and a seventh for the three southern provinces. The provincial governors, however, did not belong to the innermost ruling coterie. At the close of 1959, the junta comprised one full general, one major general, and five brigadiers; by 1962 the brigadiers had all risen to the rank of major general.

All the members of the SCAF sat in the cabinet under the premiership of General 'Abbud, who held the defense ministry and served as head of state with the title of president. Through vaunting their dual role as minister and officer, the military commanders brought the army's coercive influence to bear directly on governmental policy. To help administer the country, the SCAF enlisted the services of the inherited bureaucracy and of the technicians, but categorically shunned the former politicians. The cabinet thus included five civilians, mostly civil servants, to run the nonsensitive branches of government. The civilian ministers took no basic decisions, but simply implemented the policies laid down by the army's commanders. Still, the Sudanese military oligarchy was on the whole mild-mannered. The armed forces in 1958 consisted of 12,000 officers and men; by 1964 their number climbed to about 15,000, still a very small army for so large a population in a country nearly one million square miles in size. The growth of the army under military rule was closely related to the uprising in the south that began in 1963, as was the mounting cost of the armed forces, which doubled between 1958 and 1964. Even then, the sum set aside for defense in the last full year of military rule just topped £S 15.0 million, representing approximately 3.3 per cent of the GNP, far below the world average in 1964 of 7 per cent. The soldier rulers clearly did not succumb to the temptations of purchasing modern military hardware on the cheap. Consistently in these years they invested more in development than in defense. (See Table 5.)

The junta formally disbanded the political parties and confiscated their assets. The paramount politicians of parliamentary days, though recurrently arrested, did not as a rule remain long under detention, and the two former prime ministers even received lifetime government pensions. The military rulers came from ex-

TABLE 5. Sudan: Force Levels, Government Expenditures, and GNP, 1956/57–1965/66

| | Population (at Mid-year in millions) | Force[d] Levels (thousands) | Government Expenditures (millions of Sudanese pounds) | | | GNP (millions of pounds at current prices) | Defense Expenditures (as % of GNP) |
			Defense (including internal security and justice)	Development	Total		
1956/57[a]	10.2	5	4.1	12.6	45.3	324	1.3
1957/58	10.7		5.7	21.3	62.6	323	1.8
1958/59	11.1		5.8	22.9	64.3	333	1.7
1959/60	11.5		7.0	22.9	67.8	373	1.9
1960/61	11.8	12	7.8	26.0	74.2	380	1.8
1961/62	12.1		11.8	40.5	95.9	388	3.0
1962/63	12.5		13.6	47.7	117.6	451	3.0
1963/64	12.8		15.0	58.7	128.9	456	3.3
1964/65[b]	13.2		16.1	33.9	102.6	463	3.5
1965/66[c]	13.5	18.5	21.3	32.0	111.0	483	4.4

SOURCES: Primarily IMF, *International Financial Statistics*; AID, *Summary of Basic Data: Sudan*

[a] Fiscal year ends 30 June.
[b] Provisional.
[c] Estimates.
[d] Excluding police and other paramilitary forces.

actly the same class as the politicians whom they had supplanted, and they were protesting not so much against social and economic discrimination as against political inefficiency. Accordingly, the generals hardly tampered with the economy and the society. Even in the south, the military rulers did not alter the policies of their civilian predecessors, but simply attempted to carry them out with fewer inhibitions. The military regime replaced Christian missions with Muslim educational centers without, however, making any measurable inroads among the pagan tribesmen, except perhaps by harsh policy to widen the political gap that separated the south from the north. In 1961 the southern leaders reacted by organizing the Sudan African National Union (SANU), a secret society to protect the political and cultural interests of the south. In 1962, southern tribesmen, once again demanding autonomy for their provinces, created a guerrilla movement which the military rulers found it impossible to suppress. The imposition of martial law, the harsh handling of the tribal population, the expulsion of the missionaries, and the exile of the southern leaders enhanced SANU's influence and helped spread the insurrection. Over half of the enlarging Sudanese army by 1964 was assigned to duty in the three rebellious provinces. It was this sectional hostility that later contributed to the junta's downfall.

More significant in the end was the opposition to military rule secretly organized in the north, particularly by the Communist Party, which had formed in Sudan during World War II. Though banned by the military officers, as they had been earlier by the civilian politicians, the Communists were accustomed to working underground and more than held their own under military rule. The party appealed especially to students and intellectuals as well as to urban labor with whom professional societies combined to form the focus of dissidence with military rule. The dissident groups were concentrated in Khartum, the capital, which, as in other nonindustrial states, was the very source of national power. This was the one locality where the regime could not brook any challenge to its authority. Yet it was in Khartum that the dissidents lived, and it was there that they planned a program of civil disobedience to wring concessions from the junta. Their tactics proved so successful that they toppled the regime.

The general strike originated on 21 October 1964 in a student demonstration in Khartum that had first been authorized and then disallowed. By the time the order reached the student leaders, they were unable to call the demonstration off, and the police, in trying to suppress it, killed one student. With General 'Abbud out of the country at the start of the strike and most of the security forces tied down in the south, the civil disobedience was not checked in time. The movement swiftly grew into a mass movement, attracting even civil servants and bringing all public life in the capital to a standstill. Within five days, General 'Abbud announced the resignation of the SCAF, with the apparent initial intention of simply replacing some of its members. Having intimidated the generals, the civilian protesters, however, insisted on the transfer of total power to a civilian coalition government as the price for lifting the general strike. This, they finally achieved on 30 October, when General 'Abbud accepted the terms and the nominees of the coalition.

With the return of power to the civilians, Sudan provided the only example of the postwar Middle East of a civilian coup d'état that brought down a military regime.

Civilian Rule Revitalized

Once the military regime collapsed, the northern politicians quickly resumed plying their craft, despite the six years of enforced inactivity. The religious orders in the north, which had enabled the political parties to reach out from the few small and slowly expanding urban centers into the rural and nomadic interior, also survived in full vigor. Before the political realities could sort themselves out, the northern politicians had to capture the instruments of government, which were initially entrusted to a caretaker coalition cabinet under the neutral premiership of Sirr al-Khatim al-Khalifah. A civil servant, Khalifah had found his career in the ministry of education, rising to the rank of permanent undersecretary after having served for ten years in the southern provinces, where he earned high respect for his promotion of education. With Khalifah sat representatives of the main political parties, which were formally reorganized, and of the professional societies, the labor unions, and the bureaucracy. Among the ministers were two acknowledged Communists and two fellow travellers—one a delegate of the party, and the others representing the bar association, the labor unions, and the tenant farmers.

The caretaker cabinet turned first to a clarification of its relaitonship to the army. General 'Abbud's reputation as a public servant of high personal integrity outlasted the removal of the junta. He was therefore retained at the start as head of state, though shorn of executive powers. He served in this uncertain period as mediator between the coalition and the officer corps in the army. His former colleagues on the SCAF were arrested on 9 November; 'Abbud himself resigned six days later, after having helped find an apolitical commander-in-chief of the armed forces. By then, it was clear, in principle at least, that the army under the new command had accepted civilian supremacy. Whether the army would thereafter remain in the barracks could not be wholly foreseen, for much would depend on the quality of civilian political leadership. Within the officer corps itself, apparently only the members of the junta had been politicized. Unlike the junta in Egypt, the Sudanese generals of the military regime were not reformers, and therefore since the need and the opportunity for new kinds of public employment did not arise, they did not recruit other officers for government service except as provincial administrators. This gave the civilian leaders good prospects of keeping the army out of politics during the critical period of refashioning the civilian governing agencies and readjusting the country to civilian rule.

After the resignation of 'Abbud, the caretaker cabinet reinstated with amendments the provisional constitution, pending the preparation of a permanent organic law by a projected constituent assembly. A five-member executive, now called the Supreme Council of State, was created to serve as a ceremonial collective presidency, under the chairmanship of a neutral civil servant with one member each from the Ummah, the NUP, the PDP, and the three southern provinces. With inclusive political and geographic representation, the Supreme Council bought time for the reactivators of civilian rule by delaying what could have become a divisive issue until permanent arrangements were made in an agreed constitution. The caretaker cabinet, which vested in itself legislative as well as executive powers, saw its major reponsibility as organizing and supervising the election at the earliest practicable date of a constituent assembly that would also sit as a regular parliament. The main obstacles to an early and orderly election were two: the sharpening dissension in the cabinet with the Communists and their supporters; and the irrepressible uprising in the south.

The Communists, who had participated in the general strike that had forced the military junta to step down, created a National Front of Professional Organizations, thereby uniting the societies and the labor unions which the party had infiltrated. With the formation of the caretaker cabinet, the Communists lost no time in founding a Workers Party and a Tenants Party and then demanded representation in the cabinet for both. The other political ministers parried this tactic by forming a United National Front, which included the Professional Front and the resuscitated parties of the earlier civilian period. These were country-wide parties, in contrast to the Communist Party and the Communist-infiltrated groups, whose members came almost entirely from Khartum. In the reorganization of the cabinet late in February 1965, the Ummah Party and the Nationalist Union Party (which by then had re-absorbed the Khatmiyah), with the support of the *Ikhwan al-Muslimun* (Muslim Brethren), formed a loose coalition called the Islamic Charter Front, which more than doubled their portfolios to seven, while those of the Communists and their sympathizers were reduced from four to three. Thereafter, the non-Communist political ministers easily curbed the Communist maneuvers to defer the election until a settlement of the crisis in the south.

The return to civilian rule had an initial unsettling effect on the south. Southern spokesmen were still demanding proportional representation, as they had before November 1958, which, they believed, entitled the south to a third of the seats in the caretaker cabinet. Instead of five of the fourteen seats, the south received only two. The southerners were also insisting on the replacement of northerners in the administration of the three provinces, the release of political prisoners, the grant of amnesty to all rebels, and the evacuation of the army units.

The rebellion had united the south against the military regime; now the southerners themselves divided into rival groups, with seemingly different objectives, the cooperative politicians calling the rebellion a struggle for autonomy and the rebels calling it an independence movement for the creation of the state of Azania. The Sudan African National Union in November 1964 spawned the Southern Front and the People's Progressive Party, each designed to organize popular support for the autonomy movement, and the *Anya Nya* ("the poison that spreads," in Moru-Madi) as the guerrilla branch. An attempt to hold a north-south conference in February 1965 at Juba, the capital of Equatoria, the southernmost province, revealed a split between the SANU and its offshoots. The Anya Nya disregarded a SANU appeal to suspend the fighting. Nor did the north-south talks in Khartum in the second half of March reach an agreement, since the southern spokesmen would consider nothing less than virtual independence. They did, however, consent to sit on a joint committee that was instructed to settle the differences between the south, which insisted on a plebiscite for federation or full autonomy (including its own army and police force), and the north, which offered autonomy for agriculture and education alone.

This gesture liberated the caretaker government to proceed with the election, which it was determined not to delay because of the urgent need to procure a mandate from the people that would help, among other things, to clarify the civilian relationship to the army. Elections to the 156 seats in the unicameral constituent assembly that were assigned to the north took place on a staggered schedule in April–May 1965; the 60 seats assigned to the south were left vacant until elections there could be organized. The Ummah returned 85 deputies, and the NUP 56; smaller factions and independents accounted for the rest. The new parliament elected Ibrahim al-Azhari of the NUP the permanent president of the Supreme Council of State, pending the adoption of a constitution. His colleagues were chosen from the other major political parties and from the south. As prime minister of a coalition cabinet, the parliament designated Muhammad Ahmad Mahgub of the Ummah, who also remained the minister of defense. Mahgub named six colleagues each from the Ummah and the NUP parties. But the Southern Front and the SANU refused to join the coalition, each claiming sole representation of the south.

The Communist Party, which had been legalized in October 1964 after the overturn of the junta, was once again banned in November 1965, when the constituent assembly amended Article 5 of the draft constitution relating to civil liberties so as to exclude the Communist Party and any others that preach atheism. The 11 Communist members of the constituent assembly were immediately unseated. All represented the special constituencies for university graduates, of which there were 15. The ban on the Communist Party threatened further to alienate the urban intellectual elite.

Sudan furnished landing rights in the summer of 1965 to Algerian and Egyptian planes that were transporting arms to the Congo. After the failure of the Congolese rebellion, many of the weapons found their way back to the southern Sudan, enabling the Anya Nya to step up their own attacks on the Sudanese security forces. By then the guerrillas had brought into being their own Anzania Liberation Front.

Nearly three-fourths of the expanding Sudanese armed forces were committed by mid-1965 to restoring order in the south. The first signs of restiveness in the army appeared as early as August, when junior officers circumvented their military commanders to address directly to the cabinet their appeal to end shortages of food, supplies, and even weapons. The memorandum signed in the name of the Liberal Military Front must have conjured up visions in Khartum of an impending military coup, for within forty-eight hours the government raised the salaries of all officers in the armed forces. At the end of October 1965 a mutiny broke out in the Juba garrison, the Sudanese army's headquarters in the south. This time the estimated sixty officers, mostly of junior grade, were led by the garrison's deputy commander. In addition to the shortages, they complained about the lack of military or political direction from Khartum and the failure to rotate units. For three days the mutinous officers kept captive in a hotel the commander-in-chief of the Sudanese armed forces and the acting minister of defense (also a general), who had been decoyed to Juba by the complaints, until assurances were given of corrective measures. Within a few weeks, many of the officers were reassigned to the north, and two senior officers were imprisoned.

The cost of the civil war steadily mounted, and the defense budget for 1965–66 exceeded £S 21 million, an increase of about 42 per cent over highest allocation to the armed forces of the military junta. The armed forces, which numbered 18,500 by 1966, were scheduled to increase to 25,000.

Parliament withdrew its confidence from the Mahgub cabinet in July 1966 and designated as the new prime minister al-Sayyid Saddiq al-Mahdi, the Oxford-educated president of the Ummah Party. The elections in the south in areas under military control were held under the new cabinet early in the spring of 1967. The cabinet also approved a draft constitution which would have replaced the collective presidency with an executive president and which it was hoped the parliament would adopt. But the cabinet fell in May because of a division in the Ummah Party over its candidate for the presidency, to which al-Sayyid Saddiq aspired. Mahgub was recalled to the premiership.

After the Six Day War, Sudan became the first new Arab military client of the U.S.S.R. and its Communist allies in Europe. In the barter agreement, which was announced in August 1967, Sudan undertook to pay with cotton exports for MiG-17s, armor, and other weaponry from the U.S.S.R. and Czechoslovakia, and naval equipment from Yugoslavia. Previously, Sudan had purchased its arms exclusively in the West, primarily from West Germany and Britain.

The second try at democracy seemed far from rooted after three years. The sponsors of the regime were hobbled by the same kinds of problems that faced other Middle East states with plural societies. As in Iraq, the dominant community in Sudan had alienated the cultural minorities, and instead of seeking a stable communal balance, the northerners were hazarding the continuation of civil war. Even in the north, the politicians, though engaging in competitive politics among the old-line parties, nonetheless outlawed the Communist Party. The fact that the civilian politicians gave scope for the Sufi orders to participate in the political system helped bridge the traditional and the modernizing institutions. But the split in the Ummah Party in the spring of 1967 seemed to harden in the months that followed, threatening the unity of the Mahdiyah which provided the party its mass following. It also threatened the survival of the post-military experiment in democracy.

Whatever the future held in store, this much was clear: In Sudan, the civilians managed to overturn the military regime. In Pakistan and Turkey, as we shall see, the military regimes were terminated by the military officers themselves; but in both instances the restoration of civilian rule was not complete.

Military-Civilian Coalitions

10

JUNIOR PARTNERS: PAKISTAN AND ALGERIA

Military republics in the postwar Middle East, as we have seen, were far from uniform. They did, however, share a number of traits: The military presence was manifest, the soldiers dominated the policy-making process, and the civilians brought into policy management were technicians and bureaucrats. There were yet other kinds of regimes, those in which soldiers shared the powers of government with civilians. Such civil-military partnerships in the postwar Middle East were of two varieties: in one the senior partners were civilian politicians; in the other they were military officers. Although the degree of military participation in the formulation of political policy varied in both categories, the military presence was always concealed. These I call the quasi-military republics.

With the exception of Egypt, the quasi-military condition has appeared at one time or another in every Middle East country where the army has intruded into politics. Thus, in Syria in 1948 and in Sudan a decade later, civilian politicians invited military commanders to support civilian regimes on the verge of collapse. The partnerships did not long endure; officers swiftly seized power and established military regimes.[1] In the Yemen Arab Republic the military-civilian coalition lasted considerably longer. Yet, until the fall of 1967 Republican Yemen remained the ward of the U.A.R., which had failed to show that it could build or even help build a political system in other than its own image, insofar as local conditions permitted.

Civilian politicians court trouble when they summon soldiers to restore domestic order. Admittedly, with military aid, politicians may enhance the power of the executive at the expense of other branches of government. But they pay dearly for what is often only a short-term advantage, since in accepting such aid the politicians admit the inadequacy of civilian authority and their dependence on the armed forces. They are thus enlarging the function of the military establishment to defend the regime against its internal as well as its external foes. The soldiers, in the process, may develop political ambitions, especially when the problems that the military are called upon to help solve resist easy solution. In their civil-military partnership, military officers at the summit are becoming politicized, since they are given opportunities to participate in the political system in varying nonmilitary capacities.

The pattern of the civil-military partnership is established in situations where the soldiers do not initially have strong political ambitions and develop them only slowly. When such partnerships become institutionalized, their particular nature is revealed. In the postwar Middle East, durable alliances of this sort appeared in Pakistan (1953–58) and in Algeria (1962–65). In both, undeniably, quasi-military regimes gave way in the end to full military rule. Yet there was no advance certainty of the outcome in either land.

In making comparisons, we must remember that Pakistan and Algeria are disparate countries. With an estimated 100 million people, Pakistan ranks as the world's sixth most populous country. Less than one-eighth as many people live in Algeria, which, however, has an area (roughly 920,000 square miles) more than twice that of Pakistan (365,000 squares miles). Both countries are Muslim, and both have linguistic minorities. Perhaps as many as 30 per cent of the population of Algeria are Berber speakers, largely concentrated in the Kabylia and the Aurès mountains in the east. West Pakistan (310,000 square miles and 45 per cent of the population) is united in name only, for despite the unification decree of 1955 and the adoption of Urdu as the official language, its residents still speak vernaculars corresponding to the earlier administrative divisions, notably Punjabi, Sindhi, Baluchi, and, in the tribal district of the Northwest Frontier, Pushtu. Separated by a thousand miles of Indian territory is East Pakistan (55,000 square miles and 55 per cent of the population), where Bengali is almost the exclusive language. The division between the two provinces of Pakistan is reflected in military politics as, in fact, in all other aspects of public affairs to a more vigorous extent than is the Arab-Berber split in Algeria. Moreover, the civil-military partnership in Algeria began at birth, molding the political system from its inception. In Pakistan, the alliance came into being gradually after a half-dozen years of independent institutional growth.

In the circumstances, the analogies must not be drawn too fine; yet if we probe deeply enough, the similarities should become clear. Let us begin with the civil-military partnership in Pakistan, which lasted for more than five years before the creation in October 1958 of the martial-law regime.

The Governor-General (President) and the Soldier

For more than a decade after independence, the Pakistani political elite seemed bent on finding a viable political system. To judge from the deliberations of the two Constituent Assemblies and from the kind of regime that emerged in form and, less perfectly, in practice, the consensus of articulate political opinion favored parliamentary democracy. This seemed wholly natural, since such institutions were precisely the ones that the British rulers had tried to implant. However, although the institutions were those of parliamentary democracy, the practice was that of benevolent despotism, because the imperial power had given the population of the subcontinent few real opportunities before partition to develop democratic government.

While the politicians (primarily landlords, lawyers, and a sprinkling of orthodox religious spokesmen) frittered away their opportunity in intense personal rivalry, the technicians stepped into the breach. As administrators and technicians, the senior civil servants in Pakistan had inherited from the British a tradition of selective recruitment, careful training, and high standards of performance. In almost every sphere of public institutional life, including the senior civil service but notably excluding the military, Pakistan had received in the partition of the subcontinent far less than its due share. This unequal division was not attributable to a design in favor of India over Pakistan; rather, it reflected the fortuitous birth of the Islamic state, for the idea of such a state took shape only late in the struggle for independence. In the event, the Indians, who constituted the bulk of the total population, inherited the lion's share of the political apparatus and experience.

The first Governor-General of Pakistan, Muhammad 'Ali Jinnah, was known as the Qaid-i 'Azam (Great Leader), a title later borne by no other Pakistani. Jinnah could endow his office with whatever powers he desired. He therefore governed, not as a formal head of state, but as British viceroys had before him. When Jinnah died in September 1948, just thirteen months after independence, Prime Minister Liaqat 'Ali Khan was the obvious legatee. He chose to remain prime minister in the expectation, later fulfilled, of exercising paramount political power through that office, while the gover-

nor-generalship went to Khwaja Nazimuddin, Pakistan's first and
only ornamental head of state. In this period, too, the practice of
assigning the governor-generalship and the prime ministry on a
geographic basis, so that if one office went to a West Pakistani, the
other went to an East Pakistani, seemed to be the aim. When
Liaqat died prematurely in October 1951 from the wounds of an
assassin's bullet, political leadership went begging.

The Liaqat-Nazimuddin relationship had as its objective the
shaping of a parliamentary democracy on the British model. It was
thus expected that the governor-generalship would become essentially a ceremonial office, with all effective political authority vested
in the cabinet, which in turn would be responsible to an elected
legislature and would remain in office as long as it continued to
enjoy that body's confidence. Such a system works efficiently in a
society whose leaders receive their mandate through popular elections and compete for office through parties that provide them
with means of organizing popular support. In Pakistan these essential conditions did not obtain.

Thus, even if the Liaqat-Nazimuddin precedent had grown into
a convention, parliamentary democracy might nevertheless not
have survived. The absence of popular political parties deprived
the electorate of an institutionalized means to make known their
views and to select their candidates for office, while the legislators
in reality represented no one but themselves. This accounted in
part for the failure of the first Constituent Assembly (1947–54) to
complete the framing of a constitution and for the failure of that
assembly, in its role as legislature, to establish its supremacy over
the council of ministers. In the circumstances, the cabinet assumed
authoritarian powers since the defective parliament did not hold
the ministers accountable for their actions. But after the death of
Liaqat, the cabinet proved no more effective than the assembly.
With little or no prior experience under British rule in the management either of national politics or national government, the
politicians simply floundered. They relied to a considerable degree
upon the senior civil service to direct the ministries, and even
began to name senior civil servants to the cabinet.

When, on the death of Liaqat, Khwaja Nazimuddin vacated the
office of governor-general to assume the premiership, he had every
reason to believe that he was ascending the political ladder from a
ceremonial post to an executive one. This was confirmed by the
appointment as governor-general of a former senior civil servant
with a chronic illness, Ghulam Muhammad, who was finance min-

ister at the time. By the fall of 1951, however, parliamentary democracy in Pakistan was well on the way to becoming a sham, even though the fact was not yet generally acknowledged. Nazimuddin proved incompetent to deal with the West Pakistan politicians who were on home ground and more numerous than the Bengali (East Pakistani) politicians who were operating in a less familiar political terrain. Instead of holding a tight grip on affairs of state, the prime minister allowed the situation to deteriorate swiftly. Hundreds of thousands of refugees from India were still not resettled. Bengalis leveled ever more insistent complaints against alleged discrimination in the central government by the West Pakistanis. Religious spokesmen raised demands for the safeguard of Islam in the projected constitution and for the establishment of Sunni or orthodox Muslim supremacy. Indeed, Sunni fundamentalists in Lahore, the largest city in the Punjab and the cultural center of the divided country, staged riotous demonstrations in March and April 1953 against the Ahmadiyah sect, focusing in particular on Sir Muhammad Zafrullah Khan, an Ahmadi who was foreign minister.

The crisis in Lahore revealed that Ghulam Muhammad, once installed as governor-general, conducted himself as neither a figurehead nor an invalid. Hitherto, the governor-general was a nominee of the prime minister, though formally appointed by the crown, as was customary in the British Commonwealth. Ghulam Muhammad now reversed the roles by dismissing Nazimuddin and replacing him with a Bengali, Muhammad 'Ali (Bogra), the Pakistan ambassador to Washington, thus preserving for the time the principle of geographic distribution. Significantly, it was not the prime minister designate, but the governor-general himself who formed the new cabinet. His act was clothed with authority, because he dealt firmly and effectively with the riots in the Punjab. Allegedly on the advice of the director general of the defense ministry, Iskandar Mirza, the governor-general invoked martial law for the first time in independent Pakistan, calling upon the armed forces to suppress the disorders in Lahore. The reversal of roles was not challenged by the Constituent Assembly, which was not in session at the time of Nazimuddin's dismissal and which did not even discuss the issue on reconvening five months later.

Although from the army's viewpoint the intervention in Lahore was not more than a police action, it produced a permanent political effect by helping convert the governor-generalship into an executive office. However, this was a contribution of the army, not of General Muhammad Ayub Khan, its commander-in-chief. Liaqat had originally chosen General Ayub as top commander ahead of other officers senior in rank because of his reputation as a nonpolitical soldier. From the moment that he assumed the top command in January 1951, the general nevertheless managed with finesse the internal and external politics of the army. He raised the morale of his officers by generous salaries, allowances, and pensions, which assured their loyalty to his leadership and to the government. Nor had the government interfered when Ayub, apparently without seeking prior cabinet approval, seized the initiative as early as 1952 in opening negotiations with the United States for a military aid agreement.

The governor-general dissolved the Constituent Assembly in October 1954. Ghulam Muhammad took this action as a riposte to the assembly's amendment of the 1935 Government of India Act, depriving the governor-general of the right to dismiss a cabinet that still held the legislature's confidence. Instead of asserting its new authority by withdrawing its confidence from the Muhammad 'Ali government, the assembly merely adjourned, thereby affording the governor-general an opportunity for his counterstroke. Ghulam Muhammad found a pretext for his drastic step in the contention that the assembly had not fulfilled its purpose either as a constitution framer or as a lawmaker. It was not a popularly elected body to begin with, but one chosen by indirect electors held over from the days before independence. They were for the most part politicians of the stripe who became ministers.

In support of his unprecedented initiative, Ghulam Muhammad also reshuffled the cabinet, summoning to Karachi Prime Minister Muhammad 'Ali and General Ayub Khan, who were then negotiating the basic military aid agreement in Washington. The general turned down Ghulam Muhammad's offer of the prime ministry but consented to come into Muhammad 'Ali's remolded cabinet as defense minister. Ten months of service in the cabinet without having to surrender command of the army furnished Ayub Khan an invaluable political apprenticeship. It enabled him to manage government-army relations from both ends and to widen his political perspective. Even before becoming defense minister, he had reportedly drawn up a "short appreciation of present and future problems of Pakistan," [2] in which he favored the unification of West Pakistan, a presidential system of government, indirect election of the president and the lawmakers, a supreme commander of the armed forces (with an *ex officio* seat in the cabinet) appointed by the president and responsible to him, and radical reform of the systems of law, administration, and land tenure. Most of these ideas were later put into effect when Ayub became president.

Significantly, the general remained in the cabinet until after the Supreme Court, with a dissenting vote by the sole British judge, conditionally upheld the governor-general's right to dissolve the legislature, thereby fixing that office as the executive head of state to whom the legislature and the cabinet were both responsible. The second Constituent Assembly, like the first, was brought into being by indirect elections. It existed on the governor-general's sufferance and relatively swiftly approved a constitution in March 1956. The constitution itself provided for parliamentary democracy and, despite Pakistan's continuance in the British Commonwealth, for a republican form of government. But the head of state, now styled president, continued conducting his office as an autocrat. Ghulam Muhammad's successor after September 1955 was Iskandar Mirza, an alumnus of the Indian Political Service with a long assignment in the Northwest Frontier Province. President Mirza was never effectively challenged by the politicians, whom with very few exceptions he manipulated at will. Without a popular base for his power, Mirza confided administration to the senior civil service and the maintenance of order to the armed forces.

General Ayub took no ministerial portfolio after August 1955, although he continued without interruption what was probably intended as a rotational post of supreme military commander. Ayub's primary interest in those years still seemed to be that of strengthening the military establishment and securing it against political meddling. With generous aid from the United States, he was able to enlarge the armed forces, modernize their equipment, and improve their efficiency. Meanwhile, the more autocratic President Mirza became, the more he undermined the authority of the ministers and the more he had to lean on the general—all of which strengthened the public's conviction of the irresponsibility of the politicians. On 7 October 1958 Mirza finally tore up the constitution, closed the federal and provincial legislatures, abolished the political parties, and set up a martial law regime with General Ayub Khan as chief martial law administrator. Two days after the coup d'état, the general disclosed that in the preceding year he had repeatedly urged President Mirza in private to take decisive action to save the country "from ruin through misrule of corrupt politicians." In his account, the martial law administrator reported,

I said to the President: "Are you going to act or are you not going to act? It is your responsibility to bring about a change. If you do not, which Heaven forbid, we [the armed forces] shall force a change." [3]

That Mirza and Ayub were not pulling in harness after their joint coup became apparent from their contradictory statements to the press. One week after the overthrow of the first republic, Mirza predicted an early end of the martial law regime and revealed that he viewed his martial law administrator "much in the same light as a constitutional prime minister." [4] On the following day Ayub let it be known that

> whereas Martial Law will not be retained a minute longer than is necessary it will not be lifted a minute earlier than the purpose for which it has been imposed has been fulfilled. And that purpose is the clearance of the political, social, economic and administrative mess that has been created in the past.[5]

The fact that Ayub's appointment as commander in chief was due to expire on 16 January 1959 no doubt contributed to his removal of Mirza on 27 October 1958.

The partnership in Pakistan between the head of state and the army's commander-in-chief was clearly one that benefited both sides. With Ayub's cooperation, Ghulam Muhammad proved able progressively to enlarge his power over the political system. In return, Ayub enjoyed full autonomy in the management of the military establishment. This freedom enabled Ayub, with American assistance, to rev up the military machine. By the time Iskandar Mirza inherited the mantle of political leadership, the powers of the office and the terms of the partnership with the general were already laid down. Mirza simply carried on, after March 1956, under the new title of president. Minimal at the start, Ayub's political ambitions developed only slowly as the partnership weakened, partly under the pressure of the military establishment whose exercise of autonomy began to encroach on the political domain and partly because the autocratic civilian head of state could not be entirely satisfied with the exclusion of the armed forces from his jurisdiction. As the mutual confidence waned, the general, largely in self-defense, finally deposed his civilian partner altogether.

This scenario was later re-enacted in Algeria. There, however, the origins of the partnership were obfuscated by the near chaos that attended the birth of sovereign Algeria.

The Ben Bella–Boumedienne Partnership

Following the cease-fire agreement signed at Evian on 18 March 1962 and the referendum on Algerian self-determination on 1 July, France in theory transferred sovereignty to a Provisional Executive. The word "sovereignty" did not appear in the enabling French decree, which simply stipulated that "a Provisional Executive . . . shall be responsible [Article 2] for the conduct of public affairs specifically pertaining to Algeria" until the elections that the "Executive shall organize [Article 24] . . . for the designation of the National Assembly to which the Executive shall hand over its powers." [6] The French government conceived of the Provisional Executive, to judge from its composition, as a neutral body that would represent the entire Algerian population, Europeans as well as Muslims, and among the latter the top rebel leaders were conspicuously absent.

However, with the collapse, on the eve of self-determination, of the secondary Algerian rebellion—the one staged by the European settlers and French Army dissidents—the flight of the colons from Algeria became a rout. Whatever claims the colons might have pushed with French blessings had thus nearly evaporated. The Provisional Executive made almost no contribution to the creation of an Algerian regime. It could not administer the country in the crucial interval between the French political departure on 3 July and the Algerian election on 20 September, even though the Provisional Executive held the purse strings, since the French government doled out to it funds set aside for Algeria in the residue of the calendar year 1962. Actually, the central administration all but broke down, until it was reconstructed by the former Muslim rebels.

In the contest over who would pick up sovereignty in the name of Muslim Algeria, few if any questioned the claims of the *Front de libération nationale* (FLN), as the Muslim insurrectional movement had styled itself. The FLN in 1956 created, as its supreme policy-making body, the *Conseil national de la révolution algérienne* (CNRA), which later became an embryonic legislature when, two years later, it named a *Gouvernement provisoire de la république algérienne* (GPRA) to serve as the executive from its station in exile at Tunis. The GPRA, under the premiership of Ben Youssef Ben Khedda, represented the FLN in negotiating the cease-fire instruments with France and thus had every right to assume that it would become the custodian of Algerian Muslim in-

terests, pending the completion of formal arrangements for acceptance of Algerian sovereignty by elected spokesmen. Despite the
internal and external recognition that it had received in the final
years of the insurgence, the GPRA was forcibly displaced from
Muslim leadership during the tricky transition from dependence to
independence. The key to an understanding of the political collapse of the GPRA lies in the partnership that Ahmad Ben Bella
formed with Colonel Houari Boumedienne [Muhammad Ben
Brahim Boukharouba].[7]

Ahmad Ben Bella rose to power neither through the rebel army
nor through the the GPRA but through prison. In the opening
years of the rebellion, he and three colleagues had set up headquarters in Cairo where they organized external support for an independent Algeria, Ben Bella himself handling the acquisition of military equipment and its clandestine shipment to the guerrillas. The
French in October 1956 kidnapped the four and imprisoned them
in France—ultimately in the Chateau d'Aunoy on the Isle d'Aix—
until after the conclusion of the cease-fire. These four, together
with five others, were the fathers of the Muslim insurrection and
collectively came to be labeled "the historic leaders." For this reason the prisoners were granted seats in the original GPRA of September 1958 and retained them after its reorganization in August
1961. In fact, Ben Bella was one of three deputy premiers. His
enforced retirement assured him widespread popularity among Algerian Muslims but deprived him of opportunities for exercising
leadership. While he languished in prison and reflected on politics
in the abstract, the active ministers in the GPRA were gaining experience in statecraft by running the politics of the insurrection.

Almost from the moment of his release on the morrow of the
Evian agreement in March, Ben Bella refused to cooperate with
other civilian politicians unless he could sit in the driver's seat.
Thus, in essence, he could elect one of two courses: replace Ben
Khedda as premier of the GPRA, or replace that body altogether
by another of his own creation. In little more than a month Ben
Bella managed to amass enough political support to persuade the
provisional government to convene the CNRA to frame post-
independence policy. Conveniently, and presumably on Ben Bella's
insistence, the CNRA met not in Tunis but in Tripoli, Libya, away
from the moderating influence both of the seat of the provisional
government and that of its host, President Habib Bourguiba. Almost half of the seventy delegates in attendance consisted of mili-

tary officers; the GPRA and the underground political leaders within Algeria made up the rest.

The delegates manifestly did not alter the provisional government. Ben Bella accordingly resorted to his second tactic by reportedly proposing that the FLN become the sole "party of the masses," with a Political Bureau as its policy-making directorate. The projected bureau would include the four prisoners of Aunoy and would omit altogether the key leaders of the GPRA. Ben Bella's proposal was voted down, as was also the counterproposal of Ben Khedda who, while accepting the principle of a Political Bureau, urged the creation of a smaller body that would include Ben Bella and himself. Thus, the split between Ben Bella and Ben Khedda crystalized nearly a month before the referendum on self-determination on 1 July. Ben Bella's scheme had not yet worked, but Ben Khedda could no longer claim leadership of a united FLN.

In those early weeks Ben Bella found an ally in Colonel Boumedienne. The Muslim insurgency had spawned two kinds of soldiers: the internal army or the guerrillas, numbering at the war's close some 90,000 survivors; and the external army or the conventional forces, trained and garrisoned in Tunisia (about 25,000) and Morocco (about 15,000) but prevented from re-entry into Algeria as a group by French counterguerrilla measures, although many individuals shifted from one army to the other, in some instances more than once. The internal and external armies together formed the *Armée de libération nationale* (ALN). Boumedienne, the commander of the inactive external army since 1960, also claimed supreme command of the ALN, although in the spring of 1962 he was as uncertain of his future as was Ben Bella. In retrospect, it seems clear that Boumedienne was bent on converting the external army under his command into the nucleus of sovereign Algeria's regular army; yet such an outcome was by no means assured.

One major consequence of the elaborate French counterinsurgent action was the division of the guerrilla forces among six *wilayas*, or military regions, each commanded by a colonel and four majors who enjoyed broad discretionary powers in view of the fragile communications and the dictates of secrecy. Bearing the brunt of the war, which had become three-sided after the colons in Algeria were joined by French Army deserters, the guerrillas had little time for more than district politics. Moreover, they developed growing suspicion of the external army. The leaders of the latter organization, in their enforced idleness, had become preoccupied with post-independence national politics in which they saw a central role for themselves as a "people's army." Like the guerrilla commanders in the wilayas, Colonel Boumedienne had acknowledged his responsibility to the GPRA during the rebellion. Five days before the referendum on self-determination Premier Ben Khedda announced in the name of the GPRA the formation of a Political Bureau under his leadership as a means of spiking Ben Bella's ambitions. The Ben Bella group, with the backing of Boumedienne and two other members of the external army's general staff, rejected the Premier's proclamation.

The first public intimation of Boumedienne's insubordination came on 30 June 1962, when the GPRA announced the dismissal of the external army's general staff because of "criminal activities." The act of dismissal also directed the soldiers of the external army to obey no orders but those issued by the GPRA or its authorized representatives and expressly prohibited obedience to the deposed officers. The general staff, however, openly defied the GPRA, as did also the officers of the troops encamped in Morocco, who declared that they would continue "to execute, as in the past, only orders coming from the Chief of Staff or passing through him." [8] Boumedienne and his colleagues insisted that the GPRA had no authority to dismiss them, contending that that power belonged to the CNRA from which, the general staff argued, they had received a vote of confidence at its Tripoli session. Without resigning the deputy premiership, Ben Bella refused to accept the actions either of setting up a Political Bureau of Ben Khedda's choice or of dismissing the external army's general staff. He also let it be known that he would not enter Algiers with the GPRA after the grant of independence.

The failure of the GPRA to assert its supremacy over the external army's general staff marked a turning point in Muslim Algeria's military politics. Not only did the GPRA mortally undermine its own position of political leadership, but it also destroyed the principle of civilian paramountcy over the armed forces. In the light of later developments, Boumedienne, in joining Ben Bella, must have insisted on the continued freedom of the military establishment from civilian control as a condition for cooperation.

Sovereignty thus came to Algeria with Muslim leadership split and the major contestants engaged in a battle for political keeps. Neither side had public funds. Party organization was nonexistent. With the hasty dismantling of the colonial regime and the Provisional Executive exercising little more than nominal authority, central government had almost completely vanished. In the circumstances, military support became decisive. Ben Bella won the first round when he detached the external army from the effective jurisdiction of the GPRA. Following the referendum, the GPRA and the external army re-entered Algeria. There the struggle for political supremacy continued, in the first instance, as a struggle for the armed forces, as each side tried to win over the guerrilla commanders. By this time the commanders in each wilaya had assimilated the political and administrative powers surrendered by the French counterguerrilla commanders at the time of the cease-fire.

The support of the guerrilla commanders was thus indispensable, even though they themselves were at a distinct disadvantage insofar as they might have made their own bid for national power, for the very strength of the guerrillas in the insurrection became a serious weakness in the opening post-independence political struggle. Inured to self-reliance, the guerrilla officers and their men had for the most part forgotten how to take orders and had in any case narrowed their political horizons to the affairs of the wilaya in which they had been fighting. By contrast, what the external army may have lacked in field experience it more than made up in discipline; and its recruits represented no individual district but the country as a whole.

The GPRA, meanwhile, established itself in Algiers on 3 July 1962, proclaiming that it spoke for the entire Muslim population. The commanders of Wilaya IV (Algiers and its hinterland) placed themselves at the disposition of the GPRA, as did also those of Wilaya III (the Kabylia)—the Berber district which had the most rebel-hardened units of all—and part of Wilaya II (Constantine). Ben Bella returned to Algeria a week later, staging his entry as a hero's homecoming after twelve years' absence and setting up political headquarters in Tlemcen. By then Boumedienne had won to his banner the commanders of the remaining wilayas into which the two branches of the external army moved.

With the political-military lines of battle thus drawn, the Tlemcen group announced on 22 July the formation of a Political Bureau composed of five of the surviving "historic leaders," plus two politicians loyal to Ben Bella. The Political Bureau, it was stated, would supplant the GPRA in administering the country and preparing for the elections to the Constituent Assembly. Two historic leaders—Hocine Ait Ahmad and Muhammad Boudiaf, both Berbers—refused to serve on the Political Bureau and went into hiding. On 30 July Ben Bella's troops captured Boudiaf, who consented reluctantly to accept the bureau seat only on condition that the CNRA formally approve the creation and composition of such a directorate and the definition of its powers and that the Tlemcen and Algiers groups jointly prepare the election list. On these terms the GPRA withdrew from Algiers on 3 August, permitting the Political Bureau to take its place as Muslim custodian.

Since the guerrilla commanders of the wilayas of Algiers and the Kabylia persisted in opposing the Political Bureau, the Tlemcen coalition, for its own safety, introduced some 900 loyal guerrillas into the old city of Algiers by mid-August. Meanwhile, the Political Bureau was resolved to draw up the single list of candidates in such a way that the domination of the Constituent Assembly by Ben Bella and Boumedienne would be assured. The GPRA protested against these maneuvers. Moreover, throughout the period, Hocine Ait Ahmad resisted all efforts at reconciliation, while Muhammad Boudiaf formally resigned from the executive on 25 August. Four days later, after Ben Bella and other bureau members had left the city, Algiers became the scene of bloody fighting between the Political Bureau's guerrillas and those of the two wilayas, and for a full week independent Algeria was threatened by a general civil war. The cease-fire, negotiated on 4 September by Muhammad Khider, the bureau's secretary-general, and Colonel Mohand Ou al-Hadj, the commander of the Kabylia wilaya, signified the final collapse of the GPRA opposition. Boumedienne and his colleagues on the general staff entered Algiers on 9 September at the head of some 4,000 soldiers of the external army to pledge loyalty to the reassembled Political Bureau.

The election to the Constituent Assembly, deferred five times, was finally fixed for 20 September 1962. Its outcome was a foregone conclusion. On 28 September Ahmad Ben Bella became prime minister of the first government of sovereign Algeria, and Colonel Houari Boumedienne its minister of defense.

The Sparring Partners

The Muslim rebels of Algeria had overturned the colonial government, and turned it out altogether. The civil-military coalition that seized power in the Muslim community acquired formal title through the device of a carefully screened single list of candidates to the Constituent Assembly, thus offering the voters no choice but endorsement or protest. Even after the election, Ben Bella and Boumedienne still had to consolidate their power. Since the

French had done almost nothing to prepare the Muslims for self-government and since the experience of the Muslim revolt was largely inapplicable, the consolidation of power also required its institutionalization. The victors thus found themselves literally creating the instruments of government, including the army. In all the turmoil of setting up a new regime, two lines of policy remained constant: Ben Bella's determination to fashion a political system that he could dominate, and Boumedienne's equal dedication to shaping a professional army that he could master without civilian restraint. This was roughly reminiscent of the earlier experience in Pakistan.

Ben Bella, like Ghulam Muhammad and Iskander Mirza, was clearly the senior partner with an explicit goal of uncontested political leadership. As a tactician, he became flexible in the search for power; the perimeter of his pragmatism, however, was described by his dependence on Boumedienne. Only an army loyal to the central government could discipline the unruly guerrillas, round up the political dissidents, and help impose law and order and thereby establish the new regime's authority. As a junior partner with only a limited but no less explicit goal, Colonel Boumediennne, like General Ayub, became inflexible in safeguarding the autonomy of the armed forces under his command. The key to the colonel's policies and actions lay in his insistence on remaining the chief commander and the defense minister, so that in the two roles he might best superintend from within and without the affairs of the military establishment in its formative period. In brief, the civil-military partnership in Muslim Algeria was one in which the civilian leader enjoyed the initiative, so long as he honored the inviolable character of the military domain.

Primary authorship in shaping the Democratic and Popular Republic of Algeria could thus be ascribed to the civil-military alliance. It was not an easy relationship, precisely because almost every decision in the beginning had a double significance, for the making of policies and of institutions. Yet the partners sparred behind closed doors. The nature of the competition and the undertakings given by either side can be deduced mainly from the policies and political structures that became public. In the first year after the election, Ben Bella served as prime minister of a regime that was a parliamentary democracy in form. He then became president of the republic in September 1963, after the adoption of a constitution that the partners wrote and that provided for a presidential system, enabling Ben Bella to assimilate the title and the

duties of head of state and of government with a cabinet designed
not as an executive, but as an advisory, council. Because the deputies in the National Assembly elected in 1964 under the new constitution, no less than those in the Constituent Assembly, were
handpicked, the legislature could not be expected to balance the
executive in the emerging political system.

Outside the government, Ben Bella's political position was much
weaker. Following the election and the creation of the first cabinet,
the Political Bureau was retained to serve as the executive of the
envisioned single socialist party. In totally displacing the GPRA,
the bureau inherited the right to form a government and a regime
and to try to transform the insurrectional movement into a political party. Ben Bella sought to make the FLN the country's single
party, but the effort fell short of the goal. The FLN became the
only legal party in the country, it is true, and the National Student
Union, the General Union of Algerian Workers, and even the
Communists were forced by January 1963 to surrender their independence of action and affiliate with the government party. Despite these measures, the FLN did not develop into a vigorous
party. Ben Bella contrived, for reasons that we shall presently explore, to alienate not the members of the GPRA alone but all the
surviving historic leaders and, because of his association with
Boumedienne, a majority of the former guerrilla commanders.
Many politicians had their own groups of followers, while many
commanders continued to enjoy the loyalty of men in their former
guerrilla units. Yet all who withheld endorsement of the regime
were prohibited from forming legal opposition groups. Those who
persisted in criticism faced arrest or exile or went underground
where their years of experience were put to effective use.

Ben Bella used the FLN to mobilize mass support for his evolving regime and its program of pragmatic Marxism. The Political
Bureau was advertised as the party executive, in theory executing
policies framed by the party conference or central committee; but
the bureau was not an elected party executive. As originally constituted in the summer of 1962, it was Ben Bella's private instrument.
In September it was reshaped, Boudiaf and Ait Ahmad were
dropped altogether, for these Berber leaders showed no inclination,
even after the election, to accept Ben Bella's primacy. Boudiaf in
fact ignored the government's orders to abolish his *Parti de la révolution socialiste*. He was subsequently imprisoned for a short period for allegedly plotting to overthrow the regime and, on release,
went into hiding. Even more brazen was Ait Ahmad's defiance

from his mountain stronghold in the Kabylia, when he refused to dissolve his revolutionary *Front des forces socialistes* or to disband its associated guerrilla units. Muhammad Khider, as the bureau's secretary-general, launched the scheme of converting the FLN into a political party. But Khider himself was expelled from the party post in April 1963, when Ben Bella took over as secretary-general.

Meeting in Algiers a year later, the first party conference of the FLN approved the creation of a central committee, whose 80 members and 23 alternates were named by Ben Bella and Boumedienne. The coalition partners also selected the members of the enlarged Political Bureau, eight taken from the cabinet (among them Ben Bella and Boumedienne) plus nine others (including the entire general staff of the armed forces). The line of demarcation between the cabinet and the Political Bureau was thus blurred, and who made what policies where never became clarified; nor did it seem to make much difference so long as all decisions directly or indirectly affecting the armed forces carried Boumedienne's stamp of approval. All other political decisions originated with Ben Bella, or were endorsed by him before execution.

These arrangements were reflected in the unfolding of Algerian politics. From the outset Ben Bella demonstrated that he could abide no political competition. On the ascent to paramount leadership and after arrival, he removed actual and potential competitors, developing a low tolerance for energetic, independent-minded politicians whom he sent, one after another, scurrying for cover. If Ben Bella appeared incapable of sharing honors and powers with civilian politicians, he seemed equally incapable of denying them to soldiers for whom he developed a high if reluctant tolerance in the opening year of independence and beyond. Colonel Boumedienne held on to the supreme military command even after becoming defense minister in the first cabinet. One of his intimate aides, Ahmad Medeghri, headed the interior ministry, making Boumedienne absolute master of the country's security. Moreover, sixty army officers, one-third the Muslim total, sat as deputies in the Constituent Assembly, where they acted as guardians of the military interest. Nor were the military deputies required to surrender their commissions, and when the brief war with Morocco broke out in October 1963, Ben Bella suspended the assembly to enable them to join their army units.

The alliance that bound Ben Bella and Boumedienne palpably promoted their respective causes. The two men rose to power by mutual assistance, and neither one could have made it alone. Ben

Bella furnished the political leadership and Boumedienne the military. They cemented their ties in jointly flouting the authority of the GPRA, and then in destroying that executive altogether before the first election. In the process, Boumedienne brought the external army into Algeria, assimilated two-thirds of the guerrilla units and militarily neutralized most of the others. He went a long way in the first year of sovereignty toward remaking the rebel *Armée de libération nationale* into the new state's *Armée nationale populaire* (ANP), as Muslim Algeria's armed forces were labeled in September 1962. Nor was it surprising that he gradually sloughed off a majority of the guerrillas, who were initially brought into the ANP, but preserved almost intact the erstwhile external army.

In the second year Ben Bella showed signs of trying to subordinate the ANP. But the colonel parried the presidential thrusts. Boumedienne, of course, continued as chief commander of the armed forces and as defense minister, and to these titles was added that of first vice-president of the republic in the presidential cabinet of September 1963. It requires little imagination to ascertain the authorship of the constitutional provisions (Articles 67–68) entrusting the formulation of military policy to a *Conseil supérieur de la défense* (CSD), comprising the ministers of defense, the interior, and foreign affairs, the chairman of the assembly's national defense committee, as well as the president of the republic and two others designated by him. The CSD seems never formally to have been brought into being. Still, Boumedienne took no chances. Into the presidential cabinet came Medeghri again as interior minister and another loyal aide, Major Abdulaziz Bouteflika, as foreign minister. In addition, the chairman of the assembly's national defense committee, Major Ali Mendjili, had been a member of the external army's general staff. To balance this constitutional arrangement, meanwhile, was another under which soldiers as soldiers were not simply permitted to take part in politics. They were required to do so. Article 8 laid down that

> The National Army is a popular army. Faithful to the traditions of the struggle for national liberation, it serves the people under the orders of the government.
>
> It assures the defense of the territories of the Republic and participates in the political, economic, and social activities of the country within the framework of the party.[9]

While Boumedienne was negotiating a military-aid agreement in Moscow on the eve of the Algerian-Moroccan war, Ben Bella named as chief of the (ANP's) general staff Colonel Tahar Zbiri, a former guerrilla commander and outspoken friend of the president, and later as a member of the general staff another ex-guerrilla leader, Colonel Muhammad Chaabani. Though by no means a presidential henchman, Chaabani seemed to have been even less fond of the defense minister. Boumedienne finally acquiesced in these changes in March 1964, relinquishing to Zbiri the post of chief of general staff, but significantly changing the staff's character. It remained under Boumedienne's control but was shorn of command duties and left only with those of organization, planning, and recruitment. Besides, Boumedienne retained for his own appointees the two remaining slots. Similarly, in the enlarged Political Bureau, formed at the first national conference of the FLN at Algiers in April, nine of the seventeen seats went to army officers, and of these six represented the Boumedienne group.

The ANP, moreover, enjoyed a privileged status. The government's austerity program bore down heavily on the civil servants who suffered reductions in salary and arrears in payment, while the soldiers, enlisted men as well as officers, received increases in their relatively lavish scale of pay. Despite high unemployment in the towns, army officers maintained an ostentatious club on the Algiers waterfront, where they could buy custom-exempt imports. The army monthly, *al-Jaysh*, appearing in French and Arabic, enabled the army officers to make known their views on public issues. Furthermore, nearly one-fifth of the open budget, and substantially more that was not disclosed, was allocated to the ANP in 1964 and 1965. A career army, the ANP in the summer of 1964 consisted of some 65,000 men, or nearly twice the number that the Political Bureau had originally planned, and was undergoing rapid modernization with Soviet and U.A.R. aid. As a means of softening the resistance of former guerrillas in the Kabylia in 1964, the ANP left on its payroll nearly a thousand demobilized soldiers from that recalcitrant district.

The ANP cleaned up the last major pockets of resistance to the regime in the summer and fall of 1964. Colonel Chaabani, who refused to give up his private army of veteran guerrillas in the Aurès mountains even after he was appointed to the general staff and to the Political Bureau, went into open revolt in June. He was captured in July and executed in September. In the following month the ANP cornered Ait Ahmad in his mountain hideout, bringing to a halt the organized Berber opposition. Meanwhile, between the two ANP domestic campaigns, all prominent political foes of the regime still in the country were placed under arrest.

By this time, Ben Bella was making a determined effort to clip Boumedienne's wings. Ben Bella relieved Medeghri of the interior ministry in July 1964, transferring to the president's office the supervision of the provincial prefects (governors). Army officers were deliberately kept off the list of candidates for election to the second National Assembly in September. The president in December further reduced the size of the Boumedienne contingent in the cabinet by removing from the ministry of tourism Ahmad Kaid, a close associate of the commander in chief from earlier days. Ben Bella's attempt in the spring of 1965 to drop Foreign Minister Bouteflika from the cabinet brought the issue to a head. Boumedienne and his military colleagues refused to acquiesce in the president's proposal, and on 19 June, five days before the scheduled opening in Algiers of the Afro-Asian Conference which Ben Bella had taken such a prominent part in organizing, staged a coup d'état.

While he was taking steps in the spring of 1965 to curb Boumedienne's influence, the president also began systematically to pardon those politicians whom he had earlier alienated, giving evidence that he recognized the high price he had paid for uncontested political leadership. But the endeavor to organize a more broadly based civilian political structure, if such it was, to hold the ANP and its supreme commander in check came too late. Up to the very dissolution of the partnership, Boumedienne pursued what might appropriately be termed reactive politics. He revealed no positive aspirations for political office, other than that of defense minister. The partnership that linked Ben Bella and Boumedienne in the first three years of Algerian sovereignty, giving freedom to each in his domain and providing for common action in the zone of overlap, had produced a relatively durable arrangement. It lasted as long as it did precisely because Boumedienne's ambitions were circumscribed and he was able to prevent Ben Bella from subordinating the military establishment.

Yet durability is not a synonym for stability, and civil-military partnerships of this variety are inherently unstable. The ambitious political leader uses the army to enable him to achieve mastery over the political system, the military institution excepted. Once he has reached this goal, to judge from the experience of Pakistan and Algeria, he seems impelled to assert his mastery over the armed forces as well. This, however, the military leader, who has come to enjoy the fruits of his autonomy, views as a betrayal of the partnership. Thus only when Boumedienne became persuaded that his autonomy was in jeopardy did he finally strike back, not to restore the balance as he had done on many earlier occasions, but to elevate himself to the presidency of the Revolutionary Council as custodian of the coup d'état regime.

11

CONCEALED PARTNERS: PAKISTAN AND TURKEY

Civil-military partnerships may come into being either by civilian rulers asking soldiers to participate in government or by soldiers inviting civilian politicians to join them. Their relations differ perceptibly in the two types of arrangements. Military rulers, it is true, invariably appeal to civilians to help run governments; commonly they are technicians expressly assigned such tasks as managing foreign affairs, finance, communications, and education. This has occurred, as we have seen, in all postwar military republics in the Middle East. Quite different are the coalitions that the soldiers form when they invite politicians to participate in militarized political systems. In these circumstances the soldiers write the rules of the game. They do not give the civilians full freedom, for the politicians responding to their normal aspiration to govern will almost certainly try to eliminate the soldiers from politics altogether. This is precisely what happened in Sudan in the fall of 1964, when General Ibrahim 'Abbud tried to keep political power after requesting civilian politicians to set up a government. A fortnight later 'Abbud himself was thrown out and the politicians became masters of the regime. More momentous examples are the long-lived military-civilian coalitions in the second republics of Pakistan (from 1962) and Turkey (from 1961).

Pakistan: The Martial Law Regime, 1958–62

The civil-military partnerships in Algeria and Pakistan shattered in essentially the same way. In each it was the commander-in-chief who seized power, and, with a loyal military establishment behind him, neither man was distracted by an immediate need to cleanse his military house by removing potentially disloyal officers. Boumedienne and Ayub differed, however, in political personality and skill. The Algerian supervised the execution of the coup with remarkable precision, but he took a long time to decide on the structure of government and even longer on the general lines of its future policy. This suggested inadequate political preparation for the overturn. Moreover, Boumedienne's shyness, bordering on total self-effacement, made Ayub's outgoing manner look almost exhibitionist. Politically decisive at the time of take-over, Ayub held firmly to the course of overhauling the structure of politics and infusing a new spirit into government.

Ayub was already prime minister and minister of defense and of Kashmir affairs on the day that he sent Mirza packing. As prime minister, Ayub had placed high army officers in charge of key ministries (interior, rehabilitation, and health and social welfare) and civilian technicians in charge of the others. He had also co-opted as deputy martial law administrator in each of the two provinces and in Karachi an officer of the rank of lieutenant general, and to them the civilian governors and officials became accountable. Military officers of the rank of colonel or lower were assigned to most civilian ministries and departments in the federal and provincial governments to provide close liaison with the work of the civil administrators and, not infrequently, to handle business directly. But the military presence grew progressively less pervasive as the authority of the martial law regime became fixed.

Like many military rulers, Ayub concentrated in his person all supreme power. In assuming the presidency of Pakistan, he became its chief executive; by keeping the title of martial law administrator, he also remained chief lawmaker and chief justice; and by not giving up command of the armed forces, he performed his multifarious duties with the authority of the military arm. Martial law regulations, issued as presidential orders, were enforceable in military courts—summary (one-man) or special (three-man)—erected primarily for rooting out corruption in public affairs as well as the black market and hoarding, for curbing an irresponsible press, and for introducing reform. Martial law did not abolish civilian courts; it simply narrowed their jurisdiction and bound them to uphold the presidential orders. Moreover, the Laws (Continuance in Force) Order of 10 October 1958 expressly stipulated that Pakistan "shall be governed as nearly as may be in accordance with the late Constitution."

The stiff judgments of military courts were not subject to civilian review. But criticism of martial law, which began soon after it was inaugurated, did not subside until it was lifted. The West Pakistan High Court disapproved of the military court procedures and attempted to assert the right of determining whether individual cases fell under civil or military jurisdiction. While withholding this right, Ayub nevertheless confirmed his belief in the rule of law and the independence of the courts.

Other than in politics and government, the martial law regime sought action in four broad areas: land reform as a base for agricultural development, reorganization of the legal system, formulation of a plan for national education, and prompt refugee resettlement as an earnest of a comprehensive program of social welfare. Ayub set up one or more expert commissions to examine and present recommendations in each area. The recommendations furnished the substance of presidential orders which were then put into immediate effect, sometimes under the supervision of implementation commissions.

Among the regime's more dramatic accomplishments were the revitalization of local government and the settlement, after more than a decade of neglect, of refugee claims. For the most part, however, the record was spotty, since Ayub was not a social radical. He came from the same level of society as the senior civil servants whom his government was determined to discipline, and as the politicians whom it was determined to crush. Indeed, the martial law regime from the start became preoccupied with political and administrative reform, which was in many respects revolutionary and whose effects were durable. In Ayub's textbook, good government was efficient and honest government, not popularly elected government. Civil servants were temporarily deprived of their traditional security of tenure by a presidential order of March 1959, which provided the legal basis for the screening committees that had begun the preceding November to evaluate the integrity and performance of government employees. Of more than 1,600 dismissed or forcibly retired for misconduct, corruption, or inadequacy, almost all fell in the middle or lower echelons of the civil service hierarchy, although a handful of the seniors were also affected. The politicians were even more vigorously handled. An initial Public Officers (Disqualification) Order of March 1959 stipulated that politicians found guilty of misconduct or corruption would be barred from public office for fifteen years. In August the Elective Bodies (Disqualification) Order, which introduced "ebdonian" and "ebdoed" as new terms in Pakistan's political vocabulary for disfranchised politicians, defined public misconduct more broadly and transferred the investigative function from the police to a special tribunal.

These measures were preliminary to the basic recasting of politics. As President Ayub observed,

> The British parliamentary system which we inherited and later adopted in the Constitution of 1956 is largely an unwritten law and takes for granted too many prerequisites which do not really exist in a country like Pakistan. Our rate of literacy is appallingly low. Our means of communication are poor, even primitive. The rural population which constitutes over 80 percent of the total is hardly touched by the world outside the villages.[1]

Ayub accordingly sought to create a political system that would bring the peasantry and the urban masses constructively into politics, and that would continue employing the electoral principle while avoiding the need for political parties, which he was persuaded were a source of much evil. "To my mind," President Ayub wrote,

> there are four prerequisites for the success of any democratic system in a country like Pakistan:
>
> 1. It should be simple to understand, easy to work and cheap to sustain.
> 2. It should put to the voter only such questions as he can answer in the light of his own personal knowledge and understanding without external prompting.
> 3. It should ensure the effective participation of all citizens in the affairs of the country up to the level of their mental horizon and intellectual calibre.
> 4. It should be able to produce reasonably strong and stable governments.[2]

With these considerations in mind, Ayub had put into effect in the fall of 1959 "basic democracy," a pyramidal scheme designed to give expression to the "genius" of Pakistan by mobilizing popular support without politicians. Each province was divided into 40,000 constituencies, and each constituency elected by universal suffrage one "basic democrat." The 80,000 basic democrats and half that number of government nominees sat in 8,000 union councils (each representing a cluster of villages) or in their urban equivalent called town or union committees. Above the union councils were successive levels of county, district, division, and provincial councils. Each of these consisted of members elected indirectly from the councils of the next lower tier and of civil servants sitting *ex officio*, so that at the summit only a small portion of the members reflected popular choice, those originally elected by the union councils or the town committees.

The first election took place in December 1959–January 1960. The basic democrats, constituting themselves an electoral college, formally elected Ayub president for a five-year term. As his first act after the inaugural ceremony at Rawalpindi on 17 February, Field Marshal [3] Ayub Khan appointed a constitutional commission of ten, five from each of the two provinces, with a former justice of the Supreme Court as chairman. The constitutional commission circulated a questionnaire to seek selective opinions on the kind of political system that would be most appropriate. This gave rise to a vigorous public debate among the few former ministers, lawyers, and religious leaders who received the questionnaire. It was no secret that Ayub favored the presidential system so as to assure a strong executive and to avoid legislative indecision. Most of those who responded to the questionnaire, however, advocated parliamentary democracy. When the public debate threatened to get out of hand in the summer of 1960, the government warned that action would be taken against those who persisted in using the discussion of the projected constitution as a pretext to "play politics." [4]

The commission submitted its proposals in the spring of 1961 to the president, who referred the draft for appraisal to a cabinet committee, an administrative committee, and a governors' conference. The constitution that Ayub promulgated on 1 March 1962 incorporated the central ideas that he espoused and advanced under the martial law regime: a presidential system and basic democracy. The 80,000 basic democrats, functioning as the electoral college, elected the deputies to the National Assembly on 28 April and to the provincial assemblies on 6 May. Martial law was lifted on 8 June, and two days later the first "civilian" cabinet was formed.

Constitutional Government on Sufferance

The transformation of Pakistan's martial law regime into a constitutional one after forty-four months appeared to repeat the Egyptian pattern. There, the Revolutionary Command Council (RCC) six years earlier had proclaimed the end of military rule with the endorsement by referendum of a republican constitution forty-seven months after the deposition of King Faruq. But, as we have seen, the RCC did not really civilianize the political system. President Muhammad Ayub Khan, admittedly, surrendered few powers in the constitution that he bestowed upon his country in 1962, and he reinforced his reserved powers in the presidential system by keeping the defense ministry, the supreme military command, and the active rank of field marshal. Ayub took no constitutional chances of permitting in his effective lifetime the restoration of civilian control over the armed forces. For a period of twenty years the president was required (Article 238) to name as a ministerial adviser on the country's defense "a person who has held a . . . rank . . . [not lower than that of lieutenant general in the army or its equivalent in another arm of] the Defence Services of Pakistan, unless the President has himself held such a rank in those Services." Moreover, the political and military capitals were no longer to be so widely separated, as Karachi had been from the national headquarters of the armed forces during the first republic. The constitution stipulated (Article 211) that the "principal seat of the Central Government shall . . . be at Islamabad," a still unbuilt city within easy distance of Rawalpindi, and until the erection of the proposed capital the central government was to be located at Rawalpindi. The closing of the geographic gap between the political and military centers of power did not suggest the president's full confidence in the reliability of attempted personal longdistance control over either.

Nevertheless, the similarities between Pakistan and Egypt in the delicate transition to constitutional government do not run deep. The successive Egyptian constitutions after 1956 represented at best no more than a façade so far as responsible popular participation in government was concerned, only thinly disguising the survival of military rule. Despite the organic instruments, the governmental powers were never separated, so that the junta continued exercising full executive, legislative, and judicial, as well as military, authority. The junta never tired of reminding the public that the armed forces were still playing a primary role in the planning and implementation of the unfinished revolution. 'Abd al-Nasir and those colleagues of the original junta who acquiesced in his leadership alone made policy. They entrusted policy management to a compact but steadily growing bureaucracy of active and veteran military officers on whom the much larger civil bureaucracy depended. The army also buttressed the internal security system to uncover and apprehend counterrevolutionaries, as all the regime's opponents were labeled. Civil liberties were never reinstated. The civilian politicians of the supplanted monarchy never regained their franchise, nor was the absolute ban on political parties relaxed. Yet the military regime failed to develop a sturdy framework for mass political participation.

In Pakistan, on the other hand, with the enactment of the constitution, the authoritarianism of the regime was reduced and its military character substantially ended. Martial law, once lifted, was not later reimposed. Civil liberties were restored, except to a handful of politicians, and in December 1963 the National Assembly amended the constitution to make civil rights enforceable in the courts. Yet the government could exercise ample discretion to detain persons on the basis of its judgment of a threat to national security or public safety. The press still bridled at the tight governmental surveillance. As late as October 1963, a special ordinance reaffirmed the constitutional regime's wide powers of suppression and punishment for any action that tended to bring the government "directly or indirectly into hatred or contempt." The political parties were resuscitated, but this did not prevent the government in January 1964 from banning the Jamaat-i Islam (religious fundamentalist) Party and imprisoning its leaders. The one branch of government, other than the executive, that gained from Ayub's constitution was the judiciary, whose independence became more securely fixed than ever before, a matter that we shall explore in greater detail below.

What is important here is the transformation of the military role in politics from a direct to a recessive influence. The experience with military rule had left an indelible impression and had vested the president's authority with a military halo. What remained chiefly was the memory of the martial law regime and its ceaseless flow of presidential orders that transcended civilian legal jurisdiction. It was a memory of military courts and stiff penalties, of the suspension of civil liberties, of the abolition of political parties and the disfranchisement of politicians, and of the civil servants' loss of tenure. This memory could not be erased as long as the man who symbolized the martial law regime filled the presidency in a political system and under a constitution both of his invention. Since Ayub combined in his own person the supreme political and military positions, there was no way of drawing a clear line between the two.

Thus fear of the reactivation of military rule constantly lurked in the background and increased public respect for the presidential office. Yet Ayub himself left no doubt that he was determined to keep the armed forces as such out of politics. He retired the three lieutenant generals who sat in the martial law cabinet from the army as well as from their ministerial posts. He did not later bring other senior military officers into civilian activities. Former senior officers, it is true, were given top managerial posts in government industrial enterprises. But the hundred or more active officers assigned to nonmilitary duties, mostly as teachers but some as civil servants, were drawn only from the junior ranks. It made little difference that Ayub may have been motivated in these policies partly by a desire to eliminate potential rivals. Whatever the intent, senior army officers were assigned military duties only. The army itself, though a career army, did not expand at a faster rate than the population, as Table 6 shows. Nor was Ayub pampering the armed forces. The defense budget, it is true, nearly doubled in the decade ending in 1965–66, but this could be ascribed largely to the rising cost of modern weaponry. More meaningful comparisons were outlays for defense in relation to outlays for development and for over-all governmental operations. The sums allocated to development in 1956–57 hardly overtopped those for defense by as much as one-fourth; by 1956–66 they were more than three times as large. In the same period, defense expenditures declined from one-third of the total government budget to less than one-seventh. At no time through 1965–66 did Pakistan's defense budget reach 4.5 per cent of the GNP, and for most years it fell below 3.5 per cent, or less than one-half the world average.[5]

The National Assembly, in theory, was independent. It became, in fact, subservient to the president and seemed destined to remain so under the scheme of basic democracy and its system of indirect elections. Nevertheless, the few politicians of the First Republic who were elected national assemblymen, with the support of public pressure by the larger number of such politicians who were not, were able as early as July 1962 to push through the legislature an enactment permitting the formation of political parties without restriction on the use of past names. In making this concession, Ayub exacted another in return. The law prohibited from party membership for a period of five years those whom the martial law regime had either disqualified as politicians or dismissed as civil servants, governors, or ministers, because of gross misconduct. In May 1963 Ayub joined the Muslim League (Conventionist), one of three factions that claimed to be the sole legatee of the original pre-martial-law party, and became its president in December. The Pakistan Muslim League, the name it later adopted, became the most powerful party in the country. The other parties proved little more

TABLE 6. Pakistan: Force Levels, Government Expenditures, and GNP, 1953/54–1965/66

	Population (millions)	Force Levels (thousands)	Government Expenditures (millions of Pakistani rupees)			GNP [c] (millions of rupees)	Defense Expenditures (as % of GNP)
			Defense (including internal security and justice)	Development	Total		
1953/54 [a]	80.1		646.9	790.0	1,905	19,447	3.3
1954/55	80.2		639.3	649.2	1,799	19,857	3.2
1955/56	82.4	200	814.3	810.0	2,140	19,516	4.2
1956/57	83.6		777.7	958.7	2,266	20,785	3.8
1957/58	84.5		743.7	1,581.7	2,993	20,987	3.5
1958/59	86.8		837.3	1,305.5	2,911	20,839	4.0
1959/60	88.8		1,003.5	1,724.1	3,502	26,100	3.8
1960/61	92.7	225	1,044.3	1,787.7	4,670	32,510	3.2
1961/62	94.5		1,023.9	1,904.1	5,246	36,360	2.8
1962/63	96.6		960.7	2,599.9	5,912	38,170	2.5
1963/64	98.6		1,210.8	2,989.2	7,479	40,470	3.0
1964/65 [b]	100.8		1,321.4	3,503.0	8,031	43,480	3.0
1965/66 [b]	102.9	253	1,360.9	4,568.6	9,270	52,630	2.6

SOURCES: Principally IMF, International Financial Statistics.
[a] Fiscal year ends 31 March, up to and including 1958/59; thereafter 30 June.
[b] Estimates.
[c] National income, 1953/54–1959/60; GNP, 1960/61–1965/66.

than pressure groups, because of almost complete lack of representation in the central or provincial assemblies.

The elections in October and November 1964 of basic democrats, who were to choose the president in January 1965, underlined the weakness of the opposition parties. Five of them in July 1964 had joined together to form a Combined Opposition Party (COP). In September the COP named as its presidential candidate Miss Fatima Jinnah, who shared with the president the stigma of West Pakistan origin, but her national reputation was above reproach, since she was the sister of Pakistan's founder and, having never held public office, she escaped all charges of inefficiency, corruption, and maladministration. The presidential race proved spirited. The COP gave voice to demands for full freedom of political organization, for release of all political detainees, and for amendment of the constitution by replacing the presidential with a parliamentary system, and indirect with direct elections. However, those who ran for election as basic democrats were not party candidates, despite the party affiliation of some. By presenting a platform that proposed to do away with basic democracy altogether, the COP alienated many successful candidates who obviously benefited from the system. The electoral college on 2 January 1965 returned Ayub to a second five-year presidential term by an over-all majority of more than 62 per cent, East Pakistan even giving him an absolute majority of nearly 53 per cent.

Ayub's performance in East Pakistan was better than anticipated even under basic democracy, for he ran there under a handicap: He personified the traditional British practice of recruiting mainly Punjabis and Pathans into the military establishment. As late as 1955 no more than 14 of the 900 army officers above the rank of major, 60 of the 700 air force officers, and only 7 of the 600 naval officers were Bengalis. Although Ayub deliberately tried under the martial law regime and later to recruit East Pakistanis, they still represented only a small portion of the officers and enlisted men in the career forces. Nevertheless, Ayub had taken great pains in his constitution, while adhering to the plan for a strong central government, to cater to provincial sentiments by reaffirming the principle of geographic distribution. Dacca was declared (Article 211) the second capital and the principal seat of the National Assembly. Moreover, Ayub's rural works program in East Pakistan contributed to his popularity, which was already high among the Hindu minority (about one-fifth of the population of the province) and the refugees.

With the National Assembly little more than a debating club packed with the president's friends, and with Ayub's continuing grip on the armed forces, only the judicial power was effectively separated from the executive under the new constitution. Actually, the courts had never wholly lost their independence even under the martial law regime. Justices of the supreme court and the provincial high courts consistently spoke out against martial law and brought ceaseless pressure to bear for its termination. The president invited sitting and retired justices to draft the constitutional proposals, and although he did not accept all their recommendations, he modified least those on the judiciary.

The new constitution, as amended, provided for judicial review, with the exception of matters relating to federal-provincial relations. The courts were bound to uphold the fundamental law, and they did not shrink from holding the president accountable to its provisions. When Ayub tried to amend Article 104 so as to enable six of the eight members of his cabinet and more than a dozen ministers in the provincial cabinets to continue serving as assemblymen, the supreme court in May 1963 ruled his act unconstitutional, compelling the ministers to resign from the several legislatures. Indeed, Ayub was persuaded formally to retire from the army as a result of the COP's threat in the presidential election campaign of 1964 to take the issue to court. The opposition had challenged Ayub's eligibility as a presidential candidate, charging that as a field marshal he was violating Article 115 by occupying another "office of profit in the service of Pakistan." To forestall the COP, the government announced on 8 November 1964 Ayub's retroactive retirement from the armed forces as of 16 February 1960, the day preceding his first inauguration as president. The surrender of his commission, however, did not deprive him of the supreme command, since the constitution (Article 17) gave that responsibility to the president with power "subject to law . . . to appoint chief commanders [of the services] . . . and determine their salaries and allowances."

The judiciary thus served to hold the executive in line. Manifestly, within the rigid constitutional framework there were still loopholes that discerning lawyers could use to whittle away at the power of the president. Because the lawyers and the judges in domestic affairs tended to side with the politicians of the opposition, the judiciary could be expected to try to strengthen the case of these politicians in their struggle for the restoration of the parliamentary system.

Turkey: The 1960 Military Coup

The military intrusion into politics in Turkey ran a course parallel to that in Pakistan. The National Unity Committee (NUC), as the Turkish military junta that staged the coup d'état on 27 May 1960 styled itself, brought down the First Republic by abrogating its constitution and used the interval of its self-appointed martial rule to lay the foundations of the Second Republic. The military conspirators had no over-all program for social and economic reform before they seized power, nor did they develop one while exercising it. A majority of the NUC conceived of their mission as almost wholly political and, in this respect, proved remarkably conservative. They preserved the inherited parliamentary system—just as Ayub had simply converted the extraconstitutional presidential system of the First Republic in Pakistan into a constitutional one —but contrived new modes of protecting it.

In the fourteen months that passed between the military seizure of power in Turkey and the plebiscitary approval in July 1961 of the new constitution, the original junta gradually and quietly surrendered control over the armed forces, and then over the military regime, to the top commanders whom the junta itself had appointed. The experience of Turkey in this respect did differ from that of Pakistan. The supreme command, however, did not deviate from the original junta's main political purpose. It launched the Second Republic on the basis of the constitution framed under its predecessor's sponsorship and devolved the management of the new political system upon the civilians within eighteen months of the coup d'état, which was sooner than Ayub had done. The Turkish military commanders placed less reliance than Ayub did in the formal safeguards of a new constitution. Yet, like Ayub, the second junta reserved for itself the role of concealed custodian of the refurbished republic.

In outline, the experience of Turkey looked much like that of Pakistan. In detail, the differences were significant.

Turkey is not a new state, being heir to a tradition of self-rule that has endured for more than 600 years. When General Mustafa Kemal took over the leadership of the nationalist insurrectional movement in 1919, his act exemplified an earlier military intervention into the politics of a dying empire, but the political revolution to which the intervention gave rise was a departure from empire. It was a struggle against the triumphant allies of World War I for the survival of a truncated Turkish state. Under Mustafa Kemal's leadership, the Turkish nationalists accommodated themselves to the loss of non-Turkish territory up to the linguistic and ethnic frontiers of what became a relatively homogeneous Turkish Republic. The Association for the Defense of the Rights of Anatolia and Rumelia, which had rallied the Turkish nationalists to the war for political survival in an integrated Anatolia, became the People's Party at an inaugural congress in August 1923, and in the following year the Republican People's Party (RPP). Two experiments with opposition parties in 1924–25 and 1930 proved abortive. The single-party system lasted until after World War II. Following the death in 1938 of Atatürk, as Mustafa Kemal was called by then, he was succeeded as permanent head of the party and as president of the republic by İsmet İnönü, the victorious general in the war for independence. Immediately after World War II, İnönü permitted the development of a multiple-party system. The first free election under the new system which brought the Democratic Party (DP) to power in May 1950, was greeted throughout the Western world as an example of orderly change from authoritarianism to democracy. The United States in particular found it congenial to foster close relations with an industrializing democratic country.

The DP victory brought basic political changes. Atatürk's constitution, while theoretically vesting supreme power in parliament, nevertheless enabled Atatürk to convert the system in practice into one dominated by the president, and the president had used the RPP to mobilize mass support and the party organization to frame governmental policies. The single party thus reinforced the president's power, enabling him through the RPP's growing membership to press his influence forward into the provinces. Even in the provinces, however, the RPP remained essentially an urban party. Without formally modifying the constitution, the DP Prime Minister, Adnan Menderes, substantially reduced the role of the presidency and developed what appeared on paper as a parliamentary system but represented in reality his own brand of authoritarianism.

Beginning in 1953 the DP, under Menderes' leadership, pushed through the legislature a succession of laws designed to stifle public criticism, cripple the opposition parties, and bring the administrative and judicial branches of government firmly under the party's command. Civil servants became subject to dismissal, without right of appeal, thus enabling the government to get rid of those who failed to hew to the party line. The retirement of judges after 25 years' service became mandatory, making it possible to pack the courts with loyalists. Progressively stringent press laws inhibited free discussion of public issues. University professors were deprived of the right of leadership roles in the political parties. As early as 1953 the government confiscated most of the assets of the RPP, its most formidable rival. Thereafter the DP made it almost impossible for the opposition parties to engage in free electioneering. They were, for example, practically barred from access to the state radio, the only facility of the kind in the country. On the eve of the 1957 election, new electoral laws disallowed coalitions and stipulated that the party winning no more than a plurality in any province return all its deputies.

In retrospect, it is puzzling to understand why Menderes and the DP resorted to restrictive policies, which did not seem necessary for victory at the polls. In the Democratic decade a new revolution was launched. The Atatürk revolution had reached primarily the urban areas in the interwar decades. Until after World War II a majority of Turkey's 35,000 villages, many strewn among the mountains, were isolated from one another because of the absence of roads and transportation facilities, and the country's agricultural economy hardly rose above the subsistence level. Thus the rural revolution awaited the construction of a nationwide highway system which in fact came as part of the American aid program during the Menderes administration. Opening up the hinterland helped integrate the peasant economy into the national economy. The Menderes government relieved the peasants of taxation, and granted special favors to those provinces whose peasants supported the government's policies. This all formed part of Menderes' program for rural modernization.

Although Atatürk had declared Turkey a secular republic, the disestablishment of Islam greatly changed life in the cities, but it did not penetrate deeply into the rural districts. Islamic institutions and practices retained their full vigor in the villages, which accounted for three-fourths of Turkey's population. As more and more peasants poured into the cities and towns to escape the effects of economic and social lag in the agricultural sector, they brought their dedication to religious conservatism. Moreover, Menderes catered to the peasants by relaxing restraints on religion and providing government support for the rebuilding of mosques.

The DP thus could count on the support of the urban masses in many places. It also won the endorsement of the new and swiftly growing class of entrepreneurs and merchants in the cities and towns by its favoring private enterprise over state enterprise (*étatisme*), on which Atatürk had relied for industrial develop-ment. From Menderes' standpoint this was prudent politics, since in any freely competitive election the peasants and the urban masses assured a majority. The Republicans for the most part con-tinued faithful to secularism, one of the basic doctrines of Atatürk's modernization program.

On these substantive issues most military officers tended to ally themselves with the Republicans. Their choice was reinforced by purely private considerations. In the Democratic decade the social and economic status of military officers in the country at large de-clined, because as a fixed-income group they were adversely affected by inflation, while that of the manufacturers and shopkeepers rose. The experience in Turkey was directly the reverse of that in Pakis-tan. Although it was Menderes who, like Ayub, had found a way of reaching the peasants, it was the military establishment in Turkey, like the politicians in Pakistan, who felt their position threatened by the political recognition given to the rural masses. The govern-ment's policies reinforced the conviction of many Turkish military officers that Menderes and his Democratic Party had made a trav-esty of what started out as a genuine experiment with democracy. The disenchantment of these officers with the Menderes govern-ment on military matters added another dimension to their agony. As was to have been expected, Menderes did not neglect the armed forces. He promoted officers freely, no doubt hoping thereby to gain in popularity, but he chose officers for the top com-mands on the ground, not of merit, but of fidelity to the prime minister and his party. Many officers were alienated by what they came to view as the politicization of the top command and the suborning of officers to serve the private interests of the party in-stead of the public interest of the state. Anger rose sharply early in the spring of 1960, when Menderes ordered infantry units to sup-press meetings of the political opposition and the student protest demonstrations that followed, and imposed martial law on Istan-bul and Ankara.

The crisis in confidence sprang from a conviction among the dis-gruntled officers that the armed forces had lost status under the Democrats. The military establishment, it is true, had undergone a more rapid modernization under the Democrats than in any equivalent period in its history, and had acquired respectability in the world community, thanks to American largesse and to Turkey's admission, on American insistence, to membership in NATO. Nevertheless the feeling was widespread in officer ranks that the army was no longer the favored agency, the source of candidates for cabinet ministers and for lawmakers. Gone was the intimacy that linked the officers to the head of state in the RPP administration under the leadership of victorious generals—Atatürk and İnönü, his successor—in the first 27 years of the republic.

Atatürk had been the first Turkish ruler to attempt as a matter of principle to keep the armed forces out of politics, as Ayub was later to do in Pakistan's Second Republic, for essentially the same reason: fear of displacement by popular generals who opposed him. Yet Atatürk did not prevent military officers from entering civilian governmental careers, either at the ministerial level or below, provided the officers first surrendered their commissions. In any case, in the republic as in the antecedent empire the officers were still largely recruited in the urban centers, from the same educated class that filled the ranks of the civil service and the professions and among which Atatürk had found strong support for his revolution.

The combination of the DP's rural popularity, the attempted suppression of the opposition, the subordination of the civil service and the bench, and the controls over the electoral system seemed to assure Menderes permanent entrenchment. In the absence of any ostensible legitimate means of changing leaders and policies, the military conspirators were persuaded that they had no choice but to intervene. This accounts for the preoccupation of the National Unity Committee with the restoration of democracy and with the introduction of adequate safeguards to prevent the recurrence of authoritarianism of the Menderes stripe. The Turkish armed forces had seized power, it was stated, "for the purpose of extricating the parties from the irreconcilable situation into which they had fallen and for . . . having just and free elections . . . as soon as possible under the supervision and arbitration of an above-party administration, and for handing over the administration to whichever party wins the election." [6] On the very day of take-over, the NUC appointed a committee of law professors to write a new constitution. General Cemal Gürsel, the chairman of the NUC, made known the basic reforms that the junta had in mind: a bicameral legislature, an electoral system based on proportional representation, and judicial review. When the constitutional commission failed to fulfill its assignment, the NUC created a constituent assembly, which began meeting in January of 1961, and in which the NUC sat as an upper chamber so as to have a commanding voice in framing the instrument. On the first anniversary of the coup d'état the assembly approved the draft of the new constitution, which on 9 July 1961, received public endorsement by 62 per cent of the voters in a national referendum.

The military intervention in Turkey, as in Pakistan, had as its primary purpose the reconstruction of the political system. Whereas Ayub was persuaded that the entire system of Pakistan's First Republic was discredited, the NUC in Turkey blamed only the Democratic Party for suppressing civil liberties, rigging elections, manacling the opposition, straying from Atatürk's revolution, and above all—from the purely military viewpoint—using the armed forces to promote the interests of the party. Good government, in the NUC handbook, was government that excluded the DP altogether and restored to a central role the urban educated class, especially the civil service and the army officers. Thus it was not surprising that in the constituent assembly the RPP was prominently represented, and spokesmen of the Republican Peasants Nation Party, another holdover of the First Republic, were also invited. Furthermore, the NUC allowed other parties to organize in anticipation of the restoration of a multiple-party system.

In the interregnum between the First and Second Republics, the military governed Turkey by fiat with the cooperation not of the politicians but of civilian technicians. The NUC, as a body, took over the legislative function. The cabinet, created under the prime ministership of General Cemal Gürsel, who also served as his own national defense minister, included only two other army officers, one as interior minister and the other as communications minister. The rest of the cabinet consisted of civilian technicians. For more than fourteen months martial law was limited to the cities of Ankara and Istanbul. Only on 31 July 1961, after the less-than-enthusiastic response of the electorate to the new constitution, did the military government extend martial law to the entire country. The step was taken as a precautionary measure in anticipation of the execution of Prime Minister Menderes. It was also taken to ease the policing of the first election in October and the later transfer of powers to the new civilian government.

A majority of the junta were determined to stick to the purposes of the coup, or, as they referred to it, the 27 May Revolution. This was forcibly illustrated by their expulsion from the NUC of fourteen members who sought in November 1960 to seize power and establish on a permanent basis a military authoritarian regime that would retain power in perpetuity to carry out radical social and economic policies. The military officers completed the political task in the summer and fall of 1961, submitting the new constitution to a national referendum in July, executing Menderes and two ministerial colleagues in September, holding the first election of the Second Republic in October, and forming the first civilian government in November.

Yet even before the adoption of the new constitution in July 1961, the NUC had already surrendered effective political power to the top command of the armed forces, although it was never formally acknowledged, then or later. To understand how and why this transfer of power had taken place and to evaluate its consequences, we must first examine the NUC itself more closely.

Disguised Junta: Custodian of the Second Republic

The seizure of political power by the original NUC proved a relatively simple matter, as military coups often do. Once power was seized, however, the stubborn problems presented themselves. The Turkish military conspirators did not as a group plunge into politics for personal ends. They did so for the express purpose of erasing what they were persuaded was a political evil. But what is more germane to our present inquiry, they did so in the name of the armed forces. The original NUC, however, did not include the top commanders. In fact, the chief of the general staff, who under the constitution was also the supreme commander of the armed forces, was General Rüştü Erdelhun, a Menderes appointee who had cooperated intimately with the overthrown regime and who obviously had no sympathy for the conspiracy. The leader of the NUC, General Cemal Gürsel, had served as commander of the land forces —second in rank only to the chief of the general staff—from 1957 until 3 May 1960, less than a month before the coup, when he was given "forced leave" because of his protest to the government over the police action in the student demonstrations and the employment of the army for domestic political ends. As NUC chairman, Gürsel became head of state and of government after the coup. To assert and hold NUC mastery over the armed forces whose support was indispensable to the success of the military regime, he also became national defense minister and chief of the general staff. However, management of the NUC, a heterogeneous and oversized junta of 38 officers in all, ranging in rank from full general to captain, proved at times more difficult than management of the government. Soon after the coup, Gürsel handed over the supreme command to General Ragip Gümüşpala, until then commander of the Third Army in eastern Turkey. In October Gürsel also gave up the national defense ministry, naming to the post a fellow general.

Indeed, the members of the NUC seemed preoccupied with their new non-military roles. It must be assumed that any who so elected could have retained their regular or equivalent positions in the armed forces. Actually, after Gürsel's withdrawal, only two members clung to active commands, although both significantly were located in the nation's capital. Major General Cemal Madanoğlu, a veteran of the Korean War and the third highest officer in the junta, headed the Ankara garrison, and Colonel Osman Köksal stayed on as commander of the elite Presidential Guards Regiment.

As a group, the members of the NUC represented the responsible section of an officer corps that in the preceding decade had been subject to contradictory pressures. The Turkish military establishment was the most professionally trained one in the Middle East, benefiting as it had from American aid and from membership in NATO. The high standards of officer performance that such an organization demanded were, however, being gradually debased by Menderes' studied policy of fast promotions and slow retirements, which expanded all upper ranks far beyond need and assigned many officers duties beyond their training and talent.

In paring down the officer corps, the NUC attempted to resolve the professional and the political problems simultaneously. The army's table of organization, Gürsel disclosed, had called for only 50 generals, not close to 250 as there actually were, and for some 1,200 colonels, not 2,600. The junta therefore aimed to restore the officer corps to its proper numerical balance, by terminating the commissions of an estimated 5,000 officers. The only figures released were those for officers of general rank (or its equivalent in the navy), of whom there were 244 before the purge, and only 9 after it. The more populous lower grades were also thinned, but none so drastically. The "rejuvenation" of the officer corps was thus accomplished in a single act. Along with the deadwood, however, went much live timber, selected according to political criteria. Those known to favor Menderes or suspected of doing so headed the political list, which also included many (among them General Gümüşpala) thought to be not wholly in sympathy with the objectives of the coup, as variously understood by the junta's members.

On the other hand, it was a testament to the professional pride of the officers in the junta, if not necessarily to their political wisdom, that they did not themselves seek the highest commands as a reward for having taken part in planning the coup d'état. This had happened elsewhere in the Middle East, and would doubtless continue to happen, in armies of inferior training and poor morale: in

Syria in 1949, when Colonel Husni al-Za'im elevated himself to field marshal within a few weeks of his overturn of the civilian regime; or in Egypt in June 1953, when 'Abd al-Hakim 'Amir jumped from major to major general on the day of his appointment to the supreme command; or a decade later in Yemen, where 'Abdallah al-Salal rose from colonel to field marshal in less than a year after the birth of the republic.

It would have been remarkable, however, if so cumbersome a junta as that in Turkey could have pulled in harness for a prolonged period while fundamental decisions were being reached on the future structure of the country's politics and on the future role of the armed forces. Because of insistent advocacy of permanent military rule, the so-called fourteen radicals under the leadership of Colonel Alparslan Türkeş were expelled in November 1960 from membership in the NUC, involuntarily retired from the army, and sent into political exile as counsellors of scattered Turkish diplomatic missions. In taking this action, the moderate majority found it necessary to call for the cooperation of General Cevdet Sunay, who had become chief of the general staff in August as part of a reshuffle of the top command that accompanied the purge. The junta thereby demonstrated that its grip on the armed forces was loosening. In the months that followed, the reorganized NUC consulted General Sunay with growing frequency, as he assumed the role of spokesman for the armed forces.

The issue of divided authority over the military establishment came to a head in June 1961, when, in an effort to keep Lieutenant General Madanoğlu and Colonel Köksal in their active command positions, the NUC tried to reassign as adviser to the Turkish military mission in Washington Lieutenant General İrfan Tansel, the chief of the air force and a vigorous advocate of the complete separation of the NUC from responsibility for the armed forces. In openly rejecting the NUC directives, Tansel on 9 June ordered F-86 jets to fly low over Ankara and Eskişehir. The planes continued buzzing the two cities for six hours until the NUC finally reversed its directives. Madanoğlu and Köksal stepped down from their commands, the first withdrawing from the NUC altogether; Tansel kept his command; and Sunay took to meeting regularly with the NUC.

The showdown was typically Turkish. It was not Tansel seeking either the top military or the top political slot or both. It was a reassertion of Atatürk's principle that the army must be separated from politics and of the further principle, enunciated in the 27

May coup d'état, that the armed forces were the final custodians of the country's democracy. Though the two principles may appear contradictory, in the Turkish context they were not. In any case, this was not Tansel's decision; it was the collective decision of the Supreme Military Council (SMC), a body that had been created in the early years of the First Republic to review problems of the armed forces with the national defense minister for the guidance of the cabinet. Larger than the general staff, the SMC comprised the staff chief and his deputy, the three force commanders, the three army area commanders, the prime minister, and the defense minister.[7]

As originally constituted, the SMC furnished, in essence, yet another civilian shield against any military incursion into politics. Under the military regime, however, the line dividing the armed forces from politics vanished, so that by asserting its advisory role and then insisting on the autonomy of the armed forces, the SMC was in fact assuming an executive and supervisory role. When the senior commanders compelled the NUC to capitulate, they were in effect mounting their own coup d'état, even though it has never been designated as such. "So far as I am concerned," as one senior commander put it at the time, "there is no [National Unity] Committee. There is only the army. After all it was the army that carried out the revolution [of 27 May]. The Committee depends on us, not we on the Committee." [8] Thereafter, it was the SMC that administered the successive steps in the transfer of political power from the armed forces back to the civilians, for the SMC stuck to the original resolve of the planners of the coup that its purpose would be fulfilled when a new constitution with adequate safeguards against a recurrence of personal or party authoritarianism was framed, approved, and put into effect. The almost mystical fidelity to democracy and to civilian rule, at least among the older men in uniform, derived from the Atatürk tradition. It was also reinforced by the Council of Europe to which Turkey belonged but from whose consultative assembly in Strasbourg it had been disbarred in the period of the interregnum because of the requirement that all assembly members be designated by their respective parliaments.

The enforcement of countrywide martial law in the summer of 1961 enabled the SMC to tighten military controls until after the first election and the formation of the first civilian government. At a meeting convened by the NUC in Ankara early in September, leaders of the four contesting parties signed a National Declaration that laid down the campaign rules that all participants pledged to uphold, proscribing, in particular, laudatory comments on the Menderes regime or adverse ones on the military regime. The returns of the election on 15 October confirmed that the voters followed their own preferences, for the two new parties that fell heir to the suppressed Democratic Party did well in the districts that had formerly supported the Menderes regime in strength. The larger of the two, the Justice Party (JP), returned 158 deputies to the assembly (or only 15 fewer than the leading RPP) and 70 senators to the upper house (or nearly twice as many as its rival). The Grand National Assembly, as the two houses were collectively called, elected Gürsel president of the republic on 26 October, but only after the SMC had persuaded Ali Fuat Başgil, an Istanbul University law professor who had been closely identified with the Menderes government, to withdraw his candidacy, which was supported principally by the Justice Party. On entering office as president, Gürsel formally retired from the army, as did the other NUC members, who received *ex officio* seats in the Senate.

Even before his election as president, Gürsel met with the general secretaries of the four parties and with the commanding officers of the three services to sign yet another declaration on government policy. The party spokesman reportedly agreed neither to challenge the sentences meted to the Democratic Party leaders, nor to request an amnesty for the members of the Menderes regime serving prison terms, nor to seek the reinstatement of those officers who lost their commissions in the massive purge of August 1960. There followed nearly a month of intense negotiations between the SMC and the party leaders for the creation of a government that would enjoy the confidence of the Grand National Assembly. To the success of the negotiations, which brought together the basically incompatible Republican and Justice parties, the two strongest in the election, the SMC's contribution was decisive. The military commanders left no doubt of their preference: a coalition government under the premiership of İsmet İnönü and dominated by the RPP; and to these terms, which it could view only as ignominious, the Justice Party capitulated on 20 November.

After the formation of the first government, the SMC withdrew from the center of the stage to play its guardian role from the wings. Two further elections were held in the first three years (of village and municipal councils in November 1963 and the rotating third of the Senate in June 1964) and by common accord both were unimpeded. Yet, ironically, by adhering to its pledge of free elections, the senior officers found themselves in a quandry. They were dead-set against the resuscitation of the Democratic Party or the policies that it had come to espouse under the leadership of Menderes. The spirit of Menderes and of the defunct DP, however, had been largely reincarnated in the Justice Party, one of two new ones among the four (later six) that constituted the Second Republic's multiple-party system. Despite divided leadership, the JP ran first in the local elections of 1963 and held its overwhelming lead in the subsequent senatorial elections.

The secret of the party's success lay in the growing political articulateness of the peasants and their overflow into the towns. Their memory of Menderes had lost none of its vigor. The conversion of the Grand National Assembly into a bicameral legislature made it possible to use two electoral systems, proportional representation for the lower chamber and a simple majority for the Senate. Still, under the new complex electoral system, as under the old, the peasants and urban masses were bound to predominate in any free election, and, as Menderes had learned, any party that appealed to their interests could hardly fail to win.

The one feature common to the first three cabinets of the Second Republic was the commanding position of the RPP in each, with İnönü as prime minister. Each time a coalition broke down, the SMC stepped in to mediate the negotiations for a replacement. The second government (June 1962–November 1963) united the RPP with the two smaller parties that had participated in the first election, the Republican Peasants Nation Party (a survivor of the First Republic) and the New Turkey Party (a lesser legatee of the DP). The third government (January 1964–February 1965) consisted of Republicans and independents. Though the leading party in 1961, the RPP had tallied less than 37 per cent of the popular vote, and in the later contests trailed far behind the Justice Party. The SMC was thus, in effect, keeping a minority party in power. The senior officers must have believed in this period that the welfare of the Second Republic depended on the policies and aspirations of the urban educated elite who ran the RPP. This military-civilian partnership regarded itself as the custodian of Atatürk's revolution. The partners seemed determined to establish a self-sustaining democracy, but the principles of the Atatürk revolution on which such a democracy was supposed to be founded failed to inspire the peasant majority. Yet the senior officers let it be known that they would not countenance a "counterrevolution." The SMC thus faced irreconcilable alternatives. Any party system designed to uphold the aims of the 27 May coup could not rest on a free electoral system; any electoral system permitting freedom of choice to the population at large was likely to bring to power men who would undermine the original purposes of the coup.

Once the RPP was dropped, as it was from the fourth coalition formed in February 1965, partly because of İnönü's refusal to cooperate with the JP, the military-civilian partnership changed character. The new governing combination consisted of the JP and three smaller parties. The first head of the Justice Party was General Ragip Gümüşpala, who had briefly been chief of the general staff before the massive purge. Relations between the general and the two juntas grew frigid when Gümüşpala consented to lead a party that frankly identified itself with the defunct DP. Gümüşpala, however, died in mid-1964, immediately after the Senate elections. At a conference called in the fall to locate a new party president, the delegates whipped up normal partisan sentiment by unflattering references to the senior military officers, who were charged with having "sold themselves" to the RPP. A Justice Party newspaper at the time impugned the honor of the armed forces in a series of articles. General Sunay in November took the unusual step of sending a blunt letter to the speaker of the lower house, warning that if JP spokesmen did not cease their provocation, the military might have to warm up their tanks. After secret meetings between President Gürsel and the party leaders, a joint declaration reaffirmed their loyalty to the 27 May revolution. Significantly, Suat Hayri Ürgüplü, the prime minister of the fourth government, was an independent, and the new Justice Party leader, Süleyman Demirel, who was only lightly tainted by the Menderes brush, accepted the deputy premiership. By the fourth year the SMC clearly seemed willing to experiment with the Republicans in the opposition and the Justice Party sharing the government with other parties and politicians, on the basis of the latest promise of political good.

Meanwhile, in addition to restraining the politicians, the SMC also restrained the officer corps. The very act of intrusion into politics in May 1960 had contributed to the politicization of the officers, for once defiance of established authority succeeds, the example breeds further defiance. The summary expulsion of the 14 radicals from the NUC in November 1960 brought to light the first serious political division within the officer ranks. Such divisions multiplied in the 1961 election, as many victims of the purge joined political parties. An estimated 175 former officers ran as candidates for both houses, and of these 36 were seated.[9] Continued disgruntlement among the officers and former officers resulted in attempts at military coups, led by Colonel Talat Aydemir, in February 1962 and again in May 1963. After the first failure, Aydemir was removed from his post as commander of the Ankara War College and discharged from the army. After the second, he was brought to military trial and executed along with six fellow conspirators; 29 other defendants received life sentences; and all the cadets were expelled from the war college for complicity in the abortive putsch. Moreover, martial law, reimposed in Anakra and Istanbul in May 1963, was not lifted for fourteen months.

The quasi-military regime in Turkey was thus performing a dual function. The army officers had approved the creation of a competitive political system that required managing, and the SMC took over the management. The military presence also defended the Second Republic against possible conspiracy by dissident military officers. Still, as the 1960 coup receded in time, the less clear became its original political purposes. Though extraconstitutional, the SMC was nevertheless rotational in membership, despite the survival of Generals Sunay and Tansel beyond the customary three-year terms. New commanders, like new political leaders, might be expected to yield new policies.

The fourth coalition, which excluded only the RPP, augured such a change. The prime minister was an independent politician, but the Justice Party held the deputy premiership and otherwise predominated. The leaders of all the parties signed an advance declaration pledging to safeguard the purposes of the second Republic. In particular, the declaration reaffirmed Turkey's absolute loyalty to international treaties and to the collective security systems in which it took part, thereby precluding in effect the possibility of a shift to neutrality or to an alliance with U.S.S.R. Nevertheless, it was emphasized that within this broad context Turkey would pursue its own foreign policy. The latest coalition was the first indication of the army's preparedness to set İnönü aside and experiment with a government in which the Justice Party, as the main legatee of Menderes, was to have a primary voice in governing the country. The coalition also served as a caretaker government to organize and oversee the second election. In the election of October 1965, the Justice Party won an absolute majority and thus could set up its own government without need for partners.

The SMC clearly continued viewing itself as the guarantor of an open society by insisting on free elections and assuring the victors, even the deeply suspected JP, the right to form a single-party government. Hence, in less than a half-dozen years, the military custodians of the Second Republic had gone full circle. Yet appearances were deceiving, for it was clear that the army's top command, while continuing to remain in the background, had not abandoned its custodial politics. The SMC seemed prepared to tolerate the JP only on the officers' own conditions. The party had to accept without question the legitimacy of the 27 May revolution and uphold its principles. It was not an accident that the SMC favored Süleyman Demirel over Sait Bilgiç, who led the JP's conservative wing which advocated the revival of the Menderes policies.

That the SMC was not willing to abandon its supervisory politics, even after the JP came to power, was disclosed in the election of a new president in March 1966. As soon as Gürsel's presidency was terminated on medical grounds, the SMC reportedly notified the government and the leaders of the opposition parties that its candidate for the succession was General Cevdet Sunay, the chief of the general staff ever since the 1960 army purge. Sunay thereupon resigned as supreme commander, so as to take a seat in the Senate to which the acting president of the country appointed him. It is the parliament that elects the president in Turkey, and on 28 March 1966 the only bloc of votes against his candidacy were those of the small conservative Republican Peasants' Party. As head of state, Sunay, who held the respect of the top commanders, mediated between the SMC and the civilian politicians, particularly the leaders of the JP. The new president quietly but firmly clung to the alliance with the United States against its detractors, civilian and military. On these matters, as on all questions relating to the armed forces, the Demirel government acquiesced in the wishes of Sunay and the SMC. Or, to put it differently, Demirel willingly accepted military leadership.

After the 1960 coup, it is worth noting, the armed forces expanded, and so also, at a more rapid rate, did military expenditures. Yet both trends must be viewed in perspective. The Turkish armed forces by 1947 had been reduced to 600,000 from a wartime mobilization level of some 800,000. Under the American aid program, the size was further streamlined to about 400,000, remaining relatively stationary for about a dozen years. The smaller establishment more than made up in modern organization and weaponry what it lost in manpower. After 1960 the forces gradually enlarged to a total of about 480,000 by 1965; yet even then there were only 15 men in uniform for every thousand inhabitants, or about the same number as in 1956. Defense expenditures ran somewhat higher than government investment in development in the decade ending in 1965, and from an average of 4.0 per cent of the GNP in the five years ending in 1960, as Table 7 reveals, the sums allocated to defense jumped to an average of more than 5.0 per cent in the first five years following the military coup. The Turkish forces were thus consuming national resources at a relatively faster pace than was Pakistan in the same period, yet at a considerably slower pace than the world average.

Meanwhile, the RPP late in 1966 began to split into a majority who remained faithful to the indomitable İnönü, their octogenarian leader, and the program of socialism that the party had espoused in the 1965 election campaign. The faction led by Turhan Feyzioğlu that separated from the party in the spring of 1967 initially included some fifty deputies and senators who formed their own Güven (confidence) Party, subscribing to a platform based on the original principles of the RPP.

Still, the governing Justice Party, while enjoying a strong mandate from the people and a majority in the legislature, rendered even more powerful by an economic growth rate of 9 per cent in its first full year in office and by a divided opposition, nevertheless handled only timorously the issues raised by the progressively assertive nationalism in an opening society. Antiforeignism grew steadily more articulate and collided with the prevailing sentiments of the senior military officers who appeared as determined as ever to preserve close working relations with the United States. Most senior officers did not wish to lose the reinsurance of American support against the still lively threat to Turkish security from the north. These officers were also pressing for further military modernization and believed that the equipment and the training could come more cheaply—and safely—from the United States. On the other hand, part of the antipathy toward the United States in the late 1960s seemed to be disguised antipathy for the residual supervisory powers that the top military officers exercised over the political system.

While the senior military officers had demonstrated that they could work in harmony with the legatees of the discredited Democratic Party, even as late as the start of 1968 there was no evidence to suggest that the army's top command was contemplating an early return of civilian control over the armed forces. The SMC may well have been more fearful of attempted revenge than of the attempted reanimation of the spirit of Menderes. Moreover, the

TABLE 7. Turkey: Force Levels, Government Expenditures, and GNP, 1956–66

	Population (millions)	Force Levels (thousands)	Government Expenditures (millions of Turkish lira)			GNP (millions of lira)	Defense Expenditures (as % of GNP)
			Defense (including internal security and justice)	Development	Total		
1956	24.8	400,000	1,074	920	3,444	24,330	4.4
1957	25.5		1,273	1,240	4,144	30,530	4.2
1958	26.3		1,313	1,300	4,627	38,510	3.4
1959	27.0		1,600	1,725	6,232	47,730	3.4
1960	27.8	400,000	1,844	2,350	7,640	50,970	3.7
1961	28.5		2,800	2,358	9,035	53,720	5.2
1962	29.3		3,288	2,247	10,468	60,300	5.5
1963	30.0		3,667	2,835	12,563	68,490	5.4
1964	30.7		3,813	3,246	14,021	74,198	5.1
1965	31.4	480,000	3,997	3,479	15,195	79,687	5.0
1966	32.1			4,228		89,546	

SOURCES: U.N. Yearbook of National Account Statistics; U.N. Statistical Yearbook; AID, Summary of Basic Data: Turkey; OECD, Economic Surveys: Turkey; see also Frederic C. Shorter, "Military Expenditures and the Allocation of Resources," in Four Studies on the Economic Development of Turkey (London, 1967), edited by Shorter, tables on pp. 38, 41, and 43.

army officers by and large continued to identify with the urban educated elite and to hold in contempt the peasants (including the growing mass of semi-urbanized émigrés from the villages to the cities and towns), the private entrepreneurs, and the spokesmen for religious conservatism.

Before leaving the military-civilian coalitions, we might well compare the experiences of Pakistan and Turkey in yet another context. The president of Pakistan had not developed any basis of confidence in the politicians and the lawyers, who were the main upholders of urban interests. Ayub's poor showing in the cities and the towns in the presidential election of January 1965 deepened his suspicion of the old-line politicians and especially of the lawyers with whom they were allied. How sensitive Ayub remained to their politicking he betrayed at the height of the election campaign by retroactively resigning his commission as field marshal.

Thus in neither country did the disguised military custodians of politics appear able to close the widening urban-rural gap. But the fact that Ayub was building his political power on organizing the peasantry, while the SMC was fighting a rear-guard action in defense of the political supremacy of the urban educated elite, suggested that the military politicians in Turkey and Pakistan had ceased running a parallel course.

Traditional Monarchies

12

LIBYA: TRIUMPH OF
SANUSI LEADERSHIP

Libya proclaimed its independence in December 1951, less than a decade after the expulsion of the Italians. As late as 1960, Libya was still one of the poorest independent Arab countries. Though nearly 680,000 square miles in size, the new North African state had a population in 1954 no larger than 1.1 million, about a quarter of it huddled along the 1,000-mile Mediterranean coast whose geographical place-names had fleetingly become familiar to newspaper readers in the early years of World War II when the seesaw battles placed the Italian colony alternately under Axis and British control. The population density of Cyrenaica in the east, nearly 350,000 square miles in size, or more than half the country's total, was less than one person per square mile. More sparsely inhabited was the Fazzan in the south, where 60,000 residents rattled around in 220,000 square miles of desert. Of these, less than 10 per cent were beduin. But even Tripolitania in the west, where two-thirds (738,000) of the country's inhabitants lived, had a population density of less than seven per square mile.

The most significant political reality of sovereign Libya was the dominant role of the beduin tribes of Cyrenaica, who in 1954 made up about 45 per cent of the district's population of 291,000. The Cyrenaicans had suffered most from Italian imperialism (1911–42), since they had resisted stubbornly the Fascist attempt to consolidate Italian power in the colony. For a decade (1922–31) they bore the brunt of an increasingly brutal Fascist program of subjugation. The advent of World War II interrupted at an early stage Mussolini's ambitious program of Italian colonization. In the eight years of the British paternalistic military administration (1943–51), a majority of the Cyrenaican tribes reassembled from their dispersion and recovered from the shock of Italian brutality.

Tribesmen live according to a rigid, unwritten code of social conduct, dictated by the austere conditions of survival in the desert; and so, too, do other tribes, who live in equally inhospitable mountains, as seminomadic or even settled population. In Islam the Shari'ah, or Muslim canon law, binds all the faithful, rulers and ruled alike. It is a devotional and ethical as well as a legal system that embraces all aspects of life. In theory, when Islamic law conflicts with tribal custom in the tribal areas, Islamic law prevails. In practice, the reverse is almost always true. Tribal society, moreover, is collective. Beduin share such benefits as their forbidding life may bestow in material wealth, food, clothing, shelter, and employment. They also share such obligations as it may demand. In the past the beduin often lived beyond the effective reach of the central government; but even when they did not, they still assumed responsibility for their own security, a duty which every adult male bears. Each tribe thus has a built-in military organization, a rudimentary citizen army, capable of rapid mobilization when needed. Though individual tribes constitute highly integrated social units, tribal areas, more often than not, are torn by intertribal feuds. Tribes therefore tend to form federations or alliances for mutual defense in the incessant warfare. Tribes became known by the federation they kept, and membership in one often invited the enmity of another. As a rule, such federations could be broken easily, unless the primary harnessing agent was religion.

The beduin in Libya were Sunni or orthodox Muslims. But a majority of the tribes of Cyrenaica in the past had claimed membership in the Sanusiyah, a Sunni mystical order with an appeal for the restoration of the original purity of the faith. Al-Sayyid Muhammad ibn 'Ali al-Sanusi (1787–1859) selected in 1856 the isolated oasis of Jaghbub near the Egyptian frontier as the headquarters of the Sanusi brotherhood that he had transferred to Cyrenaica thirteen years earlier. In the decades that followed, the Sanusi movement spread throughout the desert interior, as the beduin formed lodges that became an intrinsic part of the tribal system. The movement also spread, though less intensively, to the Fazzan and southern Tripolitania as well as to Egypt and Sudan. "Bedouin are hardheaded people," observed E. E. Evans-Pritchard,

> and they expect a return for their labour and gifts. The neighbouring tribesmen considered that they were adequately rewarded for their support of their zawiya [lodge] by the services it rendered, for, like the Christian monasteries of Europe in the Dark Ages, Sanusiya lodges served many purposes besides catering for religious needs.

They were schools, caravanserai, commercial centres, social centres, forts, courts of law, banks, besides being channels through which ran a generous stream of God's blessing. They were centres of culture and security in a wild country and amid a fierce people, and they were stable points in a country where all else was constantly on the move. . . . But the chief benefits the lodges conferred on the Bedouin were . . . that they and their children might learn from scholarly and pious men the faith and precepts of Islam, that they might have the opportunity to worship in a mosque, and that by charity to their lodges they might earn recompense hereafter.[1]

The movement, which began disintegrating in the early years of the twentieth century, was revived and politicized in the struggle against Italian conquest and rule. Leadership of the Sanusiyah was hereditary. At the close of World War I the grandson of the founder, al-Sayyid Muhammad Idris (1889–   ) was the Grand Sanusi, whom the Italians recognized in 1920 as the hereditary amir of an autonomous Cyrenaica. In the coastal villages and towns and in the beduin zone of Tripolitania, where the Sanusi movement was weakest, the resistance to the Fascist program of subjugation in the 1920s quickly fell apart. But in the Cyrenaican desert the Sanusi guerrillas proved so determined that the fighting dragged on for more than eight years. The Italians eventually forced nearly half the population and their livestock into concentration camps, taking a high toll of beduin and beasts and all but snuffing out the tribal society. The Sanusi lodges were shut, their properties confiscated, and their leaders imprisoned or dispersed.

Just before the new Fascist regime embarked upon its repressive campaign, Sayyid Idris had taken refuge in Cairo at the end of 1922, where he remained for more than two decades. Soon after Italy entered World War II in June 1940, he began with British help to organize through loyal tribal shaykhs and other fellow political exiles in Cairo a Libyan resistance movement. Unconvinced in the early war years that Britain would triumph, the Tripolitanian leaders responded with less enthusiasm to appeals from the sayyid for participation in the British war effort. The Cyrenaican tribal chiefs, however, had a score to settle with the Italians and seized the opportunity for taking military action against the common enemy.

The organization of Libyan military resistance was thus essentially a Cyrenaican effort, even though the volunteers forming the five infantry battalions were called the Libyan Arab Force (LAF). Once the Italians and Germans were finally driven out of Libya in

February 1943, a British military administration governed Cyrenaica and Tripolitania, and a Free French administration governed the district of Fazzan. The British demobilized three LAF battalions and transformed the two others into the basic units of a gendarmerie. The Cyrenaica Defense Force, as the gendarmerie was known, comprised in 1945 about 900 Arabs, commanded by some 50 British officers. In Tripolitania, on the other hand, there were so few LAF veterans on whom to draw that the Sudan Defense Force was brought in to perform police duties until the Tripolitania Police Force, a mixed force of Muslims and Jews, could be raised and trained. Recruitment into the force proceeded slowly, and many candidates were dismissed before the completion of their training.

"His Majesty's Government are determined," Foreign Secretary Anthony Eden assured Sayyid Idris in January 1942, "that at the end of the war the Senussis in Cyrenaica will in no circumstances again fall under Italian domination." [2] In the Italian peace treaty of 1947 the four powers (Britain, France, the United States, and the U.S.S.R.) pledged that they would accept the recommendation of the United Nations General Assembly if they could not agree on the disposal of the former Italian colonies within one year of the treaty's coming into effect. The issue thus appeared on the agenda of the General Assembly, which proposed in November 1949 that the three districts of Libya should "be constituted an independent and sovereign state . . . not later than January 1, 1952." A United Nations Commissioner was appointed to assist the Libyans in drafting a constitution, which was approved in December 1951.

The constitution provided for a federal government of a United Kingdom of Libya, with Idris as first king. Federalism represented a compromise, reached in two years because of the General Assembly's deadline, but it was the Tripolitanians who did most of the conceding. As spokesmen for the most populous district, the urban politicians of Tripolitania favored a unitary state under their hegemony. Just as they had been lukewarm toward Britain during the war, they continued lukewarm toward Idris and the Cyrenaicans after the war. The slickers of Tripoli, the largest city in the three districts, tended to look down on the illiterate and unsophisticated beduin of Cyrenaica as bumpkins and on their amir, Sayyid Idris, as the leader of an outmoded and depleted religious order. Admittedly, the Sanusiyah, though resuscitated, never recovered its lost vigor. Yet it counted for some political worth among key tribal shaykhs, particularly when combined with the memory of the Sanusi political and military leadership in the struggle against the

Italians. The tribal support of Idris in Cyrenaica was thus larger than the Sanusi movement. What is more, Idris's reputation as a political leader was reinforced by his continuing close relations with Britain, for his alliance outlived the war and assured him invaluable political, economic, and military props. Meanwhile, the politicians of Fazzan had also flocked to his banner, as a means of escaping French rule. Even without Fazzani backing, however, the political unity and power of the tribesmen in Cyrenaica encountered no effective competition in Tripolitania, whose politicians were united on no issue except a conviction of their superiority.

Idris I thus became a constitutional monarch reigning over a federal government with two capitals, Tripoli and Benghazi, and over three provincial governments. The representative institutions functioned relatively smoothly because they were adjusted to local conditions. The cabinet was stronger than the parliament, because of the absence of political parties. An oligarchy of wealthy townsmen and important tribal shaykhs formed the small circle from which the king chose the prime minister, who in turn chose his colleagues. The cabinet was responsible in theory to parliament, but in practice, to the king. Besides, as a man of religion, Idris tended to behave like a traditional ruler. The firmest loyalty to the crown came from the Sanusi tribesmen, who accepted Idris as the religious as well as political head of state. But the very weakness of the Sanusiyah in the postwar decades also made the king less objectionable to the rest of the population precisely because he did not appear formidable. To them, however, Idris was essentially a temporal ruler, even though this was a contradiction in Muslim terms; he was defender of the faith only in relation to the external, non-Muslim world. Yet the performance of his office in the traditional style proved acceptable even beyond Sanusi ranks. Though not an absolute monarch, Idris thus subtly exercised executive, legislative, and judicial powers that exceeded those given him in the constitution. Even more significant was his uncontested control of the armed forces, since he served by constitutional right as the supreme military commander. King Idris was thus a traditional monarch in modern constitutional dress.

At birth the life expectancy of the new kingdom was not high. There was no certainty that the union of the three districts would endure, and if it did, that the public revenues would be able to finance such elaborate governmental machinery. The infant country had few resources. Its principal asset was its strategic location in the Cold War. Still incapable of paying its own way as late as 1960,

Libya depended substantially for balancing its budget on grants from Britain and the United States and on rental for military bases leased to the two powers. The Western military presence also assured Libya further premiums in technical assistance and defense against external aggression.

Britain concluded a twenty-year preferential alliance with Libya in July 1953. In return for an annual subvention of $2.8 million for development, an annual contribution of $7.7 million to the budget, and an agreement to help the new government raise and train its armed forces, Britain was given access to bases for its ground forces and for the RAF. In the early years the British military mission, consisting of fewer than 60 officers and men, was wholly advisory and limited its training program to expanding and modernizing the gendarmerie and police—the tribal levies inherited from the days of British military administration. The king favored the Cyrenaica Defense Force with its nucleus of World War II veterans. Cyrenaica traditionally produced the best warriors in the country, and they were intensely loyal to the king. He kept their levies the strongest, giving them special instruction and the best available equipment. Until Libyan officers could be trained in Britain, Turkey, and Iraq, the tribal forces were placed under the supreme command first of a Turkish officer and later of an Iraqi. The tribal levies were united into a single establishment in 1962, but the experiment was abandoned two years later, when each of the old units was reconstituted and given a simple geographic name. In 1965 the Eastern Force included about 6,000 officers and men, the Western Force about 5,000, and the Southern Force about 700. All British troops withdrew from Tripolitania by 1966, and the remaining British garrisons with fewer than 1,600 men regrouped in Cyrenaica; and even this small force finally pulled out after the Six Day War in June 1967.

King Idris dragged his feet in developing a regular army. After eight years of organization and recruitment, the regular forces in 1965 did not exceed 6,500. In addition to the infantry battalions of about 500 men each, there were two small artillery battalions, an armored car squadron, and one engineer company. The king also had a minuscule navy (with about 100 men), composed of two patrol craft and two minesweepers, and a somewhat larger air force (with about 200 men), composed of light aircraft and American jet trainers. Libya imported its military hardware chiefly from Britain and the United States but also from Czechoslovakia, Germany, Thailand, and the U.A.R., and the variety posed formidable problems of maintenance. By then, the phenomenal oil income enabled the kingdom to pay its own military way, as it began to develop a regular army and to invest in modern equipment (see Table 8). Between 1952 and 1960 the defense budget rose slowly from 1.1 million Libyan pounds to 3.9 million, and in the latter year the outlay represented 5.6 per cent of the estimated GNP. By 1966 the defense allocation had swollen to 25.9 million pounds, yet the annual average after 1962 hovered around 5.0 per cent of the GNP. The garrisons of the regular army were about equally divided between the two capitals, separated on land by more than 700 miles without a rail connection. The king's formula for effective handling of his soldiers thus seemed to consist in keeping the tribal forces and the regular forces divided and especially in insulating the elite Eastern Force, the most powerful in the land, against political contamination from steady exposure to the others.

In the spring of 1948 the United States Air Force reactivated Wheelus Field near Tripoli—an air base that it had abandoned at the end of 1945—as a stop on the global Military Air Transport Service then being established. Wheelus Field was integrated in the early 1950s into the Strategic Air Command. Not until September 1954, however, did the United States and Libya finally conclude an agreement formalizing the Air Force presence. By then, Wheelus Field had become a primary training base for NATO and a refueling station, and because of its year-round utility, it swiftly grew into the largest American air base outside the continental United States. In the initial agreement the United States undertook to pay Libya an annual rental of $4 million in the first six years and $1 million in the next eleven years. In addition, the United States gave Libya economic and technical assistance. The annual rental for Wheelus was increased in 1960 to $10 million. Moreover, an American military aid program was instituted in 1957 to train and equip a 1,000-man unit of the army in handling modern transport and the toy air force, which eventually would inherit the mammoth Wheelus installations.

With the discovery of oil in 1959, Libya ceased overnight being a penurious desert kingdom. By the end of 1965 the proved oil resources had soared to approximately ten billion barrels, and their rate of development was unsurpassed in the Middle East. Commercial production began in 1961, and by December 1967 the concessionaires were exporting some 2.2 million barrels of crude per day. The government's income from direct payments rocketed from $5.6 million in the first year to nearly $550 million in the

TABLE 8. Libya: Force Levels, Government Expenditures, and GNP, 1952/53–1966/67

	Population (millions)	Force Levels (thousands)	Government Expenditures (millions of Libyan pounds)			GNP[d] (millions of pounds)	Defense Expenditures (as % of GNP)
			Defense (including internal security and justice)	Development	Total		
1952/53[a]	1.04		1.1	0.3	6.6		
1953/54	1.05		1.5	0.6	8.2		
1954/55	1.09		1.8	0.8	8.8		
1955/56	1.11		2.0	4.0	13.0		
1956/57	1.12		2.5	5.1	15.4		
1957/58	1.14		2.8	5.0	17.0		
1958/59	1.15		3.5	4.4	20.0	52	6.7
1959/60	1.17		3.8	2.4	20.6	61	6.2
1960/61	1.19	11[b]	3.9	9.7	28.3	70	5.6
1961/62	1.22		5.4	6.4	34.5	82	6.6
1962/63	1.24		7.0	9.0	44.4	91	7.7
1963/64	1.50		11.5	12.8	62.8	245	4.7
1964/65	1.56	18.2[c]	16.7	22.8	91.8	337	5.0
1965/66	1.62		21.9	86.8	165.8	427	5.1
1966/67	1.68		25.9	90.9	177.7	539	4.8

SOURCES: AID, Summary of Basic Data: Libya; IMF, International Financial Statistics.
[a] Fiscal year ends 31 March.
[b] Tribal levies, 10,000; regular forces, 1,000.
[c] Tribal levies, 11,700; regular forces, 6,500.
[d] GDP, 1958/59–1962/63; GNP, 1963/64–1966/67.

seventh. Oil production in Libya was expanding at a faster rate than in the first postwar decade in Kuwayt and Saudi Arabia, the two largest oil-producing countries in the Middle East, and the outlook for the immediate future seemed even more promising. Libya's success lay in the low cost of production (partly because of high yield at the wellhead) and of transportation (because of proximity to the European markets), the high quality of the crude, and, above all, the kingdom's oil policies.

The oil law of 1955 offered concessions to foreign companies on attractive yet competitive terms. Instead of awarding an exclusive concession to a single bidder, as had been government wont in the Middle East a generation earlier, Libya issued relatively small fragments (on a regional scale) to many bidders. Between November 1955 and December 1959, Libya distributed 84 concessions to 16 companies, requiring each concessionaire to give up one-fourth of its plot within five years of the date of award and another fourth within the next three years. The companies were thus under pressure to speed up the exploration, but the government in turn permitted the companies to amortize their outlays for exploration and development at an annual rate up to 20 per cent of the profits. Seventy per cent of the revenues were set aside for use by the Development Council, an autonomous body that was vested with power to finance projects of federal or provincial interest. The residue was earmarked for the regular budgets, half going to the federal government and the other half to the government of the province from which the share of the revenue derived.

The sudden onset of massive income from oil could hardly fail to bring drastic changes to a pre-national and pre-industrial society, where trade, finance, and the professions were still primitive and more than 80 per cent of the population was illiterate. A middle class was bound to spring up where none existed before, and with it would come the demand for widening the political participation of the citizenry and the welfare services of the state. The political system, fashioned with the paternalistic cooperation of the international community, outlasted the first decade because of its happy combination with a king who made relatively few mistakes in his chosen mediatory role among the competitive politicians. Idris skillfully utilized the help, internally, of the loyal tribes and the military forces that they placed at his disposal, and externally, of powerful allies. But he was a childless septuagenarian in declining health. The king selected in 1955 as heir apparent his grand-nephew, al-Hasan al-Rida (1928–   ), whose qualities as a leader many doubted. Moreover, in the early years of independence the royal family was deeply divided into two branches. The ruling branch had only six adult males; the other had more than five times that number. Idris had suppressed recalcitrant members of the second branch after one of them had assassinated his principal advisor in October 1954. Clearly the succession posed many uncertainties which could only complicate Libya's future problems.

It was still too early in 1968 to know how these problems would work themselves out. Nevertheless, we may find some guidelines by examining the experience of Saudi Arabia, which came into being earlier in a comparable context. To do this we need only substitute Najd for Cyrenaica, Hijaz for Tripolitania, and the Wahhabiyah for the Sanusiyah; and combine with these ingredients a generous measure of oil.

13

SAUDI ARABIA: THE PENINSULA UNDER NAJDI RULE

Saudi Arabia had a population in the mid-1960s larger than Libya's; how much larger was unknown, since no census had ever been taken. Estimates ranged from about 3.0 million to 7.0 million and even higher. The population of the kingdom, however, may well have been less than 3.5 million. Moreover, Saudi Arabia had undefined borders on the south and east, contested borders on the north, and a partly unsurveyed and nearly uninhabited district appropriately named the Empty Quarter (*al-Rub' al-Khali*) in the south. The exact size of the country was not yet determined. Little wonder that area estimates start at 618,000 square miles and end at 870,000. There was thus no way of learning the size or the population of the several provinces into which the country was divided. Nevertheless it was known that the Eastern Province (formerly Hasa), home of the oil installations, had a substantial Shi'i minority. The Red Sea coastal provinces were two: Hijaz in the north, where Jiddah, the diplomatic capital of the country, and the holy cities of Mecca and Madina are located; and to the south 'Asir, the Kingdom's most populous province. The Empty Quarter apart, the landlocked residue of the realm was generally designated Najd.

At the dawn of the twentieth century the Arabian Peninsula was still splintered into tribal principalities of varying size and description, some loosely tied to the Ottoman Empire as vilayets (provinces), others more securely tied to the British Empire as protectorates or quasi-protectorates, and still others either lying in the shadow of the two empires or wholly independent. An observer surveying the fragmented peninsula at that time and contemplating the prospects of political union might well have selected Hijaz as the likely center of unification.

Even more than Tripolitania, Hijaz was cosmopolitan. Year after year it received thousands of pilgrims from everywhere in the Mus-

lim world, piously paying obeisance at the birthplace of their religion and the residence of their Prophet. The numbers mounted as
the growing ease of international travel made it possible for more
and more Muslims to observe one of the requirements of the faith.
From the endless traffic a small but steady deposit of fresh talents,
skills, and knowledge enriched the Hijazi middle class, unique in
the Muslim world because it existed wholly to serve—or, according
to less kindly observers, to fleece—the pilgrims. Exposure to the
pilgrims and catering to their wants broadened the horizons of
many Hijazis. Thus Hijaz, or the vilayet of Madina as it was ad-
ministratively known as part of the Ottoman Empire, seemed
chosen by history and religion to become the peninsula pacemaker.
Sharif Husayn ibn 'Ali, the vali (governor) of Madina, proclaimed
the independence of Hijaz in 1916, after concluding an alliance
with Great Britain. But he proved militarily incapable even of keeping the state that he had erected, let alone assimilating more territory. In Arabia, as in Libya, the beduin with their built-in citizen
army furnished the victorious warriors. Here, too, religion knit the
tribes into an effective political union. Yet the observer in 1900
would not have seen 'Abd al-'Aziz ibn 'Abd al-Rahman Al Faysal
Al Saud [Su'ud] (1881–1953) as the peninsula's man of destiny.
The son of a dispossessed shaykh, 'Abd al-'Aziz was then living in
exile in Kuwayt. In 1902 he managed to retake by guile and daring
the capital of his ancestral shaykhdom, the oasis of Riyad. Within
five years he pushed his influence out slowly in all directions to
place the heart of Najd solidly in his grip. From then on, with his
patrimony regained, he could realistically sport the inherited title
of amir. Each victory facilitated the next one, as success battened
on success, and his influence moved out radially to absorb more
sandy waste and more tribal population.

The Rise of the Muslim Unitarians

With the capture of Hasa, in the east, in 1913, 'Abd al-'Aziz became a Persian Gulf shaykh, and since the new district was one
that the Ottomans had occupied in 1871, he was caught between
the conflicting claims of the Ottoman and British empires. That
was the era of complex international bilateral negotiations affecting
the Middle East, spurred by the plans for the construction of the
famed but never completed Baghdad Railroad. As part of this series of instruments, intended in the end to dovetail, a segment of
the Anglo-Ottoman accord was initialed in the summer of 1913,

placing 'Abd al-'Aziz and his enlarging estate squarely in the projected Ottoman zone.

'Abd al-'Aziz, it is true, accepted British protected status in 1915, when he was still only the amir of the remote and inconsequential Arabian principality called Najd, Hasa, and their Dependencies. The government of India concluded the arrangement on Whitehall's behalf to enlarge the Anglo-Indian system of quasi-protectorate shaykhdoms on the eastern shore of the Arabian Peninsula and to convert the Persian Gulf into an Indian appendage. In the dozen years of the Anglo-Saudi treaty's validity, the only investment that Britain made in the amirate was a monthly stipend of $25,000. This was originally designed to encourage the amir to engage Ottoman forces in World War I, but it was later continued until March 1924 to discourage him from engaging other Arabian princely states in varying conditions of dependence on Britain. By May 1927, when 'Abd al-'Aziz severed formal ties to the British Empire, he was master of the Arabian Peninsula (except for Yemen and the British dependencies) and carried the several titles of King of Hijaz, Sultan of Najd and its Dependencies, and Protector of 'Asir. Five more years elapsed before he consolidated the districts of his realm as the Kingdom of Saudi Arabia.

It ought not be overlooked that 'Abd al-'Aziz moved ahead as fast as he did because Britain, by agreement with its allies, had sealed off the peninsula as a pre-emptive sphere of influence. Whitehall had no plans of its own to push into the interior of this vast expanse of desert. Yet it would have found disconcerting the intrusion there of another European power. Insofar as new European positions were staked out in the peninsula in World War I, they were British coastal positions. After abortive attempts in the opening interwar years to bring King Husayn of Hijaz into treaty relations, Britain finally gave up, allowing the internal peninsular situation to take its natural course. Preliminary skirmishes in 1919- between 'Abd al-'Aziz's men and Husayn's demonstrated that beduin fighting their own cause are militarily superior to beduin fighting the cause of another master. Better equipment and more diversified skills did not bring victory to Hijaz in the final contest of 1924–25, for Husayn's tribal forces developed no zeal and devotion that could begin to match that of the Wahhabiyah.

The Wahhabiyah, like the Sanusiyah, became the tribal unifier. Both were Sunni movements, and the Sanusiyah was related in origin to the Wahhabiyah. But the Sanusiyah was a Sufi or mystical order, and the Wahhabiyah, a variety of Muslim puritanism. This fundamentalist sect was founded by Muhammad ibn 'Abd al-Wahhab (1703–92), who preached against innovations in Islam of a date later than the third Muslim century and inveighed particularly against the cult of the saints as a form of polytheism and contrary to the principles of early Islam. Viewing all fellow Muslims as polytheists (*mushrikun*), the adherents of the movement called themselves unitarians (*muwahhidun*), for Wahhabi was the name given them by opponents and became the accepted one outside Islam. As religious fundamentalists, the Wahhabis forbade smoking, discouraged shaving, and disallowed the decoration of mosques, even with minarets. To the Wahhabis the Sufi orders, like all other groups in Islam, were polytheist. The Wahhabiyah and the Sanusiyah were thus not parallel, and they were analogous only as revivalist movements and in their roles as tribal unifiers. The Wahhabiyah had become entwined with the Saudi amirate in the middle decades of the eighteenth century. Thus, in the twentieth century 'Abd al-'Aziz could justify conquest as well as resuscitation of the religious cause, whose original adoption had enabled his namesake (1765–1803) to spread Saudi power in the peninsula from coast to coast in the last third of the eighteenth century.

Beduin are notorious for upholding Islam while straying from its principles. The overriding reason is the transcendence in practice of tribal custom over Islamic law. The moment Islamic law, so central to the faith, loses its paramountcy, the way is open to all kinds of innovation, not least the worship of saints and prophets. The beduin of the peninsula thus became for the Wahhabis fair targets for conversion. The genius of 'Abd al-'Aziz lay in his use of religious fundamentalism as a state-building and state-expanding instrument. He developed the Wahhabiyah in 1912 into a program for transforming nomadic beduin into settled farmers, and the farmers into soldiers of the cause, providing them with missionaries to propagate the faith. The devotees turned farmers called themselves *ikhwan* (brethren) and subordinated tribal affiliations to their newly discovered religious affiliation. Some fifty ikhwan and their families founded in 1912 the first fraternal settlement at Artawiyah, a minor oasis on an inland caravan route from Kuwayt.

Artawiyah became the model for Wahhabi settlements, which spread swiftly in all directions, each dedicated to uphold the unitarian principles of the sect. 'Abd al-'Aziz financed the new villages, giving the settlers money, seed and agricultural implements, religious teachers, and the wherewithal for building mosques, schools and dwellings: and, last but not least, arms and ammunition for the defence of the faith, the basic article of which was the renunciation of all the heathen customs and practices of the old tribal code. . . . ['Abd al-'Aziz] Ibn Sa'ud [soon] found himself in command of a voluntary territorial army . . . of Badawin turned yeoman, on whose loyalty he could count to the death, though their undisciplined courage always needed a backing of steadier troops from the towns and villages to make them an effective force, while their fanatical zeal for the destruction of the infidel (a term liberally interpreted by them to include . . . all Muslims who did not share their fundamentalist conception of the true faith) had often to be kept in check in the hour of victory, and in times of peace. Henceforth the armies of Ibn Sa'ud always included a contingent of Ikhwan levies, marching under their own banners in company with the still unregenerate Badawin and the steadier yeomen of the old citizen army. Each category had its special function to perform in the ensuing operations; but it was the Ikhwan who leavened the whole lump with that cachet of ferocity, which often stood Ibn Sa'ud in good stead in dealing with his enemies.[1]

With the annexation in 1926 of the district of 'Asir, the Saudi state reached its furthest expansion. The remaining territories in the peninsula or adjacent to it were British, with the exception of Yemen, which was ruled by the Zaydiyah, a Shi'i sect. In assessing the political realities in the peninsula, 'Abd al-'Aziz recognized that he had exhausted his expansive capabilities and that missionary activity in these areas could only embroil him in conflict that might prove disastrous. In promoting Wahhabism in the first place, 'Abd al-'Aziz had suffused tribal life with fresh religious purpose. Now it became essential, forcibly if necessary, to abandon the missionary objective while keeping intact the religious and political doctrines that united the tribes. 'Abd al-'Aziz therefore sought to redirect the loyalty of the tribes from the Wahhabiyah to himself. The king still needed the tribal forces to consolidate domestic power and to safeguard the realm against external enemies. When 'Abd al-'Aziz first directed the ikhwan in 1929–30 to cease their military conquests, some tribal shaykhs refused to obey the king's orders. The decisive defeat of the most stubborn shaykhs brought an early end to the civil war, from which 'Abd al-'Aziz emerged with solid authority and his new principle firmly established.

From Personal to Clannish Rule

In Saudi Arabia, as in Libya, political unity resulted from the triumph of pastoral nomads over culturally more advanced townsmen. The accidents of history, however, gave each a different political system. The default of the great powers induced the premature birth of Libya, and with the aid of United Nations midwifery it started life with a written constitution. Libya was a traditional monarchy by virtue, not of its formal political system, but of the society over which the king ruled and of the central role of the tribal troops. By contrast, the Saudi regime was built in the classical Muslim image.

A self-made monarch who forcibly expanded his realm by his own exertions, 'Abd al-'Aziz reached his prime a generation before it became fashionable to invite from the industrial countries technical aid for political, economic, or social development. He governed the kingdom, as he had earlier governed the amirate, by vesting in himself full executive, military, legislative, judicial, and religious powers. 'Abd al-'Aziz did not establish discrete organs of administration. He simply ruled his domain directly without ministerial intermediaries, employing the customary tribal techniques of governance with the aid of a small group of royal advisers, a few of whom were brought in from neighboring Arab states. He did not even create a separate judiciary to handle extra-religious litigation, but dispensed justice himself on appeal from his subjects, with the advice of the religious legal establishment which managed the routine legal process. The king delegated limited and variable powers in the provinces to sons and relatives.

The political system was first modified, more in form than in fact, at the provincial level, and significantly in Hijaz. The defeat of the Hashimis in 1924–25 obviously delighted the Wahhabis, but it must also have embarrassed them. In conquering Hijaz, 'Abd al-'Aziz could no longer evade the limelight. Pious Muslims everywhere riveted their attention on the new custodian of the holy cities and on the future regime. It was one thing for 'Abd al-'Aziz to try to impose unitarianism on his own subjects; it was something else again to seem to be trying to do so on the world of Islam by laying down new rules for the pilgrimage.

In an effort to quiet external Muslim fears, 'Abd al-'Aziz as early as August 1926 promulgated a constitution for the "kingdom" of Hijaz that provided for "autonomous" institutions modeled after existing Ottoman ones, among them a small advisory body on legislative matters, called a Consultative Council (*Majlis al-Shura*), and local municipal, village, and tribal councils. Administration of provincial affairs was allocated to six departments or agencies, and the heads of these departments were collectively designated in December 1931 a Council of Agents (*Majlis al-Wukala*), or the viceroy's executive advisers. Even after Hijaz formally became a province in September 1932, and after 'Abd al-'Aziz changed the name of his realm from the Kingdom of Hijaz and of Najd and its Dependencies to the Kingdom of Saudi Arabia, the constitution continued in effect. The constitution did not give Hijaz autonomy, for the king's rule through the viceroy was no less absolute in that province than elsewhere in the realm. It did, however, give Hijaz representative institutions below the provincial summit, while the provincial agencies at the summit, over which the King's second son, Amir Faysal, presided, later grew into ministries of the Saudi Arab kingdom. Indeed, from their inception the agencies of finance, foreign affairs, and defense handled not only the affairs of Hijaz, but also those of the central government. Hijaz progressively lost its separate institutions during and after World War II, but it furnished the experience and the institutional models for ministerial government at the center, which 'Abd al-'Aziz decreed in October 1953, a month before his death. Yet it took a dozen years longer before personal rule was fully replaced by ministerial administration.

From birth, Saudi Arabia was plagued by problems of finance. The first problem was one of poverty. The poverty was as undeniable as its precise dimension was unknown, although the rough order of magnitude suggested by St. John Philby's educated guesses establishes some sense of size. In the opening decade of Saudi rule, 'Abd al-'Aziz's authority did not push out beyond the borders of Najd, and his amirate's annual revenue may well have amounted to no more than $250,000. The conquest of Hasa in 1913 probably doubled the sum. In the circumstances the monthly stipend of $25,000 from the British Government over a period of eight years (1916–24) must have appeared munificent. To 'Abd al-'Aziz, therefore, Hijaz looked highly attractive on purely material grounds, for immediately after the annexation of the district his income rose steeply, to an estimated average of about $20 to $25 million, according to Philby. But revenue from the pilgrimage, which accounted for much of the high return, declined sharply in the depression of the 1930s and then almost vanished in World War II, when normal transportation facilities were disrupted.

By this time an American company, the California Arabian Standard Oil Company (Arabian American Oil Company, or ARAMCO after 1944), which had received an exclusive concession first in 1933 and later expanded in 1939 to embrace the eastern two-thirds of the country, discovered oil in commercial quantities. But the war delayed production so that in the first dozen years of the concession the Saudi exchequer received from the concessionaire, besides token annual rentals, a total of $6.8 million in loans against future royalties. 'Abd al-'Aziz therefore relied on grants-in-aid from Great Britain, and later also under lend-lease from the United States, to balance his modest wartime budgets. The rapid Saudi transit from poverty to plenty was thus a postwar phenomenon. The king's direct receipts from the oil industry in 1946 did not exceed $10.4 million. Five years later these payments multiplied to $165 million and thereafter continued climbing, so that by 1965 they passed $650 million. The sudden rise in oil income derived after 1950 in part from a new agreement that more than doubled the payments to the government and in part from the Anglo-Iranian oil crisis, which enabled Saudi Arabia to become the region's largest oil-producing country. It yielded first place to Kuwayt in 1955 but then clung to that rank throughout the second postwar decade.

Libya had had the experience of a full decade of cabinet rule before the onrush of oil wealth, and the institutional management of public affairs brought with it rational administration. Saudi Arabia's experience was exactly the reverse. Personal rule with all its vagaries changed only slowly. Oil revenues poured into the royal coffers for nearly a decade before the formal introduction of ministerial administration. Yet another decade passed before the monarchy finally abandoned the practice of whimsical allocations for development, each project receiving the king's requisite approval without reference to other comparable projects and without benefit of an over-all plan. The funds were accordingly disbursed in the same informal manner as when the Saudis governed a tribal principality still struggling for survival. The income, like the subsoil petroleum resources from which it came, belonged to the king, who continued making no distinction between personal allowances for the numerous adult male members of the several generations of families of the Saudi clan and public allocations for the conduct of the affairs of state. In 'Abd al-'Aziz's reign the formal state budget was an alien and therefore abhorrent practice, and where the money went no one really knew, not even in every instance the king's trusted financial adviser, 'Abdallah al-Sulayman Al Hamdan, who supervised the royal till for nearly thirty years and carried many of the realm's fiscal particulars in his head. The financial mismanagement was compounded under King Saud (1953–64), when conspicuous consumption by the princes, the new king's sons even more than their uncles and their cousins, became the hallmark of Saudi Arabia in the world community. So prodigiously did they spend the revenues that the kingdom began living on advances from the oil companies, despite the steadily mounting income which by 1957 exceeded $300 million in direct oil payments.

Under pressure from the royal clan, King Saud in March 1958 named his brother Faysal viceroy and prime minister, delegating to him full political powers to reorganize the finances and the administration. The king and his sons, however, chafed under the new dispensation, and in December 1960, after a semblance of orderly fiscal management was achieved, Saud dismissed Faysal. The handling of public affairs once again deteriorated. Following Syria's secession from the U.A.R. in September 1961, Cairo focused much of its strident socialist propaganda on the "reactionary feudalism and corruption" of Saudi Arabia, a message that found willing listeners among the enlarging middle class of Hijaz and the Eastern Province. Faysal was thus brought back in March 1962 as deputy prime minister and, after the outbreak of the civil war in Yemen in the fall, as prime minister. The rivalry between the brothers sharpened and in March 1964, when the Yemeni war—which was also by extension a U.A.R.–Saudi war—was running full tide, a majority of the princes decided permanently to transfer full powers from Saud to Faysal, leaving the king with nothing but the title and a generous allowance. In November even the title was taken away.

By then ministerial administration had come to stay, but the Saudis were still not sharing their powers with the people. The political system had evolved from a personal absolutism to a clannish absolutism, and Faysal became the first member of the first clan of the kingdom. The clan's male membership probably surpassed 300, of whom perhaps one-fifth represented the effective political component. In asserting the king-making role, the princes were joined by the chief 'ulama, or religious leaders, many of whom were also related to the royal clan. Noticeably absent, however, were the tribal shaykhs, including the clan's leading clients. The prime ministry and all the sensitive portfolios such as finance, defense, national guard (tribal forces), and interior were reserved for the royal clan. Even though non-clan members, chosen on the whole by merit, received seats in the cabinet, they participated in policy-making only in the king's presence and at his pleasure.

As the political system changed under the impact of the rapidly changing economy, the military institution also changed. After 'Abd al-'Aziz in 1930 pulled the fangs of the ikhwan movement, no new settlements were established. Nevertheless all adult males in those settlements that stayed firm in their allegiance to the crown were issued weapons, and their shaykhs received government subsidies. They carried the major burden of policing the tribal areas and helping the king consolidate his authority. The ikhwan tribesmen were from Najd, as were also the tribal reserves furnished when needed by other beduin and, at their own expense, by all towns and villages in the province. These towns and villages were required to fill annual quotas fixed by the government. This in practice constituted a form of taxation, since the government collected sums equal to the cost of maintenance whenever the men were not called up. A substantial number of the levies were gathered in the vicinity of Riyad by the simple expedient of the king's having had wells dug nearby for loyal tribes. The military system proved entirely adequate for the kingdom's external as well as internal needs in the decade before World War II, as demonstrated in Saudi Arabia's decisive defeat in 1934 of the tribal troops of Imam Yahya of Yemen. By that time 'Abd al-'Aziz had created an agency of defense, which at the start was appropriately directed by Agent of Finance 'Abdallah al-Sulayman, since the military and taxational activities were interchangeable. In later years responsibility for managing all military affairs was entrusted only to members of the royal clan. 'Abd al-'Aziz had no money for modernizing his tribal forces, let alone for creating a modern standing army. He did, however, raise a Royal Guard. These elite units were normally stationed in Riyad, but in the performance of their duty to protect the king and the princes, Royal Guardsmen accompanied the Saudi clan on their periodic circuits of the kingdom.

The United States and the United Kingdom in World War II assigned small training missions to Saudi Arabia. The Americans instructed tribal officers in using and maintaining small arms and communications equipment; the British, light ordinance and military transport. But the two missions were terminated before the end of the war. A British advisory group resumed both programs in 1947, undertaking to modernize, on the model of the Transjordan Frontier Force and the Arab Legion, some 10,000 tribal troops for combined gendarmerie and military duties. A handful of Saudi

officers, mostly the king's sons, were sent to Sandhurst and elsewhere in Britain for advanced instruction. Replacing the British in
1952, the Americans became the kingdom's sole Western military
trainers for nearly a dozen years. As in Libya, the American military training mission turned exclusively to creating a regular army
and a small air force. A military academy was erected at Riyad, and
two training bases were substantially enlarged. The initial target,
an army of three to five regimental combat teams by 1956 (each
team consisting of infantry plus engineer, signal, artillery, and
other technical troops), was not reached six years later. The delays
arose in part from the difficulty of finding capable Najdis, so that
in the end Hijazis were selected to fill many of the officer slots; and
in part from the acceptance alongside the American training mission of an Egyptian training mission and even Egyptian commanders under the short-lived Egyptian-Saudi alliance of 1955–58. Similar problems slowed down the formation of an air force.

The Saudi clan suspected many officers of the regular army and
the air force of sympathizing with 'Abd al-Nasir and his Arab
unity movement. In fact, following the defection to the U.A.R. of
a number of pilots early in the Yemeni war, the Saudi government
grounded the entire air force for a time. In the circumstances, for
internal defense the Saudi clan continued placing primary confidence in the tribal forces, variously known as the *mujahidun* (jihad
warriors), or the White Army. Moreover, the Saudi Arab government in 1963 resumed formal diplomatic relations with Britain and
France, interrupted six years earlier because of the Suez crisis. A
British military mission on invitation from Faysal resumed in mid-
1963 the training of the tribal forces, renamed the National Guard,
with primary responsibility for domestic security. As part of the
program the British also developed a scheme for settling nomadic
beduin on the land without weakening the tribal communities, a
scheme that recalled the ikhwan movement, stripped of its religious puritanism. France took over once again management of a
small arms and ammunition factory, which it had first erected in
the early 1950s and operated until the Suez rupture.

The armed forces in 1965, not including the Royal Guardsmen
and the small air force, probably did not surpass 45,000, about
equally divided between the regular army and the National Guard.
At the time of the transfer of full powers to Faysal in March 1964,
the Royal Guards Brigade was permanently attached to the regular
army, which otherwise consisted of four widely dispersed regiments, still trained along Western lines by the United States. The

integration of the Royal Guard, it was hoped, would improve the morale and the loyalty of the officer corps. The regular army (including the small air force and tiny navy) was responsible to the ministry of defense and aviation, which had its separate budgetary allocation and princely management. The National Guard, responsible to another Saudi prince, who was designated the amir (commander) of the mujahidun, comprised more than twenty units of battalion size with their own command and equipment. The National Guard was still associated with the practice of annual subsidies to the shaykhs of loyal tribes, from which the recruits were drawn; moreover, their number could be expanded substantially in time of crisis by calling up, as in the past, the untrained tribal reserves.

14

YEMEN: TEST OF
ZAYDI DURABILITY

In Yemen we encounter many of the symptoms that have by now become familiar: an unintegrated society in which warlike tribes, united by religious doctrine, have subordinated a less bellicose and partly urban population of a rival Muslim sect and whose leaders are a shade less parochial by reason of their superior education and their contacts with the external world. We must not pedantically seek a one-for-one correlation, however, since Yemeni society in the late 1960s was still visibly more primitive than that of Saudi Arabia and Libya. Yemen remained almost completely cut off from the outside for a much longer period than either of the two other traditional monarchies. Yet, true to form, the most isolated community of the isolated society has dominated the country in the present century. Settled tribesmen of the interior highlands, rather than nomadic tribesmen as in the two other monarchies, furnished nearly the exclusive source of military power. When the external influence finally came, it literally came with a bang. Yemen's extreme isolation was terminated not by the discovery of oil, as in Saudi Arabia and Libya, but by a coup d'état in September 1962 and by the arrival of troops from the most revolutionary Arab country of the day, the U.A.R. The years of inconclusive struggle for republicanism that followed forcibly altered the pace and the pattern of political change. Yet despite the prolonged fighting, the traditional society was not vanquished; and if the Yemeni royalists were rudely awakened, so too were the Egyptians.

Yemen's political system did not conform to the usual variety of traditional Islamic monarchies. At the apex, admittedly, stood the imam as the leader of the Zaydiyah, which began at the end of the ninth century and formed a unique sect among the Shi'is. Like other heterodox Muslims, the Zaydis had repudiated the Caliphate and became partisans of the family of the Prophet, taking their name from Zayd, the grandson of the Prophet. The Shi'is believed that the Prophet's descendants were the only true leaders (imams) of Islam. There were two main Shi'i sects, one which subscribed to the doctrine of twelve prophetic imams, and the other, to the doctrine of seven. The Zaydis for their part held that the prophetic power passed on without interruption to their imams of the present century. Succession by inheritance was forbidden, each imam in Zaydi theory reaching office on his own merits. The Zaydiyah thus accommodated itself to periods without an imam and to others with more than one. Thus, in one sense, the reigning Hamid al-Din dynasty, which passed the religious and political throne from father to son to grandson, violated a basic tenet of the faith. By the same token, the challenge to the imamate from the republicans was not unprecedented or necessarily fatal to the sect, since its religious doctrines provided for such contingencies. The Zaydi imam was absolute sovereign of his kingdom, which contained the most fertile soil and the loftiest and most rugged mountains in the Arabian Peninsula. The precise size of Yemen cannot be determined, since its eastern Saudi boundary had never been agreed. The area of Yemen, usually rounded off at 75,000 square miles, probably does not exceed 10 per cent of the size of Saudi Arabia. There are no reliable population statistics for Yemen, although a commonly accepted estimate of 4.5 million may be somewhat high. The imam, moreover, ruled over a mixed population that was about equally divided between Zaydis and Shafi'is (or orthodox Muslims).

Technically, the imam himself was elected by the sayyids, or claimed descendants of the Prophet, a closed class of religious leaders to which he belonged. The sayyids must have established themselves in Yemen through conquest, but over the centuries they lost all their original martial functions. Under the reign of the Hamid al-Din dynasty in the twentieth century, founded by Imam Yahya (1904–48), the sayyids alone supplied the administrators, the royal advisers, the district governors, the judges, and the tax collectors. The sayyid class, which may have numbered some 2 to 3 per cent of the total population, was unique in many respects. The influence of the sayyids derived from neither land ownership nor commerce but from their privileged status, and even those not actively in the imam's employ nevertheless received his royal dole.

Although the imam ruled the country with the cooperation of the religious class, the power that the sayyids commanded derived from the imam himself, who manipulated the large Zaydi tribal confederations in the interior highlands of north and east Yemen and the connecting plateau. The two largest confederations, the Hashid and the Baqil, were known as the wings of the imam. Like the Saudi Arab kings, the Yemeni rulers granted regular subsidies to the loyal shaykhs. But whereas 'Abd al-'Aziz had pacified the tribal areas and, to cement the ties of the Najdi tribes to the royal family, instituted the practice of marrying daughters of the principal shaykhs, the imams by contrast traded on tribal dissension and sought to assure the fidelity of the Zaydi tribes by continuing the age-old local practice of retaining the shaykhs' sons and brothers as hostages in the royal citadel. There they were well-housed and educated, but they were not allowed to leave.

As in Saudi Arabia and Libya, the tribal levies in Yemen formed the basis of the imam's military power. These forces, varying in number according to need, were brought into active service by impressment and remained always at the imam's call, so long as he enjoyed the shaykhs' allegiance or could compel it by punitive action against the hostages. In addition, Imam Yahya in the 1930s sent a handful of young men to Iraq for officer training and before the outbreak of World War II began to form a royal guard with the aid of a short-lived Italian mission and, briefly after Italy's entry into the war, of an Iraqi one. Imam Ahmad (1948–62) expanded the royal guard into the nucleus of a regular army, roughly organized on Western lines, to perhaps three to four thousand troops. An Egyptian military mission took over the training of the regular forces from 1954 to 1961, and in this period there was a steady trickle of officer candidates to Egypt for technical training. Moreover, Yemen began in 1957 to purchase Soviet-bloc military hardware, mostly Czech small arms and Russian machine guns and armored cars, and, to instruct Yemenis in their use and maintenance, accepted a Soviet mission, which at one time was believed to include perhaps as many as 150 technicians but which reportedly was reduced to a third that number by the time of Imam Ahmad's death in 1962. In the early 1950s the imam even experimented, with Swedish help, in creating an air force; the experiment, however, never got off the ground. Significantly, Imam Ahmad carried on his person the keys to the arsenals, and his regular soldiers never reached the level of training or equipment of the other Arab armies.

The secret of the imam's political power thus lay in the complete separation within the dominant Zaydi community of the kingdom's administrative and military functions, between the sayyids or religious elite and the tribesmen; and in the further separation of the economic function, which was chiefly the property of the subordinate Shafi'i or orthodox Sunni community. The Shafi'is, in fact, probably constituted a slight majority of the population, and their urban merchants managed the kingdom's domestic as well as external commerce. Bunched in the southern highlands and in the coastal plain, the Shafi'is were undeniably by local standards the sophisticated segment of Yemeni society. Many had relatives outside the country, since most Yemeni émigrés were Shafi'is: in Aden, where some 80,000 played a prominent role in the progressively assertive labor movement; in Saudi Arabia, where by the early 1960s perhaps as many as 50,000 or more found seasonal employment each year; and in Cairo, where the small colony became highly politicized. Among the tribesmen, the Shafi'i lowlanders (many of them seminomads) were, as a rule, more peaceable and less cohesive than the Zaydi highlanders. Still, a minority of the Shafi'is could be found among the imam's tribal levies, as for example the Zaraniq federation south of Hudaydah. For the most part, however, the Shafi'i tribesmen were less responsive to the imam than to the Shafi'i merchants who dominated the Sunni community.

The plot that led in September 1962 to the attempted overthrow of Imam Muhammad al-Badr, who had ascended the throne a week earlier, and to the creation of the Yemen Arab Republic brought Zaydi officers of the regular forces into partnership with Shafi'i merchants. Long before the appearance of the republican regime, Cairo had served as a haven for political refugees from Yemen, as from many other Arab lands. The refugees from the Zaydi imamate formed a Free Yemen movement in the Egyptian capital with the blessings of 'Abd al-Nasir's government. Whether or not advance joint planning between the U.A.R. and the Yemeni conspirators actually took place was not publicly disclosed. What did become common knowledge was the U.A.R.'s prompt recognition of the Yemeni rebels. The U.A.R. followed almost immediately with military, material, and technical aid on a grand scale for the inconclusive struggle against the royalists, who won the lingering material support of Saudi Arabia.

Since neither army officers nor civilians could acquire political experience under the imamate, the Egyptians found themselves on arrival in need of fighting a war and establishing a viable political regime. In the absence of a local base on which to build, the Egyptians actually conducted the nascent government. The Egyptian administrators did double duty, serving also as technicians and training Yemenis ultimately to take over the management of the new government services. Measurable if slow progress was made in this sphere. By the start of 1965, Yemeni republicans were running routine matters in many ministries under the supervision of Egyptian advisers. The advisers occasionally took executive action on complex questions, however, and the ministries of presidential affairs, defense, interior, foreign affairs, and finance were still in the charge of U.A.R. personnel.

The supplanting of the imam's bureaucracy evoked widespread support in the zone under republican jurisdiction. In addition to the hostility that the oppressive practices of the sayyids had aroused, they were still regarded, a millennium after their arrival from the north, as foreign invaders. Yet although the republicans —Yemenis and Egyptians—won administrative popularity in the early months, they did not automatically acquire military capability. The imam's tribal levies, particularly in the north and central interior highlands, rallied to the defense of the Zaydiyah against the Sunni foreigners and their puppet republic. The U.A.R. was therefore compelled to retrain the regular forces and to try raising their own tribal levies among disaffected Zaydis, including a few Hashid shaykhs still smarting under the memory of Imam Ahmad's cruelty, and among the less martial Shafi'is. While a number of tribes became steadfast republicans, others (perhaps a majority) proved in time less reliable, not a few finding it profitable to take arms and money from both sides. The new republican army, as distinct from the tribal levies, was slow in building, and as late as the spring of 1967 still numbered fewer than 10,000 troops, three-fourths of them trained in Egypt. In the circumstances, the Egyptians had to assume nearly full responsibility for the major campaigns.

By mid-1964 the Egyptians had amassed some 40,000 troops in Yemen and seemed determined to push ahead to total victory against the royalist tribesmen, whom Saudi Arabia upheld with weapons and funds. In a vigorous summer offensive the Egyptians drove many tribesmen across the Saudi frontier and felt sufficiently encouraged to enter into political exchanges with Saudi Arabia in September 1964, agreeing in principle to a cease-fire. By the time the republican and royalist tribal shaykhs framed acceptable terms and a project for further negotiations that might lead to a political settlement, the military situation once again had changed in royalist favor. Most Zaydi tribesmen had returned by then to their mountain strongholds and resumed harassment of the Egyptian army's tenuous lines of highland communication that linked San'a to Sa'dah in the north. Little wonder that the cease-fire broke down even before the political negotiations could be launched, and the buildup of Egyptian troops to nearly 60,000 by mid-1965 suggested that the Egyptians were planning yet another offensive to strengthen their bargaining position and possibly even to push on to final victory. When Egypt and Saudi Arabia signed a fresh agreement in August 1965 for ending the hostilities in Yemen, it was President 'Abd al-Nasir who proceeded to Saudi Arabia to negotiate with King Faysal on his home ground. Under the cease-fire concluded at Jiddah, Saudi Arabia pledged to stop its aid to the royalists, and Egypt to evacuate its troops from Yemen within ten months.

The republicans by this time had split into a pro-Egyptian faction and another that favored the progressive withdrawal of Egyptian forces from Yemen. The pro-Egyptian faction was led by 'Abdallah al-Salal, an Iraqi-trained Zaydi army officer who had helped organize the republican conspiracy in September 1962 and who became the first president of the republic. He also became the commander-in-chief of the army, promoting himself from colonel to field marshal by April 1963. At the outset, the Yemeni republicans, with Egyptian blessings, tried to establish and maintain a Zaydi-Shafi'i balance in the governing apparatus. Thus, a Cairo-born and educated Shafi'i, 'Abd al-Rahman al-Baydani, became the first prime minister. But as the fighting dragged on, Zaydis came to dominate the new regime. By January 1965, when General Hasan al-'Amri, a Zaydi also trained in Iraq, took over the premiership of a staunchly pro-Egyptian government, Zaydi military officers dominated the Yemen Arab Republic (Y.A.R.).

At this juncture, many republican civilians in both communities started pressing the Egyptians to reduce their military and political presence and transfer to the Y.A.R. more and more responsibilities for the management of its own affairs. The Egyptian government seemed prepared to experiment with such a proposal, perhaps because of disillusionment in Salal and his intimate military aides, who seemed incapable of uniting the republicans, and perhaps also because of the inability of the Egyptians to defeat the royalists. Accordingly, the Egyptians late in April brought Salal to Cairo, where he was held in custody. The Egyptians also ousted his then deputy, General 'Amri, and named Ahmad Muhammad Nu'man, a Shafi'i civilian, prime minister. The appointment was intended as a gesture to redress the sectarian balance and to enable the civilians to demonstrate their capacity to manage the government. Yet even Nu'man, the first civilian prime minister of the Y.A.R. with a substantially civilian cabinet, had to acquiesce to a majority of Zaydi ministers. Still, he attempted to reduce U.A.R. influence, by convening the cabinet without Egyptian participation and by excluding Egyptian advisers from the several ministries. It was in this period that the first evidence appeared of Yemen republican interest in working out its own settlement with the royalists at a tribal conference of republican and royalist shaykhs called by the Nu'man government early in May at Khmir. The government also attempted to raise a tribal force to supplement the regular army being trained by the Egyptians, so that the enlarged force might replace the Egyptian troops altogether.

The experiment with the civilian government came to an abrupt end late in June 1965 when the U.A.R. changed its mind and reinstated Salal and 'Amri, who restored Egyptian influence in San'a. It was at this time that 'Abd al-Nasir and Faysal signed the Jiddah agreement, which called for a conference of republicans and royalists at the end of November. In the preliminary negotiations between the parties for acceptable delegations, the hardliners led by Salal refused categorically to treat with the imam or with any of his Hamid al-Din clan. The royalists on their side refused to accept Salal or any of his intimates. Accordingly, the Egyptians again locked Salal up in Cairo. However, the conference at Harad, opening on 23 November as scheduled, failed to reach an accord because of differences over the structure of the proposed interim government and over the question of Egyptian troop withdrawal. By the start of 1966 'Abd al-Nasir had enlarged the size of his expeditionary force to its peak, estimated at 70,000 troops, with a warning that it would remain in Yemen until a final settlement. Nevertheless, the Egyptian forces were withdrawn from Sa'dah and regrouped within a more tenable triangular enclave that included San'a, Hudaydah, and Ta'izz, thereby leaving two-thirds of the country in the north and in the east to the royalists. At this time, too, the U.S.S.R. apparently forgave a large part of the Egyptian debt—amounting, according to one estimate, to the equivalent of $460 million—for equipment and supplies used in Yemen.

With Salal in Cairo, General 'Amri served as acting president and supreme commander, continuing the close cooperation with the U.A.R. 'Amri reduced the number of civilians in his cabinet and permitted the Egyptians to resume their management of the army, the currency, and the sensitive ministries. It was in the spring of 1966 that the U.A.R. began to cut back the size of its expeditionary force. Meanwhile, republican hostility toward Egypt hardened, and to check the trend, the U.A.R. sent Salal back to Yemen, this time having to reinstate him forcibly, even against the wishes of General 'Amri, who now sided with the anti-Egyptian faction. The outgoing government, which the faction dominated, was invited by the U.A.R. to come to Cairo and protest directly to President 'Abd al-Nasir. On arrival, the Yemeni delegation of forty-two ex-ministers and army officers, including 'Amri, were placed under house arrest, thus giving Salal freedom of action.

Naming himself prime minister, Salal proceeded to dismiss large numbers of civil servants and army officers who opposed his policies, imprisoned hundreds of others, and executed a handful. Even before the war with Israel, Egypt had become disenchanted with the inconclusive struggle in Yemen, as attested by the steady contraction of its expeditionary force, which fell below 40,000 by the spring of 1967. But not until the summit meeting of the Arab League, which met at Khartum in August to coordinate the members' policies on the consequences of the Six Day War, did the U.A.R. finally release the two score republican leaders who had been held in custody in the Egyptian capital for nearly a year. The summiteers also created a mission consisting of Iraq, Morocco, and Sudan to mediate the dispute over Yemen between the U.A.R. and Saudi Arabia. Such was the price that 'Abd al-Nasir had to pay for Saudi participation in the consortium of the oil-rich members of the Arab League which helped Egypt and Jordan balance their budgets after the defeat in June. This time, the U.A.R. carried out its pledge to evacuate Egyptian troops from Yemen, completing the operation before mid-December. A month earlier, a joint military-civilian coup d'état had overthrown the Egyptian puppet regime, while Salal was visiting Baghdad. The new junta experimented once more with a civilian prime minister and a largely civilian cabinet. But the experiment lasted only a few weeks, for General 'Amri resumed the premiership at the end of December 1967.

Following the Egyptian departure, the civil war in Yemen entered a new phase. The republicans still leaned heavily on outside props. The U.S.S.R. now furnished military weaponry directly, and with it technicians. At the start, Soviet pilots flew planes as air cover for the republican troops that were defending San'a against royalist encirclement in December 1967. When one of the planes was shot down, the U.S.S.R. became more cautious. Volunteer pilots were recruited in Syria to constitute the republican air force, while other volunteers from Algeria and from South Yemen, which won its independence from Britain in November 1967, reinforced the officer corps of the ground troops. Even Chinese Communist technicians, who had remained behind after the erection of the Hudaydah-San'a road, helped shore up the republican military machine by constituting a trained engineer unit.

In the circumstances, Saudi Arabia continued to back the royalists. Their tribesmen were still undergoing training in Saudi Arabia by expatriate French officers in Saudi pay, while British and German expatriates developed and operated a radio communications system for the tribal soldiers. The failure to invest San'a by early 1968 revealed basic cleavages in the royalist ranks. The rivalry between the imam and two young cousins divided the royalist camp at least three ways. Yet, even then, the royalist cause could not be written off, for the Zaydi millennial tradition infused the highlanders with a religious fervor that in the end gave their cause greater unity of purpose than the republicans could hope to achieve in a few short years.

There was thus no way of telling what political system might arise from the turmoil of prolonged civil war. Too many questions remained unanswered, even after the Egyptians had decided to cut their losses. If the external props were removed from both sides and the Yemenis were permitted to express their preferences, would the Zaydi tribal shaykhs demand the retention of the Hamid al-Din dynasty, or, minimally, the imamate under new management? After all, were not the tribal forces emerging from the civil war more powerful than ever, since they could claim major credit for holding the republicans to a stalemate despite the heavy U.A.R. military commitment? If the tribal shaykhs proved stubborn, as they had in the past, would their demands be acceptable to the Shafi'is and to the Zaydi republicans? Even if the imamate were restored, the administrative monopoly of the sayyids had almost certainly been broken. They were not popular with either the indigenous Zaydis or with the Shafi'is. But neither was republicanism, to judge from the frequent changes of constitution. Many Shafi'is believed the republic to be no more than a mask for continuing Zaydi hegemony, while Zaydi royalists seemed convinced that it placed the country under alien suzerainty.

Modernizing Monarchies

15

AN AMERICAN CLIENT: IRAN

In the Middle East, monarchies have survived only in countries where tribal populations remained assertive. This is not to say the converse: that wherever tribal populations remain assertive, monarchical government will be found. Iraq's monarchy disappeared in 1958: and Syria was republican at birth, despite the tribal and sectarian divisions of its society. Still it is notable that the military regimes in these two countries ran into difficulty precisely because of their societies.

The traditional monarchs, as the preceding chapters have shown, relied heavily on tribal forces for the internal defense of their regimes. Though designed in theory to safeguard the state against external aggression, the small "modernized" armies that were brought into being in these countries in the postwar years mainly served to enhance prestige. The modernizing monarchs for their part gave up tribal levies altogether and employed the modernized forces largely for upholding the regime against domestic opposition.

By the second postwar decade even the resistance of the traditional monarchies to modernization began to give ground, and the process, once begun, quickened in pace. In the small but growing towns the traditional middle class was starting to change into a modernizing one. Still, their societies remained relatively stable, with an overwhelming peasant and beduin population. The societies of the modernizing monarchies, by contrast, were more clearly transitional. They had already moved some distance away from the traditional patterns of organization, but the process was uneven, so that traditional and modernizing institutions and practices existed side by side.

The category of modernizing monarchies lost and gained members. If the traditional monarchies lasted, they tended to move into the modernizing category, as Kuwayt and Afghanistan did in the second postwar decade. This is not meant in any social Darwinian sense, which might suggest that the more modern society is the better one. Modernizing societies are more complicated, it is true, but complication is hardly a mark of quality. Once a society becomes modernized, the gap between political power and economic power that opens in the transitional society with the emergence of a modern middle class will tend to close, thus restoring stability to society. But stability, too, is not necessarily an index of quality.

The outcome of a military seizure of government at the traditional level, it might also be noted, may differ measurably from that at the modernizing level. The republican insurgents in Yemen in 1962 demonstrated that the regular forces had no modernizing middle class on which to erect public support for their regime, dispite the widespread discontent with the imamate. As has been seen, the U.A.R. had to furnish its Yemeni republican allies not only soldiers but also managers, technicians, and bureaucrats. No such difficulties faced the soldier politicians after their overturn of the modernizing monarchies of Egypt and Iraq, where in each case there was an established urban middle class. These military regimes could build up their own loyal bureaucrats and attract a popular following without summoning outside help. One key to a modernizing monarch's success seemed to lie either in his taking over direct command of the armed forces or in entrusting it to a close relative. If he failed to do so, as kings Faruq and Faysal did, he invited military intervention. Such monarchs became increasingly dependent on the armed forces for defense of their thrones; and the reliability of the security arrangements, no matter how ingenious and how tight, depended upon the ambitions of the most cunning army officer.

Reza Shah's Legacy

When Muhammad Reza Shah and Queen Suraya fled Iran on 16 August 1953, many experts predicted that the secret and hasty departure marked the end of the Pahlavi dynasty and perhaps of the monarchy. In less than a week the shah returned to Tehran in triumph, his political opponents vanquished. The shah's reinstatement brought to an end Iran's second experiment in limited monarchy in the twentieth century, giving way once more to royal absolutism. The abrupt change in the political system could not be explained convincingly without taking into account the Iranian army. The opponents of the Pahlavi dynasty, in their own year of triumph that preceded the crisis, had tried to reshape the organization and replace the management of the armed forces in the hope of redirecting their loyalty from the crown to an undefined alternative. The antiroyalists bungled the opportunity, however, and the very attempt to reduce the prestige of the army by curtailment of its budget and dismissal of senior officers reinforced the military ties to the dynasty. These ties in any case were vigorous and intimate, for the father of the shah had also been the father of Iran's modern army.

The Pahlavi dynasty, established in 1925, grew out of a military intrusion into politics in 1921 under the leadership of Reza Khan, a colonel in one of several uncoordinated military establishments in the country. But the monarchy itself, with interruptions of outside rule, claimed to reach back 2,500 years. In modern times Persia, as Iran was still known until 1935, never really lost its sovereignty, although it suffered several decades of political anarchy in the eighteenth century and found its independence almost snuffed out by Anglo-Russian occupation in the two world wars of the twentieth.

The first census ever taken in Iran (1956) revealed that some 19 million people lived in nearly 50,000 settlements. The census-takers had fixed places of settlement with populations greater than 5,000 as urban. For purposes of studying civil-military relations in a modernizing polity such as Iran, however, a more realistic dividing line between urban and rural would probably be towns with populations of 25,000 or more. On this reckoning the urban population in 1956 amounted to about 4.4 million, or 23 per cent of the total in forty towns and cities, nearly 1.5 million in the capital, Tehran. The approximately 14.6 million people, or 77 per cent, rural population included about 2.5 million nomads and seminomads, or 17 per cent of the rural total. Nomadism was thus prevalent in Iran, as was tribalism among the settled highlanders.

The atomistic condition of society was reinforced by the ethnic and linguistic diversity of the population. Probably no more than three of every five Iranians used Farsi (Persian) as their mother tongue, and among them were sizable numbers who spoke such discrete dialects as Gilaki and Mazandarani. On the details the census was unclear, since the government classified as Persian all settled inhabitants, peasants and townsmen alike, so long as they spoke one of the Iranian languages such as Kurdish, Luri, and Baluchi—all related to one another and to Persian from ancient times. The nearly two million Kurds chiefly lived in the western district of Kurdistan;[1] an estimated quarter-million Kurds, however, were living in the eastern district of Khurasan. Fewer than half the Kurds were nomads, and most of the rest, mountain peasants. South of Kurdistan in the Zagros Mountains in Luristan, and like the Kurds the half-million Lurs were partly settled, as contrasted with some 600,000 Bakhtiyaris farther south, who were still largely nomadic. Though tribally organized, the more than half-million Arabs of Khuzistan were not beduin. Predominantly nomadic were the approximately 400,000 Baluchis in the Makran highlands of the Zagros range in the extreme southeast, adjacent to the Baluchi communities of Pakistan and Afghanistan. The estimated quarter-million nomadic Qashqais speak their own Turkic dialect. So, too, do the four million almost wholly sedentary Azarbayjanis in the northwest, who are the largest Turkic-speaking ethnic group in the kingdom.

Ethnic and linguistic differences were more significant than the religious. Nevertheless it should be noted that at least 85 per cent of the population adhere to the established Shi'ah Islam of the Ja'fari rite, which embraces the doctrine of the twelve lineal descendants of Muhammad as the true imams, or leaders of the community of Islam, and therefore the only true successors of the Prophet. Set apart from the Shi'ah were the Kurdish, Arab, and Baluchi communities, all three adhering to Sunni Islam.

Under the Qajar dynasty (1795–1925) Persia suffered progressive decline in the second half of the nineteenth century as it was caught in the path of Russian and Anglo-Indian expansion, which gave rise by the turn of the century to the first nationalist movement in the kingdom. Indeed, only in response to such an external threat to sovereignty could nationalism in a country with a plural society like that of Persia become a unifying force. By 1906 the nationalists, who temporarily won to their banner in Tehran the religious elite, the merchants, and the small educated class forced the shah to promulgate a constitution providing for an elective *Majlis*, or legislature. They hoped that by checking the absolutism of the crown they would also be able to check the further advance of European imperialism.

Before constitutional government struck root, the country had been divided in 1907 into Russian (north) and British (southeast) spheres of influence separated by a buffer, under the terms of an Anglo-Russian convention. The arrangement, in effect, interposed the two European imperial powers between the shah and the constitutionalists, limiting the activities of each. Tsarist troops, who entered the Russian sphere in 1908 in support of the shah's abortive attempt to destroy the Majlis, thereafter remained in the

country. With the coming of the war in 1914 the influencing powers ignored the Persian declaration of neutrality and intervened more visibly in the domestic affairs of Persia, with Russian
and Russian-commanded Persian troops fighting Ottoman forces
in the north and Anglo-Indian-commanded Persian troops trying
to pacify tribes aroused by German agents in the south. The Majlis,
meanwhile, was suspended in 1915.

Instead of a single unified army, Persia had by the war's close at
least four distinct kinds of forces, established at different times and
functioning in varying states of organization and efficiency: the
Nizam, or "regular" army, the Persian Cossack Division, the gendarmerie, and the South Persia Rifles. The Nizam, composed of
provincial troops under the command of Qajar princes and levies
of tribes friendly to the dynasty under the command of their
khans, represented the remnant of a traditional Muslim army as
modified by more than a century of exposure to various and often
conflicting European military doctrines and weapons. The force
had long since lost its place as the shah's exclusive or even primary
military prop. By 1919 the Nizam fell below its stated size of
10,000, the morale of officers and men slackened because of salary
arrears, and weapons and uniforms were far from standard. Only
the Nizam's Central Brigade, expressly organized for duty in Tehran, was kept at its full operational strength of some 2,000 officers
and men, including cavalry and artillery as well as infantry.

Russian officers and NCOs trained and commanded the Persian
Cossack Division, which had been created in 1879 as an elite force
to safeguard the shah's person. The Persian Government financed
the division until 1916, when tsarist Russia took over its upkeep
and used the force for auxiliary wartime duty in the Russian-occu-
pied Persian north. When the Bolsheviks rose to power in the following year and repudiated tsarist policy in Persia as elsewhere, the
United Kingdom absorbed the financing of the Cossack Division
and its White Russian officers. The division survived the war as the
most efficient force in the land.

Meanwhile, the Persian Government in 1911 had employed
Swedish officers and NCOs to form a gendarmerie or rural con-
stabulary for keeping order and collecting taxes in the provinces.
The Swedish-commanded gendarmerie in World War I responded
to initiatives of German agents who were stirring tribes in the Za-
gros range to action against the Russians and the British. The
Swedish-German collusion accounted for Britain's decision in
March 1916 to raise, train, and finance in the British sphere the

South Persia Rifles (SPR) and place the force under Anglo-Indian command. The SPR actually came into being in the face of sustained opposition from the Persian Government. Indeed, between May and October 1918 the SPR was engaged almost wholly in suppressing uprisings among the Qashqais and other tribes in the south, provoked by German agents and by the Swedish officers of the gendarmerie.

At the war's close Britain was thus financing the SPR, still under Anglo-Indian command, and the Persian Cossack Division, still under White Russian command. By such measures and by the addition of a small Anglo-Indian force, based on Qazvin, the second influencing power tried to step into the breach, opened by the disappearance of the tsarist regime. While the war lasted, the British still had to contend also with Ottoman troops in the north; after the Ottoman armistice, the British turned to preventing Communist Russia from subjugating Iran or dismembering it or even filling the tsarist vacuum. With these ends in view, Britain signed an agreement with Persia in August 1919 which in effect would have converted the Muslim kingdom into a preferential or dependent ally.

An Anglo-Persian commission, which submitted its report on a proposed unified army in 1920, estimated the over-all size of the European-trained forces as exceeding 22,000 men: 6,000 in the SPR, 8,000 in the Persian Cossack Division, and 8,400 in the Swedish gendarmerie. The commission recommended the fusion of the three forces into a single army under a ministry of war, and the separation of the police under the ministry of the interior, proposing a combined strength of some 40,000 men as an initial target and ultimately one of 60,000. The chief military adviser was to be British, and the chief staff officer Persian. The South Persia Rifles, it was understood, would form the nucleus of the projected unified army.

In preparation for the change, the British Embassy induced the imperial Persian government in October 1920 to dismiss the White Russian officers still commanding the Cossack Division. But the embassy proved too weak to persuade the imperial government at the same time to fill the command slots with British officers, as recommended by the mixed commission. Persia was not a country in which the prosecution of the war had called for a buildup of large Anglo-Indian forces, as occurred next door in the conquest of Mesopotamia (later Iraq) from the Ottoman Empire. With only marginal military capability in Persia at the war's close, and with the public in Britain clamoring for retrenchment, the prospect of sending British or Anglo-Indian reinforcements to the scene was almost nonexistent. Britain was unable to prevent the Bolsheviks from occupying Gilan and Mazandaran in 1920, thereby reviving among Persian nationalists the traditional fear of their powerful Russian and Anglo-Indian neighbors.

Since the British officers attached to the Cossack Division remained advisers even after the discharge of the White Russians, the top command of the kingdom's most effective military establishment was virtually thrust on its Persian officers. Among them was Reza Khan, a third-generation officer originally from the Caspian province of Mazandaran who had risen to the rank of colonel by 1920. The Persian government by this time had all but broken down, and its two imperial neighbors were too distracted by their own problems to exploit their advantages. With the country literally begging for leadership, Reza Khan with some 3,000 Persian Cossacks joined civilian conspirators at their invitation to stage on 21 February 1921 a coup d'état that encountered no resistance and that brought a crusading journalist, Sayyid Ziya al-Din Tabatabai, to the premiership and Reza Khan to the supreme military command. Five days later the new Persian regime signed an agreement with Communist Russia repudiating all tsarist privileges in Persia. This act virtually killed the unratified 1919 Anglo-Persian instrument, and with it disappeared the British sphere of influence. Reza Khan also refused to ratify the Soviet treaty until the Red Army troops were withdrawn from Gilan at the end of 1921, thus eliminating any prospect of a renewal of the Russian sphere in the north. Late in April 1921, meanwhile, he had become minister of war without surrendering the military command, and a month later Sayyid Ziya was forced out of the premiership and out of the country.

As minister of war (1921–23) and later also as prime minister (1923–25), Reza Khan integrated the motley military establishments into a unified army, in general accord with the proposal of the mixed commission, merely ignoring those provisions that would have made the army an instrument of British policy. Consequently, the Persian Cossack Division became the core of the national army, which assimilated officers and men from the gendarmerie. The South Persia Rifles were dissolved altogether. As early as 1922 Reza Khan began, with Majlis approval, to send officer candidates each year to military academies in France and later elsewhere in Europe. By 1925, when he had an army of 40,000 troops with a nucleus of European-trained officers, he persuaded the pliant Majlis to enact a law calling for two years of compulsory military service for all men reaching the age of twenty-one. On completion of active duty, the conscripts remained for twenty-three years longer in the reserves, though with progressively declining obligations. As *sardar sipah*, or supreme military commander, Reza Khan kept the machinery of the central government firmly in his grip by the simple device of retaining martial law, Which enabled him to develop a personal military dictatorship. In the capital he gradually replaced the politicians of the old regime with "technicians" of his own choice, and to the provinces, as he pacified them, he sent loyal army officers as governors. The Majlis formally ended the Qajar dynasty in the fall of 1925 and, sitting as a constituent assembly six weeks later, elected as monarch the sardar sipah, who styled himself Reza Shah Pahlavi.

By 1930 the army comprised an estimated 80,000 men plus a gendarmerie, known as the Highway Patrol, of 12,000. As an emergency measure, after the outbreak of World War II, the gendarmerie was absorbed into the regular army, and their combined ranks had grown by 1941 to about 125,000. There were in addition an air force and a navy with about 1,000 men each. In creating his armed forces, Reza Shah placed heavy stress on amassing large numbers of professional officers, of whom some 300 by then had been trained in France and Germany. Two military schools in Tehran were directed in the 1930s by French officers and Iranian alumni of the European academies. The shah deliberately made the Iranian Army officer-heavy so that he might, in case of need, rapidly mobilize the reserves. To cement the allegiance of the officers to the crown, Reza Shah gave them unusual privileges, and to many he transferred titles to large tracts of land.

Reza, it was commonly held, was an Iranian Atatürk, and indeed there were certain superficial similarities between the two men. Both brought new leadership to their countries, repudiated imperialism, and reduced to a minimum their dependence on Europe; both attempted to refashion the governmental administration on the European model; and both dedicated themselves to modernization by building schools, factories, and railroads and by forcibly changing social practices. There the parallel ends, however, even though Reza, in his program for modernizing Persia, emulated the founder of the Turkish Republic. In 1924, Reza also entertained the hope of converting Persia into a republic, but he bowed to the strong opposition of the religious leaders by keeping the monarchy.

The Turkish Republic became a relatively homogeneous country, after accepting the loss of the Arab provinces of the former dynastic Ottoman Empire and by negotiating an agreement with Greece in 1923 for the exchange of populations. By contrast, Persia remained fundamentally a country of minorities, and Persia's plural society continued plaguing Reza Shah as he sought to use his unified army to unify the people.

From the outset, when Reza first created a united army, he was determined to discipline the troublesome nomadic tribes. He dealt with them singly and successively, usually timing his action as punishment for brigandage or some other transgression of the law. The shah had two motives in his tribal policy; to destroy potential political and military opposition to the central government, and to restore order in the provinces. As he imposed central authority on the tribes, he disarmed the men and sent the khans, or leaders, for enforced residence in Tehran, where some were imprisoned, others brought to trial, and not a few executed. A small number of tribes were even transplanted from the Zagros mountain districts to the north. But the Shah's policy of compelling the tribes to give up nomadism and settle down as farmers aroused such fierce resistance that throughout the 1930s he had to contend with revolts among such major groups as the Bakhtiyaris, the Kurds, and the Qashqais.

By the time Reza became shah he had already created a personal military dictatorship. He did not abrogate the constitution, however, nor did he destroy the institutions for which it provided. They were simply bent to serve his purposes. The cabinets consisted wholly of the shah's factotums, the Majlis of servile deputies drawn chiefly from wealthy landowners (not a few hand-made by himself), and the bureaucracy of submissive civil servants.

Experiment in Limited Monarchy

Reza Shah's determined efforts to escape entanglements with the U.S.S.R. and Britain led him by the end of the 1930s to establish close relations with Nazi Germany, which outlasted the start of World War II. Understandably, the peacetime foreign policy asset turned into a wartime liability once the U.S.S.R. and Britain became allies. Soviet and British troops entered Iran late in the summer of 1941, less than three months after the Nazi invasion of Russia, and swiftly crushed Iranian military resistance. British forces occupied the south and Soviet forces the north, except for Tehran, which continued occupation-free as the Iranian capital. The occupiers declared that their action was designed to round up

Axis agents and to prevent possible Nazi seizure of the country. The British also desired to protect their oil interests in the south. But, above all, the occupiers were set on opening up an all-seasonal supply route to Russia, for the Turkish Straits were closed to such traffic because of the war.

The unexpected Soviet-British military presence traumatized Iran. It called vividly to mind the Anglo-Russian occupation in the First World War, when the European imperial powers believed that they had come for keeps, and aroused genuine fears among politically articulate Iranians that this time their northern and southern neighbors would not depart. The occupation could hardly have been expected to arouse enthusiastic Iranian cooperation. The occupiers substantially abridged the kingdom's external sovereignty, and Iran had no choice but to sever diplomatic relations with Germany and Italy.

To save the self-made dynasty when the occupation started, Reza Shah abdicated in favor of his son, Muhammad Reza. The new shah, to dispel his own anxieties and those of his people, pressed the U.S.S.R. and Britain to place the occupation on a legal basis with firm assurances of its eventual termination. Accordingly, in January 1942 Iran signed a treaty of alliance in which Britain and the Soviet Union pledged (Article 1) "jointly and severally . . . to respect the territorial integrity, sovereignty and political independence of Iran." They also promised (Article 5) that their "forces . . . shall be withdrawn from Iranian territory not later than six months after all hostilities between the Allied Powers and Germany and her associates have been suspended by the conclusion of an armistice or armistices, or on the conclusion of peace between them, whichever date is the earlier." [2]

To expedite the delivery of war matériel to the U.S.S.R. under the Lend-Lease Act, the United States entered Iran in mid-1942, later setting up in the British zone a Persian Gulf Command that at its height consisted of nearly 30,000 troops. The shah sought to formalize the American military presence, but the United States refused to adhere to the tripartite treaty of alliance or even to sign a special bilateral agreement on American troops in the kingdom. Washington preferred instead the status of a nonoccupying power, with rights acquired for American soldiers by special arrangement with Britain. Muhammad Reza's perseverance paid off, for the United States, in the Tehran Declaration signed on 1 December 1943 by Roosevelt, Churchill, and Stalin, also subscribed to the pledge of maintaining "the independence, sovereignty and territorial integrity of Iran" and promised it economic aid during and after the war.[3]

The external politics of Iran subtly interplayed with domestic politics. Reza Shah's imperious policy had restored monarchical absolutism in a strong military cast; he used his army to unify a fractured country and to discipline the population while he attempted, often by ill-advised means, to modernize the society and the economy. Even before he became shah, he had silenced almost all the politicians, but he failed to form any political party in support of his policies and throughout his reign tolerated no political opposition. Reza Shah's departure turned the clock of domestic politics back to the eve of his personal rule. Muhammad Reza at twenty-one reached the throne prematurely, his education for rule far from complete. He had studied in Switzerland and underwent military training in Iran and a brief royal apprenticeship by observation at his father's court. However, the young shah inherited not a functioning regime, but one that had been gravely damaged by rough handling in the Soviet-British occupation. He could never hope to fill his father's boots so long as the occupation forces were around, yet he had no intention of abnegating his royal prerogatives, and for a dozen years he remained uncertain of his political identity.

The 1942 treaty of alliance stipulated (Article 4) that the Soviet and British troops "will disturb as little as possible the administration and the security forces of Iran, the economic life of the country, the normal movements of the population and the application of Iranian laws and regulations." Practice, especially by the Russians, violated the letter no less than the spirit of the formal agreement. The Soviet authorities treated the Iranian provinces as occupied enemy territory; they seized for their own use agricultural produce and the output of the few factories, and thereby exacerbated the serious food shortages and the uncontrolled inflation. The Russians released Iranian Communists imprisoned by Reza Shah, and less than a month after the start of the occupation inspired the formation of the Tudeh (Masses) Party, which grew steadily in size. The U.S.S.R. locked up its zone to all but Soviet nationals and resident Iranians, denying entry even to British and American officials charged with expediting American aid to Russia. The British never tried to shut their zone. But, together with the Russians, they confiscated trucks and took over the operation of the Trans-Iranian Railroad in their separate spheres, redirecting transport facilities to serve the corridor for sending aid to Russia. Iranian interests were subordinated to the safeguard of this activity, and when the Iranian government became petulant, neither occupier seemed averse to compelling the dismissal of ministers and a change of policies.

The government of Iran manifestly exercised no more than residual powers. Even within the crippled polity, Muhammad Reza did not command public affairs. The occupation destroyed the shah's absolutism, shattered the army on which it was based, and thereby put an end to centralized rule. It cleaved the unified country into north and south and, in effect, chopped both zones into smaller districts by releasing from house arrest in Tehran the khans, who reasserted traditional rights of autonomy upon rejoining their tribes. To compound the confusion, the Soviet and British authorities in their several zones took advantage for their own ends of restiveness and hostility to the central government, especially in the tribal districts. Their censorship and arbitrary intrusion into domestic politics in the name of the war effort stifled political liberties. Still, despite the imposed fragmentation of the country and the meddling, the Iranian politicians enjoyed considerable freedom of political action under the reactivated 1906 constitution. A surprising number of them, including Shi'i religious leaders and tribal khans who had outlived the ordeal of two decades of enforced political idleness, came out of hiding at the first opportunity to resume participation in Iranian competitive politics.

For the duration of the war, the dynasty was protected by the mutual suspicions of the occupiers, and, more positively, by the support of the United States after the Tehran Declaration. However, the shah's role was drastically circumscribed: what he lost in the transfer of political power the Majlis undeniably gained under the revived 1906 constitution. The fourteenth Majlis, elected in 1943, seized the purse strings, as was its constitutional right, and began insisting, also in accordance with the constitution, that all cabinets and even individual ministerial appointments receive its vote of confidence. The antiroyalist politicians, however, seemed even less prepared for organizing political parties in the revitalized democratic system than the new shah for assuming the responsibilities of the crown. The Majlis proved less consistent and less successful in asserting its powers of ministerial appointments and dismissals than on budgetary matters; however, in 1947, Muhammad Reza proved unable to persuade the friendly fifteenth Majlis to amend the constitution by making the prime minister responsible to the crown. As time wore on, the shah's struggle with the antiroyalist politicians focused on ministerial appointments, especially, as we shall see, on the designation of ministers of war, since the constitution vested in the crown the supreme military command and exclusive powers to grant commissions and promote officers. In any case, Muhammad Reza enjoyed a two-year respite—time to begin to find his bearings, since a majority of the deputies in the thirteenth Majlis, elected while Reza Shah still sat on the throne, remained faithful to the dynasty to which they owed their privileged status. But the shah's friends in the Majlis had no party of their own at the time of the occupation and formed none until the late 1950s. In planning for the future, Muhammad Reza was thus compelled to fall back on the prestige of the crown and to invoke its powers under the constitution, including the formal appointment and dismissal of ministers.

The young shah inherited a decimated, demoralized, and denuded army. Reza Shah had cultivated the myth of his army's invincibility, but made the mistake of advertising defense against external aggression as its primary mission. That mission, at best, was an ostensible one; the army was never intended to stand up against the forces of a major power. Its real mission was the domestic, political one of uniting the country and building up and protecting the shah's influence. The army's disgrace after defeat was magnified by the antipathy of large segments of the population, particularly in the tribal areas, toward the main instrument of the shah's despotic power. The army simply fell apart, as thousands of troops deserted, and became immobilized by the occupiers' seizure of its motor transport. Much of the military equipment that the invaders had not captured was abandoned and later retrieved by tribesmen. The rebuilding and refitting of the army to which the shah soon addressed himself required the aid of a foreign government acceptable to the U.S.S.R. and to Britain. Fortunately, from the shah's standpoint, the logical candidate was at hand—the United States.

Muhammad Reza's appeal to the United States formed part of a larger program that he and his aides fashioned to shore up Iran's political defense against the occupying powers. As early as 1942 the United States accepted the invitation to send to Tehran, at Iranian expense, financial, military, and other technical advisory missions to help rationalize the administration of his realm. The small military mission limited its advisory activities to the supply and other noncombatant branches of the army. The mission's initial report "specified four necessities as basic to Army reorganization: limiting total strength to 88,000; retaining only the best officers; providing a reasonable scale of pay; and providing adequate motor transport." [4] The United States also sent a second mission to advise in transforming the imperial gendarmerie into an efficient constabulary for the rural and tribal areas, although the army was still to handle major tribal security problems. The military and gendarmerie missions were arranged with Britain's blessings, because the British in their zone, unlike the Russians in the north, eschewed responsibility for domestic security even when tribal revolts against the central government interfered with the safety of the supply route to the U.S.S.R. The Soviet Union, in fact, confiscated for use by its own troops the only substantial barracks in the north outside Tehran, permitted in its zone only token units of the Iranian army and gendarmerie, and wholly excluded the American advisors. Little wonder that even before the end of the war, the United States began to suspect the motives of Soviet policy in northern Iran.

During and immediately after the war, American policy had two purposes: to uphold the integrity and independence of Iran, and to strengthen its armed forces. Since the shah had taken the initiative in the pursuit of such a policy, it was he who received the accolade and the censure in Iran. For the United States, the dual purposes of its Iranian policy were inseparable; for Iran, they were not.

The United States honored its pledge to safeguard Iranian sovereignty, at the United Nations and through normal diplomatic channels, by firmly resisting the Russian-organized secessionist movements in Azarbayjan and Kurdistan in 1945–46 and by insisting on the withdrawal of the Red Army units that lingered in the Soviet zone beyond the contractual date. The Majlis in October 1947 also found the courage to repudiate, by a vote of 100 to 2, the draft agreement on oil that the U.S.S.R. had exacted from Iran in 1946 as the price for terminating the occupation. The near-absence of dissent could be ascribed in part to the Tudeh's boycott of the election of the fifteenth Majlis. While there is no way of knowing with certitude how many Tudeh deputies might have been returned in 1947, the virtual national consensus in opposition to the Soviet sledge-hammer policy in Iran could not be denied. The pro-Soviet party leaders must have taken their decision not to enter the contest because of fear of losing one or more of the eight seats that they had won four years earlier.

The decision to prolong the American military and gendarmerie missions had been taken by the cabinet without referral to the Majlis but under its original enabling act of October 1943, and the signing of the new military mission agreement of 6 October 1947 escaped primary notice at the time because of the preoccupation of the politicians with the Majlis debate on the draft Soviet oil contract. Public political reaction was therefore delayed until early in 1948, when the Majlis considered the terms of a loan from the United States for the purchase of war surplus. After heated debate, the Majlis finally approved acceptance, not of the $25-million credit that the United States originally proffered, but of only $10 million, and even then the vote of endorsement was 79 to 6 with 10 abstentions. The difference between the votes in the Majlis rejecting the Soviet oil agreement and accepting the American loan could not be attributed solely or even largely to the vigorous campaign of the Tudeh Party and to the thinly disguised threats of the U.S.S.R.

No deep probing was necessary to ascertain underlying reasons for the non-Communist hostility in Iran to American military aid. Many antiroyalist politicians objected to the American missions and military equipment, not because of objection to a strong Iranian army as such or fear of the growth of excessive American influence, but because they feared that such an army might become the private political instrument of the shah. The tribal khans could greet only with deepest apprehension the decision to prolong the American missions, for in their view a powerful army almost assured a return to the type of autocracy and the hated tribal policies that the shah's father had framed. But even the urban politicians, among them the 'ulama, were no less perturbed, for they too recalled their earlier disfranchisement and were afraid that an efficient and well-equipped army might encourage the shah to destroy their regained political liberties.

On these ambivalences, doubts, and hesitations the Tudeh Party traded. The party had admittedly begun to tarnish in the wake of the embarrassing Soviet defeats in the north. Yet it remained, as the kingdom's only ideological party, the embodiment of a protest movement against the Pahlavi dynasty and its record of harsh rule under its founder, against the gross social inequalities inherited from the remoter past, and against the obscurantism of the re-enfranchised religious leaders. Because the United States and Britain assisted the shah in the early postwar years, they were identified with reaction by the war-expanded urban educated class that resented its continued exclusion from national politics, since the antiroyalist deputies were almost wholly drawn from the same landowning, religious, and tribal elites as were the royalist deputies.

Of greater pertinence was the altered political system after the restoration of full sovereignty in 1946. Iranian politics had acquired by then a surrealist quality, with the shah quietly trying to play an absolutist role while publicly pretending to be the very essence of a constitutional monarch. In reality, he had to compete with the Majlis and the antiroyalist politicians because his powers were constrained. In their rediscovered freedom, the antiroyalist politicians were determined to entrench themselves as the real rulers of the country, for constitutional politics in Iran under Muhammad Reza Shah had become in the early postwar years the politics of mutual destruction. Either the politicians would progressively take over the machinery of government and in so doing reduce the shah to a figurehead, if not eliminate him altogether; or the shah would triumph and in so doing again cut the politicians down to puppet size. Given the mood of the country and of the political rivals, no middle solution seemed possible. What little confidence the shah had come to reciprocate with the antiroyalist non-Communist politicians in the common struggle against the occupation was later swiftly dissipated in their own struggle for power. In this phase of the contest the shah did not attempt to form a political organization. He simply continued to rely on his claimed constitutional powers, however fuzzy these had become, and he appealed for popular support by seeking to project an image of a nationalist, forward-looking reformer, who nevertheless favored a strong modern army to hold his realm together against the machinations of foreign-supported conspirators.

The shah's attempt at modernizing the armed forces with American aid was hampered by Majlis control over government finances. The Majlis closely scrutinized requested miilitary outlays, in part because the deputies tended to be suspicious of the armed forces and in part, in the war years at least, because the deputies themselves were held in check by the American Director General of Finance, Arthur Millspaugh, who until his dismissal early in 1945 exercised the executive powers that the Majlis had conferred on him in a vain effort to balance the Iranian budget. During the Soviet crisis in 1946, the shah and the top command began pressing the United States to expand the scope of the American mission to encompass the entire military establishment.

Unlike Turkey and Greece, Iran did not initially qualify under the Truman Doctrine for grant military aid because its Soviet crisis had been "resolved." Nevertheless Iran was authorized to purchase war surplus and, although it started its procurement of such matériel on a modest scale, the army for the first time was given the prospect of acquiring military hardware of recent design. Under the revised terms, the new mission focused on developing a comprehensive, integrated army school system on the United States model, and, beginning in 1950, Iranian officers were sent to the United States for training as instructors. The size of the army nearly doubled from 65,000 in 1946 to 123,000 (among them nearly 8,000 officers) five years later. Similarly, the air force was increased from about 1,400 to nearly 3,300 in the same period, and the navy from 440 to nearly 1,200. The American gendarmerie mission also survived World War II, but the size of the gendarmerie was kept essentially at a level of 20,000 men in the early postwar period.

The contest between the shah and the politicians reached its climax in 1952–53 over the issue of responsibility for management of the armed forces. By then, the antiroyalist politicians had succeeded in bolstering the power of the Majlis by adding to its control over the budget, control over appointment and dismissal of all ministers except the minister of war. In April 1951 Dr. Muhammad Musaddiq, the leader of the antiroyalist opposition, had become prime minister as paramount spokesman for the nationalization of the British-owned Anglo-Iranian Oil Company. To his banner flocked the antiroyalist National Front that he had helped form in 1949; the pro-Soviet Tudeh Party that had been outlawed in 1949 after an unsuccessful attempt on the life of the shah and later became, with undisguised Soviet backing, a protagonist of republicanism; and the conservative 'ulama who looked for leadership to Ayatallah Sayyid Abu al-Qasim Kashani. Before requesting a confidence vote for his new cabinet in July 1952, Prime Minister Musaddiq sought from the seventeenth Majlis full powers for six months to legislate reforms by decree and from the shah the right to become minister of war in his own government. When the Majlis and the shah turned these demands down, Musaddiq resigned in a test of power. The National Front, with the support of the religious leaders and of the Tudeh Party, staged popular demonstrations in Tehran that threatened to become uncontrollable. Fearing civil war, the shah recalled Musaddiq to the premiership within five days of his resignation and acceded to his request for the war ministry portfolio. In August, the Majlis approved the bill granting Musaddiq the right to legislate by decree for the next six months.

At the time that Musaddiq became war minister, there were an estimated 240 generals and 500 colonels in active service. In Musaddiq's year of management of what he came to designate the ministry of national defense, he systematically discharged scores of older officers originally recruited by Reza Shah and loyal to his son. The prime minister also substantially reduced the budget of the armed forces and the size and activities of the American mission. In the spring of 1953 an eight-man committee of the Majlis determined that the shah was only the titular commander-in-chief and that the national defense minister would direct the army and execute the shah's constitutional powers of appointment and promotion of army officers. As the lines of conflict between the royalists and the antiroyalists sharpened, the dismissed officers rallied to the shah and overturned the Musaddiq regime in August.

Musaddiq's manifest inability to put an end to the Pahlavi dynasty could be attributed to many causes. He had mastered the art of bringing out the urban masses, especially the students of the University of Tehran and of the high schools in the larger cities. But he never channeled these masses into continuing political endeavor. Musaddiq formed no political party either on his ascent to the premiership or in his twenty-seven months in power. He even ignored the National Front, which, in his last months in office, disintegrated into rival factions. By then he also lost the backing of the fiery speaker of the Majlis, Ayatallah Kashani, who dominated conservative religious opinion. Musaddiq, moreover, spurned the offers of further cooperation from the Communist Tudeh Party. Musaddiq's hard-core but organized followers belonged to that segment of the urban educated class who opposed the traditional landed oligarchy, whether royalist or antiroyalist.

Constitutional Absolutism, Iranian Style

The removal of Musaddiq did not immediately usher in personal rule, for after shackling the politicians, the shah was beholden to the generals and the army. He was also beholden to the United States, whose discreet intervention helped put an end to the Musaddiq regime. At this juncture the United States and the shah shared fully the desire to root out the Communists who had penetrated major government ministries and infiltrated the officer and NCO ranks of the armed forces. Already the largest and best disciplined political party in the kingdom, the Tudeh Party continued growing during the stubborn Anglo-Iranian oil crisis. The pursuit of containment dictated that the United States take action to arrest the spread of communism in a weak country that barely escaped Soviet domination. Otherwise, the interests of the United States and of the shah overlapped only moderately.

The Eisenhower Administration might have been able, for example, to accommodate itself to Musaddiq, if he had shown some practical political sense. He appeared at the start of his premiership to unite nationalist sentiment behind him, but he neglected the opportunity for institutionalizing his popular support and left his followers dangling. Nor was he able to disengage the military establishment from its ties to the shah or even neutralize it while trying to mobilize a paramilitary substitute loyal to himself. As an alumnus of Reza Shah's school for the enforced idleness of politicians, Musaddiq in truth was still waging the struggle against Reza Shah. Musaddiq failed altogether to adjust his techniques and his aims to the swiftly changing political realities of postwar Iran.

At the outset, the reinstated shah leaned heavily on the United States for funds to replenish an empty exchequer and for an oil settlement that would satisfy Iranian nationalists and the operating oil companies. Nor did he overlook his armed forces. Iran did not have to enact new legislation or negotiate new enabling instruments for the resumption of military aid. The American mission, though hamstrung by Musaddiq, never ceased functioning, and an agreement with the United States of 23 May 1950 had already made Iran eligible for grant aid. Prime Minister General Fazlallah Zahidi, who organized the royalist coup d'état against Musaddiq, did not have to introduce martial law. Zahidi simply prolonged the state of emergency that had already been in effect since March 1951. As the first order of business, he started rounding up the enemies of the shah. A military court sentenced Musaddiq in December 1953 to three years in prison, and his army chief of staff, General Taqi Riyahi, to two years.

The military government prohibited Kashani and the 'ulama from engaging in politics, but its main efforts were dedicated to smashing the Tudeh Party. The assault on the party was directed by the military governor of Tehran, and later by Brigadier Timur Bakhtiyar. With the aid of Captain J. J. Leonard, a veteran of the Chicago police force who had served as counterintelligence chief in Hawaii and later in Korea, Bakhtiyar assembled and trained a staff in the use of FBI techniques for penetrating civilian subversive organizations. The army, meanwhile, undertook its own self-cleansing operation. Military counterintelligence uncovered hundreds of officers (mostly below field grade) and of NCOs who belonged to military cells of the Tudeh Party. All were arrested and tried by military courts and some two dozen officers were executed. By 1955 the back of the Tudeh Party, as then constituted, was broken, and in the decade that followed it proved unable to regain its vigor. Muhammad Reza lifted martial law in September 1956, and two months later converted the counterespionage office into a permanent agency of the government. Bakhtiyar, by then a major general, became the first director of the State Organization for Intelligence and Security (*Sazman-i Ettela'at va Amniyat-i Keshwar*), or SAVAK, as the new agency was commonly known. Attached to the office of the prime minister, SAVAK exercised jurisdiction only over civilians. The United States helped design the counterespionage agency primarily to uncover Communists, but the shah utilized it against all his political opponents.

Following the removal of Communist and antiroyalist officers from the armed forces in 1953–54, the shah, with American cooperation, finally put into effect an accelerated program of military modernization and expansion. With the psychological and political barriers removed, the shah tossed caution to the winds. No longer accounting in detail to the Majlis, he abolished the legislative restraints on the size of the American military and gendarmerie missions. He invited and accepted whatever level of military aid the United States was prepared to give Iran. Even more than in the past, the shah's demands exceeded the liberality of the United States, which paid much of the cost of new equipment and training—more than $400 million in the first seven years.

In these years the army grew from 120,000 officers and men to 190,000; the air force doubled to 8,000 and the navy to more than 4,000. An economic crisis in the early 1960s, which marked the start of an economic stabilization program, coincided with a projected progressive decline in American aid and forced the shah to accept the counsel of his advisers and of the American military mission to substitute quality for quantity. The armed forces were accordingly cut back from 205,000 in 1961 to 185,000 five years later. Only the air force continued expanding to an estimated 10,000 in mid-1965. But the cost of defense rose steadily (see Table 9) from 2.5 billion rials in 1953–54 to 14.2 billion in 1960–61 and then to 23.9 billion five years later. Until 1962–63 defense expenditure exceeded or roughly kept pace with investment in development but thereafter fell progressively behind, as the Third Five-Year Plan induced an unprecedented growth of the economy. In the circumstances, in the peak years of military spending (1959–60

TABLE 9. Iran: Force Levels, Government Expenditures, and GNP, 1953/54–1966/67

| | Population (millions) | Force Levels (thousands) | Government Expenditures (billions of Iranian rials) | | | GNP (billions of rials) | Defense Expenditures (as % of GNP) |
			Defense (including internal security and justice)	Development	Total		
1953/54 [a]	17.9 [d]		2.5	1.6	12.1		
1954/55	18.2 [d]		4.0	1.8	14.1		
1955/56	18.5 [d]	135	5.0	4.4	20.5		
1956/57	18.9		6.2	7.8	27.0		
1957/58	19.3		8.4	11.7	34.5		
1958/59	19.7		11.3	12.5	39.9		
1959/60	20.1		14.0	12.8	45.8	292.5	4.8
1960/61	20.2	202	14.2	14.8	48.6	331.3	4.3
1961/62	20.7		14.7	14.6	50.2	322.0	4.6
1962/63	21.2		16.1	17.5	59.7	334.9	4.8
1963/64	22.2		17.1	21.8	64.2	356.7	4.8
1964/65 [b]	22.9		19.8	30.6	79.1	390.0	5.1
1965/66 [c]	23.4	185	23.9	55.4	112.7	441.6	5.4
1966/67	23.7					485.6	

SOURCES: IMF, *International Financial Statistics*; C. Issawi, "Iran's Economic Upsurge," *The Middle East Journal*, Vol. 21 (Autumn, 1967), p. 460.

[a] Fiscal year ends 20 March.
[b] Provisional.
[c] Budget estimates.
[d] Rough estimate based on 1956 census.

—1965–66) the government devoted no more than an average of 4.8 per cent of the GNP to the armed forces.

Muhammad Reza, in the mid-1960s, was the real as well as the constitutional commander-in-chief of the revitalized army. The shah alone made appointments to the general staff and selected the commanders of all major units and of the military schools. He made all senior promotions on his own, and the junior promotions, while recommended by the unit commanders, required his approval. He treated the top commanders as personal friends. To hold the confidence of the officers, Muhammad Reza pampered them with high salaries and special perquisites such as free housing and luxury imports, including cars and refrigerators at generous discounts, and a lavish officers' club in Tehran. Nor did the shah neglect the junior officers. He took a personal interest in their training, even attending graduation exercises at all the military schools.

In the decade and a half after 1950, some 2,000 Iranian officers were sent to service schools in the United States. Others went to France and Germany. Training abroad whetted the appetite of these officers for the latest and most expensive hardware, and the shah in turn became an enthusiastic and tireless proponent of their interests in his annual appeals to Washington. The quality of Iranian military leadership steadily improved, as the incompetent and the corrupt officers were weeded out. Some 300 colonels with no prospect of promotion were dismissed in 1961 after 25–30 years of service; somewhat later a handful of generals were brought to trial by Prime Minister 'Ali Amini as part of his anticorruption drive. By the mid-1960s, it was Muhammad Reza Shah's army, no longer that of his father.

The shah clearly dominated the army, and the army, in turn, dominated all the security services. The director of SAVAK, all his principal aides, and much of their highly trained staff were either army officers or NCOs. Major General Hasan Pakravan (1961–65), who succeeded Bakhtiyar as director, was generally believed to have tried to reduce at least the visible military influence on the counterespionage service. Despite his efforts, SAVAK's military core showed through its civilian casing.

Similarly, the commanders of the gendarmerie and of the national police were always generals, and many of their subordinate officers were also borrowed from the army. Below the officer level, the gendarmerie and the police consisted only of volunteers, but these for the most part were veterans of the conscript army. The gendarmerie were the rural, the tribal, and, after 1963, the frontier police, for in that year the Border Guard of some 5,000 men was transferred to it from the army. The American gendarmerie mission focused on teaching the gendarmes the proper use and care of equipment and on staffing the force school with officers trained in the United States, so that the improving standards of performance might become self-perpetuating. The force itself nearly doubled in size to about 35,000 by 1966. Radio networks were progressively linking the more than 1,750 widely dispersed gendarmerie posts to Tehran, enabling the central headquarters to direct major operations. The national police, a force of more than 25,000 officers and men in the mid-1960s, supervised routine security problems in the urban areas. Nearly one-third of the police were stationed in Tehran, attesting to the problems of law and order in the capital where high-school and university students as often as allowed joined unemployed workers in street politics. Whenever such demonstrations threatened to explode into riots, the army intervened, as it did also when the gendarmerie were unable to restore order in tribal areas.

The army also dominated the war ministry, which handled only the administrative and financial affairs of the armed forces. The war minister was a general of Muhammad Reza's choice who presented for royal endorsement the names of all officers he wished to assign to the ministry. The non-operational affairs of the gendarmerie and the police fell under the jurisdiction of the interior ministry, always headed by a man, occasionally a general, in whom the shah reposed high confidence. Nor was it uncommon for Muhammad Reza to call upon general officers to accept troublesome portfolios in the cabinet. The top officers of the armed forces, the commanders of the gendarmerie and the national police, and the director of SAVAK reported directly to the shah, who also took all major operational decisions of the several security services.

If the shah's rule stopped here, it could doubtless be said that he had established by the mid-1960s a police state even more efficient than his father's. That Muhammad Reza had in fact fashioned such a regime, with American help, was the insistent refrain of the antiroyalists. But when examined in full, the evidence showed that the shah had redressed the balance in part by a program of benevolent economic and social reform.

The shah remained unalterably suspicious of party politics. Like his father, Muhammad Reza did not abrogate the constitution, preferring instead to keep a democratic façade. He used the security forces to block his political enemies. He discouraged, forcibly when necessary, all political activity that did not conform to his system of "constitutional absolutism." This meant, in effect, that the parties did not compete for power, since all power resided in the shah. Nor did they necessarily compete for office, since the prime minister and his colleagues, severally and jointly, were accountable not to the legislature but to the monarch. In 1957 Muhammad Reza permitted his friends to establish two parties. The Mardum, or People's Party, appeared in May as a loyal opposition under the leadership of a boyhood friend of the shah, Asadallah Alam. Somewhat later, Prime Minister Dr. Manuchihr Iqbal (April 1957–September 1960), former chancellor of the University of Tehran, created his own Milliyun, or Nationalists Party.

In the election of the 20th Majlis in August 1960 the Mardum and Milliyun parties alone were allowed to run candidates in the hope that a legislature might be structured wholly of the shah's friends. With the shah's program of economic austerity and radical reform in mind, the parties by advance agreement tried to shut out the conservatives—the older army officers, the tribal khans, the wealthiest landlords and merchants, and the 'ulama. The balloting as usual took place piecemeal over several weeks, and the returns in the provinces by mid-August disclosed that the scheme of pre-cooked elections was working well. But the ballot managers lost control of the contest in Tehran later in the month, when many conservatives, heartened by the breach in the provinces, presented themselves as candidates. Iqbal, with the aid of the interior ministry, then tried to manipulate the vote in his party's favor. The prime minister's ploy alienated Alam, and the Mardum Party reinforced the conservatives' denunciation of the election as a fraud and constrained the shah to nullify the election at the end of August. Uplifted by the negative victory in frustrating the shah's original scheme, the conservatives presented themselves in larger numbers in the re-run election in the opening weeks of 1961, when they polled sufficient votes to deny either royalist party a majority.

Unwilling to embark upon a program of austerity and reform with a Majlis that seated so many conservatives, the shah called to the premiership Dr. 'Ali Amini (May 1961–July 1962), one of His Majesty's outspoken critics who nevertheless agreed to execute the projected policies that were calculated to arouse the conservatives' wrath. The shah dissolved the legislature, as Amini had insisted, and placed the country under martial law, so that the royal decrees became law without legislative endorsement, carrying the final enforcing authority of the security establishment.

For two decades, Muhammad Reza had spoken about reform almost without surcease; but the many projects that were minutely framed and noisily proclaimed were quietly abandoned, with little cumulative impact. It was hardly astonishing, therefore, that the shah's latest and most grandiose plan should be greeted with incredulity by those who were called upon to surrender privilege and property, as well as by those who were to become the beneficiaries. No less was the skepticism of Muhammad Reza's reform-minded domestic opponents and his American advisers who had been badgering the shah for years to translate his words into deeds. This time, at the dawn of his third decade as monarch, Muhammad Reza really launched his White (or bloodless) Revolution. He aimed at nothing less than a complete transformation of an agricultural society of illiterate and disease-ridden landless peasants into a modern, literate, and healthy society.

From the start, Amini made clear his fixed purpose of eradicating corruption in high places. He put on trial for embezzlement and other abuse of power former civilian ministers and top army officers, among them a recent army chief of staff. These trials had the desired effect of softening the resistance of the landowners and the 'ulama to the proposed changes. Land redistribution lay at the heart of any basic overhaul of an agricultural country where peasant owners worked no more than one of every five cultivated acres. The shah's first major edict, promulgated in January 1962, was a land reform law that required all owners of two or more villages to transfer title of all but one to the government for resale to the peasants. To supervise the land redistribution, Amini named as minister of agriculture Dr. Hasan Arsanjani, a vigorous advocate of radical agrarian policies.

In the absence of a cadastral survey, Arsanjani marked his slide rule with the village as the unit and guessed that perhaps one-fifth of the more than 50,000 villages belonged to landlords with more than seven villages each. One in Shiraz was said to own as many as 168 and another in Khurasan 136. Another 6,000 villages were reportedly held in perpetuity under the system of *awqaf*, or religious endowments, with the revenue earmarked in theory for the upkeep of mosques, schools, shrines, and other religious institutions. In practice, it also financed the conservative politics of the 'ulama. The state itself owned some 1,800 villages, while Muhammad Reza inherited more than 2,100 villages from his father. Title to the latter in the first dozen years of the son's reign passed back and forth between the state and the crown. The shah disposed of only a small number of villages under his own scheme after 1953, so that most of his inheritance was still available nine years later for the massive reform program.

The gross inequalities of traditional land tenure in Iran are hard to imagine. These were certainly not all corrected by the changes that the shah sponsored and insisted on carrying out. Nevertheless, the achievement, objectively measured, was impressive. In the first phase of land distribution, ending in mid-1964, it was estimated that about 15,000 villages had passed to peasant ownership, with some 600,000 families or about one-fifth of the rural population as beneficiaries. The peasants undertook to pay the government for the land over a fifteen-year period, starting one year after purchase. In the second phase, smaller holdings in nearly 18,000 additional villages were redistributed by March 1967; the landlords were given wider options than before, and mechanization was encouraged by permitting the landlords using such equipment to retain up to 1,250 acres above the statutory limit. The government assisted in the formation of agricultural cooperatives among the new peasant owners, and by 1967 there were an estimated 7,500 cooperatives in which over 1.1 million families in about 18,800 villages took part. Nature also eased the adjustment to the sudden transformation of the economic and social structure of the villages by providing in biblical rhythm three fat crop years (1965–67) after three lean ones.

Before the lifting of martial law and the restoration of parliament, Prime Minister Asadallah Alam (July 1962–March 1964) received popular endorsement by referendum in January 1963 of the shah's reform program. In addition to the land distribution scheme, the reform program called for the nationalization of forests, the sale of state-owned industries to the public, a profit-sharing plan for industrial workers, amendment of the election law by providing for parliamentary elections in a single day and including the grant of female franchise, and the creation of a Literacy Corps. Patently modeled on the American Peace Corps, Iran's Literacy Corps was conceived late in 1961. It permitted high-school and university students to escape two years of compulsory military service by agreeing to spend an equivalent time teaching peasants to read and write in outlying villages that had no schools. Close to 15,000 Literacy Corpsmen were pushing into the countryside in

September 1965, and it was estimated at the time that the proportion of rural children receiving some form of education had risen to perhaps 35 per cent. The Literacy Corps was an inspired idea; yet there was no denying that it was also a political move. It was political because it thinned the ranks of the students, who were the most implacable critics of the shah, and channeled their energies into constructive endeavor for the state; because it was designed to win popularity for the shah; and also because the Corpsmen were not simply teaching peasants to read and write but to read and write Farsi, thus creating the basis for cultural unity and the prospect of reducing linguistic frictions in domestic politics.

The Literacy Corps, by its very success, spawned in 1964–65 a Health Corps and a Rural Extension Development Corps. The Health Corps could hardly have been expected in the first two or three years, to make a serious dent in the massive problem of educating the peasants to change their individual and group habits. But the very existence of the Corps was an earnest of the government's interest, and even if the problem were eased, a thousand new and subtle ones would take its place, all derivative of the inescapable consequences of continued high birth rates and sharply declining death rates. In military-political terms, the rapid population growth, an accelerating exodus from the villages to the towns, and the uncontrollable expansion of the towns would compound the difficulties of security for the crown and therefore of security management for the armed forces.

Likewise, the Rural Extension Development Corps was elementary by all standards, and could not be otherwise. There were no miracles in the offing. But even a fractional rise in land-use standards represented achievement; perhaps little more than that could be expected in the first decade. If the peasants could be persuaded that loans were best used for production and not for consumption, that would be net gain. If they also learned that crop rotation was good for the land and for revenue, that too would be net gain. If the second lesson was accompanied by the issuance of simple tools with instructions in their care and use, the Development Corps would have exceeded valid anticipation. But whatever the fraction of growth, it was a growth not only in the rural economy but in the politicization of the peasantry.

In preparation for the election to the twenty-first Majlis, SAVAK and the interior ministry disqualified all candidates who opposed the shah's radical reforms, enabling the shah finally to secure in September 1963 a cooperative Majlis. Of the 200 deputies, about 140 belonged to the New Iran Party (NIP), formed with the shah's blessing on the eve of the election. The NIP originated in a semipolitical group called the Progressive Center, founded in 1961 by Hasan 'Ali Mansur, the secretary-general of the High Economic Council, at the time the government's policy-recommending body for reform. The shah designated the slowly expanding center in June 1963 as his personal agency for social and economic research, and in the following month permitted it formally to enter politics. The NIP consisted primarily of superior government technicians, mostly engineers and economists, who had supervised the reform program from its inception. After the election in September 1963, Mansur became prime minister. The only non-NIP members in his cabinet were the security ministers. Incidentally, for the first time in Iranian history, six women deputies sat in the Majlis, and the shah appointed two others to the Senate. At last the shah had fostered the organization of a political party that could call upon the necessary technical skills to oversee the program and that shared with him a vested interest in the success of his wide-ranging reforms.

By then the shah had clearly alienated the conservative leaders who traditionally supported the crown: the landowners, the wealthy merchants, and the 'ulama. The National Front also still looked back to Musaddiq for inspiration and found few words of praise for the shah's social and economic innovations. Throughout the period of martial law the army frequently had to intervene to restore order in Tehran and the other major cities, chiefly because of student demonstrations that the police could not handle. The most serious defiance came in June 1963 when religious leaders, using as a pretext the enfranchisement of women, staged riotous protests in Tehran and Shriaz, which the army forcibly quelled with possibly as many as 3,000 civilian casualties. Large-scale arrests of the 'ulama and the exile to Turkey of the principal leader seemed to put an end to open religious hostility to the shah for the time being. But the murder of Prime Minister Mansur in January 1965, and the attempt on the shah's life three months later, suggested that antiroyalism had not been entirely eradicated.

Oil revenue, meanwhile, soared from less than $10 million in 1954 to some $600 million in 1966. In fact, during the period of the Second Five-Year Plan (1962/63–1966/67) over three-fourths of the government's revenues, $2.8 billion out of a total of $3.7 billion, came from oil. In view of the spectacular rise in oil income, the

United States in December 1965 declared Iran a "developed" country, no longer in need of economic and military grant aid, which formally came to an end two years later. Once the United States ceased paying for much of the new equipment, the shah was almost certain to start enlarging his army again. The pressure for expansion was almost wholly domestic, since the external threats to Iranian security, for the time being at least, were contained.

Relations with the Soviet Union steadily improved in the 1960s. By the end of 1965 Iran had accepted Soviet credits amounting to the equivalent of $330 million for a variety of economic projects. A Soviet-Iranian agreement of 1967 called for the annual sale of 10 billion cubic meters of natural gas, or two-thirds of the total, to the U.S.S.R. on completion in 1970 of a trans-Iranian pipeline. By 1966 Iran even began to purchase from the Soviet Union nonsensitive military hardware—primarily automotive equipment. The shahdom could be expected to become an even more venturesome military customer of the U.S.S.R., but there was very little evidence in mid-1968 of a desire to engage in a shopping spree in Moscow for sophisticated weapons.

Although the ice was thus breaking, the old anxiety did not entirely vanish. If no Iranian army could ever hope to erect an adequate defense against so powerful a neighbor, the bilateral military alliance with the United States seemed to furnish an effective deterrent. Anglo-India had disappeared as an expansive neighbor, although the ancient image retained its vividness for many Iranians because of Britain's slowness in departing from the Persian Gulf. Iran's remaining neighbors were all closer in size and military capability to itself. As allies in CENTO, Turkey and Pakistan presented no threat. Nor did Iraq and Afghanistan individually stir grave anxiety, since the Iranian army was more powerful than that of either. Still, the shah became sensitized to the unabating attacks on himself and his regime by the Arab military governments, particularly by the U.A.R., Syria, and Iraq. Spokesmen of the three commonly referred to the Persian Gulf as the Arab Gulf, and to Khuzistan with its Arab majority as an Arab irredenta. Khuzistan, after all, was the site of the major proved crude oil resources in the kingdom and of the single most elaborate rural development project that the shah had sponsored in his reign. Little wonder that he supported the royalists in Yemen and the Kurds in Iraq as counter-irritants.

The domestic mission of the army as final peacekeeper and

guarantor of the shah's writ, to be used when needed for enforcing his will, was thus still the overriding one in the late 1960s. This mission appeared to have the twofold character of maintaining law and order in the tribal districts and in the cities, particularly Tehran. While occasional tribal disorders still occurred, no large punitive expedition against an unruly tribe was undertaken after March 1963, when the army suppressed a Qashqai uprising. By 1966 the army was better organized and equipped than any army in Iranian history. The tribes seemed to acquiesce by then in the military superiority of the crown, and so long as the army remained faithful to the shah, the likelihood of tribal outbreaks grew progressively smaller. The police responsibilities in the tribal districts were accordingly being transferred to the gendarmerie. The two antiroyalist groups of students and urbanizing peasants seemed destined for years to come to multiply faster than the government could realistically hope to convert them into productive citizens. The peasants were still politically inert in the late 1960s, but their awakening did not appear too distant; and when the peasants came to political life, the rural areas were likely to enlarge the breeding grounds of antiroyalism.

For the moment, the success of the shah's policies, including his dealings with the Soviet Union, invigorated his position among the silenced nationalists. Technicians who once belonged to the National Front and even to the Tudeh Party were now working for the White Revolution. The hard core of the shah's foes had been weakened and fragmented. The disaffected and disenfranchised conservative elite were divided among themselves and, despite a common hostility to the crown, were even more widely separated from that segment of the urban educated class, consisting largely of the second generation of disciples of Musaddiq, who were associated with the still limping National Front. These men had not personally known the dictatorship of Reza Shah and, in any case, were persuaded that there was no essential difference between the father's regime and the son's. They tended, even in the late 1960s, to idealize Musaddiq's crusade against Muhammad Reza as a crusade for political freedom. Whatever else Musaddiq had exemplified in the early 1950s, political freedom was neither an achieved reality nor an avowed practical objective of his two governments. He utilized the same authoritarian instruments—martial law, rule by decree, and even attempted development of his own private security agency—as those for which he condemned the shah. This was perhaps wholly natural, for Musaddiq was, after all, an anachronism in postwar Iran, a survivor of the frustrated political struggle against Reza Shah. The replacement of Muhammad Reza, if that were to occur, was not likely to yield political freedom, to judge from the postwar record in the Middle East.

16

COLD WAR BENEFICIARY: AFGHANISTAN

The formula in Afghanistan looked familiar: a rugged terrain, primitive communications, a plural society of minority communities, a largely tribal and illiterate population with a relatively high number of nomads, a subsistence agricultural economy, a dynasty which still exercised almost absolute powers under a constitution designed to satisfy the demands of the growing but communally disunited urban educated class, and a postwar modernizing army which progressively subordinated refractory tribes to the crown. A new element in the formula was the supplier, for the Afghan army's weapons were made in the U.S.S.R. and the technicians who trained the Afghan officers in their use and maintenance were Russians. The source of the weapons and the nationality of the technical instructors had little bearing on the practical results, which looked remarkably similar to those in next-door Iran.

Though hardly competing with the military republics in quantities purchased, Afghanistan nevertheless was the lone Middle East monarchy that modernized its armed forces exclusively with Soviet equipment—a fact that provides a handy analytical control for evaluating non-military consequences of military modernization in a traditional society.

A Landlocked Kingdom

Afghanistan is a landlocked, poverty-stricken, Sunni replica of Iran. An even more rugged country than its Western neighbor and less than half its size, Afghanistan encompasses some 250,000 square miles. The massive Hindu Kush mountain range, stretching laterally from the northeast to the southwest, descends from a height of 25,000 feet. Together with the longitudinal spurs, the mountains spread across 70 per cent of the country's surface. At no point does any valley drop lower than 500 feet above sea level. Until the second postwar decade there were no paved highways in the kingdom. The steep mountains and the underdeveloped communications in

Afghanistan, as in Iran, sustained the cultural heterogeneity of the population.

The Pushtuns, who speak their own Persian-related language, Pushtu, make up nearly half the total population—an informed guess only, as are all Afghan demographic statistics, because no census has ever been taken. The government itself in 1964 revised its population estimate from 15 million to 11.5 million, and even this figure may have been excessive. It was generally assumed that perhaps no more than 5 per cent of the Afghans could read and write. Distributed throughout the south, and especially the southeast along the Pakistan frontier, the Pushtuns were a partly nomadic people, whose paramount tribes supplied the dynasties of the kingdom after Afghanistan won its independence in the mid-eighteenth century. If the Pushtun community gave the country its rulers, its administrators, and its soldiers, the largely urban Tajik community gave it the civil servants, the merchants, and the members of the professions. About a fourth of the population, the non-tribal Tajiks, could be found in all the major cities, particularly Kabul, the capital, where they formed the majority of literate Afghans. Because of their prominence in the kingdom's administration, the Farsi-speaking Tajiks helped keep Persian the language of the government. The Hazaras and the Uzbeks, the next two largest communities, were roughly equal in number and perhaps amounted together to some 15 to 20 per cent of the kingdom's total. Also Farsi-speaking, the Hazaras were almost wholly illiterate, tribal peasants of Mongolian origin subsisting in the central part of the kingdom. Bunched in the north were the Turkic-speaking Uzbeks, a tribal, peasant, and partly nomadic population. The four major communities altogether probably made up as much as 85 to 90 per cent of the Afghans. The rest were splinter communities, none larger than a quarter million, and many numbering fewer than 10,000, speaking a score of languages.

The Afghans were almost solidly Muslim and predominantly Sunni. Nevertheless somewhat more than 10 per cent were Shi'is, among whom the Hazaras formed the largest group, joined by the far smaller community of urbanized Qizilbash and that part of the Tajik community living in the remote mountains of the northeast. Not fewer than 10 per cent, and perhaps as many as 20, were nomads—Pushtuns, Uzbeks, and Baluchis in descending numerical order. The urban population was still small in the mid-1960s, so that no more than every tenth citizen lived in the towns. The largest city, Kabul, probably did not exceed a quarter-million, or almost as many as the next three largest cities combined—Qandahar, Herat, and Mazar-i Sharif. Scattered throughout the country were perhaps as many as two dozen other towns with 10,000 or more inhabitants.

Afghanistan was one of the older new states of the Middle East. Before the eighteenth century it never formed an independent political unit, and in modern times it passed back and forth in whole or in part between Persia and the Mughal Empire in India. Only toward the close of the nineteenth century did Afghanistan acquire durable frontiers. The Pushtun dynasties that ruled the country after 1747 came from the Durrani (formerly Abdali) tribe that originated in the Qandahar district. But even after tearing itself away from the neighboring empires, the country did not remain united; and in the middle decades of the nineteenth century, rival khanates or principalities contended for supremacy. In these years Afghanistan, like Iran, was caught in the path of British and Russian expansion. By the end of the 1880s the tsarist southward advance stalled at the Amu Darya River, which thereafter became Afghanistan's boundary with Russia. Meanwhile, in defense of Anglo-India, British troops occupied Kabul in 1879–80 and installed 'Abd al-Rahman (1880–1901) as amir of a unitary Afghanistan, compelling him to surrender his external sovereignty to the United Kingdom. Thirteen years later Sir Henry Mortimer Durand, the foreign secretary of the government of India, shortened the eastern and southern boundaries of Afghanistan in India's favor by drawing a line through the middle of the Pushtun districts, thus placing at least half of the Pushtun population under British rule. With boundaries fixed by the turn of the century, Afghanistan was removed temporarily from the zone of Anglo-Russian contention, a condition later confirmed by a convention that the two powers concluded in 1907 in establishing the Muslim country as a buffer.

The British otherwise interpreted their protecting role lightly, giving the vigorous and imaginative 'Abd al-Rahman an opportunity to unite the martial Pushtun tribes and the several other ethnic communities under his amirate. The amir left no doubt that he was the military commander as well as ruler of his principality. "I am always ready, as a soldier, to march to a battle," observed 'Abd al-Rahman,

in such a manner that I could start without . . . delay in [an] . . . emergency. The pockets of my coats are always filled with loaded revolvers and one or two loaves of bread for one day's food; this bread is changed every day. Several guns and swords are always lying beside my bed, or on the chair where I am seated, within easy reach of my hand, and saddled horses are always kept ready with other armaments . . .

I have also ordered that a considerable number of gold coins should be sewn into the saddles of my horses in case these should be needed on a journey. On each side of the saddles there are two revolvers. I think that it is necessary in such a warlike country that the King, and especially a monarch who is a soldier himself, should always be prepared for emergencies as a soldier on the field of battle. Though my country is perhaps more peaceful and safe now than many other countries, still, one cannot be too cautious and too well prepared.[1]

Immediately after World War I Amir Amanallah (1919–29) seized full independence from Britain, and in 1921 a series of agreements with Soviet Russia, Turkey, and Iran gave international recognition to Afghan sovereignty. Amanallah, inspired by Mustafa Kemal and Reza Khan, tried to introduce reforms, including a constitution with a democratic façade that he promulgated in 1923. But conservative opponents of the attempted innovations, particularly the 'ulama, forced the overthrow of the self-styled shah in January 1929.

After nine months of anarchy, Sardar Nadir Khan, the triumphant military commander in the "war" for independence a decade earlier, seized power, restored order, and re-established the dynasty in a new line of the Muhammadzay clan with the support of Pushtun tribal levies, which remained the principal source of military power throughout his brief reign. Nadir Shah (1929–33) had himself formally invested as monarch in November 1929 and named one brother prime minister, and a second one war minister. Nadir Shah issued his own constitution in 1931, copying its main provisions from that of his predecessor. However, the new shah was murdered two years later, and his nineteen-year-old son, Zahir, (1933–) ascended the throne. Rallying behind the youthful shah, the ruling clan displayed unusual solidarity in an Islamic kingdom, where the male members of a royal family often contended for the succession. The two uncles served in essence as regents, preserving political continuity by keeping the titles of premier and war minister. By this means the royal family assured sovereign Afghanistan its longest period of political stability. In the first three decades, the premiership was held by three princes: the

shah's uncles, Sardar Muhammad Hashim Khan (1929–46) and
Sardar Shah Mahmud Ghazi Khan (1946–53), and his first cousin
Sardar Muhammad Daud (1953–63). In this period the princes
ruled, while the shah reigned.

Military Transformation

Afghan amirs in the middle decades of the nineteenth century attempted, with Anglo-Indian help, to develop a regular force alongside the tribal levies. These modest efforts were carried forward by
'Abd al-Rahman. But the first durable changes had to await the
interwar years of the twentieth century when Afghanistan employed advisers from Turkey to reorganize the army and successively from Russia, Germany, Britain, and Italy to create an air
force. A law of conscription, unsuccessfully introduced by Amanallah in 1923, was reactivated by Prime Minister Sardar Muhammad
Hashim a decade later. But the primitive communications and the
paucity of vital statistics made it impossible to enforce the law, so
that the army remained a tribal force with high reliance on Pushtuns for the main military units. While Afghanistan as a neutral in
World War II escaped the inconveniences of foreign military occupation, it was also denied the benefits of Great Power assistance.

"I am convinced that America's championship of the small nations guarantees my country's security against aggression," declared
Prime Minister Shah Mahmud Khan Ghazi in 1946.

> America's attitude is our salvation. For the first time in our history
> we are free of the threat of great powers' using our mountain passes
> as pathways to empire. Now we can concentrate our talents and re-
> sources on bettering the living conditions of our own people.
>   I propose to reduce the army in size to that of a small but well-
> trained internal security force charged with maintaining order among
> the nomadic tribesmen. Money once used in maintaining a large
> army will find better use in the already started national improvement
> program.[2]

The Afghan army, numbering 45,000 officers and men on Zahir
Shah's accession in 1933; was doubled by 1945, largely under the
stimulus of war and with the aid of a Turkish advisory mission.
During World War II the Afghan government had also brought
into being a quasi-military gendarmerie commanded by army officers. As in Iran, the gendarmerie relieved the regular army troops
of rural security duties for the duration of the international crisis.
The military ranks were reduced in the first postwar decade by

more than half, while the gendarmerie was expanded to approximately 20,000 officers and men.

Manifestly inspired by Iran's experience, Afghanistan turned to the United States for help in modernizing the armed forces. Afghan appeals to Washington for military aid in World War II and for a decade following, yielded no results. When General Sardar Muhammad Daud Khan assumed the premiership in September 1953, Afghanistan still lay claim to Pakistan's Northwest Frontier Province, which fell on the Indian side of the Durand Line of 1893 and which contained as many Pushtuns as Afghanistan itself. In his decade as prime minister, Daud became the most vocal advocate of the redemption of "Pushtunistan," for his rise to the premiership coincided with Pakistan's rapprochement with the United States. Although in 1954 Afghanistan became the first Middle East state to accept Soviet economic aid, it was the formation the next year of the Baghdad Pact, to which Pakistan adhered, that conditioned Afghanistan for acceptance of Soviet military aid. (By then Egypt had become the first Soviet military client in the Middle East.) Daud regarded Pakistan's participation in the regional security system sponsored by Britain and the United States as a hostile act.

The U.S.S.R., which had viewed with anxiety earlier Afghan overtures to the United States for military aid, made a determined effort under Stalin's successors to take advantage of official Afghan disappointment over the negative American response. During the Bulganin-Krushchev visit to Kabul in December 1955, the Soviet leaders signed an economic aid agreement with Afghanistan and renewed the treaty of neutrality and nonaggression as a means of giving the widest publicity to the new Soviet policy. The U.S.S.R. pledged a credit of $100 million repayable in thirty years, with interest at 2 per cent starting eight years after the issuance of the loans. This was one of the largest Soviet credits to a non-Communist state up to that time. The proffered sum must have appeared massive to a government whose annual budget did not exceed $25 million.

Prime Minister Daud confirmed the first arms agreement with the U.S.S.R. in August 1956. The agreement, it was understood, provided for the sale at substantial discount of the equivalent of $25 million of modern hardware, including jet planes, tanks, and heavy guns as well as light weapons. The terms of the arrangement, according to Foreign Minister Sardar Muhammad Na'im Khan, stipulated repayment to the U.S.S.R. in cotton, wool, and oilseeds.

The Soviet deliveries were prompt. As early as October 1956, Western observers reported the appearance at the newly built airstrip at Mazar-i-Sharif, close to the Soviet frontier, of a dozen MiG-15s together with an IL–14 for King Zahir and a small number of helicopters. Later agreements provided for the sale of steadily more sophisticated and larger quantities of weapons, although neither donor nor recipient ever disclosed the precise details. By 1965 it was estimated that Afghanistan had received perhaps as many as 100 tanks, reconditioned T-34s and postwar T-54s, and that the air force had been equipped with MiG-17 fighters, IL-28 bombers, and a small number of helicopters, perhaps numbering altogether about 100 planes. Soviet military technicians helped the Afghan army assimilate the new weapons, until Afghan officers and NCOs, after special instruction in Soviet and Eastern European military schools, could take over. At the same time, the work of the Turkish military mission substantially tapered off, although the Afghan government sent a small number of officers to the United States for training. Under the Soviet-managed program of modernization, the Afghan army was enlarged, essentially to the 1945 level of 90,-000 officers and men. The modernized air force consisted by 1965 of an estimated 1,500 officers and men.

The sums allocated to defense in the 1960s were still nominal even by Middle East standards. From less than $2.0 million in 1949–50 they grew to about $23 million by 1965, representing on the average about 14 per cent of the total annual budget. Investments in new equipment over a ten-year period, based on actual payments rather than the "retail value" of the weaponry probably amounted to about $5 million to $10 million a year.

Unlike Iranian officers who were chosen from many ethnic and linguistic communities, the senior officers in Afghanistan were mostly Pushtun tribesmen closely associated with the dynasty, while the administrative officers, usually at lower levels, were mainly Tajiks. The selective conscripts, who served for two years, were largely Tajiks, Uzbeks, and Hazaras.

Afghanistan did not become a satellite of the Soviet Union, as many Western observers feared. Despite the decision to purchase military equipment from the U.S.S.R., Afghanistan did not automatically turn its back to the West. Afghan spokesmen, among them Prime Minister Daud, the Afghan architect of the arms deal with the Soviet Union, insisted that Afghanistan was still pursuing a policy of nonalignment in the Cold War. The Afghan Government did not view its status as a Soviet arms client as one that automatically required its terminating all American-financed aid programs. The royal government visualized its new relationship to the U.S.S.R. as an opportunity to play successfully on American anxieties in the Cold War and to encourage ever more bounteous grants. In the decade ending in 1965, Afghanistan received altogether some $350 million in American economic aid.

In the process the Cold War opponents became friendly rivals. The Soviet Union and the United States helped Afghanistan to build a basic, integrated highway system: the United States planned and financed the construction of the main highway from Kabul to Qandahar and the major spurs to the Pakistan frontier while the U.S.S.R. built the main highway from Qandahar to Herat and its continuation to the Soviet frontier, as well as other highways in the north. In the chill of the Cold War, American and Soviet technicians maintained the most cordial relations in Afghanistan. "On the third floor of the Royal Afghan Planning Ministry," wrote an American newsman,

> Russian and American advisers use the same teacups and telephones (both are in short supply in Afghan government offices) and lecture the Afghans with equal vigor on the blessings of economic progress. At noontime Russians, Americans, and Afghans all queue up for GI style hamburgers and chocolate pie at the chrome-lined Khyber Cafeteria, one of the showplaces of the Afghan capital.[3]

Especially significant was the contrast in Soviet aid to Afghanistan and to the Arab states. To Afghanistan, the Soviet Union between 1954 and 1965 extended credits valued at $552 million for economic assistance, primarily for roads, industries, and prospecting. The book value of the military equipment in this period was estimated at $275 million (between 10–15 per cent of it from Czechoslovakia), while its actual repayment value was probably less than half that sum. By contrast, 80 per cent of Soviet (and Czech) military aid to the Middle East in the second postwar decade went to three Arab countries: Egypt, Syria, and Iraq. These Soviet-bloc arms clients also accepted economic aid, including some from other East European countries. Yet here the ratio was reversed. The value of Soviet arms sent to the three Arab states (estimated at well over $2.0 billion) exceeded the value of economic projects (estimated at less than $1.7 billion) sponsored there by the U.S.S.R. and its associates. Moreover, in Egypt and Syria, as later also in Iraq, Algeria, and even Yemen, Soviet military aid seemed designed to encourage economic and social revolution at home and hostility abroad, particularly to those immediate neighbors that were Western military clients.

The planners of Soviet military aid to Afghanistan clearly must have been looking over their shoulders at Turkey, Iran, and Pakistan for purposes, not of arousing Afghan enmity to the allies of the West, but of demonstrating to them that even military aid from the U.S.S.R. need not be feared. No doubt, with its arms the U.S.S.R. bought the usual tactical advantages: Afghanistan became dependent on the Soviets for spare parts and replacements, to say nothing of new equipment; the Afghan army adopted Soviet military doctrine; Afghan officers trained in the U.S.S.R. and Soviet technicians and instructors in Afghanistan cemented official personal relations at all officer levels; and Russian became the military language of the new Afghan army. Yet the Russians did not appear to exploit these advantages. In brief, they made no attempt to overturn the Afghan regime and seemed unperturbed by Communist sponsorship of a prenationalist, traditional, absolute monarchy.

Soviet military aid, in fact, increased the power and influence of the central government over the recalcitrant tribesmen. As the modern army came into being, conscription was more systematically and equitably enforced in urban and rural areas. The fact that the royal government exempted many Pushtun tribes from the draft while continuing to give them financial subsidies and other benefits suggested that, for the time being, the government was doing everything possible to avoid arousing their antagonism while developing its own independent military capability. Still, in the tribal areas the central government continued to raise tribal levies for frontier duty. Use of such irregular units also provided the basis for payment to the tribes.

As the central government progressively subordinated the tribal areas, the slowly emerging urban educated class in the handful of cities became the focus of the organized opposition. Centered in Kabul, this class represented an amalgam of Tajiks and Pushtuns. The more important families tended to intermarry, and it was from the newly mingled group that many of the key politicians and top administrators were drawn. Essentially detribalized, the new urban elite in the postwar years moved into more and more key positions in the kingdom's administration. As a group, the educated elite brought mounting pressure to bear on the monarchy for political modernization. The military changes of Daud's decade were directed at pacifying the tribal areas. The political changes that Zahir

Shah inaugurated in 1963 were intended to pacify the urban educated class.

Political Transformation

In Daud's decade, Afghanistan benefited from the inversion of the
Cold War. Usually the U.S.S.R. and the United States were
ranged in negative rivalry; if a new state became an arms client of
one, it was as a rule held in suspicion by the other. Among the
Middle East states, only in Afghanistan did there develop a remarkably stable co-existential rivalry, long before co-existence became fashionable. Daud could take some of the credit for this. He
had negotiated the economic and the military aid agreements,
which brought to Afghanistan from the U.S.S.R. the equivalent of
well over half a billion dollars in credits, grants, capital goods, and
military equipment. American grants and loans pumped half as
much into the landlocked kingdom. Foreign aid in this period was
channeled to economic and social overhead, such as the building of
roads, airfields, and telecommunications. With American assistance, the educational system at the primary and secondary levels
was steadily expanded, and the University of Kabul further developed. Any country that would entrust the reorganization of its
armed forces to the U.S.S.R. and the reorganization of its educational system to the United States at the height of the Cold War
must have taken calculated risks. But the risks paid off.

From 1929, when the dynastic line started, until 1963, the prime
ministry and the most sensitive portfolios were distributed among
the king's uncles and cousins. The remaining portfolios were assigned to "commoners." When Zahir Shah dismissed Daud in
March 1963, the ruling dynasty for the first time designated as
prime minister someone outside the royal family. He was Muhammad Yusuf, who had received a Ph.D. in physics at Göttingen and
taught at Kabul University before entering Daud's cabinet as minister of industrial production and mines. Yusuf in turn structured
the first cabinet made up entirely of commoners.

The year and a half between Daud's dismissal and the adoption
of the new constitution proved a tricky transition. As modernizer
of the army, Daud kept the armed forces tightly in his grip by
serving as commander-in-chief and top administrator of the pertinent ministries (national defense and the interior) that managed
and financed the changes. Many observers believed that the army
would remain faithful to Daud and might resist the king's determination to remove the author of the military reorganization. In the

event, Daud acquiesced in the shah's wishes, and the army transferred its loyalty to the crown.

In the very same month, the king named a committee to draw up a new constitution. The proposed instrument was reviewed in the spring of 1964 by a royal constitutional advisory commission, which presented its revised version to the king, who summoned a Loyah Jirgah, or Great Assembly, to deliberate on and approve the final draft. An outgrowth of the Pushtun tribal assembly, the Loyah Jirgah represented all communities and all districts in the realm and gave the monarch a means of reaching a consensus among his subjects in time of crisis. The Loyah Jirgah convened in September 1964 to sit as a constituent assembly, the fifth time since the end of World War I that it had been summoned; on three of the occasions (in July 1924, August 1928, and September 1964) it met to consider constitutional proposals. The Loyah Jirgah, as the record shows, was not a rubber stamp. In 1924, the assembly had forced Amanallah substantially to modify his draft constitution. Forty years later, it demonstrated its independence in devoting twelve days to a paragraph-by-paragraph review of the draft constitution, before giving its endorsement to the entire instrument.

The 1964 constitution went a long way toward creating an institutional structure that might eventually satisfy the demands of the urban educated elite for greater political participation, while not immediately abridging the crown's powers. Article 9 invested in the king the supreme command over the armed forces, with the right to declare war and conclude an armistice. He was authorized at his discretion to summon the Loyah Jirgah, to convene parliament in ordinary and extraordinary sessions, and to dissolve parliament and order new elections. The council of ministers was in effect responsible jointly to the crown and to the legislature, but the power of appointing the prime minister was wholly the crown's. The king also appointed and dismissed all judges, the top civil servants, and military officers. Finally, Article 9 gave him the power to proclaim and terminate a state of emergency.

The constitution also formalized the king's assertion of his royal powers by expressly excluding (Article 24) members of the Royal House from political parties and from holding ministerial office or sitting in the legislature or on the Supreme Court. The Royal House was defined as comprising the sons, daughters, brothers, and sisters of the king, their husbands, wives, sons, and daughters, and the king's paternal uncles and their sons. By this means, the king's cousins, Daud and Na'im, were explicitly debarred from future political activitity.

The bicameral legislature for which the constitution provided was elected, as agreed, twelve months after the promulgation of the constitution on 1 October 1964. Dr. Muhammad Yusuf, who had shepherded the drafting and the endorsement of the constitution and overseen the first election, faced a student demonstration soon after the convening of parliament. Called to restore order, the troops killed more than a score of students. As a result, the legislature withdrew its confidence from Yusuf, who was replaced by Muhammad Hashim Maiwandwal, a former ambassador to the United States. The Maiwandwal government won its initial vote of confidence in November 1965. Organized parties were prohibited until the legislature enacted the political parties law in the spring of 1967. Nevertheless, the membership of the lower house in the intervening period had begun to split along recognizable lines. The landowners and tribal chiefs formed the traditional bloc. The urban educated elite were divided into moderate reformers and "radicals." The last group comprised those deputies from Kabul and a small number of socialists who, while supporting the reforms, opposed the pro-Western policies of the government.

There was little evidence that the king had in fact surrendered his absolute powers, despite his willingness to engage in an apparent experiment with broad popular participation. Still, whatever the future held in store for the political system of Afghanistan, it was clear by 1968 that the trend in politics had moved away from the clannish supremacy of the royal family toward the personal supremacy of the shah, with a constitutional façade that gave the growing educated urban class an opportunity for expressing its views.

17

JORDAN: KEEPING A NONVIABLE STATE ALIVE

On April Fool's Day of 1957, the premium for insurance on the life of King Husayn ibn Talal Al 'Abdallah Al Hashim (1952—) may well have been 100 per cent. The eleven-year-old nonviable monarchy that had grown out of a quarter-century-old artificial amirate appeared on the verge of blowing up in chaos. King Husayn had been experimenting with the consequences of a free election based on adult male suffrage for the first truly representative government in the country's history. With the encouragement, and probably connivance, of Egypt and Syria, the prime minister had already joined the chief of the general staff of Jordan's crack army in a plot to replace the monarchy with a republic. The plot was foiled by a combination of the king's courage and the loyalty of key officers and units. After three weeks of uncertainty, the twenty-one-year-old, diminutive monarch brought the situation under control. By the month's end King Husayn had allowed the army's commander and his immediate successor to flee the country, and placed the treasonous prime minister under house arrest. He prorogued the parliament, abolished the political parties, suspended the constitution, clamped a strict censorship on the press, and imposed martial law throughout the land. Most important, he appointed as the army's commander-in-chief an officer of unquestioned reliability and instructed him to remove all colleagues of doubtful allegiance.

In April 1967 King Husayn was still around and still living dangerously. The hostility of many of his subjects had been tempered in time by respect for his mettle (or fatalism as he has called it), tenacity, and accomplishment against overwhelming odds. But his subjects were still responsive to long-distance incitation by his external foes—primarily the military regime of Egypt, joined at times by successive military regimes of Syria and Iraq—who had not given up the practice of attempting to goad Jordanians into the murder of their sovereign. Jordanians were urged, as late as the spring of 1963, to "tear the dwarf in pieces and hang him on the gates of the British embassy." [1] This continued even after Israel's destructive, punitive raid on the West Bank village of al-Samu' in November 1966, when the 'Alawi-dominated regime of Syria led the "revolutionary" Arab states' campaign of invective against Husayn's "conservative" monarchy. Despite the persisting restiveness, the king resumed the experiment in representative government, on the basis of controlled elections. He released most of the political prisoners, reinstated the prime minister to public life by appointing him a member of the upper legislative chamber, the Senate, and readmitted to the Kingdom the once treasonous Chief of Staff. The nonviable economy was still nonviable, but the gap was narrowing, and a few optimistic economists were beginning to believe that it might even be closed. The army continued to play an indispensable role in shoring up the king's constitutional absolutism.

Then came the crushing defeat in the Six Day War. Husayn's soldiers fought more bravely and with greater discipline than did the Egyptian or the Syrian soldiers. But half of his population and perhaps more than half the kingdom's resources fell into enemy hands. His army lost much of its equipment, and the casualties were steep. His dangers multiplied. Yet somehow he held the rest together—at least into mid-1968.

East Bank, West Bank

A key to the puzzle could be found in a comparison of the population estimates of 1952 and the census returns of 1961. Fully to appreciate the importance of the demographic trends we must first bear in mind that as late as 1945 the nearly landlocked amirate of Transjordan, then under British mandate, had encompassed an area of some 34,500 square miles with a population generously estimated at 450,000. The amirate was little more than a fertile patch east of the Jordan River attached to a hinterland desert four times as large. At the mandate's end in 1946 the ruler, Amir 'Abdallah ibn Husayn, was proclaimed king. The armistice with Israel assigned some 2,000 square miles of the adjacent remnant of Arab Palestine to the kingdom's custody in April 1949. A year later 'Abdallah formally annexed the district with the approval of a submissive legislature and thereby tripled the kingdom's population. By that time Transjordan had already abbreviated its name to Jordan.

The resident population had risen to 1.7 million by 1961, yet significantly, nearly 900,000, or more than half, lived on the East

Bank, as the Transjordan segment is known. It was thus no longer accurate to speak of the East Bank as if it consisted solely of the kingdom's pre-merger population. About 300,000 West Bankers had crossed over from Palestine by 1961. Most of the transplantation took place soon after the merger, but continued in the years that followed. Before the Palestine war, Transjordan was probably the least urbanized country in southwest Asia, except for the tribal principalities of the Arabian Peninsula. By 1961 almost 650,000, or about 38 per cent, of the Jordanians, nearly two-thirds on the East Bank, were concentrated in nine cities and towns with more than 20,000 inhabitants each. Meanwhile, the nomadic and seminomadic population may have declined by more than half in nine years, yet four of every five among the 95,000 nomads and seminomads enumerated in 1961 pitched their tents on the East Bank, one-third of them in the settled zone. Moreover, the number of refugees steadily mounted, through natural increase, from 470,000 in 1952 to 631,000 in 1961, when they represented 37 per cent of all Jordanians. Refugee camps in urban areas such as 'Amman, Zarqah, and Jerusalem had been assimilated by the expanding cities, but the remaining camps preserved their special character as settlements that were neither urban nor rural in any economic or social sense.

The population had thus moved eastward, for displaced and unrooted refugees in search of temporary or permanent anchorage migrate more easily than does a settled population. As a result of the migration, the East Bank was no longer identifiably Transjordanian in the political, social, and economic connotation of a largely nomadic and seminomadic society with few and only small urban communities. The West Bank, however, substantially kept its Palestinian purity. 'Amman, the capital of the enlarged kingdom, underwent the most significant political transformation. It exploded from a town of no more than 30,000 in 1948 to one approaching a quarter-million thirteen years later, thus making it the largest city in the realm. Perhaps two-thirds of the 'Ammanis or more were former Palestinians. Like capitals in many newly sovereign states, 'Amman lured workers looking for jobs in the swelling bureaucracy and in the commercial, financial, and public institutional enterprises collecting at the source of political power. As residents of the capital, the Palestinians could bring their grievances directly to the government's attention. But restiveness at the seat of authority could be tolerated only at the risk of overturn of the government or even the regime.

The former Palestinians could hardly have been expected to abandon demands for the "liberation and reintegration of their national patrimony." They were the ones who had suffered the material consequences of the defeat. Far from accepting defeat, however, the Palestinians seemed determined to recoup their losses and, above all, to regenerate their political life in their own country. They thus had compelling reasons for insisting on a renewal of war with Israel. However, the government had no less compelling reasons for deferring such a war, for Jordan could hardly contemplate going it alone against Israel in the foreseeable future. Military victory would require manpower, more sophisticated training and equipment, and better organization than the monarchy could furnish. Still the Palestinians represented an overwhelming majority of the kingdom's population, and if allowed, they were strategically located to make their demands hurt, as a majority in the capital and as the almost exclusive residents of the West Bank. Since the government could not satisfy the demands, it had either to ignore them or to suppress them. Hence the regime was beleaguered by a discontented mass, larger than the kingdom's original society, which the new citizens, though still substantially unassimilated, were threatening to overwhelm. Nor was there any prospect in sight of removing the psychological basis of the Palestinians' discontent.

The very existence of unrequited and unrequitable demands created ideal conditions for external intervention into Jordan's domestic politics by Arab neighbors. All had participated in the Palestine war and, after it was over, took to blaming one another for the defeat. But Jordan was the most vulnerable Arab state and became in time the major victim. Three other states had also, along with Jordan, become host to Palestine refugees: By June 1965, through natural population growth, Egypt had some 297,000 in the Gaza Strip; Lebanon had 160,000; and Syria, 136,000. The three governments, each for its own reasons, refused to grant the refugees citizenship, thus nurturing the refugees' aspirations for the recovery of Palestine.

From the common policy Jordan had strayed. It was not King Husayn, of course, who took the decision to annex the Palestine fragment on Jordan's side of the armistice line, nor did he invent the policy of assimilating its population. He simply inherited the condition from his grandfather, who in turn had been seeking ways of enlarging his realm in the hope of constructing a more substantial state than the one allotted him. The acquisition of a part of

Palestine first came into practical consideration in 1937 when a British royal commission proposed division of the mandated country between Jews and Arabs and the union of the envisaged Arab state with Transjordan. When the union finally took place a dozen years later 'Abdallah wasted little time in conferring citizenship on all residents and refugees in the Palestine district in his charge. Pro-Hashimi Palestinians promptly received equal representation in the legislature and one-third of the ministerial portfolios. Jordan's Arab neighbors thus baited the Hashimi Kingdom for its alleged failure to support the Palestine Arab cause, and disgruntled Palestinians— the overwhelming majority of the new citizens—proved highly susceptible to this line of propaganda.

The quarrel over Palestine policy also became entangled with other issues. From the mid-1950s Egypt and Syria promoted republicanism in Jordan as part of the crusade for terminating British (and French) imperialism everywhere in the Arab world. In Egypt this crusade was linked to an expansionist policy thinly disguised by 'Abd al-Nasir's commanding role in the Arab unity movement. The Syrian antipathy to Jordan, on the other hand, was reinforced by private rivalry with the Hashimi Kingdom reaching back to the days of 'Abdallah, whom many Syrians viewed as a competitor for leadership in the multiple schemes for Arab unity in the Fertile Crescent. Saudi Arabia at first joined Egypt and Syria in promoting the overthrow of the monarchy in Jordan because of the durable dynastic quarrel with the Hashimis that sprang from the Saudi conquest in the mid-1920s of Hijaz, then ruled by 'Abdallah's father and older brother. After the overthrow of the Hashimi dynasty in Iraq in 1958, the nascent military republic became Jordan's implacable enemy, while Saudi Arabia turned ally in common defense of the surviving Arab monarchies. Husayn thus seemed to be seated on a throne fixed to high explosives whose fuses reached as far afield as Cairo, Damascus, and Baghdad. When Egypt, Syria, and Iraq signed a pledge in the spring of 1963 to unify the three socialist military republics, all three fuses were lit but fizzled after the pledge failed to materialize.

Husayn met the threat of his Arab enemies by reinstating controlled constitutionalism, or, more accurately, monarchical absolutism, which enabled him at his own discretion to tighten or loosen the controls as changing conditions warranted. The basic political system, like the basic political condition, was one that his grandfather had shaped. Yet the assumption that the political system had not changed in transit would be erroneous. To measure the change, we must remember that the Hashimi dynasty had been grafted on the local society in the 1920s. The country itself was artificially contrived, so that within its boundaries were encompassed two culturally distinct Arab populations: those in the south, mostly nomads and seminomads, who spoke the dialect of the Arabian Peninsula; and those in the north, mostly settled, who spoke the Syrian dialect. 'Abdallah surmounted the internal opposition in the south before 1939, for there he was accepted as a fellow Arabian, and as he succeeded in settling the tribal feuds, the tribal shaykhs one after another acquiesced in his rule. With their backing, 'Abdallah could continue to overlook the opposition of the northerners, townsmen and beduin alike, who tended to respond sympathetically to Syrian initiatives and Palestinian moods, a condition that persisted into the reign of Husayn.

'Abdallah accepted a treaty with Britain in 1928 confirming the mandate over Transjordan and the mandatory's conduct of the amirate's external sovereignty. He also accepted a constitution to regulate his exercise of domestic sovereignty under a regime that provided in form for representative government but in practice for amiral rule on the Islamic tribal model. His was personal, not clannish, rule since three of the four sons of King Husayn of Hijaz, the Hashimi patriarch, had been distributed by the settlement of World War I among as many countries, each forming a separate dynasty. To help administer the amirate, 'Abdallah over the years recruited a handful of aides in Syria and Palestine as well as Transjordan, who provided the candidates for the Council of Ministers, a policy-implementing and administrative agency that was responsible to the king alone. The Legislative Council, in which the ministers also sat, served in effect as an advisory body. The king was of course bound to follow the guidance of the small group of British advisors, who were principally concerned, however, with foreign affairs, defense, and finance. The monarchical constitution of 1946, replacing the amiral one, re-enshrined the practice but altered the form of government, by creating a bicameral legislature with an appointive Council of Notables, or Senate, half the size of the elective Council of Representatives.

The addition of the West Bank introduced a population that was better educated, politically more sophisticated, and accustomed to higher living standards. However, the once thriving middle class and the peasantry of the Palestine mandate were literally dumped into a political system that was ill-adapted to absorb them. Even more than the Hijazis in Saudi Arabia, the Palestinians in

Jordan believed themselves superior to the ruling community. The West Bankers had come to take for granted many public services that their fellow citizens across the river had never known, and criticized the Jordan government for its primitiveness. In demanding that the political system be changed, the anti-Hashimi Palestinians were concerned less with the principle of replacing personal rule with democracy than with the substantive goal of undoing the evils of the war that had resulted in the rise of Israel and in their own displacement. They were convinced that, if they could capture the Jordan regime, they could at the same time redirect policy on Israel and settle the Palestine issue in their own favor once and for all.

Glubb's Legion

The Palestinians thus had numbers, sophistication, motivation, and the support of influential Arab governments, yet they failed to seize the political controls. In part this could be attributed to their lack of political organization and leadership. The absence of both had accounted for the shambles to which the Palestine Arab cause had been reduced after the expiry of the mandate. In larger measure it could be attributed to the vigor of the regime under 'Abdallah, to the presence of the British until 1956, to American support after 1957, but above all to the loyalty of the army. That loyalty was not really tested in 1951 when a Palestinian murdered 'Abdallah. Many of his opponents, it is true, welcomed the king's murder, but it was not the act of a well-planned conspiracy with a large organized following, nor was it accompanied by an attempted coup d'état. For success, such a coup would have required the participation of the armed forces. Yet there was no prospect whatsoever of effective collusion between those who plotted the murder and the commanders of the elite units of the army, for the commanders at the time were all British officers and all were proved servants of the monarchy.

The Arab Legion, as 'Abdallah's army was known in English, remained under British command even after the termination of the mandate, which gave way in 1946 to a preferential alliance. The altered condition of dependence removed visible signs of British hegemony, leaving invisible ones that enabled the preferred ally to frame and execute military policy. A Joint Defense Board was created to coordinate Anglo-Jordan plans and training. Under the alliance it was also stipulated that British officers would fill the top positions in Jordan's army. Some officers, including John Bagot

Glubb Pasha, the commander-in-chief who ultimately rose to the rank of lieutenant general, served the Jordan government under contract. But others had simply been seconded to the Arab Legion for three-year tours of duty by the British Army and the RAF.

As a modern military force, the Arab Legion was essentially a by-product of World War II. From its creation in 1922 until 1956 the Legion integrated the police with the armed forces, originally for economy reasons. As late as 1941, the police were three times as numerous as the "soldiers," and both combined did not exceed 1,350. The successful use of the minuscule mobile force in the brief Iraqi and Syrian campaigns in 1941 encouraged Britain to enlarge for war service the Legion's military arm, and by the war's close Transjordan had 8,000 men under arms, the police included. Though modernized and equipped with military hardware of recent design, the enlarged army was nevertheless deprived of battle experience, because by the time the new units were trained the war had receded from the Middle East. Still, until May 1948 the Legion constituted an integral part of the imperial forces under the British Middle East Command. The size of the Arab Legion, meanwhile, had been cut back in the early postwar years to 6,000 men, only to undergo swift expansion to 10,000 in the first five months after the expiry of the Palestine mandate. Its record in the Palestine war was superior to that of any other Arab army.

Political discontent among the Jordanian officers at the time of 'Abdallah's murder could hardly have been more than minimal, for throughout 'Abdallah's reign the officers had been carefully chosen and closely watched. "In some ways," wrote Glubb Pasha,

> the Arab Legion was even more thorough than the British Army itself. . . . The character and antecedents of every recruit were checked by the police before his acceptance. Then again, in the Arab Legion, a confidential report was submitted on every officer and man every year.[2]

Political reliability, it may safely be assumed, was a major criterion for enlistment as well as for promotion. Little wonder, then, that the allegiance of the armed forces to the dynasty in the succession crisis was unwavering.

In the search for ways of preserving its military power in the Middle East at a reduced cost to the exchequer, Britain gambled on a program of enlarging the British-commanded Arab Legion and more than doubled its ranks to 23,000 by 1956. The infantry and artillery received initial consideration, followed in 1952 by the creation of an armored corps. A small air force was also established. But the Legion remained essentially a ground force supported by British armor, based at 'Aqabah, and British air power, based at 'Amman and Mafraq. Although Britain bore the entire cost of Jordan's military establishment, the total outlays ($30 million annually by 1955) reached only a fraction of the cost of maintaining a comparable number of British troops in the area. Moreover, the presence of some 65 to 70 British officers lodged the Arab Legion firmly in Britain's grip. The Jordanian officer corps expanded from 300 in 1948 to 1,500 eight years later, but only a handful of the Jordanians rose above the rank of first lieutenant. Before and during World War II almost all the Legion's soldiers were recruited from the southern trans-Jordan beduin. In the opening phase of rapid postwar growth many were also drawn from the trans-Jordan north and the West Bank.

Almost all the recruits for the National Guard, which Glubb Pasha raised between 1951 and 1956 as a static defense against reprisal raids along the Israel armistice line, were Palestinians. It was Glubb's feeling that the Legion could not properly perform functions of static defense. The National Guard was trained and commanded by Legion officers and NCOs. But the guardsmen at first went unpaid, and Britain and the Arab League shared the costs of training and equipment. Later, part of the National Guard was organized for mobile defense, and all guardsmen received token salaries.

The National Guard clearly constituted no threat to the Legion. Nor did the National Guard contribute significantly to the Jordanization of the Palestinians, as its sponsors hoped it would. The British-commanded Legion buttressed the monarchy in the crisis precipitated by the death of 'Abdallah and the uncertainty that followed. To judge from available evidence, 'Abdallah's choice for the succession, in the event of the incompetence of Crown Prince Talal, was Talal's oldest son, Husayn. Glubb Pasha remained faithful to 'Abdallah's preference, as did the internal custodians of the Hashimi dynasty, who worked closely with Glubb also because of gratitude to the regime that gave them their careers. The Legion thus stabilized the environment, while 'Abdallah's aides took over the conduct of political affairs.

The custodians of the Hashimi regime numbered four, constituting the inner core of the small circle of the late king's aides. At the time of 'Abdallah's death, Samir al-Rifa'i (a pre-partition Palestinian) was prime minister. His cabinet designated Amir Naif as regent, owing to the absence in Europe for medical treatment of his older brother Talal. Because of the lack of political training, the regent became more a ceremonial than an executive acting head of state, so that the cabinet actually inherited the management of affairs in the interregnum. A new cabinet was selected with the experienced Tawfiq abu al-Huda (a Transjordanian Arab) as the new prime minister and Sa'id al-Mufti (a Transjordanian Circassian) as interior minister. The two men held the same key positions in the three cabinets that spanned the twenty-two months between the death of 'Abdallah and Husayn's attainment of majority, thus assuring continuity. Moreover, in the last twelve months Ibrahim Hashim (another pre-partition Palestinian), president of the Senate, also chaired the Regency Council that performed the ceremonial duties of the crown, for Amir Naif in the interval took up residence outside of Jordan, apparently by cabinet design.

'Abdallah's aides presided over twelve of the sixteen governments formed between July 1951 and May 1959. Four men were exercising power not in their own names but in the name of a dead king, a demented one, and, after August 1952, one who had not yet identified himself. They thrust themselves to the summit of the Jordan political system not in their own interest, although they manifestly enjoyed the fruits of office, but in the interest, as they understood it, of the dynasty and its external prop. As early as May 1953, when Husayn reached his majority, his grandfather's system of personal rule had already been modified, even though its custodians would not have acknowledged the change and its opponents would not have recognized it. The custodians were taking the decisions, not receiving instructions. Admittedly, they tried to frame policy in 'Abdallah's spirit; but the same line of policy, after its inventor's death, did not ring true. Husayn, though imprisoned by the consequences of his grandfather's nonconformity in the Arab world, was bound nevertheless to bring to bear on his handling of public affairs the influence of his preparation for kingship, which differed markedly from that of 'Abdallah. No less binding on Husayn's range of choice was the rapidly transforming regional and international setting.

'Abdallah was the son of an Ottoman provincial governor, at home in Istanbul and in Mecca by education and public service. His broadened outlook had enabled him to become an effective mediator between Britain and his trans-Jordan subjects. When he incorporated Arab Palestine into the realm, his domestic problem was compounded by the need to rule two seemingly immiscible communities while attempting to weld them into one. He did this, moreover, at a time when Britain, his European sponsor, was swiftly losing its political supremacy in the Middle East. Husayn was schooled in Egypt until he reached fifteen, then underwent accelerated training for roughly equal periods of less than a year each: as apprentice to 'Abdallah until his death, as crown prince at Harrow, and as uncrowned king at Sandhurst. The compressed experiences gave Husayn a base on which to refashion the Hashimi system of royal absolutism to fit the evolving realities. As British influence in the Middle East waned, not only did American influence there wax but the multiplying newly sovereign Arab states acquired growing freedom of action.

In those years of rapidly shifting power, Husayn made his first experiments with a policy of compromise, designed to win the allegiance of his recalcitrant Palestinian subjects and their external Arab patrons. A contest ensued. The king and his friends were determined to preserve the primacy of the crown while the anti-Hashimi Palestinian advocates of change and their Arab proponents abroad were no less determined to establish the primacy of the parliament. The failure in the opening year or two to adapt the political system to the Palestinians' liking induced the new citizens to step up their demands for repudiating the preferential alliance with Britain. The condition of continued dependence on Britain angered most Palestinians who viewed the treaty as the old imperialism in a new guise. Many of them became persuaded that to limit the king's powers, the alliance first had to go, since in their belief the Hashimi monarchy derived its power and its vitality wholly from the British presence. This was an exaggerated belief, as events later proved, but there was enough truth in it to enable the opponents of the Hashimis by acting on that belief to come close to destroying the dynasty.

After a year of mounting hostility stirred by propaganda from Egypt and Syria and generously financed by Saudi Arabia, Palestinian 'Ammanis staged their first successful street politics at the turn of 1956. The Arab Legion forcibly restored order. But the street politicians brought down three governments in a month and won their point: Jordan did not join the Western-sponsored Baghdad Pact. Without losing momentum, now that Britain had suffered a major political defeat, the anti-Hashimi Palestinians and their foreign Arab allies demanded the dismissal of the Arab Legion's British officers. Swept along on the Palestinian tide of praise for having kept Jordan out of the Western collective security system, King Husayn discharged General Glubb without notice on 1 March 1956, and replaced him with a Jordanian. As commander since 1939, Glubb had transformed the Arab Legion from a minor police force into the best-trained and, for its size, best-equipped army in the Arab world.

With Glubb out of the way, the Palestinians stepped up their campaign for representative government. Along with the demand for parliamentary supremacy came demands for freedom of the press and political assembly and organization, abolition of emergency laws, and guarantee of personal liberties. The issuance of licenses for the formation of political parties, begun selectively late in 1954, was now extended even to groups such as the Ba'th, a branch of the Syrian Arab unity socialist movement, that endorsed the cause of republicanism. Three-fourths of the deputies returned to the house in October 1956 in the country's first free election represented six parties. The king called upon Sulayman al-Nabulsi, an East Bank opponent of the monarchy and the leader of the National Socialist Party, which represented nearly a third of the deputies, to form a coalition government.

With the enthusiastic support of the Palestinians and the close cooperation of Egypt, Syria, and Saudi Arabia (the signatories of an Arab Solidarity Agreement that was intended as an Arab nationalist answer to the Baghdad Pact), the Nabulsi government conducted itself as if a parliamentary regime had in fact been established and the king had been reduced to a constitutional monarch. Even after the dismissal of Glubb and the departure of the other British officers, the Anglo-Jordan treaty remained in abbreviated effect, since Jordan continued receiving its annual British subsidy for the upkeep of the Legion and units of British armor and the RAF were still stationed in the kingdom. In January 1957 Jordan formally adhered to the solidarity agreement, and its three other members undertook to give Jordan grants-in-aid of $35 million a year for a ten-year period. With this financial pledge in hand, the Nabulsi government in March 1957 negotiated the formal termination of the alliance with Britain.

The experiment with representative government coincided with the Jordanization of the army's officer corps. This meant that at a time when Husayn was agreeing to surrender basic political powers to the cabinet and to the parliament, he was also undermining his capacity to reimpose the traditional full powers of the monarchy, should he feel threatened by the experiment. He had already weakened the army's officer corps, abandoned a tested mode of financing the entire military establishment for an untested and uncertain one, and voluntarily attenuated his personal control over that establishment. The withdrawal of the British officers brought to the top command men of doubtful military ability and, from the dynasty's viewpoint, of doubtful political loyalty. In May 1956 King Husayn had appointed as chief of staff Lieutenant Colonel 'Ali abu Nuwwar, whom he promoted to the rank of major general. Abu Nuwwar proceeded to form a Fourth Infantry Brigade, whose officers and men were composed largely of Palestinians, to furnish the military nucleus for a coup d'état. To this end he also organized a group of "Free Officers," presumably as the nucleus of a future regime. Into this conspiracy Nabulsi was drawn, by reason not of joint authorship but of close cooperation with the Egyptian Embassy in 'Amman, a practice shared with the chief of staff.

The battle between Husayn and his republican opponents was joined over the king's exercise of executive powers without consulting his government, whose policy decisions he tried to countermand. The conflict came into focus over foreign policy. The government favored external aid from Arab countries only, "positive neutralism" as practiced by Egypt, and the establishment of diplomatic relations with the U.S.S.R. The king, by the start of February 1957, let it be known that he unalterably opposed communism and the exchange of relations with the U.S.S.R., welcomed the Eisenhower Doctrine and its promise of economic aid (provided it came "without political strings"), and invited the signers of the solidarity agreement to convene with the heads of the other Arab states in a summit meeting on Arab unity in the Cold War. As the conflict reached its climax early in April, the government sought guidance from the Egyptian Embassy, while the king turned to the American Embassy and to 'Abdallah's surviving protégés. When Nabulsi was forced to resign on 10 April, abu Nuwwar was apparently still unclear about his own position within the army and therefore did not go to Nabulsi's defense. The showdown with abu Nuwwar occurred three days later, when the king learned that the chief of staff was plotting a military overturn of the monarchy. In abu Nuwwar's presence, Husayn rallied to himself loyal officers and men of the pivotal armored brigade stationed at Zarqah, a brigade consisting of southern trans-Jordan tribesmen. The king nevertheless saved abu Nuwwar's life and allowed him to escape to Syria. The refusal of Major General 'Ali al-Hayyari, the next chief of staff, to purge the officers corps resulted in his exile on 20 April. Husayn now chose as chief of staff Colonel Habis al-Majali from the southern town of Karak, with tribal ties in that district. It took the king until 25 April and at least four unsuccessful tries to create a cabinet of proved fidelity. He turned to two of 'Abdullah's aides, who had conducted the regency during his minority; the bland Ibrahim Hashim served as prime minister and as his deputy and foreign minister the decisive and occasionally overweening Samir al-Rifa'i.

Reassertion of Royal Absolutism

To surmount the domestic and external threats to Hashimi rule, King Husayn reinstated royal absolutism in April 1957 while keeping the democratic façade. He governed the country for eighteen months under martial law with the customary restrictive apparatus and practices: military courts, wholesale arrests without preferment of charges, prohibition of public meetings, strict censorship of the press and mails, internal travel with identity cards only, entry and exit of all cities and towns and larger villages and movement on all major highways subject to clearance at military barricades, and permits to leave the country issued only after investigation by the interior ministry. Parliament, which did not meet after March, was suspended in June 1957 by royal decree for three months. When the king reconvened parliament in October, it was a chastened and truncated body that could do no more than endorse the royal will. The king's power was tested in November, when Egypt and Syria mounted a shrill radio offensive, heaping personal insult and abuse on "that stunted lad, sucking the blood of his people, who calls himself a king," while Palestine refugee demonstrators in Damascus carried placards calling for the death of Husayn "like the dog his grandfather." [3] But the campaign stopped in a fortnight as suddenly as it had started, without visible consequence in Jordan, for martial law ruled out street politics. The king finally lifted martial law in November 1958, but the lists of political exiles were not shortened and the prisons remained crowded with political detainees, despite the steady release of minor offenders.

For the first time in five years the king permitted a parliamentary election in October 1961; yet it took two more elections in less than 21 months until he finally erected a reliable legislature. The third election, held in July 1963, was dictated by the action of the house, which for the first time withheld confidence from a government appointed by the king. This one was headed by Samir al-

Rifa'i, who had master-minded the martial law regime of 1957–58. The vote of no confidence occurred in mid-April 1963, when riots and student demonstrations were staged in 'Amman, Jerusalem, and other urban areas in response to appeals from Egypt, Syria, and Iraq, which had just agreed to unite in a federal state. Prime Minister Rifa'i ordered the army to disperse the street politicians, advocates of Jordan's affiliating with the three military republics. The king replaced Rifa'i less than a month after naming him, dissolved parliament, and proclaimed a state of emergency in urban areas and along all frontiers with a dusk-to-dawn curfew. The crisis did not last long, as the projected federal union dissolved into violent quarrels among its three promoters.

In the circumstances, the cabinet remained an agency of the crown, not of parliament. In the first two years of renewed absolutism Husayn continued to rely on his grandfather's disciples, as he developed his own mode of personal rule and then trained his own aides. Contrast the style of the kingdom's founder with that of his grandson: 'Abdallah had never delegated political power that was his to delegate, so that his prime ministers were little more than errand boys; but he did not exercise military power, which was entrusted entirely to Glubb. Husayn managed both the political system and the army. Husayn came to rely on three men formally to manage cabinets of his own choice. Two became the king's factotums, nominally holding the office that the king himself actually filled: Bahjat al-Talhuni, a southern East Banker, born in Ma'an on the eve of World War I, and the decade-older Sharif Husayn ibn Nasir, a Hijazi Hashimi and also an uncle by marriage. The youngest, Wasfi al-Tall, born in the northern East Bank town of Irbid just after World War I, was the most forceful of the trio and brought his graduate studies at the University of Michigan to bear in his administrations, particularly in supervising the development plans. Yet, although Tall took initiatives in policy recommendation, the king alone took the decisions.

Husayn's style of constitutional absolutism had the merit of encouraging economic and administrative modernization and, above all, of providing a durable regime, giving the two populations on the East Bank an opportunity economically and socially to begin to fuse into a single community, so that the east-west division was taking a new shape. But political integration of the Palestinians, in the sense of their acquiescing in Hashimi rule and policies, seemed almost as remote in 1967 as it had been in 1949. The king and his opponents had become prisoners of the Palestinians' preoccupation with subverting the regime and their seeming inability to form a loyal opposition. Consequently, Husayn could abide only a pliant parliament structured by elections without political parties.

Manifestly, without a devoted and modernized army, Husayn could not have imposed his will on a disunited and largely dissident populace. Under the command of Habis al-Majali, who also served in 1957–58 as military governor-general under martial law, the officer corps was recast. Soon after he took over, an estimated fifty to seventy officers were arrested for conspiracy, only two of whom were beduin tribesmen. Tribal officers whom abu Nuwwar had discharged were given back their commissions, while the mainly Palestinian 4th Infantry Brigade was broken up, many of its officers and men were discharged, and the rest were distributed among the other infantry units. Permanently stationed in the 'Amman district, the armored and Royal Guards brigades were clearly the elite troops. Their ranks, officer and enlisted, were made up almost exclusively of southern East Bank tribesmen. To the nomadic and seminomadic tribesmen, the relatively well-paid employment in the army assured security in a depressed economy, and a military uniform became the symbol of high prestige. Despite the dismissals in 1957, the army expanded from 23,000 at the time of Glubb's departure to 36,000 four years later. The rate of expansion slowed down in the four years that followed, the total strength reaching an estimated 38,000 by the end of 1964. Enlistments were again stepped up in 1965, when the largely Palestinian National Guard was dissolved and 40 per cent of the guardsmen were, after careful screening, inducted into the regular army. A roughly equal number of additional recruits brought the size of the Jordan Army by the year's end up to 45,000.

The expansion of 1965 was sparked by the Arab summit meeting at Cairo in January of the preceding year, when it was decided to create a Unified Arab Command (UAC), ostensibly to unite against Israel the armies of the four Arab members of the armistice system—the U.A.R., Lebanon, Syria, and Jordan. Of the $42 million a year that the Arab League pledged to set aside for the UAC, $24 million were earmarked for the further enlargement of Jordan's armed forces. U.A.R. efforts to persuade Jordan to adopt Soviet equipment for the sake of standardization were resisted. Similarly, Jordan opposed the formation of armed Palestine units, which the UAC had recommended. Meanwhile, following the withdrawal of the RAF in 1957, the Jordan Air Force was also measurably developed, so that by 1965 it comprised more than

1,500 men and about 50 planes, largely American off-shore purchase from Britain.

Great care was taken in filling the command posts. Majali remained commander-in-chief of the army and was promoted in May 1965 to field marshal, the first Jordan officer to hold the rank. Named as his deputy was Major General Sharif Nasir, the king's uncle, and commander of an armored brigade, who established a direct royal link to an elite unit of the armed forces, in which the king himself maintained a close personal interest. In the expanded army, the elite units and the commands remained largely tribal. Elsewhere, political reliability—not religious or geographic credentials—still constituted the overriding criterion for the acceptance of applicants in the career establishment. Palestinian officers, many of them Christians, rose to the highest administrative posts. How effectively the armed forces served the king could be gauged from the fact that in the difficult period of 1962–63, when Husayn supported the Yemeni royalists, the commander of the air force was the only officer to defect. Moreover, relatively few dismissals followed the major purge and reorganization in 1957: 17 officers in 1959 charged with conspiracy, 5 in 1961 who joined the defense minister in what might best be described as an intertribal feud aimed at the removal of Majali in favor of one of their own men, and finally in 1962 before the outbreak of civil war in Yemen some 72 officers, ranging in rank from lieutenant to colonel.

With the expansion of the armed forces, the government's defense expenditures sharply increased from about 10.5 million Jordanian dinars, or just under $30 million, in 1955, to double that sum eight years later, remaining at that level through 1965 (see Table 10). Between 1953 and 1964 defense (including internal security) received more than half the total government budget each year; in 1965, for the first time, defense consumed less than half the available public funds. Or, to view it differently, Jordan invested in its security establishment in the six-year period ending in 1958 an annual average sum equal to 22.7 per cent of its GNP, the highest such rate in the Middle East; in the next five years the annual average declined to 16.4 per cent. Even in 1965 when Jordan's expenditures on security reached a postwar relative low, it was spending on defense an amount equivalent to 12 per cent of its GNP, a rate that was substantially higher than the world average of 7 per cent.

No oil-dry Middle East state in peacetime could afford to set aside for the armed forces such a large share of its GNP and still

TABLE 10. Jordan: Force Levels, Government Expenditures, and GNP, 1953/54–1965/66

	Population (millions)	Force Levels (thousands)	Government Expenditures (millions of Jordanian dinars)			GNP[b] (millions of dinars)	Defense Expenditures (as % of GNP)
			Defense (including internal security and justice)	Development	Total		
1953/54[a]	1.4		10.2	2.7	16.9	37.8	27
1954/55	1.4		10.1	2.7	18.0	48.8	21
1955/56	1.4	23	10.5	2.8	17.7	45.5	23
1956/57	1.5		13.5	3.1	21.3	63.3	21
1957/58	1.5		13.4	4.3	23.8	64.6	21
1958/59	1.6		16.6	5.8	29.3	71.0	23
1959/60	1.6		18.0	4.7	30.7	97.4	18.5
1960/61	1.7		18.4	6.0	33.1	103.6	18
1961/62	1.7	36.5	18.7	4.6	32.8	125.0	15
1962/63	1.7		19.1	7.4	37.4	128.4	15
1963/64	1.8		21.0	6.0	39.2	135.3	15.5
1964/65	1.9		21.0	7.5	41.9	159.0	13
1965/66[c]	2.0	45	21.0	10.1	45.1	180.0	12

SOURCES: U.N., *Yearbook of National Accounts Statistics*; U.N., *Statistical Yearbook*; AID, *Summary of Basic Data: Jordan*; U.S., ACDA, *World-wide Defense Expenditures and Selected Economic Data, Calendar Year 1964* (Washington, 1966) and *Calendar Year 1965* (Washington, 1967).

[a] Fiscal year ending 31 March.

[b] Calendar years 1953 through 1965. The years 1953–58 are estimated at factor cost; those from 1959–65 at market prices.

[c] Provisional data.

expand government services and invest in development. Yet King Husayn was doing all three although the kingdom was never able to balance its accounts from internal revenue alone. The explanation lay in the fact that until 1957 Britain paid in full for the upkeep of the Jordan Army. As long as General Glubb commanded the Arab Legion, the British grant was deposited in a special account that Glubb administered. Indeed, this became a major irritant dividing Jordan and Britain in the mid-1950s. Jordan's adherence to the Arab Solidarity Agreement early in 1957 was intended in part to replace the British subsidy to Jordan's army by an Arab subsidy. But neither Egypt nor Syria kept its promise, and even Saudi Arabia made only the first quarterly payment of its $14 million share. At this juncture the United States rescued Husayn by offering Jordan as well as the other Arab states economic aid under the Eisenhower Doctrine. Once Husayn had reasserted his supremacy, he formally accepted the American offer. Thereafter the United States made an annual direct contribution to the Jordan budget. The sum climbed from $40 million in the first year to a peak of $51 million in 1960 and slowly descended to $44 million by 1965. Only a fragment reached the kingdom under the label of military assistance. Nevertheless, American aid enabled the Jordan Army to expand and modernize.

In brief, the financing of the military establishment was channeled through the Jordan government, substantially concealed by the donor and substantially controlled by the recipient. The United States thus proved generous almost to a fault, and in this case generosity paid off. It kept a nonviable state alive, enabling the monarchy to help two disparate, incompatible communities escape immediate or early self-destruction and, as time wore on, even begin fusing into a single nation. This process could not easily be separated in the minds of Arab nationalists, particularly of the Palestinians, from the Palestine problem. The Jordanization of the Palestinians, many of them were convinced, represented an Israel victory. Yet in many subtle ways, the Palestinians were gradually Palestinizing the original East Bankers and, by boring from within, might eventually subdue the political system, an eventuality that would represent an Israel defeat. For the time being, however, the American mode of payment strengthened Husayn's position against the argument of the Palestinians and their external Arab allies that American grants-in-aid represented a form of imperialism. Nor could Husayn be charged with avoiding close arrangements with other Arab states to foot his military bills, for he had given the Arab solidarity agreers their chance. Husayn continued receiving a small annual stipend from Britain, which, however, declined from a peak of $8 million in 1962 to a level of $6 million in the next two years. A British military advisory team was attached to Jordan's armed forces after 1958, while United States military aid was administered by the army attaché, assisted from time to time by temporary mobile training teams.

American and British aid tapered off with a warning from the donors that the kingdom would in time have to pay its own way. To this end the two Western powers guided Jordan in framing and executing plans for expanding its economy, but the prospects for this looked bleak. Transjordan had sprung to life as an historical accident, without prior thought to its economic foundations. On the annexation of Arab Palestine most of the East Bank population was still tribal, living at the subsistence level in a predominantly agricultural economy. The West Bank augmented the cultivated acreage and, of greater significance, introduced a population that included a ready-made urban middle class with many technical and professional skills. But the residents of the West Bank, hardly less than its refugees, were torn from the rapidly expanding economy of the Palestine mandate and thrust back into a subsistence economy, for the most part as an impoverished mass. Four of every five employed Jordanian workers in the mid-1960s were still engaged in farming, yet agriculture's share added up to less than a fifth of the gross domestic product. About a third of the labor force, which according to the 1961 census was approaching 400,000, was unemployed or largely underemployed, testifying to the consequences of a rapidly growing general population (both indigenous and refugee) in an economy of little promise.

Every state in the Middle East was searching for oil; in Jordan the continuing search had yielded no results by 1967. The development planners therefore focused on less lucrative but already-discovered natural resources. The potash industry was reactivated at the northern end of the Dead Sea, an industry that Jews had originally created in the mandatory period. Commercial exploitation of the hitherto untapped phosphate deposits was also begun. Both industries, however, were low earners: the value in 1963 of potash production was estimated at $4.5 million and of phosphate at $3.5 million. Until May 1967 tourism seemed likely, in the long run as in the short, to bring the country more income. It was early recognized that Jordan, which embraced the Old City of Jerusalem and other Biblical and post-Biblical sites, and whose variable climatic conditions for those seeking warm winters and pleasant summers could attract as many visitors as local facilities might comfortably accommodate. This was the rub, for such facilities took time to erect, experience to run, and political calm to assure foreign travelers their personal safety. Net earnings from tourism began nevertheless to move upward late in the 1950s, from about $2.5 million in 1959 to $12.3 million five years later. Jordanians temporarily employed outside the country earned even more foreign exchange currency. The 1961 census placed nearly 63,000 in this class and estimated that more than 90 per cent were Palestinian and that more than half were living in Kuwayt. The sums they sent home grew from $12.9 million in 1959 to $17.3 million in 1963.

All the encouraging economic progress of the 1960s was dissipated in less than a week by defeat in the war and Israel's occupation of the West Bank in June 1967. Even in the best of times, King Husayn could not take the initiative in seeking a settlement with Israel, for he was too vulnerable to the incitation of his Palestinian subjects by Arab politicians in the neighboring states. In the trauma of defeat, his only hope lay in a consensus among the Arab League states; such a consensus proved unattainable in the early postwar months. Yet until a settlement was reached, there was no way of estimating the long-range consequences of the war on the kingdom's military politics.

Husayn assumed personal command of his army in October 1967 and promptly dismissed about forty officers, including the commander on the West Bank in the June war. He resisted the nationalist pressure to become a Soviet military client; and the United States, after an interruption of more than half a year, resumed military aid early in 1968. But by then the king had lost authority over the multiplying *fidaiyun* ("self-sacrificers" or commandos) who were openly gathering and training in Jordan for organized guerrilla war against Israel with the avowed aim of liberating "occupied Palestine." In their view there was no distinction between the West Bank and Israel as demarcated by the 1949 armistice lines. All of it was occupied Palestine. Whether Husayn, even with the rearmament and reorganization of his forces, would be able to bring the commandos under his control before a general settlement with Israel, or without agreeing to lead the guerrilla cause, seemed highly doubtful in the opening months of 1968. Without such control, Husayn's days appeared numbered, for with each passing month of Israel's occupation of the West Bank, the Palestinians were progressively gaining the upper hand.

Even before the Six Day War, the improvement in Jordan's economy, though steady, had not been sufficient to narrow the adverse balance in international payments. The government budget, through 1966, showed an average annual deficit of approximately $50 million. This sum roughly equalled the annual grants given by the United States and Britain, which enabled Jordan to meet its international payments arrears. By quiet persistence and with the aid of the Western powers, Husayn's regime was thus able to expand the country's economy. The United States and Britain were no less anxious than Jordan itself to reduce the kingdom's dependence on them. Yet the economic expansion hardly kept pace with the cost of the military expansion, and military expansion was indispensable if Husayn was to cling to his political supremacy. Here was the irony: the economic improvement might have begun to enable the government realistically to contemplate balancing its budget, if the defense allocation could be cut back sharply. But a modernizing monarchy such as Jordan's, without an efficient and loyal military establishment, could not long endure. So it appeared before June 1967. Thereafter, there was a break in the pattern, and a rational assessment would have to await more clues on the eventual settlement of the issues left by the Six Day War.

18

CONSTITUTIONAL
ABSOLUTISM: MOROCCO

The experience of Jordan demonstrated that the determined opposition of the politically articulate citizenry could convert a traditional monarchy into a modernizing one, and that such a monarch
could become an agent for controlled economic and social modernization by tenaciously holding on to absolute powers with the coercive influence of a loyal army, selectively recruited from his apolitical subjects, armed with modern weapons, and organized and
trained along modern lines. Much that applied to Jordan also applied to Morocco, despite the fact that the latter was not a new
state but a resuscitated and refashioned old one.

Perched at the northwest corner of Africa, Morocco is the only
Arab state washed by the Atlantic Ocean. Steep mountain ranges
zigzag across Morocco's 171,000 square miles. (Peaks higher than
13,000 feet are found in the Great Atlas, the central lateral range
that roughly divides the country in half. Stretching to the northeast is the Middle Atlas rising to nearly 11,000 feet and connecting
with the lateral Rif range in the north whose tallest peak exceeds
8,000. To the south of the Great Atlas lie the Anti-Atlas mountains
which reach no height greater than about 6,500.) The plains and
plateaus of the northwest are the most fertile districts of the country, and the Moroccan Sahara in the southeast is the most barren.

The population has mounted swiftly, from 9.3 million in 1952 to
11.6 million in 1960 and an estimated 13 million in 1965. The
census of 1960 revealed that eight cities had more than 100,000
residents each and that the urban population approximated 29 per
cent of the total. The most rapidly expanding city and one of the
largest in Africa was Casablanca, the commercial and industrial
center, whose population in 1960 was thrusting toward one million;
among the three cities next in size, with populations between 200,-
000 and a quarter-million, was Rabat, the capital. Moroccan society

was still essentially tribal; and the tribesmen, for the most part mountaineers, were settled villagers or nomads and seminomads who were progressively losing their isolation as modern transportation and communications networks spread across the mountain ranges. The rugged terrain largely accounts for the survival of the Islamized yet non-Arabized, Berber-speaking community, containing perhaps as much as a fourth of sovereign Morocco's population. Most of the remaining Muslims are Arabized Berbers. With the steady departure of Europeans and Jews, the percentage of Muslims in the country's total population climbed to more than 95 in 1960.

The Political Tradition

Morocco is the oldest Arab country. It acquired its separate identity as early as the close of the eighth century, when it broke away from the 'Abbasid caliphate. The rulers of Morocco thus also served as religious leaders, exercising within their limited domain the powers of the caliphs; they also bore the title of imam, or head of the local Muslim community, and, after the fourteenth century, that of commander of the believers (*amir al-muminin*). In modern times Morocco remained the only Arab state along the North African littoral to escape subordination to the Ottomans. The 'Alawi dynasty, which ruled independent Morocco in the twentieth century, had originated in the seventeenth. Claiming descent from the Prophet through his grandson al-Hasan, the 'Alawis had migrated from Arabia to Tafilalt in southeastern Morocco at the end of the thirteenth century. Because of their lineage the 'Alawis belonged to the *shurafa* (plural of *sharif*, or noble), who formed part of the Moroccan religious elite. The *mawlay* (master), or ruler, was an absolute monarch of the traditional Islamic variety with no separation of the executive, legislative, or judicial powers.

The 'Alawi rulers rarely unified the entire realm, and never for a sustained period. Indeed, they inherited a divided kingdom and under the dynasty the divisions hardened. In general, the townsmen and the Arab and Arabized Berber tribesmen of the lowlands and of scattered mountain districts, particularly in the Anti-Atlas, recognized the authority of the mawlay and constituted the zone of governmental authority (*blad al-makhzan*), over which the sultan, as the mawlay also styled himself, ruled directly from either of the two capitals, Fez and Marrakesh. By the late nineteenth century the sultan had brought into being a *diwan* (council), headed by a grand wazir (the only member holding a ministerial title), with offices in the palace. To each tribe the sultan appointed an agent called a leader (*qaid*). The makhzani or government tribes were split into military (*gish*) and nonmilitary tribes. The gish tribes, commonly Arab or Arabized Berber, were in a feudal relationship to the crown. Their able-bodied men were on the sultan's call for military duty, occupying a status midway between regular forces and reserves, and in return they enjoyed the use of designated lands and the privilege of tax exemption. Usually Arabized Berbers paid taxes in lieu of military service. On the eve of the European conquest, meanwhile, the sultans also organized a "modern" force of regimental size.

In contrast to the blad al-makhzan was the mountain country, labeled the zone of dissent (*blad al-siba*), which encompassed mainly the Berber strongholds in the Rif and in the Middle and Great Atlas. The autonomous Berber tribes, among whom customary law prevailed over Islamic law, fell politically into two broad classes: those, mostly in the Middle Atlas, who organized local self-rule on the principle of an assembly of the adult males; and those, mostly in the Great Atlas, who were in essentially feudal and patriarchal dependence on the most powerful tribes of the area. The ceaseless tribal warfare throughout the blad al-siba induced the tribes to form federations for mutual defense. But these alliances were always unstable, with membership shifting to satisfy immediate needs. While the tribes were thus beyond the makhzani pale, they were nevertheless disunited and presented no threat to the authority of the crown, since the makhzan represented the largest, most powerful political organization in the country. The sultan was thus able to play off the warring tribes of the blad al-siba against one another and occasionally to conclude short-lived alliances with individual tribes or their chiefs. And in time of crisis, when the kingdom was besieged by non-Muslims, the sultan, as commander of the believers, could even count on the support of the dissenting tribes.

When Morocco fell under alien rule on the eve of World War I, France acquired all the territory except the Rif district in the north (about 8,500 square miles), the Ifni Enclave (about 580 square miles), the Tarfaya district in the south (about 10,500 square miles), which went to Spain; and the city of Tangier (about 150 square miles) at the entrance to the Mediterranean, which was internationalized. As was customary in protectorate arrangements, the French government pledged in the treaty of Fez of 30 March 1912 (Article 3) "to give constant support to His Sharifi Majesty against any danger that might threaten his person or his throne" and to continue giving such support to "the heir to the throne and to his successors." [1] The Spanish protectorate rested on an agreement that Spain concluded with France on 27 November 1912, and the sultan's interest was entrusted to his chosen viceroy, called a caliph. Refusing to become a client of the protecting powers, the reigning sultan abdicated in favor of his brother, Mawlay Yusuf, who by cooperating with France remained sultan until his death in November 1927. Only sixteen at the time of his accession to the throne, Sultan Muhammad ibn Yusuf (1927–61) became the first monarch of sovereign Morocco.

Under alien rule the sultan became a figurehead and the makhzan atrophied, for it exercised residual powers in the Muslim community only. Since Morocco was treated as an extension of Algeria for purposes of French settlement, the French modernized the protectorate administration for the primary benefit of the European settlers. The number of Europeans grew from an estimated 3,000 in 1912 to more than a half-million in 1956; 400,000 in the French zone, 70,000 in the Spanish, and 50,000 in Tangier. The investment of French capital occurred in spurts with cumulative effect in response largely to local inducements such as modest taxes and government subsidies and credits before 1939, and, after 1945, to political uncertainties in the metropolis and in French Indo-China. In the last decade of the protectorate, which ended in 1956, the French pumped an estimated $2 billion into Morocco, chiefly in public and semipublic funds.

Four of every five Europeans settled in the cities, and nearly half of the settlers made their home in Casablanca. In the urban areas the Europeans invested in modern light industries, such as food-processing, and textiles; and such firms employed one-quarter of the European labor force, according to the 1952 census. An almost equal number found work in the protectorate administration and in the liberal professions. In the rural areas the colons were attracted to mining phosphate, Morocco's chief export, which was to become competitive in the international market. More significant was the European investment in modernizing agriculture, for under the protectorate some 6,000 colons acquired title to about 2.5 million acres of the most fertile land in the country. The government modernized the ports and built modern highways, railroads, and communications facilities to promote public security and to serve the European economy; when France laid down its sovereignty, some 30,000 miles of highways, nearly one-third of them all-weather roads, and 1,000 miles of rails, criss-crossed the French zone.

The benefits of the modernization process were hoarded by the Europeans, yet repercussions were bound to be felt in the traditional Muslim society and economy, although most consequences, good and bad, were unplanned. The primary change in the Muslim community was the rapid growth of population, which almost doubled in the three decades preceding 1952. As one result, the rate of urbanization quickened, and by 1956 every fifth Muslim lived in the cities. However, as elsewhere in the Middle East, too many new townsmen crowded into the *bidonvilles*, or shantytowns. The internal migration was provoked by the spreading condition of fallahin, or peasants, being pushed off the land because of the lag of rural development and by the improved transportation that eased their mobility. Although 80 per cent of the Muslims still lived on the land in 1952, those gainfully employed in the rural areas represented only 70 per cent of the Muslim labor force. Moreover, a new rural group of about 60,000 former peasants were employed as salaried farmhands on the commercial farms of the colons. Not a few of these plantations, given over prominently to the cultivation of citrus and vines, were massive by any standard, since about 900 colons owned some 1.5 million acres. The urban Muslim labor force comprised, among others, nearly 300,000 who worked in traditional handicrafts and in the European-owned factories, nearly 250,000 in transportation, port administration, and longshoring, just over 100,000 in commerce, and 60,000 in the protectorate administration and in the liberal professions.

The colons clearly had displaced many peasants and, by depriving the Muslims of their most fertile lands, aggravated the rural population pressure. The jobs available for the unskilled in the towns did not multiply as quickly as the new townsmen who formed ever-larger pools of unemployed and underemployed workers. Nor did the French, for that matter, energetically develop the Muslim educational system, for as late as 1955 an estimated 77 per cent of the townspeople and 93 per cent of the villagers were still illiterate.

There were thus in effect three economies and three societies in French Morocco: the European, the modernizing Muslim, and the traditional Muslim. The modernizing Muslims created the nationalist movement, which found its first leaders among teachers, lawyers, senior civil servants, and wealthy merchants. Attempts in the mid-1930s to establish a formal organization all but foundered over personality clashes, and split the incipient movement before it could take solid shape. Some six years of repression by the protectorate regime followed. With the coming of World War II, the consequent weakening of the French position in Morocco, and the spread of independence movements in Asia and Africa, the Moroccan groups surfaced in the later war years, bolder than ever. In January 1944 the Moroccan nationalist leaders presented to the French Resident General, to Sultan Muhammad V, and to the British and American consular and military representatives in Rabat the first formal demand for Moroccan independence. The French responded by redoubling their efforts to suppress the independence movement through wholesale arrests.

Thus was launched the familiar vicious circle: popular demonstrations in the large towns, police and military repression, deaths on both sides, imperial concessions, then further nationalist demands followed by more demonstrations, repression, bloodshed, and concessions. The nationalists steadily advanced their cause. Moroccan ranks started to close as the traditional spokesmen endorsed their actions. In 1947, when Muhammad V openly sided with the nationalists, the Arab League had begun to take up the Moroccan cause and through its exertions the U.N. General Assembly in December 1952 gave its blessings to the Moroccan nationalist demand for terminating the protectorate.

For the first time under the protectorate, the French deposed a sultan when in August 1953 they exiled Muhammad V and his oldest son, Mawlay Hasan, and named as replacement Sidi Muhammad ibn Mawlay 'Arafah, an ineffectual older member of the 'Alawi clan, whose appointment simply exposed the imperial pretense of respecting Muslim rights and traditions. Every French act of disciplining the Muslim nationalists seemed to backfire. Exile gave Muhammad V a stature in Muslim Morocco that he had never enjoyed before; to modernizer and traditionalist alike he came to symbolize the aspiration for sovereignty regained. Recurrent arrest of the leaders kept the rival nationalist groups together in the National Front that they had formed in April 1951. The order to Muslim workers to disband their recently legalized unions, as punishment for the 1952 Casablanca demonstrations for independence that degenerated into riots when the French police and troops tried to curb the demonstrators, gave the nascent Muslim labor movement the needed fillip to develop, while underground, into a mass organization. The *Union marocaine de travail* (UMT), at its formal birth in March 1955, became the largest membership

organization in Morocco. By the following November, when Muhammad V was reinstated amid a triumphal welcome by the entire
Muslim population, an irregular tribal force called the Army of
Liberation and composed of Berbers from the Rif in the northern
Spanish zone had come into being and was beginning to strike at
vulnerable French targets, civilian and military. The guerrilla action, coinciding with the French admission of error, hastened the
decision to terminate the protectorate.

As protecting states, France and Spain had been in legal theory
trustees of the sultan and his makhzan. The French administrative
apparatus, which under the protectorate remained distinct from
the makhzan, was turned over to sovereign Morocco. Morocco thus
acquired a more centralized and more modern governmental system than the one it was deprived of nearly a half-century earlier.
But of greater importance, France transferred the sovereign authority, not to the Moroccan people, but to their sultan, who was
vested with legislative as well as executive power. France, moreover, assured the sultan that he would have at his disposal a national army, which the withdrawing protector would help create.
Parallel provisions appeared in the joint declaration and protocol
on the transfer of the northern zone signed by Spain and Morocco
on 7 April 1956; two years later Spain returned the southern zone.
The international regime of Tangier, meanwhile, was abolished on
29 October 1956.

The Moroccan Style of Absolutism

The nationalist parties had their beginnings in the 1930s. But the
struggle for independence, as we have seen, was not really launched
until January 1944 when the nationalist leaders, encouraged by the
allied military presence, submitted to the Free French the first formal demand for terminating the protectorate. Even then the
struggle gathered momentum only slowly as the movement, despite
its small organized membership, cleaved into rival factions. The
original National Action Bloc in the French zone had split in two
as early as 1937. After six years of repression, both factions were
reorganized in 1943 and renamed the Independence (*Istiqlal*)
Party and the Party of Democratic Independence (PDI). Two
other groups in the Spanish zone, the Reform Party (an Istiqlal
ally) and the Moroccan Unity Party (the only one with a branch
in Tangier), retained their prewar names. With the cooperation of
the Arab League, the four parties in April 1951 formed a National
Front, which lasted until independence and which gave its corpo-

rate members scope for individual action. In the final years of the protectorate the Istiqlal Party in the French zone blossomed into a mass movement with local cells in all major towns and attracted as an affiliate the UMT at the time of its organization. Thus, by 1956, Istiqlal far outstripped its rivals in size and nationalist influence.

In view of the major contribution to the struggle for independence, it was hardly surprising that the nationalist party leaders, particularly those of Istiqlal, expected to manage the political system of sovereign Morocco; but their hopes were illusory. Theirs were political parties in name only. Since the political system that brought forth the parties was a colonial system, wholly administered by imperial technicians, the parties formed part of a protest movement which failed to develop a quasi-governmental structure. Under the protectorate, it is true, the French recognized the sultan as chief of the Muslim government; and the makhzan, even in its shriveled condition of administering the *habus* (religious endowments), the mosques, the shari'ah courts, and other purely religious affairs, still conserved more than a spark of life. But the makhzan administrators were drawn from the traditional elite and not the modernizing one that dominated the protest movement. In the struggle for independence no nationalist party explicitly demanded that Moroccan sovereignty be transferred to a revitalized makhzan, for, manifestly, the nationalist leaders did not consider the makhzan a training ground for self-rule or the nucleus of an independent Moroccan regime.

Yet, what a majority of the nationalist leaders did not want actually came to pass. The protecting states transferred sovereignty to the sultan, which meant more than a simple revival of the makhzan, since the sultan also inherited the instruments of government fashioned by the imperial rulers. The first cabinet that the sultan named in the French zone with French approval on 7 December 1955, the first Muslim cabinet in the land, combined the functions of the makhzan and of the protectorate regime, even though full powers to perform these functions had to await the formal termination of the protectorate. Muhammad V successfully resisted Istiqlal demands for a "homogeneous government" (that is, an Istiqlal government) and for immediate sharing of political power, selecting instead as prime minister a man who belonged to no party, Mbarak Lahbil Bekkai (1907–61), a Berber veteran of the French Army who rose to the rank of colonel. The sultan structured a government of national union, that is, a coalition of all parties in the French zone—Istiqlal, the PDI, and the Liberal In-

dependents (a recently organized group of the sultan's friends)—
and insisted that the cabinet as a whole and its individual members
serve at his pleasure. In this precedent-making test of power between the sultan and the nationalist leaders, the sultan's position
was upheld, though this merely marked the start of the contest and
not its end.

Thus the modernizing elite found itself moving without interruption from the struggle for independence to the struggle for responsible political participation. The political modernizers in the
independence period seemed to have three basic choices: They
might acquiesce in the resuscitation of a traditional monarchy,
based on the classic Islamic practice of royal absolutism but applied
to modernizing agencies of administration, managed by party politicians and by independents, all chosen and delegated policy-
executing powers by the crown. They might demand conversion of
the monarchy from absolutism to constitutionalism under a system
of true parliamentary democracy. Or they might organize a conspiracy to overthrow the monarchy altogether and establish a republic, which could range in form from a multiple-party democracy
or a single-party dictatorship to military authoritarianism.

The development of a constitutional monarchy, an aspiration
which seemed to enjoy the support of a majority of the party politicians, was probably the least likely outcome, for neither the party
leaders, nor their followers, nor the country at large were ready for
a meaningful trial of democracy, as the postwar record in the rest
of the Middle East bore eloquent testimony. Constitutional planners have the merit of working in the open, so that their activities
are usually well charted. Conspirators, on the other hand, must
operate secretly. Consequently, the social scientist learns about
them only after the event, when they succeed or fail. For success in
Morocco, conspiracy needed the cooperation of the armed forces
or, at the very least, of its elite units. But this was precisely where
lay the strength of the king, a title that Muhammad V adopted in
August 1957. In any case, if the Moroccan monarchy were overthrown, the most likely outcome would be some variety of military
regime.

The three choices, it is obvious, were not mutually exclusive.
Most of the politicians of the pre-independence parties (except the
Liberal Independents) did not support in the revival of traditional
Islamic absolutism, but they grudgingly consented to take part in
the system, while directing their energies toward its transforma-
tion. Neither Muhammad V nor Hasan II, who succeeded to the

throne in March 1961, seemed willing to share, let alone surrender, any real powers. Yet neither king interfered unduly with the parties or the politicians, despite the politicians' avowed aim of curbing the royal office or, in a few instances, of even eliminating it. Actually, the number of parties, some short-lived, increased after independence. Although the Moroccan political system looked different from the Jordanian, the differences were more apparent than real.

Central to the survival of royal absolutism in Morocco, as in Jordan, was the king's reliance on a dedicated army to impose his will. Morocco's political system, perhaps even more than Jordan's, resembled a traditional Islamic monarchy with a modern veneer. But the two kingdoms were distinguished from the traditional monarchies by their armies, which were modern, career, apolitical forces with powerful attachments to the crown. When sovereignty was handed back to Morocco in 1956, Muhammad V could not have restored the pre-protectorate military organization even if he had so desired. The French policy of enabling the colons to procure the most fertile land resulted in uprooting most of the military, or gish, tribes that had in the past furnished the Moroccan sultans with the bulk of their fighting men. As France and Spain progressively pacified the mountain districts, the heartland of the old zone of dissent, they put an end to intertribal warfare while destroying the resistance to European imperial authority. The pacification thus erased the old division between the highlanders and the lowlanders and placed the two, at least in French Morocco, under a unified administration.

Meanwhile, even before World War I France began recruiting troops in Morocco for service in the French Army and continued the practice almost to the end of the protectorate. Spain did the same in its zone. In seeking the most martial candidates, the imperial powers favored the mountain tribesmen from the erstwhile blad al-siba. The Berbers for their part regarded service in the French and Spanish armies not as a political act but as a means of improving their economic condition, for they earned a handsome salary by local standards to do precisely what many tribesmen like best— to become experts in the care and use of modern military equipment. As tribesmen, they were born soldiers and easily accepted service in the French and Spanish armies as lifetime careers. On transfer to the Royal Moroccan Armed Forces (*Forces armées royales marocaines*, or FAR), they simply changed employers, thereby providing the Moroccan monarch with a professionally trained, partly combat-hardened army. Moreover, in the Moroccan service the loyalties were reinforced by Islamic ties, as the soldiers acknowledged the religious leadership of their king.

The FAR formally came into being in May 1956, when the French Army transferred to the newly independent kingdom some 15,000 Moroccan soldiers, among them a handful of officers and NCOs. Many of the soldiers were veterans of World War II with service in Europe and in the French empire, where they had battle experience in a modernized military establishment. A few months later the Spanish Army released to the FAR, 9,000 Moroccans most of whom had no exposure to modern warfare. To the French and Spanish transfers were added nearly 4,000 alumni of the Army of Liberation, mostly tribesmen from the Rif. In the splintered Moroccan nationalist movement, the Liberation Army took its place alongside the other political factions as the only militarized one. Probably for this reason the fledgling government of sovereign Morocco did not induct into the FAR all former guerrillas, who may have totaled 10,000.

By agreement with France in 1956, Morocco employed 150 officers, 550 NCOs and 190 enlisted men of the French Army for instructional and command service in the FAR, pending the training of Moroccan officers in French and Spanish military academies and in a new Royal Moroccan Academy for officers at Casablanca and a school for NCOs at Ahermoumon. By mid-1959 the FAR comprised some 880 Moroccan officers, 3,800 Moroccan NCOs, and approximately 26,000 enlisted men. The command was Moroccanized in 1960. Over the next three years the size of the FAR slowly expanded to some 35,000, including nearly 2,000 in the air force and about one-fourth that number in the navy. As a primary mission in the early years of independence, the FAR helped the king establish his authority in the highlands by suppressing insurgent tribes before they could assert their autonomy. The most serious crisis of this sort occurred in the winter of 1958–59 in the Rif, where militant tribes used dissatisfaction with the policies of the government as a pretext for openly defying the king's orders for peaceful submission. Such missions tested the allegiance of the troops to the king, for Berbers in the FAR's infantry battalions were sent into action against Berber tribesmen. The FAR thus enabled the king to keep the tribal areas pacified and the traditional society, as distinct from the modernizing one, united under his leadership.

The brief war in the fall of 1963 showed that the FAR was superior to the Algerian Army. The Moroccans seized their limited objectives and smashed the counterattacks. The Moroccan commanders, moreover, proved resourceful in overcoming logistical problems by employing their few transport planes to carry troops, munitions, and supplies from Marrakesh to isolated areas on the southern front and to evacuate the wounded. They also improvised a solution to an expected shortage of manpower by hastily mobilizing local "reserves," much in the pre-protectorate manner. The king's appeal to friendly shaykhs and his issuance of small arms to supplement tribal stores made it possible to enlarge the FAR by more than 75 per cent in less than three weeks. Once the crisis had passed, the tribal reserves were demobilized. The Moroccan armed forces in 1965 once again began to expand, reaching a peak of standing strength that approached 44,000 men in the three arms: some 40,000 in the FAR, 1,000 in the navy, and the rest in the air force. Perhaps as many as 80 per cent or more of the enlisted men and a high proportion of the officers were Berber tribesmen, among whom military service in sovereign Morocco, as in the French and Spanish protectorates, was still eagerly sought because of continuing widespread unemployment. The few urban Muslims in the armed forces, Arabs and Arabized Berbers, usually preferred administrative assignments either at headquarters or in noncombatant technical units, leaving to the Berber officers the top command slots.

The king held a tight rein over the armed forces. At the very inception of the military establishment in 1956 Muhammad V named as chief of staff Crown Prince Hasan, who became the actual supreme commander even though the king carried the title. Hasan relinquished neither the title nor the active command when he ascended the throne; indeed, he took a closer interest in the security forces than ever before. The commanders of the major military units reported to the king directly and also indirectly through the ministry of national defense. The paramilitary forces, which included the police and which numbered more than 30,000 men in 1965, were commanded by army officers, whom the king supervised personally as well as through the ministry of the interior. Besides, for the safety of his person the king organized elite troops as a Royal Guard. King Hasan continued relying heavily on France for matériel and for the training of his military and paramilitary forces. Nevertheless, he also seemed to be reviving the makhzan's pre-protectorate habit of seeking hardware and training missions from many countries, among them the United States,

Spain, Britain, and even the U.S.S.R. The military budget (see Table 11), which exceeded 300 million dirhams (about $60 million), or only 2.5 per cent of the estimated GNP in 1963, soared in the next year because of the Algerian war to 565 million dirhams (4.5 per cent of the GNP), declining in 1965 to 515 million (3.9 per cent).

Little wonder that the politicians, as a tactical objective in their unabating struggle to persuade the king to surrender some of his powers, tried to gain control over the management of the sensitive ministries. But Hasan, even more than his father before him, refused to modify the practice of appointing the loyal Berbers as ministers of defense and occasionally of the interior. Berber officers from the FAR filled, moreover, at times, many of the key posts in the two ministries. They were also sent by the ministry of the interior, which managed the centralized administration of the kingdom, to the provinces as governors and as *qaids* (governors' deputies) in the local districts.

The attempt of the modernizing politicians to capture the sensitive ministries was not an end in itself but only a means to the end of curtailing the king's powers. They demanded a written constitution that would rest on the principle of popular sovereignty, that would stipulate a separation of powers, and that would vest full executive authority in a council of ministers, reflecting popular, and not royal, choice and accountable to an elected legislature. It was an unequal struggle from the start. The politicians could not bargain with the crown. They had nothing to offer, because they still represented only a minority of the population. At least two-thirds of the citizenry belonged to the traditional society that as yet was not pressing for such changes. While not united behind a positive program, the traditionalists were nonetheless bound together in their mistrust of the advocates of change. Concentrated in the coastal cities, the modernizers may be said to have constituted a new zone of dissent. Although they were a steadily growing minority, they were also disunited, just as the old blad al-siba had been, and became progressively splintered into competing groups. The king skillfully played the groups off one against the other, and to compound the confusion he also sponsored the formation of political factions faithful to himself.

A constitution, framed at the king's request by French and Moroccan technicians, received popular approval by referendum in December 1962. The constitution guaranteed civil liberties and political rights to all citizens and provided for an elected bicameral

TABLE 11. Morocco: Force Levels, Government Expenditures, and GNP, 1956–65

| | Population (millions) | Force Levels (thousands) | Government Expenditures (millions of Moroccan dirhams) | | | GNP (millions of dirhams) | Defense Expenditures (as % of GNP) |
			Defense (including internal security and justice)	Development	Total		
1956 [a]	10.6	28	80.0	309.0	918.0	7,490	1.1
1957	10.8		118.0	270.0	991.0	7,640	1.5
1958	11.0		170.0	377.0	1,185.0	8,510	2.0
1959	11.3		197.0	315.0	1,287.0	8,310	2.4
1960	11.6	30	201.0	351.3	1,395.0	9,090	2.2
1961	11.9		234.0	451.1	1,616.3	9,040	2.6
1962	12.0		271.3	502.3	1,823.0	10,620	2.6
1963	12.3		301.5	720.3	2,035.0	11,950	2.5
1964	12.6		565.0	860.1	2,191.0	12,580	4.5
1965	13.0	44	515.0	791.0	2,098.0	13,180	3.9

SOURCES: IMF, *International Financial Statistics;* AID, *Selected Annual Statistics;* ACDA, *Selected Data, 1964 and 1965.*
[a] Fiscal year ends 31 December.

legislature. But under the instrument King Hasan II surrendered no real powers. The king alone (Article 65) named all the members of the government, which remained responsible to him. Although the House of Representatives, or lower chamber, in theory could force the collective resignation of the government by withholding confidence or by censure (Articles 80–81), the chamber itself to all intents and purposes (Articles 75 and 77) existed on the king's sufferance. If the house were dissolved by royal decree, it is true, new elections were required within forty days and the newly elected house might not be dissolved in less than a year (Articles 78–79). But the king was empowered (Article 35) to suspend the legislature altogether by simply decreeing a state of emergency. This is precisely the action that Hasan took in June 1965. After more than two months of fruitless negotiations with the opposition politicians to form a government of national union, he became de facto prime minister and, with the exception of three ministers who belonged to royalist factions, selected independents (technicians and nonparty politicians) as his colleagues. At the same time he proclaimed a state of emergency and prorogued parliament indefinitely.

The proximate cause of the drastic action had occurred late in March 1965. High-school students in Casablanca demonstrated in protest against the government's impending sharp reduction in the number of those who would be permitted to continue their education beyond the age of 18. This touched off riots which produced large-scale destruction of property by pillage and arson, as unemployed, half-urbanized peasants from the bidonvilles of the realm's largest city joined the demonstrators. The regular police, including auxiliaries, could not cope with the situation and were chiefly responsible for the high toll of deaths (more than two hundred). Order was finally restored by Mobile Intervention Companies (MICs), especially trained and equipped elite units of the national police stationed in the largest cities and intended for swift deployment in emergencies. The MICs proved their effectiveness not only in the prompt re-establishment of order in Casablanca but in keeping the sympathy demonstrations in Rabat and in some of the larger interior cities such as Fez, Marrakesh, and Ujda peaceable. More than that, the efficiency of the MICs made it unnecessary to employ units of the FAR.

King Hasan later weathered the crisis precipitated by the kidnapping and probable murder in Paris in October 1965 of Mehdi Ben Barka, the leftist opponent of the monarchy who, in exile, conducted a vigorous campaign for Moroccan republicanism. The minister of the interior, General Muhammad Ufqir, along with French intelligence and police officers, was charged by a French court with complicity in Ben Barka's disappearance. The king's refusal to surrender Ufqir, a Berber veteran of the French Army and former aide de camp to French residents-general and later to Muhammad V, led to difficulties with France. President de Gaulle in 1966 suspended direct economic and military aid to Morocco; the French commitment had been estimated at $100 million. Throughout the months of tension in domestic Morocco politics and in the relations with France, the king stood by his minister. Even after Hasan relinquished the premiership in July 1967, he did not dismiss Ufqir.

In Morocco, as in the other modernizing monarchies of the region, the king was reverting to a neoclassical Islamic political type. The cabinets resembled more closely the traditional Islamic wazirial diwan, or an absolute monarch's privy council, than the Western democratic ministerial council, for the prime minister and his colleagues individually and collectively served at the pleasure of the crown—and King Hasan served as his own prime minister in nearly five of the next seven years of his reign. To parliament, when in being, the king surrendered circumscribed powers only, and even these powers he entrusted to the lawmakers on a permanently probationary basis. King Hasan confirmed this when he dissolved parliament in June 1965 and ruled by decree for more than two years. Though filled with royalists, the bench nevertheless enjoyed independence in ordinary litigation whether civil (religious), commercial, or criminal. But in view of the continuing high rate of political crime, the king fell back again and again on summary arrest and military trial.

Royal authority in Morocco derived in the final analysis from the modernized armed forces. Over the years the king tightened the military (and civilian) counterespionage services, expanded the armed forces, improved the instructional methods, modernized the weaponry, and established himself as the real supreme commander of the security services. In them the king cultivated a close personal interest. Cabinet control, as we have seen, was no more than nominal, for even though the cabinet was an instrument of the crown, the king took special pains to place his own carefully selected aides in administrative charge of the security forces, the police no less than the soldiers. The police, in any case, were little more than an extension of the FAR and were commanded by its officers. All the top officers in the sensitive ministries and the security services reported directly to the king. The political allegiance of the officers to the crown had a powerful economic base—good pay and special benefits in what became a prestigious occupation. It also had a social and ethnic-linguistic base, for the Berber officers who predominated were recruited in the countryside to help uphold the king's will in the cities, largely Arab, and the primary zone of political dissent.

19

KUWAYT: AN AFFLUENT AMIRATE UNDER POLITICAL SIEGE

Kuwayt came under political siege by way of substantial oil revenues and the large foreign population that it attracted. In 1945 it was still a traditional tribal principality under British protection, and its domestic politics were the exclusive preserve of the shaykhly clan. By the time Britain returned external sovereignty to the amirate a decade and a half later, its ruler was already struggling to preserve his clan's paramountcy.

Kuwayt is an oddity, not in the Middle East alone, but in the world at large. Less than 6,000 square miles of unrelieved desert to which may be added more of the same waste in the undivided half of the 2,000-square-mile Kuwayti-Saudi Neutral Zone, the Sunni amirate floats on the largest known pool of oil. Kuwayt ranked in the 1960s among the half-dozen largest oil-producing, oil-exporting countries. By 1963 its oil concessionaires on land and offshore were hoisting to the surface more than 100 million metric tons of crude a year, and at that rate of production it was estimated that the proved resources would not be exhausted in fewer than eighty years. The annual oil revenues already overtopped a half billion dollars and were still climbing; a dozen years earlier, the government's oil income had not reached $20 million. The growth could be attributed in part to the accident of Iran's nationalization in 1951 of the then exclusive oil concession owned by the Anglo-Iranian Oil Company (AIOC), a British firm in which the British Government owned a controlling interest. As it happened, the AIOC together with the (American) Gulf Oil Company also owned the Kuwayt Oil Company, the exclusive concessionaire in Kuwayt proper, where most of the country's proved reserves were located. The AIOC thus took the natural step of substituting Kuwayti for Iranian crude to meet the demand of its clients. The scheme for company-government equal sharing of the profits, trebling the rate of payment to the shaykhdom, coincided with the sudden rise in production.

The size of the population of Kuwayt as late as 1945 is not precisely known, but it could not have exceeded 100,000 and may have been much lower. The preliminary returns of the census of 1965, the third census in eight years and indeed in the country's history, disclosed a population of 468,000. The startling population increase in two decades, which could hardly fail to unhinge the traditional society, resulted from a combination of extraordinary circumstances: not only the sudden and sustained massive income, but the unpreparedness of the native population for its rational use, the absence of natural resources other than oil, and the presence on the throne of an enlightened yet self-interested ruler.

Kuwayt was essentially little more than a city-state, since every second resident lived in Kuwayt City, the capital. Though of beduin derivation, many townsmen before the discovery of oil had earned their living as fishermen, builders and sailors of dhows, and pearl divers. A handful of international traders (and smugglers) formed, by local standards, a wealthy merchant class. With the coming of the unending oil boom and the shaykh's investments in transforming his principality into a welfare shaykhdom, in modernizing Kuwayt City, and in attempting to build a modern economy, the demand for labor of all qualities—unskilled, technical and professional—became insatiable, and the only way to meet it was to import it. The government alone, it was estimated in 1963, employed 53,000 civil servants (or one for every seven or eight residents), but not more than a third were citizens of the state. The registered expatriate labor force in 1963 surpassed 122,000 and may well have reached 150,000 two years later.

Kuwayt received its independence from Britain in 1961. Shaykh Mubarak al-Sabah Al Sabah (1896–1915), who had seized power by murdering his older half-brother in 1896, joined Britain's quasi-protectorate regime in the Persian Gulf three years later by surrendering the shaykhdom's external sovereignty. The unratified Anglo-Ottoman convention of 1913 introduced an element of ambiguity into the Anglo-Kuwayti relationship. It recognized Kuwayt as an autonomous Ottoman provincial district while simultaneously confirming the validity of the instruments that defined Kuwayt's status as a British-protected shaykhdom. This ambiguity was removed by a new Anglo-Kuwayti agreement of November 1914, concluded when the Ottoman Empire entered World War I as Britain's enemy. Britain then recognized Kuwayt as "an independent Gov-

ernment under British protection." To each of the protected
shaykhdoms in the Persian Gulf, Kuwayt included, a political
agent was assigned, and the agents in turn reported to a Political
Resident, the area coordinator of British affairs. In 1937 management of Britain's Gulf interests passed from the India Office to the
Foreign Office, and the Political Residency moved from Bushire in
Iran to al-Manamah on the Bahrayn Archipelago. The United
Kingdom helped defend Kuwayt against attack by Saudi forces in
1920–21 and again in 1929–30 but, aside from upholding the
Mubarak line of the Sabah clan, refrained from interfering in the
shaykhdom's domestic affairs.

Shaykhly rule in Kuwayt, like its counterparts elsewhere in the
Arabian Peninsula, was personal, and insofar as the shaykh delegated authority, he did so at his own discretion and only to his
Sabah relatives. The succession, however, did not necessarily pass
from father to son but was determined by the clan. The first attempts to break the Sahab political monopoly were made by the
wealthy merchants, who at the time of the accession of Ahmad al-
Jabir (1921–50) and 'Abdallah al-Salim (1950–65) persuaded the
shaykhs to create advisory bodies on which merchants sat. But the
new organs of government proved ineffective and short-lived.
What did take root, however, were government departments set
up late in the 1930s to divide the administrative labor, and, characteristically, supervision of the departments was entrusted only to
Sabahis. The political system was not modified again for a decade
and a half, until the paternalistic policies of the first oil-rich shaykh,
'Abdallah al-Salim, compelled further rationalization. To coordinate the activities of the several departments, Shaykh 'Abdallah
created a Supreme Council, consisting of the departmental heads,
or presidents, as they were called.

Like the kings of Saudi Arabia, Shaykh 'Abdallah al-Salim
viewed the income from oil as his to dispense without further accounting. Yet in marked contrast to his contemporary, King Sa'ud,
Shaykh 'Abdallah was personally frugal and handled his multiplying revenues wisely. With few exceptions—the most egregious was
the ruler's uncle, 'Abdallah al-Mubarak, who presided over the departments of defense and the interior of the 1950s—the Sabahis
avoided conspicuous spending in the earlier years, although they
could hardly escape it in the later ones. Instead, the ruler transformed the newly affluent principality into a welfare state and each
year invested much of the oil income in overseas securities, which
poured additional millions annually into the state's coffers. He

offered all residents in his principality, whether citizens or not, free education, free medical care, and subsidized housing. In the absence of a natural water supply, he had desalination plants erected with a daily production by 1965 of 12 million gallons.

Meanwhile, in June 1961, Britain and Kuwait replaced their 1899 agreement with a treaty of mutual support and consultation, which bound Britain "to assist the Government of Kuwait if the latter request such assistance." [1] In the period of the British protective presence the otherwise shattering impact of a rapidly modernizing society and economy on the traditional political system could be cushioned. Following the British withdrawal, the ruler had to devise new ways of preserving political continuity while encouraging further social and economic change. The political threat was not a wholly internal one. No sooner had the 1961 treaty been signed than Prime Minister Qasim of Iraq laid claim to Kuwayt, which he charged had been stolen from Iraq by British imperialists. The legal basis of Qasim's claim was murky at best. However, the issue was settled not by legal proceedings but by the prompt military action of Britain under the 1961 agreement, and of the Arab states, particularly Saudi Arabia and the U.A.R., which rallied to Kuwayt's side. Admission to membership in the Arab League in August 1961 and to the U.N. two years later also helped shield the amirate, as Kuwayt had already begun calling itself. Besides, the amir himself tried to win Arab friends and influence their governments by founding in 1963 the Kuwayt Fund for the Economic Development of the Arab Countries, with capital resources amounting to $840 million. The Fund was expressly designed to issue loans to Arab governments for development projects. Early loans were granted to Sudan for modernizing railroads, to Jordan for expanding agriculture and industry, to the U.A.R. for improving the Suez Canal, and to Tunisia for extending land settlement and increasing electric power. Moreover, in February 1965 Kuwayt gave the U.A.R. a loan of $98 million in hard currency to help it surmount a financial crisis.

In retrospect, the foreign threat proved a blessing in disguise. More complex was the internal threat to Sabah hegemony, and checking it dictated action of a different sort. In less than a decade the Kuwaytis had become a minority in their own country. The first census, taken in 1957, showed that of the 206,000 residents 56.2 per cent were citizens. The population rose to 322,000, according to the 1961 census, but the proportion of Kuwaytis had declined to 50.4 per cent. The breakdown of the census returns of

1965 was not available, but the relative number of Kuwaytis continued its sharp descent to possibly as little as 40 per cent. The foreign population, however, was largely transient—seasonal and short-term workers from nearby Arab countries and from Iran, Pakistan, and India. Three-fourths of these workers came without wives or families. Had they been encouraged to settle permanently in the country, many might have responded; but the original Kuwayti population, no less than the ruler, seemed convinced that their interest lay in protecting themselves against the resident aliens. When Shaykh 'Abdallah al-Salim issued the first naturalization decree in December 1959, stipulating that only those living continuously in Kuwayt from 1920 on would be recognized as citizens, the measure won the plaudits of an overwhelming majority of his subjects. Foreigners seeking naturalization were required, under an amendment of 1960, to reside in the country from the date of promulgation for ten years if they were Arab nationals, and for fifteen if they were not.

Though inhibited from acquiring citizenship, the resident aliens were carriers of political and social ideas as well as technical skills. They brought with them first-hand knowledge of other forms of government and of economic and social organization. The Egyptians in particular, with a considerable assist from the Jordanians (former Palestinians), who together formed the most numerous element among the teachers in Kuwayt's school system, introduced a strong element of social and political discontent by instilling concepts of Egyptian republicanism in the youth. Economic expansion brought into being a new middle class with increasing economic power but deprived of opportunities to acquire political power. As late as 1961 the Sabah clan still governed the country as their private domain. Only the relatives of the amir sat on the Supreme Council.

Under the growing pressures, the amir slowly recoiled from the traditional system of personal and clan rule. In the interest of national solidarity during the quarrel with Iraq in 1961, the amir co-opted ten merchants into the Supreme Council. In December he authorized the election of a Constituent Assembly of twenty, and eleven months later promulgated a constitution that provided for a National Assembly of fifty and a council of ministers. Kuwayt was declared (Article 4) a hereditary amirate of the descendant of Mubarak al-Sabah Al Sabah, and the amir was empowered to designate his successor. Amir 'Abdallah named as heir and first prime minister his brother Sabah. The first cabinet took over substantially the membership of the replaced Supreme Council, so that it was composed exclusively of Sabahis and wealthy merchants. However, about a fourth of the deputies in the first Assembly, elected in January 1963, were Arab unity nationalists who looked to the U.A.R. for political inspiration. This faction opposed the formation in December 1964 of a new cabinet because of the retention of so many merchants. In the ensuing struggle for the political power that the amir was gradually relinquishing, the merchant class found support in the reigning Salim branch of the Sabah clan, and the middle class in the 'Ahmad al-Jabir branch. The amir responded in January 1965 to the opposition in the Assembly by dropping from the new cabinet most of the merchants and appointing in their place for the first time spokesmen of the middle class. Under the constitution (Article 58) the council of ministers, individually and jointly, were responsible to the amir. By acquiescing in the demands of the opposition, he had opened the door to the Assembly's eventually sharing with him mastery over the cabinet.

The constitution and the organs of democratic government, however, were still little more than a façade, since all the principal ministries were assigned to Sabahis alone, the heir-designate retaining the prime ministry in the successive cabinets. The authority of the amir and the Sabah clan was sustained by the steadily enlarging, modernized military establishment. So long as Kuwayt had remained a British dependency, the shaykh had assumed minimal domestic police duties with the close guidance of the protecting power. Once Kuwayt became a major oil producer, the shaykh expanded his armed forces from some 600 in 1954 to about 2,500 seven years later. They were trained by British officers and Palestine Arab émigrés and equipped with British hardware, mostly light arms but also Centurion tanks. In the first four years of independence Amir 'Abdallah nearly trebled the size of the army (see Table 12). The top officers were Sabahis, some trained at Sandhurst. It was a career army, whose officers and ranks were carefully recruited and were given higher pay than soldiers in any other Middle East army. On good behavior and continued loyalty to the amir, they were assured permanent employment. Little wonder that service in the army was prestigious, and the morale of the men high. In addition to the army, there were a paramilitary national police force and volunteer military reserves, each consisting of more than a thousand men. Their commanding officers, like those of the army, were members of the amiral clan. A British mission

Table 12. Kuwayt: Force Levels, Government Expenditures, and GNP, 1959/60–1965/66

| | Population (thousands) | Force Levels (thousands) | Government Expenditures (millions of Kuwayti dinars) | | | GNP (millions of dinars) | Defense Expenditures (as % of GNP) |
			Defense (including internal security and justice)	Development	Total		
1959/60 [a]	219		15.2	29.9	158.6 [b]	296.0	5.1
1960/61	223	2.5	16.4	26.8	135.2	350.0 [c]	4.6
1961/62	322		15.0	26.3	160.7	400.0 [c]	3.8
1962/63	321		21.7	26.8	165.0	460.0	4.7
1963/64	371		26.4	36.8	176.3	500.0	5.3
1964/65	426		25.7	44.9	201.3 [c]	542.0	4.7
1965/66	467	7	25.6	47.0	211.0 [c]	612.0	4.2

SOURCES: IMF, International Financial Statistics; United Nations, Statistical Yearbook; AID, Selected Annual Statistics; ACDA, Selected Data, 1964 and 1965.

a Fiscal year ends 31 March.
b The 1959/60 budget covered the 15-month period from January 1, 1959, to March 31, 1960. Budget data shown here are adjusted to cover a 12-month period.
c Budget estimates.
d Rough estimate.

still supervised the over-all training program. The allocations to defense and security in the annual budgets rose from 15 million dinars or less than 4 per cent of the GNP in 1961–62, the first year of independence, to nearly 26 million dinars or 4.5 per cent of the GNP three years later, reflecting the ruling clan's anxieties.

Under the constitution (Article 67), the amir was supreme commander of the armed forces with exclusive power to commission and discharge officers. Amir 'Abdallah delegated responsibility for managing the armed forces to his minister of defense and for managing the police to his minister of the interior, and in the cabinet created in January 1965 he assigned both portfolios to his oldest son. On 'Abdallah's death in November, his brother Sabah al-Salim Al Sabah, the prime minister and heir apparent, succeeded to the amiral throne. By pre-arrangement, the new amir's cousin, Jabir al-Ahmad Al Sabah, was named prime minister and heir apparent. There was no immediate break in the policy of reserving the sensitive ministries for members of the Sabah clan, and 'Abdallah's son remained minister of defense and of the interior. The election of January 1967 reduced the number of opposition deputies from 8 to 4 in an assembly of 50 deputies, but, later in the year, the amir, for the first time, entrusted a sensitive ministry to someone other than a relative, when he named 'Abd al-Rahman 'Atiqi minister of finance and oil.

Non-military Republics

20

GARRISON DEMOCRACY: ISRAEL*

The Six Day War in June 1967 disoriented Israel's external military politics. It appeared almost certain that the remnants of the 1949 armistice system had been shattered beyond repair. What might take its place could not be foreseen. Israel insisted that it would not give up the territories occupied in the war, unless the Arab states were prepared to negotiate a formal peace, with full recognition of Israel's right to exist and with the unconditional guarantee of free naval and maritime transit through the Suez Canal and the Straits of Tiran. The Arab states, for their part, insisted on the prior return of the occupied territories before they were even willing to consider the remaining issues. Equally deep were the differences over the mode of settlement, with Israel demanding direct negotiations, and the Arab states, indirect. The diplomatic stalemate left too many questions unanswered to permit a meaningful evaluation of the future of Israel's external military politics.

In many subtle ways Israel's internal military politics were also changing. The June 1967 war reopened political options that the armistice system of 1949 had closed. For reasons of historical and religious sentiment, it is true, the prompt annexation of Jordanian Jerusalem even before the end of June 1967 stirred little controversy among Israel's Jews. For reasons of national security, the Israel government seemed likely, also with wide popular support, not to release its grip on Syria's Golan Heights. But on policies toward the remaining occupied districts—the West Bank, the Sinai Peninsula, and the Gaza Strip—there were wide differences of view. The political parties, dusting off their pre-independence doctrines about the future size and nature of the state that they aspired to build, divided along lines reminiscent of the debate on partition that had begun with the original proposal of the British

* This chapter is based in part on my paper on Israel in *The Military in the Middle East: Problems in Society and Government*, edited by Sydney Nettleton Fisher (Columbus: Ohio State University Press, 1963), pp. 89–104.

357

Royal Commission on Palestine in July 1937. The new debate, like the old one, focused not only on boundaries but on the political system, since former Jewish binationalists, who had all but abandoned their cause, revitalized the program for a Jewish-Arab state. Of no less significance, with the continuing failure of the Arab governments to frame fresh policies toward Israel to cope with the new realities, the Palestine Arabs, for the first time since the mandate's expiry, were taking matters into their own hands. After confining their exploits largely to rural and frontier districts, the Palestine Arab guerrillas in the late summer of 1968 became bolder and started planting time bombs outside movie houses, bus stations, and cafes in Jerusalem and Tel Aviv. These acts of violence, which threatened to upset the Jewish-Arab communal balance within Israel proper, recalled the tactics of the guerrillas in the Palestine Arab revolt of 1936–39.

Because of the uncertainty of Israel's external and domestic politics, pending a durable settlement of the issues created by the latest Arab-Israel war, the analysis in the present chapter is primarily limited to the conditions that prevailed before 5 June 1967.

The Jewish community of Israel in May 1948 could boast an estimated literacy rate of 93.7 per cent; by 1961 that rate had fallen to 87.9 per cent, thus making the community the only one in a sovereign state of the postwar Middle East with declined literacy. Yet, even including the country's Arab minority, whose estimated literacy rate by 1961 had climbed to 48.3 per cent, the proportion of people in Israel above the age of 14 who could read and write exceeded that of any other state in the region. Declining literacy was, of course, only a passing phenomenon that reflected the condition of many adult Jewish immigrants from Middle East countries who had received no formal education. This condition was being corrected among the second generation, for children between the ages of 5 and 14 were required by law to attend school.

Of all the region's oil-poor countries, Israel has the highest estimated per capita GNP, over $1,300 in 1965 or double the sum at the nation's birth. Israel started sovereign life with an economy that was still in an incipient stage of development, with material resources that were far from bountiful. Its human resources, by contrast, were highly unusual. Many scientists, engineers, technicians, entrepreneurs, and managers immigrated into the country under the mandate and after independence. Outside grant aid averaged more that $200 million a year in the first two postwar decades. In those twenty years American Jews contributed about $1.0 billion, purchased about $0.5 billion worth of Israel bonds, and invested perhaps $0.25 billion in Israel industry. In the same period the United States gave the new state about $800 million in economic aid, nearly half as grants. The next largest source of external support, West Germany, contributed a total of $750 million in reparations in the dozen years ending in 1965. Skilled manpower and foreign aid enabled Israel to expand its economy at an annual average rate of more than 9 per cent in the decade and a half ending in 1965. The expansion came to a sudden halt in 1966, as the country suffered its first severe depression, with at least one-tenth of the workers unemployed by May 1967.

By the mid-1960s Israel seemed more comparable to the states of Western Europe than to its regional neighbors. The Jewish population was overwhelmingly urban, 86.8 per cent in 1964 living in the towns and their immediate suburbs. Two of every three Christian Arabs were also townsmen, while four of every five Muslim Arabs were fellahin. Israel's industrial condition is reflected in the following tabulation of the distribution of national income and of the labor force in 1964:

	National Income	Labor Force
Agriculture	10%	13%
Industry	25	25
Services	65	62

The economy was a mixed one, combining governmental, private, and socialist enterprise. Three of every four Jewish villages were either cooperatives or collectives, which jointly owned purchasing and marketing cooperatives. Agriculture was thus the most thoroughly socialized section of the economy. Private investment in industry exceeded that in agriculture. The Histadrut, or General Federation of Jewish Labor, which consisted in 1965 of nearly 900,000 members, or all but 10 per cent of the organized workers, owned many factories and most transport, banking, and insurance firms. The government, too, participated in essential undertakings that did not promise early or certain profits, and it owned outright those plants intimately associated with national security.

The depression of 1966–67 underscored the country's vulnerability, for Israel led the most dangerous life in the Middle East. In the twentieth year of independence, Israel was still a beleaguered country. All its immediate neighbors were political enemies, formally committed to put the Jewish state out of existence. The threat from the Arab League was real. The Unified Arab Command that the League created early in 1964 was advertised as a measure that would prevent Israel from using its share of the Jordan River waters. The League also established at that time, under Palestine Arab leadership, the Palestine Liberation Organization (PLO), which, as its title suggested, aimed at Israel's destruction. To these organizations, based in Cairo, was added a third, al-Fatah, sponsored by the government of Syria. The PLO and al-Fatah recruited among Palestine refugees, chiefly in Syria and Jordan, guerrillas who stepped up acts of sabotage in 1966–67 on the highways and in the villages of Israel close to the Arab frontiers, with mounting numbers of wounded and dead. These incidents intermixed with others staged by the Syrian army over unsettled disputes in the Israel–Syrian demilitarized zone. Israel's counterraids, such as the spectacular one at al-Samu' in Jordan in November 1966, recurrent consideration of the border violence by the United Nations Security Council, and the supersonic dogfights between the Israel and Syrian air forces, starting in the summer of 1966, all illustrated the unabating tension along the Arab-Israel armistice lines.

The tensions on the frontier induced Israel to accelerate its arms rivalry with the eastern members of the Arab League, particularly Egypt. The armies in this zone were going sophisticated, and supersonic aircraft, missiles, tanks, and electronic gear carried steadily higher price tags. The double-tiered races, which paired off the suppliers and the clients, pushed Israel into ever sharper competition. In the search for self-generative military capacity, Israel diverted a large share of its industry to military uses. One of the most energetic and resourceful customers for war surplus in the world, Israel created workshops for the rehabilitation and upgrading of heavy weapons considered obsolete in Europe and North America. Moreover, Israel produced almost all its needs in light and medium weapons, developing in the process the most elaborate military industry in the region. For research and engineering in new weaponry, Israel summoned technicians and scientists from the major industrial countries of the world. In the depression of 1966–67, the military industry did not lay off personnel.

The Israel government at that time admitted spending as much as 11.3 per cent of its GNP for external and domestic security (see Table 13). While much of the cost of the military industry and of the associated research and engineering was incorporated into this

TABLE 13. Israel: Force Levels, Government Expenditures, and GNP, 1952/53–1968/69

	Population (millions)	Force Levels[c] (thousands)	Government Expenditures (millions of Israel pounds)			GNP (millions of pounds)	Defense Expenditures (as % of GNP)
			Defense (including internal security and justice)	Development (less debt repayment)	Total		
1952/53[a]	1.63		60.3	108.8[d]	295.6	1,062	5.7
1953/54	1.67		70.2	164.2[d]	406.4	1,334	5.3
1954/55	1.72		73.3	257.0	648.2	1,762	4.2
1955/56	1.79	250	81.8	347.3[d]	777.8	2,124	3.9
1956/57	1.87		173.1	276.4	827.4	2,534	6.8
1957/58	1.98		221.8	404.9	1,132.3	2,943	7.5
1958/59	2.03		256.3	438.4	1,295.7	3,373	7.6
1959/60	2.09		283.9	506.5	1,336.5	3,861	7.4
1960/61	2.15	300	357.8	399.4	1,728.8	4,346	8.2
1961/62	2.23		372.7	548.7	2,271.9	5,208	7.2
1962/63	2.33		474.1	688.3	2,476.4	6,243	7.6
1963/64	2.43		616.8	890.7	3,113.8	7,528	8.2
1964/65	2.52		838.9	894.0	3,676.0	8,692	9.6
1965/66	2.60	375	947.8	1,015.0	4,373.0	10,202	9.3
1966/67[b]	2.66		1,340.0	900.0	5,046.6	11,863	11.3
1967/68[b]	2.72		1,518.0	1,151.0	6,226.9		
1968/69[b]			1,559.0	502.0	5,897.0		

SOURCES: Israel, Central Bureau of Statistics, *Statistical Abstract of Israel*; Government of Israel, Annual Budgets.
a Fiscal year ends 31 March.
b Estimates.
c Including reserves in the citizen army; the regular service probably consisted of about 100,000 in 1965.
d Figures for debt repayment not included; figure given shows only development budget.

budgetary figure, some of the expenses undoubtedly were not, so
that the total outlays for security were probably understated in the
1960s. They may well have been closer to 14 per cent of the GNP
or even higher in the last fiscal year before the June war. Though
relatively one of the highest military spenders in the world, Israel
found ample company in the immediate neighborhood. At least
five Arab states (Iraq, Jordan, Saudi Arabia, Syria, and the U.A.R.)
were spending relatively as much on arms in 1966. Yet despite the
steep sums set aside for security, Israel managed to keep up its high
investments in development which, after debt repayment,
amounted to about 10 per cent of the GNP in 1965–66 and 7.7 per
cent in the next fiscal year.

The proliferating military industries, the multiplying stockpiles
of local and imported weapons, and a citizen army converted Israel
into a garrison state under David Ben Gurion, prime minister in
thirteen of the state's first fifteen years. As his successor in 1963,
Ben Gurion selected Levi Eshkol, a man who rose to political-
military leadership after eleven years of managing the ministry of
finance. Like Ben Gurion, Eshkol also held on to the defense portfolio. The economy-minded prime minister in the first three years
of his tenure approved for defense an ever-bigger slice of the annual government budgets. The continuity of defense policies could
be attributed largely to the country's security position and to its
stable political system.

Israel's Vulnerability

An appreciation of the magnitude of Israel's security problems was
indispensable to an appraisal of the state's defense efforts. A frontier of 750 miles, four-fifths of it on land, was uncommonly long for
a country less than 8,000 square miles in size. The central and
coastal plains were scarcely wider than 12 miles, for a distance of
some 35 miles. No point within the country was more than ten
minutes by slow plane from a hostile land frontier. With the exception of the Mediterranean coast, Israel has no permanent boundaries. By resorting to economic and political blockade, the Arab
governments continued to seek the isolation of Israel; and by sponsoring the unified command and the saboteurs, the Arab states
continued to try to frighten Israel into submission. The state was
born in a war for survival, and its neighbors seemingly refused to
give up the aspiration of wiping Israel off the Middle East map. Of
this objective, responsible Arab spokesmen reminded the Israelis
almost daily on the air and in the press.

Israel's security planners argued that their country could not afford to lose a war since it might never have a second chance. The menacing realities went far to explain the government's undiminished suspicion toward its Arab minority, which, located in part along the armistice lines, remained basically sympathetic to the state's enemies and thus formed a potentially subversive community. Yet some Israelis, among whom the Marxist but non-Communist Mapam (United Labor Party) was the largest group, disagreed with the government's Arab policy, particularly with the treatment of the Arab minority. On doctrinal grounds, Mapam never tired of insisting that Israel take the initiative in abandoning the residual military administration. To these pressures the government responded gradually, allowing the Arabs in 1959 free daytime movement in the cities, ending night curfews in Arab areas three years later, when the government also gave the Arabs the right of appeal from military court convictions, and finally, in November 1966, abolishing military government altogether.

Continued mutual distrust contributed to interlocking arms races in the Arab-Israel zone.[2] If the rivals had been left to their own devices, Israel would still have enjoyed a technological lead over its neighbors. But the new states in the postwar Middle East, like those farther east in Asia and those in Africa, turned to the industrial states for arms. Early in life Israel developed a sense of isolation that reached its greatest intensity in the winter of 1955–56, when the Soviet bloc began competing with the Western countries in courting the Arab states by the sale of modern military equipment at high discount. The importation of military hardware that Israel could neither make nor buy had the effect of a technological breakthrough by its Arab enemies. The isolation came to an end in the summer and fall of 1956 as a result of the Suez crisis, which aligned France and Britain against Egypt and brought Israel early delivery of jets and other heavy equipment long on order from France. Israel's pre-emptive strike in Sinai in the fall of 1956 might be attributed largely to its fixed purpose of restoring a qualitative weapons lead by the destruction or capture of much of Egypt's Soviet-bloc equipment, which was conveniently, if threateningly, stockpiled along Israel's southwest frontier. The Arab-Israel arms rivalry in the 1960s became steadily more costly, as Israel made a determined effort to buy sophisticated weapons in all major Western states.

Internal difficulties further jeopardized Israel's security. For the most part, Israel was a land of immigrants who arrived after the declaration of independence. To the 650,000 Jews living there in May 1948 were added 1.25 million newcomers by 1965. Nearly three-fifths poured into the country in the first three and one-half years. Until the settlers were integrated into the society and the economy, they represented a liability more than an asset. They did not know the terrain; they spoke different languages; and their dedication to the country's mission of sponsoring the Jewish national renaissance and to the sacrifices that state-building entailed was uncertain. At the end of 1948, nearly 55 per cent of the Jews in Israel had immigrated from Europe and the Americas; more than 35 per cent were born in the country; and slightly less than 10 per cent came from Asia and Africa, mostly the first. The Western preponderance lasted little more than a decade, for by the end of 1959 the *sabras*, as the Israel-born Jews are known, outnumbered the Europeans. By the end of 1964, the sabras were approaching 40 per cent of the total, while the Europeans had fallen to less than 32 per cent, the Africans had risen to nearly 15 per cent and the Asians to nearly 14 per cent. Most Asians and Africans hailed from countries of low living standards, and not a few were illiterate. Their assimilation was costly. Advance assurance of whether the standards of the Asians and Africans would be lifted or those of the Europeans lowered was lacking.

In the circumstances, Israel faced the need to create a military establishment that would provide greatest use of its technical and managerial skills at lowest cost in manpower and funds, so as not to hamper the expanding economy. It would have to be capable of rapid mobilization and demobilization. It would have to achieve and preserve a qualitative superiority in weapons over the armies of its neighbors, and do so with the least dependence on the outside, in view of the unreliability of external sources of supply. As many foreign powers as possible had to be cultivated in the outer non-Arab zone of the Middle East and in Asia and Africa, no less than in Europe and the Americas. The army would have to furnish a means of integrating into the society the heterogeneous multilingual polyglot immigrants, and of populating the repellent districts on the frontier and in the desert. The founders of Israel's defense establishment sought to obtain all these ends, and to a remarkable degree they succeeded. What techniques did they employ?

The Citizen Army

Israel found its primary answer in a citizen army. The structure of the Israel Defense Forces (IDF)[3] is more typical of Europe than of the Middle East, and among the European armies the IDF, particularly in the organization of the reserves, most closely resembles the citizen army of Switzerland, after which it was originally patterned. Yet, in time, the IDF developed its own distinctive qualities partly inherited from a pre-independence, semilegal militia, and partly adapted from British, French, American, and Russian practices to meet the special security needs of the country.

In 1948 a hodgepodge of military units that had come into being in the Jewish community under the the mandate fought what has since been designated the War for Liberation. The largest group, Haganah (defense), was essentially a secret militia organized by the Jewish quasi-government in 1921, and enlarged in later years in cooperation with, and at times in defiance of, the Palestine government, so that by 1948 it could place about 45,000 troops in the field. Two smaller dissident guerrilla groups—the National Military Organization (*Irgun Zvai Leumi*), formed in 1938 and numbering about 3,000, and the Fighters for Israel's Freedom (*Lohamei Herut Israel*) formed in 1940 and numbering fewer than 500 —did not acknowledge the quasi-government's jurisdiction, although on occasion after the summer of 1945 they cooperated with Haganah. In less than a fortnight after the declaration of independence, the Provisional Government of Israel issued a special ordinance establishing the IDF. Within the area assigned to the Jewish state by the United Nations General Assembly's partition resolution, the Irgun and the Freedom Fighters were declared illegal and their members compelled to join the IDF. The terrorist groups, however, continued their independent action in the Jerusalem area, where they were finally disbanded in September 1948, immediately after the murder of Count Folke Bernadotte, the U.N. Palestine Mediator. The depoliticization of the armed forces was completed early in November with the dissolution of the headquarters of Palmah,[4] Haganah's commando troops, who were closely identified with the collective villages of the non-Communist Marxist *Ahdut ha-'Avodah* (Labor Unity) Party.

On 8 September 1949, less than two months after the consummation of the Arab-Israel armistice, the *Kneset* (unicameral legislature) enacted a comprehensive Defense Service Law which, with later amendments, established the legal basis of Israel's citizen army. The IDF embraces the ground troops, the navy, and the air force. The Regular Service (*Sherut Sadir*), or the troops on active duty, consists of the career forces and the conscripts. The career forces constitute what is called the Permanent Service (*Sherut*

Qevah). In the army the Permanent Service is composed of a nucleus of commissioned and noncommissioned officers who form the cadre for the conscripts and for the reserve units and carry out functions of command, planning, administration, technical service, and instruction. Because of the need for constant preparedness and special servicing and maintenance, the Permanent Service of the navy and air force, however, represents a much larger proportion of their total manpower.

The rank and file of the Regular Service is made up of the Conscript Service (*Sherut Hovah*) which, under the law, all men and women[5] on reaching 18 must enter, the men for 26 months and the women for 20.[6] In the early years of independence, because of the large number of immigrants of military age, liability for the draft continued until the age of 29, although the term for recruits above 26 was reduced for men to 24 months and for women to 18. The army conscripts form infantry components which, when not in training or on maneuver, are normally assigned to the border patrol. Upon completion of their terms, the draftees enter the Reserve Service (*Sherut Miluim*), which is composed of all able-bodied men under 45 and unmarried women under 35. Based on designated military districts, the reserve formations are issued emergency equipment, including vehicles. Men under 40 are liable to an uninterrupted month of training each year and older men to two weeks, with each age group reporting for duty the equivalent of one day a month. All officers, including NCOs, must serve additionally one consecutive week each year. After 1 June 1953, all men between the ages of 45 and 49 constituted the Civil Defense (*Hitgonenut Ezrahit*).

Israel developed a military doctrine that called for the fusion of strategic, economic, and Zionist ideological purposes by erecting fortified villages, inhabited by especially chosen and prepared personnel, along the exposed frontier. Comparably recruited were volunteers for settling the uncultivated farmland and other areas in the country that might be uninviting for reasons of climate or remoteness. Before independence, this function had been performed by the Zionist-socialist youth movements, whose members reached Palestine after protracted training in their native lands, often of six or more years' duration. The Defense Service Law of 1949 simply allocated this task to the army.

In the early years all recruits except those electing to serve in the air force and the navy were sent to frontier villages for agricultural training after basic military training. They also underwent instruction in socialism for living in cooperative and collective villages. These trainees were called the Fighting Pioneer Youth (*No'ar Haluzi Lohem*) or Nahal. Because of nonsocialist resistance to the use of universal military service as an agency for propagating socialism, Nahal was transformed in the mid-1950s from an obligatory to a voluntary instrument. Nahal trainees were instructed as airborne infantry, who shored up the defense of the exposed frontier by assuring a steady, if rotational, supply of soldiers. It provided candidates for permanent residence in existing but understaffed border villages; and funneled recruits into new security villages (he-Ahzuyot). Until these villages become economically viable, their members remain under army command and subject to Nahal discipline. Every male farmer in an Israel frontier village is thus a disciplined soldier. Every village is equipped with appropriate defense weapons and essential stores of food, fuel, medical supplies, and underground shelters. Neighboring villages in exposed districts are organized for mutual support, and reinforcements are swiftly available from the nearest towns in an emergency.

Volunteers for Nahal and for the air force and navy are sought among members of Gadna (*Gdudei No'ar*, or Youth Battalions), a premilitary movement first established early in World War II and placed in 1949 under the combined direction of the Nahal and the ministries of defense and of education and culture. Gadna attempted to reach all youngsters between fourteen and seventeen, whether in school or already employed. Apart from weekly unit meetings, periodic camp exercises, and an eleven-day basic training program, Gadna members could volunteer for help in afforestation, road building, archaeological excavations, and auxiliary projects in the security villages. By such means, the government endeavored to instill patriotism and a sense of loyalty to the purposes of the citizen army. When Israel developed its technical aid program to Asia and Africa, and also to Latin America in the second postwar decade, it met with growing interest in adapting Nahal and Gadna principles to local needs.

Israel's navy operated almost wholly in the Mediterranean. Although the Gulf of 'Aqabah was opened to Israel shipping in 1956, it had limited practical use since it lacked adequate maintainance and repair facilities and was inaccessible for joint maneuvers or action with Israel's Mediterranean vessels. Modest in size, the navy was reported to consist in 1965 of two destroyers, one frigate, two submarines (with two more on order from Britain), nine torpedo boats, and two landing craft. The air force in that year was estimated to have 450 planes. These included Mirage IIIC supersonic fighters (some carrying French air-to-air missiles), Super Mystère interceptors, Mystère IVA fighter-bombers, Vautour tactical reconnaissance bombers, and Noratlas, Stratocruiser, and C-47 transports.

The government did not divulge the size of its armed forces. However, a semiofficial publication estimated the manpower potential of the IDF in 1961 at about 250,000. Almost the same estimate was given in 1967 by a British publication evaluating the military balance in the Arab-Israel zone during the Six Day War, also adding that there were 3,000 officers and men in the navy and 8,000 in the air force. But in 1961 there were 166,000 of both sexes in the 15–19 age group in the Jewish community, and four years later the number in this group had risen to 245,000. This would suggest that the average number of recruits inducted each year had risen from perhaps 30,000 to more than 40,000 in the period, and the annual figure was steadily growing. A Reserve Service of 200,000 appeared somewhat low for 1967 (see Table 13). Actually, such arithmetic is probably meaningless, since a citizen army may be expected to call upon as many trained men and women as an emergency might require.

The army, the navy, and the air force are represented in a single general staff, headed by a chief of staff who may be an officer from any one of the three branches but who until 1967 at least was drawn from the army. Of the seven officers (four belonging to the dominant Mapai [Israel Labor Party], two independents, and one General Zionist [later Liberal] Party) who rose to the rank of chief of staff, all except the first were younger than forty on appointment, and were retired into civilian employment in the early forties.

The ministry of defense owns and runs all factories producing military equipment, and conducts a technical school for training its workers. From these plants come a growing variety of products, including components, spare parts, and ammunition for each new type of imported tank or plane adopted by the IDF. The military industry deliberately cultivated an export market and on the average, it was believed, sold some 30 to 40 per cent of the output abroad, earning hard currency for the purchase of strategic raw materials and capital equipment for further expansion. The ministry's research and planning department, which boasts the largest laboratories in the country, while primarily concerned with weapons research and engineering, has also developed electronic devices for military and civilian use. A modest aircraft industry was created in the second postwar decade and employed about 4,000 workers in 1965. Starting out as an agency that serviced the air force and local and foreign air lines, the industry manufactured jet trainers under French license. It also became a hard-currency earner and thus could take care of its own replacements and expansion needs.

Druzes and Circassians were the country's only non-Jews who joined the IDF from the very outset. The Druzes of military age, at their own request, became subject to compulsory service in 1956; the practice was later extended to the Circassians. Wholly exempt from the draft were Christian and Muslim Arabs, who were finally permitted in 1965 to volunteer for the IDF. Only a handful of Arabs responded. Nor was their lack of enthusiasm startling, since they could not have been expected to approve the state's central purpose of fostering Jewish nationalism.

Until November 1966, the IDF remained ultimately responsible for administering the areas of concentrated Arab settlement where four-fifths of the total lived. The Arabs in 1965 numbered about 212,000 Muslims and 57,000 Christians (plus nearly 30,000 Druzes). Under the military administration the Arabs in these districts did not enjoy free mobility and had to carry identification cards. Civilian police progressively took over the supervision of the regulations. Still in effect in 1965 were drastic emergency laws, originally promulgated by the mandatory government to hold in check political violence by Arabs and Jews. For crimes committed under these laws, Arabs were tried by military courts. The sentences required the commanding general's endorsement, from which there was no appeal. Under Kneset legislation, first adopted in 1954, unauthorized movement in either direction across the armistice lines was an offense judged by a one-man military court, from which appeal might be made not to a civilian court but only to a three-man military one.

In Israel's citizen army there are easy working relations between the officers and the recruits, an eschewal of formalistic discipline, and a high degree of individual initiative even among the ranks. In these respects the IDF parallels the Swiss army. "Though the tactical and operative doctrine of the I.D.F. is offensive," according to Colonel Mordechai Bar-on, its director of education, as befits a modern and efficient army and particularly a small army which must stand up against far larger forces, Israel's citizens are profoundly convinced that the I.D.F. is a definitely defensive instrument from the political and moral viewpoint.[7]

The capabilities of the IDF offensive operations were tested in Sinai in 1956. Israel could mobilize for action within seventy-two hours five reserve brigades in addition to three conscript brigades; and the men of one of the reserve brigades were back at their farms within eleven days of call-up.

Decisive Leadership in Coalition Politics

Israel is a democratic republic with a ceremonial president and an executive cabinet, responsible to a 120-member unicameral Kneset, or parliament, from which the prime minister and most of his ministerial colleagues are drawn. Israel has no written constitution, although it is committed to one under a resolution adopted on 13 June 1950 by the Constituent Kneset, which also served as the first legislature. Meanwhile, the Law and Administration Ordinance of 19 May 1948 and the Transition Law of 16 February 1949 provided basic constitutional guidance on the allocation of powers among the presidency, the executive, the legislature, and the judiciary. The projected written constitution is to consist of basic laws adopted by the Kneset; these laws, of which many had been framed in later years, may be modified or replaced by a simple majority, so that they are in no way privileged. The Kneset elects the president for a five-year term. The life of each Kneset is limited to a maximum of four years.

The system of proportional representation was developed in the mandatory period to give voice to all shades of political opinion. In the six Kneset elections held in the first seventeen years of independence, between seventeen and twenty-four lists of candidates were entered, although fewer than a dozen parties seated deputies. Because no party ever won a majority, the country was governed by coalitions. In the first five Kneset elections the moderately socialist and pragmatic Mapai (Israel Labor Party), the most powerful single party, polled between 32 per cent and 38 per cent of the votes, returning between 40 and 47 deputies. After the formal separation from the party of Ben Gurion and a small group of his dedicated followers on the eve of the sixth election, to found the Rafi (Israel Workers List), Mapai entered into an alliance with the Marxist non-Communist Ahdut ha-'Avodah. The Alignment, as the alliance was known, seated 45 deputies in November 1965.

In the first nineteen years there were fifteen governments. This suggested greater instability than in fact prevailed. Only 50 people filled some 275 incumbencies in the period. A multiparty system with doctrinal parties should have undergone, it would seem, an experience like that of the Fourth Republic in France, where the cabinet was subordinate to the legislature and plagued by *immobilisme*, or paralysis. In fact, however, Israel's parliamentary system functioned more like the British two-party system, in which the cabinet, far from being a creature of the legislature, actually dominated it. This condition in Israel suggested a cohesive cabinet with decisive leadership.

David Ben Gurion invented the principles of cohesive coalition government with the formation of the first cabinet in 1949. Mapai had won only 46 of the 120 seats, or less than 36 per cent of the total. Yet it represented nearly three times the number of the next largest group, the religious bloc, comprising three parties which together sent 16 deputies to the Kneset. As the acknowledged head of Mapai, David Ben Gurion was invited to form the government, and with three other parties he was able to erect a coalition in which Mapai was assured a majority of the seats. The conditions that he laid down for participation in the coalition were two: cabinet decisions by majority vote; and collective responsibility of all coalition partners for all cabinet decisions. After six weeks of intensive negotiations, Mapai's coalition partners acquiesced in these principles, which enabled the contending doctrinal parties n the government to reach agreement in advance on a formula of compromise. The compromise arrangements, agreed on by the coalition partners, are brought together in a statement called the basic principles of the government, which are presented to the Kneset when the coalition seeks its initial vote of confidence. Since almost invariably parliamentary discussion and ballots are based on party discipline, cabinet decisions can fail to receive Kneset endorsement only by ministerial or party defection. Such defection, however, would violate the principle of collective responsibility. These precedents, once established, became the immutable procedure.

In brief, with a majority of the seats, Mapai could dominate all cabinet actions. By the same token, the parties that consented to take part in the coalition exacted their price in advance. This accounted for the time that it invariably took to nail together a new government after a parliamentary election, rarely less than six weeks, and in 1955, after the election of the third Kneset, as long as

fourteen weeks. The stiff bargaining with the doctrinal parties behind closed doors was crucial to the formation of a workable coalition. No less crucial was the pragmatism of Mapai, which enabled
the dominant party to mediate between the clashing doctrines. It
eventually became necessary to enshrine the principle of collective
responsibility in a formal law. The two Marxist non-Communist
labor parties, Mapam and Ahdut ha-'Avodah, violated the principle of collective responsibility in 1959 by declining to uphold the
government decision to sell arms to West Germany, while refusing
to withdraw from the government. It took the Kneset more than
six years to adopt the relevant amendment of the Transition Law.
The amendment obligated every minister and his fellow-deputies
to vote for government proposals in every ballot of the plenary
Kneset. A negative vote or an abstention, without prior cabinet
approval, made it possible for the cabinet to force the resignation
of the offending minister after notice to the Kneset. Coalition
partners, as parties, were also bound by similar rules.

The constant party partners in all coalitions of the state's first
two decades were Mapai, the national religious bloc, and those
Arab factions affiliated with Mapai. The constant opposition parties until June 1967 were Herut,[8] which joined the right wing of
the Liberal Party in 1965 to form Gahal,[9] and the Communists,
who in 1965 divided into two parties: the Communist Party of Israel, which retained the old name but only a fraction of the original
membership, primarily Jewish; and the Raqah,[10] which was overwhelmingly Arab. The two Communist parties were pro-Soviet,
and neither seemed unduly influenced by the Sino-Soviet dispute.
The remaining parties (Mapam, Ahdut ha-'Avodah, and the Liberal Party) moved back and forth between coalitions and the opposition. In the first two decades of independence immigrants of
East European origin dominated the political establishment, largely
accounting for the doctrinal parties and rigidly centralized party
organization.

The Arabs have from the outset enjoyed the franchise, which is
universal, and have returned to the Kneset between four and eight
deputies in each of the first six elections. Two or three of the deputies invariably belonged to the Communist Party, and the others to
small factions affiliated with Mapai. No Arab ever sat in a cabinet,
and in the Kneset neither the Arabs nor the Communists were
allowed to sit in the sensitive committees on finance and on foreign affairs and security. Still, the Arabs enjoyed opportunities
of education and employment. The educational system basically

promotes Israel nationalism, and to this the Arabs can hardly be expected to develop an enthusiastic attachment. As long as the economy was expanding, Arab workers in the towns found ready employment and Arab peasants good prices for their agricultural products. In the depression of 1966–67, the Arab urban workers—along with Jews of African and Asian origin—were often, as unskilled workers, among the first to lose jobs in industry and the services.

The Army and Politics

Neither the Law and Administration Ordinance of 1948 nor the Transition Law of 1949 shed light on the question of civilian control over the armed forces. The defense minister is responsible, under all legislation on the IDF, for executing the laws and issuing attendant regulations. Moreover, all proposed legislation, that on the defense establishment included, while drafted in the pertinent ministry or ministries, must receive cabinet approval before it is sent to the Kneset. There ample opportunity obtains, in the three plenary readings and in the intervening committee review, for rejection or modification. While the annual budget of the defense ministry, which manages all allocations to the IDF, does not reach the floor of the Kneset for reasons of security, it must nevertheless receive the approval of the Kneset's committees on finance and on foreign affairs and security. All parties in the coalition government thus have a voice, at the cabinet level, in framing legislation on the armed forces; and, at the Kneset level, while the larger opposition parties as a minority in the committees cannot in fact control the military budgets, they may at least get to know the contents. Informed Israelis sharply disagreed on whether or not such civilian checks on the military establishment were adequate.

The key to the puzzle is the defense minister, who serves, in effect, as the commander-in-chief of the armed forces, although his office does not expressly carry the title. Under the law, the defense minister need not consult his cabinet colleagues or procure Kneset endorsement before making major decisions, even the decision to mobilize the reserve brigades. He must, it is true, immediately bring such a mobilization order to the attention of the Kneset Committee on Foreign Affairs and Security, which may confirm the order, or modify it, or withhold confirmation, or refer it to the plenary Kneset. However, in the event of a situation that seems to demand mobilization, is the Kneset likely to reverse the order of the defense minister?

Ben Gurion, the almost perennial defense minister until 1963, towered above all Israel politicians and held the allegiance of a substantial part of the civilian population and of the military officers. Even among Ben Gurion's political enemies, respect for his judgment in crisis was widespread. The precedents that Ben Gurion established in running the defense ministry and the armed forces tended to limit institutional control over the military establishment. As a forceful leader, Ben Gurion was prone to take decisions and then inform the cabinet, and sometimes the Kneset, too. Israel's constant state of siege gave him sufficient grounds for such freedom of action. Surrounded by hostile neighbors with populations far more numerous than its own, Israel had no alternative to its policy of vigilance. Vacillation might be not only costly but fatal. One reason why Israel managed to safeguard its security so well lay precisely in the steady, uncontested, and decisive leadership of the defense establishment.

Yet a lack of broader civilian control did not mean a lack of civilian supervision. Ben Gurion was a political leader, elected to office by popular franchise and subject to removal by popular will. The public outcry over the Lavon Affair illustrated the kind of political pressures brought to bear on Ben Gurion to change his policies and to modify his manner. His refusal to do either yielded prolonged political deadlock in 1961 and contributed to the split in Mapai in 1965. The precedents of bypassing checks and balances found in other democracies might conceivably complicate the future introduction of such checks and balances into Israel's governmental system.

In a symposium on Israel's army in state and society held at Tel Aviv late in 1953, S. M. Eisenstadt, one of the country's most gifted sociologists, suggested that the prime minister's unbroken retention of the defense ministry represented a serious danger to Israel's democracy. Eisenstadt thought that such a combination, normal in a democracy at war, was abnormal "in time of peace and even in time of relative peace." [11] He felt that for one person to hold the two offices was to involve the army with the authority that attaches to the prime minister. Shortly afterward the offices were in fact separated in the first cabinet of Moshe Sharett, when Pinhas Lavon was named minister of defense and Sharett retained the foreign ministry.

The experiment, however, was hardly successful. The Lavon Affair arose from a dispute in the winter of 1954–55 over responsibility for an abortive act of sabotage in Cairo that Israel's military intelligence organized. Lavon sought to dismiss the director-general of the defense ministry (Shim'on Peres) and the chief of intelligence (Lieutenant-Colonel Benjamin Gavli) who had issued the original order for the Cairo action. If the prime minister had supported his defense minister, he would have lost the ministry's chief of the general staff branch (Colonel Joseph Avidar) and other high-ranking officers. Sharett chose to support Peres and the army officers; Lavon resigned; and Ben Gurion returned to the defense ministry. The Lavon Affair scarcely provided conclusive evidence either for or against the separation of the defense ministry from the prime ministry "in times of relative peace." But it did emphasize a problem that apparently had never been adequately examined up to that time.

With its many ramified activities, the Israel defense ministry must maintain almost constant liaison with all other major ministries: with foreign affairs over the delicate problems imposed by the ceaseless enmity of the Arab states and its repercussions in other countries; with finance, over the progressively large bite out of the government's annual appropriations that a swiftly modernizing military establishment must take; with commerce and industry, over questions of military imports, purchases, and sales; with labor, over the most appropriate use of manpower; with education and culture, over the instructional program of the army and its premilitary training scheme; with interior and police over the administration of the Arab areas; and with the ministry of agriculuture over the program of Nahal. It would seem that the prime minister is much better able than any other member of the cabinet to coordinate so many liaison efforts.

It is significant that when Eshkol succeeded as prime minister in June 1963 he retained the defense ministry. He kept as deputy minister Shim'on Peres, who had been Ben Gurion's stand-by almost from the beginning. Peres was finally removed in 1965, when he joined Ben Gurion to withdraw from Mapai. Eshkol named as replacement his former deputy at the finance ministry.

Clearly, Eshkol differed in political style from Ben Gurion. For one thing, in relation to the defense ministry and the IDF, he hardly commanded the respect and adulation enjoyed by his predecessor, the father of both the ministry and the forces. For another, Eshkol was inclined to seek the counsel of his colleagues. In the circumstances, the Ministerial Security Committee (MSC), created in November 1961, under the chairmanship of the prime minister, received wider powers than it ever exercised under Ben

Gurion. Eshkol's practice reduced the tension over defense affairs among the coalition partners in the cabinet, with some unavoidable loss of decisiveness.

The mounting tension between the Arab states and Israel in May 1967, particularly after the withdrawal of the United Nations Emergency Force from the Gaza Strip and the Sinai Peninsula at 'Abd al-Nasir's request and his later closure of the Straits of Tiran to Israel shipping produced a domestic political crisis over Eshkol's management of the defense ministry. For the first time in the country's history, the pressure of public opinion forced a prime minister to surrender the defense ministry, not to a man of his own choice but to a man of the public's choice, one who no longer even belonged to the Mapai Party. The prime minister implicitly acknowledged his own uncertainty in managing the ministry by first offering the portfolio to Yigal Allon, who had been commander of the Palmah at the birth of Israel and soon thereafter became a leader of Ahdut ha-'Avodah, which by 1967 had affiliated with Mapai in the Alignment. The public's choice, however, was Moshe Dayan, the chief of staff of the IDF at the time of Israel's preemptive strike against Egypt a decade earlier. Dayan had retired from the Permanent Service of the IDF in 1958, and after a brief interval of graduate study at the university, entered the Kneset as a Mapai deputy in 1959 and became the minister of agriculture in Ben Gurion's new government. Dayan held on to the same ministry in Eshkol's first government, only to resign in 1964. In the following year he left Mapai altogether to become with Ben Gurion a founding member of the Rafi Party.

On taking over the defense ministry on 2 June 1967, Dayan invigorated the morale of the troops and the public, and the foreign press later gave him primary credit for the massive victory. This sharpened the personal rivalry between Eshkol and Dayan and embittered the political rivalry, which was inescapable in Israel's political system. The separation of the two offices, as has been seen, courted friction. In a lingering national emergency, the two men were tripping over each other in the conduct of routine business. As effective commander-in-chief and spokesman for security policy, Dayan was also an interministerial coordinator for security policy, and such coordinating activity impinged on the prime minister's office. Less than a month after the war, Eshkol was already disclosing his irritation to the press when he stated that in his view "logic dictated" that the premier should be his own defense minister at least "until lasting peace is achieved." [12] As the months of postwar political stalemate dragged on, the issue became blurred. In January 1968, Mapai reintegrated with Ahdut ha-'Avodah and Rafi to form a united Israel Labor Party. The merger transformed the political competition between the two men into an intraparty affair, and it was certain to become accentuated in the election of the seventh Kneset, scheduled to take place in 1969, if the party remained united until then.

However, it still left unresolved the question of responsibility for the framing of defense policy. Under the law, this responsibility belongs wholly to the defense minister. The practice, whether under Ben Gurion or under Eshkol, did not endanger Israel's democracy. A citizen army, by definition, is the best assurance against that. The Permanent Service of Israel's ground forces, as has been seen, is a very small career nucleus. Its officers, commissioned and noncommissioned alike, did not form a separate political group, but represented instead a cross-section of Israel's many parties. Even Dayan's appointment as defense minister in 1967 did not alter this condition, for he had separated from the Permanent Service nearly a decade earlier. Thus there appeared little danger of a military overturn of the civilian regime.

The shoe seemed to be on the other foot. The danger was not one of military interference in politics, but of partisan political interference with the management of the defense establishment. In a multiparty system with sharp doctrinal differences on society, the economy, and the government, indecision is an ever-present prospect, and it can affect security matters no less than the others. Such indecision had been obviated in the past by the principles of cohesive coalition laid down by Ben Gurion and acepted by the coalition parties. If the enlarged Labor Party did not fall apart before the election of the seventh Kneset, it might become the first majority party in the state's history. Such an outcome could hardly fail to transform the political system, for the party would be able to form its own government. Failing such a victory at the polls, the Labor Party was certain to continue exercising its leadership by coalition government on the established precedent.

Many academic and diplomatic observers have noted that the presence of Israel in the Middle East contributed much to the movement for Arab unity. It might also be noted in reverse that the very minatory manner and attitude of the Arab states toward the unwanted neighbor in their midst served as a potent unifying force in Israel, enabling the new state to make a virtue of its necessity. It helped close the ranks of a doctrinally divided country behind the security policies first of Ben Gurion and then of Eshkol. There was no reason to believe that it would not continue doing so in the future.

CONFESSIONAL
DEMOCRACY: LEBANON *

Except for a border that runs for 49 miles, Lebanon and Israel appear to share little in common. Israel is pre-eminently a country of immigration, and Lebanon one of emigration. Israel parades the largest per capita army in the Middle East, on which it spends relatively one of the highest sums each year; Lebanon has one of the smallest armies in the region and denies it modern weaponry. Politics in Israel is party politics; in Lebanon it is confessional and clannish politics. Israel discovered the secret of cohesive coalitions and decisive leadership. Lebanon thrives on loose coalitions and a constant state of near political paralysis.

These are the visible signs. Dig beneath the surface and you also encounter a number of similarities. The two political systems are democratic. The two societies are substantially urban, literate, and world-minded. In part, this is a function of size. The next-door neighbors are small states. Lebanon, in fact, encompasses less than half the area of Israel, and in 1965 had a population almost as large, some 2.4 million (Palestine refugees included). A third of the Lebanese were crowded into Bayrut, which together with four other cities (Tripoli, Sidon, Zahlah, and Tyre) accounted for about half the population; the rest was distributed among some 2,200 villages, many of them semiurban, because of the smallness of the country and the excellent communication and transportation facilities. The urbanization was also suggested in the high literacy rate, since more than three of every four Lebanese could read and write in 1965. Lebanon is an oil-poor country, and among the Arab states in this group, it boasts the highest per capita GNP,

* This chapter draws heavily on my paper on "Lebanese Democracy in its International Setting," in *The Middle East Journal*, vol. 17 (Late Autumn 1963), pp. 487–506; see also *Politics in Lebanon*, edited by Leonard Binder (New York, 1966), pp. 213–38.

estimated at approximately $375 in 1965. Even the distribution of GNP (but not of the labor force) did not look unlike that of Israel.

	GNP	Labor Force
Agriculture	15%	50%
Industry	24	24
Commerce, finance, rent	46	14
Professional services	15	12

Parallels may also be found at the regional and international levels. Lebanon and Israel are non-Muslim states in a predominantly Muslim zone. Israel turned to the Jewish communities abroad for continuing support and future population. The ties of Lebanon with its emigrant communities in the Americas, Africa, and Europe remained vigorous in the second and third generations. In the Cold War both leaned toward the West, Israel emphatically and Lebanon hesitantly, but the direction of their foreign policies was unmistakable.

Military politics in the two countries have been dominated by civilians. The IDF is basic to the survival of Israel, but in Lebanon the army is basic to the survival of democracy. Lebanon possessed relatively the largest middle class of any Arab state and the highest literacy rate of any Middle East state, except Israel. Yet while in other countries in other regions of the world these objective criteria suggest conditions favorable to the growth of democracy, in Lebanon they hardly begin to illuminate the problems.

The Political System

The Lebanese political system has become an oddity, not in the Arab lands alone where representative government has almost vanished, but among the world's democracies. It beggars summary analysis. The cabinet is responsible, in constitutional theory, to the unicameral chamber of deputies. Yet in more than forty years only one government has fallen (as long ago as 1930) because of the loss of the legislature's confidence. The right of appointing the premier and all the members of his cabinet has been wholly the president's by original design. To this has been added, by the legislature's default, his exclusive power of ministerial dismissal. Lebanon's president stands in relation to the cabinet, the premier included, as the American president does in relation to his. But the chamber has become the president's creature in a way that the Congress never has. Should the chamber fail within forty days to reach a decision on an impending bill deemed urgent by the cabinet, the president may enact it by decree. His also are the prerogatives to dissolve the chamber, with cabinet approval, before the expiry of a normal four-year term; to name public officials whose manner of appointment is not otherwise specified in the law; and to enter into executive agreements with alien governments. The system might thus be labeled a parliamentary system in theory, since the chamber also elects the president for his six-year term, but a presidential system in practice. Still, with all his power, the Lebanese president remains essentially a lame duck, since he may not stand for immediate re-election and, of greater importance, he must function within the context of confessional politics.

In the unwritten National Pact (*al-mithaq al-watani*) of 1943, the major religious communities reached a compromise accord that has proved thus far impervious to modification. Under the arrangement, the president of the republic must always be a Maronite (whose Uniate church, though in communion with the Vatican, nevertheless uses Syriac as its liturgical tongue); the prime minister, a Sunni Muslim; and the president of the chamber, a Shi'i Muslim (belonging to the sect of the Matawilah, who remain loyal partisans of Muhammad's son-in-law, 'Ali, and his descendants, hailed as the only true successors to the Prophet). The apportionment of deputies in the chamber rests on an immutable numerical formula for sectarian representation, six Christians to every five non-Christians. This explains why the legislature, though varying in size (so far from 33 to 99) according to the wishes of the outgoing chamber, always comprises as its number of deputies some multiple of eleven. The element of electoral chance and the degree of sectarian displeasure with the outcome, however, have not been entirely eliminated. They have merely been reduced. Within each confessional community more than one candidate is almost certain to run for every available seat.

The common tendency to divide Lebanon's population into Christians and Muslims is misleading. The two so-called major communities are not monolithic; they are fractured. Among the ten or more Christian communities, three account for nearly 90 per cent of the total: the Maronite, the Greek Orthodox, and the Greek Catholic (a Uniate church, also affiliated with the Vatican, but employing Greek as its language of worship). To the Muslim communities, divided principally between the Sunnis and the

Shi'is who together represent more than 85 per cent of the non-Christians, may be added the post-Islamic Druzes. In the circumstances, no individual sectarian group can claim a majority or ever hope to attain one, since the Maronite community, the largest, numbers less than 30 per cent of the country's over-all population; and the Sunni community, the second largest, less than 25.

Lebanon, like Iran and Afghanistan, is thus a country of minorities. Its system of confessional politics rests on principles inherited from premandatory, Ottoman institutions and practices that have lost little of their traditional vigor. Lebanon cannot claim uniqueness among Middle East states in keeping alive elements of the Ottoman *millet*, or confessional regime, under which each recognized religious group—and in Lebanon all religious groups are recognized—enjoys cultural, legal (in matters of personal status), and religious autonomy. Even Israel's democracy, which otherwise is the most Westernized political system in the region, has retained millet features in the dominant Jewish community no less than in the minority Christian, Muslim, and Druze communities. In Israel, however, candidates may stand for election to the unicameral Kneset only on party lists. Even the expressly religious parties, which exist in the Jewish community alone, are doctrinal parties, and they have rarely won a combined total of more than 10 per cent of the votes. In Lebanon, by contrast, candidates for the chamber continue for the most part to be recruited among the strongest clan leaders (*zu'ama*), who normally run as independents. They exercise influence through traditional ties to the clannish landed properties and, in the towns, to the proliferating clannish commercial enterprises. Those who become deputies try to retain their hold on popular following through easy accessibility for granting favors and distributing government patronage. They do so in a manner more closely akin to that of traditional societies in the Middle East.

Confessional politics tends to make political parties essentially meaningless, although parties as such do exist. Maronite leaders began forming political organizations during the mandatory period to pool their resources. They carried the names of political parties —such as the National Bloc Party of Emile Eddé (1886–1949), one of mandated Lebanon's presidents, and the Constitutional Union Party of Bisharah al-Khuri (1890–1963), the first president of the sovereign republic—but were intrinsically clannish interest groups. Other political organizations—such as the Maronite *Phalanges Libanaises* Party and the Sunni *al-Najjadah* (helpers) Party

—started out in the mid-1930s as youth clubs and developed, after independence, into formal political parties with some programmatic content, chiefly on external affairs. Both were represented in the chamber for the first time after the election of 1960. The Maronites favored policies of cooperation with France, while the Sunnis sought closer ties with Arab unity movements in nearby countries.

These four parties managed to survive because they trimmed their sails to the confessional winds. But even the avowedly doctrinal and cross-confessional Progressive Socialist Party, founded in 1949 by Kamal Jumblatt (1920–   ), has contrived to limp along despite its small formal membership, primarily because its Druze leader has been able to eke out the doctrinal appeal with the patronage available to a well-established, landed clan.[1] Still to be tested was the reliability of the Lebanese branch, founded in 1956, of the Ba'th Party, the doctrinal Arab unity socialist movement that spread in the 1950s from Syria to Iraq, Jordan, and other Arab countries. The earlier bans on the Communist Party and the Syrian National Social Party (a quasi-fascist organization calling for the unity of the Fertile Crescent, more as a geographical than as an Arab goal) offered no firm precedents. Both parties were also driven underground by neighboring authoritarian Arab regimes.

The arrested party life has deprived the Lebanese body politic of a basic mechanism for political integration. Most deputies do not belong to any party whatsoever. Their competition for office with candidates of the same sect, in effect, splits the confessional communities. Even the formal parties produce the same divisive results, since the appearance of one in a particular community is likely to spark the creation of at least one rival sectarian group. On the other hand, most electoral districts, rural as well as urban, have from the very first election in the 1920s embraced enough eligible voters of more than one sectarian community to require the presentation of mixed confessional lists. Voters in such districts cast their ballots for any candidates of their choice, regardless of the religion of the voter or the candidate. Out of election campaigns in such districts sometimes grow cooperative arrangements among zu'ama of differing communities, which may lead to collaboration in the chamber among the winners. The low-level party activity has thus placed a premium on this less formal and less durable subparty or bloc action, which, in the aggregate, courts legislative indecision.

Hardly less indecisive are the cabinets, which suffer from the absence of discipline and unity, especially in times of domestic crisis. "Lebanon lived under some forty-six cabinets in twenty-eight years . . . from 1926 to February 1964," it has been observed,

> or an average of less than eight months per Cabinet . . . [But] this fact is mitigated by the tendency toward carry-over in membership from one Cabinet to the next, and by the stable character of the circle of eligible ministers within Parliament (and, to a small extent, outside it). From 1926 through 1963 a total of 333 ministerial posts were occupied by only 134 individuals . . . and eleven individuals . . . alone accounted for 95 of the 333 posts.[2]

The ministerial council expands and contracts in direct proportion to the changing size of the chamber, since this seems to be the only way of procuring and holding the confidence of a majority of the deputies. The number of ministers has thus varied from three to eighteen. Commonly, there is an equal number of Sunnis and Maronites. Even the undersized compromise cabinet of 1958 (with only four ministers), which clinched the settlement of the civil war, consisted of two Sunnis and two Maronites. The smallest cabinet size to accommodate the six largest confessions appears to be eight, with the Sunnis and the Maronites represented by two ministers each and the Shi'is, Greek Orthodox, Greek Catholics, and Druzes by one minister each.

In the circumstances of legislative and ministerial indecision, it is the president who must exercise leadership. The mark of a president's success lies in his capacity to mediate the clashing positions of the communities and forge an interconfessional consensus. This procedure broke down, in 1952 and again in 1958, when the first two presidents tried, in defiance of the constitution, to succeed themselves. In both instances, they failed; and in both the army stepped in, once by itself and once accompanied by external intervention.

Lebanon's singular brand of democracy is doubly wondrous. It works, and, for its continued growth and functioning, has depended heavily, since birth, on the international community and, since independence, on the army as well.

The International Setting

Despite intermittent breaks in the continuity, Lebanese democracy grew progressively through four successive, easily identifiable stages of development and conditioning, and entered its fifth in 1958, with each phase essential to the one that has followed. The system sprang from nondemocratic origins, and its many authors contrived to fashion democratic institutions that could operate, however clumsily, within the traditional confessional structure of the society and, as time passed, with an apparently indispensable complex of static fictions. The central fiction, from which all others spring, is the presumed stationary relative size of each major religious community.

Jurisdiction over the Mountain, as Ottoman Lebanon was commonly known, was still exercised by the Sublime Porte until 1832 (when the district fell under temporary Egyptian rule) through a system of authoritarian autonomy that could scarcely be labeled democratic or even representative. The authoritarian regime came to an abrupt halt as part of the European-sponsored Ottoman-Egyptian settlement of 1841. In two decades the government of the Mountain had passed from uncontrolled to controlled authoritarianism, and the change together with abortive experiments in launching representative institutions constituted progress.

The second stage, persisting longer than a half-century, saw the creation of durable representative institutions on the confessional pattern, under the guarantee of the European concert. In this period, moreover, the start of true confessional politics established precedents essential to the later appearance of Lebanon's unusual democracy. In the third stage (1920–41), spanning most of the mandate, the late Ottoman representative institutions were built into a democratic system extending throughout the country, the area of which was now double in size. The enlargement of Lebanon destroyed its relative demographic homogeneity and brought into being a land composed of sectarian minorities. Democracy proved in these years more nominal than real. Full self-government and sovereignty had to await the fourth stage that commenced in 1941, underwent five years of incubation and a dozen more of maturation, and gave no firm assurance that the confessions would stick together within a Greater Lebanon. The present, fifth stage originated in the 1958 civil war that periled Lebanon's democracy until the settlement restored the system to its original vitality.

International politics made an indispensable contribution to each of these stages. We need not concern ourselves with the developments before 1943 since they are not entirely relevant to an appreciation of the problems of civil-military relations in the confessional democracy. It was in the fourth stage that Britain interposed itself between the Lebanese and the French, as a result of the joint military action of Britain and Free France in 1941 in destroying the Vichy administration over the mandated territory. For the war's duration Britain remained the keeper of security and, by drawing Lebanon (with Syria) into the operational zone of the Anglo-American Middle East Supply Center, also a major supervisor of the mandate's economy. Military exigencies had thus transformed a simple mandate under the control of one European government into a dual control, enabling Britain to hold Free France in check. Under the dual control, whose formation launched the fourth stage, Lebanese democracy rose in five years to the level of genuine self-government and then full sovereignty with no strings attached.

The Free French and British statements proclaiming the independence of Lebanon (and Syria) that accompanied the military action in 1941 had been no more than promissory and conditional, for the Free French announced, with British approval, their intention of converting the mandated lands into preferential allies. Britain's presence, however, proved indispensable to the further development of confessional democracy in Greater Lebanon, as the French-enlarged country was called after 1920. The Lebanese seized the opportunities of World War II to achieve their sovereignty. The British literally pushed the Free French into restoring the constitution and affording real self-government to the Lebanese for the first time. Without British prodding, the elections might not have taken place as early as 1943. Without the mediation of the British Minister, the Lebanese politicians might not have reached an understanding on the ratio of six Christian deputies for every five non-Christians. This settlement, a basis for one of the hallowed principles of the National Pact, broke the deadlock between the Maronites and the Sunnis that threatened to delay interminably the election of the chamber and the formation of a government that were to proclaim independence. Moreover, without British firmness toward the Free French, the Lebanese government and chamber in November 1943 would not have succeeded so soon in unilaterally expunging from the constitution those articles that reserved transcendent powers to the mandatory. The clumsiness of the Free French in attempting, first to use the offer of elections and then to hold on to residual mandatory controls as bargaining levers for wringing preferential treaties out of the Lebanese, served to unite the confessions behind the program for keeping Greater Lebanon intact and weakened the resolve of Sunnis to fuse Lebanon with Syria immediately and unconditionally.

The Free French arrest of the Lebanese president and the cabinet in November 1943 so enraged every confessional community that it created for the first time a consensus for preserving Greater Lebanon (at least for the time being). As the price for winning the support of the other communities in saving an expanded Lebanon, the Maronites, with the Greek Catholics tagging along, had to agree to the unconditional French withdrawal. This merely reaffirmed the National Pact, negotiated a few weeks earlier by President Bisharah al-Khuri and Premier Riyad al-Sulh, and outlined by Sulh in his cabinet's program which won the chamber's unanimous approval. The Free French action produced precisely the reverse of the intended effect, since it sharpened the desire of the Christians and Muslims alike for proclaiming independence and their determination to prevent France from salvaging any privileged status in the land.

With British garrisons and economic controls in Lebanon, Whitehall's pressure on Charles de Gaulle and his French Committee of National Liberation (CFLN) at Algiers yielded the release of the Lebanese president and ministers before the confessional unity and outrage could spark nationalist rebellion. The consequent loss of Free French prestige eased Britain's task in encouraging the CFLN in 1944 to transfer by agreement to the newly elected government all sovereign powers except control over the *Troupes spéciales*, or nucleus of the later Lebanese army. Before the year ended the U.S.S.R. and the United States became the first major powers unconditionally to recognize the nascent state's sovereignty. Lebanon's admission in February 1945, on American and British invitation, to charter membership in the United Nations gave the confessional republic powerful international legal credentials, and support for resisting the final French efforts immediately after the war to negotiate an unequal alliance. By 1946 Lebanon attained full independence without having had to pass through an intervening period of indirect imperialism, as had Egypt, Iraq, Jordan, and Libya. The big question still remained, of course, whether inner vitality and unity would survive the withdrawal of British and French troops.

At the Arab unity conference in Alexandria late in 1944, Lebanon profited from having French and British garrisons still in the country, because their presence endowed its claims with the heady appeal of anti-imperialism. The Lebanese delegation insisted on the insertion into the Protocol of a special resolution solemnly pledging the unanimous respect of the Arab states for the "inde-

pendence and sovereignty of Lebanon within its present frontiers."
The same assurance was later generalized in the Arab League Pact
as one in which each member state undertook (Article 8) to reserve "as the exclusive concerns" of the other member states their
respective "systems of government" and "to abstain from any action calculated to change" such established systems. Any schemes
for erecting "closer cooperation and stronger bonds" than those
visualized in the pact were expressly left (Article 9) to the voluntary decision of the individual members.[3]

Lebanese confessional democracy thus entered upon its sovereign career with a National Pact that laid down fixed rules for external no less than internal behavior. The National Pact dictated,
in effect, the full depoliticization of the country's relations with
France and the Christian West and the limited depoliticization of
its relations with the neighboring Arab states. As an Arab land,
Lebanon was expected to participate in Arab regional politics but
not to the point of sovereignty's abridgement. These rules placed a
premium on policies of neutrality in the Arab community of nations as in the world at large. As long as disputes among Arab states
did not rise above the essentially dynastic level on which typically
Egypt, Saudi Arabia, and Syria ranged themselves against the
Hashimi kingdoms of Iraq and Jordan, Lebanon's customary neutral, mediatory stance in the Arab League proved relatively fruitful.
But the moment the quarrels turned doctrinal, as they began to do
after 1954, neutrality lost its protective charm.

Similarly, in the Cold War between the Soviet bloc and the
West, Lebanon through the early 1950s faced no serious difficulty
in adhering to a course of nonalignment with a manifest preference
for the West. Of all the Arab states, Lebanon took least offense at
the Tripartite Declaration of 1950, which seemed admirably suited
to Lebanon's subdued foreign policy objectives. Among the modernizing Middle East states, Lebanon was one of the least active
buyers in the arms market and, as a nonirredentist country, could
only welcome the unilateral guarantees for the safeguard of its borders against external aggression.

The real danger to Greater Lebanon's integrity and therefore to
the survival of its democracy came from Syria, where the sentiment
prevailed, especially in the dominant Sunni community, that Lebanon really formed part of an envisaged Greater Syria. That danger
was intensified by the other Arab states' active promotion of one or
another scheme for Arab union; and it grew acute when they divided sharply over the Baghdad Pact of 1955. The failure at that

time of the United States and its trans-Atlantic allies to invoke the Tripartite Declaration to prevent the export of Soviet military equipment to Egypt automatically destroyed the efficacy of the three-power instrument for arms control and for preserving existing national boundaries against forcible change. Throughout the Arab East, 'Abd al-Nasir, following his successful repudiation of the Tripartite Declaration, came to personify the aspirations for union and, in foreign policy, the doctrine of "positive neutralism," under which the Egyptian president accepted material help from both sides in the Cold War but formally joined neither. However, as Egypt's dependence on Soviet arms rose in those years, positive neutralism tipped progressively in favor of the U.S.S.R. and hostility to the West grew more vocal.

The Iraqi-Egyptian dispute over the Baghdad Pact became so savage that the Lebanese president's mediatory efforts simply evoked the disdain of Egypt and its Arab allies, Syria and Saudi Arabia, which charged the Lebanese president with secretly favoring "defectionist" Iraq. Egypt and Syria began supporting the internal Lebanese opposition to President Kamil Sham'un, thus invalidating the assurances in the Arab League charter against intervention into the domestic affairs of any member state. In the Suez crisis of 1956, Sham'un reciprocated by naming a new cabinet that refused to join other Arab League states in severing diplomatic relations with Britain and France, and then, early in 1957, publicly endorsed the Eisenhower Doctrine. As the Maronite president and his Sunni premier, Sami al-Sulh, placed Lebanon behind the American shield, the domestic Lebanese opposition drew closer to Egypt and fell under the spell of 'Abd al-Nasir's Arab unity leadership.

The removal by mid-1957 of the regional and international props to Lebanon's security temporarily nullified the integrative National Pact. Deep grooves and fissures began to separate Christian from non-Christian and one sect from the next and to split the major confessional communities apart. The mounting crisis was polarizing the population of the country over issues of external policy, between the supporters of Sham'un and his pro-American policies and the proponents of more intimate ties with Egypt and the positive neutralists. Following the outbreak of civil war in May 1958, the United Arab Republic, from radio stations in Cairo and Damascus, incited the Lebanese to overthrow the Sham'un regime. The U.A.R. also organized gun-running from Syria to arm the Lebanese rebels. At the same time much of the United States military equipment airlifted to Lebanon's armed forces found its way to government partisans. Observed in this light, the civil war of 1958 represented the supreme test of whether a confessional democracy so cumbersomely conceived and so infirmly dedicated could long endure. Lebanon's confessional democracy,—indeed, the country itself—might never have outlasted the civil war without United States intervention, with which the fifth stage of political development started.

The arrival of American troops in mid-July 1958 on President Sham'un's invitation could be seen, in the context of Lebanese politics, only as a demonstration of the United States favor to the sole Arab head of state who had subscribed to the Eisenhower Doctrine. But the issue of the Lebanese civil war had been placed on the agenda of the U.N. Security Council as early as May 1958 and had already been magnified into a major international crisis before the American intervention occurred. The American military initiative stirred vocal Soviet protest. The two superpowers, for opposite reasons, sponsored in the Security Council the request for an emergency session of the General Assembly. President Eisenhower, in ordering the American units to Lebanon, had invoked Article 51 of the United Nations Charter, claiming that the United States action was taken in support of the international organization, even though outside its framework. President Eisenhower assured the General Assembly on 13 August that American forces, which he had dispatched to Lebanon solely to uphold its sovereignty and territorial integrity, would be withdrawn at once "whenever this is requested by the duly constituted government . . . or whenever through action by the United Nations or otherwise" Lebanon was "no longer exposed to the original danger." [4]

Before the American soldiers departed in the fall, however, the United States employed its military presence to sustain the diplomacy that settled the dispute between the champions of the West and the champions of United Arab Republicanism and that arranged for the election of a new Lebanese president, one avowedly neutral on foreign as well as on internal issues. In fact, as commander of the armed forces, General Fuad Shihab had earlier approved neither the American intervention nor Sham'un's policy of close cooperation with the United States. What is more, Shihab appointed a cabinet recruited almost wholly among erstwhile rebels. To put it crudely, one might say that Lebanon had learned, in independence, how to elect a president but not how to get rid of one, as the crises of 1952 and 1958 seemed to attest.

The election of Shihab to succeed Sham'un enabled the U.A.R.

to save face. It joined the other Arab states in sponsoring a resolution that the U.N. General Assembly adopted on 21 August 1958 reiterating the appeal for the "early withdrawal of foreign troops" but explicitly reaffirming the original Arab League principles of nonintervention by member states in the internal affairs of other member states. Shihab's neutral presidency swiftly reinstated the National Pact in its full vigor. The parliamentary elections of 1960 and 1964 disclosed that confessional politics had returned to normality. Thus, in the fifth stage, the memory in the Arab East of the American military intervention provided the new external prop so necessary to the survival of Lebanon's democracy.

The Army in Politics

Lebanon's reliance on the international community, while seldom acknowledged, is reflected in its eschewal of oversized armed forces. Lebanon has almost brandished its toy army, which scarcely sufficed before 1958 for the maintenance of domestic law and order, let alone defense against external aggression. Yet even with the hardening of its armor during the civil war and again under the Unified Arab Command (1964–67), the diminutive state could not be charged with investment beyond its means in martial hardware. In this respect, among the newly sovereign Arab nationalist lands, Lebanon and also Tunisia, as we shall see in Chapter 22, resembled the prenationalist traditional monarchies that appeared content, at least until the 1960s, with comparatively small armed forces.

The Lebanese army in 1950, it was estimated, comprised some 5,000 officers and men; by 1965 it had grown to no more than 13,000. There were in addition in 1965 a tiny air force of fewer than 1,000 officers and men and 18 planes, among them 8 helicopters and 4 trainers, and an even tinier navy of about 200 men and a handful of coastal patrol boats. The gendarmerie, or rural police, which numbered 2,500 men in 1950, essentially did not vary in size over the next decade and a half, while the urban police nearly doubled in these years to about 1,000.

The Lebanese army was basically an extension of the gendarmerie and the urban police. The mission of the army was almost wholly a domestic one in a sect-ridden country whose government machinery was prone to break down in the face of intercommunal quarrels. The primary population stock is mountain peasantry, and in a land where traditionalism flourishes, it is perhaps not unnatural that the peasants and their city cousins consider sidearms indispensable to a man's wardrobe. In times past, the gun protected his person, his honor, and the honor of his family, his clan, and his tribe. Under democratic self-rule it also protected the honor and the interests of his confession. "The Lebanese are likely the most prolific weapons carriers in the world," a student of the area noted;

> every Lebanese acquaintance will tell you that he is the only one in the country who does not have a weapon—which makes him even more suspect. The keeping of arms was, of course, essential to the society in the past . . . It is still a part and parcel of traditional village life with its vendettas of honor and its fanfares of firing on any occasion from birth through marriage to death . . . [The civil war of 1958] proved to what extent everyone was armed. . . .[5]

In the circumstances, it is not astonishing that, when under the spell of confessional elections the rival candidates traduce one another and tempers rise, pistols come out of the holsters. The Lebanese voter, it is facetiously said, is not required to carry a gun on his way to the ballot box, but it helps. The life he saves might be his own.

City life in Lebanon is dominated by businessmen who believe in little government. They practice what American Republicans preach. Only small sums are allocated for public services. With modest budgets, even the security services (gendarmerie and urban police included), which consistently received between 15 and 20 per cent of the total, have been starved. Lebanon's annual security budget rose only modestly, from 38 million Lebanese pounds ($12.3 million), or 2.2 per cent of the GNP, in 1956 to 90.1 million pounds ($29 million), or 3.3 per cent of the GNP, in 1965 (see Table 14). In these years the military budgets of Lebanon's neighbors grew by geometric progression. The Lebanese army, which expanded only slowly, was by the mid-1960s not even one-fourth the size of Jordan's army, the next smallest army in the Fertile Crescent; yet Jordan's population was even smaller than Lebanon's.

One of the essential and most visible political functions of the Lebanese army was to umpire elections to see that the voters cast ballots and not hand grenades. Even so, elections were hazardous affairs. Invariably men were hurt, and not infrequently a few were killed. The elections had to be staggered, usually on four successive Sundays, because the security forces were not large enough for countrywide assignment on a single day. The choice of Sunday seemed to reflect the businessman's preference. The security super-

Table 14. Lebanon: Force Levels, Government Expenditures, and GNP, 1954–66

	Population [c] (millions)	Force Levels (thousands)	Government Expenditures (millions of Lebanese pounds)			GNP (millions of pounds)	Defense Expenditures (as % of GNP)
			Defense (including internal security and justice)	Development	Total		
1954 [a]	1.66		40.2	11.2	111.2	1,507	2.7
1955	1.73	6.2	26.7	24.8	132.4	1,650	1.6
1956	1.79		38.0	33.1	162.3	1,700	2.2
1957	1.85		39.1	36.2	192.5	1,800	2.2
1958	1.90		45.6	15.0	181.6	1,590	2.9
1959	1.95		43.0	35.0	198.6	1,900 [f]	2.3
1960	2.01	10.8	47.7	45.7	243.1	2,000 [f]	2.4
1961	2.07		56.4	98.2 [d]	325.6	2,150	2.6
1962	2.13		80.6	138.4 [e]	415.3	2,280	3.5
1963	2.20		68.9	156.3	430.3	2,325	3.0
1964	2.28		76.6	190.5	473.0	2,434	3.1
1965 [b]	2.40	13.0	90.1	190.4	526.2	2,723	3.3
1966			114.3	219.5	585.3		3.3

SOURCES: U.N. *Statistical Yearbook*; AID, *Selected Annual Statistics*; and ACDA, *Selected Data, 1964 and 1965*.

a Fiscal year ends 31 December. b Budget estimates.

c Population for 1954–62 represent roughly adjusted estimates, based on 1963–65 rate of growth.

d Beginning with 1961, development expenditures of the "Fund for Large Works" (about L £50 million in that year) were incorporated in the budget. Data on expenditures by this Fund for the years preceding 1961 are not available.

e Beginning with 1962, development expenditures include Chapters 2 and 3 of the budget and may include some recurring expenditures on completed projects.

f Rough estimates.

vision of elections in Lebanese style called for the deployment of troops in the pertinent district, where they remained on alert in barracks or out of sight until the gendarmerie and the police lost control, if they did. Precautionary measures were not lifted until after the post-election celebrations of the victors.

The Lebanese army is a career army, and its commander-in-chief until 1958, Brigadier Fuad Shihab (1902–   ), a graduate of St. Cyr who married the daughter of a French colonel, was the army's only general officer. Though a practicing Maronite, Shihab could claim mixed confessional ancestry, including Sunni strains, thus fixing a cross-confessional image. The general demonstrated his own political neutrality and that of the army in the presidential crisis of 1952. Bisharah al-Khuri, sovereign Lebanon's first president, rigged his own re-election more than a year before the end of his term. Late in May 1948, when the Palestine war deeply distracted the public, he persuaded the chamber to amend, "as an exceptional case," the constitutional prohibition against a president's succeeding himself. Halfway through Khuri's second term, the political opposition, even in the president's own Maronite community, exploited the widespread unemployment, rising prices, and general corruption to organize popular demonstrations in Bayrut that forced his resignation on 18 September 1952. General Shihab, who refused, even at the president's command, to order his troops "to shoot their fellow citizens," was named prime minister of a caretaker cabinet (consisting, besides himself, of two civilian ministers) to hold the reins of power until it could be transferred to a new president. Characteristically, Shihab retired when the chamber within five days elected Kamil Sham'un. Despite the difficulties in finding a prime minister who could construct a viable cabinet, the general resolutely resisted the temptation to continue in political office.

Even more dramatic was the test of political neutrality of the confessional army and its commander in the civil war of 1958, when a presidential crisis over the issue of re-election became enmeshed with larger issues of the Cold War in the region and beyond. The army at that time consisted of fewer than 10,000 men, recruited on a proportional basis in the major confessional communities. The officers, who reportedly were fewer than 200, also reflected a sectarian balance, although Maronites filled the top slots. The Shihab clan, in fact, dominated the security services, supplying the chief of the Sûreté Générale (the Lebanese equivalent of the FBI) and the director-general of the interior ministry.

Shihab conceived his role in 1958 as mediator between the government and the rebellious communal leaders. The two most redoubtable were Kamal Jumblatt, the fiery Druze socialist who had organized mountain tribesmen from his headquarters at al-Mukhtarah in the Shuf, the center of Druze settlement southeast of Bayrut; and Rashid Karamah, who organized the rebel resistance in Tripoli, the main center of Sunni settlement in the north. The general mediated with consummate skill, and what enabled him to do so was his use of a confessional army for police patrol among the quarreling confessions by cautious commitment. He refused to go further than to keep the warring confessions apart, being "content to hold the ring in the bigger towns, and to chivvy the bands in the countryside with a view to reducing their nuisance value." [6] By midsummer General Shihab emerged as the only neutral candidate to break the confessional deadlock, and the chamber elected him president late in July. Immediately after taking office two months later, he faced the problem of how to accommodate the rebel leaders who insisted on participating in the government without dissolving the chamber that had been constructed by rigged elections in the spring of 1957 and that included many deputies who remained loyal to Sham'un's discredited regime or at least vigorously opposed to the rebel cause. In preparation for naming Rashid Karamah prime minister, the erstwhile Sunni rebel leader in the north, Shihab dismissed a number of high-ranking army officers, ostensibly because they had planned a military coup d'état. The newly elected president also replaced the chiefs of the gendarmerie, the urban police, and the Sûreté Générale with reliable military aides. Sham'un's followers finally acquiesced by mid-October in a four-man cabinet, headed by Karamah and comprising with himself two Sunnis and two Maronites, only after President Shihab threatened to hand over the ministerial powers to army officers and civilian technicians.

Although Shihab surrendered the supreme military command upon taking political office, he nevertheless continued to use his high prestige in the armed forces and among its top command to bring the politicians into line. Following the staggered parliamentary elections of June-July 1960, and only on the express appeal of 90 of the 99 newly elected deputies, President Shihab agreed to continue in office, after threatening to resign and to hand over to army officers the management of the defense ministry and internal security. With that degree of endorsement, Shihab exercised his considerable powers as a model president by not stepping out of bounds. He avoided extreme decisions and simply kept the un-wieldy governmental mechanism working. Toward the end of his term, moreover, he adamantly refused to give in to the mounting pressures from all confessions to run for a second term.

When the government, late in the fall of 1958, pardoned all citizens arrested during the civil war, it also announced the pro-posed cancellation of all licenses for firearms. This proposal, how-ever, never went into effect. In the election of the spring of 1960 and again four years later, and indeed even in 1968, the security forces were once again patrolling the streets leading to the polling booths.

So long as confessional democracy survives, the army is likely to continue as a neutral and, in times of stress, neutralizing agency in a country whose very existence amid the conflicting regional and international pressures depends upon pursuing a neutral course. Lebanon's creeping democracy still harbors many residual frailties. Yet with each passing domestic and external crisis, confessional politics becomes more firmly entrenched. Christians and Muslims learned lessons from the near disaster of 1958. Neither side, it would seem, found it profitable or desirable to cultivate alterna-tives to the existing scheme. Continued alliance with the West might have given many Christians a feeling of security, but the price they would have had to pay was much too high. Now that Arab socialism has fattened the doctrine of the most potent Arab unity movements, many Lebanese Muslims apparently are reluc-tant to give up free enterprise for merger with other Arab states. Beyond those reservations, the longer confessional democracy en-dures, however artificial and fictional its contrivances, the more the participants are likely to think of themselves as hyphenated Leba-nese rather than simply as Maronites, Sunnis, Shi'is, Greek Ortho-dox, Druzes, and Greek Catholics. Still, the large Christian popula-tion, even if no longer a majority, has created this opportunity. The process, even late in the 1960s, is far from complete. Despite the lessons of 1958, the Arab unity slogans wafting in from Cairo, Da-mascus, and Baghdad still titillate many Muslims and even some Christians (particularly those who happen to be socialists) of Bay-rut, Tripoli, and Sidon, just as many Christians in the Mountain find pleasurable excitement in their continuing depoliticized com-munion with the West.

Lebanese democracy has checked the effects of external inspira-tion and redirected the loyalties of Muslims and Christians to a political system in whose functioning all confessions have won a voice and in whose very viability all communities, as distinct from individuals or groups, have begun to acquire a vested interest. By partly integrating Christianity and Islam in such delicate balance, Lebanon endowed its democracy with an inner vibrance, often concealed by its imperfect apparatus, that was not shared in intensity or kind with any other Arab state. Given these conditions, which grew out of the Ottoman and French precedents, little wonder that nationalism in Lebanon, insofar as its political system holds together, must remain an Arab nationalism with stunted aspirations for Arab unity.

The fashioning of democracy in Lebanon and its continued growth and survival, it is clear, can be understood only by examining the interactive forces at the domestic, regional and international levels. The very condition of being a neither-Christian-nor-Muslim nonsocialist state at the edge of a predominantly Muslim Arab region that seems to be striving for a larger socialist unity has made Lebanon a natural target for regional intervention. What is more, the internal social and cultural structure of Lebanon, which binds it to the West and to the Arab East, also renders the country with its essentially defensive foreign policy subject to recurrent intervention from beyond the region.

In these circumstances, the Lebanese army's unique domestic role of mediation and policing amid the clashing confessions is likely to persist into the foreseeable future. Nor is such an army prone to develop political (or even military) ambitions and therefore to succumb to the temptations of acquiring modern military hardware on the cheap, as have all the other armies in the neighborhood.

22

TUNISIA: STABLE
ONE-PARTY SYSTEM

The armed forces in Tunisia in the first decade of sovereignty were a government agency in neglect, attributable to the pre-protectorate legacy, to the later changes introduced by the French, and above all to the decisive leadership of Habib Bourguiba and the powerful one-party rule that he instituted. The neglect could be attributed also to the structure of Tunisian society. At the domestic level, there was need neither for military umpirage in confessional disputes as in Lebanon nor for unification of a polyglot immigrant community as in Israel, since the population of Tunisia was substantially homogeneous. Almost all visible traces of Berber culture in Tunisia had been obliterated, by contrast with the Berber strongholds in Morocco and Algeria. In the mid-1960s the Sunnis of Tunisia, representing more than 95 per cent of the total population, were nearly all Arabs. Tunisia even escaped a tribal problem, since the relatively small number of beduin at the start of the protectorate further declined under French rule.

For external defense, Bourguiba and his colleagues relied on the international community even more palpably than did the confessional leadership in Lebanon. The Tunisian president refused to be drawn into the inner quarrels of the Arab League states. Denied the role of neutral, which Lebanon was assured from the outset, Bourguiba preferred to withdraw his delegation from the activities of the League whenever its policies appeared detrimental to his country. An authoritarian, yet paternalistic, single party, renamed in 1964 the Socialist Destour, dominated the Tunisian political system. One of the keys to Tunisia's political success was the pragmatism of the Socialist Destour leadership, and in this respect Tunisia compared favorably with both Israel and Lebanon.

Twelve times the size of Lebanon with double its population, Tunisia encompasses an area of 48,300 square miles and had an estimated population in 1967 of 4.7 million. The Atlas Mountains, stretching across the Maghrib from Morocco, terminate in Tunisia, where the tallest peak (Jabal Shambi) rises only slightly above 5,000 feet. The country is divided into the fertile *Sahil*, or coastal plain, along the north and east, the comparatively well-watered Tall, or forested mountains, in the northwest, the semi-arid steppes in the center, and the arid Saharan zone in the south. The Majardah in the northwest, the country's major river, more than 200 miles long, flows from its source in Algeria northeastward into the Gulf of Tunis. While unimportant for transportation, the Majardah has been used increasingly for irrigation and hydroelectric projects. The Tall in the northwest provides good land for grain, fruits, and animal husbandry, the semi-arid and arid south for dry farming and livestock in the interior, and olive production along the coast.

One of every three Tunisians lives in an urban area. Tunis, the capital, and its urban suburbs perhaps accounted in 1967 for 15 per cent or more of the total population. The European immigrants had for the most part settled in the towns, where they were conspicuously engaged in commerce, the professions, and—if French —the bureaucracy. They totaled in 1956 about 255,000, over 70 per cent French by birth or naturalization and 25 per cent Italian; their number declined after ten years to perhaps fewer than 30,000. No more than one in ten French immigrants settled on the land, whereas every fifth Italian immigrant became a farmer, typically first as an employee on a massive, French-owned commercial farm and then, as he accumulated savings, on a small plot of his own. The colons in 1956 held nearly 4 million acres, or approximately one-fourth the cultivated zone, almost all of it located in the fertile north. A decade later, their holdings amounted to less than 10 per cent of the farmed land. The Tunisian government, which, beginning in 1960, progressively forced the colons to sell their land at fixed prices, re-assigned it to Muslim peasants. Similarly redistributed were the estimated 3 million acres under *habus*, or religious endowment. At the same time, the government tried to rationalize the ownership of nearly 6 million acres of grazing land held by the beduin, who were being encouraged to engage in sedentary agriculture. Although two-thirds of the Tunisians in 1966 earned their living from agriculture, they contributed only one-third to the national income.

France modernized the transportation and communication networks throughout the Maghrib, and Tunisia thus acquired 1,300 miles of railroad that runs along the coast, with connecting spurs to all important mining and agricultural centers in the interior. In 1963, four-fifths of the 5,500 miles of highway, mostly built under French rule, were paved. French industrial investment, which never grew large, was attracted chiefly to mining—particularly of phosphates—rather than manufacturing; but the deposits of phosphate rock were of relatively low quality. A modest fertilizer plant, erected in 1962, began processing phosphate prior to shipment. A small Bessemer steel mill, managed by the national railroads, was the only other major industrial enterprise. Far more significant were the crafts, which in 1963 were said to employ about 600,000. Moreover, with the shifts in land ownership and the internal migration from rural to urban areas, it was estimated as late as 1963 that some 300,000 were unemployed. On the other hand, the existence of a well-established middle class made Tunisia comparable to Lebanon and Israel. While rising steadily after independence, the literacy rate among those older than 14 in Tunisia probably did not exceed 40 per cent in 1966, a rate still much lower than that of Lebanon. Nevertheless, in that year the government was approaching its goal of universal elementary education.

As a protectorate, Tunisia, like Morocco, escaped the political surgery that Algeria suffered because of its legal integration into metropolitan France; but whereas the 'Alawi dynasty in Morocco seemed to acquire in independence a new lease on life, the Husayni dynasty in Tunisia did not long outlast the French political departure. The explanation could be found in the contrasting political institutions, which were reflected, in turn, in the instruments by which France in March 1956 conferred sovereignty on the two protectorates. In the protocol on Morocco, France transferred full legislative, executive, and military powers to the sultan; in the protocol on Tunisia, France simply agreed that Tunisia would exercise its responsibilities in matters of foreign affairs, security, and defense, and that a Tunisian national army would be constituted.

Before we examine military politics in sovereign Tunisia, we might find it useful first to consider briefly the transformation of Tunisian society and politics under the protectorate.

The Beylical Tradition and the Protectorate

Tunisia was still loosely attached to the Ottoman Empire in 1881 under an autonomous arrangement that originated soon after the Ottomans had seized the territory late in the sixteenth century. The Husayni dynasty that the French found in Tunisia, and later preserved, was thus a provincial dynasty, established in 1705 by Husayn ben 'Ali Turki (1705–35). As each "Pasha Bey, Possessor of the Tunisian Kingdom" (*basha bay, sahib al-mamlakah al-tunusiyah*), succeeded to the "throne" of Tunisia, known in Europe as a regency, he sought a *ferman*, or decree of investiture, from the Ottoman sultan. On demand, the bey also sent military and naval aid to his suzerain, as he did in the Greek war for independence in the 1820s and in the Crimean war three decades later. The Bey of the Camp (*bay al-amhal*), as the heir apparent was styled, commanded the troops, whom he led periodically into the local districts "to assert the authority of the central government and to overawe tribes who might refuse to pay their taxes." [1]

Until after the Congress of Vienna the bey of Tunis earned much of his revenue from the tribute levied on the major maritime powers for his curtailment of piracy by Tunisian corsairs in the Mediterranean. In the middle decades of the nineteenth century the beys, like the Muslim sovereigns of the day, tried to modernize the institutions of government. An enlightened despot, Ahmad Bey (1837–55) abolished slavery, attempted to reorganize his army with the help of French instructors, and enlarged the rights of the resident Jews, the only native non-Muslims in the province. Muhammad Bey (1855–59) brought into being in 1858 a municipal council for Tunis, the first in the territory. In response to pressures from the British and French governments and with the drafting assistance of the French consul, Muhammad al-Sadiq (1859–82) became in 1861 the first Muslim ruler to promulgate a constitution. The bey retained almost exclusive executive power but consented to share the legislative power with a Grand Council of 60 nominated members who also, in theory, managed the finances. The experiment in responsible government came to an early end when the constitution was suspended in 1864.

The level of education in Tunisia was relatively higher than in most Arab and Muslim countries, even before French rule. Quranic schools existed in all towns and many villages, and al-Zaytunah Mosque University was one of the three most prestigious universities in the Arab world. General Khayr al-Din, a Circassian mamluk who served as the bey's principal adviser, founded in Tunis in 1875 Sadiqi College, the first secular institution of higher learning in the Maghrib. The equivalent of a French lycée, Sadiqi College under the protectorate became an unplanned center for training the rising political leadership.

Ahmad Bey, who started the practice of borrowing from European banks to finance modernization projects, left to his successors in 1855 a large foreign debt. Muhammad al-Sadiq Bey lost his fiscal sovereignty in 1869 to an international financial commission on which sat French, Italian, and British representatives. Twelve years later, overwhelmed by a French invasion force of 30,000, he surrendered external sovereignty to France. The protectorate, however, did not formally come into effect until a second expedition two years later. At its conclusion, 'Ali Bey (1882–1902) signed the Convention of La Marsa, pledging (Article 1) "to undertake such administrative, judicial, and financial reforms as the French Government should deem useful." [2]

The protectorate, in theory, preserved the beylical institutions insofar as they related to domestic jurisdiction. The bey, in practice, exercised only residual powers. To advise him in administering internal affairs, the protecting power at first permitted the bey to create a wazirial diwan, or ministerial council of two: a great minister (al-wazir al-akbar), or principal adviser, aided by a minister of the pen (wazir al-qalam), or minister of the interior. France added a minister of justice (wazir al-'adliyah) to the council in 1921. Each of the three served under a French "adviser." Governors called qaids, or leaders, appointed by beylical decree, administered the provinces, with limited functions, under the supervision of superior French civil controllers. Each qaid maintained a native gendarmerie, whose primary duty seemed to be tax collection. The districts of the south, with the country's only tribal population, remained under French military administration. France allowed the bey himself to keep a personal military guard no larger than 600 men.

France superimposed on the beylical institutions gradually more elaborate governing agencies, whose purposes were to promote the economic development of Tunisia through the encouragement of French (and European) immigration, and to protect the interests of the settlers. The French Resident General, accountable to the foreign ministry in Paris, enjoyed full executive powers in political, economic, and military affairs. The only other French officers with ministerial rank, the ministers of war (after 1881) and of marine (after 1942), were responsible to the Resident General. Below them, French officials ran the slowly proliferating government departments, known as directorates general, largely staffed by French civil servants. A beylical decree as early as 1883 stipulated that Muslims might be recruited for mixed army companies. Ten years later all Muslims became liable for military service; but the men, chosen by ballot, could easily arrange for substitutes. This practice lowered the standards of Muslim induction, making it almost certain that the recruits came from the illiterate and the poor sections of society, and established a precedent that survived the first decade of independence. French settlers, on the other hand, were subject to the same laws as citizens in metropolitan France. Still, of the 60,000 Tunisians who served in mixed army units in World War I, more than half had to be Muslims, since the total French settler population as late as 1921 was less than 55,000. The number of Tunisian Muslims in the French army in later years was sharply cut back and by 1956 seemed not to exceed 1,300.

The Rise of a New Political Elite

The chance existence of Sadiqi College, where French was the instructional language, benefited the French administration, for it enabled the protecting power to recruit literate native personnel for the lower echelons of the burgeoning administrative service. The protectorate regime therefore placed the college under its patronage. But the college produced more graduates than the bureaucracy absorbed. Within a decade and a half, Sadiqi alumni, now formed into a modernizing elite, called Young Tunisians, became public advocates of Muslim reform. The Young Tunisians at first primarily aimed at cultural modernization; as early as 1896 they helped create the Khalduniyah College, the first secular institution of higher learning in the Maghrib using Arabic as the teaching medium. At the start of 1912 the Young Tunisian movement organized a boycott of the tramlines in Tunis in support of their demand for equal pay for Muslim workers and equal treatment of Muslim passengers, and then protested the arrest of seven of their leaders, four of whom were deported. Tension persisted for several months until finally the Resident General imposed martial law.

Martial law continued in force for nine years. The Young Tunisians, driven underground, became politicized; and when they surfaced in 1920, they founded the first political party in the country, the Tunisian Liberal Constitutional Party (*al-hizb al-hurr al-dusturi al-tunisi*). The Destour Party, as it was commonly known, was a protest movement that called for political autonomy, guaranteed by a written constitution. Accommodating gestures of the protecting power, which created in the Muslims an illusion of greater political participation without actually enlarging their political rights, kept the party's continuing protest muted. But the number of Sadiqi alumni multiplied, and because they had been admitted to the college on the basis of countrywide competitive examinations, all the towns and many villages sent their most promising youngsters to Tunis for higher education. Many later became local Destour leaders. But the top leaders, though brought up on French secular education, were still recruited from the "best families" of the former beylical establishment. After World War I, as a leading American historian of Tunisia has observed,

> the cumulative effect of many French innovations (not necessarily planned for such a purpose) in land tenure, economic policy, transportation and communication, capitalistic exploitation of resources, all served to give Tunisians greater mobility, greater openings that had once been the closed preserve of the Tunis elite. . . . By the 1920's the sons of modest, frugal provincial Tunisians were climbing into the role of the new elite—through the sole device of Western education.[3]

Among the new leaders was Habib Bourguiba (1903–   ), the son of a former lieutenant in the beylical guard from the small, ancient town of Monastir on the eastern coast. Fresh from Sadiqi College, he joined the Destour Party in 1922; later he went to Paris for a law degree, returning in 1927 to set up his practice in Tunis. Bourguiba threw himself into party activity and soon won a wide audience among the rising generation by a steady flow of articles in the nationalist press; and in 1932 he began publishing his own journal, L'Action tunisienne. The party machine, however, remained firmly in the grip of the traditional elite, who barred bright young men from reaching the top. Bourguiba attracted to his banner those Sadiqi alumni imaginative and fortunate enough to study in France, who as a group separated in March 1934 from the Destour, forming their own Neo-Destour Party.

The Neo-Destour thus came into life full blown by the simple process of fission, with delegates from three-fifths of the parent's eighty local committees taking part in the organizing congress. Nor could the protecting power suppress the Neo-Destour movement, which fed on the resident general's ban, imposed six months after the new party's birth and enforced with varying degrees of rigor until the start of the negotiations for independence twenty years later. Bourguiba spent half that period in the enforced, and apparently meditative, seclusion of political imprisonment, and the other half developing oratorical skills of a remarkable quality.

The Bourguiba and Neo-Destour Take-over

By the time of the negotiations for independence, following the decision by Premier Pierre Mendès-France on 31 July 1954 to give the Muslims self-rule, al-Amin Bey (1943–57) and the leaders of the old Destour Party had receded into the political background. Instead, Bourguiba and the Neo-Destour organized the resistance to French rule. The Neo-Destour by then had become a mass political party with branches in the towns and villages throughout the Sahil. Scattered through the rural areas were Sadiqi alumni, sons of wealthy olive growers. These educated farmers provided the party in the villages with leadership of as high quality and *esprit de corps* as in the provincial towns. Also at the middle level of the party leadership were graduates of the traditional Zaytuniyah University, who served as a vital link with the artisans and the workers in the towns, the peasants, the landless day laborers on the massive French-owned farms, and the beduin. The party, on its legalization in the summer of 1954, claimed more than 100,000 members, and it reportedly trebled in size before the year was out.

The party structure was centralized and hierarchical. Each of the estimated 1,000 branches was managed by an executive, chosen by an assembly. The branches, grouped into 32 federations, sent delegates to federation congresses, each selecting its own executive. The branch assembly and the federation congress in theory met annually, but in practice as regularly as the protecting power permitted. The branches also sent delegates to the National Congress, in theory the supreme party organ, which also met irregularly under the protectorate—and legally in November 1955 for the first time in seventeen years. Between sessions, the National Congress delegated its powers to the smaller National Council, on which sat members chosen partly by the Congress and partly by the branches. The Political Bureau, or the party's central executive, became from the outset the real party manager. Varying in size from five to ten members, the Political Bureau reached the rank and file through permanent functional committees and through the geographical federation and branch executives.

With such a tightly knit party that penetrated so deeply into the society, Habib Bourguiba could hardly fail, provided he kept his hand on the central controls and provided the party became the real government, whatever the formal institutions of state. The issue was decided, in retrospect, in the twenty months of negotiations with France that followed the Neo-Destour's acceptance of

Mendès-France's offer of autonomy in the midsummer of 1954. The guerrillas of the Liberation Army never grew numerous (probably at no time exceeding 3,000 men), and, in the absence of serious fighting, their commanders received no opportunities for cultivating political ambitions. As it was, the guerrillas for the most part were recruited among the Neo-Destour youth, with some toughening of their ranks in the south with beduin volunteers. The principal rival to Bourguiba was Salah ben Yusuf (1910–61), who stayed in Cairo as a member of the Maghrib Liberation Committee. Like the Moroccan and Algerian committeemen who were distraught by the Neo-Desturian "defection," ben Yusuf was an inflexible advocate of militancy, betting on the guerrillas as the surest and swiftest route to full independence, and he adamantly rejected all compromise arrangements. As secretary-general of the Neo-Destour and second only to Bourguiba in the party command, ben Yusuf could not be ignored.

The issue came to a head in June 1955 on the signature of a half-dozen conventions by which France simply formalized the practical arrangements made the preceding September, when it transferred for the first time in the protectorate's history internal autonomy to a cabinet comprising only Muslims. Half of the ten ministers, including the premier, however, were independents, and only four represented the Neo-Destour. The protecting power retained full management of the country's external sovereignty. Bourguiba returned to Tunisia from three years of political imprisonment and exile two days before the signature of the instruments that made up the proposed accord between Muslim Tunisia and France. He received the tumultuous welcome of a hero and his endorsement of the conventions established his position as a moderate. Bourguiba's strategy and tactics are clear in retrospect. He, like ben Yusuf, sought full independence, and the dignity and self-respect that it conveyed, but he saw the overwhelming problems the modernizing Muslims faced because of their political inexperience and the paucity of their material resources.

Bourguiba recognized that the Tunisians of the Neo-Destour stripe had had no experience in self-rule, and that the instruments of autonomy available to the bey in his severely limited role under the protectorate bore no relevance to the needs of a new state that would have to struggle for survival in a country whose national income was low and whose economy, still largely agricultural, was only in the incipient stages of modernization. Besides, Bourguiba was wedded not only to a French wife but also to French culture.

In his view, the modernization of Tunisia would take place most assuredly by building on the base that France was bequeathing to sovereign Tunisia. He therefore elected to move toward his goal step by step, preferably in cooperation with France. He was unafraid of defying France, but he did so only when domestic politics required it or regional and international politics favored it. In brief, the moderate Bourguiba was more of a realist than the militant ben Yusuf.

These views and tactics ben Yusuf fought with the vigor and determination of a dedicated nationalist who subscribed to the favored Arab nationalist doctrine of the day: that the only defeat an imperial power understood was total defeat of the kind that France had suffered in Indo-China in the spring of 1954. Accordingly, he advocated mounting violence and an expanding guerrilla war, which he calculated, correctly, would be popular on the streets of Tunis and throughout the Sahil among the varied opponents of the Neo-Destour, the traditional first families who still clustered around al-Amin Bey. He could, in particular, count on the support of the Jarbis of his native island who "formed a powerful class of small shopkeepers and large retailers who virtually monopolized the food trade throughout Tunisia." [4] With their financial backing he hoped to organize the opposition to Bourguiba's policies and to his leadership. On 7 October 1955 ben Yusuf, whom Bourguiba had persuaded to return to Tunisia, launched his public bid for political leadership with an inflammatory sermon in the Zaytunah mosque in Tunis. Bourguiba's uncontested mastery of the Neo-Destour Political Bureau enabled him to obtain the dismissal of ben Yusuf as the party's secretary-general and to expel him from the party altogether. Ben Yusuf fled into exile as early as January 1956 and until his murder in West Germany in 1961 never ceased stirring militant opposition against Bourguiba and the Neo-Destour.

In retrospect, ben Yusuf's campaign, and its political terrorism partly supported by Egypt, weakened neither Bourguiba's primacy in the party nor the party itself, which had no political peers on the eve of independence. The influence of the Neo-Destour was reflected in its massive victory, five days after the grant of independence, in the first general and only free election. This brought Bourguiba to the premiership and the party to exclusive management of public affairs at a time when decisions were taken not alone on issues of the day but on the creation of the permanent machinery of government. Al-Amin Bey (1943–57) remained a figurehead until 25 July 1957, when the Constituent Assembly deposed him and proclaimed Tunisia a republic and Bourguiba its first president.

The bitter quarrel with ben Yusuf over basic political strategy in the first five years of sovereignty persuaded the Neo-Destour Political Bureau that Tunisia's welfare lay in unifying the country behind the party leadership. The insecurity bred by ben Yusuf's militancy thus reinforced the inherent authoritarianism of one-party rule. In June 1959 the assembly endorsed Bourguiba's constitution that enshrined what had already come into being: a one-party presidential system. The cabinet, which served at the president's pleasure, dominated the National Assembly; the basic policy discussions, however, took place in the party executive and not in the cabinet. The party structure had been reorganized to conform to the governing structure of the country. In October 1958 the 1,800 party branches were reduced to about 1,000, one for each *shaykhat*, or local district. At the same time the 41 federation offices were reduced to 14, one for each governate. Each governate office was in turn directed until October 1964 by a political commissioner and thereafter by a coordinating committee. The National Council and the National Congress became organs for the approval of decisions taken by the party executive, as did the Political Bureau in October 1964, when it was more than doubled in size to 32 members. A presidium of about a half-dozen members appointed by Bourguiba constituted the executive of the Socialist Destour, as the party was called thereafter. It was thus in the executive of the Socialist Destour that the sole leader of the party, the state, and the nation framed public policy with his self-appointed colleagues. The Socialist Destour Party was undeniably authoritarian, but its one-party rule made no allowance for a strong army.

The Army in Bourguiba's Politics

Although in Tunisia and Morocco the mode of transfer of security responsibilities from France was similar, Tunisia's end product looked more like Lebanon's. France's conferral of sovereignty on Tunisia on 20 March 1956 represented more of a promise than a reality. France still exercised most powers, pending the negotiation of pertinent agreements. The framing of agreements on the conduct of external and judicial affairs by the new state encountered no obstacles. Even the transfer of responsibility for internal security in April 1956 took place smoothly. Still, the French adverted in the negotiations to the question of "unifying responsibilities," by which they could only have meant joint responsibilities by the two countries for Tunisian security. The building of an army created many problems. Its small size at the start could be explained partly by the small number of Muslim volunteers in the French army, in contrast to the much larger number recruited in Morocco by France and Spain.

More significant than comparative statistics was the contrast in military political style. The Moroccan dynasty from the outset built up the army as a political instrument, while taking every precaution to keep it from becoming politicized. The army was designed primarily to bolster and protect the authority of the crown. In Tunisia, the Neo-Destour Party required no strong army as domestic backstop. The party leadership seemed determined to avoid using the army as a political instrument expressly because of the fear that it might become politicized. Instead, Bourguiba's steps to develop the Tunisian army served as opportunities for lessening Tunisian dependence on France, and enabled him to formulate a policy of benevolence toward the Algerian rebels without actively involving Tunisia in the rebellion.

Many French leaders saw in Habib Bourguiba, who did not conceal his strong preferences for the West, an ideal ally among the new states. France was seeking in Tunisia interdependence—rhetoric for continuing French dominance in the former protectorate, on the pattern later developed by France in West Africa. High dependence on economic and military aid, it was apparently assumed in France, would give France powerful levers in Tunisia.

French assumptions were tested in the clash over Algeria. The French commitment to a counterguerrilla war in Algeria permitted no weakness in the defense structure. Tunisia, for its part, could not afford to oppose the rebels, with whom Tunisian nationalists sympathized. Moreover, Tunisia owed the early termination of the protectorate to the rebellion in Algeria. The mounting rebellion forced Tunisia into mounting support for the rebels. Tunisia gave them a haven for escape and for training and afforded such material aid as could be spared. France was determined, however, to prevent the conversion of Tunisia into a privileged sanctuary, to block the Tunisian conduit for the flow of arms into Algeria, and to strengthen French bases in Tunisia. Domestically, the pressures were generated by Salah ben Yusuf, the advocate of action, total goals, and alliance with Egypt and the anti-Western leaders in the Arab East. Habib Bourguiba could brook no cracks in the political party nor could he tolerate rival parties. To preserve his image of vigorous leadership, he was forced to move forward.

This was the setting for military politics in Tunisia. Bourguiba's realism and his nimble tactics could be measured by his success in dispensing with a large army, and in whittling away his dependence on France by cultivating the partnership of other Western powers, particularly the United States. The timetable demonstrated how Bourguiba contrived to construct an army while denying it the opportunity to grow overbearing. In June 1956, shortly after ben Yusuf had proclaimed himself "generalissimo" of "a Tunisian Liberation Army," organized and commanded from Egypt and Libya, France finally transferred from its army some 1,300 Muslim officers and men to form the nucleus of the projected independent Tunisian army. Although Bourguiba in the following month raised the question of the evacuation of French forces, the first crisis over this issue was delayed until the summer of 1957, when France threatened to cut off aid unless its terms for a continued military presence were accepted. The Algerian war, however, focused Tunisian attention on its military nakedness.

The Tunisian search for arms, though modest, was real. The Franco-Tunisian crisis that reached its climax in November 1957 appears in retrospect no more than a large outcry over small arms. The *immobilisme* brought on by the loose coalitions denied the Fourth Republic effective policy toward Tunisia no less than effective leadership in Algeria. The lack of tolerance for Bourguiba's vulnerability pushed the Tunisian government into erecting a National Guard, as the gendarmerie or rural and border police were called, without French aid. For this paramilitary force some 3,000 former *fallagha*, or rebels, were recruited, bringing the total size of the forces, including the regular army, to about 6,000. It is ironical that while Bourguiba wanted to create a border patrol at that time to help prevent Algerian rebels sympathetic to ben Yusuf from assembling in Tunisia in large numbers, rightist politicians in France were persuaded that Bourguiba's appeal for light arms was simply a pretext for buying military equipment for the Algerian rebels. After fruitless efforts to consummate the deal with France, Bourguiba finally turned, early in September 1957, to the United States, where he received courteous attention by simply mentioning that he had accepted an Egyptian offer of military aid while rejecting a Soviet one.

The United States responded to Bourguiba's gentlemanly blackmail first by trying to convince France to fill the order. When this tactic failed, Washington next suggested that a small NATO ally such as Belgium, Italy, or one of the Scandinavian countries might become the supplier. When French counterpersuasion ruled that choice out, the United States, still insisting on the company of a NATO ally, persuaded Britain to join it. Meanwhile in France, the government of Maurice Bourgès-Maunoury reached an impasse over Algeria. The counterguerrilla war was going adversely and was draining the last ounce of vitality from the leftist coalition, as the rightist politicians and army spokesmen charged the government with responsibility for the defeats in North Africa. Foreign Minister Christian Pineau acquiesced in insistent demands from the United States and Britain to sell Tunisia a modest amount of light arms, accepting Tunisian assurances that the weapons would not reach the rebels. At the same time, the French government tried to conciliate the rightist opposition by acquiescing in the military demand for the "hot pursuit" of Algerian rebels into Tunisia. This debate took place in the context of the National Assembly's consideration of an Algerian reform bill, and brought down the Bourgès-Maunoury government.

In the five weeks when France had no government, Tunisia stepped up its pressure on the United States and Britian, which in turn had accepted the appeal of the French caretaker government to delay a decision until its successor came into being. When Félix Gaillard finally strung together a new coalition on November 6, retaining Pineau as foreign minister, the United States and Britain gave France one week to decide whether it or they would fill Tunisia's order. The Gaillard government failed to meet the deadline, and on November 14 the State Department and the Foreign Office announced that 500 rifles and 50,000 rounds of ammunition from the United States, and 350 submachine guns and 70 Bren guns and ammunition from Britain would be airlifted to Tunisia before the expected arrival of Egyptian military aid. The United States and Britain stressed in their public statements that they sought to avoid embarrassing France or disturbing the normal supplier-client relation between France and its former protectorate. But France, having walked out of a meeting of NATO's permanent council in protest, received assurances from the United States that future arms shipments to Tunisia would not be made except after consultation among the three major Western powers.

Once the arms issue had been settled, Bourguiba began insisting on the evacuation of French troops before 20 March 1958, the second anniversary of Tunisian independence. The next major crisis, however, occurred in February 1958 when French planes bombed a Tunisian border village in pursuit of Algerian rebels. The raid caused an immediate rupture of relations with France. Western reporters at that time noted that Tunisia had in fact become a corridor of arms aid from Egypt to Algeria, a sanctuary for rebels, and a training site for their external army. By February 1958 there may have been as many as 10,000 rebels in Tunisia. The multiplying Algerian rebels undoubtedly represented a major factor in the Tunisian military buildup at that time.

Meanwhile, Bourguiba's views on the French military presence hardened. He recognized that the massive facilities at Bizerta represented a French interest and also a larger NATO interest. In 1942, France had integrated Bizerta into a network of naval bases that included Brest and Toulon. Bizerta was more than a naval base, however, since it consisted also of a complex of air bases, and in the over-all installation France had invested over the years an estimated $200 million. A legacy of the protectorate, Bizerta by 1958 was of potential use to NATO in the Mediterranean area, and of active counterguerrilla use to France in Algeria. More than half the French troops in Tunisia, an estimated 12,000, were concentrated at Bizerta; the rest were scattered among five air bases throughout the country. After failing to persuade Tunisia to establish joint border patrols, France unilaterally withdrew its troops from the Tunisian side of the frontier and erected an electrified barbed-wire barrier on the Algerian side from Bône to Tebessa to impede the arms traffic. France also evacuated the air bases, concentrating its residual force at Bizerta.

Tension had subsided sufficiently by the time of the Congo crisis of 1960–61 to enable Tunisia to respond to the U.N. request for volunteer troops; four battalions, or 3,200 men, were assigned to duty with the international force. The Tunisian troops remained in the Congo until the summer of 1961, when they were airlifted back to Tunisia, as a result of the Bizerta crisis that broke out in July. By then Tunisia had become host to the Provisional Government of the Algerian Republic (GPRA) and to the smaller part of the Algerian External Army. Bourguiba sought a middle path between the demands of the rebels for closer cooperation and the needs of domestic development. Bourguiba's tactics were ingenious. He simultaneously insisted on the complete French evacuation of Bizerta and a rectification of the Algerian boundary in the south. Civilian Neo-Destour volunteers and military reservists blockaded the French naval and air force installations at Bizerta early in July 1961. Bourguiba also announced that a patrol of army volunteers would "plant a flag at Marker 233," twenty-eight miles south of

Tunisia's southern limit at Fort Saint. In attempting to "rectify" the Algerian border by unilateral action, Bourguiba declared:

> We see it as our duty to claim our Saharan space today rather than start a conflict tomorrow with our Algerian brothers. I pledge myself not to fix our Saharan limits except with the government of an independent Algeria. I hope, nevertheless, that the National Council of the Algerian Revolution will bring back to reason those elements who, while we were crouching in French jails, were asking themselves if Algeria was part of Africa or part of Europe.[5]

At this juncture the United States airlifted the return of the 3,200 Tunisian officers and men from the Congo. Although Bourguiba announced that the Arab League states had offered volunteers, the dispute over Bizerta subsided in September, when Bourguiba declared that France might retain the base until the settlement of the Berlin crisis. France finally pulled out of Bizerta in October 1963, about 18 months after the Evian accords on Algeria, terminating the French military presence in Tunisia. However, the Tunisian-Algerian border problem was not resolved, although Tunisia temporarily withdrew its claims.

Meanwhile, Bourguiba made public his view of the role of the army in politics after an attempt on his life late in 1962, in which Tunisian Army officers, including one of his own bodyguards, were implicated. In a speech to the students at the school for noncommissioned officers in March 1963, the president stressed civilian primacy in state-building. "Officers must also realize that these tasks [of state-building] are matters for the political authority and for it alone. It can only perform them if it knows that the State's existence is secure." He also went on to allude to "a series of *coups d'Etat*, sometimes bloody ones, in other countries formerly under the yoke of foreign powers." He suggested that such military intervention into politics could be attributed generally to the political immaturity and the "state of disorder and political instability" that characterized these countries. "It is easier to get rid of a man than to replace him," declared the Tunisian president.

> Whether inspired by socialism, communism or any revolutionary doctrine, the authors of *coups d'Etat* always claim to be concerned for social improvement and human dignity. They promise the moon and the stars. But what results do we have? A series of *coups* with everyone pushing aside the slight gains of the previous one. Socialism is always for tomorrow. Insecurity paralyzes all long-term creative

efforts. In the light of these endemic *coups d'Etat*, the stability and solidity of the Tunisian State ought to have greater value for us.[6]

Bourguiba, it is clear, deliberately kept his army weak. The Socialist Destour commanded mass support for the regime throughout the country, thus dispensing with the need for elaborate and costly internal security arrangements. Until 1965, at least, Bourguiba preferred to rely on diplomacy for external defense. The party imposed a stable civilian management on the security forces: Bahi Laghdam, who replaced ben Yusuf as the party's secretary-general, also served as the minister of national defense; and Tayyib Mehiri, another party stalwart, directed the interior ministry until his death in 1965. Nevertheless, the military establishment slowly expanded in response to the successive disputes first with France and then, after 1962, with Algeria.

By 1965 the armed forces had grown to nearly 17,500 officers and men. Of these, some 15,000 constituted the army, and the rest, the navy and the air force, which were of roughly equal size. The cadre of the army consisted of fewer than 3,000 officers and NCOs plus an approximately equal number of privates. The officers and a handful of the NCOs entered the army for career employment; most of the NCOs and all the privates in the cadre enlisted for five-year, renewable terms of service. Some 9,000 conscripts were inducted each year, about a third of the total every four months. After undergoing a four-month basic training, the conscripts were assigned to regular duty, which included participation in civic-action projects, for the remaining eight months of service, when they formed the main body of troops. The selective system of conscription, with liberal allowance for exemption, lowered the quality of the inductees, bringing in a majority of illiterates; and in any case, all conscripts were discharged at the end of a year, just at a time when the army could begin to benefit from their training. The conscription law was amended in June 1967, so as to reduce the opportunities for exemption and to improve the quality of the reserve units.

The Tunisian armed forces were hardly an impressive military machine, and investment in weaponry in the first decade of independence never reached as much as 2 per cent of the estimated GNP (see Table 15), undoubtedly the lowest rate of expenditure in the Middle East. Even the military slice of the government budget was consistently under 10 per cent. Until the dispute over Bizerta in 1961, almost all the Tunisian officers received French

TABLE 15. Tunisia: Force Levels, Government Expenditures, and GNP, 1956/57–1965

| | Population (millions) | Force Levels (thousands) | Government Expenditures (millions of Tunisian dinars) | | | GNP (millions of dinars at current prices) | Defense Expenditures (as % of GNP) |
			Defense (including internal security and justice)	Development	Total		
1956/57 [a]	3.80	1.3	1.8	17.5	58.4		
1957/58	3.81		2.7	17.5	58.4		
1958/59	4.05		5.0	14.0	60.8		
1959/60	3.94		5.0	21.0	69.6		
1960 [b]	4.17	8.0	3.7	17.9	85.0	335.0	1.1
1961 [c]	4.25		4.8	20.2	76.0	365.8	1.3
1962	4.29		4.8	25.7	82.5	370.7	1.3
1963	4.49		4.3	46.8	106.8	385.6	1.1
1964	4.56		7.8	46.1	114.2	428.1	1.8
1965	4.59	17.5	7.3	46.3	121.6	462.3	1.6

sources: *Annuaire Statistique de la Tunisie*; IMF, *International Financial Statistics*; AID, *Selected Annual Statistics*; and ACDA, *Selected Data*, 1964 and 1965.

[a] Fiscal year ends 31 March.
[b] Last nine months.
[c] Fiscal year ends 31 December.

instruction; thereafter they were sent largely to NATO countries, including Turkey and Greece, and also to the United States. Not until 1967 did the Tunisian government institute its own instructional program for officers. As French aid declined, small missions from Sweden and Italy helped train the air force. American economic aid to Tunisia, through June 1965, amounted to $444.5 million, of which two-thirds represented grant aid. By contrast, United States military aid in this period did not exceed a total of $16.5 million. An American military survey mission, invited by the Tunisian government, proposed in December 1965 that the United States sponsor a program of modest military growth in Tunisia. Tunisia's desire for American military aid stemmed largely from fear of Algerian military expansion, after the border war with Morocco in October 1963, when Algeria became a Soviet military client.

At the start of 1968, the United States program for modernizing the Tunisian armed forces was still a low-cost project, even by Tunisian standards. It could thus be said that Bourguiba had contrived, by skillful use of internal and external pressures and crises, to maximize the external help in building a military establishment which, though adequate for domestic needs, did not seriously challenge the supremacy of the party. The test would come at the time of the political succession, since advance arrangements, even in a paternalistic authoritarian system, cannot always be guaranteed.

Regional Consequences

ARMIES AS AGENCIES
OF SOCIAL CHANGE

Now that we have examined at close range military politics in its evolutionary perspective, we are able to evaluate the effects of military modernization on differing societies in the nonindustrial states of the region. There is manifestly a direct link between politics and military change. We must now explore the relationship between military change and economic and social change, a theme which social scientists working on nonindustrial states have favored. But many of their hypotheses do not stand up under close analysis of the Middle East experience. Too many of the hypotheses have rested not on the realities of the postwar Middle East but on abstract logic, and on the premise of military rule.

At this point we are able to consider the role of armies in social and economic change not only where they have seized power but even where they have not. Military modernization, as we have seen, is taking place everywhere in the Middle East, although the pace varies from country to country. Not all military rulers, for example, are lavish spenders on new weapons, as Sudan well illustrated in 1958 to 1964. Nor is there a necessary correlation between democratic government and low military spending. In the mid-1960s Israel, the region's most vigorous democracy, was allocating perhaps as much as 12–14 per cent of its GNP annually to its armed forces for training, hardware, research and engineering, and industrial production.

Let us start with an analysis of the widely held assumption that military politicians in nonindustrial states make the best, the most thoroughgoing, and perhaps the only reliable managers of social change. Implicit in this assumption is the argument that the army in a nonindustrial state is the most effective supervisory agency for directed development because it is itself, as a rule, the most modernized and most highly disciplined nationwide institution, and its officers are expressly trained for dedicated public service. A comparison of the record of the two men who by common accord have been the most successful of the region's Muslim military social changers in the twentieth century—Mustafa Kemal Pasha, as Atatürk was known before 1935, and Gamal 'Abd al-Nasir—should help test the validity of this hypothesis and clarify the relation between military politicians and planned social change.

Turkish and Egyptian Experiences

Military officers are likely to become revolutionaries if social and economic conditions they hold oppressive continue without improvement. If the officers are denied participation in the political system and the opportunity to modify by constitutional means its institutions and its policies, they may become convinced that the abuses can be corrected only through "disinterested" military intrusion into politics. The two Middle East leaders fit this description admirably, and their careers were roughly parallel.

Both men came from the lower middle class, and in attaining supreme political leadership reshaped the political, economic, and social systems and suppressed traditional privilege. Mustafa Kemal's father was a government clerk and his mother a peasant. 'Abd al-Nasir's father was a deputy postmaster. The two leaders early in life became ardent foes of the privileged classes. As heads of state, both continued to live simply. In each case the army gave the future leader his start in public service, and both turned to politics after their countries suffered major military defeats, the Ottoman Empire in World War II and Egypt in the Palestine war of 1948–49. The wartime records of the two men were beyond reproach. Mustafa Kemal's reputation as a brilliant commander was established at Gallipoli in 1915. He organized the triumphant nationalist resistance (1919–22) against the European occupation armies and the related efforts by the Greeks, Kurds, and Armenians to grab chunks of what remained of unoccupied Anatolia. 'Abd al-Nasir had far more limited martial experience but he nevertheless showed bravery in the al-Falujah pocket in the first war against Israel.

Once the two men reached the top, they clutched their political leadership tightly. Mustafa Kemal never relinquished the presidency of republican Turkey, a post he held from its birth in October 1923 to his death in November 1938. 'Abd al-Nasir also revealed remarkable staying powers, for no one seriously challenged his supremacy once he became prime minister in 1954 and president two years later. Even after the military disaster in June 1967, he contrived to reassert his popularity by the stratagem of a formal "resignation" and "resumption" of office by "popular acclaim." Each man entered his political career without prior training in civilian leadership. Both cultivated flamboyant styles and proved superlative pragmatists. Not until 1931 did the congress of Turkey's sole political party of the day adopt the six guiding principles, or "arrows," of the regime—republicanism, nationalism, populism, statism, secularism, and revolutionism. Similarly, not until the summer of 1961 did 'Abd al-Nasir proclaim the creed of Arab socialism.

Neither man could claim primary authorship of his modernization program. The urge to Westernize the Ottoman Empire—that is, to seek acceptance by Europe as a European state—had gained currency among the Muslim Ottoman elite eighty years before Mustafa Kemal appeared on the political scene. By the mid-nineteenth century Westernization (modernization) provided the central theme of a public dialogue among the army officers, the bureaucrats, and the intellectuals. 'Abdülhamid's repression did not end the dialogue; it simply drove the urban educated elite underground. The major ideas received clear formulation before the Young Turk Revolution in 1908, from which military intervention into Turkish politics in the twentieth century dates. Mustafa Kemal's genius lay in an ability, not to coin ideas, but to put them into effect. 'Abd al-Nasir, on his side, did not write the social doctrines that found their way into the 1956 Egyptian constitution. As early as 1950 the Syrians began incorporating such principles into constitutions from which the Egyptians later drew freely. To the Ba'th Party of Syria, similarly, might be attributed the invention of Arab socialism. But the Ba'this never learned how to translate their doctrines into action. By the mid-1960s 'Abd al-Nasir had converted Egypt's economy into a socialist one. Though pragmatically conceived and applied, Atatürk's program became ideological after his death. 'Abd al-Nasir's equally pragmatic program automatically became doctrinal on export to other Arab lands.

Among the economically privileged class in pre-revolutionary Turkey and Egypt were foreigners and non-Muslim minorities. This simplified the problem of reform, for it is always easier to arouse public feeling against foreigners, particularly those tied to imperialism, and against the minorities associated in the public mind with the foreigners. In any case, the minorities, through the performance of special economic functions, had come to enjoy their own economic privileges. With the minorities and the foreigners were allied the Muslim upper classes, for whom political rights and power formed a private monopoly. The two soldier presidents, therefore, suppressed the traditional Muslim political elites and toppled the Europeans and the non-Muslims from their economic perches. In 1923, the Turks negotiated the end of the capitulations, the legal basis of European economic domination, and arranged with Greece for the exchange of populations, thus reducing the minority problem to tractable size. Mustafa Kemal then turned to the creation of a Muslim commercial and industrial middle class in the towns and, when Muslim private capital proved insufficient, promoted statism, or state enterprise. In preparing the ground for Arab socialism, 'Abd al-Nasir after 1956 liquidated the economic power first of the foreigners and the minorities and later of the Muslim commercial, industrial, and landowning elite.

Finally, the two presidents espoused neutrality in foreign policy to avoid alliances, or even fixed identity, with any single great power. From this practice 'Abd al-Nasir seemingly departed after 1965, as he alienated the United States and placed his reliance increasingly on the U.S.S.R. Yet despite high dependence on Soviet aid after the Six Day War in June 1967, 'Abd al-Nasir's capacity to wriggle loose from the Soviet grip was not to be discounted.

A review of the gross analogies does not begin to come to grips with the central issue, which is how the officers in the armed forces, after intruding into politics, became instruments of social change. Here the similarities between Atatürk and 'Abd al-Nasir grow faint and the differences striking, because the conditions in Turkey and in Egypt were not wholly comparable. The differences should be viewed against the background of the transformation of international politics and of the international mood between the interwar years, when Western Europe dominated the nonindustrial world, and the postwar years, when the Western European imperial powers were retreating from Asia and Africa. A generation earlier the industrial states hardly shared their wealth or their skills with the nonindustrial states, most of which were still dependencies. Under the impact of the Cold War after 1945, the industrial states, often in rivalry, offered growing economic and technical (including military) aid to the nonindustrial states.

Atatürk's dedication to modernization in his day was innovative. After 1945, all sovereign states of Asia and Africa became devotees of rapid modernization. The unique quality of 'Abd al-Nasir's achievement was thus neither his dedication to the social transformation of Egypt nor his skill in procuring aid simultaneously from the U.S.S.R. and the United States. Rather was it his ability, until 1965, to procure such aid on a continuing lavish scale.

When General Mustafa Kemal took over the leadership of the nationalist resistance in 1919, he was intervening in the politics of a dying empire. The political revolution arising from this military intervention moved away from empire, struggling for survival as a truncated but integrated Turkish state. Under Kemal's leadership, the Turkish nationalists accommodated to the fact that their non-Turkish provinces had been lost. A relatively homogeneous republic accordingly emerged from the ruins of an empire, and, despite the territorial contraction, Turkish sovereignty was never entirely eclipsed.

Egypt under military management moved in precisely the opposite political direction, from dependency to empire builder. The Free Officers overthrew the dynasty in 1952, while Egypt was still Britain's reluctant preferential ally, conducting its foreign and military affairs under the coercive shadow of the massive British base in the Suez Canal Zone. On replacement of the preferential alliance, Egypt assumed with more vigor than imagination the leadership of the Arab unity movement. The role was cut out for the most populous Arab state, which was also the cultural center of the Arab world and the one state that might hope to lead the Arabs toward their cherished goal. Even before 1952, Egypt used the Arab unity movement as an instrument for the conduct of Egyptian foreign policy. After experiments in Arab political merger began to look feasible, as they did with the formation of the United Arab Republic in 1958, 'Abd al-Nasir used the movement also as an instrument for territorial expansion.

The political objectives of Atatürk and 'Abd al-Nasir clearly differed. Atatürk strove to create a homogeneous nation-state. 'Abd al-Nasir, after 1954, tried to weld the Arab countries into a single united nation-state with Cairo as its capital. The divergent political objectives were reflected in the divergent attitudes of the two men toward their armed forces. One premise implicit in much of the political sociology on soldiers as instigators of social change in Asia and Africa seems to be that such politicians in uniform indulge the armed forces, on the ground that the soldiers as custodians of the public welfare must also lead and oversee the enterprise of modernization. Those who subscribe to this view seem to be saying that the larger and the more modern the military establishment, the faster and the more thorough the pace of societal change. Whether or not there is an optimum relative size for a military establishment playing such a custodial role may be worth examining. But as this is not our present purpose, suffice it to say that soldiers do not always pamper the establishment which gave them their start.

'Abd al-Nasir, it is true, favored his military forces and equipped them with spanking new hardware and the latest gadgets on land, under the sea, in the air, and even sought those for outer space. For this, there were sufficient explanations, but an essential link to modernization was not one of them. His feverish efforts at military modernization sprang from a desire to win acceptance of Egypt by the international community as a leading world power, alone if necessary, but preferably as the core of an enlarged Arab state. From modern arms, he appeared to be saying, flowed prestige, authority, and international leadership. Such equipment, too, would help the Arabs overtake Israel. Not to be ignored, of course, was the availability of up-to-date weaponry at attractive prices.

In Atatürk's day, such equipment was just not that easily available. Nor did Turkey face hostile neighbors. Communist Russia did not follow an expansionist policy toward Turkey in the interwar years. Greece was the only country that might have aroused anxiety in Turkey, but following the exchange of populations, Greece and Turkey in 1930 reached an accord that survived Atatürk's death. When to these conditions was added the absence of irredentism, Atatürk's calculated neglect of Turkey's armed forces after the war for independence and the inauguration of his comprehensive modernization program became wholly understandable. At a time when most European armies were being motorized, the Turkish army still relied on horse-drawn vehicles and an outmoded railroad system that hardly began to meet his country's true defense needs. At a time when the industrial states were developing air forces, Turkey did little to imitate them.

Yet who would question that Atatürk in his day was the most forceful, imaginative, and persistent military modernizer in the Middle East? It might have been argued, of course, that from the moment Mustafa Kemal Pasha resigned his commission in July 1919 he had become a civilian. Still, he continued wearing his uniform throughout the war for independence, and even after he switched to mufti, he left no doubt in the minds of the active military officers who their real supreme commander was. When necessary to invoke public respect, he summoned the memory of his reputation as an infallible military leader, and many of his statues and pictures showed him in military posture. Admittedly, he instituted and enforced the rule of separating the army from politics. After 1924, no army officer could run for election to the legislature without first surrendering his commission; the chief of the general staff no longer was named to the cabinet. Indeed, all ministers recruited from the officer corps had to sever their ties to the armed forces. That Mustafa Kemal's primary motive in civilianizing the government was not fidelity to the principle but fear of displacement by other popular generals who vocally opposed him in the legislature is irrelevant. Retired army officers represented a high proportion of the members of successive cabinets and of the legislatures under Mustafa Kemal's presidency.

From the outbreak of the war for independence in 1919, Mustafa Kemal paid close attention to the organization of civilian support for his policies. The Association for the Defense of Rights grew into the Republican People's Party (RPP) in August 1923, on the eve of the inauguration of the republic's national parliament. Although Mustafa Kemal could abide only the RPP, having given short shrift to the opposition parties in his experiments of 1924–25 and 1930, he nevertheless strove to enlarge its membership. 'Abd al-Nasir and the Free Officers who formed the Revolutionary Command Council simply did away with the political parties altogether in 1953–54. Thereafter they went through the motions of creating under various names a government-sponsored party which was never allowed to take firm shape. Instead, the military continued to hold the civilians—especially those technicians who were given ministerial posts—in tight harness.

Finally, the Egyptian and Turkish revolutions differed in scope. 'Abd al-Nasir's new order reached simultaneously into the rural and urban areas, whereas Atatürk's was essentially an urban revolution. The fact that the Egyptian revolution was taking place a generation later than the Turkish may go far to explain the difference, but other considerations must also be taken into account. From the beginning of recorded history, Egypt has had a market economy, and the peasants were united by a natural riverine communication system. In such an integrated economy, changes in economic organization and activity penetrate into the villages as well as into the towns. The Turkish agricultural economy, in contrast, remained until after World War II primarily one of subsistence or barter, and the country's thousands of villages, many scattered among the mountains, were largely isolated from one another by inadequate means of communication and transportation. The rural

revolution in Turkey, therefore, had to await the construction of a
road system in the 1950s. One generation's revolution may become
the next generation's conservatism. The Turkish military coup of
1960 bore this out.

What conclusions may we draw? Atatürk made a rigorous point
of civilianizing his regime. The military influence on modernization was thus an indirect one. 'Abd al-Nasir and his fellow Free
Officers manifestly preferred direct military domination of the government and, through it, of the society and the economy. This was
true, at least until June 1967, when Field Marshal 'Abd al-Hakim
'Amir was forced to retire after Israel's victory. With 'Amir's removal and later suicide, 'Abd al-Nasir destroyed his vital link to
the armed forces. Unless he reforged a facsimile link, his choices
were narrowed to weakening the army or courting political disaster.
Moreover, the diversion of so much of the public resources to military investment jeopardized the experiment in social revolution.
The shattering defeat by Israel, following on the heels of Egypt's
dismal showing in Yemen, destroyed the army's reputation for infallible leadership of the government, to say nothing of the morale
of its officers. The preoccupation with military modernization,
which yielded largely negative results, brought into serious question its value as an avenue of social and economic change. It was
scant comfort that that preoccupation and the accompanying in-
dulgence of the armed forces sprang from Egypt's frustrations ever
since the mid-nineteenth century. Each time an attempt to expand
the army was frustrated by outside powers, as it had been in 1841
and again in 1882 and after the two world wars, the interest in
military expansion and modernization seemed to reassert itself with
ever mounting vigor.

The Turkish officers, on their side, in the late 1960s continued to
behave as guardians, but less of Atatürk's revolution than of the
Second Republic. After the 1965 election, however, political leadership in the republic was transferred from the minority governments of the Republican People's Party to the majority government of the Justice Party. But the latter was the lineal descendant
of Menderes' Democratic Party, which had been forcibly overthrown and dissolved by the 1960 coup. Thus, ironically, within a
half-dozen years the military custodians of the Second Republic
also became indirect sponsors of Turkey's second revolution in the
twentieth century, for, under Menderes, runaway change had begun to overtake the rural areas. The consequent outpouring of villagers into the towns compounded the problems of modernization.

Modernization in Plural Societies

The first presidents of the Turkish and Egyptian republics, living a generation apart, were both radical reformers; both devoted their political careers to the social and economic as well as political transformation of their countries. Still, Turkey and Egypt were exceptional in the Middle East. Their societies were homogeneous, by Middle East standards, for the Turks in the one and the Muslim Arabs in the other represented over nine-tenths of the total population. The dominant communities in each society so thoroughly subordinated the others, that for all practical purposes the residual minorities could no longer even marginally influence social and economic policies. It may also be noted that in interwar Turkey and postwar Egypt the military-political elites and the overwhelming majority of their officer following belonged to the dominant communities. The experiences of the two countries, while comparable, can nevertheless hardly form the basis of a general hypothesis because in all other Middle East countries where the military have intruded into politics there are, not homogeneous societies, but heterogeneous or plural ones.

Cultural pluralism is used here not in the American sense of a culturally diverse population which enjoys freedom to express itself in its own diverse media while all participate in a common culture. Instead, it is used in the Middle East sense of ethnic, linguistic, and sectarian communities that have traditionally coexisted and survived into the twentieth century as distinct units, with traces of the old communal division of labor, in the largest cities long after these have become "modernized." Even the so-called homogeneous countries have sizable minorities. The Kurds in Turkey and the Copts in Egypt each represent an estimated 8 per cent of the total population. The Arabs in Israel before June 1967 represented nearly 12 per cent. Saudi Arabia, Libya, and Jordan, it might be argued, are wholly Arab. But, as we have seen, the divisions in Saudi Arabia and Libya are sectarian, while in Jordan before June 1967 the population was divided between the pastoral and the settled and between the East and West banks. Perhaps the only truly homogeneous country in the Middle East is Tunisia, whose original Berber population has been thoroughly Arabized.

Those who argue that officers of modernized armies are modern men leading their countries into the modern world assume that the social cleavages in these countries follow the normal lines of lower, middle, and upper classes. In the plural societies of the Middle

East, however, such horizontal cleavages are criss-crossed by vertical cleavages among differing ethnic, linguistic, sectarian, and even at times nomadic communities. When class changes take place in these countries, they normally occur in more than one community at a time. Intercommunal barriers persist, and the communal middle classes in a plural society tend to perpetuate their competitiveness in most spheres, economic and social no less than political and military. The criss-crossing cleavages help explain why the military rulers of Syria and Iraq, for instance, failed to develop durable regimes like the one in Egypt, and why the interrupted programs of modernization often have had retrogressive economic, social, and political effects. No less significant, the modernizing monarchies under admittedly retrogressive political regimes, even in countries with plural societies, have been able to carry out progressive economic and social reforms.

In plural societies, therefore, officers by and large are not in fact social revolutionaries, even where they have seized political power. In Algeria, Egypt, Iraq, and Syria the soldier-rulers proclaimed their fidelity to Arab socialism and paraded themselves as radicals. After 1963 they were prone to speak of the need to "liberate" the remaining Arab countries, a euphemism for destroying the monarchical and the non-military republican regimes. Yet what are the facts? There is no doubt that Arab socialism was an asserted reality in Egypt before the Six Day War. But in Syria after 1964, when socialism was first introduced under direct Ba'thi inspiration, the soldier-rulers showed little competence in making their policies work. Much of the difficulty derived from the fact that the junta's officers came from the 'Alawi community, a schismatic minority in a plural society whose numerically dominant Sunni Arab community constituted some two-thirds of the total population. The 'Alawis were the backwoodsmen of Syria, less educated and less wealthy as a group than the Sunnis and thus probably underrepresented in the country's middle class. Yet they wrested substantial control over the army from their fellow politicized officers in the coup d'état of February 1966. Before then, ever since the beginning of military rule in 1949 (excluding the interval of union with Egypt), the 'Alawis had shared the top military positions with Kurds and Druzes. The 'Alawis continued the minority practice of deliberately discouraging Sunni Arabs from entering the military academy at Homs so as to keep their numbers down, gave the few Sunni officers slow promotions, and assigned them to the least sensitive posts. There thus seemed to be little prospect of an early Sunni Arab military coup. By the same token, to keep themselves in power, the 'Alawi rulers appealed for popular support in Syria and in the Arab world at large by advertising their espousal of socialism, which, like their espousal of Arab unity, was more extreme than that of the Sunni Arab socialists in Egypt or even Iraq.

In Iraq, it is also necessary to look at the communal as well as social origins of the soldier-politicians in assessing their performance as social reformers. 'Abd al-Karim Qasim, the first military dictator after the removal of the monarchy, was a Sunni Arab. He came from the lower middle class, it is true, but he favored in national policies the Sunni Arab community and seemed to trust only Sunni Arab officers whom he sent as district officials even to Shi'i and Kurdish zones, down to the township level. He thus exercised power in much the same way as had the monarchy, which also discriminated in favor of the Sunni Arabs. Once Qasim precipitated civil war with the Kurds in 1961, he upset the delicate communal balance: in the opening months of the military republic the Kurdish middle-class leaders in the northern towns, particularly in Sulaymaniyah, had sided with the regime; after the outbreak of hostilities they joined the rebels and thereafter ceased to identify with the Sunni Arab middle class.

In this connection, it is instructive to contrast the military republican achievement in social reform with that of the modernizing monarchies. Some social scientists seem to accept uncritically the military republican propaganda that all Middle East monarchies, whether modernizing or traditional, are outmoded and ripe for displacement. Yet those monarchies with modernized armies, while governing with a repressive hand, nonetheless began introducing more and more liberal economic and social policies, as best exemplified by Iran after 1961, when Muhammad Reza Shah launched his "White Revolution." The Shah devoted the major part of the multiplying oil revenues to expanding the economy and developing welfare services. By the late 1960s, as we have seen, the economy was growing at an unprecedented rate. No military republic could show a comparable achievement. In next-door Iraq, where the per capita prospects for economic expansion on the basis of cultivable land, plentiful water, and generous oil income probably exceeded those of Iran, the Arab-Kurdish civil war plunged the economy into such deep and prolonged crisis that development projects other than schools and roads received only scant attention.

Even such an unpromising economy as that of oil-poor Jordan was growing, until June 1967, at a rate faster than any predicted by the informed economists a decade earlier.

Dual-Purpose Investment

Modernizing armies, whether they intervene in politics or not, are often said to be modernizing agents at large in their societies, because military investment in men and machines invariably produces positive non-military side effects. Military training upgrades the quality of workmanship, for instance, and thus prepares the men for better jobs when they return to civilian life. Machines are exported to nonindustrial countries for the armed forces but they may frequently be put to general use as well. In addition, the modernizing army itself is commonly employed in civilian projects, thus making a direct contribution to non-military development. Therefore, this argument goes, a dollar invested in modernizing the army is worth three dollars or more in the country at large, because it does double duty. Such a claim may be good sales talk but it is poor social science. It might have been ignored but for its endorsement by reputable social scientists. Let us first look at the proposition piece by piece and then see how the pieces fit into the Middle East jigsaw.

The transferability of military skills to non-military employment is always at least partly true. Retired officers, it is said, put their army-learned skills to use in the advancement of society and the enlargement of the economy by becoming engineers, managers, and entrepreneurs. In the army, moreover, many illiterate enlisted men are taught to read and write, and all, whether literate or illiterate, are given opportunities to learn how to operate and maintain modern machinery and communications systems. Veterans of such armies enrich the civilian labor force. "If the young man returning from the army . . . remained within the village," it is noted,

> he might be the driving force behind both technical and social innovation, such as the purchase of modern agricultural equipment and the organization of a local youth society. . . . In other words, the absorptive capacity had increased by reason of the military development program.[1]

The double-duty enthusiasts trip over hard facts. They resort to deductive reasoning and tend to overlook the empirical evidence.

Their arguments sound plausible, if the armies are conscript armies. Actually, however, two of every three Middle East armies are career armies, a fact which slows down and restricts the feedback to civilian life. Occasional retirements from career armies enable skilled personnel to find civilian employment, but their over-all number is too small to have more than minor importance. Yet even in those countries with conscript armies—Afghanistan, Egypt, Iran, Iraq, Israel, Tunisia, and Turkey—the results are grossly uneven. Army-acquired skills were neither invariably nor easily transferable. A soldier who learned to read and write in the army often discovered after returning to his native village that he could not put literacy to effective use in a locality with no newspapers and few books. A veteran might also discover that such technical skills as driving and maintaining a jeep or repairing a telephone would earn him no livelihood, if there were no demands for such services in his native village or too few of them in the town where he might have resettled. Even in Turkey, where tractors became common in the 1950s, mechanized farming was often not feasible in hill country, where most Turkish villages are located. In any case, before valid generalizations on the actual transfer of skills from the army to the civilian economy and society can be framed, country studies must be made to ascertain whether conscripts are actually learning the supposed skills in military service. The contribution of the Turkish armed forces to literacy in rural areas, for example, seems to have been exaggerated. No more than about 3 per cent of the literate rural males, according to one survey, learned to read and write in the army.[2]

In Egypt, on the other hand, army officers, active and retired, were deliberately employed after 1961 in managing the multiplying enterprises that the government sponsored in its program of Arab socialism. The soldier-rulers had started this process earlier with the seizure of the Suez Canal Company and the confiscation of British and French commercial, fiscal, and even educational establishments in 1956–57. The use of such officers was designed, however, even more for political security than for redirecting army-acquired talents to civilian occupations. Still, it could not be denied that the army managed Egypt's proliferating Arab socialist program.

The Israel Defense Forces probably best illustrated in the Middle East an army designed for more than a simple military mission. The IDF is a citizen army. The professional cadre excepted, all the officers and men are reservists who, after compulsory military service, are expected to seek their careers as civilians and to undergo annual refresher training in their units. From the very outset the authors of the IDF conceived of it as an educational agency to help transform the polyglot immigrant population into Hebrew-speaking Israel nationalists. These objects, the IDF later substantially realized. Yet when the IDF is judged as a modernizing agency, the results are less impressive. Technicians were absorbed in all branches of the economy, which in the second postwar decade expanded at an average annual rate of about 9 per cent, yet the demands through 1965 exceeded the available skills. Those conscripts who joined the IDF with the best educational preparation were the ones selected for the most specialized training that the army offered. The others were funneled to the less skilled branches, which often had little civilian application. Clearly, those conscripts of European parentage coming into the army with better education enjoyed more options. They sometimes developed technical expertise for which there was a civilian demand. In brief, the IDF excelled as a unifying agent for the immigrant population and, in effect, as a finishing school for the socially privileged conscripts; but it was not an equalizing agent, for it hardly offered to the socially less favored conscripts comparable opportunities for learning new skills. Thus, most citizen soldiers of Asian and African parents left the IDF as they had entered it—as candidates for unskilled labor.

Many Middle East armies, like armies elsewhere, directly sponsor non-military projects, putting their special equipment, facilities, and technical experience to civilian work. In Morocco, for example, the king employed his army in civic action programs, often tied in the early years of sovereignty to a military campaign for the restoration of order in rural and mountain districts. In Pakistan, too, the planning commission, which was trying to make the best use of its limited funds, formulated a civic action rationale for the army's employment in road construction. "When a given expenditure," observed the commission,

> can serve the dual purpose of defence and development substantial economies can be achieved. . . . The armed forces utilise men during significant portions of their useful lives but the nation is concerned with their entire period of usefulness. New skills, habits of discipline, and familiarity with group organisation are required during terms of military service. These attainments are national assets to be conserved after discharge and fully utilised in the civilian work of development.[3]

It is only one short logical step from the argument for civic action to the argument that social and economic benefits are hidden in every defense appropriation. The annual military budgets of most armies provide for the purchase not only of weapons and uniforms but also of trucks, bulldozers, air transport, telephones, and radios, and for the civilian construction of highways, airstrips, harbor and navigational installations, as well as barracks. These facilities undeniably serve national strategic purposes. But, it is contended, they also help transform the social and economic institutions. The introduction of modern highways where none existed before increases the mobility of the population and hastens the modern integration of the society and of the economy. A comparison of the social and economic conditions in Turkey in 1965 with those in 1950 will show that the country's face-lifting is more than skin-deep. The highway network, which grew out of an original need for modern roads simply to deliver American weapons to the Turkish armed forces, contributed measurably to integrating the subsistence rural economy into the national monetary economy. More peasants than ever before were moving back and forth between village and town in the mid-1960s, and their demands for manufactured goods and for improved public services in education, health, and welfare steadily multiplied.[4] What applied to Turkey, it is sometime insisted, could be generalized for most of the Middle East.

That many military investments also served non-military purposes cannot be denied. Yet it is sometimes impossible to tell whether the modernization of a transport or a communications system was motivated exclusively or even chiefly by military or by non-military considerations. The fact remains that such systems, when completed, serve both the armies and the civilian societies. Who pays the cost is basically immaterial. In the former French North African dependencies, as in British India, the metropolitan powers developed such networks primarily to "pacify" the countries. The basic systems were inherited at independence from the former alien rulers. Other countries such as Iran and Afghanistan, which never became European dependencies, lagged far behind in this type of construction. Moreover, postwar building of highways in Middle East countries was not motivated exclusively or even largely by military considerations and in any case the construction itself was often executed and financed by civilian agencies. This is true even in Turkey where, according to one economist, "only about one per cent of the expenditure on highway development in

1948 to 1960 was in some way made by the military establishment." [5] It is manifestly impossible in the absence of reliable studies to determine with mathematical precision what proportion of government investment in public works in any country represents purely military outlay or purely civilian outlay.

The double-duty hypotheses seem to emanate from the offices of the professional armers, those men in the American government and in the governments of other industrial states who are managing foreign military aid programs. An arms salesman understandably wants to make his product attractive, to package his swords to look like plowshares. It is also quite natural for professional armers to describe military aid to nonindustrial states in the best possible light. Thus, although this aid is intended to serve political ends, rarely do they even mention politics. The social scientist, however, has no commodity to sell but the truth, and there is no excuse for his uncritical acceptance of such arguments. "The more the army was modernized," argues one,

> the more its composition, organization, spirit, capabilities, and purpose constituted a radical criticism of the existing political system. Within the army modern technology was eagerly welcomed and its usefulness and power appreciated. By contrast, the political system showed greater inertia, inefficiency, skepticism, and greed in utilizing the products of modern science. Within the army, merit was often rewarded. In civilian politics, corruption, nepotism, and bribery loomed much larger. Within the army, a sense of national mission transcending parochial, regional, or economic interest, or kinship ties seemed to be much more clearly defined than anywhere else in society.[6]

This theory hardly applies to the armies that have seized power in the Middle East, and even less to the career armies, whether or not they had intervened in politics.

The notion that the military institution is usually the only one in nonindustrial states that is truly national in character is relatively widespread. The military, according to a well-known political sociologist, "is ubiquitous, it recruits from all parts of the country and, most important of all, it is national in symbolism." [7] The verity of the statement depends on how national solidarity is defined. Most Middle East career armies recruit officers and enlisted men from particular communities or particular districts. The Pakistan army still consists chiefly of West Pakistanis (Punjabis and Pathans, the latter from the northwest frontier districts), so that the standard grievances of the East Pakistanis that they are severely underrepresented was shared by Baluchis, Sindhis, and other West Pakistanis. Probably three of every four officers and soldiers in Morocco are Berbers, yet the national language is Arabic and the Arabs constitute the numerically and culturally dominant community. Before June 1967, the commanders in Jordan and most of the officers and enlisted men were Muslim East Bankers from the South; deliberately kept small in number and out of the sensitive units were the former Palestine Arab volunteers, who represented the numerically preponderant community. This is the common condition in the Middle East career armies. Similar discrimination often characterizes the conscript armies as well. In Iraq, the top officers are invariably Sunni Arabs, as they are also in Egypt. In Turkey, they are Sunni Turks. In Israel, Muslim and Christian Arabs hardly ever volunteer for the armed forces, and the only non-Jews liable to compulsory service are the Druzes and the Circassians. Still, within the dominant communities of Egypt, Turkey, and Israel, the conscript armies promote national solidarity.

The typical Middle East army, it is observed, "has become the principal political actor and instrument of a new middle class." The army, it is alleged, has been transformed "from an instrument of repression in its own interest or that of kings into the vanguard of nationalism and social reform." Incompetence and corruption prevailed everywhere in the Middle East, according to this thesis:

> Countries therefore do not always need the shock of a Palestinian War to set their army officers plotting *coups d'état* or to grow more sensitive to poverty, disease, exploitation, and ignorance that constitutes the daily defeats of Middle Eastern life. . . . As the army officer corps came to represent the interests and views of the new middle class, it became the most powerful instrument of that class. The army's great strength lay in the kind of men who joined it, the opportunities at their disposal, and the weakness of competing institutions.[8]

One might go on extolling the virtues of military investment by noting the direct employment that it provides, and the generous salaries that the officers in most Middle East armies receive. This would be as relevant to the conscript as to the career armies. Little wonder that some social scientists believe these officers represent the vanguard of the new salaried middle class.

Rising Costs of Military Modernization

At the other end of the spectrum from those who rationalize the value of military aid, stand the American professional disarmers and their counterparts in other countries, those men in and out of government who are convinced that all investment in military equipment wastes public resources. Particularly is this true, they claim, in the nonindustrial states where such resources are already insufficient to meet the unlimited demands of development. In their view, all military investment is harmful, since they are certain that modernizing armies will of necessity promote tension and breed war.

This position, while undeniably virtuous, is also unrealistic. Implicit in it is the suggestion of stopping the flow of all weaponry to the nonindustrial states. This in turn would lead logically to the further premise that armies in nonindustrial states are no longer necessary. Clearly, no substitute for armed forces has yet been devised, and pending the invention of such a substitute, no states, large or small, can dispense with armies. That being the case, whatever the side effects, good or bad, all sovereign states simply must have armed forces or depend on others to assure their security. It is precisely the insistence of the nonindustrial states on preserving their sovereignty that dissuades them from primary reliance on others for external defense.

There is yet another argument built into the position of the American professional disarmers: the United States ought unilaterally to suspend all arms shipments to the nonindustrial world. This, too, is unrealistic, since the United States was drawn into the business of selling arms to the nonindustrial countries for political, not commercial, reasons. The political conditions that induced the United States and its European allies to engage in the arms traffic have not been corrected. It would therefore follow that political considerations must still weigh heavily in decisions on the transfer of weapons by sale or grant to the nonindustrial states.

If the nonindustrial states must have arms, serious thought must nonetheless be given to the reservations about the high price of military modernization. Yet even here it must realistically be recognized that the cost of defense and security in the postwar Middle East, as elsewhere in the world, rose after 1945—moderately in the first postwar decade, dramatically in the second. All new states found much of the initial expenditure unavoidable, since they often had to build and equip armed forces almost from scratch; and more than two-thirds of the region's states reached sovereignty after World War II. Besides, the older states—especially Turkey, Iran, and Afghanistan—also became military modernizers. Trucks, tanks, and piston planes of World War II vintage went begging in the first postwar decade. Even the obsolescing jet planes and electronically equipped tanks, not to mention radar systems and missiles, to which all modernizing armies in the Middle East formed fond attachments in the second postwar decade, carried spiraling price tags. Manifestly, the high cost of military equipment is one of the facts of sovereign life late in the twentieth century.

However, the professional disarmers cannot be ignored when they point to the investments of many nonindustrial states in more sophisticated weaponry than they require. Most armies in the Middle East, while pretending to have external defense missions, are preoccupied with domestic security. In these states, the procurement of sophisticated weaponry, which happens to be the most expensive class, is therefore motivated more by prestige than by defense. The symbolic value of such weapons is enhanced, once they appear in the region, since officers' appetites tend to be whetted by the weapons diets of fellow officers in the immediate neighborhood. The further fact that the supplier rivalry in the second postwar decade was sharpened by the lingering Cold War in the region went far to explain why the Middle East amassed larger amounts of sophisticated weaponry than any other nonindustrial region in the world.

More significant, the United States served as principal peacekeeper in the second postwar decade among the region's quarreling states, providing them with an umbrella of security. Since Soviet use of massive military aid served as a means of influencing the policies of clients toward their neighbors and toward the United States, it was largely to enable American military clients to defend themselves against the Soviet military clients that the United States was drawn into the arms races in the Middle East.

24

ARMS RACES
IN THE REGION

The competitive military aid of the Soviet Union and the United States in the Middle East, an area—as defined in this book—that stretches from Morocco to Afghanistan and Pakistan, was intended to serve their political purposes, and in limited ways it did. Through military assistance programs the United States was able to help keep alive Middle East regimes that were, if not invariably formal allies of the West, at least proclaimed enemies of communism and opposed to the spread of Soviet influence. If the U.S.S.R. nevertheless met obstacles in building up its own direct military and political influence in the region through military clients, it diminished the military and political influence of the West and perhaps laid the basis for the growth of Soviet influence. Competitive military aid had one disturbing effect: it spurred arms races in the Middle East, in keeping with the structure and the scale of postwar arms traffic.

The mode of transfer of weapons and weapons technology from industrial to nonindustrial countries has changed markedly in the twentieth century. Before World War I, private weapons manufacturers, particularly in the United States, could often sell their products direct to foreign governments, with the knowledge of their own government but often without its interference. In the interwar years, government licensing of private manufacturers became the Western norm, and in the Middle East it represented a form of European governmental management of the arms traffic for imperial ends. After 1945 the transactions in weapons, most commonly a government-to-government activity, were designed to serve disimperial and postimperial purposes, with some hang-over of imperial practices in the disposal of war surplus in the first postwar decade. Since the U.S.S.R. can deal in such equipment only through state enterprise, even if the international arms traffic

438

from industrial to nonindustrial countries had not been so deeply affected by the larger issues of the Cold War, the competition between the U.S.S.R. and the West would nevertheless have demanded a substantial measure of governmental action and control by the major Western powers.

No less important was the scale of the traffic. Never before had the movement of weapons into the Middle East been so brisk. The value of military imports from all external sources jumped from perhaps $2.0 billion in the first postwar decade to $9.25 billion in the second, and the pace was still quickening at the start of the third,[1] for the retail value of arms exports to the Middle East from all external sources exceeded $1.5 billion each year in 1966 and 1967. These estimates do not include such windfalls as installations and stores abandoned by departing imperial powers or seized by the successor states or sold to them for token sums. Nor do they encompass the share of economic aid, particularly from the United States, which, though classed as economic, was primarily military in inspiration: the modernization of harbors, roads, and communications, or the grant of budget support that was really military in intent, or even the sale of agricultural surplus that released hard currency which the receiving country could divert to military imports.

It must not be assumed that the sudden appearance of so much modern weaponry did nothing but nourish arms races. The Middle East, after all, was a region where armies were being created afresh, as was inescapable in most new states. So long as they were building from the ground up, they naturally sought spanking new merchandise to match that of their neighbors. Of greater importance was the spiraling price of modern weapons. Fighters, bombers, and tanks of World War II vintage could in the first postwar decade often be picked up as war surplus or as "demilitarized" scrap. In the second decade tanks with improved fire-control systems, jet planes, guided missiles, and radar became standard gear for Middle East armies and carried far higher price tags.

The United States became the region's paramount supplier in the second postwar decade, sending to its thirteen clients probably as much as $5.5 billion worth of modern arms, and to this its major allies (Britain, France, and West Germany) may have added another billion dollars worth. The U.S.S.R. ran second, funneling to six Middle East countries weapons with a market value of more than $2.25 billion, and when shipments from Czechoslovakia (and, on a marginal scale, Poland) are included, the total value of arms reaching the region from the Communist bloc was raised by another $0.5 billion.

A closer look at the gross statistics reveals that more than 75 per cent of Western (mostly American) regional military aid was destined for three countries: Turkey, Iran, and Pakistan, all of them members of CENTO, the "northern tier" alliance. The CENTO members took part in the Western collective security system, benefiting from American aid, and receiving with every three dollars' worth of arms more than four dollars' worth of economic assistance

TABLE 16. The Frontier Zone:

Western and Soviet Bloc Economic and Military Aid,

1 July 1955—30 June 1965

(in millions of $U.S.)

	Economic		Military	
	Western Powers [a]	Soviet Bloc [b]	Western Powers [c]	Soviet Bloc [c]
Turkey	2,050	210	1,950	0
Iran	730	330	1,100	0
Pakistan	2,750	94	900 [d]	0
CENTO total	5,530	634	3,950	0
Afghanistan	350	552	3	275
Zonal total	5,880	1,186	3,953	275

SOURCES: AID, U.S. *Overseas Loans and Grants and Assistance from International Organizations, Obligations and Loan Authorizations, July 1, 1945–June 30, 1965* (Washington, 1966); OECD, *Geographical Distribution of Financial Flows to Less Developed Countries (Disbursements), 1960–1964* (Paris, 1966); Leo Tansky, "Soviet Foreign Aid to the Less Developed Countries," in U.S., 89th Congress, 2d session, Joint Economic Committee, *New Directions in the Soviet Economy*, part iv, *The World Outside* (Washington, 1966), pp. 947–74, especially table, p. 974; *The New York Times*, 19–21 July 1967; see also U.S., 90th Congress, 1st session, Senate Committee on Foreign Relations, *Arms Sales and Foreign Policy* (Washington, January 1967), a staff study, and its subcommittee on Near Eastern and South Asian Affairs, "Hearings on Arms Sales" (14 March, 13, 20, 25 April, and 22 June 1967); and Leo Heiman, "Moscow's Export Arsenal: The Soviet Bloc and the Middle Eastern Arms Race," *East Europe*, vol. 13 (May 1964), pp. 3–10.

[a] Includes credits, grants, and surplus food sales, and assumes U.S. share as 90%, and that of its allies as 10%.

[b] Total credit offered; variable portions obligated as of June 1965.

[c] Includes sales as well as credits and grants.

[d] Assumes U.S. share as 85%, and that of its allies as 15%.

(see Table 16). Significantly, in the Soviet aid program for Afghanistan, which like Turkey and Iran bordered on the U.S.S.R., the economic projects were twice as costly as the military.

In contrast, 80 per cent of Soviet (and Czech) military aid to the Middle East in the second postwar decade went to three Arab countries: Egypt, Syria, and Iraq. The economic aid to the Soviet-bloc clients was in reverse ratio to the military aid (see Table 17): the value of Soviet arms, in fact, exceeded the value of the economic projects sponsored by the U.S.S.R. and its associates. Altogether, the U.S.S.R. and Czechoslovakia pumped into the three Arab countries in a single decade military hardware that would probably have been priced in the market at more than $2.2 billion.[2] What is more, the hardware was almost always delivered promptly, whereas the economic commitments sometimes took years to fulfill. To the remaining countries in the Arab-Israel zone —Israel, Jordan, Lebanon, and Iraq, the last only until 1959 as a member of the Baghdad Pact—the United States and its allies in the second postwar decade sold or granted matériel, possibly worth about $1.625 billion, which was less than the sum devoted to economic ends.

Arms races in the postwar Middle East first appeared in the Arab-Israel zone at the region's center. These were interlocking bilateral races that traced back to the early 1950s, and the number of participants contributed to their complexity. At the close of the second postwar decade, arms races began at the eastern and western ends of the region. In the east the race between Pakistan and India spilled over the Middle East frontier; nonetheless, its consequences were a matter of concern to the region. The race in the region's west, precipitated by Algeria with its immediate neighbors in the former French-managed Maghrib, was on a much smaller scale.

Arms rivalry in the subcontinent grew only in part out of the dispute over Kashmir. Because of India's superiority in numbers, size, and economic capability, Pakistan's military aid agreements with the United States and its participation in CENTO and SEATO had aroused India's anger but did not drive India to any competitive military activity. The competition as such in the subcontinent was touched off by India's border war with China in 1962. India's military expansion, with the cooperation of the two superpowers, enlivened Pakistan's fear and, because the United States did not respond to requests for supplementary aid, weakened Pakistan's ties to the West. The tempo was visibly stepped up after the short, inconclusive war over Kashmir in 1965. The United

TABLE 17. The Arab-Israel Zone:
Western and Soviet Bloc Economic and Military Aid,
1 July 1955—30 June 1965
(in millions of $U.S.)

| | Economic | | Military[c] | |
	Western Powers [a]	Soviet Bloc[b]	Western Powers	Soviet Bloc
Egypt (U.A.R.)	1,650	1,250	0	1,500[d]
Iraq[e]	75[e]	220	150[f]	400
Jordan	100	0	450[g]	0
Lebanon	75[h]	0	25[i]	0
Syria	135[j]	200[k]	0	350[l]
Arab total	2,035	1,670	625	2,250
Israel	1,500[m]	0	1,000[n]	0
Zonal total	3,535	1,670	1,625	2,250

SOURCES: Same as for Table 16.

[a] Includes credits, grants, and surplus food sales.

[b] Total credit offered; variable portions obligated as of June 1965.

[c] Includes sales as well as credits and grants.

[d] Assumes 80% from the U.S.S.R., 20% from Czechoslovakia.

[e] Almost all from U.S., before July 1958.

[f] Assumes more than 70% from Britain, the rest from the U.S. (before July 1958).

[g] Assumes 85% from the U.S., 15% from Britain. U.S. share formally given as budget support, which enabled the government of Jordan to finance its armed forces.

[h] From the U.S. only.

[i] Assumes 40% from France, 35% from the U.S., 25% from Britain.

[j] Almost all from the U.S.

[k] Three-fourths from the U.S.S.R., the rest from Czechoslovakia and Poland.

[l] Assumes 90% from the U.S.S.R., and the rest from Czechoslovakia.

[m] Excludes private remittances and assumes nearly 40% from West Germany and most of the rest from the U.S.

[n] Assumes one-half from France, one-fifth from West Germany, and the rest from Western Europe and the U.S. To this must be added perhaps as much as $250 million or more in purchases of weapons surplus, and scrap that are not classified as aid.

States, it is true, suspended delivery of new equipment to the contestants and did not resume the shipment of spare parts until 1966. India simply turned to the U.S.S.R. and to Britain for new weapons, while Pakistan turned to Communist China and to France, as well as to the surplus market in Europe, chiefly West Germany and Italy. Thus Pakistan's defense budgets, which averaged about 1.0 billion rupees a year from 1959 to 1962, jumped to an annual average of 1.3 billion between 1963 and 1965 and to more than 2.2 billion in 1966 and 1967.[3] India's defense budget after 1962 was about four times the size of Pakistan's, and India's spirited rearmament was incited by fear more of China than of Pakistan. Still, India reacted sharply in 1968 to the Soviet Union's first large-scale arms agreement with Pakistan.

Much different was the race in the Maghrib among France's former dependencies. In Algeria, the U.S.S.R. together with Czechoslovakia followed the same arms export policies as in the Arab East, selling huge quantities of sophisticated equipment at large discounts. Between 1964 and 1967, Algeria may have received from the two Communist countries military hardware worth $300 million and probably more. The sudden accumulation of so much modern weaponry disturbed Morocco, which tried to wheedle compensatory weaponry primarily out of France, and when that source dried up after 1965 because of the Ben Barka affair, out of the United States. When shipments from the United States lagged in 1967, Morocco accepted arms on a small scale from the U.S.S.R.. Also aroused was the anxiety of Tunisia, which in 1965 became primarily an American client. The arms contest in the Maghrib was still in an incipient stage in 1968, and looked modest alongside the races that beset the Arab states and Israel.

Since exploration of all the races in the Middle East lies beyond the scope of the present work, the analysis that follows is limited to the races in the Arab-Israel zone. If we can unravel their tangled skeins, the lessons of the testimony should ease the difficulty of assessing the less confusing rivalries that later appeared elsewhere in the Middle East. Before we turn to the races in the Arab-Israel zone in Chapter 25, we shall first have to ascertain how arms rivalry among the nonindustrial states differs from that among the industrial states.

Arms Races Among Industrial States

Arms races in general are only imperfectly understood, for theorizing, as far as it has gone, has concentrated on the experience of the industrial countries, or their equivalent in earlier periods. These states are militarily self-sustaining, actually or potentially. Their political and economic organization permits effective mobilization of manpower and effective use of raw materials to satisfy the demands of an arms buildup in competition with states of comparable size and capability. Most new states in the twentieth century are states of a different order. Their political systems are shaky, their economies pre-industrial, their societies sometimes unintegrated, and their armed forces often even incapable of handling problems of domestic security which, for most, is their primary mission.

An arms race has been defined as "a progressive, competitive, peacetime increase in armaments by two states or coalitions of states resulting from conflicting purposes or mutual fears" and reflecting "disagreement [over] . . . the proper balance of power between them." Such races, it is argued,

> are an integral part of the international balance of power. From the viewpoint of a participant, an arms race is an effort to achieve a favorable international distribution of power. Viewed as a whole, a sustained arms race is a means of achieving a dynamic equlibrium of power between two states or coalitions of states. Arms races only take place between states in the same balance of power system. . . . Within any such system, power may in general be balanced in two ways: externally through a realignment of the units participating in the system (diplomacy), or internally by changes in the inherent power of the units.[4]

The bipolarized balance-of-power system breeds arms rivalry. Balancing power under it by rearranging the units is difficult, so that the accumulation of military force tends to replace diplomacy. So far, the definition of an arms race and the role that it plays in an international or a regional balance of power would hold for all states, industrial and nonindustrial. But on closer examination we begin to encounter inherent differences.

Take, for example, the basic distinctions between the quantitative and the qualitative races among the industrial states. Expansion of the military power of a state, it is observed, may be accomplished quantitatively by multiplying the number of men under arms and enlarging their supporting arsenals, or qualitatively by introducing new and more effective weapons. Qualitative races became common in the nineteenth and twentieth centuries as the tempo of military technology began to accelerate; after 1950 the pace stepped up fantastically. Military expansion and innovation are really two varieties of arms races. "In a quantitative race," it is held, the decisive ratio is between the resources which a nation devotes to military purposes and those which it devotes to civilian ones. . . . [In a qualitative arms race] the essential relationship is not between the military and the civilian, but rather between the old and the new forms of military force. . . . [The] principal issue is the extent to which the new weapons system should replace the old "conventional" ones. In a quantitative race the key question is "How much?" In a qualitative race, it is "How soon?" A quantitative race requires continuous expansion of military resources, a qualitative race continuous redeployment of them. . . . In the long run, a quantitative race makes extensive demands on a broad segment of the population. A qualitative race, however, tends to be a competition of elites rather than masses. . . .[5]

Much of this analysis clearly applies to arms races among established industrial states, not among states that are either pre-industrial or in an incipient stage of industrialization.

Innovational competition among the industrial states requires each competitor to pass through four stages between the decision to adopt a new weapons system and its actual assimilation: research and engineering, production, training men to use the new weapons, and modification of the military organization and doctrine to absorb the weapons system. The balance is restored when both reach the last stage. This was well illustrated by the American-Soviet nuclear competition. The American expansion of nuclear weapons dictated the invention of an appropriate delivery system that could encompass the strategic targets in the U.S.S.R., and the development of the Strategic Air Command later made the doctrine of massive retaliation credible. The U.S.S.R., which lagged behind the United States in its development and production of nuclear instruments, did not have access to convenient bases for a SAC counterpart and therefore concentrated on the development of long-range missiles as its delivery response, thereby compelling the United States to undertake a crash missile program. When both sides emplaced their ICBMs in hardened launch pads by the mid-1960s, they had erected a new balance, which was again upset a few years later by Soviet research into an antiballistic missile (ABM) system, which compelled the United States to follow suit.

Arms Races Among Nonindustrial States

No Middle East state could produce all the weapons that its armed forces demanded, and very few of the states could vaunt more than the most primitive factories that made only small arms and ammunition. Even Israel, which had developed with the help of foreign technicians the most elaborate military industry in the region, imported sophisticated hardware and many components for locally manufactured items from the industrial countries of the West. All Middle East states, in brief, leaned on external suppliers. Without such sources of military wares the regional races would have been reduced substantially in scale.

The very dependence on the outside inevitably affected the shape, the dimension, and the rhythm of the races among the new states. Initial import of the sophisticated conventional arms from abroad dispenses with the need for the first two stages of the qualitative race (research and engineering and production). This tends to foreshorten the time of assimilating a new system. Still, although in theory the problems of training and assimilation remain identical for the nonindustrial states as for the industrial, in practice these problems work themselves out differently. Among the nonindustrial states the use and the maintenance of the new weapons are less effective than in the originating state, and their absorption is less complete, for the armed forces in such states are recruited largely among illiterates, actual as well as scientific and technological. On the other hand, the army of a semi-industrialized country that manages to train men to handle and maintain, even with limited effectiveness, supersonic jets, various families of missiles, and the latest generation of the progressively versatile tanks and to absorb these instruments if only partly into its military organization and doctrine should nevertheless be able to challenge the army of a more industrialized country that does not have such instruments at all. Whether or not this may in truth be actually so makes little difference, so long as the rulers think it is so.[6]

There is yet another major difference. In a quantitative race between industrial states, numbers of men and weapons count. But in the Arab-Israel area, where the countries are in varying stages of military industrialization, there is wide diversity of military capability and potential. A recognizably quantitative race could occur in such an area only between states or coalitions with populations of roughly comparable size and at roughly comparable levels of industrialization. For example, the population of Egypt exceeds that of all the other states in the Arab-Israel zone combined. Nevertheless, Israel's citizen army could at any time between 1949 and 1967 put into the field within two to three days a force larger than the Egyptian, Jordanian, and Syrian armies combined. The Israel army, moreover, was supported by a population that was substantially literate and that could boast the highest per capita GNP in the zone (indeed, second in the Middle East as a whole only to oil-logged Kuwayt), the highest relative number of students in technical schools and workers in manufacturing industries (a sizable proportion devoted to military needs), the highest per capita production of electric energy—and the highest per capita expenditures on defense. All neighboring Arab states fell far behind Israel on each of these scales. In the Arab East, Egypt had relatively the highest number of students in technical schools and workers in manufacturing industries but was still a poor second to Lebanon in 1965 in per capita electric energy production, had the second lowest literacy rate, and the lowest per capita GNP. With the largest actual expenditure on defense in the zone, exceeding even Israel's, Egypt's per capita defense expenditure was the second smallest, indeed only one-eighth that of Israel. Similarly, although Egypt had the biggest Arab army in the zone, its per capita force level in 1965 was the second smallest. Table 18 attempts to reflect the realities without trying to project any value judgment on the political quarrels that abound in the zone or on their outcome. In such a heterogeneous neighborhood, military competition tended to become qualitative, since it was not manpower as such but effective manpower that mattered.

War as the outcome of arms rivalry, international or regional, is less likely if the challenged state remains militarily stronger than the challenger. Only then, in any system, does power stay balanced. In the Arab-Israel contest, which traced its antecedents to the mandatory period, the Palestine Jews were initially the challengers and the Arabs the challenged, since the Jews refused to accept the status quo of an integrated Palestine if that prevented them from achieving independence. The roles were reversed after 1949. The Arab states became the challengers and Israel the challenged, for Israel accepted the new status quo of the armistice, whereas the Arab states did not. They vowed the "liberation of Arab Palestine" and left no doubt that that meant the extermination of Israel; they seemed determined not to budge from this stance, which shaped Arab military policies toward Israel. The essentially defensive character of Israel's arming under the armistice system helped explain why Israel insisted on preserving its military primacy, for its security planners were persuaded that only a military lead could assure the survival of the state. "Israel cannot allow itself to be overtaken," its delegate to the United Nations informed the Security Council as early as August 1949. "It cannot in

TABLE 18. The Arab-Israel Zone: Economic, Social, and Military Indicators

	Population (millions)		Literacy		Students Enrolled in Technical Schools (per 10,000 population)		Electric Energy Production (per capita kwh)		Workers in Manufacturing Industries (per 10,000 population)	
	1955	1965	1948[a]	Early 60s	1959	1964	1955	1965	1955	Early 60s
Egypt	22.9	29.6	20	27	39	47	60	180	115	305
Iraq	6.0	7.4	10	18	11	10	95	170[e]	270	110
Jordan	1.4	2.0	5	33	8	13	n.a.	80	100	140
Lebanon	1.4	2.4	70	n.a.	4[e]	5	160	380	460	210
Syria	3.9	5.6	20	36[b]	12	14	40	100	n.a.	n.a.
Israel	1.8	2.6	94[b]	87[b]	75	135	740	1600	920	1500

	Force Levels (thousands)		Force Levels (per 1,000 population)		Defense Expenditures (in millions of $ U.S.)		Defense Expenditures[g] (per capita in $ U.S.)		Per Capita GNP (in millions of $ U.S.)	
	1955	1965	1955	1965	1955	1965	1955	1965	1955	1965
Egypt	80	180	4	6	286.91	461.84	12.53	15.60	134	171
Iraq	40	82	7	11	56.00	243.60	9.33	32.92	160	259
Jordan	23	45	6	23	29.40	58.80	21.00	29.40	91	252
Lebanon	6.2	13	4	5	12.19	29.35	8.58	12.23	530	370
Syria	25	60	6	11	29.47	95.50	7.55	17.05	145	194
Israel[f]	250	375	134	144	45.46	315.93	25.39	121.50	659	1308

SOURCES: U.N. Statistical Division, *Demographic Yearbook; Statistical Yearbook; Yearbook of National Account Statistics.*   [a] Estimates.   [b] Jewish community only.   [c] 1961.   [d] Provisional.   [e] 1964.   [f] Including citizen reserves; the regular services consisted of about 75,000 in 1965.   [g] Including internal security and justice.

any circumstances suffer itself to reach a state of military inferiority which might be a temptation to renewed assult." [7] This estimate remained constant thereafter. In the Sinai campaign of 1956 and the Six Day War of 1967, Israel demonstrated the lengths to which it was prepared to go in safeguarding its military advantage. The two pre-emptive strikes, moreover, show how thin is the line that divides defense from offense.

The concept of balanced power in support of the armistice status quo, which was the Western policy, rankled in the Arabs. "When they [the Western powers] give the 70,000,000 Arabs one rifle, they give the 1,000,000 Zionists two rifles," as 'Abd al-Nasir put it in his speech announcing the nationalization of the Suez Canal Company in July 1956,

> so that the Zionists can always maintain supremacy over the Arabs and so that they can threaten the Arabs. This is "the balance of power." If they give all the Arab countries one aircraft—if they give any Arab country one aircraft—they give Israel one aircraft and they call it "the balance of power." What sort of balance of power, and who appointed you [the Western powers] our guardians so that you can maintain the balance of power in this region? [8]

Israel was not born an industrial state; it did have, however, a high industrial potential—in human rather than material resources —which it realized more swiftly than expected precisely because of the stubborn military threat to its existence. In the early years of the arms competition, when Israel was still struggling with the massive problems of industrializing its economy, the Western powers did not allow more than a trickle of sophisticated weaponry to reach the Arab states and Israel. By the time the Soviet bloc put an end to the Western monopoly and made the newfangled hardware available to Arab states at cut-rate prices, the foundation for Israel's inventive military industry had been well laid. Throughout the first two postwar decades Israel's citizen army remained the largest in the zone (Table 19).

Among the new states the "qualitative" race becomes a race, not in technology as in the old states, but in imports of weapons. This held true in the 1950s even for Israel. Israel in the 1960s became an industrial state and began behaving like one in military politics, thereby complicating what might otherwise still have conformed to a relatively simple pattern. Israel differed from the normal European industrial state, however, because it had so small a popula-

Table 19. The Arab-Israel Zone:
Rising Force Levels, 1948–67
(in thousands of soldiers)

	1948	1950	1955	1960	1965	June 1967
Egypt (U.A.R.)	25–30	80	80	100	180	200
Iraq	25	30	40	70	82	82
Jordan	6–10	10	23	36.5	45	55
Lebanon	3.5	5	6.2	10.8	13	15
Syria	7–8	10	25	45	60	60
Arab total	66.5[a]–76.5[b]	135	174.2	262.3	380	412
Israel	49[c]–90[d]	125[d]	250[d]	300[d]	375[d]	400[d]

[a] On 15 May 1948.
[b] On 1 October 1948.
[c] On 8 June and mid-October, 1948; Netanel Lorch, *The Edge of the Sword: Israel's War of Independence, 1947–1949*, p. 324.
[d] Including reserves in the citizen army.

tion, which severely limited its technological potential. Its continued import of tanks, planes, missiles, and all products of heavy industry basically conditioned the country's role in the international community. Though technically a candidate for membership in the nuclear club after 1960, Israel, unlike other candidates, could never aspire also to the status of a major power through that route or any other. By contrast, Japan and West Germany seemed almost certain to go nuclear, since they already had the other attributes of a major power.

Nonetheless, Israel could use, and indeed did use, its industrial capacity to full advantage in the arms race with the Arab states. Lack of faith in the reliability of external sources of military supply was reflected in the ever-widening range of light weapons and repair parts that Israel manufactured, of vehicles that it assembled, and of heavy equipment that it upgraded and adapted to its special military needs. With each import of this class, Israel procured both the product and the technology, for once its technicians learned how to overhaul a piece of equipment, its military industry also learned how to manufacture a domestic version. So long as the item in question was in high military demand and could be produced locally, a domestic copy was likely to appear in Israel's arsenal and in its military industrial catalogue for sale abroad, wherever politically and militarily feasible, to help the expanding military industry maximize its economies. More than that, Israel's industry, wherever militarily significant, upgraded automotive equipment and improved the firing power of tanks by adding or substituting larger guns, to say nothing of standardizing the "furniture"—as the engines and parts were called—of military vehicles and other complex martial machinery of diverse origins.

Israel's requirements for a favorable power balance in the Arab-Israel system, and therefore for political survival in a hostile environment, provided the very psychological stimulus to the race. "The army opposing us is obtaining arms from various parts of the world," charged 'Abd al-Nasir in September 1955 when he disclosed the arms deal with "Czechoslovakia" (actually, the U.S.S.R.);

> Israel's army has been able to obtain arms from England, France, Belgium, Canada, Italy and from various other states. It can always find someone to supply it arms, while we read in the foreign press— in the British, American or French newspapers—that Israel's army can defeat all the Arab armies combined. . . .
>
> When we saw this . . . domination . . . this influence which was being used against us, we decided to ask all the states of the world to supply us arms without conditions. . . .[9]

Egypt denied that it was planning to make war, despite its inflexible rejection of all proposals for a negotiated settlement with Israel and its endorsement of the Arab nationalist doctrine of "dumping Israel into the sea." Still, as 'Abd al-Nasir shopped around for arms, he assured his potential suppliers that they would be used only for defense, and never for aggression.

Double-tiered Arms Races

The Arabs so far outnumbered the Israelis, that there was never any prospect of achieving numerical equality. The equilibrium, rather, was fixed by Israel's scientific, technological, and industrial superiority, which the Arab states could not reasonably expect to match in the foreseeable future. In the circumstances, the existing balance could be upset only through supplier intervention, as indeed it was when the Soviet bloc began exporting advanced military equipment to Egypt and Syria in 1955–56. It recurred in later years, as the U.S.S.R. permitted its Arab clients, Egypt in particular, to climb up the conventional ladder to select sophisticated weapons from steadily higher shelves. Since the imbalancing weapons were ones that Israel did not, and for the most part could not, produce, the equilibrium was restored in each instance largely by purchase, first from France and later from elsewhere in the West, including the United States, and in time reinforced by Israel enterprise and skill.

Egyptian threats to fellow Arab regimes, as to Iraq and Jordan in the mid-1950s or to Saudi Arabia in the 1960s, reflected an arms race of a different genre. Egypt was still the challenger, for at times it hardly concealed its desire to overthrow the Arab monarchies, to which the U.S.S.R. gave its blessings, sometimes muted but never absent. The race was an unequal one in every respect. The population differential, more than three to one between Egypt and Iraq, was nearly ten to one between Egypt and Saudi Arabia, and surpassed fifteen to one between Egypt and Jordan; and the military-industrial levels of the three kingdoms ranked well below that of Egypt. As upholder of the Middle East status quo (except when peaceably modified), the United States signaled to the Soviet clients its support of the existing regimes in Jordan and Saudi Arabia, in effect playing the role of discreet balancer in the Arab East system. It went time and again to the rescue of the two American military wards either by a show of American force (as in the appearance in April 1957 of the Sixth Fleet in the eastern Mediterranean in support of King Husayn and the deployment in 1963 of a United States Air Force unit of interceptors in Saudi Arabia); or by an upgrading in the quality of arms offered the two United States clients; or by both.

Important to observe is the pairing of supplier and client, for it was their special relationship that upset and righted military balances. It was client against client in the original quarrel that gave rise to the regional races; but it was supplier and client against supplier and client at the later stage, since the suppliers were responsible for the changes in the balance. The willingness of the suppliers in the second postwar decade to play this role was a function of their own arms race. It is a matter of record that the progressively imbalancing involvement of the U.S.S.R. induced the comparable balancing involvement of the United States. To put it differently, the arms races in the postwar Middle East were composite races, since the suppliers were as deeply entangled as their clients. Nor could it always be discerned who depended on whom, since in many subtle ways the suppliers became captives of their clients.

The regional arms races among nonindustrial states thus differed from the major global contest by virtue of the participation of both the suppliers and their clients. Until 1955, in the Arab-Israel zone, there was in effect a single supplier, the United Kingdom. In the second postwar decade, when the U.S.S.R. became a major supplier to selected Arab states, the pattern became much more complicated because of the simultaneous competition at the supplier and client levels. The competition between the United States and the Soviet Union as suppliers after 1955 was wholly political, while among the Western allies it became in time increasingly economic. The suppliers, of course, firmly denied that they were taking part in the regional contests. The quarrels, they implied, were not the suppliers' quarrels, and the regional disputants would continue their disputes whether or not the supplies flowed in. Thus from the moment that the U.S.S.R. became a major arms vendor in the Middle East, it insisted that arms sales of the Soviet bloc were simple commercial transactions. The U.S.S.R., in fact, realized a financial as well as a political return on the original investment in equipment that had quickly become obsolescent. But when Egypt, the U.S.S.R.'s largest nonallied client, began requesting nonconventional weapons, as it did in 1965 when it appeared that Israel had acquired a nuclear option, the Egyptian request was patently turned down, not on commercial, but on political grounds.

The Soviet rationalization had one incontrovertible merit: simplicity. Until 1955 the U.S.S.R. was not burdened by commitments to Arabs or to Israelis; it was therefore free to take sides in that dispute and in any of the disputes that wracked the Arab world. Yet by injecting itself into the situation as a partisan arms merchant with no stake in preserving the existing regional military balance, it deliberately disturbed that balance to annoy the Western powers, the United States above all. The U.S.S.R. could also hope to develop a basis for striking a bargain with its Cold War rival by offering an arms embargo in the Arab zone in exchange for the United States termination of its defense arrangements with the Middle East states that bordered on the Soviet Union—as indeed Khrushchev began doing publicly in 1957, in response to the Eisenhower Doctrine.

The Western powers, on their side, kept alive the fiction that they were not participants in the Middle East arms races. During their monopoly of the market, they could plausibly argue that they were merely doling out arms to states in the Arab-Israel zone in accordance with the needs of internal security and local self-defense, as spelled out in the Tripartite Declaration. As dolers, however, they were also balancers. They warned the zonal states that, in the event of an attempted forcible change of the military balance by violation of frontiers and armistice lines, the suppliers would intervene to uphold the existing balance. In retrospect, until 1955 the Western powers kept the Arab-Israel arms rivalry at a low pitch. Yet as sole suppliers they were nonetheless taking part in the double-tiered race. Clearly, the Western powers in this period were not competing with one another. They were, however, supplying or offering to supply selected states—primarily Britain's preferential allies—quality weapons that exceeded purely local security or defense demands, as payment for their association with Western plans for the general defense of the Middle East. This in turn stimulated those states that did not receive or accept such offers (notably Egypt and Israel) to find comparable weapons elsewhere.

The Western powers were determined insofar as possible to uphold the military status quo in the Arab-Israel area, unless it was modified peaceably and by mutual agreement. The military balance in that area was not merely one between the Arab states and Israel but also among the Arab states themselves. Once the Soviet bloc adopted Egypt and Syria, and later Iraq, as its chosen clients and gave them opportunities to accumulate massive amounts of quality weapons, the hand of the Western powers was forced, if they were to keep the remaining Arab states within the Western fold and prevent a renewal of Arab-Israel hostilities. American military aid, under the Eisenhower Doctrine, was manifestly designed to help Arab states fend off Soviet and Egyptian encroachment. Yet, clearly, by offering these states military weapons and other forms of military assistance, the United States was contributing to the races in that area, even though striving to uphold a military balance. Nor did the Western powers abandon their endeavors to curb races, even after the U.S.S.R. demanded too high a political price for re-establishing, in effect, an arms cartel under an enlarged directorate that included the Soviet Union. In brief, the Western powers could not escape participation so long as they furnished, on political grounds, weapons not otherwise available.

After the U.S.S.R. began dumping highly prized weapons into Egypt and Syria, and later into Iraq and Algeria, beyond the actual defense needs of the clients and their early capacity to assimilate them, it was establishing new ground rules. The United States had to play the game accordingly, even as it continued trying to hold the line on rising levels of armaments, in order to prevent a further loss of Western clients. In explaining why Britain and the United States agreed in the fall of 1957 to supply arms to Tunisia, after France, its military sponsor, had withheld equipment because of problems arising from the Algerian revolution, Foreign Secretary Selwyn Lloyd reported to the House of Commons that

> it would be most unfortunate if the Tunisian Government should be forced to rely upon arms coming indirectly or directly from the Soviet *bloc*. . . .
> The United States and United Kingdom Governments in agreeing to supply these arms, have been particularly concerned to prevent a situation arising in Tunisia like that which has arisen in certain other countries where, by their readiness to supply arms, the Communist *bloc* have acquired a dominant position. Far from being "contrary to the principles of Atlantic solidarity," this action by the United States and United Kingdom Governments is designed to protect the interests of the West as a whole. There is nothing in it which would prevent France from supplying the main arms requirements of the Tunisian Government.[10]

Among allied suppliers in double-tiered races, another principle that often prevailed was the mutual recognition of established clients. France, observed Lloyd, "is the traditional supplier of arms to Tunisia, and, as we made clear to both the French and Tunisian Governments, we believe that France should continue by agreement with Tunisia to be the main supplier." [11]

A single supplier or allied group of suppliers trying to freeze the military balance in a clients' market proved about as useful as an oil company's efforts to raise prices on crude when production far outstrips effective demand. In the circumstances, both sets of major suppliers lost maneuverability. The U.S.S.R. allowed its clients to move up the conventional ladder perhaps more quickly than it had intended, particularly in Egypt, which in the mid-1960s received progressively more frequent relief in paying interest on credits and even in repaying principal. Besides, the U.S.S.R., as all other suppliers in double-tiered races, acquired a stake in the success of its clients' test of military power. When the Egyptian military campaign in Yemen stalled, the U.S.S.R. found itself saddled with mounting costs in an inconclusive war. The United States for its part had to meet the challenge to stay in the contest, by furnishing equipment to its clients corresponding in quality to that sold by the Russians. One false step by a Western client might mean the end of the regime, and the slippage of the state into the slowly expanding orbit of the Soviet arms market in the Middle East.

Double-tiered races were complicated enough. In the Arab-Israel zone there were three interlocked and inseparable races going at once: a multilateral race between the Arab participants in the Palestine war and Israel; a bilateral race between Egypt and Israel that began basically in 1955 when Egypt became a Soviet client; and a wholly Arab contest that on occasion in the mid-1960s threatened to pit the military republics against the other Arab states.

25

RACES IN THE
ARAB-ISRAEL ZONE

Most observers have tended to treat the Arab-Israel arms race, the oldest and most widely advertised one in the zone, as a simple contest between the two sides that had taken part in the Palestine war. Without a formal settlement, the basic issues left by the war—particularly refugees and boundaries, blockade practices and economic boycott—were left dangling. The armistice system, originally framed in 1949 as a provisional mechanism, stiffened into permanence, giving little satisfaction to either party. Mutual suspicions multiplied as the armistice arrangements wore thin, encouraging militancy and vigilance up and down the zone.

Israel came into being in a country that split according to the fortunes of war. Israel applauded the results, for the war had enlarged the territory originally proposed for the Jewish state by the United Nations General Assembly resolution. Much of the enlargement grew out of the rescue of Jewish Jerusalem where one-sixth of Palestine's Jews had lived. Besides, the emotional attachment of Jewish nationalists to Jerusalem, the symbol of ancient sovereignty, ran deeper than to any other relic in that relic-ridden district. The Arabs had tried to starve Jerusalem's Jews into submission in the interrupted war. In meeting that threat the Israelis forged a corridor to the mountaintop city, seizing strategic points along the way such as Lydda, which had housed the largest airport in undivided Palestine, and nearby Ramlah. If partition could not be achieved peaceably, and if no formal settlement could be reached within a reasonable period, the armistice lines, which (with the exception of the demilitarized zones) Israel viewed as the boundaries of the state, provided more rational contours for defense than those in the General Assembly's original proposal, which had assumed cooperation between the successor states. Israel thus welcomed the new status quo of the armistice, which carried the endorsement of the United Nations insofar as that organization arranged the cease-fire between the combatants.

The Arab states condemned it. The Arab League Council had proclaimed in May 1948 the determination of its members "to save Palestine for its rightful owners"; or to use the legal formula of the League's Secretary General, the end of the mandate left "no legally constituted authority behind to administer law and order in the country and afford the necessary and adequate protection of life and property" in a war that had been launched by "aggressive . . . Zionists" with "imperialist motives." The Arab states proposed to restore peace and security, establish law and order, and then hand the government over to the Palestine Arabs.[1] The League members had laid their prestige on the line. Yet they could not by military action prevent the state of Israel from coming into being. Instead, they had suffered a humiliating defeat and grudgingly acquiesced in the existence of Israel, giving it the recognition only of a belligerent, not of a political entity. Later they argued that since an armistice is not a peace, the unfinished war permitted them to introduce such warlike measures as a blockade of shipping to and from Israel through the Suez Canal and the Tiran Straits at the entrance to the Gulf of 'Aqabah, and an economic boycott which included blacklisting those firms across the globe that sold goods and services to Israel.

In order to examine comprehensively the origins and growth of the arms races in the Arab-Israel zone, we shall have to retread political ground with which the reader may already have become familiar. However, some of the testimony given in earlier chapters was used to make other points; in the present chapter, it is used to clarify the problems of arms rivalry.

Fixing the Pattern

Israel first called attention to the arms race as a menace to its security in 1949, when its delegate to the United Nations, after the armistice system had formally come into being, warned the Security Council of an impending arms race between the Arab states and his country. "Iraq and the Hashemite Kingdom of Jordan have treaty connexions with the United Kingdom," he observed,

> which, unless the Security Council will decide otherwise would involve the immediate renewal of heavy arms supplies to these countries.
> It is not difficult to imagine what Israel's attitude must be in the

event that its neighbours would embark on large-scale rearmament. . . .[2]

The Israel spokesman accordingly urged that the Security Council reaffirm the arms embargo which, imposed during the Palestine war, was about to be lifted. "Such an authoritative ruling by the Security Council," he continued, "would of itself by the influence which it would exert on the arms-supplying States, insulate the Near East against the worst dangers of an armaments race." Israel was sensitive to its disadvantages in any arms race with the Arab states, which were important to the Western powers in their policy of containing Communist expansion into the vulnerable Middle East. Israel feared that the United Kingdom, in its effort to stop the imperial rot under pressures of the Cold War, would accelerate the flow of arms to the Arab states, while impeding it to Israel. Without formal arrangements, comparable to those of its Arab rivals, for the procurement of modern weapons, Israel was driven into the open market, where trading in armaments of postwar design was severely restricted at the time. It was therefore natural for Israel to try to save the embargo since, if enforced, it would have hardened the post-armistice Arab-Israel military equilibrium.

Egypt and the other Arab states, however, opposed the continuance of the embargo, which had hurt them more than Israel. The Arab states had depended mainly on regular sources of military supply in Western countries, which suspended shipments in accordance with the Security Council resolution. But national and international controls over war surplus, especially over scrap, were loose, once the wares had passed from government to private ownership. Private entrepreneurs could scarcely be expected not to gravitate to that market which assured the highest returns. New states seeking banned equipment would naturally be willing to pay much higher prices than individuals wishing to put the surplus to private civilian use. The Arab states and Israel invested heavily in such matériel. The Palestine Jews had developed workshops for the recovery of scrap in the mandatory period, when it was a principal variety of available heavy armament. The Arabs generally were ill prepared for quick salvage. Besides, Israel was also getting equipment from Czechoslovakia, mostly light arms and ammunition, despite the embargo. The Security Council, in fact, formally lifted the arms embargo in August 1949, raising Arab hopes and Israel fears, although in retrospect both were overstated. What is more, from the outset Israel viewed Egypt as the primary Arab adversary.

Yet almost throughout the period of the Western arms monopoly, Egypt was influenced in its arms procurement policies by the desire more to liberate itself from the political burdens of the British military presence and of the military dependence on Britain than to build up Arab military might in the dispute with Israel.

The Egyptian government was early persuaded that Britain was using military aid as an instrument for safeguarding British supremacy. The 1936 Anglo-Egyptian treaty had placed a premium on Egyptian military expansion and modernization as the only way of terminating Britain's military privileges in the country. The failure of Anglo-Egyptian negotiations in the final years of the monarchy could be attributed largely to the crisis in confidence over the British promises in 1936 to evacuate its troops and to hand over the defense of the Suez Canal when the Egyptian army was able to assume the responsibility.

When, after the overthrow of the monarchy in 1952, talks shifted to Egyptian participation in a Western security system, the military leaders in Egypt still nourished unyielding suspicions of military collaboration with military suppliers. The junta argued that if the only way to procure modern arms lay in agreement on regional defense, such responsibilities would have to be vested in an Arab system under Egyptian leadership without formal ties to the West. It had in mind the joint defense treaty which all the Arab League members had signed in 1950 in the wake of the Palestine defeat and which went into force two years later. This treaty did not effectively bring into being either a permanent military mission drawn from the general staffs of the armies or a joint defense council consisting of the foreign and defense ministers to serve as a military-political directorate of the League. In any Arab League security system, Egypt was bound to play a dominant role, and Egypt's newly found consecration to Arab unity compounded the belief, on the one hand, that an Egyptian-led Arab security system would enlarge Egypt's military power and the fear, on the other, that divided ranks among the Arab states (with some of them adhering to a Western system) would permit European imperialism to regain entry through the back door.

Early in 1955 Egypt had tried to discourage Iraq from joining Turkey in the creation of a Middle East security system under Western sponsorship. "The source of arms is the West," contended Fadhil al-Jamali, the Iraqi delegate to a meeting of Arab foreign ministers in Cairo, so long as we do not want to cooperate with Communism. The West will not supply these arms for the sake of our black colored eyes, but only if we come to an understanding with it. We cannot obtain arms from the West without agreements. The Foreign Ministers were told, "Wait and the West will give you arms. The West will need you and give you arms without commitments." Certain Arab countries got in touch with the United States and Britain in this regard and they found that their information was wrong and that the West would not give arms freely.[3]

Iraq, too, was trying to build up its own and Arab military might. If Iraq's terms for cooperation with the West seemed more relaxed than those of Egypt, this could be attributed to a less stormy record of postwar Anglo-Iraqi relations. Britain's military interest in Iraq was far more expendable than its military interest in Egypt. Besides, the promise of modern weapons, comparable to those that Turkey and Iran were receiving, proved irresistible, especially when it was accompanied by the British promotion of Iraq as a rival to Egypt in Arab regional affairs. Indeed, the bitterness of the Egyptian-Iraqi dispute, no less than that of the Arab-Israel dispute, could not fully be appreciated without examining the arms-purveying policies of the Western powers.

As principal supplier with cooperative allies and quiescent adversaries, Britain in effect managed the arms market in the Arab-Israel zone until 1955. With the tradition of using military aid as a political instrument well established in the Middle East, Britain tried to exact a political price for the sale of modern weapons and for instruction in their use. British arms-dispensing policies, as it turned out, agitated Israel and Egypt above all others in the area, inducing each to embark upon its own arms-procurement course beyond the market manager's control. The policy toward Israel was simple but final: to mollify Arab mistrust, Britain held to a bare minimum the sale of new weapons to the Jewish state. By contrast, Britain muddled its arms-dispensing policies toward Egypt, using them as adjuncts to the stormy negotiations for treaty revision.[4]

In grooming Iraq as a rival to Egypt for leadership in the Arab East and for participation in a Western-sponsored Middle East security system, the United Kingdom probably hoped that the threat of rivalry together with the other pressures would suffice to bring Egypt around. It was with this goal in mind that the United States concluded a military assistance agreement with Iraq in April 1954. American willingness to supplement arms grants with offshore procurement was intended as much to preserve weapons continuity in the British-equipped Iraqi army as to assist Britain's military industry. The more cooperative Iraq became, the more obdurate Egypt grew. When finally Britain took the plunge in encouraging Iraq and Turkey to inaugurate in February 1955 a military alliance, to which it adhered a few weeks later, and which grew into the Baghdad Pact before the year's end, Britain still tried to attract to the venture the other Arab countries in the Fertile Crescent and perhaps ultimately Egypt itself. But the response in the Arab East, following the lead of Egypt, was solidly negative, despite the prospect of American military aid.

The Soviet-Egyptian arms deal of 1955 abruptly ended the Western monopoly of the Middle East arms market. By then, the races in the Arab-Israel zone had been launched. Modern weapons, it is true, were only trickling, not flowing, into the zone. But the emotions were high, and the lines of cleavage sharp. With the sudden appearance of an uninhibited supplier, the rules of the game changed overnight among the suppliers and the clients, and the swift rise in the level of sophistication intensified the mutual fears.

Changing the Rules

The Soviet-Egyptian arms deal dumbfounded the Western powers. Did Soviet issue of modern military hardware, first to Egypt and soon thereafter to Syria and Yemen, constitute the opening stage in an attempted subordination of the Arab clients? Was it simply a device for stockpiling weapons for later use by Soviet troops? Was it designed primarily to slip subversive agents disguised as technicians into client countries? Whatever the motives, the Western powers had no way of estimating the damage to their interests in the Arab-Israel zone. Even if the U.S.S.R. could not directly build up its military might in the Middle East through arms sales, it began to benefit indirectly from the progressive destruction of Britain's primacy in the Arab East.

It was the formation of the Baghdad Pact on British initiative with American encouragement that had thrown the U.S.S.R. and Egypt together. For Britain, the pact held out the hope of transforming the mode of its military-political leadership from imperial domination into paramountcy in a regional organization. The promoters were persuaded that, if the system proved workable, Britain would be able to protect its investment in Middle East oil, contribute its share to the containment of "international Communism," and cling to its status as a major power. In the context of the regional arms races, the British bait to Arab–East candidates for membership in the Baghdad Pact was the promise of military modernization. At this, Egypt balked.

The U.S.S.R., for its part, viewed the Baghdad Pact as an "aggressive bloc," whose further growth it was determined to check. It easily outbid the West by offering Egypt and the other Arab states modern military weapons without haggling over types such as offensive or defensive, strategic or tactical, and without compulsory participation in any alliance. The arms deal insured that Egypt would stay out of the Baghdad Pact. Whether Syria or Yemen might ever have joined had Soviet military aid not been forthcoming, we shall never know. In any case, as Soviet military clients they did not join, nor did Saudi Arabia, which followed the Egyptian lead in Arab politics without ever becoming a Soviet arms customer. In October 1955 Egypt began organizing through bilateral agreements with Syria and Saudi Arabia a joint Arab command, as a rival to the Western-sponsored system. Under Egyptian leadership the Arab opponents of the Baghdad Pact won their greatest triumph at the turn of 1956 by intimidating Jordan from joining, despite the high-powered British salesmanship—the designation of the chief of the Imperial General Staff as principal negotiator, the immediate gift of ten Vampire jet fighters, the promise of substantial expansion of the Arab Legion at British expense, and the proposed termination of the preferential alliance. Egypt, with Syria and Saudi Arabia in tow, continued riding the crest of its defiance of Britain by encouraging King Husayn in March 1956 to Jordanize the Legion command and a year later to end the alliance with Britain altogether. From these blows to its military paramountcy in the Arab East, Britain never recovered.

The three Western powers, not having planned in advance for the crisis precipitated by Soviet one-upmanship in arms sales, were unprepared to meet it. Instead of facing up to the new realities, once the U.S.S.R. became a major supplier in the area, the Western leaders sought refuge in a reaffirmation of the Tripartite Declaration. The declaration, it is true, had laid down guidelines for arms distribution and for peacekeeping in the Arab-Israel zone so as to discourage arms races and wars. But the guidelines rested on the assumption that military rivalry in the zone would continue, essentially as in the past, to range the Arab states against Israel. From the start, however, the Arab states lacked cohesion, and Britain's political use of the disunity stimulated arms rivalry between Iraq and Egypt, even before the U.S.S.R. entered the competition.

Anger over the Anglo-American arrangements for the military modernization of Iraq, no less—and probably more—than fear of Israel's military might, helped condition Egypt for the initial acceptance of Soviet weapons. From the moment of that acceptance, the Western guidelines on arms control among the Arab states and Israel became outmoded, since the whole purpose of the Soviet initiative was to wean the Arab states away from their arms dependence on the West.

John Foster Dulles, joined by his British and French colleagues, lost no time in exploring informally with Foreign Minister Vyacheslav M. Molotov the implications of the Soviet-Egyptian arms deal. No understanding was reached, and the details of the discussion were not released. In England, the Labor opposition tried badgering the Conservative government into initiating quadripartite talks with the Soviet Union for imposing an arms embargo on the Arab-Israel zone. Sir Anthony Eden later reported that he had raised the issue of arms control in the Arab-Israel area with Bulganin and Khrushchev on their visit to England in April 1956, only to learn that they did not "wish to take any initiative in the matter themselves, though they were ready to hear any proposals others might have to make." [5]

Meanwhile, the Western powers were not pulling in harness. France did not take part either in the Baghdad Pact or in formulating, after the Soviet-Egyptian arms deal, a counterstrategy to check rising Soviet influence in the Arab world. Instead, the United States and Britain consulted alone. They enlarged the quantity and upgraded the quality of the military hardware allocated to their Arab clients—Iraq, Jordan, Saudi Arabia, and Lebanon. But the real pressure was prospective, not immediate. Iraq's needs were already attended in the Baghdad Pact. Saudi Arabia, strictly speaking, lay outside the armistice regime, and its demands for weaponry, still only modest, were met by the United States, although not without incident. Lebanon simply neglected its armed forces and was not tempted by Soviet overtures. This left as the most urgent problem of the Western powers in the Arab East the kingdom of Jordan, which under pressure of the Soviet clients was breaking away from dependence on Britain. In the opening weeks of the crisis, Britain was still confident of guiding Jordan safely into the Baghdad Pact, despite the delicacy of the operation; and the strong pro-Arab position of the Eden government reflected a desire to strengthen the resolve of the youthful King Husayn and his advisers to accede to the pact.

On the other hand, since the U.S.S.R. supported the Arab side in the dispute with Israel, the two Western allies did not wish to become identified as military aiders of Israel. This in itself, it was feared, would ease the further penetration into the Arab East of the Soviet Union as arms dispenser. Since spokesmen of the two Western governments would not admit this publicly, they resorted to rationalizations that failed to satisfy Israel and its supporters in the United States and Britain. The allies, it was explained, were determined to avoid contributing to an arms race, which "could only increase tensions in the area" [6] and which would not "be in the true interest of any of the participants." [7] While Secretary Dulles in February 1956 acknowledged that "a disparity in armed force between Israel and its Arab neighbors" had been created by Soviet arms shipments to Egypt, he doubted that the disparity could

be adequately offset by the additional purchase of arms by the State of Israel. Israel has a population of under two million, whereas the Arab population amounts to tens of millions, and they apparently have been offered access to huge stores of Soviet bloc material. Under this circumstance the security of Israel can perhaps better be assured by means other than an arms race.[8]

The United States and Britain shared the judgment that Israel still enjoyed a military lead that allowed room for maneuver because of the time lag between the procurement and the assimilation of new weapons. Israel's security planners, however, must have believed that they could ill afford such risks. In arms races, what rivals believe about each other's military policies is often more powerful than the reality. Each is under constraint to take precautionary steps, because it must undergo the assimilative phase. The challenged regime is under more pressure than the challenger as it tries to preserve the existing balance. Israel could not have been expected to concur in the expressed British and American concern over arms races, which rang hollow in view of their own participation as suppliers. Israel's overriding anxiety was survival, and its appeals for hardware of compensatory quality were insistent. In response, the United States and Britain tried to find a formula that would simultaneously furnish Israel a neutral guarantee of its security, and enable the Western powers to elude the label of arms purveyors to the Jewish state.

Instructively, the references to the Middle East in the joint

Anglo-American statement issued at the close of the Eisenhower-Eden talks in Washington on 1 February 1956, did not even mention the provision on arms control in the Tripartite Declaration but focused instead on its provision for allied action within the United Nations and outside it to prevent forcible changes of boundary or armistice lines in the Arab-Israel area. The two powers expressed a hope that was bound more to provoke fears and anger than to dissolve them:

> We believe that the security of states in this area cannot rest upon arms alone but rather upon international rule of law and upon the establishment of friendly relations among neighbors. The action of the Soviet bloc in regard to arms supplies to Middle East countries has added to tensions in the area and increased the risk of war. Our purpose is to mitigate that risk.[9]

Israel's restiveness, as leaders of the Labor opposition had been arguing since Soviet arms sales to Egypt became a critical issue, derived from the Western refusal to supply Israel compensatory weapons and to give it a territorial guarantee like the one Britain gave to Jordan. In October 1955, Anthony Nutting had admitted that "we do not think that this is the moment to give the guarantee . . . because what we wish to do is to guarantee a settlement in that area and not guarantee the existing unsettled state of affairs." [10] This was still the government's position the following March, at the time of the parliamentary review of General Glubb's summary dismissal in Jordan. Previously, the prime minister had suggested, in his well-publicized Guildhall speech, that an Arab-Israel settlement could be reached by Israel's surrender of territory to the Arabs. At least, that was Israel's reading of Eden's Solomonic proposal for dividing the territory that Israel had acquired under the armistice system of 1949.

Even more disturbing to Labor M.P.s than the Eden government's refusal to give Israel a territorial or security guarantee was the threat to peace posed by the Arab-Israel weapons imbalance. Hugh Gaitskell, leader of the opposition, called attention to the significance of the prospective military superiority of the Arab states on the ground and in the air. "The result is that two grave dangers emerge," Gaitskell stated.

> The first, which is the most obvious one, is that the Arabs, whose feelings on this matter we know, are bound now to be encouraged to

hope that in the not very distant future they will have their revenge and will have their opportunity to eliminate Israel. The second danger is that the Israelis, realising that the balance is tilted against them and will be more and more tilted, will take the opportunity while things are not so bad from their point of view to go in for preventive action.[11]

The Conservative government, however, held firm in its resolve not to give the Soviet Arab clients and their nationalist sympathizers in adjacent Arab lands a basis for levelling charges against Britain as a military ally of Israel.

For identical reasons on the American side, Secretary Dulles parried the thrusts of pro-Israel Congressmen and newsmen who urged equipping Israel with matching quality weapons. Dulles never said yes; but he also never said no. While the United States refused to sell modern arms direct to Israel, it did not object to Israel's getting them elsewhere. In a press interview in spring 1956 Secretary Dulles stated his views on Israel's request to Canada for jet planes:

The Canadians are aware of the fact that there is no intention or desire of the United States to try to establish a worldwide boycott of the Government of Israel as far as arms are concerned. Our own policy is based on certain considerations which are, in some respects at least, distinctive to ourselves, and not necessarily a pattern which we think all the world should follow, certainly not a pattern which we are trying to impose upon other countries of the world.[12]

Israel had already contracted to buy, reportedly with United States knowledge and approval, the latest model of Mystère jets from France. But the delivery date was mid-1956, and their number was limited. The IL-28 bombers that the U.S.S.R. released to Egypt caused Israel security planners great anxiety and prompted them to seek, in addition to the French interceptors, United States F-86 Sabrejets from Canada. Israel had to pay the full price in hard currency for the jets that it contracted to purchase from France and Canada, whereas Egypt procured all its hardware at a discount and paid for it either in agricultural products or in Egyptian currency. Moreover, the Egyptians received prompt delivery from the Soviet bloc, whereas Israel had to wait for production schedules.

As it turned out, Canada unilaterally suspended the F-86 contract immediately after word reached Ottawa of Israel's invasion of

Sinai in October 1956, and later cancelled it altogether with Israel's consent. By then, however, Canadian support no longer seemed essential to Israel. Common grievances had cemented an Israel entente with France. France and Israel found themselves isolated in international and regional politics. Both were alienated by the U.S.S.R. and Egypt, and both were barred from the Baghdad Pact. The British government, which clearly felt that the membership of France in the Baghdad Pact would almost certainly frighten the Arab states away, simply had not invited its European ally to join. French policies toward its Arab dependencies in North Africa provided at the United Nations General Assembly a target annually attacked by the Soviet and Arab blocs, the latter under Egyptian leadership. French sensibilities were further scraped by the haven and the material support that Egypt gave North African political refugees, specifically in 1956 to Algerian rebels. The nationalization of the French-managed Suez Canal Company was the last straw.

The Sinai-Suez war marked a turning point in the Arab-Israel arms races. It temporarily dissolved the Anglo-American partnership in the Arab East. Since Britain had already been toppled from its political-military pre-eminence in the area, the decision to join France in gunboat diplomacy in the Suez crisis of 1956 represented a desperate British attempt to recapture its position of dominance. Anglo-French cooperation proved short-lived. By the time the Anglo-American partnership in the Arab-Israel zone was reconstituted in 1957, Britain had become the junior partner. In the meantime, the United States had asserted its paramountcy in the area by introducing its own measures to discourage the Soviet Arab clients from subverting the regimes of the West's Arab clients. It had taken more than a year for the United States, engaging in its own style of one-upmanship, to outsmart the U.S.S.R. through the Eisenhower Doctrine. No longer was enrollment in a Western security system the prerequisite for military aid. Under the doctrine the president could peddle military (and economic) grant aid to any Arab East state that asked for it.

Application of the Eisenhower Doctrine helped the United States to rally those states in the Arab East that were not Soviet clients. Iraq, already formally attached to the anti-Communist coalition, received no special handling. Saudi collaboration with Egypt and Syria against Jordan in 1955–56 was influenced as much by anger against Britain over the Buraymi dispute as by the traditional dynastic quarrel with the Hashimis. The United States succeeded

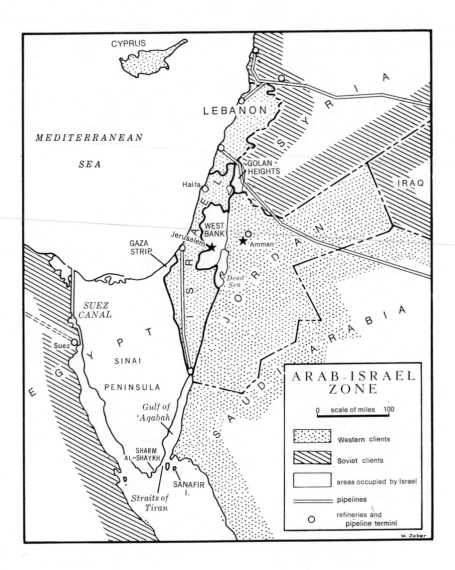

CYPRUS

LEBANON

S Y R I A

MEDITERRANEAN

SEA

GOLAN
HEIGHTS

IRAQ

Haifa

WEST
BANK

Jerusalem

J O R D A N

Amman

GAZA
STRIP

Dead
Sea

SUEZ
CANAL

S A U D I   A R A B I A

Suez

E G Y P T

SINAI

PENINSULA

Gulf of
'Aqabah

SHARM
AL-SHAYKH

SANAFIR
I.

Straits of
Tiran

ARAB-ISRAEL
ZONE

0   scale of miles   100

Western clients

Soviet clients

areas occupied by Israel

pipelines

refineries and
pipeline termini

W. Jaber

in snatching the Arabian kingdom from the Egyptian grip as early as February 1957, even before the doctrine received Congressional endorsement. King Saud on a state visit to Washington renewed the Dhahran base agreement for five years in return for promised military assistance. In April the United States went to the rescue of King Husayn by declaring the sovereignty and territorial integrity of Jordan "vital" to American security. The United States assumed at that time an open-ended obligation to balance the Jordan budget, primarily in support of its modernizing and enlarging military establishment. Paradoxically, Lebanon failed to develop a hefty military appetite, even though it was the only Arab country that formally endorsed the Eisenhower Doctrine.

While detaching these Arab states from the Egyptian sphere, Dulles's diplomacy contrived to keep American flexibility in the Arab-Israel area. The United States was simultaneously in and out of the Baghdad Pact: it sent observers to the periodic meetings of the council, sat on the several committees, yet never formally acceded to the system. Of the four Arab East states that initially escaped Egyptian domination in regional politics, only Saudi Arabia and Lebanon could be designated American clients. But both had small and only slowly growing armies. While a beneficiary of the American military aid program, Iraq nevertheless continued, as in the past, mainly to rely on Britain for new hardware and replacements. Jordan, too, with American counsel, used its annual American subvention of close to $50 million partly for the purchase of modern weapons in Britain. Thus, the United States avoided becoming a major military supplier in the Arab East. Moreover, the United States had passed Israel off on France. On the eve of the Sinai-Suez war, the tentative supplier-client relationship, which had grown out of and would outlast the Algerian war, was welded into a durable Israel-French understanding. Thus, the Eisenhower Doctrine, for the time being, enabled the United States to escape becoming a major supplier to Israel. The United States, however, as we shall see, bought its flexibility in the Arab-Israel zone on the deferred-payment plan.

The supplier tier in the Arab-Israel races at first had a single market manipulator, Britain, which managed by the tactics of divide and rule to cultivate inherent differences and thereby fracture the client tier. It played off the Arab states against Israel and, within the Arab zone, Iraq against Egypt. In 1955–57, the supplier tier itself was divided, so that three competitive market manipulators replaced the single one, and each was paired off with competitive clients: Britain was left with the Hashimi contingent; Russia with Egypt, Syria and, later, Iraq; and France with Israel. Into this murky situation the United States reluctantly moved as a sort of supermanager, trying to check the arms races in the Arab-Israel area. It did so, not by negotiating with the major suppliers, since the Soviet conditions were still too stiff, but by dealing with its two allied suppliers and with friendly clients to restore uneasy weapons balances that Soviet shipments continually upset. Until 1955 the arms races that quickened under the armistice system had been essentially quantitative races in rehabilitated war surplus, interlarded with small amounts of weapons of postwar design that primarily reached Britain's preferential allies in the Arab East. The armies of all the armistice signers except Lebanon expanded steadily.

Between 1955 and 1960 weapons of postwar design began to pile up in the zone. Egypt became the only country to sport heavy tanks, the Josif Stalin-3, added to its inventory in 1955–57; and once Egypt bought sixty copies, it stopped investing in the noncompetitive model. On the other hand, the medium tank—whether the Soviet T-34 or the British Centurion or the American Patton—became standard fare in the zonal armies except those of Jordan and Lebanon. In armor, troop carriers mounted on half-tracks, tank transporters, and self-propelled assault guns were favored. The infantry of all armies was substantially motorized by 1960; their vehicles consisted of jeeps and trucks of most dimensions and purposes; and their weapons included bazookas, recoilless guns, antitank rifles, and light mortars. The air forces had converted to jets by 1960. While most of the planes were still subsonic, the three Soviet clients and Israel were moving into transonic aircraft. Most of the planes were interceptors (fighter-bombers) and transports, but Egypt, in acquiring IL-28 bombers, and Israel in acquiring Vautours, the French equivalent, showed a growing interest in attack aircraft. Radar screens began to take their place in national air defense systems. Radio and telephonic equipment united the units with area commands, and the latter with the supreme command. Egypt and Israel were the only states in the area to build up naval power, and by 1960 Egypt had purchased nine submarines and six destroyers; of these types of naval craft Israel had assembled only two each, obviously relying on air power to repel possible Egyptian naval attack. What Britain and the United States had started as cautious enticement for cooperation with the West thus developed in the second half of the 1950s into open rivalry, as the Soviet Union lifted most limits on quantity and many on quality, thus requiring the Western suppliers to do the same.

The armies of the Arab states and Israel had been modernized in less than five years; once aroused, their desire for ever new military gadgets that rolled off the assembly lines of the major supplying countries became insatiable. Any hope of reduction demanded at the very least the common action of the suppliers. "Perhaps the nations involved in the 1948 hostilities may, as a first step," President Eisenhower appealed to the clients in the summer of 1958 at the United States General Assembly, then meeting in emergency session on the Lebanese dispute,

> wish to call for a United Nations study of the flow of heavy armaments to those nations. My country would be glad to support the establishment of an appropriate United Nations body to examine this problem. That body would discuss it individually with these countries and see what arms-control arrangements could be worked out under which the security of all these nations could be maintained more effectively than under a continued wasteful, dangerous competition in armaments. I recognize that any such arrangements must reflect these countries' own views.[13]

This tentative suggestion was not accompanied by any concrete proposal and met with no response, for neither the U.S.S.R. nor its Arab clients found in it any positive inducement to acceptance of arms control.

A test of power in the Arab-Israel zone came in the pre-emptive strike that Israel mounted against Egypt in Sinai in 1956. The results were clouded, it is true, because of the French (and British) collusion with Israel. This enabled the Arabs to rationalize that without Western imperial aid, Israel would never have triumphed in the field. Still, the Sinai campaign demonstrated the power and the punch of Israel's citizen army. The war clearly chastened Egypt. It ceased stockpiling new weaponry in Sinai, as it had done provocatively in 1955–56, for the later convenience of capture by Israel. Egypt seemed in no hurry after 1956 to challenge Israel's citizen army again. Thus, to all intents and purposes, the Arab states continued acknowledging Israel's military superiority. In the climate of suspicion and fear that the rising level of armaments engendered, the private middlemen who had figured prominently in the war-surplus stage gave way to government officials as the traffic in weapons became increasingly a government-to-government activity.

Going Sophisticated

The arms races in the Arab-Israel zone, it was manifest by the 1960s, were following a predictable pattern. After the Palestine war, three of the five Arab states were still saddled with problems of disimperialism, which distracted them from attending freely to their arms wants. This was the phase of rehabilitated war surplus, spiced with token handouts of postwar models. The second phase, which began when the U.S.S.R. became a major vendor to selected Arab states, led to the diffusion of the out-of-date postwar hardware from the supplying countries; and with it even Egypt and Israel, to say nothing of their neighbors, were more than reasonably happy, for it surpassed in quality the armaments in their arsenals before then. In the third phase the U.S.S.R. still set the supplier pace, just as Egypt set the client pace among the Arab states and Israel. Since Egypt did not reach its military goals—developing the most powerful army in the neighborhood, uniting under its command the armies of the Arab states, and destroying Israel—the Egyptians continued climbing the conventional ladder as far as their generous Russian patrons allowed them. Israel in this period enlarged its sources of supply and, of no less importance, greatly expanded the range and output of its military industry. Armaments throughout the area in these years grew more and more sophisticated and tended to become uniform, for this is one of the major attributes of arms racing.

In the first half of the 1960s supersonic fighters came into vogue in the Arab-Israel zone. The MiG-21 appeared in its several editions first in Egypt and then in Syria and Iraq; and the French counterpart, the Mirage III, also in several editions, showed up in the Israel air force. Jordan and Lebanon trailed behind the others. Not until the start of the third postwar decade did Jordan arrange to buy from the United States an early model of the F-104 Starfighter, the American version of this extended family of supersonic fighters. Egypt, and on a smaller scale Iraq, began supplementing their IL-28 light bombers with the TU-16 medium bomber. Israel, to eke out its Vautours, negotiated a contract with the United States in 1965–66 for the purchase of the A-4, or Skyhawk, attack bombers. For attack aircraft the remaining states of the zone were still restricted in 1966 to fighter-bombers.

The most enterprising military establishments of the area, meanwhile, began enriching their armor with diesel-driven tanks, of which the best models could cruise much farther than the earlier gas-driven models without refueling; the newer tanks, moreover, were equipped with improved fire-control systems. But above all, in the first half of the 1960s the armed forces in the countries of the area, except those of Jordan and Lebanon, started adding guided missiles to their inventories. The surface-to-air and air-to-air missiles proved the easiest to obtain; and on independence day of 1966 the Egyptian air force put on display for the first time under the wings of TU-16s Soviet air-to-surface missiles. Egypt and Syria also bought Komars, or missile-firing vessels, the postwar Soviet class of the former torpedo boats. But there was no evidence in the mid-1960s that they had procured from the U.S.S.R. surface-to-surface missiles of the desired 200- to 500-mile range.

The arsenals of the Arab states and Israel in 1965 were still bulging with recently outmoded arms, interspersed with sizable and swiftly growing quantities in current style. Several states were manufacturing small arms and ammunition, and all were attempting to establish facilities for the maintenance and repair of the imported hardware. Egypt and Israel, however, had developed more elaborate industrial plants than any of their neighbors. The two armies were competing not only in the accumulation of the latest cycle of arms but also in the search for military self-generating capacity in sophisticated weapons. Each worked out the consequent problems in a characteristic way.

Egypt seemed under compulsion to demonstrate its maturity and to realize, according to its own lights, its full military industrial potential. The junta accordingly aspired to produce the prestigious weapons of the day. After modest experimentation, Egypt began recruiting on a large scale in 1958 scientists, engineers, and skilled workers in West Germany among the alumni of the development and production of World War II rockets and aircraft. Other technicians came from Austria, Switzerland, and Spain. Most of the European expatriates, eventually numbering about 500, were employed in the jet plane program, which was directed to design and manufacture a trainer (designated the HA-200) and a fighter (HA-300). The manufacture of both was hobbled with difficulties. Even with British engines, in test runs as late as 1965, the Egyptian planes were unable to fly faster than Mach 1, or the speed of sound (roughly 745 miles per hour at sea level or 660 mph at 35,000 feet), although they were intended to reach supersonic speeds of Mach 2 to 2.5. At the same time the Egyptian government, with the help of the European expatriates, also tried to develop surface-to-surface missiles with a range of more than 250 miles. In the summer of 1962 they tested prototypes of two one-stage rockets with payloads varying between 500 pounds and a ton; they also planned to combine both in a two-stage rocket, but, so far as was publicly known as late as 1968, the more complex weapon was not tested. The supporting industry in Egypt could not furnish essential components, especially for the guidance systems, and these proved difficult or impossible to get in the East or West, so that the missiles, too, probably never went into production.

The cost of the two projects was still mounting in 1965, when it was conservatively estimated that Egypt was spending no less than $50 million a year. Significantly, the Egyptian experiments in the manufacture of sophisticated weaponry were undertaken with the cooperation of West Europeans as individuals (but not of their governments), which suggested an Egyptian search for release from total arms dependence on the Soviet bloc. Even when Egypt broke off diplomatic relations with West Germany in 1965, 'Abd al-Nasir did not accept East German offers to replace West German skilled labor on advantageous terms, including payment in soft currency.

The test models of the rockets and jets appeared to disturb Israel security planners. Nor could they later be certain that either or both weapons systems were not actually going into production. By the mid-1960s there was no way of telling whether the accelerating Israel program of arms purchase and production was motivated more by these fears or by the urge to remain militarily as far ahead of the Arab enemy as possible. From Egypt's style, however, Israel's rival activities differed significantly, as is best exemplified by Israel's handling of jet plane production and the procurement of medium-range surface-to-surface missiles. Israel manufactured jet trainers under French license, repaired all jets added to its air force, and used the same facilities to service civilian jets of airlines that operated in Israel. But it contracted to buy fighters and bombers from the major Western suppliers.

As early as 1961, Israel tested its own rocket, the Shavit (Comet) 2, and labeled it a meteorological rocket. In theory, Israel could have developed missiles of all types domestically. But the local editions, particularly of the desired surface-to-surface missile, were certain to show far rougher edges and poorer performance than the imports. In this respect, Israel and Egypt shared the same difficulties, since many components, particularly for the guidance systems, had to be imported. Instead of merely importing talent from the West, Israel also invested in 1966 in the government-supported industrial talent of France, which lagged well behind the superpowers and Britain in missile production. Indeed, Israel sent its own scientists to France to cooperate in the venture. Since President de Gaulle appeared determined to achieve missile and plane as well as nuclear independence from the United States, France probably welcomed Israel investment of capital and scientific skill and research and engineering for a mobile medium-range surface-to-surface missile. Israel's share in the missile development project took the form of a small advance order, with a reported delivery date of 1970. As a carrier of high explosives that would make up in guaranteed penetrability what it might lose in accuracy, the French missile would, seemingly, give Israel a psychological edge in the competition with Egypt. It would also constitute an obvious delivery system for an atomic bomb.

If Israel wished to make its nuclear option credible to Egypt and the Arab states, the promise of a missile large enough to accommodate the bomb would do it. At Dimona in the Negeb in 1960 Israel began the construction, with French assistance, of a 24-mW(th) nuclear research reactor, which, on completion, would be able to produce enough plutonium for one bomb a year, with fissile material to spare. Israel tried to keep the project a secret, despite the scale of construction, and when its existence became known, "American officials were given, in total, seven different explanations of what the factory was, none of them accurate." [14] The France-Israel agreement, under which the reactor was built, was never published. Eventually Israel permitted Americans to visit the Dimona installation, and Israel insisted that it was intended to serve peaceful purposes. In the Israel budgetary context, however, the experiment's probable cost of $75 million or more seemed excessive for a research project. Attempts to find a domestic source of uranium as a by-product of the phosphate industry at the Dead Sea produced negative results, so that Israel did not become self-sufficient in the raw material needed to feed the reactor. Nor was there any public evidence as late as 1968 of the construction of a chemical separator, without which the bomb could not be made.

Yet by deliberately blurring the precise purposes of the Dimona reactor, Israel was able to assure itself an open nuclear option, and at the same time claim that no bombs were being produced. But the Israel experiment undeniably pushed the arms race with Egypt up to the threshold of unconventional weapons. According to reports in the press, Egypt approached the U.S.S.R. in December 1965 for nuclear weapons in defense against Israel. The Soviet Union, it was alleged, turned down the Egyptian request but promised 'Abd al-Nasir a guarantee of nuclear protection if Israel developed or obtained such weapons. "If Israel proceeds with the production of an atomic bomb," the Egyptian president told journalists in February 1966, "then I believe the only answer to this is a preventive war." [15]

Israel, like Egypt, was torn between the need to import heavy, sophisticated hardware and the desire to become militarily self-sufficient. The ambivalence helps explain why in the second post-war decade, they seemed bent on freeing themselves from high dependence on a single supplier. From the start of the partnership with France, there was a residual fear in Israel, as there was a residual hope in the Arab East, that the close working relations would not survive an Algerian settlement. Israel fears could hardly escape reawakening when France returned in the mid-1960s as weapons purveyor to the Arab East, offering to sell supersonic fighters and other hardware to Jordan, Lebanon, and even Egypt. Meanwhile, Britain, following the collapse of its position in the Arab East after Suez, discarded some of its inhibitions about arms sales to Israel. Thereafter Israel became one of Britain's steady customers for naval and other martial equipment.

Moreover, after a modest start in 1955 with the purchase of spare parts, Israel finally concluded a secret arms agreement with West Germany. The precise terms were not formally released; but enough information was leaked at various times for reconstruction of the major outlines. Apparently, Prime Minister David Ben Gurion and Chancellor Konrad Adenauer reached an understanding in principle, when the two met in New York City in March 1960. Shim'on Peres, Israel's deputy defense minister, and Franz Josef Strauss, West Germany's defense minister, worked out the details in Bonn in the following summer. Under the agreement West Germany early in the 1960s furnished Israel a wide assortment of new and used hardware ranging from helicopters, submarines, and transport planes to anti-aircraft guns and antitank rockets—items manufactured in various Western European countries and the United States as well as in West Germany. What is more, West Germany absorbed the cost as part of its reparations payments to Israel.

In its plans for diversifying the sources of imported arms, Israel gave high priority to persuading the United States to abandon its restraints about selling heavy weapons direct to Israel. From the Israel standpoint, it was a slow, tough battle. But in the 1960s, perseverance began yielding results. Israel arranged for the purchase from the United States of Hawk anti-aircraft missiles in 1962–63, of Patton tanks in 1965, and of Skyhawk attack bombers in 1965–66.

From Marginal to Balancing Supplier

The United States had tried to preserve the flexibility of its arms policies toward the Arab states and Israel by keeping alive the American image as a nonsupplier, or at the very most as only a marginal supplier, in the multiple races of the Arab-Isarel area. In doing so, the United States tried to avoid becoming identified, among the Soviet Arab clients and their sympathizers in the surrounding states, as an upholder of the status quo against the forces of social and political change; and, among the Arab states generally, as a patron of Israel in the Arab-Israel dispute. Consequently, the Kennedy Administration, and Johnson's until June 1967, did not modify the inherited policy of annual budget support to Jordan, principally for financing its allocations to defense, including the purchase of new equipment from Britain. The United States could continue to claim, as indeed it did, that it was not a major supplier of arms to the Hashimi kingdom. The Kennedy Administration, admittedly, departed from the inherited norm when it consented in principle in September 1962 to sell Hawk missiles to Israel. That this was regarded as an exception at the time may be seen from President Kennedy's public statements in the following spring.

Pressed to explain American policy on Israel's appeals for arms in the light of its "growing concern over the manufacture of missiles in Egypt," the President took refuge in the technicality that the Hawk missile agreement had not been formally concluded when he declared: "As you know, the United States has never been a supplier of military equipment directly to the Israelis. We have given economic assistance. The Israelis themselves have bought equipment, a good deal of it from France." [16] Nevertheless, Kennedy made it clear that the United States "would be reluctant to see a military balance of power in the Middle East which was such as to encourage aggression rather than discourage it." The President went on to note that "we have expressed our strong opposition to the introduction or manufacture of nuclear weapons in the Middle East, and have indicated that strongly to all of the countries." In response to a question, a few weeks later, about American policy toward Israel and Jordan if they were threatened, President Kennedy replied:

The United States supports social and economic and political progress in the Middle East. We support the security of both Israel and her neighbors. We seek to limit the Near East arms race, which obviously takes resources from an area already poor and puts them into an increasing race which does not really bring any great security. . . .

This Government has been, and remains, strongly opposed to the use of force, or the threat of force, in the Near East. In the event of agression, or preparation for aggression, whether direct or indirect, we would support appropriate measures in the United Nations and adopt other courses of action on our own to prevent or put a stop to such aggression, which, of course, has been the policy which the United States has followed for some time.[17]

The West German–Israel tank deal of 1964 indicated the continuing reluctance of the United States to become a major arms supplier to Israel, while at the same time trying to preserve "some sort of reasonable balance in the armed forces in that area," as Secretary of State Dean Rusk later explained.[18] It all began with Israel's approach to the United States in 1963 for the purchase of medium tanks of the M-48, or Patton, class to match in quality, not in number, those that the U.S.S.R. had made available to its Arab clients. After several months of consultation the United States apparently accepted Israel's contention that it needed the tanks, since, as a spokesman of the Department of State later acknowledged, the United States authorized West Germany to transfer from its arsenal to Israel an undisclosed number of M-48s. In the West German–Israel contract, presumably signed in October 1964, the tanks were added to those earlier Israel weapons orders that were still unfilled, and payment was arranged in the customary way by charging it to the reparations account.

The West German–Israel arms traffic was a porly kept secret from its inception. The addition of the Patton tanks, which West Germany undertook to deliver before the end of 1965, aroused immediate domestic opposition. Among the public foes of the policy was Dr. Eugen Gerstenmaier, a leader of Chancellor Ludwig Erhard's own Christian Democratic party and president of the Bundestag, or lower house, who explored the matter with 'Abd al-Nasir on a visit to Egypt in November 1964. Meanwhile, Egypt, which had known for some time about West German arms sales to Israel, blew the issue up into a *cause célèbre* early in 1965, first by seeking, at an Arab League summit meeting, punitive action against West Germany, and then by threatening to recognize East Germany. West Germany, accordingly, canceled all its arms contracts with Israel. As we shall presently see, Egypt in effect pushed the United States and Israel together.

Indeed, from Israel's standpoint the most important consequence of West Germany's default was the opportunity it afforded to persuade the United States to fill the canceled order. Sometime after the visit to Tel-Aviv at the end of February 1965 of a high-level American mission headed by Ambassador-at-large W. Averell Harriman, the United States consented. Parallel talks, it was reported, were held in Jordan. The United States thus modified its ten-year-old policy of encouraging pro-Western Arab states and Israel to buy their heavy weapons from Western Europe, and itself became, in 1965–66, a selective supplier to the zone. At the same time, the United States sought a new type of flexibility in limited balanced sales to friendly Arab states and to Israel as a counterpoise against continuing immense sales by the U.S.S.R. to its Arab clients. By then, too, the Department of Defense was able to arrange sales on easy-credit terms, for with a revolving fund of close to $400 million at its disposal it could guarantee such credits from the Export-Import Bank. In 1966–67, for example, Saudi Arabia procured loans worth $143 million; Israel, $88 million; and Jordan, $9.0 million. On the other hand, the United States tried unilaterally to dampen the races by delaying delivery and by delaying public disclosure of sales to Israel until the Department of Defense could also report sales to Arab states.

A trilateral agreement that Saudi Arabia concluded for the purchase of supersonic Lightning fighter-bombers from Britain and Hawk surface-to-air missiles and related communications and radar gear from the United States was announced in December 1965. The American sale of Patton tanks to Jordan to help modernize its army was divulged also before the year expired. In February 1966 the Department of State formally made known the sale of Patton tanks to Israel. "The established United States policy has been to refrain from becoming a major supplier of arms in this area," ran the release on Israel,

> while retaining the option of helping the countries of the area through occasional, selective sales.

These exceptions to our general policy have been based on careful case-by-case examination and a determination that such a sale would not be a destabilizing factor.

The United States has made over the years repeated quiet efforts to encourage limitations on arms buildups in the area. Until those bear fruit, however, the United States cannot be indifferent to the potentially destabilizing effect of massive Soviet sales of arms to the area.[19]

The Department of State confirmed in April 1966 the sale to Jordan of "a limited number of military jet aircraft for its air defense system to replace older models," but refused "to go into the details of the equipment," [20] although it later became known that the United States had agreed to sell to Jordan 36 F-104 Starfighters. In May the Department admitted that Israel also had been permitted to purchase "a limited number of tactical aircraft," a decision that "reflects our due regard for security in the Near East, our wish to avoid serious arms imbalances that would jeopardize area stability and our general restraint as to military equipment supplied to that area." [21] The United States, it was subsequently learned, had contracted to sell to Israel 48 A-4 Skyhawk bombers. Neither Jordan nor Israel, it might be added, received the planes until 1968. Thus, by the start of the third postwar decade the United States was forsaking its sheltered role in the Arab-Israel area of arms balancer by remote control. This arrangement had enabled the American government to watch closely the levels of weaponry that were steadily rising in sophistication but to lean on its major allies to do the actual compensating. Step by step the American government shifted to the exposed position of becoming a direct balancing supplier in the multiple arms rivalries in the Arab-Israel zone.

The race between Egypt and Israel, as we have seen, perceptibly sharpened in the 1960s. American arms sales to Saudi Arabia and Jordan illustrated the two other races in the Arab-Israel zone. These races were a function of the alternating unity and disunity of the Arab East. It made no difference whether the Arabs were united on Israel or disunited; both conditions spurred military modernization.

The formation of the Unified Arab Command (UAC) in 1964 represented the first forward movement in Arab unity, after Syria had seceded from the United Arab Republic more than two years earlier. The UAC grew out of a summit meeting of the Arab League, by which 'Abd al-Nasir contrived to head off what he viewed as ill-advised military action in an endeavor to prevent Israel from completing its scheme for the diversion of the Jordan waters. The summit conferees decided in January 1964 to superimpose the UAC on the commands of the armies of Egypt, Iraq, Jordan, Lebanon, and Syria under the supreme command of Egypt. The UAC was instructed to modernize the armies, standardize the equipment and installations, and improve the defenses along the Israel frontier. The Arab League members, assessed according to ability to pay, committed by September 1965 about $600 million to the venture, for allocation over a ten-year period, mostly for the modernization of the Jordan, Lebanese, and Syrian armies.

Since the three largest participating armies were Soviet clients and the supreme command was Egyptian, the attempted introduction of Soviet weapons into the armies of Jordan and Lebanon might have been expected. The governments of Jordan and Lebanon, however, greeted Egyptian calls for uniform weaponry with intensifying suspicion. The U.S.S.R. allegedly offered MiG-21s to Jordan and Lebanon at a fraction of the cost of comparable planes in the West. Although King Husayn and the Lebanese government probably had no intention of succumbing to the temptations, doubly great, since the funds for the plane purchase came from the UAC budget, they did not object to engaging in bazaar bargaining, a practice favored by all arms buyers. This netted Husayn, in the end, the promise of F-104s, despite United States efforts to persuade the king that F-5s, a somewhat slower and less complicated plane for flying and maintenance, would be more suitable. The essential point, however, was the king's success in shifting from British aircraft to American and from subsonic to supersonic fighters. There was almost certainly no likelihood of King Husayn's jeopardizing his annual grants from the United States by accepting Soviet equipment. But he was angered by Egyptian insistence that he recruit into the army large numbers of former Palestine Arabs, whom he regarded as politically unreliable. While consenting at UAC prompting to transfer National Guardsmen, all former Palestinians, from the reserves to the active forces, Husayn took the occasion in 1965 to dissolve the National Guard itself, while closely screening the transferees and severely limiting their number.

Even angrier was Husayn over the efforts, which he believed were taken at Egyptian instigation, of Ahmad al-Shuqayri, the director of the Palestine Liberation Organization (PLO) and its "army" to organize Jordan's citizens of Palestine birth. The PLO, like the UAC, was a product of Arab League summitry and also received its finances from the UAC budget. Any effort by the PLO to treat the citizens of Palestine birth as a separate entity struck at the very heart of the Hashimi kingdom, and Husayn at the time refused to contemplate any scheme that called for the transfer of allegiance of the Jordanized Palestinians to the PLO. Lebanon's response to comparable pressures from Egypt was far less dramatic, for it had the smallest army in the Arab East and until 1965 showed almost no interest in military modernization. Nevertheless, under UAC pressure, the Lebanese air force went shopping for advanced supersonic fighters in France, Britain, and the United States. The none-too-subtle Egyptian moves to subordinate the armies of Jordan and Lebanon proved counterproductive, as the two governments devised their own modes of resisting Egyptian domination. This tended to keep alive the spirit of disunity in the Arab East, at the very moment of its latest unifying project.

Far more serious was the sharpening enmity between Egypt and Saudi Arabia over the inconclusive war in Yemen. Egypt's refusal to withdraw its forces, despite two cease-fire agreements, touched off the vigorous quarrel that began splitting the Arab world once again toward the end of 1965. This took the form of ranging the Soviet clients under Egyptian leadership against the Western clients, overspilling the Arab East into North Africa and non-Arab Iran. The disunity represented the latest phase of the arms race in which Israel was not involved, even though it was the chief short-run beneficiary. The race acquired doctrinal overtones, for the Soviet customers were revisionists who proclaimed their determination to "liberate" the remaining Arab states from their "servitude" to imperialism. By implied definition, any Arab state in which the military had seized political power and had agreed to purchase weapons from the U.S.S.R. was a liberated state. Only Soviet arms clients, it followed, belonged to the Arab "progressive movement," which spearheaded the Arab "revolution"; the arms clients of the West, it also followed, were the "reactionary allies of imperialism." There was greater unity of sentiment than of action among the self-styled revolutionaries. But even this modicum of unity exceeded that of their adversaries. Efforts in 1966 by King Faysal of Saudi Arabia to rally the Muslim monarchs, including non-Arabs, yielded no durable results, not even an appeal "to rally the spiritual power of Islam" and, through shared political action among Muslim rulers, to check further inroads into the Muslim world of communism and "other atheistic movements," such as Arab socialism in Egypt and Syria.[22]

The doctrinal conflict among the Arab states tended to favor the Soviet position in the Cold War, since the Soviet Arab clients, largely without Soviet prompting, had taken propaganda and political initiatives against the Western clients, who felt compelled to seek greater security in military modernization. The Western clients were thus on the defensive. Yet in the Arab East the U.S.S.R. acquired no new clients after 1958; nor did it lose any either. So long as its clients were satisfied with obsolescent equipment, the Soviet Union could get a commercial return from the sales and a political return by reducing Western influence in the receiving countries. Once the U.S.S.R. in the mid-1960s began selling at high discounts and on easy-credit terms late models of planes, tanks, missiles, and other expensive equipment that it was still using in the Soviet Union and furnishing to its Communist allies, the arms export policies to the Arab East grew steadily more burdensome. The U.S.S.R. replenished Egyptian supplies in the Yemeni campaign and reportedly absorbed the costs when Egypt proved unable to make even token payments of principal and interest on past credit purchases. More costly still, as we shall next see, was the massive rearmament of Egypt after its defeat in June 1967.

Toward a Fourth Round?

In the Six Day War, the Brezhnev-Kosygin team upheld Khrushchev's policy of avoiding a direct confrontation with the United States in the Middle East, and thus resisted the pressure of Russia's Arab clients to intervene. The Soviet leaders took no chances, for as soon as word of the outbreak of war reached Moscow, they put the hot line to use for the first time to notify President Johnson of their resolve to remain onlookers. Egypt's losses in the war were staggering—some 340 planes, or three-fourths of the best planes in their possession, and about six hundred tanks, or two-thirds of the total, to say nothing of vehicles and communications and other electronic equipment. Comparable Syrian loses were somewhat smaller—about fifty planes, or half its air force, and about fifty tanks, or one-quarter of those that were operational. The replacement value of the Egyptian equipment amounted to $500 million or more, and the Syrian to no less than $100 million.

To compensate for failure to go to the military aid of its clients and to retain its influence in the Arab zone, the U.S.S.R. apparently felt impelled to make good the Egyptian and Syrian losses at breakneck speed. It even sweetened the deliveries by adding such new items as the Styx short-range cruise missile which had not appeared in the Egyptian inventory before the war. The U.S.S.R. was suspected in the West of trying to exact greater political and military influence as the price for the crash replenishment. Along with the rearmament, particularly in Egypt, went increased numbers of Soviet technicians. For the first time in more than a decade, their presence aroused suspicions in the West of Soviet officers' assuming more than instructional and advisory functions and of the U.S.S.R.'s seeking base rights for Soviet ships and planes. At the same time the Soviet Union tried to wean Jordan and Lebanon away from their total reliance on Western arms suppliers.

The U.S.S.R. still held the supplier initiative in the arms races of the Arab-Israel zone. Moreover, the United States faced many new complications, for while its arms export policies remained reactive, the relatively stable Western supplier-client pattern of the second postwar decade changed dramatically at the start of the third. The American government, as we have seen, lost diplomatic flexibility by becoming a selective supplier to Arab clients and to Israel. France abandoned its role as special arms purveyor to Israel and began courting Israel's adversaries. As political ties between the United States and the major powers of Western Europe loosened, they became competitive arms exporters for economic as well as political reasons. At home, moreover, the Johnson Administration's handling of arms exports came under Congressional fire as part of a larger revolt over foreign policy; though provoked by the war in Vietnam, the Congressional revolt also affected American action in the Arab-Israel zone.

The United States and the U.S.S.R. were playing their own game. The Soviet Union seemed determined to polarize the suppliers and the clients in the Arab-Israel zone by establishing itself as the exclusive champion of the Arab states and the United States as the exclusive champion of Israel. These tactics the United States countered with its own, by continuing to furnish military supplies to selected Arab states along with Israel; and the Soviet-American bid for Arab favor threatened to polarize the Arab East. Neither superpower was responsible for the disunity in the Arab world, but their military aid policies tended to harden the divisions. What is more germane to the present analysis, Soviet action and American counteraction were stimulating the interlocking Arab-Israel arms races.

No less disconcerting was France's abrupt repudiation of the entente with Israel. The predicted shift from a pro-Israel to a pro-Arab stance, once the Algerian dispute was settled, took five years

to materialize. Nevertheless, France did begin to look for Arab customers as early as 1965, offering planes and other equipment to Lebanon and Jordan at competitive prices. Nothing came of these first
efforts. Up to June 1967, France filled Israel's orders and allowed it
to buy spare parts in unlimited quantities. But on the outbreak of
war, President de Gaulle announced a policy of neutrality and suspended shipments of arms to all belligerents. Since Israel was still
France's only customer in the zone, the net effect of the embargo
was to deprive Israel of its primary source of sophisticated weaponry and to send it scurrying for substitute suppliers. In the spring
of 1968, moreover, France agreed to sell to Iraq three squadrons of
Mirage Vs, without lifting the embargo on Israel.

The French attempt to develop a market in the Arab East was
motivated in part by de Gaulle's desire to liberate France from all
forms of dependence on the United States, economic as well as military and diplomatic. France was anxious to capture a share of the
worldwide non-Communist arms market in sophisticated weaponry, particularly planes, which the United States had substantially
cornered. If successful, the French aircraft industry stood to earn
handsome profits. Even Britain, the steadfast ally of the United
States in the Middle East, entered the competition after it set up in
June 1965 its own government arms sales agency, corresponding to
the office of International Logistics Negotiations in the Pentagon,
which managed foreign arms sales for the Department of Defense.
The American government was investing from $3 billion to $4 billion each year in weapons research and engineering, while France
and Britain together with West Germany were investing less than
$1 billion. The annual exports of arms from the United States were
averaging $3 billion by 1966, two-thirds in sales and the rest in
grants. France, Britain, and even West Germany could hardly
compete with such a giant and thus were driven to seeking entry
into marginal markets, such as those of the Middle East. The
Western economic rivalry thus also tended to enliven the Arab-
Israel arms races.

The United States could await further difficulties in the early
1970s as the NATO members of Western Europe phased out their
obsolescent tanks and planes. It was estimated that by the early
1970s some five to seven thousand M-47 and M-48 tanks and a
thousand jet planes, mostly F-104s, would glut the surplus market,
which caters to the nonindustrial states and is managed as a rule
not by governments but by private middlemen. The United States

concluded end-use agreements with all its NATO allies, binding them not to dispose of American arms, once obsolescent, without the express approval of the United States. Similar arrangements were made with foreign manufacturers who produce American weapons under license. The kind of problem that might arise was demonstrated in 1966 when West Germany agreed to sell ninety Canadian-built F-86 Sabrejets ostensibly to Iran but in reality to Pakistan, which was striving to evade the United States arms embargo slapped on the subcontinent at the time of the Kashmir war in September 1965. This evasion suggested to some Congressional observers that the United States might not be able to exercise sufficient controls over end use when the surplus stocks began to bulge. Besides, other Western suppliers, such as West Germany, Italy, Canada, Sweden, Switzerland, and Belgium, might also begin to be attracted to potential sales in the Arab-Israel zone.

There was the further danger of economic pressures, for the United States in the 1960s increasingly shifted from grants to sales in its foreign military aid program. This was designed in part to help balance American international payments. The offset agreements with West Germany after 1961, for example, were intended to provide the United States with the necessary hard currency to defray the costs of maintaining American troops in that country. In purchasing so many American arms, West Germany was under mounting temptation to realize a return on earlier equipment now becoming obsolescent. This accounted in part for West German willingness to sell Sabrejets to Pakistan, even though the sale violated the end-use agreement. Similarly, United States sales to Saudi Arabia seemed to be motivated in part by purely economic considerations, since the Department of Defense tended to view the oil-rich kingdom as one that could afford to pay for expensive air-defense equipment.

Given the Soviet inclination to coddle its Arab clients and to wean away other Arab states from the West, given the economic rivalry among Western suppliers with a potential enlargement of their number, and given also the prospective opening of the surplus market in the early 1970s, the likelihood of framing arms export controls in the Arab-Israel zone did not look promising in the late 1960s. Among the five principles of Arab-Israel peace that President Johnson enunciated in June 1967 was one that dealt with the "danger of the Middle Eastern arms race of the last twelve years." In a broadcast to his nation, the President recognized that the responsibility must rest not only on those in the area, but on the larger states outside the area. We believe that scarce resources could be used much better for technical and economic development. We have always opposed this arms race, and our own military shipments to the area have consequently been severely limited. . . .

As a beginning, I should like to propose that the United Nations immediately call upon all of its members to report all shipments of all military arms in this area and to keep those shipments on file for all the peoples of the world to observe.[23]

The President appealed to Russia for joint action in imposing such restraints, repeating the request to Prime Minister Kosygin at Glassboro a few days later. Bent on rearming Egypt and Syria and trying to win new clients in the Arab East, the Soviet government rejected the President's proposal, and Secretary Rusk in July explained that without Soviet cooperation the United States would have to continue its policy of arming friendly Arab states as well as Israel; the Department of State accordingly lifted the embargo against Israel and selected Arab countries[24] in October 1967 and against Jordan before the year's end. Because of Soviet opposition, the unanimous resolution adopted by the Security Council in November 1967 made no reference whatsoever to the regulation of arms exports to the Arab-Israel zone.

The quickening of the races thus seemed assured. The United States could not take unilateral action, not even in reporting, for this might stimulate the races, not slow them down. Mention of sales to any states in the area was bound to encourage the others to seek compensatory deliveries. Moreover, if the United States refused to provide weaponry, the Middle East states could easily procure supplies elsewhere. Clearly, the U.S.S.R. was not yet under compulsion to stop its dumping policies and agree to some form of regulation. However, even if the U.S.S.R. and the United States were to concur in such controls, they would still have to persuade other suppliers in the West and even in the Communist sphere (notably, China) to make the arrangements firm.

26

CHANGING MILITARY POLITICS
AND UNITED STATES OPTIONS

The Arab-Israel arms races in the 1960s were the most feverish in the nonindustrial world. The replacement value of equipment lost in the Six Day War probably exceeded $750 million, and much of it was replaced in less than six months. The entanglement of the United States in these double-tiered races that were threatening to get out of hand was only one of many symptoms indicating that American military policies in the Middle East were losing their relevance. The policies had been framed in the first two postwar decades, when bipolarity conditioned international politics the world over, including the Middle East. By 1968, despite the invasion of Czechoslovakia, the bipolar security systems were visibly falling apart. Soviet perplexities over Chairman Mao and Communist China matched American perplexities over General de Gaulle and France's Fifth Republic.

The military policies of the U.S.S.R. and of the United States toward the Middle East had originally been designed to serve the interests of the superpowers in their global competition. So long as one Cold War contestant persisted in pursuing these policies, its adversary had little choice but to do the same. Sticking to such a course, however, when the underlying structure of international politics in the Middle East no longer sustained it, basically served the interests of neither the United States nor Russia.

This was convincingly shown in the spring of 1967 by the Soviet brinkmanship that encouraged Egypt and Syria to bait Israel for the manifest purpose of gaining Soviet influence in the zone by embarrassing the United States. The weakening of ties with Arab military clients, especially after the near-destruction of the kingdom of Jordan, indeed embarrassed the United States. But these were dubious Soviet gains, for the Arab regimes that were friendly to the United States before the Six Day War were still friendly after it. The U.S.S.R., which did not expect the war, failed to rescue its friends from disaster when war broke out. Instead, Russia sat nervously on the United Nations sidelines, seeking to avoid a military confrontation with the United States, while Israel, a Western arms client, thrashed into submission Egypt and Syria, Russia's oldest arms clients in the Middle East. The lightning pace of the war gave the General Assembly and the Security Council no time to interpose the United Nations between the belligerents, as had been done in 1956–57, when Israel was forced back to the earlier armistice lines once the U.N. Emergency Force was installed on the Egyptian side and Israel was assured free transit through the Straits of Tiran. In June 1967, even the cease-fires that the United Nations negotiated came after Israel's military triumph, this time without extraregional participation in the fighting. For at least a year thereafter, Russia could not maneuver resolutions through either principal organ of the world body that would induce Israel to retire from the occupied Arab territories without firm security guarantees.

The United States position was also weakened. Ever since 1950 the United States had firmly opposed the use of force between states in the Middle East or violation of their boundaries. The United States support of the political independence and territorial integrity of the states in the Arab-Israel zone was later reaffirmed on many occasions, and again by President Johnson in May and June of 1967. Yet as the principal guardian of peace in the Middle East, the United States could not prevent either the Arab action or the Israel reaction that brought on the war.

The first two postwar decades had been characterized by the struggles for independence and the progressive transfer of sovereignty from Britain and France to their wards. The two processes, during the Cold War, gave the Soviet Union a psychological advantage among nationalists in the dependencies, since the departing imperial powers were allies of the United States. This tended to offset the psychological advantage of the United States in the frontier zone, where memories of Soviet threats and pressures immediately after World War II faded only slowly. By the late 1960s, the only dependencies left in the Middle East were the quasi-protectorates in the Persian Gulf, and Britain announced its forthcoming retirement from the last imperial outpost in the Middle East no later than 1971. Now that disimperialism had run its course and the U.S.S.R. was lifting the pressures on its southern neighbors, the old psychological advantages on both sides were dissolving, even though Arabs still condemned the United States for favoritism to Israel, and the invasion of Czechoslovakia in 1968 rekindled, in the frontier zone, fears of Russian expansion.

The Soviet Union along with the United States, moreover, became burdened with commitments in the Middle East and lost its freedom of choice. In becoming an arms purveyor to Pakistan in 1968, the U.S.S.R. alienated India, much as the United States had done fourteen years earlier. In the Cyprus dispute of 1967, Moscow guardedly cultivated Turkey and turned a less than attentive ear to the appeals of Greece and the Greek Cypriotes. With the impending departure of Britain from the Persian Gulf, Russia would have to choose between Iran and the Arab states in their likely scarmble for influence over the shaykhdoms after the British withdrawal. Even the significance of the Suez Canal in the strategic calculations of the outside powers was changing. The peacetime strategic value of the waterway to Britain steadily diminished, after surrender of the canal base in 1954. Following the Six Day War the value to Britain and Western Europe of the canal as a trade route also diminished, because crude oil, which accounted for more than two-thirds of the traffic, was being transported in ever-larger tankers around the Cape of Good Hope. Meanwhile, the Suez Canal was growing more and more useful to the Soviet Union for commerce with East Africa and South Asia and potentially also for the mobility of the expanding Soviet fleet. Russia's growing interest in the canal was bound to condition its later policies toward the eastern Mediterranean.

For Russia, straddling issues in the Middle East was a relatively new experience. For the United States, it was not. Throughout the region, except in Turkey and Afghanistan where the point was not relevant, the United States strove from its first acceptance of commitments in the Middle East soon after World War II to find a middle position between the imperial powers and the nationalists, and in the Arab-Israel zone also between the Arab states and Israel. In the 1960s the United States was still trying to establish itself as a friendly neutral in all regional quarrels in which it had an interest and which by then almost invariably involved only local states. In the Cyprus dispute of 1967, Turkey and Greece, both American allies, were principals, and the United States mediated between them, and between both and the Greek Cypriotes, to avert war. Similarly, in the irrepressible Arab-Israel conflict and its many ramifications, including the arms races, the United States sought credentials of nonpartisanship by offering material favors to both sides. But the unqualified Soviet endorsement of the Arab cause compelled the United States to engage in a juggling act. Somewhat less complicated was its support of those Arab states under attack by Soviet Arab clients, because in a crunch the United States helped its own clients forthrightly. Yet even in this contest, at least in the first half of the 1960s, the United States made the grand gesture of liberal economic aid to Egypt, despite recurrent Egyptian propagandist forays against Arab friends of the United States.

The military policies of the regional and extraregional powers were shaping the political systems in the Middle East. With the exception of Pakistan, Israel, Turkey, and Tunisia, armies in the region were needed primarily for internal security. Before World War II, the governments in countries with a large beduin population faced continual resistance from the tribal areas. As the governments modernized their armies in the postwar years, they used the armies to centralize the administration. No sooner had the incumbent regimes pacified the beduin districts than they encountered new resistance in the enlarging cities from students, workers, and semiurbanized peasants.

The military influence was most visible, however, in those countries where the soldiers seized power. As we have seen, there was some movement in and out of the class of military republics in the second postwar decade. But the group finally shook down to a cluster of Arab states—Egypt, Syria, Iraq, and Algeria. (Though also a military republic by name, the Yemen Arab Republic was still too precarious and primitive to be classed with the others.) Here, military oligarchies replaced landed oligarchies, but only in Egypt and Algeria were army officers systematically infused into the bureaucracies and into the multiplying state-owned enterprises. The constitutions of the second republics of Turkey and Pakistan were framed under the close supervision of military officers, who continued to view themselves as custodians of the new regimes, even though they exercised no more than residual powers. In the modernizing monarchies, the kings employed their armed forces to reinforce royal authority as they experimented with programs of economic and social modernization. By contrast, Saudi Arabia and Libya, as traditional monarchies, were still only grudgingly engaged in military modernization, although at the start of the third postwar decade they began investing heavily in ultramodern air defense. The oil-rich kings could afford the high expense, which in part at least seemed motivated by economic considerations of the suppliers. In all authoritarian regimes, whether military republican or monarchical, the rulers governed with the aid of apolitical technicians or technocrats and suppressed past and future civilian politicians.

After the restoration of civilian rule, ironically, Sudan expanded its armed forces and defense allocations, because of the failure to reach an accommodation with the non-Muslim tribesmen in the three rebellious southern provinces, or to reimpose the government's authority there. Tunisia remained the lowest military spender in the region but seemed likely to gain on its rivals. At the other end of the military spending scale stood Israel, which was investing on a per capita basis more money each year than any other state in the region except Kuwayt. Although the Israel Defense Forces after June 1967 were engaged in administering occupied territories, they were chiefly absorbed even then with external defense.

The military republics—Algeria, Egypt, Iraq, and Syria—were the most prominent candidates for military coups d'état in the late 1960s. All faced rising domestic opposition, and none could relax its vigilance. Like most authoritarian regimes, moreover, they were plagued by problems of succession, which authoritarian monarchies could often escape. This is not to suggest that coups d'état would not take place elsewhere in the region. Clearly, monarchies would also be overthrown in the future, as they had been in the past, and among the likely candidates in the late 1960s were Libya, on the death of the septuagenarian King Muhammad Idris I, the dynasty's founder; and Jordan, unless King Husayn regained possession of the West Bank.

The rival military policies of the outside powers, particularly the United States and the Soviet Union, must be evaluated in the perspective of the region's heterogeneity. The policies of the two superpowers were variable in the Middle East as a whole. In the Arab-Israel zone, the United States and Russia avoided formal alliances. Otherwise their styles differed. The U.S.S.R. engaged in arms dumping in selected Arab countries; the United States first encouraged its Western European allies to engage in, before turning itself to, pre-emptive and balancing arms sales to friendly Arab states and to Israel. The Soviet arms policies were designed to stir up tensions, to polarize the Arab states and Israel, and to promote a settlement favorable to the Arabs, in order to discredit the United States as the principal guardian of peace in the zone. The United States, however, tried to dampen the tensions, to prevent Arab-Israel polarization, and to urge an equitable settlement. The Soviet-American rivalry in the Maghrib reflected dimly the rivalry in the

Arab-Israel zone, with the superpowers avoiding alliances, the U.S.S.R. pouring large amounts of modern weaponry into Algeria and trying to entice Morocco, and the United States falling back on pre-emptive and balancing weapons sales to Tunisia and Morocco.

In the frontier zone, the United States concluded individual bilateral alliances with Turkey, Iran, and Pakistan over and above their participation in Western-sponsored collective security systems. The Soviet Union by the late 1960s had abandoned its bludgeoning tactics in favor of courting the friendship of the United States allies in the Middle East, which in any case were themselves beginning to loosen their ties to the West. The United States was the major arms supplier to Turkey and Iran, although it suspended military aid to Pakistan in September 1965 following the outbreak of war with India over Kashmir. In Afghanistan, the Soviet Union continued its role as exclusive arms supplier. The CENTO countries in the mid-1960s began accepting credits from the Soviet Union for specific development projects, and Iran became the first of the three to buy military equipment, although the shah authorized the purchase only of nonsensitive items. After 1965, Pakistan turned to Communist China and France and finally to the U.S.S.R. to satisfy its demands for weapons. The superpowers were becoming competitive in the frontier zone in policing and peacekeeping. In January 1966 at Tashkent, Premier Kosygin mediated a settlement of the Kashmir war between Pakistan and India. It was the United States that resolved the latest Cyprus crisis of November 1967, when President Johnson sent Cyrus Vance, a former Assistant Secretary of Defense, to mediate the dispute.

The primary military-political objective of the United States in the Middle East was deterrence of the Soviet Union, as reflected in the postwar buildup of the Sixth Fleet, the alliances with the CENTO states, the SAC and U-2 bases, the erection of electronic surveillance systems, and the emplacement of IRBMs. Soviet military policies after the mid-1950s were designed to pare down the American strategic advantage in the Mediterranean and the Middle East by undermining United States influence in the Arab and frontier areas, by establishing a continuous naval presence in the Mediterranean, and by seeking informal naval and air rights in Egypt and Syria. The military planners in Moscow clearly viewed the Mediterranean and the Middle East as falling within the Soviet security sphere of influence.

Behind the military rivalry lay qualitative choices. In selecting Middle East countries as candidates for aid, the United States did not apply the criterion of political freedom. Most governments in the Middle East were authoritarian, and therefore politically repressive. Many of them became American military clients, such as the modernizing monarchies. Yet significantly, all Middle East countries with democratic systems were also military clients of the United States. The only exception in 1968 was Sudan, which began buying weapons from the U.S.S.R. after the Six Day War. But the growth of Sudan's precarious quasi-democratic regime was stunted by the unending civil war between the Muslim north and the non-Muslim south. By supporting the authoritarian regimes and strengthening their armies, the United States helped them become even more repressive, or at least more efficiently repressive. Nevertheless, at the same time, the United States prodded these regimes to the extent possible into initiating economic and social reforms. The shah of Iran might never have embarked on his White Revolution without American insistence. The economic expansion of Jordan before June 1967 might never have taken place if the United States had not helped develop tourism and build the East Ghawr canal; however, the Six Day War wiped out all the gains and even threatened the survival of the Hashimi dynasty.

Soviet military aid to Afghanistan, it will be recalled, was modest and was accompanied by much larger economic aid without any effort to undermine the monarchy or socialize the economy. What is more, the United States and the Soviet Union worked in tandem to help modernize the Afghan economy and society. Into the Arab countries that became Soviet military clients, however, Russia pumped huge quantities of modern weapons, far beyond the early capacity of the receiving states to assimilate. Although the arms were sold at large discount, and sometimes even given away, their monetary value invariably exceeded the credits given for economic projects. The acquisition of sophisticated military hardware in large quantities proved costly to maintain and inured Russia's Arab friends to seeking ever more costly weapons, thus diverting valuable resources from economic development. Of greater importance, the Soviet Union encouraged its Arab military clients (except Yemen) to expand their socialist experiments. As an imported doctrine and mode of organization, socialism in the 1960s took no firmer hold than had democracy in an earlier period. The recurrent coups in Syria and Iraq and military rule in Algeria also disrupted the continuity, further weakening the socialist programs.

The Egyptian experiment in socialism, which seemed to be making measurable progress in the early 1960s with American economic assistance, began to run into roadblocks, even before the United States terminated its economic assistance. Part of the trouble lay in the expensive military imports and abortive but expensive research and engineering projects for the construction of missiles and supersonic planes. The Six Day War dealt a stunning blow to a socialist economy that was already in a desperate condition.

The Arab military republics came into being with promises of social revolution, only to impose greater political repression on their citizens than that of the replaced regimes, and the net effect of their economic and social policies in the late 1960s seemed retrogressive. Admittedly, these developments could not all be attributed to the Soviet Union. Yet Moscow along with its Arab clients never tired of advertising these states as the revolutionary states of the Middle East and of claiming a monopoly of progressive policies. These claims, it should be noted, were directed not against Israel, which was charged with being a tool of American imperialism, but against the other Arab states and Iran, which were dismissed as reactionary because of their ties to the United States and other Western powers.

Did the United States, in this situation, have any options? There were many Americans who advocated unilateral American disengagement from the Middle East. They saw the United States saddled with major or exclusive obligations for upholding Western interests there, for keeping the peace among the new states, and for deterring Soviet aggression. They were tired of the prolonged and costly war in Vietnam and saw many Vietnams hidden in the corners of the Middle East. Consequently, they urged the unconditional withdrawal of the Sixth Fleet from the Mediterranean, the repudiation of American alliances and commitments in the Middle East, and the cessation of arms exports to the region. Such drastic policies, of course, could hardly contribute either to the security of the United States or to international or regional peace. They would constitute, in effect, writing off the entire postwar investment of the United States government in economic and military aid to the region, which probably amounted to some $20 billion, if the cost of maintaining the Sixth Fleet were included. Clearly, with tough bargainers such as the Russians, it would make little sense for the United States to surrender any position of strength in the Middle East, and therefore of annoyance to the Soviet Union, without getting a concrete return. Hence, it was in the United States interest to hold on to these positions as long as the rivalry continued, and later to use them in the search for agreed arrangements with the U.S.S.R. and other extra-regional powers interested in the Middle East.

Indeed, unless the United States and the U.S.S.R. jointly took positive action to end the Cold War in the Middle East, it was certain to persist, despite the progressive decay in the 1960s of the bipolar coalitions that each superpower led. The lingering Cold War in the region was reflected in the survival of the old superpower policies. As early as the mid-1950s the United States had moved step by step from collective Western responsibility to a unilateral American responsibility for peacekeeping in the Middle East and for checking the expansion of Soviet influence there. The Soviet Union for its part was still conducting itself as if it were determined to drive the United States out. The Soviet policies seemed to reflect a conviction of Soviet security planners that they could not assure the defense of the U.S.S.R. without Soviet domination of the Middle East and the Mediterranean. The naval buildup was designed to achieve equality with and preferably superiority to the Sixth Fleet; and the arms dumping, to undermine American prestige and influence in the Arab area.

Meanwhile, in the frontier zone the movement toward an accommodation in the late 1960s seemed fairly steady. The movement had begun a decade earlier in Afghanistan, which did not request the United States to terminate its educational mission even after the U.S.S.R. became the kingdom's exclusive military supplier. The two superpowers, as we have seen, even framed complementary economic and technical aid programs in Afghanistan. This was followed, beginning in the mid-1960s, by the Soviet cultivation of friendly relations with the CENTO countries. The Russian aim, undeniably, was to end the alliances of Turkey, Iran, and Pakistan with the United States. With the Soviet offers of credit to the three American allies or with the elaborate plans for trade between the U.S.S.R. and Iran, the United States did not attempt to interfere, although it did not fail to take note of the implications of Russia's becoming an arms supplier to Iran and later also to Pakistan. The frontier zone, in brief, was the one section of the Middle East where the bipolar rivalry had softened into an informal but unstable limited détente. This relaxation did not mean that the Cold War had ended even there. It merely meant that the superpowers were experimenting with possible modes of accommodation, while continuing the Cold War. This was just as true of the frontier states themselves. Thus, despite the one-year notice in 1968 that the agreement for the United States communications base at Peshawar would not be renewed and despite the conclusion at about the same time of a major arms agreement with the U.S.S.R., the government of Pakistan did not repudiate its alliance with the United States.

Many American and Western diplomats hoped that the Soviet-American experience in Afghanistan after 1956 and elsewhere in the frontier zone after the mid-1960s would suggest lines of desirable political action in the Arab-Israel zone and in the Maghrib in the 1970s. These hopes, however, were dashed—at least temporarily—in August 1968 when Russia and four of its Warsaw Pact allies occupied Czechoslovakia. The Soviet resort to force reawakened dormant fears and suspicions of Soviet intentions not only in the West and among Middle East states friendly to the West, but even among Soviet military clients in the region. Nevertheless, the limited détente, as it was unfolding in the frontier zone before the Czech crisis, furnished the two superpowers ample opportunity to ascertain the uses, the limits, and the costs of a partial accommodation.

Until mutual Soviet-American confidence was restored, it could safely be assumed that in the nuclear stalemate the superpowers, as in the past, would seek to avoid direct military confrontation in the Middle East and would oppose nuclear proliferation into the region. Still, it should be noted that the dangers of an accidental confrontation were multiplying with the secret Soviet maneuvers to build land-based naval air facilities in Egypt and Syria and probably also in Algeria. Because of the deepening Soviet military presence in the Mediterranean and in selected littoral states, particularly in the Arab East, the risk of Soviet involvement in a possible fourth round with Israel was growing. Such an involvement, if not resisted, would tilt the military balance in the region unmistakably in the Soviet favor and, if resisted, could develop into a military confrontation.

The Soviet-American avoidance of a confrontation and the opposition of the superpowers to nuclear proliferation were clearly concerned more with peace among the major powers than with peace in the Middle East. American and Soviet tactics were thus reminiscent of the tactics of the Concert of Europe in the nineteenth century, which invariably aimed at avoiding war in Europe. The key to successful Concert diplomacy, however, lay in spreading

the risks and responsibilities by internationalizing both and by admitting the Ottoman Empire to active participation in the negotiations and in the agreed arrangements.

Perhaps the time would approach in the 1970s when multilateral diplomacy might once again be tried in the Middle East.
The lingering Cold War in the region, even after the end of bipo-
larity, suggested that both the United States and the Soviet Union
were lagging behind in the adjustment of their policies to the
evolving realities. So far as the Western arms policies in the region
were concerned, the system of supplier-client relations had already
eroded. In the Arab-Israel zone, as we have seen, the United States
became a major supplier, while France, after terminating its entente with Israel, was becoming a free-lance supplier. France was
also proclaiming its economic and political independence in the
Middle East, as elsewhere in the world. Britain, too, seemed to be
moving cautiously in the same direction, with its announced departure from the Persian Gulf no later than 1971. If the Soviet Union
were to begin to sense that its role as arms provider and its quest
for naval superiority in the Mediterranean had built-in limitations,
it might be willing also to recognize the value of internationalizing
the problems in the Middle East: of instituting, jointly with the
Middle East states concerned, an arrangement for arms control
and disarmament in the region and of stabilizing the Soviet-
American naval competition and perhaps even reaching an accord
on naval disarmament. There was no assurance, however, that
the United States or the other major powers would seize these
opportunities, which represented one tangible hope of forging a
stable system for international and regional military politics in the
Middle East.

NOTES

CHAPTER 1. *American Entanglement in Three-dimensional Politics*

1. See, for example, Institute for Strategic Studies, *Adelphi Papers*, No. 28, "Arms to Developing Countries, 1945–1965," by John L. Sutton and Geoffrey Kemp (London, October, 1966), pp. 27–28 and tables and graphs on pp. 35–45; see also United States, 90th Cong., 1st sess., Senate Committee on Foreign Relations, Sub-committe on American Republics Affairs, "Survey of the Alliance for Progress: The Latin American Military," by Edwin Lieuwin (Washington, 9 October 1967), particularly appendixes, pp. 33–36.
2. Such as: S. E. Finer, *The Man on Horseback* (New York, 1962); Samuel P. Huntington, "Patterns of Violence in World Politics," in *Changing Patterns of Military Politics*, edited by Huntington (New York, 1962), pp. 17–50; John L. Johnson, editor, *The Role of the Military in Underdeveloped Areas* (Princeton, 1962); Edwin Lieuwen, *Arms and Politics in Latin America* (2nd Edition; New York, 1961); Sydney N. Fisher, editor, *The Military in the Middle East: Problems in Society and Government* (Columbus, 1963).

CHAPTER 2. *The Islamic Tradition*

1. Ibn Khaldun, *The Muqaddimah: An Introduction to History*, translated from the Arabic by Franz Rosenthal (New York, 1958), vol. 1, pp. 257–58.
2. Bernard Lewis, *The Emergence of Modern Turkey* (London, 1961), p. 23.
3. A. D. Alderson, *The Structure of the Ottoman Dynasty* (Oxford, 1956), p. 27.
4. Edward G. Browne, *A Literary History of Persia*: vol. 4, *Modern Times, 1500–1924* (Cambridge, 1930), p. 98.
5. *The Cambridge History of India*: vol. 4, *The Mughul Empire*, edited by Sir Richard Burn (Cambridge, 1937), p. 252.
6. *Ibid.*, pp. 232–33.

CHAPTER 3. *The Beginnings of Military Modernization*

1. On the Wahhabiyah, see chapter 13 below.
2. This concept was used by Sultan Selim III a generation earlier; see below, pp. 16–17. In all the major Muslim states in the nineteenth century,

Nizam came to mean the "modernized" regular or standing army, as opposed to tribal and other irregulars on whom Muslim rulers had traditionally relied.
3. As cited and translated by Roderic H. Davison, *Reform in the Ottoman Empire, 1856–1876* (Princeton, 1963), p. 31.
4. George N. Curzon, *Persia and the Persian Question* (London, 1892), vol. 1, p. 589.
5. "Makhzen," *Encyclopedia of Islam*, 1st ed. (EI¹), vol. 3, p. 170.

CHAPTER 4. *European Imperial Styles*

1. J. C. Hurewitz, *Diplomacy in the Near and Middle East, A Documentary Record, 1914–1956* (Princeton, 1956), vol. 2, p. 91, hereafter cited as *Diplomacy*.
2. From *ibid.*, p. 204.
3. An English translation of the preferential alliance with Lebanon appears in Hurewitz, *Diplomacy*, vol. 2, pp. 211–14; the French text of the alliance with Syria may be found in France, Ministry of Foreign Affairs, *Rapport à la Société des Nations sur la situation de la Syrie et du Liban*, 1936, pp. 201–28.
4. As cited in George Kirk, *The Middle East in the War* (London, 1953), p. 108.

CHAPTER 5. *Military Politics and the Lingering Cold War*

1. *The Department of State Bulletin*, vol. 16 (23 March, 1946), pp. 536–37.
2. Prime Minister Churchill conceded in May 1953 that the cost of maintaining the troops at Suez was probably "over £50 [$140] million a year," House of Commons, *Parliamentary Debates*, Weekly Hansard, no. 225 (11 May 1953), col. 890. But this did not begin to take into account the cost of modernizing the inventory list of the depots in a period of rapidly changing weapons systems.
3. *The Department of State Bulletin*, vol. 22 (5 June 1950), p. 886. These principles later found their way into such instruments as: the United States–Saudi air base (Dhahran) agreement of 18 June 1951 [United States, *Treaties and other International Acts Series*, No. 2290]; the Four-Power proposals for a Middle East command, 13 October and 10 November 1951 [*The Department of State Bulletin*, vol. 25 (22 October 1951), pp. 647–48 and (19 November 1951), pp. 817–18]; the United States Military Assistance Agreement with Iraq, 21 April 1954 [United States, *Treaties and other International Acts Series*, No. 3108]; The United States Military Assistance Agreement with Pakistan, 19 May 1954 [*ibid.*, No. 2976].
4. *The Department of State Bulletin*, vol. 25 (19 November 1951), pp. 817–18.
5. *Ibid.*, vol. 28, pp. 831–35.

6. From the text of Gamal 'Abd al-Nasir's speech, 26 July 1956, announcing the nationalization of the Suez Canal Company, *Documents on International Affairs, 1956* (London, 1959), pp. 85–86, hereafter cited as *DIA*.
7. From the text in Hurewitz, *Diplomacy*, vol. 2, pp. 402–5.
8. From the text of 'Abd al-Nasir's speech of 26 July 1956, in *DIA*, 1956, p. 92.
9. Texts of the Eisenhower message and the joint resolution in *Documents on American Foreign Relations, 1957* (New York, 1958), pp. 195–204, hereafter cited as *DAFR*.
10. The first and third published Soviet notes of 11 February and 3 September 1957 may be found in *DAFR*, 1957, pp. 218–23 and 227–30; the second note of 19 April 1956 appears in Department of State, *United States Policy in the Middle East, September 1956–June 1957: Documents* (Washington, August 1957), Near and Middle East Series No. 25, Department of State Publications 6505, pp. 81–85.
11. Text of United States note of 11 March 1957 in *The Department of State Bulletin*, vol. 36 (1 April 1957), pp. 523–24; reproduced in *DAFR*, 1957, pp. 223–26.
12. *Ibid.*, p. 234, 237, 248, and 251.
13. *Ibid.*, pp. 245 and 343. In the letter to Eisenhower, Khrushchev also observed that "we do not understand by what right the United States government assumes the mantle of the arbiter and judge, and maintains that there has been some kind of indirect aggression in Lebanon"; *ibid.*, p. 344.
14. *DAFR*, 1962, p. 393.

CHAPTER 6. *Armies in Postwar Politics*

1. From the text of the coup declaration in *The New York Times*, 15 July 1958.
2. Samuel P. Huntington, "Patterns of Violence in World Politics," in Huntington, editor, *Changing Patterns of Military Politics*, (New York, 1962), pp. 32–40.

CHAPTER 7. *Egypt: Military Rule in a Rapidly Changing Society*

1. From the text in Hurewitz, *Diplomacy*, vol. 2, p. 204.
2. Charles Issawi, *Egypt in Revolution: An Economic Analysis* (London, 1963), pp. 51–52.
3. United Arab Republic, Information Department, *The Charter* (Cairo, n.d.), p. 43.
4. *Ibid.*, pp. 29–32.
5. U.A.R., Department of Statistics and Census, *nashrah ihsa muwazzafi al-hukumah wa al-hayat ('an al-halah fi awwal nawfimbir sanah 1961)* [Report: Statistics of Employees of the Government and the Agencies on 1 November 1961] (Cairo, 1962), pp. 52–53; as cited in Richard Hrair Dekmejian, *The Dynamics of the Egyptian Political System: The Inter-*

action of Charisma, Ideology, and Institutions, 1952–1966 (unpublished doctoral dissertation, Columbia University, 1966), pp. 235–36. The 1964 statistics on provincial governors, *ibid.*, p. 243.

6. Khalid Muhyi al-Din, a leftist member of the original junta who had fallen into disgrace in 1954 for siding with Nagib, was partly rehabilitated when he became a deputy in the National Assembly a decade later. In 1964 the only living members of the ten who survived Nagib and who no longer sat in government councils were Gamal Salim (dropped in 1956) and 'Abd al-Latif al-Baghdadi and Kamal al-Din Husayn (dropped in 1964).

7. As cited in *Survey of International Affairs* [SIA], *1951* (London, 1952), p. 268.

8. *Parliamentary Debates, Commons*, vol. 491 (30 July 1951), cols. 2649 (Foreign Secretary Herbert Morrison).

CHAPTER 8. *Military Roulette: Syria and Iraq*

1. *The Times* (London), 23 November 1963.

CHAPTER 10. *Junior Partners: Pakistan and Algeria*

1. In Syria, after the overturn of Za'im in August 1949, "civilian" political systems were created but they functioned on the sufferance of the military commanders: Colonel Sami al-Hinnawi (August-December 1949) and Colonel Adib al-Shishakli (December 1949–November 1951). Similarly after the removal of Shishakli in February 1954, army officers dominated the "civilian" regimes that followed until the merger with Egypt four years later, and again after the secession from the U.A.R. But none of these regimes stuck.

2. Text in Colonel Mohammad Ahmad, *My Chief* (Lahore, 1960), pp. 86–93.

3. *The New York Times*, 10 October 1958.

4. *The Times* (London), 16 October 1958.

5. From text in Mohammad Ayub Khan, *Speeches and Statements*, vol. 1 (n.p., 1961), p. 6.

6. Decree No. 62–306 of 19 March 1962; English translation in *Texts of Declarations Drawn up in Common Agreement at Evian, March 18, 1962 by the Delegations of the Government of the French Republic and the Algerian National Liberation Front* (Ambassade de France, Service de Presse et d'Information, New York, 1962), pp. 54–60.

7. Boumedienne was the colonel's *nom de guerre*; his given name is bracketed.

8. *The New York Times*, 3 July 1962.

9. The same principle was also set forth in the preamble.

CHAPTER 11. *Concealed Partners: Pakistan and Turkey*

1. Mohammad Ayub Khan, "Pakistan Perspective," *Foreign Affairs*, vol. 38 (July 1960), p. 550.

2. *Ibid.*, p. 551.

3. Ayub assumed this rank in October 1959.
4. *The Times* (London), 12 July 1960.
5. See chapter 24, pp. 7–8.
6. From the translated text of the communiqué in *The New York Times,* 28 May 1960.
7. After the formation of the National Security Council, for which the new constitution (Article 111) provided, its secretary general also sat in the SMC. The NSC integrated civilian ministerial and military representation for "the purpose of assisting in the making of decisions on national security and coordination."
8. *The New York Times* (Dana Adams Schmidt), 16 June 1961.
9. It is worth noting that the largest number of former officers who became candidates for the legislature ran, not on the JP ticket (only 44), but on that of the Republican People's Nation Party (60). Of the remainder 33 were presented by the New Turkey Party and 28 by the RPP. Of the 36 who were elected, 21 were returned to the National Assembly and the others to the Senate; 16 belonged to the JP, 8 to the RPNP, 7 to the RPP and 5 to the NTP.

CHAPTER 12. *Libya: Triumph of Sanusi Leadership*

1. E. E. Evans-Pritchard, *The Sanusi of Cyrenaica* (Oxford, 1949), pp. 79–80.
2. Great Britain, *Parliamentary Debates,* Commons, 5th series, vol. 377, col. 78.

CHAPTER 13. *Saudi Arabia: The Peninsula Under Najdi Rule*

1. H. St. John Philby, *Sa 'udi Arabia* (New York, 1955), p. 262.

CHAPTER 15. *An American Client: Iran*

1. In the absence of firm data, the statistical information on the tribes must be considered informed guesses at best.
2. From the text in Hurewitz, *Diplomacy,* vol. 2, pp. 233–34.
3. From the text of the Tehran Declaration, *ibid.,* p. 238.
4. T. H. Vail Motter, *The Middle East Theatre: The Persian Corridor and Aid to Russia,* a volume in the official history under the general title of *United States Army in World War II* (Washington, 1952), p. 462.

CHAPTER 16. *Cold War Beneficiary: Afghanistan*

1. As cited by Sirdar Ikbal Ali Shah, *Modern Afghanistan* (London, 1939), p. 50.
2. As cited in *The New York Times,* 9 August 1946.

3. Welles Hangen, "Afghanistan," *The Yale Review*, vol. 56 (October 1966), p. 61.

CHAPTER 17. *Jordan: Keeping a Nonviable State Alive*

1. As cited in *The Economist*, 4 May 1963, p. 425.
2. *Ibid.*, pp. 316–17.
3. As cited in *The New York Times*, 12 and 24 November 1957.

CHAPTER 18. *Constitutional Absolutism: Morocco*

1. From the French text in J. Basdevant, com., *Traités et conventions en vigeur entre la France et les puissances éntrangères* (Paris, 1920), vol. 3, pp. 69–70.

CHAPTER 19. *Kuwayt: An Affluent Amirate Under Political Siege*

1. Great Britain, Treaty Series No. 93 (1961), Cmnd. 1518.

CHAPTER 20. *Garrison Democracy: Israel*

1. A reverse acronym for *Harakat Tahrir Filastin* or Palestine Liberation Movement.
2. See below, chapters 24–25.
3. Literally *Zva Haganah le-Israel*, or Defense Army of Israel.
4. Palmah is an abbreviation for *Plugot ha-Mahaz*, or striking force.
5. Women may be exempt from service if they are mothers, pregnant, or married, or if they request exemption on grounds of conscience or religious conviction.
6. Under the original law of 1949, men served for 24 months and women for only 12; under an amendment of 26 August 1952, the length of service for men was extended to 30 months and for women to 24; and by further amendment the period of conscript service was reduced, when the draftees began to exceed the manpower needed by the IDF.
7. Colonel Mordechai Bar-on, "Educational Processes in the Israel Defense Forces" (Tel Aviv: December 1966), p. 10.
8. The lineal successor of the two guerrilla groups of the late mandatory period.
9. Acronym for Herut-Liberal Bloc; Gahal joined the emergency government founded on the eve of the war in June 1967.
10. An acronym for the New Communist List.
11. Beit Hillel, *Ma'amado shel ha-Zava be'Israel: ba-Mdinah uva-Hevrah* (The Status of the Army in Israel: In the State and in Society) (Tel Aviv, 1954), p. 5.
12. *Ma'ariv*, 7 July 1967, and *The Jerusalem Post*, 9 July 1967.

CHAPTER 21. *Confessional Democracy: Lebanon*

1. Kamal Jumblatt distributed many of his lands to the peasants working them.
2. Malcolm H. Kerr, "Political Decision Making in a Confessional Democracy," in Leonard Binder, editor, *Politics in Lebanon* (New York, 1966), p. 192.
3. From the text of the protocol in Robert W. Macdonald, *The League of Arab States: A Study in the Dynamics of Regional Organization* (Princeton, 1965), p. 317; and of the Arab League Pact in Hurewitz, *Diplomacy*, vol. 2, p. 247.
4. From the text in *DAFR, 1958*, p. 353.
5. Charles F. Gallagher, "In the Wake of the Revolution: Comments on Lebanese Affairs a Year after the 1958 Uprising," American Universities Field Staff Report, 30 November 1959, p. 9.
6. *The Economist*, 28 June 1958, p. 1191.

CHAPTER 22. *Tunisia: Stable One-Party System*

1. C. Samaran, "Bay," EI[2], vol. 1, pp. 1110–11.
2. From the French text in Jules de Clercq, compiler, *Recueil des traités de la France*, vol. 14 (Paris, 1886), p. 244–45.
3. Leon Carl Brown, "Tunisia," in James S. Coleman, editor, *Education and Political Development* (Princeton, 1965), p. 153.
4. Clement Henry Moore, *Tunisia Since Independence: The Dynamics of One-Party Government* (Berkeley, 1965), p. 63; this section of the chapter owes much to Moore's incisive analysis.
5. As cited in *The New York Times*, 18 July 1961. Actually, the question at issue with France over the demarcation of the border related to the southeastern extremity, which had been fixed at Fort Saint (Marker 220) in 1958. The Tunisian government claimed that the treaty with France of 1911 had fixed the southernmost border at Marker 233 (Garet al-Hamel). Between the two markers the French had in the interval erected three bases. There was also a suspicion of the presence of oil in that area, sharpening the Tunisian interest.
6. Habib Bourguiba, *The Army at the Service of the State* (Tunis, 20 March 1963), pp. 10–11; this is an official translation of a speech given at Fondouk Jadid on 15 March 1963.

CHAPTER 23. *Armies as Agencies of Social Change*

1. Richard D. Robinson, *The First Turkish Republic: A Case Study in National Development* (Cambridge, 1963), p. 250; see also Lucian W. Pye, "Armies in the Process of Political Modernization," in John J. Johnson, editor, *The Role of the Military in Underdeveloped Countries* (Princeton, 1962), pp. 76–77; and Frank Sloan, "The Role of the Military in Develop-

ment," in William R. Polk, editor, *Developmental Revolution: North Africa, Middle East, South Asia* (Washington, 1963), pp. 108–9; and SORO, Foreign Area Studies Division, *U.S. Army Area Handbook for Iran* (Washington, 1963), p. 608.

2. Frederick W. Frey, "Surveying Peasant Attitudes in Turkey," *The Public Opinion Quarterly*, vol. 27 (Fall 1963), pp. 335–55.

3. Pakistan, Planning Commission, *The Second Five-Year Plan, 1960–65* (Karachi, 1960), p. 375.

4. See, for example, Robert W. Kerwin, "The Turkish Roads Program," *The Middle East Journal*, vol. 4 (1950), pp. 196–208; and Sloan, cited, pp. 106–18.

5. Frederic C. Shorter, "Military Expenditures and the Allocation of Resources," in Shorter, editor, *Four Studies on the Economic Development of Turkey* (London, 1967), p. 57.

6. Manfred Halpern, *The Politics of Social Change in the Middle East and North Africa* (Princeton, 1963), p. 258; see also William R. Polk, "Social Modernization: The New Men," in Georgiana G. Stevens, editor, *The United States in the Middle East* (Englewood Cliffs, 1964), p. 46.

7. Edward Shils, "The Military and Political Development of the New States," in Johnson, cited, p. 32.

8. Halpern, "Middle Eastern Armies and the New Middle Class," in Johnson, cited, pp. 278–87.

CHAPTER 24. *Arms Races in the Region*

1. These are the best estimates that I have been able to make, but the reader should be warned that few statistics are quite as slippery as military statistics. The United States government has publicized in detail its foreign military aid program after World War II, so that a good deal is known about the value of equipment sent from the United States to the individual Middle East countries and the value of related services. On comparable aid from the U.S.S.R. and its allies (chiefly Czechoslovakia), there has been a good deal of speculation, some of it informed, and our estimates are nowhere as accurate as the American data. Least reliable is the information on postwar arms traffic between our major transatlantic allies (Britain, France, and West Germany) and the Middle East, since very little has been formally released. Even when the researcher can ascertain the amounts and types of weapons that the industrial states transfer to nonindustrial states by grant or by sale for cash, barter, or credit and at full price or discount, he is still in no position to place a monetary value on the transaction. He must also determine whether these weapons were new or used; if new, whether they were stripped or included extras; if used, whether reconditioned or sold as surplus or scrap. Each international arms transaction, moreover, has a political value as well as a commercial value, and the particular mixture in each transaction, even between the same supplier

and client, will tend to vary with the changing international and regional political climates.

2. To the estimates for Afghanistan, Egypt, Syria, and Iraq must be added, for the regional total by 1965, nearly $100 million to Yemen and $150 million to Algeria.

3. See Table 5, chap. 11; and the Institute for Strategic Studies, *The Military Balance* (annual).

4. Samuel P. Huntington, "Arms Races: Prerequisites and Results," *Public Policy: A Yearbook of the Graduate School of Public Administration, Harvard University, 1958* (Cambridge, 1958), pp. 41–86; for literature on arms races see the bibliography at the end of the article, pp. 85–86; see also Ciro Elliott Zoppo, "Nuclear Technology, Multipolarity, and International Stability," *World Politics*, vol. 18 (July 1966), pp. 579–606 and the bibliographical references to the intervening literature.

5. Huntington, cited, pp. 75–77.

6. See, for example, Prime Minister Ben Gurion's statement of 15 November 1955, when he called attention to "the danger that threatens Israel from Egypt's superiority in arms," in *DIA, 1955*, pp. 385–88.

7. United Nations, Security Council, *Official Records*, 433rd meeting (4 August 1949), 4th year, No. 36, p. 15.

8. From text of speech in *DIA, 1956*, p. 91.

9. From the text in Hurewitz, *Diplomacy*, vol. 2, p. 404.

10. *Parliamentary Debates*, Commons, vol. 578 (18 November 1957), cols. 34–35.

11. *Ibid.*, col. 34; see also *DAFR, 1957*, pp. 307–9.

CHAPTER 25. *Races in the Arab-Israel Zone*

1. United Nations, Security Council, *Official Records*, 3rd Year, Supplement for May 1948, pp. 83–88, Doc. S/745.

2. United Nations, Security Council, *Official Records*, 4th Year, 433rd meeting (4 August 1949), No. 36, p. 16.

3. From text in *DIA, 1955*, p. 319; Jamali was summarizing, in his report to the Iraqi Chamber of Deputies, his discussion with 'Abd al-Nasir and other Egyptian leaders.

4. See chap. 7, pp. 137–38.

5. Sir Anthony Eden, *Full Circle* (American edition; Cambridge, 1960), p. 359.

6. From the text of joint Anglo-American statement of 27 September 1955 in *The Department of State Bulletin*, vol. 33 (10 October 1955), p. 560.

7. Eisenhower press release of 9 November 1955, *ibid.* (21 November 1955), p. 845.

8. In a letter of 6 February 1956 to members of the House of Representatives, *ibid.*, vol. 34 (20 February 1956), pp. 285–86; see also President Eisenhower's statement in a news conference on 7 March 1956, *The New York Times*, 8 March 1956.

9. *The Department of State Bulletin,* vol. 34 (13 February 1956), p. 233.
10. *Parliamentary Debates,* Commons, vol. 545 (31 October 1955), col. 675.
11. *Ibid.,* vol. 548 (24 January 1956), col. 68.
12. Leonard Beaton and John Maddox, *The Spread of Nuclear Weapons* (New York, 1962), p. 171; see Chap. 11 for a treatment of Israel.
13. From text of address, 13 August 1958, in *DAFR,* 1958, p. 357.
14. *The Department of State Bulletin,* vol. 34 (30 April 1956), p. 713; see also Terrence Robertson, *Crisis: The Inside Story of the Suez Conspiracy* (New York, 1965), pp. 56–7.
15. As cited in *The New York Times,* 21 February 1966; see also *ibid.,* 4 February 1966.
16. From the text of a press interview, 3 April 1963, in *DAFR, 1963,* p. 267.
17. From the text of a press interview, 8 May 1963, *ibid.,* p. 268.
18. *The Department of State Bulletin,* vol. 42 (15 March 1965), p. 367.
19. From the text, *The New York Times,* 6 February 1966.
20. From the text of the statement read to press on 2 April 1966.
21. As cited in *The New York Times,* 21 May 1966.
22. See *ibid.,* 29 June 1966.
23. From the text in *The New York Times,* 20 June 1967.
24. Lebanon, Libya, Morocco, Saudi Arabia, and Tunisia.

BIBLIOGRAPHIC NOTE

The following selective references, chiefly in English, are designed to guide the reader to further literature on subjects of interest. Military-political studies on the Middle East—books and articles on individual states, clusters of states, and the region as a whole—are slowly accumulating although the present condition of the literature is still spotty at best, since the discipline of military politics has developed unevenly. For this reason, many entries deal almost entirely with the larger political, social, and economic environment, in which armies are modernized and often saddled with non-military duties, which give their officers opportunities for cultivating political skills and aspirations. This is, of course, the stuff of military politics. But where the scholars have not yet made systematic inquiry, the reader must fend for himself.

Useful bibliographies on military politics are frequently appended to book-length monographs. Of special merit, as regards postwar writing, are the following bibliographies: Samuel P. Huntington, editor, *Changing Patterns of Military Politics* (New York: Free Press, 1962), pp. 235–66, arranges the entries topically, with general introductory comments; Moshe Lissak, "Selected Literature of Revolutions and Coups d'Etat in the Developing Nations," in Morris Janowitz, editor, *The New Military: Changing Patterns of Organization*, (New York: Russell Sage Foundation, 1964), pp. 339–62, annotates each reference; Chalmers Johnson, "Civilian Loyalties and Guerrilla Conflict," *World Politics*, vol. 14 (July 1962), pp. 646–61, assesses the state of studies on guerrilla and counterguerrilla warfare; and Mark and Karen Wing, compilers, *Subject and Author Index to* Military Review, *1922–1965* (Fort Leavenworth, Kansas: U.S. Army Command and General Staff College, 1967), have indexed a journal in which many articles on the Middle East are listed. Supplementing the bibliographies on military politics are those on Middle East politics, such as: M. Flory, R. Le Tourneau and J.-P. Trystam, "L'Afrique du Nord: état des travaux," *Revue française de science politique* (June 1959), vol. 9, pp. 410–53; in each issue of *The Middle East Journal* "Bibliography of Periodical Literature"; Abdel Rahman el-Nasri, *A Bibliography of the Sudan, 1938–1958* (New York: Oxford University Press, for the University of Khartoum, 1962); Raphael Patai, *Jordan, Lebanon and Syria: An Annotated Bibliography* (New Haven, Conn: Human Relations Area Files [HRAF], 1957); J. D. Pearson, comp., *Index Islamicus, 1906–1955: A Catalogue of Articles on Islamic Subjects in Periodicals and Other Collective Publications* (Cambridge: Cambridge University Press, 1958) and *Index Islamicus Supplement, 1956–1960* (Cambridge: Cambridge University Press, 1962); Benjamin Rivlin, "A Selective Survey of the Literature in the Social Sciences and Related Fields on Modern North Africa," *The American Political Science Review* (September 1954), vol. 48, pp. 826–48; Paul E. A. Romeril, "Tunisian Nationalism: A Bibliographical Outline," *The Middle East Journal* (Spring 1960), vol. 14; pp. 206–15; Jean Sauvaget's *Introduction to the History of the Muslim East: A Bibliographical Guide,* revised by Claude Cahen (Berkeley, Cal.: University of California Press, 1964); UNESCO, *Middle East Social Science Bibliography: Books and Articles in the Social Sciences Published in Arab Countries of the Middle East in 1955–1960* (Cairo, 1961); Donald N. Wilber, *Annotated Bibliography of Afghanistan* (3rd ed.; New York: Taplinger, 1967). Norman Robert Bennett, *A Study Guide for Morocco* (Boston: African Studies Center, Boston University, n.d.) and *A Study Guide for Tunisia* (Boston: African Studies Center, Boston University, March 1968).

The contagion of military coups d'état in the new states of Asia and Africa aroused the curiosity about military politics of a growing number of scholars, journalists, and diplomats. Many books had already appeared on Latin America, where military intervention into politics became commonplace long before 1945. The early attempts at global generalization on military politics in nonindustrial states were often little more than extrapolations from the Latin American experience, if for no other reason than the paucity of monographs on other nonindustrial regions. S. E. Finer, *The Man on Horseback: The Role of the Military in Politics* (London: Pall Mall Press, 1962; New York: Praeger, 1962), one of the solid theoretical studies, rests on the premise that the "régime of military provenance or direct military rule is . . . a distinctive kind of régime." Finer's efforts to structure a thesis on the experience of states everywhere in the world were defeated because the available works biased the evidence in favor of Latin America. Samuel P. Huntington fell under the same influence in a paper on "Patterns of Violence in World Politics," in *Changing Patterns of Military Politics*, edited by Huntington, pp. 17–50, where he classifies military coups according to the social consequences. Morris Janowitz, *The Military in the Political Development of New Nations: An Essay in Comparative Analysis* (Chicago: University of Chicago Press, 1964), also focuses on the social significance of military rule. The RAND Corporation in 1959–60 sponsored a comprehensive symposium on military politics in nonindustrial states, including the Middle East, and the papers, edited by John J. Johnson, appeared as *The Role of the Military in Underdeveloped Countries* (Princeton, N.J.: Princeton University Press, 1962); Hugh Hanning, *The Peaceful Uses of Military Forces* (New York: Praeger, 1967), reviews the problems in selected countries, among them Iran, Israel, Morocco, and Pakistan; Wilson C. McWilliams, editor, *Garrisons and Government: Politics and the Military in New States* (San Francisco, Cal.: Chandler, 1967), unfolds his own hypotheses in an introduction and a summation to a book of readings, including two essays on the Middle East; H. Daalder, *The Role of the Military in the Emerging Countries* (The Hague: Mouton, 1962), and William F. Gutteridge, *Armed Forces in New States* (London: Oxford University Press, for the Institute of Race Relations, 1962), repeat in their brochures the generalizations in the works mentioned above. In a full-length study, *Military Institutions and Power in the New States* (London: Pall Mall Press, 1965; New York: Praeger, 1965), Gutteridge bases his judgments primarily on sub-Saharan Africa. A more analytical study is David C. Rapoport, "A Comparative Theory of Military and Political Types" in Huntington, editor, *Changing Patterns of Military Politics*, pp. 71–100. Alfred Vagts, *A History of Militarism: Civilian and Military* (rev. ed.; New York: Meridian, 1959), also discusses military politics. Military, economic, social, and political data not otherwise easily procurable may sometimes be found in a series of country studies prepared for the United States Army by the Foreign Area Studies Division of the Special Operations Research Office at the American University, published under the general title of *U.S. Army Area Handbooks* by the Government Printing Office in Washington. Such handbooks have appeared on the following Middle East countries: Algeria, Egypt, Iran, Morocco, Pakistan, Saudi Arabia, Sudan, and Syria.

One of the first postwar analyses of military politics in the Middle East, Majid Khadduri, "The Role of the Military in Middle East Politics," *American Political Science Review* (June 1953), vol. 47, pp. 511–24, also in S. N. Fisher, editor, *Social Forces in the Middle East* (Ithaca, N.Y.: Cornell University Press, 1955), pp. 162–83, attributes the military interventions into Middle East politics to the failure of democracy and to "an almost nostalgic longing . . . for a 'strong' regime." The breakdown of the imported parliamentary institutions is also the primary explanation for the military seizure of political power in H. B. Sharabi, "Parliamentary Government and Military Autocracy in the Middle East," *Orbis*, vol. 4 (Fall 1960), pp. 338–55; also in McWilliams, editor, *Garrisons and Governments*, pp. 183–202. Manfred Halpern, "Middle Eastern Armies and the New Middle Class," in Johnson, editor, *The Role of the Military in Underdeveloped Countries*, pp. 277–316, and as chap. 13 in Halpern, *The Politics of Social Change in the Middle East and North Africa* (Princeton, N.J.: Princeton University Press, 1963), propounds the thesis that the military officers representing a new salaried middle class are agents of modernization in the Islamic states of the Middle East. George M. Haddad, *Revolutions and Military Rule in the Middle East: The Northern Tier* (New York: Speller, 1965), investigates military rule in the non-Arab Muslim countries of the Middle East and finds it "modest and balanced," by contrast with such rule in the Arab states, which is to form the subject of a later volume. A country-by-country survey of an abbreviated Middle East that encompasses non-Soviet southwest Asia to the eastern frontiers of Iran, plus Egypt and Sudan in adjacent northeast Africa, Bernard Vernier, *Armée et politique au moyen-orient* (Paris: Payot, 1966), recognizes that the region's diversity yields diverse types of military politics. S. N. Fisher, editor, *The Military in the Middle East: Problems in Society and Government* (Columbus, Ohio: Ohio State University Press, 1963), reproduces the papers presented to a colloquium at Ohio State University in 1961; it consists of two general and five country essays (Turkey, Iraq, Syria, Egypt, and Israel).

Legacies

The first and second editions of *The Encyclopaedia of Islam* are an indispensable source of information on Islamic institutions, particularly for developments antedating World War I. Ibn Khaldun, *The Muqaddimah: An Introduction to History*, translated from the Arabic by Franz Rosenthal (New York: Pantheon, for Bollingen, 1958), 3 vols., sets forth a still valuable theory about the rise and fall of Islamic dynasties. Majid Khadduri, *War and Peace in the Law of Islam* (2nd ed.; Baltimore, Md.: Johns Hopkins Press, 1955), examines the theoretical legal basis for relations between Islam and Christendom but sheds less light on military politics in the Islamic dynastic states than does the same author's introduction to his translation of *The Islamic Law of Nations, Shaybani's Siyar* (Baltimore, Md.: Johns Hopkins Press, 1966), pp. 1–74. On relations among the Islamic dynastic states before the rise of European imperialism, see also Aziz Ahmad, *Studies in Islamic Culture in the Indian Environment* (London: Oxford University Press, 1964), chap. 3. A primary resource for dynastic vital statistics in the Ottoman Empire with invaluable genealogical tables is A. D. Alderson, *The Structure of the Ottoman Dynasty* (Oxford: Oxford University Press, 1956); preoccupied with authenticating the facts, Alderson does not attempt to frame a theory of succession. For a detailed history of the Ottoman Empire (1300–1774) there is still no substitute for Joseph von Hammer, *Geschichte des Osmanischen Reiches* (2nd ed.; Pest: Hartleben, 1834–36), 4 vols. H. A. R. Gibb and Harold Bowen, *Islamic Society and the West: A Study of the Impact of Western Civilization on Moslem Culture in the Near East* (London: Oxford, for the Royal Institute of International Affairs [RIIA], 1950–57), parts 1–2, also explores problems relevant to succession. A case study of military politics in the Ottoman Empire in its prime, S. N. Fisher's *The Foreign Relations of Turkey, 1481–1512* (Urbana, Ill.: University of Illinois Press, 1948), assesses the succession crisis at the close of the reign of Sultan Bayezid II. Factual detail on succession crises in the Mughal Empire may be found in *The Cambridge History of India*, vol. 4 (Cambridge: Cambridge University Press, 1957). Iftikhar Ahmad Ghauri's *War of Succession between the Sons of Shah Jahan, 1657–1658* (Lahore, Pakistan: Publishers United, 1964), provides a case study of violent succession in the Mughal Empire by showing how Awrangzib displaced his older brothers in seizing the throne while his father was still alive. V. Minorski's masterful introduction to his translation from the Persian of *Tadhkirat al-Muluk: A Manual of Safavid Administration* (Cambridge: Cambridge University Press, 1943) and the text itself explain the military-political role of the Qizilbash tribes in Safavi Iran. Further information on succession problems in Iran may be found in Sir John Malcolm, *The History of Persia from the Most Early Period until the Present Time* (rev. ed.; London: John Murray, 1829), 2 vols.; and Sir Percy Sykes, *A History of Persia* (3rd ed.; London: Macmillan, 1951), vol. 2. Eugene Aubin, *Morocco of Today* (New York: Dutton, 1906), translated from the French, outlined the early history of the gish tribes under 'Alawi monarchy in Morocco.

J. Heyworth-Dunne, *An Introduction to the History of Education in Modern Egypt* (London: Luzac, 1938), explores Mehmed Ali's military training methods; far less minute but more imaginative is the treatment of Mehmed Ali in Morroe Berger, *Military Elite and Social Change: Egypt Since Napoleon* (Princeton, N.J.: Center of International Studies, 1960). For relevant official documents, see G. Douin editor, *Une Mission militaire auprès de Mohamed Aly: correspondence des généraux Belliard et Boyer* (Cairo: Société royale de géographie d'Egypte, 1923), and *Les Prémieres frégates de Mohamed Aly* (Cairo; Société royale de géographie d'Egypte, 1926). Henry Dodwell, *The Founder of Modern Egypt: A study of Muhammad Ali* (Cambridge: Cambridge University Press, 1931), based the biography and the evaluation of Mehmed Ali's modernization program chiefly on consular and diplomatic reports in the Public Record Office. An excellent summary assessment of Mehmed Ali's economic policies appears in Charles Issawi, *Egypt in Revolution: An Economic Analysis* (London: Oxford University Press, for RIIA, 1963), pp. 18–24; see also the book of readings that Issawi edited, entitled *The Economic History of the Middle East, 1800–1914* (Chicago: University of Chicago Press, 1966), part 6, chap. 5, which consists of translated selections from 'Ali al-Giritli, *Tarikh al-sina 'a fi Misr* (Cairo, 1952). Helen B. Rivlin, *The Agricultural Policy of Muhammad 'Ali in Egypt* (Cambridge, Mass.: Harvard University Press, 1961), traces the relationship of military service to agriculture (chap. 11). Brief on the early centuries of Ottoman history, Bernard Lewis, *The Emergence of Modern Turkey* (London: Oxford University Press, for RIIA, 1961)—a classic on appearance—becomes detailed on the nineteenth and is especially recommended for its concise evaluation of military reforms under Mahmud II. Roderic H. Davison, *Reform in the Ottoman Empire, 1856–1876* (Princeton, N.J.: Princeton University Press, 1963), as the title suggests, focuses on the third quarter of the nineteenth century but opens with an historical introduction that includes a fine assessment of the Janissaries. Further factual data in support of the Lewis and Davison hypotheses may be found in Niyazi Berkes, *The Development of Secularism in Turkey* (Montreal: McGill University Press, 1964). The short-lived military reforms of Selim III at the turn of the nineteenth century are dissected by Stanford J. Shaw, "The Origins of Ottoman Military Reform: The *Nizam-i Cedid* Army of Sultan Selim III," *The Journal of Modern History*, vol. 37 (September 1965), pp. 291–305. Also helpful are the occasional references to the armed forces in Harold Temperley's *England and the Near East: The Crimea* (London: Longmans, Green, 1936), and occasional papers (especially by Chambers, Frey and Rustow) on the bifurcation of the bureaucracy into military and civilian branches in Robert E. Ward and Dankwart A. Rustow, editors, *Political Modernization in Japan and Turkey* (Princeton, N.J.: Princeton University Press, 1964). On the role of the military in the overthrow of Sultan Abdülhamid II in 1908–1909 and in subsequent Ottoman politics on the eve of World War I, see

Ferozuddin Ahmad, *The Committee of Union and Progress in Turkish Politics, 1908–1913* (forthcoming). George N. Curzon, *Persia and the Persian Question* (London: Longmans, Green, 1892), vol. 1, chap. 17 assembles copious raw materials on miiltary modernization in nineteenth-century Persia. Firuz Kazemzadeh reviews the formation and evolution of the Russian-trained force in "The Origin and Early Development of the Persian Cossack Brigade," in *The American Slavic and East European Review*, vol. 15 (October 1956), pp. 351–63; see also Edward G. Browne, *The Persian Revolution of 1905–1909* (Cambridge: Cambridge University Press, 1910).

The military experience of Anglo-India enlightens later developments in former British dependencies of the Middle East as well as in Pakistan. The Anglo-Indian military literature, however, is rich on individual regimental histories but still poor on the inclusive history, particularly in the light of partition. Nevertheless, there are a few pertinent general works: *The Army in India and its Evolution, including an Account of the Establishment of the Royal Air Force in India* (Calcutta: Superintendent of Government Printing [SGP] 1924); *India's Contribution to the Great War* (Calcutta: SGP, 1923); and Sri Nandan Prasad, *Expansion of the Armed Forces and Defence Organisation, 1939–45* (n.p.: Orient Longmans, for the Historical Section of the Combined Inter-Services of India and Pakistan, 1956), a volume in the *Official History of the Indian Armed Forces in the Second World War, 1939–1945*, edited by Bisheshwar Prasad. Specifically, on the Indianization of the officer corps on the interwar years, see William Gutteridge, "The Indianisation of the Indian Army 1918–1945: A Case Study," *Race*, vol. 4, no. 2 (May 1963), pp. 39–48.

The formation and management of armies in the individual British Middle East dependencies and their political roles have been explored with variable competence and variable detail. Great Britain, Colonial Office, *Special Report by His Majesty's Government . . . to the Council of the League of Nations on the Progress of Iraq during the period 1920–1931* (London: His Majesty's Stationary Office [HMSO], 1931), pp. 38–48, describes the beginnings of the Iraqi army; and Majid Khadduri, *Independent Iraq, 1932–1958: A Study in Iraqi Politics* (2nd ed.; London: Oxford for RIIA, 1960), chaps. 6–8, analyzes the recurrent coups d'état between 1936 and 1941. Edgar O'Ballance, "The Egyptian Army," *Journal of the Royal United Service Institution*, vol. 103 (February 1958), pp. 82–88, sketches the history from the early ninetenth century; and P. J. Vatikiotis, *The Egyptian Army in Politics: Pattern for New Nations?* (Bloomington, Ind.: University of Indiana Press, 1961), chaps. 1–2, analyzes the political context of military development under British hegemony. A. J. Knott, "The Sudan Defence Force Goes to War," *The Royal Engineers Journal* [Chatham, Kent, England], vol. 58 (1944), pp. 157–70, outlines the history of the force from its inception in 1925 to the later years in World War II. J. C. Hurewitz, *The Struggle for Palestine* (New York: Norton, 1950), analyzes the mandatory origins of Israel's citizen army and the reasons for the failure of the Palestine Arabs to acquire comparable military experience. "The Trans-Jordan Frontier Force," *4th/7th Royal Dragoon Guards Regimental Magazine* [Britain], vol. 1 (December 1946), pp. 16–17, summarizes the history of the unit. W. H. Kingsberry, "The Cyrenaica Defence Force," *Journal of the Royal United Service Institution*, vol. 88 (1943), pp. 210–14, explains the beginnings and early growth of the establishment in World War II. Charles-André Julien, *Histoire de l'Algérie contemporaine: la conquête et les débuts de la colonisation, 1827–1871* (Paris: Presses Universitaires de France, 1964), chap. 6, gives a summary account of the recruitment of Algerians into the French army. For comparable details on Tunisia and Morocco and further information on Algeria, see Great Britain, War Office, General Staff, *Handbook of the French Army*, updated annually in the interwar years. The same source sheds light on Syria and Lebanon after 1920, although more plenteous particulars may be found in France, Ministry of Foreign Affairs, *Rapport a la Société des Nations sur la situation de la Syrie et du Liban, 1925* (–*1938*) (Paris, 1926–1939). I. S. O. Playfair, editor, *The Mediterranean and the Middle East* (London: HMSO, 1954–66), 4 vols., which form part of the British official history of the Second World War, details some of the wartime expansion.

Postwar Politics

The standard work on the problems of postwar military strategy in the Middle East is John C. Campbell, *Defense of the Middle East: Problems of American Policy* (rev. ed.; New York: Harper, for the Council on Foreign Relations, 1960); for further reading, see the bibliography, pp. 369–88. Elizabeth Monroe's *Britain's Moment in the Middle East, 1914–1956* (Baltimore, Md.: Johns Hopkins Press, 1963), evaluates the rise and fall of British influence in the region. Walter Z. Laqueur, *The Soviet Union and the Middle East* (New York: Praeger, 1959), charts Soviet activities, chiefly in the postwar years, while Roger Le Tourneau, *Evolution politique de l'Afrique du nord musulmane 1920–1961* (Paris: Colin, 1962), examines the changing fortunes of France in the Maghrib as its three dependencies waged successful struggles for independence. Charles F. Gallagher pursues the same theme from a different perspective in *The United States and North Africa: Morocco, Algeria, and Tunisia* (Cambridge, Mass.: Harvard University Press, 1963), chap. 2. J. C. Hurewitz examines the regional context of postwar military politics in "Regional and International Politics in the Middle East," in Georgiana G. Stevens, editor, *The United States and the Middle East* (Englewood Cliffs, N.J.: Prentice-Hall, 1964), pp. 78–112. Inter-Arab politics is the theme of Malcolm Kerr, *The Arab Cold War, 1958–1967: A Study of Ideology in Politics* (2nd ed.; London, Oxford, for RIIA, 1967), as well as of John S. Badeau, *The American Approach to the Arab World* (New York: Harper and Row, for the Council on Foreign Relations, 1968). For the situation at the close of the second postwar decade, see the Institute for Strategic Studies, "Sources of Conflict in the Middle East," *Adelphi Papers*, no. 26 (March 1966). Curt Gasteyger, "Moscow and the Mediterranean," *Foreign Affairs*, vol. 46 (July 1968), pp. 676–87, and Thomas W. Wolfe, *The Soviet Quest for More Globally Mobile Military Power* (Santa Monica, Cal.: RAND, December 1967, memorandum RM-5554-PR), consider the strategic implications of the appearance after 1962 of a continuous Soviet naval presence in the Mediterranean: see also L. W. Martin, *The Sea in Modern Strategy* (New York, Praeger, for the Institute for Strategic Studies, 1965); F. M. Murphy, "The Soviet Navy in the Mediterranean," *U.S. Naval Institute Proceedings*, vol. 93 (March 1967), pp. 39–44; Robert Waring Herrick, *Soviet Naval Strategy: Fifty Years of Theory and Practice* (Annapolis: U.S. Naval Institute, 1968).

On theories of coups d'état, see David C. Rapoport, "Coups d'Etat: *The View of the Men Firing Pistols*," in Carl J. Friedrich, editor, *Revolution: Nomos VIII* (New York: Atherton, 1966), pp. 53–74, and the footnote references for further reading. Keith Hopkins, "Civil-Military Relations in Developing Countries," *British Journal of Sociology*, vol. 17 (June 1966), pp. 165–82, evaluates the major postwar writing on military coups in nonindustrial states, expresses preference for cautious generalizations, and concludes that the "very supremacy" of military power "prevents the growth of other mechanisms of tension management, and limits further change." F. R. van der Mehden and C. W. Anderson, "Political Action by the Military in Developing Areas," *Sociological Research*, vol. 28 (Winter 1961), pp. 459–79, examines, among other problems, the causes of military intervention into politics.

Military Republics

There have been many studies on 'Abd al-Nasir's Egypt but only two investigated at book-length the role of the military after 1952: Vatikiotis, *The Egyptian Army*, and Richard H. Dekmejian, *The Dynamics of the Egyptian Political System* (forthcoming); see also Berger, *Military Elite and Social Change* and Jean Vigneau, "The Ideology of the Egyptian Revolution" in *The Middle East in Transition*, edited by Walter Z. Laqueur (New York: Praeger, 1958), pp. 129–44. The following books on revolutionary Egypt merit consideration: Jean and Simonne Lacouture, *Egypt in Transition* (London: Methuen, 1958); Anouar Abdel-Malek, *Egypt, Military Society: The Army Regime, the Left, and Social Change under Nasser,* translated from the French by C. L. Markmann (New York: Random House, 1968); and Peter Mansfield, *Nasser's Egypt* (London: Penguin, 1965). Issawi's *Egypt in Revolution* was the first thorough analysis of 'Abd al-Nasir's Arab socialist program. On the confused and confusing history of Syrian military politics before the formation of the U.A.R., see Gordon H. Torrey, *Syrian Politics and the Military, 1945–1958* (Columbus, Ohio: Ohio State University Press, 1964), a factual study; and Patrick Seale, *The Struggle for Syria: A Study of Post-War Arab Politics, 1945–1958* (London: Oxford University Press, for RIIA, 1965), an interpretative study. The Ba'th Party is analyzed by Kamel Abu Jaber, *The Arab Ba'th Socialist Party: History, Ideology, and Organization* (Syracuse, N.Y.: Syracuse University Press, 1966), and Ba'thi involvement in military politics by Alan W. Horton, "Syrian Stability and the Ba'th," *AUFS Report Service, Southwest Asia Series,* vol. 14, no. 1 (April 1965). Caractacus [Frederick J. Snell], *Revolution in Iraq* (London: Gollancz, 1959), describes the conditions that led to the military overthrow of the monarchy, while Benjamin Shwadran, *The Power Struggle in Iraq* (New York: Council for Middle Eastern Affairs, 1960), investigates the first half of the Qasim regime. Two eyewitness accounts of the Kurdish revolt are Dana Adams Schmidt, *Journey among Brave Men* (Boston: Little, Brown, 1965), and David Adamson, *The Kurdish War* (New York: Praeger, 1964). P. M. Holt assesses the opening years of the military regime in Sudan in its historical perspective in *A Modern History of the Sudan* (New York: Praeger, 1961), chap. 13. Peter Kilner, "A Year of Army Rule in the Sudan," *World Today,* vol. 15 (November 1959), pp. 430–41, describes the army's seizure of power and its use of power in the first year; Kilner took another look two years later in article titled "Military Government in Sudan," *ibid.,* vol. 18 (June 1962), pp. 259–68.

Mohammed Omer Beshir, *The Southern Sudan: Background to Conflict* (New York: Praeger, 1968), presents an Arab view of the rebellion in the southern provinces; the rebels' view is set forth in Joseph Oduho and William Deng, *The Problem of the Southern Sudan* (London: Oxford University Press, for the Institute of Race Relations, 1963).

Military-Civilian Coalitions

Khalid B. Sayeed, *The Political System of Pakistan* (Boston: Houghton Mifflin, 1967), is a solid inquiry into the evolving politics of the Muslim state with an excellent topical bibliography (pp. 293–308), although the book does not wholly replace Keith Callard, *Pakistan: A Political Study* (New York: Macmillan, 1957). A formal, institutional study by an American-trained Pakistani political scientist G. W. Choudhuri, *Democracy in Pakistan* (Dacca, Pakistan: Green Bookhouse, 1963), surveys the making of the constitutions for the first and second republics. Hugh Tinker, *India and Pakistan: A Political Analysis* (rev. ed.; London: Pall Mall Press, 1968; New York: Praeger, 1968), contrasts the two political systems. Henry Frank Goodnow, *The Civil Service of Pakistan: Bureaucracy in a New Nation* (New Haven, Conn.: Yale University Press, 1964), helps the reader understand the major influence of the senior civil service in shaping the evolving polity. Keith Callard, *Political Forces in Pakistan, 1947–1959* (Vancouver, B.C.: Institute of Pacific Relations, 1959), deals expressly with the collapse of civilian political leadership and Ayub's rise to power. A definitive quasi-legal study of the martial law regime by a British resident lawyer is Herbert Feldman, *Revolution in Pakistan: A Study of the Martial Law Administration* (London: Oxford University Press, 1967). Mohammad Ayub Khan, with a combination of frankness and studied silence in a lively autobiography, reveals his personality and his politics in a career as soldier, politician, and father of the Second Republic in *Friends Not Masters: A Political Autobiography* (London: Oxford University Press, 1967). W. A. Wilcox, "The Pakistan Coup d'État of 1958," *Pacific Affairs*, vol. 38 (Summer 1965), pp. 142–63, makes a persuasive case for the progressive politicization of General Ayub. For military data, see also Major General Fazal Muqeem Khan, *The Story of the Pakistan Army* (Karachi, Pakistan: Oxford University Press, 1963); and Colonel Mohammad Ahmad, *My Chief* (Lahore, Paskistan: Longmans, Green, 1960). Sharif al-Mujahid, "Pakistan's First Presidential Elections," *Asian Survey*, vol. 5 (June 1965), pp. 280–94, is an informed appraisal.

For an appreciation of the military role in the transition from

Ottoman Empire to Turkish Republic, Dankwart A. Rustow, "The Army and the Founding of the Turkish Republic," *World Politics*, vol. 11 (July 1959), pp. 513–52, is indispensable. An excellent brief analysis of military politics in Turkey's First Republic is Frederick W. Frey, "Arms and the Man in Turkish Politics," *The Land Reborn*, vol. 11 (August 1960), pp. 3–14. Frey's focus on personality is balanced by George S. Harris, "The Role of the Military in Turkish Politics," *The Middle East Journal*, vol. 19 (Winter and Spring, 1965), pp. 54–66 and 169–76, which considers institutions. Daniel Lerner and Richard D. Robinson, "Swords and Ploughshares: The Turkish Army as a Modernizing Force," *World Politics*, vol. 13 (October 1960), pp. 19–44 (modified and reprinted as chapter 9 in Robinson, *The First Turkish Republic: A Case Study in National Development* [Cambridge, Mass.: Harvard University Press, 1963]), defends Prime Minister Adnan Menderes and his Democratic Party, whom the military overthrew in May 1960. Continuing in time where the preceding leave off, Walter F. Weiker probes the causes and consequences of the 1960 military intervention in *The Turkish Revolution 1960–61: Aspects of Military Politics* (Washington: Brookings Institution, 1963). Two other studies of the same subject by Turkish scholars are Ali Fuad Başgil, *La révolution militaire de 1960 en Turquie* (Geneva: Perret-Gentil, 1963); and Ergun Özbudun, *The Role of the Military in Recent Turkish Politics* (Cambridge, Mass.: Harvard Center for International Affairs, November 1966), Occasional Papers, No. 14. Insightful articles on the Second Republic are Kemal Karpat, "Recent Political Developments in Turkey and their Social Background," *International Affairs*, vol. 38 (July 1962), pp. 304–23, and "Society, Economics and Politics in Contemporary Turkey," *World Politics*, vol. 17 (October 1964), pp. 50–74. The same theme is handled differently by A. Haluk Ülman and Frank Tachau, "Turkish Politics: The Attempt to Reconcile Rapid Modernization with Democracy," *The Middle East Journal*, vol. 19 (Spring 1965), pp. 153–68. Walter F. Weiker "The Aydemir Case and Turkey's Political Dilemma," *Middle Eastern Affairs*, vol. 14 (November 1963), pp. 258–71, investigates the abortive military coups of 1962–63.

For a brief military perspective on the Algerian revolution, see Edgar O'Ballance, *The Algerian Insurrection, 1954–62* (Hamden, Conn.: Archon, 1967); Joan Gillespie, *Algeria: Rebellion and Revolution* (New York: Praeger, 1960), considers in Part 3 the stucture and performance of the guerrilla forces. After racing through the military struggle for independence, Arslan Humbaraci, *Algeria: A Revolution That Failed: A Political History Since 1954* (London: Pall Mall Press,

1966; New York: Praeger, 1966), devotes a major part of the book to the post-independence "socialist revolution." David C. Gordon, *The Passing of French Algeria* (London: Oxford University Press, 1966), starts his narrative in 1930 but moves swiftly to the period of sovereignty, in this instance concentrating on Algerian-French relations, but giving considerable attention to unfolding domestic politics in Algeria. "Algeria Against Itself," by William H. Lewis, *Africa Report*, vol. 12, no. 9 (December 1967), pp. 9–15, illumines the Boumedienne regime.

Traditional Monarchies

The most competent work on the Sanusiyah in Libya is E. E. Evans-Pritchard, *The Sanusi of Cyrenaica* (Oxford: Oxford University Press, 1949), an anthropological study that opened up new ways of looking at old institutions, such as tribal and Sufi organization. For historical background, see Nicola A. Ziadeh, *Sanusiyah: A Study of a Revivalist Movement in Islam* (Leiden: Brill, 1958). Majid Khadduri, *Modern Libya: A Study in Political Development* (Baltimore, Md.: Johns Hopkins Press, 1963), surveys at length the Libyan political system in its international setting. Britain's reintegration of Libya under military administration in World War II is considered by Lord Rennell of Rodd, *British Military Administration of Occupied Territory in Africa during the Years 1941–1947* (London: HMSO, 1948), chaps. 11–12. Useful economic and social information will also be found in the International Bank for Reconstruction and Development [IBRD], *The Economic Development of Libya* (Baltimore, Md.: Johns Hopkins Press, 1960).

Sa'udi Arabia by H. St. John Philby (New York: Praeger, 1955), is a compendious history of the Jazirat al-'Arab with primary focus on the consolidation of Sa'udi rule in the peninsula in the twentieth century by its most prolific historian. In a larger perspective, Arnold J. Toynbee, *Survey of International Affairs, 1925*, vol. 1: *The Islamic World since the Peace Settlement* (London: Oxford University Press, for RIIA, 1927), pp. 271–324, charts the career of King 'Abd al-'Aziz as he conquered the peninsula. Further information may be culled from D. van der Beulen, *The Wells of Ibn Sa'ud* (New York: Praeger, 1957); Great Britain, The Admiralty, Naval Intelligence Division, *Western Arabia and the Red Sea* (London: HMSO, 1946), Geographical Handbook Series, B.R. 527; and any edition of the *ARAMCO Handbook* by Roy Lebkicher, George Rentz, and Max Steineke. Charles W. Harrington describes the transition from informal personal rule to modern institutional administration in "The Sa'udi Arabian

Council of Ministers," *The Middle East Journal*, vol. 12 (Winter 1958), pp. 1–19.

The Zaydiyah still awaits an historian. The first systematic history of the state in the twentieth century, *Modern Yemen, 1918–1966*, by Manfred W. Wenner (Baltimore, Md.: Johns Hopkins Press, 1967), is more factual than analytical. Two other factual works that might be consulted are Arthur S. Tritton, *The Rise of the Imams of Sanaa* (New York: Oxford University Press, 1925), and Harold Ingrams, *The Yemen: Imams, Rulers, and Revolution* (New York: Praeger, 1964). More valuable than either, particularly for an understanding of the society, is William R. Brown, "The Yemeni Dilemma," *The Middle East Journal*, vol. 17 (Autumn 1963), pp. 34–67. For an outline of Yemeni history and a brief bibliography, see Jane Smiley Hart, "Basic Chronology for a History of the Yemen," *ibid.*, vol. 17 (Winter 1963), pp. 144–53. A balanced report on the civil war by a competent journalist is Dana Adams Schmidt, *Yemen: The Unknown War* (New York: Holt, Rinehart and Winston, 1968).

Modernizing Monarchies

A recent readable history of Iran is Peter Avery, *Modern Iran* (New York: Praeger, 1965). As background to the rise of the Pahlavi dynasty in the 1920s, the reader must first become acquainted with the constitutional revolution of 1906, for which Edward G. Browne's *The Persian Revolution of 1905–1909* (Cambridge: Cambridge University Press, 1910), is still valuable. The failure of British efforts to subordinate Iran into a junior ally after World War I and the coup d'état of 1921 form the theme of J. M. Balfour's polemical *Recent Happenings in Persia* (Edinburgh: Blackwood, 1922). A balanced evaluation of Reza Shah's accomplishments is Amin Banani, *The Modernization of Iran, 1921–1941* (Stanford, Cal.: Stanford University Press, 1961). George Lenczowski, *Russia and the West in Iran, 1918–1948: A Study in Big-Power Politics* (Ithaca, N.Y.: Cornell University Press, 1949), appraises the unfolding Soviet interest in the shahdom. Richard W. Cottam dissects Iranian nationalism of the Musaddiq phase in *Nationalism in Iran* (Pittsburgh, Pa.: University of Pittsburgh Press, 1964). The political system of postwar Iran receives microscopic examination in Leonard Binder, *Iran: Political Development in a Changing Society* (Berkeley and Los Angeles: University of California Press, 1962). Binder's analysis antedates the institution of technocratic administration early in the 1960s, as does also Andrew S. Westwood, "Elections and Politics in Iran," *The Middle East Journal*, vol. 15 (Spring 1961), pp. 153–64. For data on the armed forces consult:

U.S. Army Area Handbook for Iran (Washington: GPO, 1963); Great Britain, Admiralty, Naval Intelligence Division, *Persia* (London: HMSO, 1945), Geographical Handbook Series, B.R. 525; and T. H. Vail Motter, *The Middle East Theatre: The Persian Corridor and Aid to Russia* (Washington: GPO, 1952), a volume in the official history of the *United States Army in World War II*. In a lively style that is rare in official publications, Motter evaluates the work of the United States military and gendarmerie missions to Iran during the war. Any inquiry into land reform in Iran must begin with Ann K. S. Lambton, *Landlord and Peasant in Persia: A Study of Land Tenure and Land Revenue Administration* (London: Oxford University Press, for RIIA, 1953). Hossein Mahdavy, "The Coming Crisis in Iran," *Foreign Affairs*, vol. 45 (October 1965), pp. 134–46, a basically unfriendly analysis of the White Revolution, may be balanced by Charles Issawi, "Iran's Economic Upsurge," *The Middle East Journal*, vol. 21 (Autumn 1967), pp. 447–62.

Afghanistan has received far less scholarly attention than Iran. On the history of the landlocked kingdom, see Sir Percy Sykes, *A History of Afghanistan* (London: Macmillan, 1940), 2 vols.; and W. K. Fraser-Tytler, *Afghanistan: A Study of Political Developments in Central Asia* (3rd ed.; London: Oxford University Press, 1967). Donald N. Wilber, editor, *Afghanistan, Its People, Its Society, Its Culture* (New Haven, Conn.: HRAF, 1962), provides a reliable introduction to conditions before the constitutional changes of the mid-1960s. Welles Hangen, "Afghanistan," *The Yale Review*, vol. 56 (October 1966), pp. 60–75, considers at first hand the friendly Soviet-American rivalry of the second postwar decade, while Theodore S. Gochenour, "A New Try for Afghanistan," *The Middle East Journal*, vol. 19 (Winter 1965), pp. 1–19, explores the domestic political changes. So, too, does Louis Dupree, "Afghanistan in the Twentieth Century," *Royal Central Asian Journal*, vol. 52 (January 1965), pp. 20–30.

Raphael Patai, editor, *The Hashemite Kingdom of Jordan* (New Haven, Conn.: HRAF, 1956), furnishes a general introduction to Jordan. Aqil Hyder Hasan Abidi, *Jordan: A Political Study, 1948–1957* (New York: Asia Publishing, 1965), a comprehensive factual analysis, shows preference for the Palestine Arabs rather than the Hashimi dynasty. Benjamin Shwadran, *Jordan: A State of Tension* (New York: Council for Middle Eastern Affairs, 1959), is hostile to Britain but uncommitted on domestic politics. The king presents his own frank case in *Uneasy Lies the Head: The Autobiography of His Majesty King Hussein of the Hashemite Kingdom of Jordan* (New York: Bernard Geis Associates, 1963). The beginnings and growth of the

Arab Legion, as seen by the man who converted the desert patrol into an efficient army, is the thesis of Sir John Bagot Glubb, *A Soldier with the Arabs* (New York: Harper, 1957); *Politics and the Military in Jordan: A Study of the Arab Legion, 1921–1957*, by P. J. Vatikiotis (New York: Praeger, 1967), is an analytical assessment by a competent political scientist.

Georges Spillman, *De protectorat à l'indépendence: Maroc, 1912–55* (Paris, Plon, 1967), and J. P. Halstead, *Rebirth of a Nation: The Origins and Rise of Moroccan Nationalism* (Cambridge, Mass.: Harvard University Press, 1967), explore the political background of the protectorate. Stephane Bernard, *The Franco-Moroccan Conflict, 1943–1956*, translated from the French by Marianna Oliver, Alexander Baden Harrison, Jr., and Bernard Phillips (New Haven, Conn.: Yale University Press, for the Carnegie Endowment for International Peace, 1968) analyzes the decay of the protectorate and the French surrender of sovereignty. On the political system of sovereign Morocco, see I. William Zartman, *Problems of New Power: Morocco* (New York: Atherton, 1964), an original and penetrating study which also treats (chap. 3) the formation of the army. An even more comprehensive analysis of Moroccan politics, covering the first dozen years of independence with an excellent historical introduction, is John Waterbury, *The King and His Courtiers: The Moroccan Political Elite, a Study in Segmented Politics* (forthcoming). Other worthwhile analyses include Jacques Robert, *La monarchie marocaine* (Paris: Librairie générale de droit et de jurisprudence, 1963); Douglas E. Ashford, *Political Change in Morocco* (Princeton, N.J.: Princeton University Press, 1961); and I. William Zartman, *Destiny of a Dynasty: The Search for Institutions in Morocco's Developing Society* (Columbia, S.C.: University of South Carolina Press, 1964). Charles F. Stewart studies the economic consequences of French rule and the evolving economy in the early years of independence in *The Economy of Morocco, 1912–1962* (Cambridge, Mass.: Harvard University Press, 1964).

H. R. P. Dickson, *Kuwait and Her Neighbours* (London: Allen and Unwin, 1956), in a work that is part history and part reminiscence, presents an informal introduction to the desert principality when it was still under British protection. IBRD, *The Economic Development of Kuwait* (Baltimore, Md.: Johns Hopkins Press, 1965), provides much of the raw material for an economic appraisal of the fabulously oil-rich sovereign amirate, which Fakhri Shehab describes in "Kuwait: A Super-Affluent Society," *Foreign Affairs*, vol. 43 (April 1964), pp. 461–74. Kuwayt's special relation to Britain is examined by Elizabeth

Monroe in "Kuwayt and Aden: A Contrast in British Politics," *The Middle East Journal*, vol. 18 (Winter 1964), pp. 63–74.

Non-military Republics

On the multiparty democracy of Israel, see: Leonard J. Fein, *Israel: Politics and People* (Boston: Little, Brown, 1968), a lively behavioral study; Nadav Safran, *The United States and Israel* (Cambridge, Mass.: Harvard University Press, 1963), a cool analysis, despite the author's warm attachment to the state; Lester G. Seligman, *Leadership in a New Nation: Political Development in Israel* (New York: Atherton, 1964), skillful surface-scratching; Oscar Kraines, *Government and Politics in Israel* (Boston: Houghton Mifflin, 1961), a fact-packed formalistic study; and Marver H. Bernstein, *The Politics of Israel: The First Decade of Statehood* (Princeton, N.J.: Princeton University Press, 1957), the first systematic study, still valuable on the emerging bureaucracy. All competent in their several ways, these books share the common failing of dismissing the role of the Arab minority in the political system. Nor is this oversight repaired by Don Peretz, *Israel and the Palestine Arabs* (Washington: Middle East Institute, 1958), which nevertheless unravels the tangled, post-mandatory history of the Palestine Arabs, including those who remained in or returned to Israel, after 1948. Leopold Laufer reviews Israel's proliferating technical aid to nonindustrial states in *Israel and the Developing Countries: New Approaches to Cooperation* (New York: Twentieth Century Fund, 1967), which also considers the export of military expertise. On the citizen army, see Ben Halpern, "The Role of the Military in Israel," in John J. Johnson, editor, *The Role of the Military in Underdeveloped Countries*, pp. 317–58; and Amos Perlmutter, "The Israeli Army in Politics: The Persistence of the Civilian over the Military," *World Politics*, vol. 20 (July 1968), pp. 606–43. Colonel Mordechai Bar-on, "Educational Processes in the Israel Defence Forces" (Tel Aviv: December 1966), explores all aspects of recruitment and training, not merely education, as the title might suggest. The military performance of the Israel army in the first three wars with the Arab states is assayed by: Netanel Lorch, *The Edge of the Sword: Israel's War of Independence, 1947–1949* (New York: Putnam, 1961); Edgar O'Ballance, *The Arab-Israeli War, 1948* (London: Faber, 1956); Moshe Dayan, *Diary of the Sinai Campaign* (New York: Harper and Row, 1966); S. L. A. Marshall, *Sinai Victory: Command Decisions in History's Shortest War: Israel's Hundred-Hour Conquest of Egypt East of Suez, Autumn 1956* (New York: Morrow, 1958); Michael Howard and Robert Hunter, "Israel and the Arab World: The Crisis of 1967," *Adelphi Papers*, No. 41 (October 1967); Randolph S. and Winston S. Churchill, *The Six Day War* (London: Heinemann, 1967); and Walter Laqueur, *The Road to Jerusalem: The Origins of the Arab-Israeli Conflict, 1967* (New York: Macmillan, 1968). Ernest Stock analyzes Israel's military policies in its international setting in *Israel on the Road to Sinai, 1949–1956: With a Sequel on the Six-Day War, 1967* (Ithaca, N.Y.: Cornell University Press, 1967).

Leonard Binder, editor, *Politics in Lebanon* (New York: Wiley, 1966), brings together papers of high quality, first presented to a symposium at the University of Chicago in 1963. George Kirk recounts British and Free French friction over the political evolution of Lebanon in the later years of World War II in *The Middle East and the War* (London: Oxford University Press, for RIIA, 1952), pp. 272–306. Fahim I. Qubain investigates the causes and the consequences of the civil war in Lebanon in 1958 in *Crisis in Lebanon* (Washington: Middle East Institute, 1961). See also Charles F. Gallagher, "In the Wake of the Revolution: Comments on Lebanese Affairs a Year after the 1958 Uprising," *AUFS* Report, 30 November 1959. M. W. Suleiman, *Political Parties in Lebanon* (Ithaca, N.Y.: Cornell University Press, 1967), scrutinizes the confessional multiparty politics of the Christian-Muslim Arab state.

On Tunisia under French rule, see Stephen H. Roberts, *The History of French Colonial Policy, 1870–1925* (2nd printing; London: Cass, 1963), pp. 259–301; Great Britain, Admiralty, Naval Intelligence Division, *Tunisia* (London: HMSO, 1945), Geographical Handbook Series, B.R. 523; and Dwight L. Ling, *Tunisia: From Protectorate to Republic* (Bloomington, Ind.: Indiana University Press, 1967). Clement Henry Moore looks critically at the political system in *Tunisia Since Independence: The Dynamics of One-Party Government* (Berkeley and Los Angeles: University of California Press, 1965); see also L. Rudebeck, *Party and People: A Study of Political Change in Tunisia* (Stockholm: Almquist and Wiksell, 1967). On modernization since the mid-nineteenth century, see Charles A. Micaud, editor, *Tunisia: The Politics of Modernization* (New York: Praeger, 1964). Leon Carl Brown inspects education in the evolving politics of Tunisia in *Education and Political Development*, edited by James S. Coleman (Princeton, N.J.: Princeton University Press, 1965), pp. 144–68, while Douglas E. Ashford focuses on the role of the bureaucracy in the modernization process in *National Development and Local Reform: Political Participation in Morocco, Tunisia and Pakistan* (Princeton, N.J.: Princeton University Press, 1967).

Regional Consequences

Many social scientists, particularly political sociologists, in studying military politics in nonindustrial states have implicitly or explicitly subscribed to the hypothesis that modernized armies serve as modernizing agents in the larger society. This view, for instance, was exemplified by Manfred Halpern, Guy Pauker, Lucian W. Pye, and Edward Shils in Johnson, editor, *The Role of the Military in Underdeveloped Countries*; by William R. Polk in "Social Modernization: The New Men," in Stevens, editor, *The United States and the Middle East*, pp. 30–52; Marion J. Levy, Jr., *Modernization and the Structure of Societies: A Setting for International Affairs* (Princeton, N.J.: Princeton University Press, 1956), vol. 2, part 3, chap. 4, especially pp. 597–605; and Richard D. Robinson, *High-Level Manpower in Economic Development: The Turkish Case* (Cambridge, Mass.: Harvard University Press, 1967), pp. 80–85. Regarding Turkey, the Robinson contention is challenged by Frederick W. Frey, "Surveying Present Attitudes in Turkey," *Public Opinion Quarterly*, vol. 27 (Fall 1963), pp. 335–55; and Frederick C. Shorter, "Military Expenditures and the Allocation of Resources," in Shorter, editor, *Four Studies on the Economic Development of Turkey* (London: Cass, 1967), pp. 33–62. Classical formulations of the dual-purpose hypothesis are: Frank Sloan, "The Role of the Military in Development," in William R. Polk, editor, *Developmental Revolution: North Africa, Middle East, South Asia* (Washington: Middle East Institute, 1963), pp. 106–18; and Harry F. Walterhouse, *A Time to Build: Military Civic Action—Medium for Economic Development and Social Reform* (Columbia, S.C.: University of South Carolina Press, 1964). The dual-purpose theorists lay great store in the non-military activity of armed forces or what is commonly labeled civic action. D. B. Bobrow explores the theoretical premises of civic action in "The Civic Role of the Military: Some Critical Hypotheses," *Western Political Quarterly*, vol. 19 (March 1966), pp. 101–11.

In view of the phenomenal growth in international arms traffic since 1945, it is remarkable that social scientists have paid so little analytical attention to the flow of arms to nonindustrial states. Samuel P. Huntington, "Arms Races: Prerequisites and Results," *Public Policy, 1958: A Yearbook of the Graduate School of Public Administration, Harvard University* (Cambridge, Mass.: Harvard University Press, 1958), pp. 41–86, is an excellent introduction to arms races among industrial states; a critical bibliographical note is appended, pp. 84–86. John L. Sutton and Geoffrey Kemp, "Arms to Developing Countries,

1945–1965," *Adelphi Papers*, No. 28 (October 1966), makes intelligible the confused subject of postwar patterns of arms transfers by sales and grants from the industrial to the nonindustrial states; especially useful are its tables. See also Sheila Barry, *The Arms Trade and Underdeveloped Areas—Some Notes* (Cambridge, Mass.: M.I.T. Center for International Studies, for ACDA, 22 April 1964). On military technology in nonindustrial states, confer H. Roberts Coward, *Military Technology in Developing Countries* (Cambridge, Mass.: M.I.T. Center for International Studies, 15 April 1964). *The Military Balance*, issued annually since 1959 by the Institute for Strategic Studies (London), reports primarily on the industrial states but includes information on selected Middle East countries as well. In 1966 the Institute also started publishing an annual companion entitled *Strategic Survey*. David Wood, "The Middle East and the Arab World," *Adelphi Paper*, No. 20 (July 1965), and "The Armed Forces of African States," *ibid.*, No. 27 (April 1966), together provide useful data on each of the states of Southwest Asia and North Africa; that is, on the Middle East as defined in this book. Other relevant information will be found in: United States, AID Statistics and Reports Division, *U.S. Overseas Loans and Grants and Assistance from International Organizations: Obligations and Loan Authorizations, July 1, 1945– June 30, 1965* (Washington: GPO, 1966); United States, Department of Defense, *Military Assistance Facts* (Washington: GPO, several times annually); and United States Arms Control and Disarmament Agency, Economics Bureau, *World-Wide Defense Expenditures and Selected Economic Data, 1964* (Washington: January 1966), and *World-Wide Military Expenditures and Related Data, Calendar Year 1965* (Washington: December 1967), which list the information by geographic region and by country. Also worth consulting is a staff study prepared for the United States Senate Committee on Foreign Relations, 90th Cong., 1st sess., "Arms Sales and Foreign Policy" (Washington: GPO, 25 January 1967). On arms races in the Middle East, see John H. Hoagland, Jr., and John B. Teeple, "Regional Stability and Weapons Transfer: The Middle Eastern Case," *Orbis*, vol. 9 (Fall 1965), pp. 714–28; "The Arms Race in the Near East," *Near East Report*, Special Supplement, February 1967; Leo Heiman, "Moscow's Export Arsenal: The Soviet Bloc and the Middle Eastern Arms Race," *East Europe*, vol. 13 (May 1964), pp. 3–10; and Stuart H. Schaar, "The Arms Race and Defense Strategy in North Africa," *AUFS Report Service, North Africa Series*, vol. 13, no. 9 (December 1967).

Proposals for arms control in the Middle East and other nonindustrial regions include: Marina S. Finkelstein, *A Brief Survey of Proposals Dealing with Arms Questions Emanating from Africa, the Middle East and Latin America: 1959–1963* (Cambridge, Mass.: M.I.T. Center for International Studies, 3 September 1963); Catherine MacArdle, *The Role of Military Assistance in the Problem of Arms Control: The Middle East, Latin America, and Africa* (Cambridge, Mass.: M.I.T. Center for International Studies; 1964); and M.I.T. Center for International Studies, *Regional Arms Control Arrangements for Developing Areas: Arms and Arms Control in Latin America, the Middle East, and Africa* (Cambridge, Mass.: M.I.T. Center for International Affairs for ACDA, 21 September 1964). Lincoln Bloomfield, Walter C. Clemens, Jr., and Franklyn Griffiths, *Khrushchev and the Arms Race: Soviet Interest in Arms Control and Disarmament, 1954–1964* (Cambridge, Mass.: M.I.T., 1966), is preoccupied with the Soviet-American rivalry and efforts at control, with almost no reference to the impact of the superpower race on the nonindustrial states; a convenient list of bibliographies on disarmament and arms control appears on pp. 321–23.

INDEX

'Abbas I, Shah (1587–1629), 20, 24f
'Abbas Mirza, 40–41
'Abbasid Caliphate (750–1258), 17, 331
'Abbud, Ibrahim, 113–14, 167–68, 171–72, 200
'Abd al-'Aziz ibn 'Abd al-Rahman Al Faysal Al Saud [Su'ud], 48, 57, 242–48, 250, 255
'Abd al-Nasir, Gamal, 87f, 109, 115, 119, 125–27, 129f, 131–34, 138–144, 146–48, 153, 157, 166–67, 205, 251, 256, 258–60, 312, 376, 389, 449, 451, 475, 477, 479, 48lf; arms purchases, 89–91; and social change, 420–26; see also Egypt
'Abd al-Rahman, Amir (Afghanistan), 298f, 300
'Abd al-Rahman, Mawlay (1822–59), 42
Abdali tribe, 298
'Abdallah, Mawlay (Morocco), 26
'Abdallah ibn Husayn, King, 309, 311–318 passim, 320
'Abdallah al-Salim, Shaykh, 349f, 351–52, 354
'Abdallah al-Sulayman Al Hamdan, 249–50
Abdülaziz, Sultan, 39

Abdüllhamid II, Sultan, 39, 421
Abu al-Huda, Tawfiq, 317
Abu Nuwwar, 'Ali, 320
L'Action tunisienne, 404
Aden, 56, 72, 78, 256
Adenauer, Konrad, 477
Afghanistan, 9, 26, 41, 69, 265, 268, 293, 296, 382, 491, 494–95, 497–498; aid to, 440–41; and Cold War, 74f, 80, 87–88, 91–92; foreign domination, 298–99; independence and establishment of dynasty, 299–300; and Pakistan, 301; political development, 305–307; population, 297–98; social heterogeneity, 296–97.

Military modernization: 8, 47–48, 57, 64, 105–107, 296, 300–304; armed forces (composition, size, and organization), 106–107
'Aflaq, Michel, 147
Africa, 116
Afro-Asian Conference (1965), 198
Afshar dynasty, 25
Agrarian reform, 185, 290; Egypt, 130; Iran, 291; see also Land reform
Ahdut ha-'Avodah Party, 365, 370f, 372, 376
Ahmad, Imam, 255, 257

533

PUBLICATIONS

FOREIGN AFFAIRS (quarterly), edited by Hamilton Fish Armstrong.

THE UNITED STATES IN WORLD AFFAIRS (annual), by Richard P. Stebbins.

DOCUMENTS ON AMERICAN FOREIGN RELATIONS (annual), by Richard P. Stebbins with the assistance of Elaine P. Adam.

POLITICAL HANDBOOK AND ATLAS OF THE WORLD (annual), edited by Walter H. Mallory.

THE ECONOMICS OF INTERDEPENDENCE: Economic Policy in the Atlantic Community, by Richard N. Cooper (1968).

HOW NATIONS BEHAVE: Law and Foreign Policy, by Louis Henkin (1968).

THE INSECURITY OF NATIONS, by Charles W. Yost (1968).

PROSPECTS FOR SOVIET SOCIETY, edited by Allen Kassof (1968).

THE AMERICAN APPROACH TO THE ARAB WORLD, by John S. Badeau (1968).

U.S. POLICY AND THE SECURITY OF ASIA, by Fred Greene (1968).

NEGOTIATING WITH THE CHINESE COMMUNISTS: The U.S. Experience, by Kenneth T. Young (1968).

FROM ATLANTIC TO PACIFIC: A New Interocean Canal, by Immanuel J. Klette (1967).

TITO'S SEPARATE ROAD: America and Yugoslavia in World Politics, by John C. Campbell (1967).

U.S. TRADE POLICY: New Legislation for the Next Round, by John W. Evans (1967).

TRADE LIBERALIZATION AMONG INDUSTRIAL COUNTRIES: Objectives and Alternatives, by Bela Balassa (1967).

THE CHINESE PEOPLE'S LIBERATION ARMY, by Brig. General Samuel B. Griffith II U.S.M.C. (ret.) (1967).

THE ARTILLERY OF THE PRESS: Its Influence on American Foreign Policy, by James Reston (1967).

ATLANTIC ECONOMIC COOPERATION: The Case of the O.E.C.D., by Henry G. Aubrey (1967).

TRADE, AID AND DEVELOPMENT: The Rich and Poor Nations, by John Pincus (1967).

BETWEEN TWO WORLDS: Policy, Press and Public Opinion on Asian-American Relations, by John Hohenberg (1967).